ANIMAL LEARNING AND COGNITION

ANIMAL LEARNING AND COGNITION

AN INTRODUCTION

2nd Edition

John M. Pearce

School of Psychology
University of Wales
Cardiff

Psychology Press
An imprint of Erlbaum (UK) Taylor & Francis

Psychology Press, Publishers
27 Church Road
Hove
East Sussex, BN3 2FA
UK

British Library Cataloguing in Publication Data
A catalogue record for this title is available from the British Library

ISBN 0-86377-433-4 (Hbk)
ISBN 0-86377-434-2 (Pbk)

Printed and bound by BPC Wheatons Ltd., Exeter

For my family

CONTENTS

Preface   xi

1.   The study of animal cognition   1
    The distribution of intelligence   2
    Defining animal intelligence   11
    Methods for studying animal intelligence   14
    Why study animal cognition?   16
    Historical background   19

2.   Associative learning   27
    Conditioning techniques   28
    The nature of associative learning   35
    Stimulus–stimulus learning   42
    The nature of US representations   44
    The performance of the conditioned response   47
    Concluding comment: The reflexive nature of the conditioned response   52

3.   The conditions for learning: Surprise and attention   55
    Part 1: Surprise and conditioning   56
    Conditioning with a single CS   56
    Conditioning with a compound CS   60
    Evaluation of the Rescorla-Wagner model   63
    Part 2: Attention and conditioning   65
    Wagner's theory   66
    Stimulus significance   71
    Pearce-Hall theory   74
    Concluding comments   79

4.   Instrumental conditioning   **81**
      The nature of instrumental learning   81
      The conditions of learning   87
      The performance of instrumental behaviour   94
      The comparative analysis of instrumental conditioning   99
      Pavlovian conditioning as instrumental learning   100
      The law of effect and problem solving   101

5.   Discrimination learning   **107**
      Theories of discrimination learning   108
      Categorisation   118
      Relationships as discriminative stimuli   124
      The representation of knowledge   129
      Connectionist models of discrimination and categorisation   130

6.   Memory   **137**
      Part 1: Long-term retention   138
      Capacity   138
      Durability   140
      Theoretical interpretation   142
      Part 2: Short-term retention   148
      Methods of study   148
      Forgetting   158
      Theoretical interpretation   160
      Serial position effects   163
      Conclusions   165

7.   The representation of time, number, and order   **167**
      Time   167
      Number   175
      Serial order   183
      Transitive inference   189
      Concluding comments   193

8.   Navigation   **195**
      Part 1: Short-distance travel   195
      Methods of navigation   195
      Hippocampal place cells   203
      Cognitive maps   206
      Part 2: Long-distance travel   215
      Navigational cues   215
      Homing   217
      Migration   220
      Concluding comments   222

9. **Social learning**   **225**
    Diet selection and foraging   225
    Fear of predators   228
    Copying behaviour: mimicry   229
    Copying behaviour: imitation   231
    Communication   236
    Theory of mind   240
    Self-recognition   245
    Concluding comments   250

10. **Communication and language**   **253**
    Animal communication   253
    Communication and language   257
    Can an ape create a sentence?   259
    Language training with other species   271
    The requirements for learning a language   275

11. **The distribution of intelligence**   **279**
    Intelligence and brain size   279
    The null hypothesis   281
    Intelligence and evolution   285

References   **289**

Author Index   **319**

Subject Index   **329**

Preface

In writing this second edition my aim, as it was for the first edition, has been to provide an overview of what has been learned by pursuing one particular approach to the study of animal intelligence. It is my belief that the intelligence of animals is the product of a number of processes. I think the best way of understanding these processes is by studying the behaviour of animals in an experimental setting. This book, therefore, presents what is known about animal intelligence by considering experimental findings from the laboratory and from more naturalistic settings.

Although the title of the first edition, *An Introduction to Animal Cognition*, has been lengthened for the second edition, I do not attach any great importance to the distinction between animal learning and animal cognition. Research in both areas has the common goal of elucidating the mechanisms of animal intelligence and, very often, this research is conducted using similar procedures. If there is any significance to the distinction, then it is that the fields of animal learning and animal cognition are concerned with different aspects of intelligence. Chapters 2 to 5 are thus concerned predominantly with issues that fall under the traditional heading of animal learning theory. My main concern in these chapters is to show how it is possible with a few simple principles of learning to explain a surprisingly wide range of experimental findings. The second

half of the book covers material that is nowadays often treated under the heading of animal cognition. My overall aim in these chapters is to examine what has been learned from studying animal behaviour about such topics as memory, the representation of knowledge, navigation, social learning, communication, and language. I also hope to show that the principles developed in the earlier chapters are of relevance to understanding research that is reviewed in the later chapters.

Those who wish to study the intelligence of animals face a daunting task. Not only are there numerous different species to study, but there is also an array of intellectual skills to be explored, each posing a unique set of challenging theoretical problems. As a result, many of the topics that I discuss are still in their infancy. Some readers may therefore be disappointed to discover that we are still trying to answer many of the interesting questions that can be asked about the intelligence of animals. On the other hand, it is just this lack of knowledge that makes the study of animal learning and cognition so exciting. Many fascinating discoveries remain to be made once the appropriate experiments have been conducted.

One of the rewards for writing a book is the opportunity it provides to thank the many friends and colleagues who have been so generous with the help they have given me. The way in which this book is organised and much of the material it contains have been greatly influenced by numerous discussions with A. Dickinson, G. Hall, and N. J. Mackintosh. Different chapters have benefited greatly from the critical comments on earlier versions by A. Aydin, C. Bonardi, C. Heyes, V. LoLordo, E. Redhead, and P. Wilson. In this respect, a special word of thanks is due to N. J. Mackintosh who not only read and provided detailed comments on a final draft of the first edition of this book, but was willing to undergo the ordeal again for the second edition. Rohays Perry of Psychology Press has been a constant source of encouragement throughout the writing of both editions, she also contributed enormously to their presentation. And for her consistently cheerful help and secretarial support, I thank Nicola Thomas.

Finally, there is the pleasure of expressing gratitude to my wife and children, who once again patiently tolerated the demands made on them while the second edition of this book was being written. Thank you Victoria, Jess, Alex, and Tim.

January, 1996
J.M.P.

1

The Study of Animal Cognition

The study of animal cognition is concerned with questions of the following kind: What is animal intelligence? How does it differ from human intelligence? If there is a difference between the intelligence of humans and animals, why should this be? In what way do species of animals differ in their intelligence? How can animal intelligence be measured? None of these is an easy question to answer, and it is partly the difficulty of answering the first that makes it so difficult to answer all others.

In this book a particular account of animal intelligence will be developed. It presumes that animals, like humans, possess a number of mental or cognitive processes and that these collectively contribute to an animal's intelligence. Thus the way animals remember, learn, reason, solve problems, communicate, and so forth will be examined in some detail. One advantage of this approach is that it may permit relatively straightforward answers to the questions posed earlier. For instance, a scale of intelligence might be constructed by ranking animals according to the number of the intellectual abilities they possess. Alternatively, it might turn out that it would be nonsensical to construct any such scale, because a species better endowed than another with one of these abilities might be less well endowed with a second. In addition, as this account is based on a human model, it should readily permit the comparison of human and animal intelligence. The chapters that follow examine in some detail the various intellectual capacities that have been revealed in animals, and to a lesser extent look at the way animals differ in their possession of these capacities.

The purpose of this chapter is to provide a background to this discussion by considering a number of preliminary issues:

1. An extremely popular view of animal intelligence is that there is a growth of this capacity with evolutionary development; apes are therefore seen by many as being more intelligent than most other animals. Although popular, this view deserves critical analysis, as it rests on some questionable assumptions.
2. The present account of animal intelligence is by no means unique. Many different approaches to this topic have been developed, and some brief justification for favouring the present one is required.
3. Although the study of animal cognition is of interest in its own right, this may be regarded as insufficient justification for devoting a book to the topic. The study of human intelligence may be considered a more proper part of psychology. It is therefore worth identifying some of the benefits that may derive from the study of the mental life of animals.

4. The study of mental processes in animals is difficult because the subject matter is not available for direct observation. It is certainly impossible at present to point to any event that can be regarded as a mental process in animals. As a result, special methods must be employed for the study of animal cognition, and the rationale for these needs discussion.

5. Much of the research discussed in this book relates to work conducted during the last twenty years or so, but the study of animal intelligence in the laboratory has now been pursued for nearly a hundred years. By way of providing a historical background to the rest of the book, the final section of the chapter presents a brief review of the dominant theoretical themes of this work.

THE DISTRIBUTION OF INTELLIGENCE

Banks and Flora (1977) asked college students to rank the intelligence of a variety of animals on a 10-point scale. Apes were considered the most intelligent with a rating of 9.2, then followed dogs with 7.4, cats with 6.6, horses with 5.6, cows with 3.6, sheep with 3.4, and chickens with 3.4; finally, fish were regarded as least intelligent, with a rating of 1.7. In fact, this ranking was not the principal aim of the study, and it is mentioned only because it reveals what is probably a widespread assumption: That there is a progressive development of intelligence throughout the animal kingdom, culminating in our own species, which presumably would have been awarded a score of 10 on the scale.

I shall examine two popular justifications for the assumption that intelligence is distributed in this way. One is based on an interpretation of evolution that presumes that animals can be arranged in a sequence according to their phylogenetic status. The other is derived from the assumption that there is a relationship between intelligence and brain size. In fact, neither of these justifies the views expressed by the students questioned by Banks and Flora (1977).

The role of evolution

The Great Chain of Being. Attempts since the time of Aristotle (384-322 BC) have been made to represent the animal kingdom in an orderly sequence. Such a sequence has been referred to as the *Scala Naturae,* or the "Great Chain of Being". Typically, the lower rankings of these scales are occupied by formless creatures like sponges, whereas the upper echelons are reserved for humans. Ascending through the intermediate range of these scales can be found insects, fish, amphibians, reptiles, and various mammals. According to Aristotle, elephants were placed just below humans. Although these scales generally end with our own species, this has by no means been a universal practice. Occasionally the "Great Chain" has extended beyond humans to include angels and, ultimately, God.

Various justifications have been proposed for such a simple ordering. Aristotle based his scheme on whether or not the animals possessed blood and on the number of their legs. More recently, evolutionary terms have been used to justify what is now referred to as the phyletic or phylogenetic scale. Since the publication of Darwin's *The origin of the species by means of natural selection* in 1859, it has become accepted that all existing species have descended or evolved from different, earlier species. As a result, it is possible to envisage a chain of evolution in which the earliest animals are placed at the bottom, and the species they led to are placed above them in the order of their appearance. *Homo sapiens* appeared some 100,000 years ago and would be very near the top of this scale. Most would accept that humans are vastly more intelligent than the protozoa to which we are distantly related, and so it is not difficult to regard the phyletic scale as roughly corresponding to the intellectual development of the species ordered along it. This interpretation could hardly be more incorrect.

While on his voyage around South America on HMS *Beagle,* Darwin noted that the iguanas on the Galapagos Islands were different from those on the mainland in that only the former ate seaweed and swam in the sea. To explain this difference between such closely related species, he developed the principle of natural selection, which is based on two observations: (1) Many more animals are born than achieve reproductive success; some may die before reaching sexual maturity, others may fail to find a mate. (2) The individuals of a given species are not identical but differ from one another in a variety of ways. As a consequence, certain members of a species will be better suited than others to survive in a given environment, and they will be more likely to mature sexually and to leave offspring. If we assume that offspring resemble their parents, it follows that better-adapted characteristics will spread through a population at the expense of less well adapted characteristics. If members of the same species should occupy different environments, the different demands they face will favour the reproduction of animals with slightly different characteristics. Eventually their characteristics may have diverged to such an extent that they can no longer interbreed successfully, and they will constitute separate species.

Presumably, then, the ancestors of the iguanas observed by Darwin on the Galapagos Islands and on mainland South America were of the same stock. However, the radically different nature of these two environments—an abundance of seaweed and a dearth of vegetation on the islands, and a proliferation of vegetation on the mainland—would have favoured the gradual development of different characteristics in successive generations of offspring from the common ancestor.

One important implication of this account is that the notion of a phylogenetic scale is a gross oversimplification of the history of evolution. Instead of one species evolving from another in a strict sequence, as the "Great Chain of Being" suggests, it is now accepted that evolution has resulted in animals being related by a sort of family tree. The roots and trunk of the tree are composed of the early life forms such as protozoa and coelenterates.[1] The species that have evolved from these origins can be regarded as separate branches, which themselves branch out as later generations of their offspring evolve into new species.

Figure 1.1 shows the trunk and initial branches of a simplified version of the evolutionary tree. To give some idea of the time-scale involved, the fossil record provides evidence of animal life as long as 2600 million years ago, yet it was not until about 450–500 million years ago that the first true vertebrates came into existence.

Figure 1.2 depicts the main branches of the evolutionary tree for the development of the vertebrates. The mammal-like reptiles that led to the mammals branched away from the reptiles approximately 200 million years ago. The birds, on the other hand, separated from the reptiles about 150 million years ago, via the link *Archaeopteryx*. Finally, the outer branches of the tree are presented in Figure 1.3 for the four families of primates: prosimians, monkeys, apes, and us.

The structure of the evolutionary tree is of interest in its own right, but of more relevance to the present discussion is the fact that it is impossible to organise the relationship among the various species into any simple linear scale. Mammals and birds have both evolved from reptiles, and many of the reptiles that are alive today are only distant relatives of the reptiles that were ancestral to the birds and mammals. Given such a relationship, it is extremely difficult to imagine how the present-day animals could be ranked in a sequence that mimics their evolutionary history. Evolution provides an explanation for the diversity of species—it does not provide any grounds for ranking animals according to their intelligence or, for that matter, any other characteristic.

Numerous authors have recently pursued this line of argument one step further to conclude that the evolutionary process will render futile any attempt to find common mechanisms of intelligence among animals (Hinde & Stevenson-Hinde, 1973; Seligman & Hager, 1972). It is not just the physical characteristics of animals that are shaped by evolution, but also their intellectual processes. Thus it might be expected that different species, if they inhabit different environments, will differ radically in the nature of their intelligence. For example, the habitat of a bird like the arctic tern, which spends most of its time flying between the polar regions, has very little in common with the sewer in which a rat might live. It is possible that animals occupying such contrasting environments possess very different intellectual processes. Furthermore, because the last common ancestor of the rat and the arctic tern was probably alive 200 million years ago, there has been ample

FIGURE 1.1

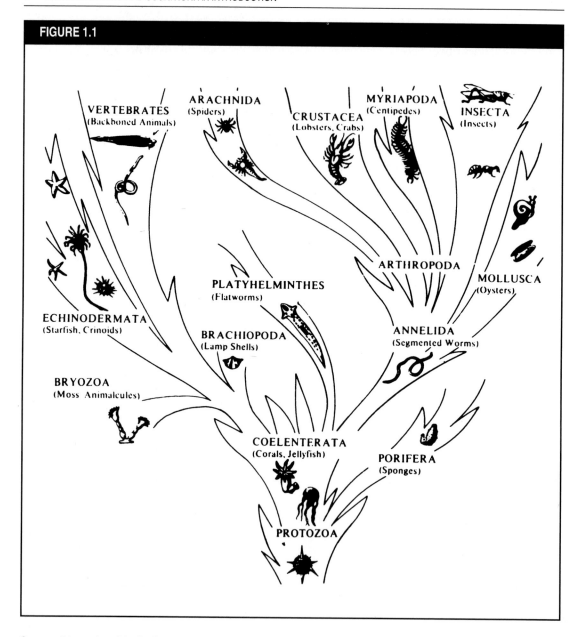

One possible version of the family tree of the animal kingdom (from Romer, 1966).

time for the evolution of different mental capacities. If this argument is correct, then it is no more possible to conclude that one species is more intelligent than another than it is to say that one is more evolved than the other. All that can be said is that the species have developed different intellectual abilities that enable them to survive in their particular environments.

There is certainly some merit in this argument. Chapter 8 shows that birds that migrate great distances possess the ability to navigate by the stars. One would hardly expect to discover this skill in the sewer rat. But, at the same time, there are good grounds for believing that animals might have much in common intellectually. Despite living in radically different environments, animals

FIGURE 1.2

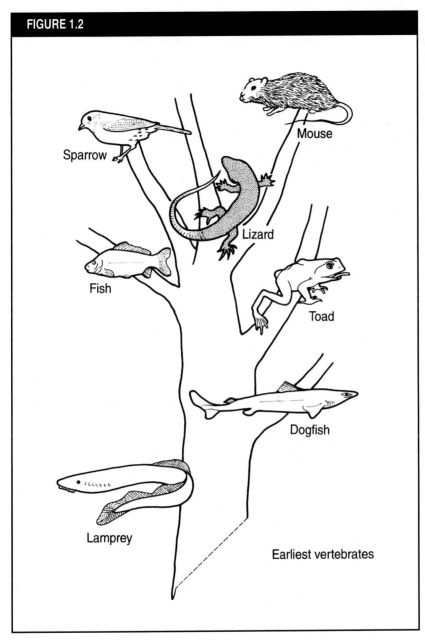

A simplified family tree of vertebrates (adapted from Romer and Parsons, 1977).

Mouse

Sparrow

Lizard

Fish

Toad

Dogfish

Lamprey

Earliest vertebrates

face a number of common problems. Many animals must learn which foods are nutritious and which are poisonous. They must learn to identify their predators and where they can be found. They must learn the location of plentiful rather than lean supplies of food, or where water can be located. If the animals raise their young in a specific location, they must remember its position in respect to local landmarks. Given such a collection of common problems, it is at least plausible that different species employ the same intellectual processes for solving them.

Animals may, for example, have the ability to learn about recurring sequences of events, particularly when one of them is of biological significance. This would enable them, in a sense, to expect future events and to behave adaptively in anticipation of them. A simple example would be

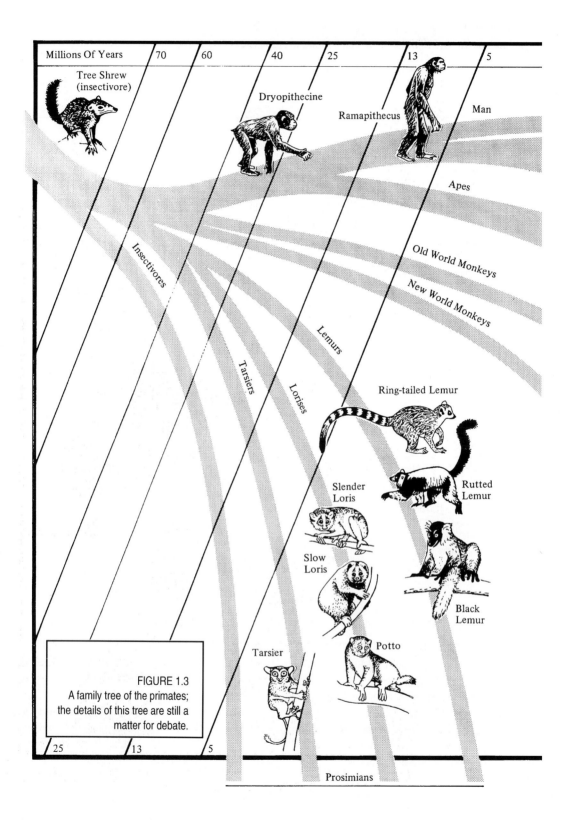

| Millions Of Years | 70 | 60 | 40 | 25 | 13 | 5 |

Tree Shrew
(insectivore)

Dryopithecine

Ramapithecus

Man

Apes

Old World Monkeys

New World Monkeys

Insectivores

Tarsiers

Lorises

Lemurs

Ring-tailed Lemur

Slender
Loris

Rutted
Lemur

Slow
Loris

Black
Lemur

Tarsier

Potto

FIGURE 1.3
A family tree of the primates;
the details of this tree are still a
matter for debate.

| 25 | 13 | 5 |

Prosimians

Australopithecus Robustus

Homo Habilis

Homo Erectus

100,000 Years

Modern Man

Neanderthal Man

Gorilla

Chimpanzee

Spider Monkey

Mandril

Cotton-top Monkey

Pig-tailed Macaque

Gibbon

Night Monkey

Rhesus Monkey

Orang-utan

Monkeys

Apes

the ability to learn about the taste of a food and its ultimate gastric consequences. Animals that can learn about this relationship would then be able to restrict their diet to foods that are not harmful. There is also an obvious advantage, for virtually all animals, in being able to learn about the consequences of their actions. This will permit behaviour that has beneficial consequences to be repeated, and that which has harmful ones to be withheld. Many species might also benefit by possessing the capacity to communicate and to solve problems. The purpose of this discussion is not to argue that all animals should possess these and other abilities. Instead my aim is to indicate that although evolution will result in animals possessing very different characteristics, the common intellectual problems that confront many species may perhaps result in their sharing the same methods for solving them. If this is correct, then there may be a considerable degree of similarity in the intellectual processes of different species. Of course, whether or not this is true can be discovered only by studying the animals directly.

Brain size and intelligence

One obvious candidate for providing an independent index of the intelligence of a species is its brain size. However intelligence is defined, few would dispute that the organ responsible for this capacity is the brain. It is thus reasonable to expect the species with the larger brains to possess the greater potential for intelligence. Perhaps this rationalisation was responsible for the replies to the questionnaire reported in the Banks and Flora (1977) study. There is certainly a high correlation between their ranking of intelligence and the brain size of the animals concerned, as Figure 1.4 demonstrates. Is it possible to rank the intelligence of species according to their brain size?

One problem that is encountered when attempting to relate intelligence to brain size is that elephants possess much heavier brains than

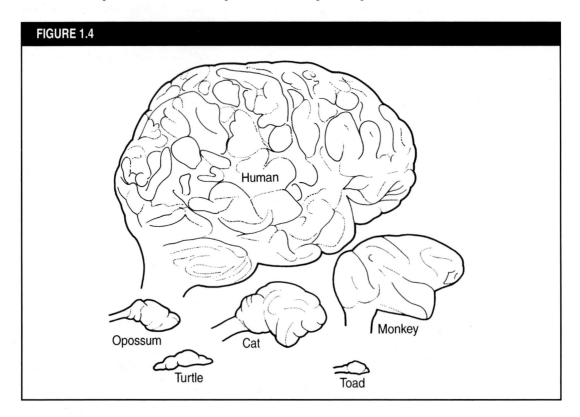

FIGURE 1.4

The size of the brain for a variety of species.

humans. Few would accept that this relationship accurately indicates the relative intelligence of these species, and a moment's reflection should reveal the fallacy in the argument. The concern of the brain is not solely with such high matters as intelligence, but also with more basic activities such as respiration, digestion, reproduction, and movement—in short, all the somatic and vegetative processes of the body. The bigger the animal, the larger the volume of the brain that will be required to control these processes. It is thus unrealistic to expect the size of the brain in absolute terms to provide an index of intelligence. A more plausible candidate is the ratio of the size of the brain to the body. If two species possess the same body size but one has a considerably larger brain, then it is likely that this extra brain will enable its owner to be the more intelligent.

Figure 1.5 shows the brain weights (vertical axis) and the body weights (horizontal axis) of a variety of species, plotted in log–log coordinates. This scale is necessary because of the extremely wide range of values that must be considered. On the basis of what has just been said, it can be concluded, with some relief, that our species should be more intelligent than the ostrich. Both

have the same body weight, but the ostrich brain weighs less than ours. The main problem is in deciding how species with different body weights should be compared.

One simple method is to draw polygons around the points for a collection of related species. In Figure 1.5, Jerison (1973), from whose book this account is taken, has drawn two polygons, one around the "higher" vertebrates (birds, mammals), and the other enclosing the "lower" vertebrates (reptiles, amphibia, fish). Because the polygons do not overlap, it is possible to conclude that in general the weight of the brain for a given body weight is greater for the higher vertebrates. In other words, the "higher" vertebrates might be expected to have a greater potential for intelligence than the "lower" vertebrates.

More precise comparisons between species can be made by computing a cephalisation index (K). This essentially represents the ratio of the brain weight (E) to body weight (P), and the larger its value—we might assume—the greater the intelligence of the species concerned. Jerison (1973) rejects the use of a simple ratio of the form E/P for determining the cephalisation index and recommends, instead, the use of the ratio $E/P^{2/3}$. [2]

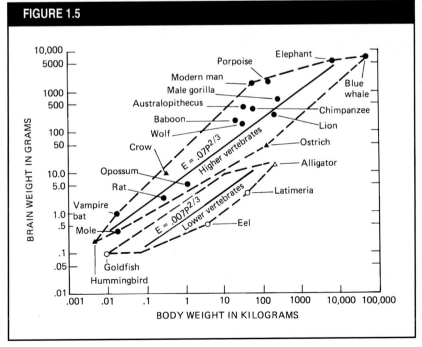

FIGURE 1.5

The brain weights (vertical axis) and body weights (horizontal axis) of a number of vertebrates (from Jerison, 1969).

The solid lines in Figure 1.5 pass through the brain and body weights that yield a K value of 0.07 (upper polygon) and 0.007 (lower polygon). Jerison (1973) assumes that all the species that lie on one of these lines possess an equivalent neural capacity for intelligence, irrespective of their body size. The magnitude of the displacement from these lines indicates the K value for a given species. Humans and porpoises possess K values that are furthest above the 0.07 line, which suggests they should be the two most intelligent species, with humans possessing a slight superiority.

Thus, by computing a cephalisation index it may be possible to rank different species according to the volume of brain they have available for intelligence. Table 1.1 indicates that this ranking is not too unlike that proposed by the students in the Banks and Flora (1977) study. On this scale the elephant has a rather average potential for intelligence.

The ranking in Table 1.1 might accord with the popular conception of the way intelligence is distributed throughout the animal kingdom, but it does not confirm this view. The most that this ranking could indicate is that some animals have less brain available for intelligence than others, once account has been taken of its remaining functions. What is needed is a detailed investigation of the intellectual abilities of animals to determine whether or not they correspond with the order summarised in Table 1.1. This in turn depends on a satisfactory definition of animal intelligence, and it is with this issue that the next section is concerned.

Before studying this problem, it is worth stating that not all authors maintain that Table 1.1 reflects accurately the distribution of animal intelligence. As early as about 500 BC, the Ionian philosopher Anaxagoras proposed that all living things possess a substance, *nous,* which is equivalent to mind. This substance has power over all things that have life; it is infinite, self-ruled, and just as good in animals as in humans. In more mundane terms, he was claiming that all animals are equally intelligent. Any apparent intellectual differences between animals were said to be due to variations in the way they can express themselves. Hence, he might have argued that worms are intelligent, but unfortunately they lack the necessary appendages to demonstrate this capacity fully. Among Anaxagoras' other novel ideas is the proposal that snow is, in part, black.

Somewhat more recently Macphail (1982) concluded, after an extremely thorough review of a vast body of experimental evidence, that there is no difference in the intellectual capacity of

TABLE 1.1

The Cephalisation Index (K) for 21 Mammals Arranged in Descending Order.

1.	Man	0.89		12.	Dog	0.14
2.	Dolphin	0.64		13.	Squirrel	0.13
3.	Chimpanzee	0.30		14.	Wild pig	0.12
4.	Squirrel Monkey	0.28		15.	Cat	0.12
5.	Rhesus Monkey	0.25		16.	Horse	0.10
6.	Elephant	0.22		17.	Sheep	0.10
7.	Whale	0.21		18.	Ox	0.06
8.	Marmoset	0.21		19.	Mouse	0.06
9.	Fox	0.19		20.	Rat	0.05
10.	Walrus	0.15		21.	Rabbit	0.05
11.	Camel	0.14				

Adapted from Russell (1979).

vertebrates other than humans. This null hypothesis of intelligence is based on the results of direct tests of animal intelligence, and thus merits serious attention. Although a major aim of this book is to outline a framework for the study of animal intelligence, a secondary aim is to evaluate the relative intelligence of different species. This should allow us to determine whether popular opinion is correct in assuming a progression of intelligence throughout the animal kingdom, or whether Anaxagoras and Macphail are correct in their claim concerning the equality of animals in this respect.

DEFINING ANIMAL INTELLIGENCE

Adaptability

Many authors consider that the defining characteristic of intelligence is that it enables animals to behave adaptively. Thus in a book entitled *Instinct and intelligence,* a zoologist, Barnett (1970, p.59), has proposed: "intelligence here means the ability to adapt behaviour to circumstances". There can surely be little to disagree with in this definition. None the less, its limitations become evident when attempts are made to compare the intelligence of different species. How it could be determined whether a rat or a dog is better at adapting its behaviour to the prevailing circumstances is not immediately apparent. Nor does this definition tell us anything about the mechanisms that enable an animal to adapt its behaviour.

One solution to this problem is to acknowledge that an animal that can profit from its experiences is likely to be better at adapting to a new environment than one lacking this capacity. For example, once the location of food, water, and predators has been identified, being able to remember where they were encountered will considerably facilitate survival. Accordingly, the animal that is faster at learning and better at remembering may be regarded as the more adaptable and hence the more intelligent. Indeed, Warren (1973) has suggested that this type of argument formed the rationale for much of the work in comparative psychology conducted during the first half of this century.

Learning

Learning is surprisingly hard to define satisfactorily. For the present discussion, however, learning can be said to take place when some experience results in a relatively permanent change in the reaction to a situation (see Hilgard & Bower, 1966, pp.2–6). Since the turn of the century there has been an enormous number of experimental studies of learning, using animals ranging from protozoa to humans, and a variety of tasks. One clear conclusion that can be drawn from this work is that there is definitely no relationship between the speed at which an animal learns and its cephalisation index. Evidence supporting this claim will be presented throughout the book, but at this juncture several examples will serve to make the point. Skard (1950) compared the speed at which rats and humans mastered a complex maze and found no difference whatsoever in the number of trials required to attain errorless performance. Warren (1965) reported that there was no difference in the rate at which goldfish, chickens, cats, horses, and rhesus monkeys learned a discrimination in which they were required to approach one of two stimuli to gain reward.

Perhaps even more surprising are the results of Angermeier (1984), who conducted a thorough series of experiments at the University of Cologne. Various animals were required to perform a simple response to obtain food: Mammals had to press a lever, birds peck a disc, and fish push a rod that was hanging vertically into their tank. Subjects were placed into the apparatus when hungry, and food was delivered only when the response had been performed. As his measure of learning, Angermeier (1984) recorded the number of rewards delivered before subjects reached a criterion of responding at a constant rate. The results from his studies are presented in Table 1.2, which also includes the results of other researchers using 5-month-old human infants, rewarded with food for turning their heads (Papousek, 1977), and bees rewarded for discriminating between different colours (Menzel & Erber, 1978). The remarkable feature of these

TABLE 1.2

Number of Rewards Delivered before Criterion was Reached in a Simple Learning Task for 11 Animals Arranged in Ascending Order.

1.	Bees	2	7.	Pigeons	10
2.	Triggerfish	4	8.	Rats	22
3.	Koi Carp	4	9.	Raccoons	24
4.	Silverbarb	4	10.	Rabbits	24
5.	Quail	8	11.	Human infants	28
6.	Hybrid chickens	18			

Adapted from Angermeier (1984).

data is that they are precisely the opposite of that expected if the cephalisation index of a species corresponded with its intelligence, as revealed by the speed of learning. Whatever the explanation for these intriguing results, they suggest that it would be unwise to look to speed of learning as an index of animal intelligence.

Another reason for being wary of using speed of learning as a measure of intelligence comes from studies showing that, for a given species, the speed of learning is greatly influenced by the means used to assess it. Bolles (1971) has shown that rats will readily learn to press a lever for food, yet they have considerable difficulty in learning to perform the same response to avoid electric shock. This difficulty does not reflect an inability to perform avoidance responses, as rats find it easy to learn to jump onto a ledge or to run from one compartment to another to avoid shock (Baum, 1966; Theios, Lynch, & Lowe, 1966). Similarly, in one of my experiments (Pearce, Colwill, & Hall, 1978) rats were shown to be much poorer at learning to scratch themselves than to press a lever for food. One of the clearest demonstrations of this type of effect was reported by Garcia and Koelling (1966) using an extremely simple technique. Thirsty rats were allowed to drink salt-flavoured water from a tube in the presence of a distinctive exteroceptive stimulus comprising a light and a clicker. For one group drinking was followed by an injection of a mild poison that induced illness; for another group the consequence of drinking was electric shock. After several sessions of this training the subjects

were returned to the apparatus for a number of test trials; on some trials drinking salt-free water was accompanied by the light and clicker, on others these stimuli were omitted but the water contained salt. Animals that had previously been shocked showed a marked aversion to drinking in the presence of the light and clicker but they were quite happy to drink the salty water by itself. Conversely, the animals that had been made ill freely drank water accompanied by the light and clicker but rejected it when it was flavoured with salt.

This aversion to drinking on certain test trials is generally attributed to animals learning about the relationships between the stimuli and their consequences. What is important to note is that the ease of this learning depended critically on the combination of these events. Certain pairings resulted in poor learning (salt with shock, noise and light with illness), whereas others produced very good learning (salt with illness, noise and light with shock). Some explanations for these findings will be considered in Chapter 3; for the present the principal conclusion to be drawn is that it is impossible to say whether rats are good or bad at learning, because this depends critically on the way in which they are tested. This conclusion is also true for many other species, and we must accept that assessing the speed of learning is unlikely to yield an unambiguous indication of an animal's intelligence.

But these are not the only problems with using speed of learning as a measure of intelligence. The inherent differences between species makes it very hard to devise a task that poses exactly the same demands on them. For example, where a subject must learn to respond for food, the speed at which it does so is likely to be influenced by its perceptual, motivational, and motor processes. Bitterman (1965) refers to such factors as *contextual variables* and, as they will undoubtedly vary from one species to another, they may be responsible for any differences in learning that are exhibited. This point can be emphasised by reconsidering Angermeier's (1984) findings. He observed that rats learned more slowly than fish to perform a response for food. This might reflect the inferior learning ability of rats, but it could equally well be due to a more trivial factor—perhaps the reward given to the fish was more effective than that given to the rats, or perhaps the fish found it easier to locate the lever. Unless we can be certain that these and many other factors were equated, it would be unwise to draw any firm conclusions from Angermeier's (1984) study about the relative intelligence of the animals concerned.

In order to deal with this sort of problem, Bitterman (1965) suggested the use of a technique known as *systematic variation*. This method, in essence, involves training animals from different species on the same task across a wide range of conditions. These conditions might involve variations in reward size, in the level of deprivation, in the nature of the stimuli employed, and so on. If it could be shown that despite all these manipulations one species is uniformly better at learning than another, then it would suggest that this species is the more intelligent. In principle this method should be successful, but in practice it is extremely challenging to implement. Identifying the important procedural details of an experiment is not easy, and it is therefore difficult to be sure that the relevant manipulations have been conducted. In addition, there is the practical problem that this method dictates the use of a large number of subjects being run in many possibly time-consuming experiments. Few psychologists have either the facilities or the patience to pursue this approach to the study of animal intelligence.

One final reason for being wary of using learning as a means for assessing the intelligence of animals is that it may direct attention away from other important intellectual capacities. In addition to being able to learn, animals must be able to remember what they have learned until it is needed; they may also be capable of reasoning, of solving problems, and so on. These and other abilities should be regarded as attributes of intelligence, yet until recently they have received relatively little study. We now turn to an alternative view of animal intelligence, which takes account of such abilities.

Information processing

The study of human cognition is characterised by the way it regards people as if they were sophisticated processors of information. Throughout our lives we are surrounded by information about the environment in which we live. Not only does this information emanate from such artificial sources as books or the radio, it is also provided by our interaction with the natural world. This information is received by all the senses, and its reception is essential for our survival. Of paramount importance is the fact that we do not receive this information passively. Of all the information that is available, we attend selectively only to a portion, and that which gains our attention may then be transformed as it passes through a variety of stages. The information may be retained so that it can be recalled on some subsequent occasion, or it may be forgotten. It may be integrated with other information, or it may be stored as a relatively discrete unit. Alternatively, it may be used as a step in a complex reasoning process. Ultimately, after passing through these stages, the information may produce a response. Given such a framework, the task of the cognitive psychologist is to identify as precisely as possible the nature and properties of the various information-processing stages. There is no good reason for confining this approach to the study of humans. Animals, too, are surrounded by information that is relevant to their survival, and it is plausible that they also possess a variety of mechanisms for analysing and storing it.

From this perspective, then, intelligence is the processing of information, and one advantage of this definition is that it points to ways of comparing the intelligence of animals other than using the speed of learning. For example, we might compare animals on the basis of the different means they have at their disposal for processing information. In this case an all-or-none comparison can be used to evaluate animal intelligence, such that species can be compared on the basis of whether or not they possess a particular information-processing mechanism. An alternative would be to focus on a specific ability, such as memory, and compare the extent to which animals differ in this respect. Thus some species may be able to store more information for greater periods than others.

In the next section the methods of investigating the information processing of animals are discussed. The remaining chapters in the book are then concerned with describing ways in which animals process information.

METHODS FOR STUDYING ANIMAL INTELLIGENCE

Physiological techniques

Perhaps the most obvious method of studying the way in which animals process information is to investigate the nervous system directly. Accordingly for about a hundred years now, researchers have been trying to identify the role that the brain plays when animals are confronted with a variety of tests of learning, memory, and problem solving. Despite the many advances that have been made, there is still a great deal to learn before the relationship between animal intelligence and brain function is fully understood.

One line of enquiry has been to identify the changes that take place in the nervous system during relatively straightforward learning tasks (see Macphail, 1993, and Chapter 2). In general, experiments on this topic have been conducted with invertebrates because their relatively simple nervous systems are more tractable for physiological investigation than those of vertebrates. This research is based on the plausible assumption that the knowledge gained from studying simple nervous systems will prove invaluable in helping to unravel the secrets of the vastly more complex nervous systems of vertebrates. We should acknowledge, however, that a full understanding of the vertebrate nervous system will require it to be studied directly.

In fact, a substantial amount of work has already been conducted on the vertebrate nervous system. Kettner and Thompson (1982), for example, have investigated the electrical changes that take place in the cerebellum of the rabbit brain during a simple learning task known as classical or Pavlovian conditioning (see also Thompson, Berger, & Madden, 1983). Another line of enquiry has been to identify the various intellectual functions that are carried out by different regions of the brain. By damaging the relevant regions, or by recording the electrical activity within them, considerable gains have been made in this respect. A hint of the fruits of this research will be revealed in Chapter 8, where a region known as the hippocampus is shown to be involved in navigation. But progress has also been made with other intellectual skills. To cite a few examples, several different regions of the brain have been implicated in memory (see Macphail, 1993, for a review); damage to the hippocampus and amygdala alters the way in which animals are able to measure the passage of time (Olton, Meck, & Church, 1987); and such regions of the brain as the amygdala (Gallagher & Holland, 1994), the hippocampus (Kaye & Pearce, 1987), and the prefrontal lobes (Dias, Robbins, & Roberts, 1996), may serve to focus attention on stimuli that are important to the animal.

As might be expected, given the complexity of the vertebrate brain, these and many other findings are fraught with interpretative problems. For instance, the precise role that a given region plays in a particular task is far from being fully understood. Furthermore, very little is known about the changes that occur at a cellular level during any task with vertebrates, which would constitute a complete physiological under-standing of animal intelligence. Thus the use of physiological techniques will without doubt be of help in unravelling the mechanisms of vertebrate cognition, but it is likely to be many years before we have a complete understanding of the relationship between brain and intelligence.

The study of unobservable processes

One alternative to studying the nervous system directly is to assume that an animal's brain constructs a perceptual world that corresponds to its environment (cf. Jerison, 1973). This then implies that information processing by the brain can be regarded as two distinct but related processes. On the one hand there is the perceptual processing, in which information provided by the senses is integrated into units that correspond to features of the animal's environment. Very little is said about this type of perceptual processing in this book, not because the topic is unimportant, but simply because of limitations of space. The second type of processing concerns the manner in which the brain deals with the information in the perceptual world it has constructed. It is this type of processing that is the concern of this book.

Thus if an animal is presented with a tone that signals food, we shall ignore the processes underlying the perception of these events. It will be taken for granted that their perception takes place and results in the formation of internal, central representations of the tone and food. The main focus of concern will be with such issues as identifying what information is encoded in these representations and understanding the mechanisms that enable subjects to learn about the relationship between them. In a sense, then, a central representation of an environmental event constitutes an essential component of animal cognition. The task confronting a person interested in this topic is to show what these representations consist of and how they function in the higher mental processes.

The obvious problem in studying animal cognition from this perspective is that there is no direct way of observing a central representation. It is impossible to point to any feature of an animal and identify it as being a representation of food or any other event. Instead, the existence of such representations and their properties must be inferred, and for the present the animal's behaviour provides the only medium by which this can be achieved. Consequently, psychologists interested in animal cognition conduct experiments in which it is hoped that subjects act in such a way as to demonstrate unambiguously the existence and operation of a central, internal mental process. Not surprisingly, this approach is not without its pitfalls.

If the operation of a central process has to be inferred from an animal's behaviour, then different theorists may well appeal to different mental processes to explain the same activity. How is it possible to choose between a variety of accounts when they refer to events that are not open to direct observation? There are two answers to questions of this sort: The first concerns the nature of theorising in science, the second relates to the value of the experimental method.

Consider a simple experiment in which a tone repeatedly signals the presentation of food to a hungry dog. At first there will be little reaction to the tone, but eventually the dog will salivate whenever it hears this stimulus. One explanation for this effect is that the tone arouses a memory of food, which is responsible for salivation. Another explanation, couched in terms of stimulus–response theory to be considered shortly, is that this training results in the dog reflexively salivating during the tone without any knowledge of the food that will be presented shortly.

At a theoretical level it is possible to choose between these accounts by employing what is known as Lloyd Morgan's canon (Morgan, 1894, p.53):

> In no case may we interpret an action as the outcome of the exercise of a higher psychical faculty, if it can be interpreted as the outcome of one which stands lower in the psychological scale.

In other words, the best explanation is the one that refers to the simplest psychological mechanisms. On this basis the second of the two accounts is to be preferred, because it does not assert, as the former does, that animals possess memory processes.

The other method for choosing between different accounts is to use them to generate novel predictions and to evaluate these experimentally. The best account is likely to be the one that provides the most correctly fulfilled predictions. In Chapter 2, I show that the first explanation yields a novel prediction that is confirmed and that the second explanation generates predictions that are disconfirmed. For this reason the first explanation is the better of the two.

The purpose of this brief discussion is to explain the strategy of theorists and experimenters concerned with the study of animal intelligence. A variety of explanations may be developed for a single experimental finding. They will be presented in the simplest possible terms, with little reference to sophisticated theoretical constructs. To test the explanations, experiments are conducted, which ideally will confirm one and contradict the others. Gradually this process will yield a substantial body of experimental evidence that supports a particular theory and, at the same time, contradicts a number of others.

WHY STUDY ANIMAL COGNITION?

Intellectual curiosity

A major source of motivation for any scientific enterprise is the satisfaction of intellectual curiosity; the study of animal cognition is no different in this respect. As pets, as sources of food, or in the wild, animals often play a prominent role in our lives, and for this reason alone it is natural to wonder about their intelligence. This curiosity is enhanced by the occasional reports of apparently sophisticated intellectual skills being displayed by animals. At the turn of the century, there was considerable interest in a horse named Clever Hans, who, it was claimed, could count. More recently, television programmes have shown dolphins allegedly engaged in a complicated dialogue that enabled one to tell the other how to obtain food. There have also been claims that apes are capable of communicating with humans, and vice versa. Pigeons are said to be able to perform remarkable feats of navigation to return home from a distant and unfamiliar site of release; indeed, this topic has been the subject of correspondence to newspapers and popular scientific magazines (see pages 17 and 18). Reports such as these are bound to arouse in many a genuine curiosity concerning the intelligence of animals.

Curiosity about animal intelligence also arises from an interest in our own evolutionary history. The very name *Homo sapiens* (literally meaning "Man the Wise") implies that intelligence has played a critical role in this history, but it is not clear how. Once the intelligence of animals is better understood, we may have a clearer appreciation of the evolution of our own intelligence.

Relevance to other disciplines

In a book on human cognition, Anderson (1985) considered the success of the study of artificial intelligence (AI) to mimic human intelligence. He concluded (pp.2–3):

Despite the fact that this has been an active area of interest for more than 20 years, AI researchers still have no idea how to create a truly intelligent computer. No existing programs can recall facts, solve problems, reason, learn, or process language with anything approximating human facility. This failure has not occurred because computers are inferior to human brains but because we do not yet know how human intelligence is organised.

There can be little doubt that the intellectual processes of animals are less complicated than those of humans and should therefore be easier to understand. Despite the obvious differences between humans and animals, it is my belief that an accurate model of animal intelligence would provide a tremendous spur to its study in humans. It is not just their simplicity that makes animals attractive for study; their lack of a natural language (see Chapter 10) also makes them useful experimental subjects. To cite one example, the role that human language plays in problem solving is a matter of considerable debate. If it could be shown that animals possess sophisticated problem-solving skills without complex linguistic skills, then this would at least lend support to the view that human problem solving does not always depend on language.

One final point: The human brain is estimated to contain 100 billion cells, each of which is in contact with many others. It has already been

Quicker by Tube (a selection of letters and a cartoon from the *New Scientist*)

I travel regularly on the London underground from Paddington into the City. The other morning I was waiting at the platform, the train arrived and everyone got on as normal, except that on this occasion the passengers included a pigeon. The bird hopped on rather nonchalantly and began to peck around inside the carriage. True to form none of the other commuters seemed to notice.

The doors then shut and I expected the pigeon to panic, knowing how birds normally react to being in a small space. But this truly urban bird didn't appear to notice, even when the train moved off from the station. A few minutes later we arrived at the next stop. The doors opened and the pigeon hopped out quite calmly.

As the pigeon seemed so unconcerned I can only imagine that it had done this little journey before. With their renowned navigational abilities is it possible the pigeon knew where it was going? I'd be interested to know if any other readers have observed these avian fare-dodgers.

Rachel Robson
Bayswater, London

During 1974—76, I regularly encountered a single pigeon of light reddish colouring boarding the underground at Paddington and disembarking at the next station. Could it be the same bird that Robson saw — perhaps now having graduated to a senior citizen's pass? Or has the habit been passed on to the next generation. And if the latter, is there a genetic component in this?

Jim Brock
London

A pigeon, calm as you please, hopped into my Northern Line carriage at King's Cross and stood quite calmly near the door. The tourists did the cooing, not the pigeon; they thought it was an added London attraction and tried to tempt it with crisps, but unusually, the bird wasn't interested. It appeared to know where it was going and as soon as the doors opened at Euston, it flew out.

The second occasion was during a Piccadilly Line journey to Heathrow three weekends ago. This time the pigeon waddled in at an overground station, Hounslow Central. A bird-phobic passenger shooed it out, whereupon it repeatedly walked back in, to be hustled out again every time. The bird appeared quite determined to make its journey and when it was shooed out for a final time, just before the doors closed, it made one final frantic swoop towards the door, rather in the manner in which some human passengers launch themselves at tube doors just before they close.

From observing the birds, I feel quite sure that travel, not food, was their purpose. Pigeons are intelligent and easily trained and I see no reason why they should not have cottoned on to the fact that travel by tube saves their wings, especially as there are so many deformed and crippled pigeons in the city.

Lorna Read
London

Passenger Pigeons (a selection of letters to the *Times*)

From Lord Greenhill of Harrow

Sir

Mr Price's letter (September 10 draws attention to the intelligence of pigeons. My wife wrote similarly in your columns in December 1968, and received supporting evidence in letters from all over the world.

May I offer a further example? Some years ago I observed a flock of racing pigeons from Calais to Dover. At about mid-point a single pigeon at the rear detached itself from the flock and alighted on a lifeboat davit. It remained resting until shortly before Dover when it rejoined, no doubt considerably refreshed, its fellow competitors. I could think of no way of betraying its intelligent deceit.

Yours
GREENHILL *of* HARROW
House of Lords
September 10

From Vice-Admiral Sir Anthony Troup

Sir

I don't know about yachting pigeons (Michael Greville's letter of September 24) but I do know about submarine pigeons.

In 1948 I took three pigeons to sea in a submarine from Gosport as an experiment. Submerging in mid-channel for several hours and after turning many circles at depth, we surfaced and released them at thirty miles, well out of sight of land.

After release they circled the submarine three times and then flew straight home to Gosport

Yours faithfully
TONY TROUP
Bridge Gardens
Hungerford
Berkshire
September 25

From Mr Michael Greville

Sir

Until I read Lord Greenhill's observations in his letter to you today (September 17) on the apparently common tactics of racing pigeons, I had thought of my experience two years ago as unique.

I was sailing a 34ft yacht from Fecamp towards Beachy Head when, shortly after dropping the French coast, a number of these birds passed and one of them proceeded to join me on watch in the cockpit.

For six hours he kept me company, refusing all offers of hospitality (biscuits and beer) and declining to indulge in conversation, until he alighted from his perch, circled the mast head, presumably in appreciation, and flew off.

Within ten minutes the Royal Sovereign Tower was sighted, and soon Beachy Head itself.

I was most impressed by this display of constructive idleness and accurate dead reckoning to boot, but not so by the mess left on the tiller.

Yours faithfully
MICHAEL GREVILLE
79a Milson Road, W14

suggested that very little is known about the neural processes underlying animal cognition, and this is even more true of the way in which this complex collection of neurons and synapses controls the thoughts, actions, sensations, and experiences of humans. One approach to understanding the way in which the human brain functions is to study how this organ operates in animals. But unless brain researchers have a clear understanding of the cognitive processes of animals, the effects of their various experimental manipulations will be difficult to assess. In other words, it is essential to know *what* the animal brain is capable of achieving intellectually before it is possible to know at a physiological level *how* it is achieved. As this knowledge is acquired with animals, it is likely that considerable insights into the working of the human brain will follow.

HISTORICAL BACKGROUND

Animal intelligence has been studied in the laboratory for about a century. A good deal of the early work on this topic was directed towards understanding how animals learn about the consequences of their behaviour. An interest in other aspects of animal cognition developed more slowly, which was due in part to the early researchers being strongly opposed to the study of mental processes in all animals, including humans.

Thorndike (1874–1949)
Towards the end of the last century, investigators such as Romanes (1882) regarded animals as possessing the intelligence to solve a problem by reasoning. This claim was not based on careful experimentation but on anecdotal evidence—for example, of cats operating the latches on gates without apparent tuition. Thorndike reacted, quite correctly, to this theorising by arguing that it provided nothing more than a sloppy anthropomorphic projection of our own mental processes onto the animals in question. He therefore began his experiments in order to discredit the idea that animals are capable of reasoning. This research entailed the study of animals escaping from puzzle

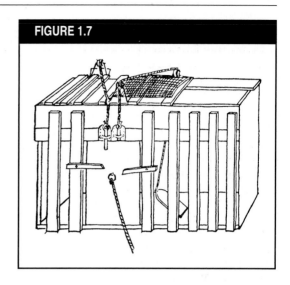

FIGURE 1.7

A sketch of a typical puzzle box used in experiments by Thorndike with cats (from Thorndike, 1898).

boxes, and the stimulus–response theory it led to was to exert a profound influence on the study of animal intelligence.

In a typical experiment, a cat was placed into a box with a bowl of food outside (see Figure 1.7). In order to reach the food, the cat had to respond in a specified way to open a door, perhaps by pulling a lever. Initially the cat would scratch and struggle in the box, and a considerable time elapsed before it responded correctly. Having made the response, the cat was allowed a few moments of access to food before being returned to the box for another trial. Thorndike's (1911) main concern was with the time it took the cat to escape from the apparatus across successive trials. The results from some typical studies are plotted in the learning curves in Figure 1.8. The vertical axis of each graph represents the time in seconds that a subject took to escape from the box on any trial. The horizontal axis represents successive trials. It is evident that the time, or latency, to escape decreased over trials. Thorndike (1911) regarded this change as evidence of learning, which raised two critically important issues: On the one hand, he was concerned with identifying what the subject had learned; and on the other, he wanted to specify as carefully as possible the conditions that promoted this learning.

Thorndike (1911) placed a great deal of emphasis on the fact that in general the decline in

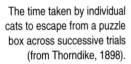

FIGURE 1.8

The time taken by individual cats to escape from a puzzle box across successive trials (from Thorndike, 1898).

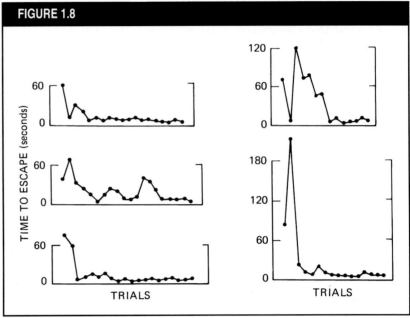

the latency to escape with continued training was gradual. This, he maintained, was clear evidence that animals did not use reason or thought to solve the problem. If these processes had been employed, then the learning curve should drop suddenly at the point where the correct solution occurred to the cat. Prior to this there should have been little improvement in performance, because the subject would be ignorant of the solution to the problem. Thorndike (1911) argued from his results that problem solving is achieved not by reasoning, but by a process of trial and error. That is, after being placed into the box, the subject eventually and quite by chance performed the correct response— perhaps by accidentally knocking the lever—and was able to escape. The subsequent decline in escape latencies was attributed to the food serving to stamp in or strengthen the correct response. This strengthening process was held to be gradual, which accounted for the progressive decline in latencies.

To say that Thorndike (1911) regarded the response itself as being strengthened is an oversimplification. In fact, he proposed that the food served to strengthen a hypothetical connection between, on the one hand, the neural centre responsible for the perception of the stimuli

that were present immediately prior to the execution of the response and, on the other, the centre responsible for the performance of the response itself. The greater the strength of this connection, or stimulus–response (S–R) association, the greater the likelihood of the animal responding correctly in the presence of the stimuli. These views were expressed as the Law of Effect (Thorndike, 1911, p.244):

> Of several responses made to the same situation, those which are accompanied or closely followed by satisfaction to the animal will, other things being equal, be more firmly connected with the situation.

This law summarises Thorndike's view of animal intelligence, and it is clear that he did not regard this capacity as involving sophisticated mental processes. The only reference to such processes is the proposal that learning consists of the gradual strengthening of a connection between neural centres concerned with the perception of a stimulus and the performance of a response. This approach is nowadays regarded as too simple, but at the time it was extremely influential and, together with the proposal that reward is essential for learning, set the stage for more than 50 years of vigorous research and theoretical debate.

The method employed by Thorndike to study animal intelligence is now referred to either as instrumental or as operant conditioning. It is characterised by the experimenter delivering an event such as food to an animal after it has responded in a certain way.

Pavlov (1849-1936)

At much the same time as Thorndike was conducting his studies, a Russian physiologist, Pavlov, was using a fundamentally different procedure to study learning in animals. Instead of waiting for his subjects to respond before delivering food, he delivered it independently of the animal's behaviour whenever a particular signal had just been presented. This procedure is now referred to as either Pavlovian or classical conditioning. The term "conditioned stimulus" (CS) refers to the signal and "unconditioned stimulus" (US) refers to the food or other biologically significant event that follows it.

The subjects in many of Pavlov's (1927) experiments were hungry dogs. They were lightly restrained in an experimental chamber, such as that depicted in Figure 1.9, and the CS—for example, the ticking of a metronome—was presented for a number of seconds before the delivery of the food US. At first the animal would show little reaction to the metronome, but as conditioning progressed, Pavlov (1927) noted that the dog salivated copiously during the CS even before the food was delivered. This response was defined as the conditioned response (CR). Because dogs do not normally salivate when they hear a metronome, such a change in behaviour can be regarded as evidence of learning.

Pavlov's (1927) account of what this learning actually consisted of was couched in neurological terms that are no longer popular. But he also provided a less physiological account, which said, in effect, that when two stimuli, such as a

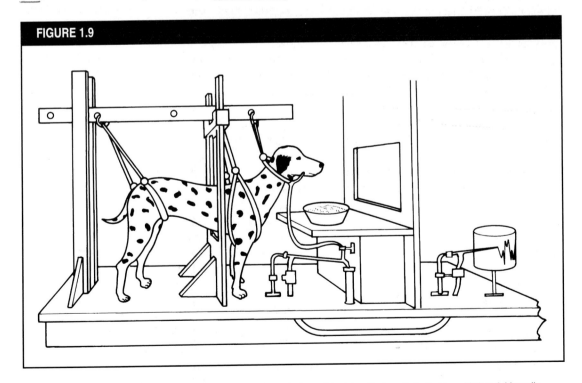

FIGURE 1.9

Diagram of the apparatus used by Pavlov for his study of classical conditioning with dogs (adapted from Yerkes & Morgulis, 1909).

metronome and food, were paired, the former came to be treated in some respects as if it were the latter. An alternative and far more influential account of the processes responsible for the appearance of the CR was provided by S–R theories of learning.

The S–R theorists

Following the publication of the work by Pavlov and Thorndike, a number of North American psychologists attempted to develop sophisticated accounts of behaviour from the premise that all learning involves the formation of stimulus–response connections. Thus despite the different methods involved in Pavlovian and instrumental conditioning, they were both assumed to result in the formation of Thorndike's S–R connections. As far as Pavlovian conditioning is concerned, these connections were held to be between a representation of the CS and a component of the response elicited by the US.

Hull (1884–1952).

A weakness of the Law of Effect is that it is vague in identifying the type of event that will strengthen an S–R connection. It merely states that satisfaction will result in the growth of a connection. But what constitutes satisfaction for an animal? Hull's (1943) answer to this question was to propose that satisfaction can be regarded as a reduction in any of the animal's needs. This led him to develop a version of S–R theory that placed considerable importance on the way needs influence both what the animal learns and what it does. Hull suggested that all needs activate a single central motivational state that he termed *drive*. An S–R connection was supposed to be strengthened whenever a response was followed by a reduction in the level of drive. Hence it was only responses that led to a reduction in a need that could be learned.

Although they provide a clearer specification than Thorndike of when learning will occur, there are still problems with Hull's proposals. For instance, Olds and Milner (1954) demonstrated that rats can be trained to press a lever if it results in the electrical stimulation of certain regions of the brain. The need that is reduced in these circumstances is hard to identify, yet learning has clearly occurred. A further property of drive is that

it can energise whatever response the animal is currently performing. If it is pressing a lever for food, then the hungrier the animal is, the greater will be the level of drive and the more rapidly will it respond. Although there is some evidence to support this prediction (see Bolles, 1975, p.95), there is much that contradicts other predictions from the theory. For example, the level of drive of an animal that is both hungry and thirsty will be greater than that of one that is just hungry. According to Hull's theory, therefore, being thirsty should enhance the rate at which an animal responds for food. In fact it is generally found that thirst has the opposite effect (e.g. Capaldi, Hovancik, & Lamb, 1975).

Guthrie (1886–1959).

One of Guthrie's (1935) main concerns was Thorndike's (1911) claim that reward, however it is defined, is essential for strengthening an S–R connection. As an alternative he made the simpler proposal that the mere pairing of a stimulus and a response is sufficient for learning to take place. Obviously when an animal is in a test chamber it makes a number of responses in addition to those that lead to reward, and it is necessary to explain why only the latter show a marked increase in frequency. Guthrie's (1935) solution to this problem was to suggest that a response will be connected to a set of stimuli only if it is the last one to occur in their presence. He further maintained that the delivery of reward will produce a marked environmental change, and this ensures that the instrumental response is connected to the stimuli that preceded its delivery. Support for this inter-pretation can be found in the surprising outcome of an experiment by Fowler and Miller (1963).

Hungry rats were trained to run down a straight alley for food. One group received only this treatment, whereas the others were given a mild shock to their feet as they were about to consume food in the goal box. For one group the shock was administered to the front paws, for the other group it was administered to the hind paws. The purpose of these different methods for delivering shock was to ensure that the shock induced different responses. When it was delivered to the front paws the rats lurched backwards, whereas they jumped forwards when the hind paws were shocked. Although the effect of such punishment in terms of the Law of Effect has not been considered, in keeping with common sense the law asserts that shock should disrupt running to the goal in both cases. In contrast, if Guthrie's (1935) claim is correct that the mere pairing of a stimulus and a response is sufficient to strengthen an S–R connection, then a different outcome is anticipated. While the rats are running down the alley for food, the lurch forward produced by shock to the hind paws will make them run faster. The pairing of this response with the apparatus cues will then strengthen an S (alley)–R (rapid running) connection, so that when placed into the alley subjects would be likely to run rapidly even before the shock is administered.

The results depicted in Figure 1.10 support this interpretation by showing that the group receiving the hind-paw shock actually ran faster down the alley than the group receiving only food in the goal box. The figure also shows that running, relative to the food-only group, was disrupted when the shock was administered to the front paws. In this instance the jerk backwards would be the response that became connected to the alley cues, and its performance prior to the shock should disrupt running.

These findings do not challenge Thorndike's claim that all learning consists of the formation of S–R connections. They do suggest, however, that reward or punishment is not essential for this learning to take place. In the aforementioned study it was found that the mere contiguity of the alley cues and the shock-elicited response was sufficient to influence what the rats learned. Many, more recent, studies also support this conclusion, and it is now accepted that reward, however it is defined, is by no means essential for learning to occur.

Tolman (1886-1959)

For Tolman, an essential feature of instrumental conditioning is that it results in behaviour that is goal-directed or purposive. If a rat has been trained to press a lever for food, then Tolman regards this response as being directed towards the goal of obtaining food. This seemingly obvious interpretation is completely lacking from S–R theory, which asserts that all an animal learns during instrumental conditioning is to respond in the presence of a given set of stimuli. It can even be said that because there is no mechanism in S–R theory that allows animals to anticipate the rewards of their behaviour, then whenever reward is delivered, it comes as a complete surprise.

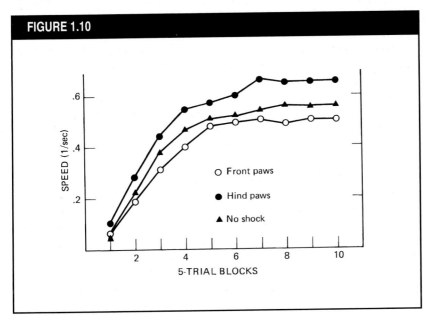

FIGURE 1.10

SPEED (1/sec) vs 5-TRIAL BLOCKS

- O Front paws
- ● Hind paws
- ▲ No shock

Speed of running down an alley for food by groups of rats that were shocked near the goal to either their front paws, or hind paws, or that received no shock in the alley (adapted from Fowler & Miller, 1963).

The S–R analysis of Pavlovian conditioning is similarly counterintuitive. When a CS and a US are repeatedly paired, the theory states that animals will learn to perform a response whenever the CS is presented. No additional learning is assumed that would enable the subject to expect, during the CS, the US that is soon to follow.

Tolman (1932) viewed these as grave shortcomings of animal learning theory and developed a purposive account of behaviour, which rejected the S–R connection as the unit of learning. As far as Pavlovian conditioning is concerned, animals were assumed to learn a CS–US connection that made the CS a sign for the forthcoming US. For instrumental conditioning, the fundamental unit of learning was a S–R–US connection. The initial S–R link in this chain is similar to its counterpart in S–R theory, but the additional, final link permits the animal to know the consequences of its actions while it is responding. The precise manner in which these units operated is not of present concern; what should be stressed is that Tolman's (1932) formulation is a radical departure from S–R theory because it enables animals to anticipate stimuli that will soon be presented to them. Thus animals can be regarded as acquiring knowledge rather than responses, and it is this that marks Tolman's approach as cognitive rather than behavioural.

Tolman (1932) also objected to the claim of S–R theory that reward is essential for learning. Instead, rather like Guthrie, he suggested that for both CS–US and S–R–US learning to take place, all that was necessary was the contiguous pairing of the appropriate stimuli and responses.

Animals were not regarded as passive learners simply acquiring a collection of CS–US and S–R–US units as they interacted with their environment. They were seen, in contrast, as active processors of information integrating previously gained knowledge, as the following quotation concerning the operation of the brain (central office) indicates (Tolman, 1948, p.192):

> We assert that the central office is far more like a map control room than it is like an old-fashioned telephone exchange. The stimuli which are allowed in are not connected by just one-to-one switches to the outgoing responses. Rather, the incoming impulses are usually worked over and elaborated in the central control room into a tentative cognitive-like map of the environment. And it is this tentative map, indicating routes and paths and environmental relationships, which finally determines what responses, if any, the animal will finally release.

This excerpt captures the essence of an extremely original view of animal intelligence that anticipated by 25 years or so contemporary accounts of information processing in animals. Thus there is now abundant evidence that Pavlovian conditioning can result in the formation of CS–US connections—or associations, as they are now referred to (see Chapter 2). There is also evidence that during instrumental conditioning animals learn about the relationship between responses and their consequences (see Chapter 4). The notion that animals form cognitive maps is also growing in popularity (see Chapter 8). During his lifetime, however, Tolman's critique and experiments led to the refinement and increasing complexity of S–R theory rather than to its downfall.

In concluding this brief history, it is worth stating that the demise of S–R theory was not brought about by its failure to explain effects with which it was principally concerned, namely, instrumental conditioning. Instead, the decline in popularity of this theory was brought about by a resurgence of interest in the 1960s and 1970s in the mechanisms of Pavlovian conditioning. It soon became apparent that attempts to explain all the effects obtained with this technique in terms of S–R learning would be unsuccessful. As a consequence, more cognitive explanations were developed to explain these findings, and this has been accompanied by a growth of interest in the cognitive mechanisms underlying behaviour in general.

NOTES

1. Protozoa are single-celled organisms of varying forms which exist wherever there is water. They are capable of performing a variety of behavioural and physiological functions. Coelenterates, of which examples are jellyfish and sea anemones, are invertebrates with a sacklike body and a single opening (mouth). They possess the most primitive functionally organised nervous systems in the animal kingdom.

2. One justification for this ratio is the assumption that body area is the major determinant for the amount of brain required for somatic processes. As the volume of an animal is related to the cube of its length, whereas its area is related to the square of its length, it follows that for larger animals the proportion of the brain required for somatic control is less than for smaller animals. The exponent 2/3 captures this relationship.

2

Associative Learning

Often in an animal's environment one event will reliably predict another. The ingestion of certain flavours will be followed by illness, whereas others will lead to beneficial consequences. Some environments will frequently be visited by predators, others will not. In addition, the action of the animal itself may result in consistent consequences: Following a certain route might take it to food or water, whereas different paths might lead to danger. Any animal that knows about these relationships will benefit because it will be able to anticipate future events and behave appropriately in preparation for them. But how can this knowledge be acquired? In an unchanging world animals could be born with it so that, for instance, the consumption of food of a certain flavour would automatically and consistently result in it being consumed or rejected. The world, however, is not unchanging. At the very least the location of food will change from generation to generation, and so too might the relationship between the taste or sight of food and its gastric consequences. Accordingly, animals must themselves discover which events reliably signal important consequences, and an important way of achieving this is by the process of associative learning.

Associative learning can be said to have taken place when there is a change in an animal's behaviour as a result of one event being paired with another. Two different methods that have proved

extremely useful for the study of associative learning were described in the historical survey at the end of the previous chapter. One method is exemplified by Pavlovian conditioning, where the two events that are paired together are a neutral conditioned stimulus (CS) and a biologically significant unconditioned stimulus (US). The other method is instrumental conditioning in which a response made by the animal constitutes one event, and the outcome of that response constitutes the second event. In this chapter, as well as the next one, we shall concentrate on what Pavlovian conditioning has revealed about the mechanisms of associative learning. We shall then turn to an examination of instrumental conditioning in Chapter 4.

At first sight there may seem to be little of interest in studying the process that enables a dog to salivate in the presence of a light paired with food, or a rabbit to blink whenever it hears a tone that signals a mild cheek shock. But once it is acknowledged that these conditioned responses (CRs) are a product of a process that is essential for learning about the sequential structure of the environment, then they become of fundamental importance. Their occurrence allows us to study in detail a fundamentally important learning process.

The first part of this chapter describes some basic conditioning techniques that have proved particularly useful for the study of associative learning. In most conditioning tasks the CS serves as a signal for the occurrence of the US, and this procedure is known as excitatory conditioning. But it is also possible for a CS to indicate the omission of a US, and here the term inhibitory conditioning is employed. Both excitatory and inhibitory conditioning are believed to be effective because they result in a relatively permanent change within the animal. In the second part of this chapter we shall look at what is known about the nature of this change. The third, and final, part of the chapter will consider the factors that determine how an animal will react to a CS that has been paired with a US.

CONDITIONING TECHNIQUES

Excitatory conditioning

Eye-blink conditioning. For eye-blink conditioning the subject, normally a rabbit, is restrained in a stock or harness, and a number of light-weight sensors are placed near its eye. Rabbits possess an outer and an inner eyelid, and this equipment can permit the recording of a small movement of either. Conditioning consists of the presentation of a relatively brief CS—say a 300-millisecond tone—followed by the delivery of a mild shock to the cheek. In most cases the intensity of the shock is just sufficient to produce a blink. After a number of CS–US pairings, the CS, which by itself should not make the rabbit blink, is often found to elicit this response. The results from a typical study are presented in the left-hand side of Figure 2.1, which shows the percentage of trials on which a blink was detected during the CS across successive blocks of 100 trials. The right-hand side depicts the effects of *extinction* in which the CS is presented but is no longer followed by shock. A term that is frequently used in discussions of learning curves is the *asymptote*, which refers to the top part of the curve that is flat and reflects a stable level of responding.

Moore (1972) describes an experiment in which rabbits first received conditioning in which a 1200Hz tone signalled the delivery of shock. Test trials were then given in which the same tone was

presented intermixed with tones of different frequencies. The results from these test trials can be seen in Figure 2.2. The percentage of trials on which a CR was recorded was maximal for the tone of 1200Hz, but when other tones were presented the likelihood of this response declined. Moreover, the extent of this decline was greater for stimuli that

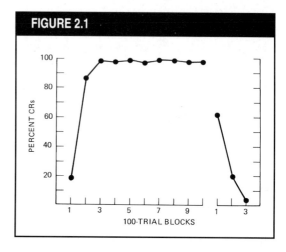

The acquisition and extinction of an eye-blink CR to a tone CS by rabbits (adapted from Gibbs, Latham, & Gormezano, 1978).

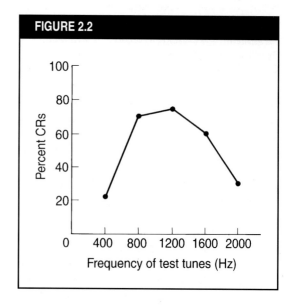

The strength of an eye-blink CR to tones of different frequencies after conditioning with a tone of 1200Hertz (adapted from Moore, 1972).

FIGURE 2.3

A typical conditioning chamber for pigeons containing three response keys.

were further removed from the training stimulus. The fact that responding occurs at all with conditions that differ from those present during training demonstrates *stimulus generalisation*, and when the extent of this generalisation is incomplete this is said to reflect *generalisation decrement*.

Autoshaping. With autoshaping, a hungry pigeon is placed in a conditioning chamber such as that depicted in Figure 2.3. At intervals of about 1 minute a response key is illuminated for about 5 seconds, and the offset of this stimulus is followed by the delivery of food to a hopper. At first subjects may be unresponsive to the key, but after a few trials they will peck it rapidly whenever it is illuminated. Note this is not an example of instrumental conditioning as the pigeon does not have to peck the key to obtain food. Instead, it is an example of Pavlovian conditioning as the mere pairing of the illuminated key with food is sufficient to engender a CR of key-pecking. A typical learning curve produced by this training is presented in Figure 2.4.

Conditioned suppression. In a procedure known either as conditioned suppression or conditioned emotional response (CER), subjects, very often rats, are first trained in an operant chamber in which they must press a lever in order to obtain food. Conditioning, which takes place in this chamber while the subject is pressing the lever, then consists of pairing a stimulus that lasts for

about 1 minute with a relatively mild shock delivered through the grid floor. There may be four such trials in each session, which itself may last for an hour or more.

When it is first presented, the signal for shock will have little influence on the rate of lever pressing. But as conditioning trials continue, so a gradual decline in the rate of responding will be

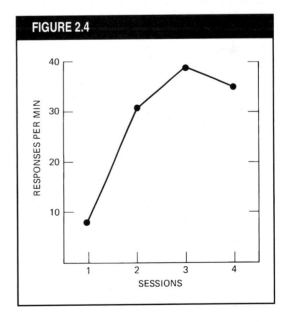

FIGURE 2.4

The rate of key-pecking by a group of pigeons for which the illumination of a response key by white light for 10 seconds signalled the delivery of food. There were 10 conditioning trials in each session (unpublished study by Pearce).

recorded until eventually the lever may not be pressed at all during the CS. As soon as the shock has been delivered, however, responding rapidly recovers to its normal rate and remains at this level until the next trial. It is important to be aware that the cessation of lever pressing has no influence on the outcome of the trial, so that shock is presented irrespective of the animal's behaviour. The decline in responding during the CS is regarded as evidence of successful Pavlovian conditioning.

The measure of conditioning is the extent to which the CS reduces the rate of lever pressing. The slower the response rate during the CS, the more effective conditioning is assumed to be. Because rats vary considerably in the rate at which they press a lever for food, it has not proved useful to look directly at the rate of responding during the CS as a measure of conditioning. Instead, a *suppression ratio* is computed according to the formula $a/(a + b)$. The value of a is determined by the rate of lever pressing during the CS, and b is the rate during a short interval immediately prior to CS onset. A ratio of 0.50 indicates that these rates are equal and that conditioning is ineffective, whereas a ratio of 0.00 shows that no responses at all were performed during the CS and that conditioning has been maximally effective. Figure 2.5 (left-hand side) presents the results from a

typical study in which the value of the average suppression ratio for a group of rats declines across successive trials. The right-hand side of this figure shows the effects of extinction, when the CS was no longer followed by the foot shock.

Taste-aversion conditioning.   The final example of a technique for Pavlovian conditioning was mentioned briefly in Chapter 1. If an animal is made ill after consuming a particular food, by being injected with a mild poison such as lithium chloride, it will develop a marked aversion to the flavour of that food. This technique has a number of characteristics that set it apart from many other methods of conditioning. It is often extremely effective with only a single trial, and very long intervals between the CS and the onset of illness can be employed with little detriment to learning. None the less, in most respects the effects of this procedure resemble those of other methods of conditioning, and for this reason it has proved an extremely useful tool for the study of the general principles of associative learning.

The need for control procedures

The examples reported earlier give some indication of the methods that can be used to engender a CR. In the introduction to this chapter, however, it was

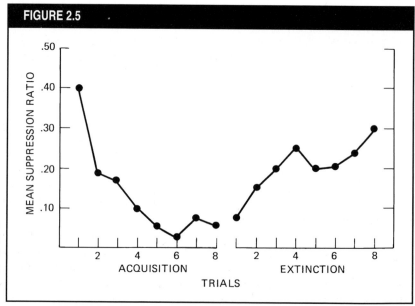

FIGURE 2.5

Acquisition and extinction of conditioned suppression by rats to a 60-second CS that was paired with foot shock (adapted from Hall & Pearce, 1979).

argued that our interest in Pavlovian conditioning lies not so much in the opportunity it offers for changing an animal's behaviour, rather this type of conditioning is important because it allows us to study the way in which animals learn about regularly occurring sequences of stimuli. Although the reported findings suggest this has taken place, there are a number of alternative accounts that must be discounted before we can conclude that a CR is a manifestation of associative learning. This point is made particularly forcefully in an experiment by Sheafor (1975). Two groups of thirsty rabbits received training in which they were presented with a brief tone and a squirt of water into the mouth. For Group T–W the tone preceded the water, whereas for Group T/W the tone and water were separated by an interval of 12 minutes.

The results from this study are presented in Figure 2.6, which shows, for each group, the percentage of trials with the tone that were accompanied by a movement of the jaw. For Group

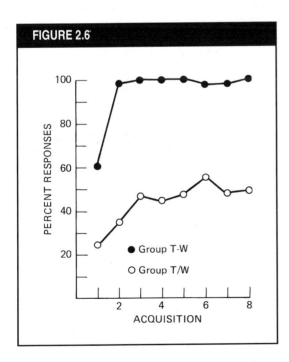

FIGURE 2.6

Percentage of trials on which a jaw movement was recorded in the presence of a tone, as a function of 6-day blocks, with 1 tone presentation each day. The tone was paired with water for Group T–W and unpaired with water for Group T/W (adapted from Sheafor, 1975).

T–W the frequency of this response increased to a substantial and consistent level across the first 48 sessions. As the tone preceded the delivery of water, this jaw movement could be regarded as a CR showing that subjects had detected the relationship between the two stimuli. From this point of view the results from Group T/W are surprising as the tone and water were unpaired and yet substantial jaw movement was also recorded during the tone.

The findings for Group T/W are worrying as they indicate that a response that can be considered to be a CR occurs to the tone, even when it is not paired with water. In these circumstances it would be unwise to regard the existence of jaw movement as evidence that rabbits had learned that the tone was a signal for water, and it becomes necessary to consider when a response can be safely used to indicate such learning.

One solution to this problem is to treat a control group in much the same way as Group T–W, by giving it the same exposure to the tone and water, but these events should not be consistently paired. If pairing the tone and water enables animals to learn that the tone is a signal for water, then such training should produce a stronger CR than for the control group. According to Rescorla (1967), a useful control treatment is to present the CS and US randomly in respect to one another; he referred to this as the truly random control. An alternative method, which was employed for Group T/W, is to ensure that the CS and US are never paired. The considerable level of responding by this group to the tone indicates that it would be unwise to attribute all the jaw movements elicited by this stimulus in Group T–W to associative learning. Nevertheless, the substantially greater level of responding by Group T–W than by Group T/W indicates that the pairing of the tone and water was responsible for at least some of the responding, and this is the necessary evidence to infer that associative learning has taken place.

There is insufficient space to speculate in depth on the reasons for the jaw movements during the tone in Group T/W, but it may be of some interest to consider Sheafor's (1975) explanation. He proposed that the experience of water in the test chambers resulted in rabbits persistently expecting this US. Normally, this expectancy does not result in a response, but one can be readily triggered if a relatively salient stimulus such as a tone is presented.

Whatever the merits of this account, the point to stress is that a response that resembles a CR does not only occur when a CS and US are paired. Occasionally, such a response may be observed when the CS is presented, either alone or unpaired in respect to the US. In view of this possibility the best way of being certain that a response is a consequence of associative learning is to compare the level of responding produced by a conditioning schedule with that engendered by the appropriate control. Unfortunately the use of control groups is time-consuming, and they are not always employed. Yet, without them, the conclusions that can be drawn from an experiment will be limited.

Inhibitory conditioning

Excitatory conditioning was said to be of interest because it allows us to study the way in which animals are able to learn that one stimulus signals another. But in an animal's environment, stimuli may conceivably signal that important events will not occur. Such stimuli are of potential importance because they might indicate places that are free from danger, or regions where food and water are not found. If Pavlovian conditioning allows animals to learn that one stimulus signals another, then we might also expect the appropriate training will allow them to learn the opposite—that one stimulus indicates another will not occur. Inhibitory conditioning refers to any method of training in which a stimulus is used specifically to signal the omission of a US and, as the next experiment shows, animals are quite capable of learning about the significance of such a stimulus.

Hearst and Franklin (1977) placed pigeons into a chamber containing a food hopper and two response keys. The keys were illuminated one at a time for 20 seconds in a random sequence, with an interval averaging 80 seconds between successive illuminations. During this interval food was occasionally delivered to the hopper, but food was never available when a key was lit. The position of the subject in the chamber was continuously

monitored throughout this training. At first, the pigeons were indifferent to the illuminated keys, but as training progressed they displayed a marked tendency to move away from a key whenever it was illuminated. This finding suggests that pigeons are capable of learning that stimuli signal the omission of food and that they may withdraw from such stimuli. One technique, therefore, for inhibitory conditioning is to ensure that the US is delivered in the absence but not the presence of the CS.

There were a number of groups in this study that differed in the frequency with which food was delivered during the inter-trial interval. When this frequency was relatively high, the movement away from the lit key was stronger than when food delivery was infrequent. This effect can be seen in Figure 2.7, which shows changes in a measure called an approach–withdrawal ratio across sessions for the groups. A ratio of 0.50 indicates that birds were unaffected by a lit key, whereas a ratio of 0.00 indicates a very strong movement away from this stimulus.

Needless to say the study of inhibitory conditioning did not start with the experiment by Hearst and Franklin (1977). Long before their

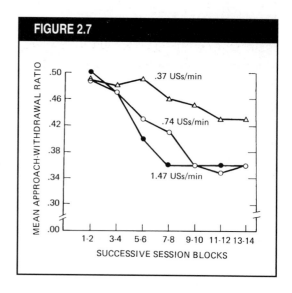

FIGURE 2.7

Mean approach–withdrawal ratio recorded in the presence of a 10-second key-light for groups of pigeons that received food at the rate of 0.33, 0.74, or 1.48 presentations per minute in the absence but not the presence of this stimulus (adapted from Hearst & Franklin, 1977).

study, Pavlov (1927) had devised an alternative method to study the effects of this type of training. An example of Pavlov's pioneering technique is provided by Zimmer-Hart and Rescorla (1974). In the first stage of the experiment a tone signalled shock for conditioned suppression training. Trials in which the tone was paired with shock were then intermixed among trials in which it was accompanied by a light and not followed by shock. Initially, the magnitude of conditioned suppression during the compound was much the same as that during the tone (see Figure 2.8), but as training progressed, the presence of the light on compound trials counteracted the suppressive effects of the tone. This pattern of responding suggests animals learned that the light signalled the omission of shock and that this opposed the properties of the tone.

The detection of conditioned inhibition

A problem that occurs in many studies of conditioned inhibition is that it is not immediately apparent that animals have learned anything about the conditioned inhibitor—that is, the stimulus that signals the omission of the US. This is because conditioned inhibitors rarely elicit a CR on their

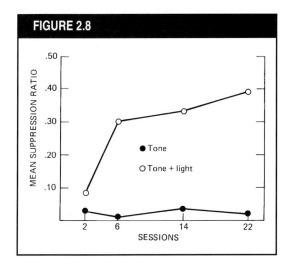

FIGURE 2.8

Mean suppression ratios for rats given excitatory conditioning with a tone intermixed among trials with a light–tone compound followed by nothing (adapted from Zimmer-Hart & Rescorla, 1974).

own. The study by Hearst and Franklin (1977) is unusual in this respect because their subjects moved away from the key light, but frequently a conditioned inhibitor by itself has no effect at all on behaviour. To return to the study by Zimmer-Hart and Rescorla (1974), had they presented the light alone rather than in compound with the tone, it would have had very little influence on the rate of lever pressing. How then can we be certain that animals have learned anything about this stimulus? One answer to this question, at least for the Zimmer-Hart and Rescorla (1974) study, would be to point to its effects on the compound trials. But on these trials it is possible that the subjects learned nothing about the light itself; they may merely have learned that the configuration of the light and tone together was followed by nothing. In order to refute this explanation, and to show that a conditioned inhibitor can have properties of its own, two techniques have been developed to reveal the existence of conditioned inhibition: the summation and the retardation test (Rescorla, 1969; Williams, Overmier, & LoLordo, 1992).

The retardation test. This test involves pairing the conditioned inhibitor directly with the US. If the initial inhibitory conditioning has been successful, then it should disrupt this excitatory conditioning. A formal explanation of this effect is elaborated in Chapter 3, but for the moment it should not be too surprising.

A demonstration of a successful retardation test is provided by Pearce, Nicholas, and Dickinson (1982). After receiving training similar to that employed by Zimmer-Hart and Rescorla (1974), Group E was given conditioned suppression training in which the inhibitory CS was paired with shock. Group C also received these pairings but without any prior training. The course of excitatory conditioning with the stimulus is depicted in Figure 2.9. Evidently the retardation test was successful because conditioning progressed more slowly for Group E than Group C. One important point to note is that on the first test trial the CS had no influence at all on responding in Group E. On this basis there would be little reason for believing that it had acquired any special properties as a result of the

FIGURE 2.9

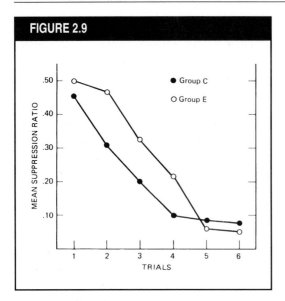

Acquisition of conditioned suppression to a CS that was novel (Group C) or one that had previously signalled the omission of shock (Group E) (adapted from Pearce et al., 1982).

prior training. This emphasises the need for special tests to reveal the effects of inhibitory conditioning.

The summation test. The experiment by Zimmer-Hart and Rescorla (1974) revealed that the light counteracted the CR elicited by the tone. This effect was attributed to the stimulus serving as a signal for the omission of the US. If this is correct, then this property of a conditioned inhibitor should be evident whenever it is accompanied by a CS that has been paired with the US in question. A demonstration of this transfer can be found in another conditioned suppression study by Pearce et al. (1982).

Rats were first trained with three types of trial: a tone paired with shock, a clicker paired with the same shock, and a clicker-light compound followed by nothing. Eventually a strong CR was observed in the presence of the tone and the clicker, but not during the clicker–light compound. In order to test whether the influence of the light on the clicker could transfer to the tone, a single test session was administered. Trials in which the tone

was presented alone were intermixed among trials with a light–tone compound. The results in the right-hand pair of histograms of Figure 2.10 show that the strength of the CR, as indexed by the suppression ratio, was substantially greater to the tone than to the compound. For purposes of comparison, the left-hand pair of histograms show the difference in responding to the clicker and the clicker–light compound for the final training session. Evidently the influence of the light transferred very well from the clicker to the tone, and this constitutes a successful summation test for conditioned inhibition.

For a variety of reasons Rescorla (1969) has argued that the ideal method for determining whether a stimulus is a conditioned inhibitor is to conduct both the retardation and the summation tests. If the stimulus passes both of these tests, then it can be concluded with some confidence that it is indeed a conditioned inhibitor.

FIGURE 2.10

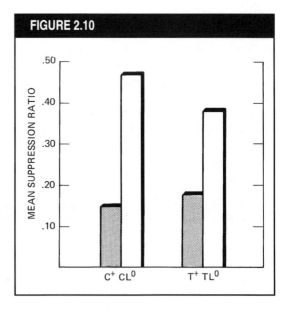

Mean suppression ratios on the final session of training for a group of rats that had received clicker–shock trials (C+) intermixed among trials in which a clicker–light compound was followed by nothing (CL⁰, left-hand pair of histograms), and on a test session when they were given a tone that had previously signalled shock (T+), and a compound composed of the tone and the light (TL⁰, right-hand pair of histograms) (adapted from Pearce et al., 1982).

THE NATURE OF ASSOCIATIVE LEARNING

Both excitatory and inhibitory conditioning can result in a relatively permanent change in the way an animal reacts to an initially neutral stimulus. In order to be effective, therefore, these procedures must produce an equally permanent change within the animal. The purpose of this section is to elucidate the nature of this change. Few would deny that successful conditioning depends on modifications that take place within the nervous system. In the first part of this section we consider briefly what is known about the physiological processes that underpin associative learning. In fact, rather little is known about these processes and a number of researchers have found it more useful to concentrate on identifying the knowledge that is acquired during the course of Pavlovian conditioning. The findings that have resulted from pursuing this line of enquiry are reviewed in the remainder of this section.

A neural model of excitatory learning

It may come as something of a surprise to discover that some of the more important advances in our understanding of the physiological basis of learning have derived from research with the rather unattractive animal shown in Figure 2.11 The figure shows two views of the large marine snail, *Aplysia californica* (the head is at the right-hand end). *Aplysia* live on seaweed, they weigh as much

as 7 kilograms, and they can grow to about 1 metre in length.

In case the reader should wonder why anyone would want to study conditioning in this creature, the answer lies in part in the structure of its nervous system. This contains a rather small number (20,000) of relatively large (1 millimetre in diameter) neurons, which makes it easy to identify individual neurons, as well as neural pathways. These properties have made it possible to understand the changes that take place in the nervous system of *Aplysia* during Pavlovian conditioning.

If a stimulus is applied to the siphon, or the mantle shelf, of an *Aplysia* it will withdraw its respiratory organ, the gill (Carew, Pinsker, & Kandel, 1972). Of present interest is the finding that the strength of the withdrawal reflex is enhanced if stimulation of either the siphon or the mantle shelf is followed by an electric shock to the tail. For example, Carew, Hawkins, and Kandel (1983) presented a discrimination in which mild stimulation of the siphon of some animals, or the gills of others, was followed immediately by a tail shock for 1 second. After 2.5 minutes, the other region was then stimulated but on this trial shock was not presented. For the sake of convenience, stimulation of the region that signalled shock will be referred to as CS+, whereas stimulation of the region that did not signal shock will be referred to as CS−.

The histograms in Figure 2.12 show the duration of gill withdrawal on a test trial with each

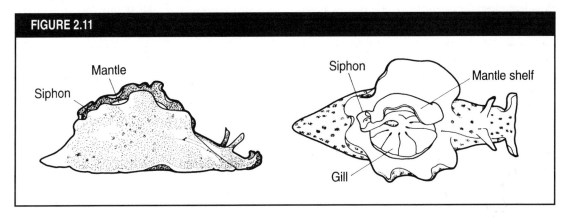

FIGURE 2.11

A view of *Aplysia californica* from the side (left-hand sketch) and from above (right-hand sketch).

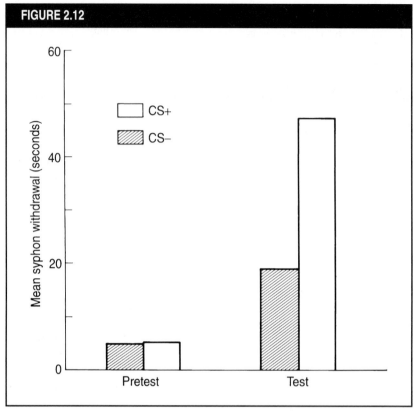

FIGURE 2.12

Mean duration of siphon withdrawal by *Aplysia* to a stimulus that was either paired with shock (CS+) or presented by itself (CS−) on test trials that were conducted before and after conditioning (adapted from Macphail, 1993).

CS prior to conditioning and on a test trial after conditioning. Shock was not presented on these test trials. At first, both CS+ and CS− elicited gill withdrawal for about 5 seconds, but at the end of conditioning this response was considerably stronger in the presence of CS+. The slight increase in responding that occurred to CS− indicates that even the unpaired experience of this stimulus and the tail shock was sufficient to enhance the strength of the response elicited by CS−. However, the fact that the strength of responding to CS+ was very much greater than to CS− demonstrates the importance of the paired relationship between CS+ and the tail shock. In other words, the stronger responding to CS+ than to CS− provides a convincing demonstration of successful Pavlovian conditioning with *Aplysia*. In one respect, this demonstration of Pavlovian conditioning is unusual because it shows a strengthening of a response that was already elicited by the CS. This type of conditioning is referred to as *alpha* conditioning, which can be contrasted with the

findings from many other studies where at least a component of the CR bears no resemblance to the responses initially elicited by the CS.

A sketch of one of the neural pathways that are involved in the conditioning that has just been described is shown in Figure 2.13 (Kandel & Hawkins, 1992). The two sensory neurons can be excited by stimulating the siphon (upper neuron) or the mantle shelf (lower neuron). These neurons make synaptic contact with a motor neuron that is responsible for gill withdrawal. Thus in normal circumstances, stimulating the siphon area will excite a sensory neuron that will then excite the motor neuron and cause the gill to withdraw. The figure also shows a third sensory neuron that can be excited by a shock to the tail. This neuron is in synaptic contact with a modulatory interneuron that in turn makes contact with synapses of the other sensory neurons. Needless to say, this sketch is a gross oversimplification of the actual circuitry as each neuron is in contact with many other neurons.

In order to identify the changes that take place in this circuit during conditioning, Hawkins et al. (1983) capitalised on the large size of the neurons, and placed stimulating electrodes in a sensory

neuron for the siphon area and for the mantle shelf. Stimulation of a sensory neuron for the siphon (CS+) was followed immediately by a tail shock, whereas stimulation of a sensory neuron for the mantle shelf (CS−) was never followed by shock. In addition, a recording electrode was placed in a motor neuron that was in contact with the two selected sensory neurons. The level of activity in the motor neuron was recorded after CS+ and CS− on a pretest trial, that was conducted prior to conditioning, and on a test trial that was conducted after five conditioning trials with each stimulus. The results from the tests, expressed as a percentage of the activity recorded on the pretest trials are shown in Figure 2.14. The figure makes it clear that conditioning enabled CS+ to increase considerably the level of electrical activity in the motor neuron, whereas CS− had little effect on the activity in this neuron.

In essence, this experiment by Hawkins et al. (1983) demonstrates that when the stimulation of one sensory neuron is followed a short time later by a tail shock, then its ability to excite the motor neuron is increased. Kandel and Hawkins (1992) have argued that this enhanced influence of the sensory neuron is due to biochemical changes that

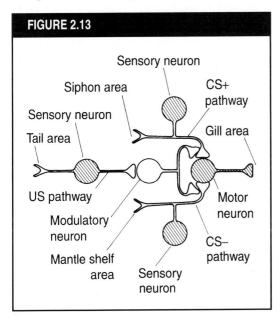

FIGURE 2.13

A simplified diagram of the neural pathways that are involved in conditioning with *Aplysia*.

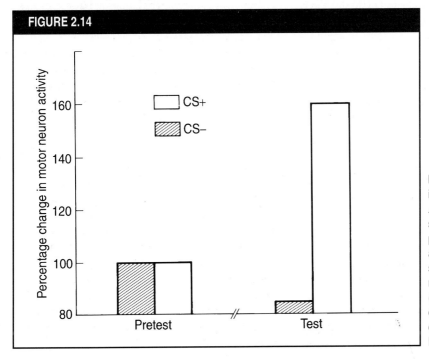

FIGURE 2.14

Mean percentage of change in motor neuron activity in *Aplysia* to stimulation of one sensory neuron that was paired with tail shock (CS+) and to stimulation of another sensory neuron that was never followed by shock (CS−), on test trials that were conducted before and after conditioning (adapted from Macphail, 1993).

take place at the synapse between the sensory and motor neuron. The catalyst for these changes is provided by the interneuron. Whenever shock is administered to the tail, the interneuron releases serotonin at its synapses with sensory neurons. If a sensory neuron should fire at much the same time as this release of serotonin, then a relatively permanent change takes place within the sensory neuron that enables it to release a greater amount of neurotransmitter than would normally occur. Subsequent stimulation of the sensory neuron will then release this abnormally large amount of neurotransmitter and result in a strong response in the motor neuron.

Thus the basis of associative learning appears to be an enhancement of the ease with which one neuron can excite another. There is no evidence to suggest that this learning depends on the growth of new neural connections, or synapses. Instead, learning simply depends on a change in the effectiveness of existing connections. We shall see over the course of the next few chapters that this finding is remarkably in keeping with current theoretical views about learning.

Stimulus generalisation can also be explained with the sort of circuit that Kandel has identified. Instead of exciting a single sensory neuron, a CS is likely to excite a collection of sensory neurons each of which could acquire the capacity to excite a motor neuron. The strength of the response to a CS would then be determined by the number of motor neurons it excites. The presentation of a slightly different CS will excite some, but not all, of the sensory neurons excited by the original CS. The new CS will thus elicit a CR, and provide evidence of stimulus generalisation; but the strength of the CR will be weaker than to the original CS. If it is assumed that the degree of similarity between two stimuli determines the number of sensory neurons that they both excite, then this account correctly predicts that the amount of stimulus generalisation will be determined by the similarity of the test and training stimuli.

A memory model for associative learning

Because the nervous system of vertebrates is very much more complex than of invertebrates, we do not yet know if the physiological changes that have

just been described also underlie associative learning in this group of animals. As a consequence, theorists with an interest in the changes responsible for learning in vertebrates tend not to talk in terms of physiological processes. Instead, they prefer to work within the framework provided by an information-processing model of conditioning. An example of such a model is shown in Figure 2.15.

Stimuli such as a CS or a US can be detected by a sensory register that excites a memory or representation of these events in a memory system. The US will in addition excite a centre in a system concerned with response generation and thus elicit an unconditioned response. As a result of the repeated pairing of a CS and a US, there are two possible changes that can take place within this model. On the one hand, a CS–R connection might develop, so that whenever the CS is presented it will directly excite the US-response centre and lead to a response that mimics the one elicited by the US. In other words, this conceptualisation is based on the assumption that Pavlovian conditioning results in the growth of S–R connections, or associations. These proposals are very much in keeping with the way in which the S–R theorists mentioned in Chapter 1 conceptualised the conditioning process. They are also consistent with the findings by Kandel with *Aplysia*. The sensory and motor neurons in these animals can be said to provide a rudimentary counterpart to the stimulus and response centres shown in Figure 2.15.

Alternatively, Pavlovian conditioning could result in the growth of a connection between the CS and US representations. Subsequent presentations of the CS will then excite the representation of the US, and this in turn will excite a response. Although the findings with *Aplysia* do not support this possibility, experiments with vertebrates lend it considerable support.

The idea that the CS retrieves a memory of the US, which is then responsible for generating the CR, can be tested in a relatively straightforward manner. If the memory of the US can somehow be altered once conditioning has been completed, then this should result in a change in the animal's behaviour when the CS is next presented. That is, the CS should elicit a response that is appropriate to the revised memory of the US. A good example

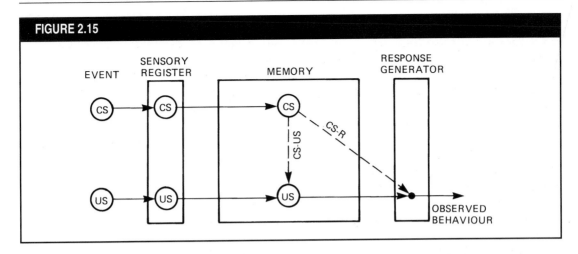

FIGURE 2.15

Two possible accounts of what is learned during Pavlovian conditioning; the solid arrows are permanent connections, the dashed arrows are a consequence of conditioning. A CS and US can be detected by the sensory register, which leads to representations of these events being activated in memory. Whenever the US representation is activated it will produce a response by activating a centre in the system concerned with response generation. According to one account, conditioning will result in the growth of a CS–US association so that the CR will be an indirect consequence of the CS activating the US representation. The alternative S–R account assumes that conditioning strengthens a CS–R association and thus allows the CS to excite the CR directly.

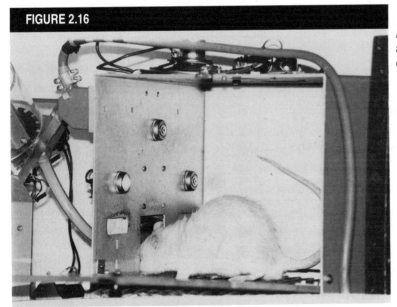

FIGURE 2.16

A typical CR of magazine activity by a rat during a CS that signals the delivery of food (from Kaye, 1983).

of an experiment that is based on this rationale is provided by Holland and Straub (1979).

Two groups of hungry rats were occasionally presented with a 10-second noise that was followed by the delivery of food in a conditioning chamber. After a number of sessions of this training the noise resulted in subjects moving towards the magazine where food was delivered (see Figure 2.16 and the left-hand side of Figure 2.17). On each of the next four days, in which noise was not presented, rats in Group E (experimental) were allowed unrestricted access to food pellets for 5 minutes in their home cages before being injected with lithium chloride to condition an aversion to the pellets. This

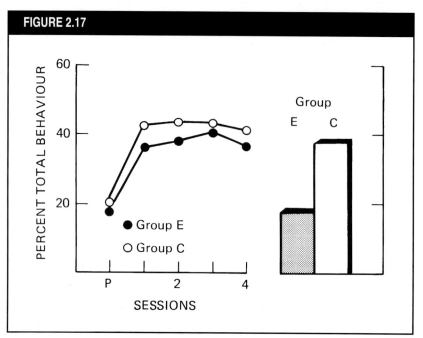

FIGURE 2.17

The amount of magazine activity by two groups of rats during a noise CS on a pre-exposure session (P), when it was presented alone, and on four conditioning sessions when it signalled food (left-hand side). The histograms show the amount of magazine activity during the noise for a test session after the food pellets had been paired with illness for Group E, but not Group C (adapted from Holland & Straub, 1979).

conditioning was successful because on the fourth session subjects consumed very few of the pellets. The treatment for Group C (control) was similar except that the lithium chloride injections and free access to food were presented on separate days so that the liking for the pellets was unaffected. Finally, both groups were returned to the conditioning chambers where the noise was again presented but this time without food. As revealed in the right-hand side of Figure 2.17, the tendency of Group E to approach the magazine on the test session was considerably less than for Group C.

These results are entirely consistent with the proposal that Pavlovian conditioning results in the growth of CS–US associations. On the test session, the noise for Group E will activate a representation of food that has been rendered unattractive by the taste-aversion training. The activation of this representation will then be unlikely to excite magazine activity, because there is little point in moving to a magazine for food that is undesirable. For Group C, on the other hand, the representation of food should be just as effective as on the final session of appetitive conditioning, and these rats should be very willing to go to the magazine during the noise.

We should also consider the implications of these results for an S–R analysis of conditioning. According to this theory, the initial training will result in an association being formed between the tone and the response of approaching food, so that whenever the CS was presented it will automatically make the animal move towards the magazine. An important feature of S–R theory is that the responses elicited by a CS can be altered only by pairing the CS with an event that elicits a different response. Because the CS was not presented in the second stage of the experiment, there was no opportunity for its influence to be altered in one group, but not the other, and both groups should thus have responded similarly in the test stage. The clear difference between the results of the two groups in the final stage of the experiment is thus very difficult for S–R theory to explain. There was, however, some responding on the test trials by Group E, which is difficult to explain if Pavlovian conditioning results only in the formation of CS–US associations. Strictly speaking, if the taste-aversion training was completely effective, then the rats should make no effort at all to approach the magazine in the test stage. Perhaps, therefore, the responses on the test trials in Group E were a consequence of S–R associations that were formed during the initial training. If this is correct, then we must conclude that the training by Holland and Straub (1979) resulted in both S–R and CS–US learning. Further evidence is presented shortly that shows that Pavlovian conditioning will, at least on occasion, permit the growth of S–R associations. But first, we shall examine two further studies that demonstrate that this training can also foster CS–US associations.

Table 2.1 summarises the design of an ingenious experiment by Holland (1990). Hungry rats in a conditioning chamber occasionally heard either a tone or white noise for 10 seconds. The tone signalled the delivery of sucrose solution flavoured with wintergreen, and the noise signalled a similar solution flavoured with peppermint. As a result of this training, Holland (1990) hoped that the rats would anticipate wintergreen-flavoured sucrose whenever they heard the tone, and peppermint-flavoured sucrose whenever they heard the noise. The rats were then allowed to drink sucrose flavoured with wintergreen for 5 minutes, in the absence of any auditory stimulus, before being injected with the poison lithium chloride. The purpose of this treatment was to condition an aversion to the flavour of wintergreen. Finally, the animals were allowed to consume plain sucrose solution in the presence of each auditory stimulus. By carefully observing the animals, Holland discovered that they reacted very differently in the presence of the two stimuli. During the noise the rats showed a typical ingestive reaction, comprising rhythmic mouth movements, tongue protrusions, and paw licking. On the other hand, in the presence of the tone they showed a marked aversive reaction, which consisted of gaping, chin rubbing, head shaking, and flailing of the forelimbs. Holland argued that this second response was due the tone retrieving a memory of the wintergreen-flavoured sucrose. The rats then reacted as if this flavour, which had been made aversive by the second stage of training, were actually present. Holland (1990) cites a number of additional findings that lend considerable support to this conclusion.

These last results imply that activating a memory of a stimulus is in many respects equivalent to presenting the stimulus itself. If this is correct, then it should be possible to conduct conditioning with an activated memory of a stimulus in much the same way as it is possible to conduct conditioning with that stimulus. A remarkable experiment by Holland (1981) provides striking support for this prediction. Two groups of rats were first placed into a conditioning chamber where every few minutes a tone was presented for 10 seconds and then followed immediately by a distinctively flavoured food pellet. In the next stage of the experiment both groups again received the tone but this time it was not followed by food. For the experimental group the tone was followed by an injection of lithium chloride, whereas for the control group these two events were presented in an unpaired fashion. Holland argued that during the second stage the tone should activate a memory of flavoured food with which it had been paired and, for the experimental group, once activated this memory would then become associated with the poison. A test of this proposal was conducted in a final session in which both groups had free access to the food. In keeping with Holland's predictions, the experimental rats revealed an acquired aversion to the food by eating rather little of it, relative to controls.

TABLE 2.1

Summary of the Design of an Experiment by Holland (1990).

Stage 1	Stage 2	Test
Tone → Sucrose + Wintergreen Noise → Sucrose + Peppermint	Sucrose + Wintergreen → LiCL	Tone + Plain Sucrose Noise + Plain Sucrose

STIMULUS–STIMULUS LEARNING

The results in the previous section show that, at least for vertebrates, Pavlovian conditioning may result in the growth of a connection between internal representations of the CS and US. There is no good reason, however, for believing that associative learning will be confined to those occasions when a US is presented. The following examples show that associations can develop between two stimuli, even when neither of them has any unconditioned properties.

Serial conditioning

In serial conditioning a sequence of stimuli precedes the US—for example, a tone might be followed by a light, which would be followed by food. Despite being rather distant from the US, the initial element of the sequence will often elicit a CR, although it may be weaker than the response observed in the presence of the element that is closer to the US. An interesting feature of serial conditioning is revealed in a study by Holland and Ross (1981), who trained rats with the sequence light–tone–food. The normal conditioned response to a light that signals food is rearing or magazine approach; for a tone it is either head jerking or magazine approach. After a number of sessions of serial conditioning it was found that during the light there was little magazine activity but there was a considerable amount of head jerking. This led Holland and Ross (1981) to suggest that during serial conditioning the presence of the first element causes animals to anticipate the second one and to respond as if it were actually present.

Sensory preconditioning

A rather different demonstration for the development of stimulus–stimulus associations is provided by sensory preconditioning. In an experiment by Rizley and Rescorla (1972), rats first received the sequence of a light followed by a tone for a number of trials. The tone was then paired with shock and, finally, the light was found to elicit a substantial fear CR when it was presented for testing. The generally accepted explanation for this finding is that during the first stage subjects acquired a light–tone association, and in the second stage a tone–shock association. When the light was then presented alone it would activate a memory of the tone, which, in turn, would activate a memory of the shock and lead to an aversive CR.

Second-order conditioning

The final method that shows evidence of associations being formed between two stimuli is known as second-order, or higher-order conditioning. We shall see, however, that depending on certain details this training can result in different outcomes.

Two types of conditioning trial are administered for second-order conditioning. Initially, first-order conditioning is conducted in which a neutral stimulus, CS1, is paired with a US until a stable CR is recorded. At this point additional trials are introduced in which a new stimulus, CS2, precedes CS1, but the US is omitted. With sufficient training a CR can be observed during CS2 even though this stimulus itself is never paired with the US.

Pavlov (1927) was the first to report this effect, although a relatively recent example will be described (Rashotte, Griffin, & Sisk, 1977). Pigeons first received autoshaping in which the illumination of a key by white light for 6 seconds signalled food; additional trials were then introduced in which the key was illuminated by blue and then white light, for 6 seconds of each colour. Food was not presented on these second-order trials. Figure 2.18 shows, for the second-order conditioning stage, the percentage of trials in any session on which at least one peck was directed towards these stimuli. The success of second-order conditioning is revealed by the increase in responding to CS2.

If second-order conditioning results in the formation of the same sort of associations as first-order conditioning, then pairing a second-order CS (CS2), with one that has already been paired with a US (CS1) should foster a CS2–CS1 association. As a consequence, the occurrence of CS2 should activate a representation of CS1, which should then activate a representation of the US and elicit a CR. There is certainly some evidence to support this proposal, but there is also some that contradicts it.

Evidence that favours this analysis can be found in a further stage of the study by Rashotte et al. (1977). An outline of the various stages of the experiment can be found in the upper half of Table 2.2. After second-order conditioning, Rashotte et al. (1977) gave Group E a series of extinction trials in which the white key-light (CS1) was presented

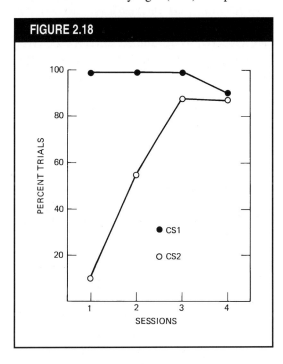

FIGURE 2.18

Number of trials in each second-order conditioning session for which at least one peck was recorded to the previously trained white CS1 and to the second-order blue CS2 (adapted from Rashotte et al., 1977).

alone. This training was intended to abolish its association with food, and it was soon found that pecking at the white key declined to a very low level. When the blue key-light (CS2) was again shown for the final test trials, it should still activate a representation of the white key, by virtue of the prior second-order conditioning. However, activation of this latter representation should no longer excite a memory of food, and pecking at blue should not take place. For Group C, which did not receive the extinction training with white, the presence of both an effective blue–white and a white–food association should allow blue to activate a representation of the food and engender a high rate of responding. In keeping with this analysis it was found on the test session that Group C responded significantly more rapidly than Group E in the presence of CS2.

Evidence to the contrary, that second-order conditioning does not enable CS2 to retrieve information about CS1, is provided by Rizley and Rescorla (1972). The design of their experiment is very similar to that of Rashotte et al. (1977) and is presented in the lower half of Table 2.2. The methods differed principally in that Rizley and Rescorla (1972) used conditioned suppression. Two groups of rats received first-order conditioning with a tone signalling shock, and second-order conditioning in which a light was followed by the tone and no shock. Group E was then given extinction training with the tone. Although this treatment abolished the CR to the tone, the subsequent presentation of the

TABLE 2.2

Summary of the Stimuli Used in the Stages of the Second-order Conditioning Studies by Rashotte et al.[a] and by Rizley and Rescorla[b].

	First-order conditioning	Second-order conditioning	Extinction	Test
Group E	White → Food	Blue → White	White	Blue
Group C	White → Food	Blue → White	—	Blue
Group E	Tone → Shock	Light → Tone	Tone	Light
Group C	Tone → Shock	Light → Tone	—	Light

[a] Rashotte et al. (1977): upper two rows.
[b] Rizley and Rescorla (1972): lower two rows.

second-order light CS elicited a very strong CR, which did not differ in magnitude from that performed by Group C. This finding makes it difficult to believe that a light–tone association was formed during second-order conditioning, for if it had been, extinction with the tone should have reduced the CR recorded during the light. Moreover, this outcome is not unique: Holland and Rescorla (1975) have obtained a similar effect with rats using appetitive conditioning.

One explanation for the findings by Rizley and Rescorla (1972) is that second-order conditioning resulted in an S–R association being formed between CS2 and the response elicited by CS1. Thus as a result of the first-order conditioning the tone may have aroused a CR of fear, for want of a better word, which was associated directly with the light. If this account is correct, then manipulations of the tone–shock association should not influence the light–fear association and hence leave unaffected the prior second-order conditioning.

What then determines the nature of the associations that are formed during second-order conditioning? According to Rescorla (1980), one answer to this question is the similarity of CS1 and CS2. When the stimuli are similar, such as the illumination of a key by different colours, then a CS2–CS1 association will be formed. When the stimuli are very different, for example if they are from different modalities, then CS2 will become associated with the response elicited by CS1. Of course, this account is incomplete. It does not explain why stimulus similarity should be so important in determining the outcome of second-order conditioning. And as it stands, it leads to the incorrect expectation that first-order conditioning will only permit S–R associations because the CS and US are so different.

THE NATURE OF US REPRESENTATIONS

Conditioned excitation

Thus far we have said that the CS is able to activate a memory or representation of the US, but what does this mean as far as animals are concerned? I do not wish to imply for one moment that when the

CS is presented to a rat it has a mental experience of remembering the US in much the same way as we may remember what we ate for our last meal. There are simply no methods that would allow us to determine whether or not animals have this type of mental experience. Holland (1990) favours the proposal that after conditioning, the CS is able to activate some of the perceptual mechanisms that are normally activated by the US. A similar idea has been proposed to account for certain aspects of human memory (e.g. Farah, 1985; Finke, 1980). One implication of this proposal is that whenever a CS is presented it will evoke a sort of hallucination of the US with which it is paired (Konorski, 1967). Whether or not this is true remains to be determined, for the present it is safe to conclude that at least in some circumstances a CS can activate, or retrieve, information about the US. All this means is that once information about the US is activated it can influence the animal's behaviour, and enable further learning about the US even though it is absent.

Given such a conclusion, it then becomes meaningful to enquire about the nature of the information that is activated. According to Konorski (1967), unconditioned stimuli possess two different characteristics—specific and affective. Specific characteristics are those that make the US unique: the place where it is delivered, its duration, intensity, and so on. Affective characteristics, by contrast, are those that the US has in common with other stimuli and reflect its motivational quality. Thus food, water, and an opportunity to mate have the common *appetitive* characteristic that animals will actively search for them. Conversely, electric shock, illness, and loud noise possess the common *aversive* characteristic that animals will do their best to minimise their contact with them. For humans, this distinction can be summarised by saying that appetitive events arouse a state of satisfaction, whereas aversive events arouse an unpleasant state of discomfort or pain.

Konorski (1967) suspected that a CS may be capable of retrieving information about the specific or about the affective attributes of the US, or indeed about both simultaneously. We can return to the study by Holland (1990) for evidence that a CS can retrieve information about the specific attributes of the US. In that study, he found that pairing wintergreen-flavoured solution with illness affected the responses during a tone that had been paired with the same flavoured solution, but not during a noise that had been paired with a peppermint-flavoured solution. Unless the noise and tone could retrieve specific information about the flavours of the solutions with which they had been paired, they should both have elicited the same responses on the test trials.

For evidence that a CS is capable of retrieving information about the affective characteristics of a US, we must consider the effects of an experimental manipulation known as blocking. In the first stage of an experiment by Kamin (1969) Group E, but not Group C, was given pairings of a noise with shock. For the second stage both groups received a compound composed of the noise and a light that was repeatedly paired with shock. Finally, test trials involving the light by itself were given. On the test trials with the light there was virtually no evidence of a CR in Group E, whereas one of considerable strength was recorded for Group C. For Group E, therefore, the original training with the noise was somehow responsible for preventing, or blocking, learning about the light during compound conditioning.

The reason why blocking occurs will be considered in some detail in the next chapter. For the present, it is important to note that blocking can be disrupted if the US is changed for the second stage of training. Thus Dickinson (1977) has found that blocking does not occur if the US is food in Stage 1 and shock in Stage 2. This type of finding has led to the informal suggestion that blocking will be most effective when the US that is delivered in Stage 2 corresponds to the memory of the US that was presented in Stage 1. But should this correspondence be between the affective or the specific properties of the US? This question is impossible to answer on the basis of the study by Dickinson, because both properties were changed. However, an experiment by Ganesan and Pearce (1988) found blocking was not at all disrupted when the US was changed from water in Stage 1 to food in Stage 2. Such a finding suggests that blocking will be effective, provided that the

general, affective properties of the US remain unchanged throughout the training stages of experiment. In other words, for blocking to have taken place in the study by Ganesan and Pearce (1988), the CS presented in Stage 1 must have become associated with a memory of the nonspecific, appetitive attributes of the water US. For a similar finding see Williams (1994).

A second reason for believing that a CS can activate an affective representation of the US comes from studies showing that conditioning can sometimes be facilitated if the CS has previously been paired with a different US of related affective value. Pearce, Montgomery, and Dickinson (1981), for instance, conducted rabbit eye-blink conditioning in which, for Group E, a brief light signalled shock to the cheek; Group C did not receive this training. Then, in the test phase of the experiment, both groups were conditioned with the light signalling shock to the opposite cheek. Acquisition of an eye-blink CR in these circumstances was considerably more rapid for Group E than Group C, which suggests that the original conditioning with the light resulted in it retrieving information that was not entirely specific to the cheek where the US was applied. The implication of this study, and this is certainly the view advocated by Konorski (1967), is that once an association has been formed between a CS and the affective properties of a US, this facilitates the learning necessary for the occurrence of specific CRs, such as eye-blink, when the US is applied elsewhere.

There are, therefore, good reasons for believing that a CS can retrieve information about either the specific or the affective properties of a US. Unfortunately, rather little is known about the circumstances that promote learning about these different properties, and that determine when information about these properties will be effective. For example, prior to our experiment (Ganesan & Pearce, 1988) we were uncertain as to whether or not blocking would be effective when the US was switched from water to food.

Conditioned inhibition

It is natural to assume in the case of excitatory conditioning that representations of the CS and US become associated, as these events are paired. But where inhibitory learning is concerned, the event associated with the inhibitory CS is less obvious. After all, this stimulus is not usually followed by any tangible event.

One possibility is that as a result of signalling the omission of a US, the presence of an inhibitory CS makes it more difficult to activate a representation of the US. This point of view has been expressed by Konorski (1948) and Rescorla (1979). Both assume that an excitatory CS is capable of activating a representation of the US with which it is paired. If this excitatory stimulus, CS_E, should be presented in compound with another stimulus and the US is withheld, an inhibitory link is assumed to be formed between the representation of the latter stimulus, CS_I, and the US representation excited by CS_E. This relationship is depicted in the upper half of Figure 2.19. The subsequent presentation of CS_I will then serve to dampen the US representation that is activated by any excitatory CS with which it is concurrently paired. A consequence of this dampening will be to reduce the strength of the excitatory CR. If CS_I should be paired with the US in a retardation test, then, although an association will grow between a representation of CS and the US, the existence of the inhibitory link will initially prevent the CS from activating the US representation, and a CR will not be recorded.

A crucial implication of this account is that a conditioned inhibitor should not have any response-eliciting properties of its own. An inhibitory link will serve only to modulate the strength of CRs whenever the US representation is activated. But we have seen that a conditioned inhibitor by itself may influence behaviour. In the Hearst and Franklin (1977) experiment a conditioned inhibitor was shown to elicit withdrawal. Whereas in other studies it has been found that rats will consume relatively large volumes of a favoured solution that has previously signalled the omission of a lithium chloride injection (Batson & Best, 1981; Best, Dunn, Batson, Meachum, & Nash, 1985). Findings such as these suggest the need for an alternative account of what is learned during inhibitory conditioning.

In his more recent theorising, Konorski (1967; see also Pearce & Hall, 1980) proposed that

p32

FIGURE 2.19

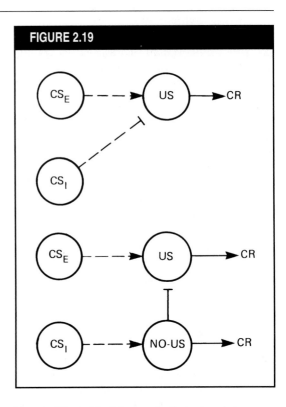

Two possible models of the learning that occurs during inhibitory conditioning. The arrows and stopped lines, respectively, depict excitatory and inhibitory links; the solid lines depict permanent links; the dashed lines depict conditioned links; and the circles denote representations in memory.

inhibitory conditioning permits the growth of a conventional association between the CS and what Konorski (1967) called a no-US representation. The activation of this representation was deemed to have two effects. It can dampen any concurrently excited US representations and thus weaken excitatory CRs, and it may also elicit responses in its own right (see lower half of Figure 2.19). If this account is to be accepted, then it is essential to specify what constitutes a no-US representation.

Superficially, the notion of such a representation might seem strange, but a moment's reflection should reveal what is meant by this term. Being told that something is going to happen and then discovering that it will not can often produce strong emotional reactions. The withdrawal of a promised reward, like a large sum of money, might result in frustration or disappointment, whereas an opposite reaction of relief or joy might accompany the news that something unpleasant, like a visit to the dentist, is no longer going to happen. Konorski (1967) proposed the no-US representation contained information about these diffuse reactions, and they are the counterpart to the affective representations formed of the US during excitatory conditioning. It is also conceivable that the no-US representation encodes precise information about the omitted US, and this would be equivalent to the specific component of a US representation. In fact there is evidence to support both proposals.

The outcome of a rabbit eye-blink conditioning study indicates the affective nature of a no-US representation (Pearce et al., 1981). Inhibitory conditioning was initially performed in which a light signalled shock to one cheek and a light–clicker compound was followed by nothing. Subsequently, to examine the inhibitory properties of the clicker, a retardation test was conducted in which it signalled shock to either the same or the opposite cheek to that used during training. The test revealed that excitatory conditioning was disrupted to the same extent irrespective of which cheek was shocked. The implication of this finding is that during inhibitory training the clicker was associated with a no-shock representation that was sufficiently general to disrupt conditioning with a US applied to any location. Perhaps, in this instance the information provided by the no-shock representation was simply that shock would not follow the clicker. If it had been more specific, then the activation of this representation would have disrupted conditioning more when the shock was applied to the original, rather than to the opposite, cheek.

An indication that, in certain circumstances, inhibitory conditioning can result in the CS being associated with a specific representation comes from a report by Cotton, Goodall, and Mackintosh (1982). Groups of rats received training in which a tone was paired with a moderately strong shock, and a tone–light compound signalled a weak shock. Thus the light signalled a reduction rather than omission of shock. Different groups were then given a summation test in which the light was paired with a clicker that had previously signalled either the strong shock (Group S), or the weak

shock (Group W). If the initial training resulted in the light retrieving an affective representation signalling, say, relief from an unpleasant event, then its properties should be evident in both groups. In fact it was only in Group S that the light passed the summation test, which implies that it retrieved relatively specific information about the strong shock that was omitted and this restricted the circumstances in which it could function as a conditioned inhibitor.

THE PERFORMANCE OF THE CONDITIONED RESPONSE

Thus far we have been concerned principally with identifying the kind of information that animals acquire during the course of Pavlovian conditioning. We now need to understand how this information is able to influence an animal's behaviour. The discussion has already hinted at the way in which a simple CS–US association can control behaviour. The presentation of a CS is believed to excite a representation of the US, which in turn will excite a response centre that will then elicit a CR. On this basis, therefore, the CS might be expected to elicit a response that is very similar to the one elicited by the US. That is, the CS might be thought to serve as a substitute for the US.

There is certainly some evidence to support this stimulus-substitution account for the nature of the Pavlovian CR. Hungry pigeons direct eating responses towards a response key that signals the imminent delivery of food, whereas a thirsty pigeon will make drinking responses to the same key if it signals the delivery of water (Moore, 1973). But, as we shall see, the way in which the US determines the nature of the CR is more complex than has just been implied. We shall also see that the CS can have an influence on the responses that are performed in its presence.

Influence of the US on the CR

Consummatory CRs.   Konorski (1967) believed that whenever a CS retrieved information about the specific properties of the US, then a consummatory

CR would be performed. Normally, such a response was expected to mimic at least a component of the response to the US. Thus in the study by Moore (1973) that has just been mentioned, the different responses of pigeons to an illuminated key that signalled either food or water provide two clear examples of consummatory CRs. Other examples can be found in the salivation by dogs to a CS that is paired with either food or the delivery of a weak solution of acid into the mouth (Pavlov, 1927). And one further example can be found in experiments where a stimulus that is followed by a mild electric shock to the cheek will cause the eye to blink in a manner similar to that seen when the shock itself is presented (Gormezano, 1965).

Preparatory CRs. Konorski (1967) further proposed that when a CS retrieved information about the affective properties of a US, it would elicit a preparatory CR. In contrast to consummatory CRs, a preparatory CR was assumed not to be intimately tied to the responses elicited by the US. An appetitive preparatory CR might consist of a general increase in activity, whereas for aversive conditioning it might consist of immobility. This is not to say that these CRs are without direction. Konorski (1967) argued that for appetitive conditioning the preparatory CR will consist of approaching the CS, and that the equivalent response for aversive conditioning is more likely to be withdrawal. Clear support for both claims can be found in a series of experiments by Karpicke, Christoph, Peterson, and Hearst (1977).

Rats were trained to press a lever for food in a chamber containing two light bulbs, one near the lever and one further away. While subjects were pressing the lever, the bulbs were occasionally illuminated, and this signalled the imminent delivery of either food (Experiment 1) or electric shock (Experiment 5). There was a decline in instrumental responding when the CS was presented in either study, but the magnitude of this effect was dependent on the position of the illuminated bulb. When the bulb nearer to the lever signalled food, there was less disruption of lever pressing than when the more distant bulb signalled this US. Presumably a preparatory CR of approach-

ing an appetitive CS is likely to be most disruptive when the CS is far from the lever. In contrast, it was the illumination of the near light bulb that produced the greater reduction in lever pressing during aversive conditioning. In this instance, a tendency to withdraw from a light signalling shock will interfere most with instrumental responding when it is close to the lever.

Compensatory CRs. Subsequent developments have indicated that Konorski's (1967) account of preparatory conditioning is too simple. Solomon and Corbit (1974) have suggested that the delivery of a US will immediately arouse what they refer to as an *a*-process. This can be regarded as an emotional state directly related to the motivational quality of the US. An electric shock may excite an *a*-process that involves the physiological changes associated with fear. Thus far the account is not too dissimilar to Konorski's (1967) views, with the *a*-process corresponding to the physiological changes necessary for a preparatory CR. Where the accounts differ is in Solomon and Corbit's (1974) proposal that a US also excites, but rather slowly, a *b*-process that opposes the *a*-process and diminishes reactivity to the US. This leads to the possibility that when a CS and US are paired, the CS may excite either of the *a*- or the *b*-processes aroused by the US. Before exploring the implications of this proposal, we must first consider the evidence for the existence of these opposing processes and examine the way they interact.

Church, LoLordo, Overmier, Solomon, and Turner (1966) recorded the change in heart rate in dogs produced by a series of electric shocks. In keeping with the opponent-process analysis, the shocks were found to have two effects. Whenever the shock was applied, there was an immediate *a*-process reaction of an increase in heart rate, but as soon as the shock ceased the effects of the opponent *b*-process became evident as a temporary reduction in heart rate. With repeated exposure to shock there was a change in this pattern. Shock onset was accompanied by only a modest increase in heart rate, and its offset led to a pronounced decline in the rate of this response. Moreover, it is not only heart rate that is influenced by the repeated exposure to the shock: Dogs also seem to be much less distressed by this event after several training sessions (Solomon & Corbit, 1974).

The explanation offered by Solomon and Corbit (1974) for these findings can be understood most readily by referring to Figure 2.20, which shows the presumed strength of the *a*- and *b*-processes to a stimulus event such as shock after a few (panel A) or many (panel B) trials. The middle row shows the effects of these trials on the underlying opponent processes. As far as the *a*-process is concerned, the amount of training has no effect. This response is always aroused rapidly by shock onset and declines equally rapidly following its offset. The amount of exposure does influence the strength of the *b*-process. At first, this response is rather weak and gains in strength only slowly after the shock is turned on, but when subjects are more familiar with the shock, then the *b*-process grows rapidly and its magnitude is considerably greater. Throughout training, once the shock has been turned off, the decline of the *b*-process is slower than that of the *a*-process.

The upper row of Figure 2.20 shows the net response that would be observed as a result of the inevitable interaction of the *a*- and *b*-processes. In principle the figure shows the impact of subtracting the *b*-process from the *a*-process and the way this would manifest itself in such measures as heart rate. The curves reflect exactly the changes in reactivity to shock that were reported by Church et al. (1966).

It is reasonable to assume that if, during conditioning, the CS becomes associated with a representation of the *a*-process, then it will elicit a preparatory CR in much the same way as Konorski (1967) envisaged. But what sort of CR could be expected if the CS should become associated with a representation of the *b*-process aroused by a US? One answer is suggested by the work of Siegel (1977) on drug tolerance.

Drug tolerance as a CR. When rats are first injected with morphine, it has a strong pain-killing (analgesic) effect. But with the repeated administration of the drug a tolerance to it develops, so that doses of increasing magnitude are required to obtain the same degree of analgesia. The development of such morphine tolerance can be understood in terms of Pavlovian conditioning (Schull, 1979; Siegel, 1977). The stimulation accompanying the injection of morphine can be regarded as a CS, and the effect of the drug as the US. In keeping with Solomon and Corbit's (1974) analysis, the CS could then become associated with the *a*-process aroused by the drug, which would consist of the typical reactions to the drug including analgesia. Alternatively, the CS could become associated with the *b*-process that opposes these effects. Schull (1979) has suggested that morphine

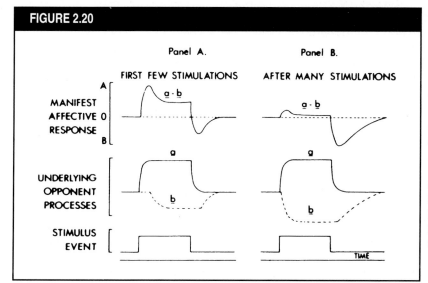

FIGURE 2.20

Panel A: The strength of the *a*- and the *b*-processes (middle row) aroused by a stimulus event (bottom row) when it is first presented, and the net reaction to this event that results from subtracting the *b*- from the *a*-process (upper row). *Panel B:* The same effects as those shown in Panel A, but for a stimulus event that has been presented for many trials (from Solomon & Corbit, 1974).

tolerance develops because the CS becomes associated with the *b*-process. After several injections, therefore, the sensations produced by the needle (CS) will activate a *b*-process CR that will counteract the subsequent analgesic effects of the injected morphine.

Support for this account can be found in an experiment by Siegel (1977). On each of six successive sessions, two groups of rats were injected with morphine shortly before a test for the analgesic effects of the drug. The test consisted of recording the weight that could be applied to a subject's paw before it was withdrawn. After the first injection rats were prepared to tolerate a considerable pressure to their paw. But with the repeated administration of morphine a weakening of the analgesic properties was revealed by a decline in the pressure that the rats were prepared to tolerate after each injection of the drug. This pattern of results is depicted in the left-hand side of Figure 2.21.

For the next 12 sessions the groups were treated differently. Group M–P–M was treated in much the same way as for the preceding sessions, except the injections contained saline instead of morphine. This training can be regarded as extinction, because the stimuli produced by the injection were no longer followed by morphine, and their association with the *b*-process should therefore be weakened. No injections at all were administered to Group M–Rest–M for this stage of the experiment. Finally, both groups were given six further injections of morphine. For Group M–Rest–M these injections can be expected to elicit a substantial *b*-process CR and counter again the analgesic effect of morphine. In contrast, for Group M–P–M a *b*-process CR should not be aroused by the injection, because of the extinction trials, and the renewed administration of morphine should be accompanied by analgesia. The results of pressure tests after these injections, which are shown in the right-hand part of Figure 2.21, confirmed this analysis.

Findings such as these reported by Siegel (1977) clearly show that properties of the US can influence the CR, but they tell us very little about the circumstances that dictate the sort of CR that will be performed. This lack of knowledge is

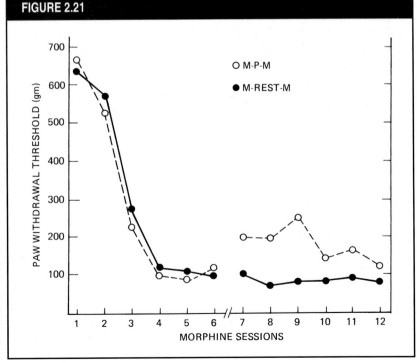

FIGURE 2.21

The mean weight that two groups of rats were prepared to tolerate on their paws shortly after an injection of morphine (M). The left-hand side shows the results for the first six daily trials, the right-hand side shows the results for a further six injections. During the interval between these stages Group M–P–M but not Group M–Rest–M had received saline placebo (P) injections (from Siegel, 1977).

emphasised by experiments that are very similar to Siegel's (1977) in design, yet have found that at least a component of the CR resembles the *a*- rather than *b*-process elicited by the drug (Eikelboom & Stewart, 1979; Sherman, 1979). For the present, the factors that determine whether a CR will mimic or oppose the response elicited by the US remain obscure. A similar state of uncertainty holds for the distinction between preparatory and consummatory CRs. Konorski (1967) proposed that the former are more likely when the CS is of relatively long duration, whereas shorter CSs were believed to be responsible for consummatory CRs. Once again, however, there is insufficient evidence to allow an adequate evaluation of these proposals.

Even if the way in which the US influences the CR were fully understood, our knowledge of the factors that determine this response would still be incomplete. This is because the nature of the CS can also influence conditioned responding.

Influence of the CS on the CR

A dramatic example of the way in which the CS influences the CR can be found in a conditioned taste-aversion study by Garcia, Rusiniak, and Brett (1977). Coyotes and wolves were made ill by feeding them chopped mutton that was wrapped in raw sheep hide and laced with lithium chloride. The effects of this conditioning episode were then examined by allowing the animals to approach live sheep. Rather than attacking them as they normally do, one coyote sniffed the sheep and then turned away retching; the reaction of the wolves was even more impressive, at first they:

> charged the sheep and made oral contact several times with their characteristic flank attack but immediately released their prey. During the next half hour, the sheep became dominant as the wolves gave way whenever the sheep threatened with short charges. Gradually the wolves withdrew and responded to the sheep like submissive pups. (Garcia et al., 1977, pp.281–282)

The response of retching by the coyote is to be expected if the US determined the CR, but the additional reactions of the wolves are clearly influenced by the fact that the CS paired with illness tasted and smelt of sheep, and that the live sheep, finding themselves not eaten by wolves, were prepared to attack their erstwhile predators.

In a different vein, Timberlake and Grant (1975) signalled the delivery of food to rats by inserting into the conditioning chamber for 10 seconds a platform on which another rat was strapped. As this event was always followed by food, an account of conditioning that assumes that the CS should elicit the same responses as the US leads to the expectation that the experimental subjects would attempt to eat the CS. Happily, there was no evidence of such cannibalism. Instead, whenever the CS was presented, the subject engaged in social behaviour with the restrained rat. This activity included pawing, grooming, and anogenital sniffing. To emphasise the importance that the nature of the CS played in this experiment, it was found that social responses were not directed towards a block of wood when it served as the CS. A further finding from the experiment was that social behaviour was not directed towards the rat on the platform, if its entry into the chamber was unrelated to the delivery of food. Thus the social response can be confidently said to be a consequence of conditioning, and it is determined by properties of the CS as well as the US.

Interpretation

By now it should be evident that our understanding of the factors that determine the nature of a CR for a given conditioning task is far from complete. On some occasions the CR mimics the response to the US, on other occasions it appears to counter the response to the US, and in other tasks the CR is determined more by the properties of the CS. Clearly the simple memory model of conditioning that was sketched on p.39 is unable to explain this complex pattern of findings. In general, learning theorists have veered away from trying to specify the circumstances in which a particular CR will be performed, but this is not to say the problem has been ignored completely.

Several authors have proposed that the determinants of conditioned behaviour are organised into functional systems that are concerned with such activities as feeding, mating, defence, and parenting (Davey, 1989; Timberlake,

1994). These systems are activated by the appropriate stimuli, and serve to coordinate patterns of behaviour that are both innate and learned. Each system is assumed to control a wide range of actions, the selection of which is determined by the stimuli that are present. Thus in the case of appetitive conditioning, many of the actions controlled by the feeding system are assumed to be available to serve as potential CRs.

To explain the finding by Timberlake and Grant (1975) that social behaviour can serve as a CR, this behaviour must be assumed to constitute one of the activities that lie within the feeding system. The question is then raised as to whether it is reasonable to suppose that social behaviour belongs to the feeding system. Timberlake (1994) has justified this assumption by pointing out that young rats have a natural tendency to follow adult rats and to eat the food that they select. That is, social behaviour with adults is an integral part of feeding in young rats. We might predict, therefore, that any animal that is a solitary feeder throughout its life will be unlikely to demonstrate social CRs when it is presented with a conspecific that signals the delivery of food. Timberlake (1983) has confirmed this prediction with hamsters who tend to eat by themselves. He actually found a decrease in social behaviour in hamsters when they were exposed to another hamster immediately before food was delivered.

Whatever the merits of the details of this behaviour systems approach to Pavlovian conditioning, there is no doubt that it has the benefit of attempting to come to terms with the complexity of the factors that determine the nature of the CR. For this reason alone, this approach deserves serious attention.

CONCLUDING COMMENT:
THE REFLEXIVE NATURE OF THE CONDITIONED RESPONSE

A common claim concerning conditioned responding is that the CS elicits the CR quite automatically, just as an innate reflex will be triggered by the appropriate releasing stimulus. As a result, whereas properties of the CS and US can influence the form of the CR, this response is often quite unaffected by its consequences. In some circumstances this does not matter, because the CR will approximate behaviour that is in the animal's best interests. Signals for food are generally found in close proximity to food itself, and a preparatory CR of approaching an appetitive CS may well lead a hungry animal to its goal. Alternatively, an animal that flees from a signal for an aversive event will very often be fleeing from that event as well. This is not to say that CRs will always benefit the animal; given the appropriate circumstances, as the following examples will show, the automatic occurrence of a CR can occasionally lead to maladaptive behaviour.

In one study by Hearst and Jenkins (1974), pigeon autoshaping was conducted in a long conditioning chamber. The delivery of food was signalled by the illumination of a response key located more than 0.6 metres from the hopper. After a number of autoshaping trials the pigeons would approach and peck the key as soon as it was illuminated. Pecking then continued until the key light was turned off, whereupon the pigeon frantically rushed down the box to collect the grain that was briefly available at the hopper. Not surprisingly, subjects got very little food to eat as a result of this training. In this example, then, the CS elicited the typical CRs of approach and pecking, and their occurrence prevented the more sensible response of going to the magazine. The automatic, or reflexive, nature of the CRs is revealed by the persistence with which they were performed, even though they interfered with the collection of grain.

A similar outcome has been demonstrated by Williams and Williams (1969) using what is known as an omission schedule for autoshaping. Pigeons were given conventional autoshaping in which the illumination of a response key signalled food. But if the birds pecked the key during a trial, the light was turned off and food was not presented. Given this arrangement, it would be in the pigeons' best interests never to peck the key. But it seems that the behaviour of these birds is not always governed by their best interests: Even with extended training they all persisted in pecking the key to some extent, thereby receiving only a fraction of the food that was potentially available. The implication of this finding is that even the intermittent pairings of the CS and food were sufficient to sustain a key-light–food association. Illumination of the key would then activate a representation of food and automatically produce a consummatory peck CR and cancel the delivery of food.

The final example of the disruptive influence of CRs comes from a study by Breland and Breland (1961), who experienced considerable difficulty in training a raccoon to pick up a coin and insert it in a money box for food. The problem did not lie with making the subjects pick up the coin, but with making them let go of it again. Boakes, Poli, Lockwood, and Goodall (1978) have suggested that this demonstration of "misbehaviour" occurs because the coin became an appetitive CS as a result of being paired with food. Consequently, the subject will be compelled to approach the coin whenever it is visible (preparatory CR) and perhaps

attempt to eat it (consummatory CR). On this basis it is quite understandable why the raccoons were unwilling to release the coin.

Pavlovian conditioning has the potential for allowing animals to learn a great deal about sequences of events that occur regularly in their environment. But if the only way this knowledge can influence behaviour is through a restricted range of reflex-like responses, then, as the studies just discussed demonstrate, its full benefits could not be realised. It now seems that in addition to eliciting stereotyped CRs, Pavlovian conditioning can exert a more flexible influence on what an animal does by modulating the vigour of instrumental responses. But we must wait until we have examined the instrumental learning process in Chapter 4 before this possibility is investigated further. In the meantime we turn in the next chapter to an examination of the conditions that determine whether or not Pavlovian conditioning will take place.

3

The Conditions for Learning: Surprise and Attention

An important conclusion to be drawn from the previous chapter is that conditioning results in the growth of an association between representations of the CS and US. Our task now is to identify as precisely as possible the circumstances that are responsible for this learning. For many years it was thought that conditioning would automatically be effective whenever a CS and US were paired, but more recent evidence suggests that this is incorrect. To be successful, conditioning is now believed to depend on the US being unexpected or surprising, and on the CS receiving the animal's full attention. In the first part of this chapter, one account of the way in which the surprisingness of the US influences conditioning is described in some detail. The way in which changes in attention to the CS can affect conditioning will then be considered in the second part of the chapter.

The reason for believing that the surprisingness of the US influences conditioning rests with the discovery of blocking, which was mentioned briefly in the previous chapter. Table 3.1 outlines the stages of a blocking study by Kamin (1969) using conditioned suppression. In the first stage Group E, but not Group C, was given pairings of a noise with shock. For the second stage both groups received identical training for a number of trials in which a compound composed of the noise and a light was paired with shock. Finally, test trials involving the light by itself were given. The suppression ratios at the right-hand side of the table indicate that on the test trials with the light there was virtually no evidence of a CR in Group E, whereas one of considerable strength was recorded for Group C. For Group E, therefore, the original training with the noise was somehow responsible

TABLE 3.1			
Summary of the Training Given to the Two Groups in Kamin's (1969) Study of Blocking.			
	Stage 1	*Stage 2*	*Test*
Group E	Noise → Shock	Light + Noise → Shock	Light 0.45
Group C		Light + Noise → Shock	Light 0.05

for preventing, or blocking, learning about the light during compound conditioning.

If conditioning merely depended on the pairing of a CS and a US, then Stage 2 should have resulted in effective conditioning with the light for both groups. To explain his finding to the contrary with Group E, Kamin (1969) proposed that in the first stage of the experiment animals learned that the noise predicted the shock, and this led to the light being followed by an unsurprising US during compound conditioning. The importance of this relationship is made apparent by the following quote (Kamin, 1969, p.59):

> perhaps, for an increment in an associative connection to occur, it is necessary that the US instigate some "mental work" on behalf

of the animal. This mental work will occur only if the US is unpredicted—if it in some sense "surprises" the animal.

This proposal led to the development of a number of formal theories of learning, all of which in various ways have stressed the importance of surprise in conditioning (Mackintosh, 1975a; Pearce & Hall, 1980; Rescorla & Wagner, 1972; Wagner, 1976, 1978, 1981; Wagner & Rescorla, 1972). In order to demonstrate the way in which these theories operate, we shall consider one of them—that proposed by Rescorla and Wagner (1972)—in detail. Some of its successors are discussed in the second part of this chapter. By way of introduction to the model, a simplified version of it is applied to conditioning with a single CS.

PART 1: SURPRISE AND CONDITIONING

CONDITIONING WITH A SINGLE CS

The Rescorla–Wagner model maintains that Pavlovian conditioning results in the formation of associations between representations of the CS and US. The capacity of the CS to activate the US representation and hence elicit a CR is held to be directly related to the strength of the association connecting them. Hence the greater the strength of the CS–US association—or associative strength of a CS as it is often referred to—the stronger will be the CR that it elicits. In order to understand associative learning, therefore, we must discover the factors that are responsible for changes in associative strength.

There are two assumptions that are basic to the Rescorla–Wagner (1972) model: The first is that the repeated pairing of a CS with a US will result in a gradual increase in the strength of the connection between them. This growth, however, does not continue indefinitely but ceases when the associative strength of the CS is equal to a value determined by the magnitude of the US. The second assumption is that on those trials when there is an increase in associative strength, it is not by a

fixed amount. Instead, the growth of an association is determined by the difference between the current associative strength of the CS and the maximum possible for the US employed. When this difference is large, such as at the outset of conditioning, there will be a substantial growth of the CS–US association, and the increase in the strength of the CR from one trial to the next will be considerable. But when the CS–US association is already strong because of extended conditioning, the growth of the association will be slight and there will be little change in the CR from one trial to the next. Equation 3.1, which expresses these assumptions formally, can be used to determine the change in associative strength that will occur on any trial.

$$\Delta V = \alpha(\lambda - V) \qquad (3.1)$$

The term V refers to the strength of the CS–US association and ΔV indicates the change in strength of the association for a particular trial. The value of λ is set by the magnitude of the US and reflects the maximum strength that the CS–US association can achieve. The parameter α does not vary during conditioning and has a value between 0 and 1; its function will be made evident shortly. Because associative strength is held to influence directly the strength of the CR, Equation 3.1 can be used to predict changes in responding during the course of conditioning. In other words, this equation can be used to generate theoretical learning curves and, if the theory is correct, then these curves should be similar to those found in reality.

The application of Equation 3.1 is extremely simple. Assume for the present that α is 0.20 and that the CS is novel. On the first trial of conditioning the CS will possess no associative strength, and the value of V will be zero. The value of λ can be arbitrarily set at 100. For the first CS–US pairing the growth in the association between them will be given by Equation 3.2, which is derived by substituting the values given into Equation 3.1.

$$\Delta V = 0.20(100 - 0) \quad (3.2)$$
$$= 20$$

Thus on the first conditioning trial there will be an increase of 20 units in associative strength. On the second trial the increment in associative strength will be determined by a new set of values. Specifically, it will be determined by Equation 3.3, because the associative strength of the CS will no longer be zero but will instead have a value of 20 units. The effect of this change will be to produce a smaller increment in associative strength on the second than on the first trial.

$$\Delta V = 0.20(100 - 20) \quad (3.3)$$
$$= 16$$

$$\Delta V = 0.20(100 - 36) \quad (3.4)$$
$$= 12.8$$

On the third trial (see Equation 3.4), the associative strength of the CS will be 36 (20 + 16) units, and this will result in an even smaller change than on the previous trials. It should now be clear that with continued training the increments in associative strength will be progressively smaller and result in the curve depicted by the solid line in the left-hand side of Figure 3.1. Eventually a point will be reached where the sum of the increments will equal 100; at this juncture the expression $\lambda - V$ will equal 0 and, according to Equation 3.1, no further changes in associative strength will be possible. This equation thus predicts that the growth in associative strength—and hence increase in CR strength—should be extremely rapid on the initial trials but decline and eventually cease with continued training.

Equation 3.1 can be used just as easily to account for extinction when a CS that has been presented for conditioning is no longer followed by the US. Suppose there has been sufficient training to ensure that the strength of a CS–US association equals the value of λ (100 units). If we then present the CS without the US, what does Equation 3.1 predict? Before answering this question, the value to be substituted for λ on these nonreinforced trials

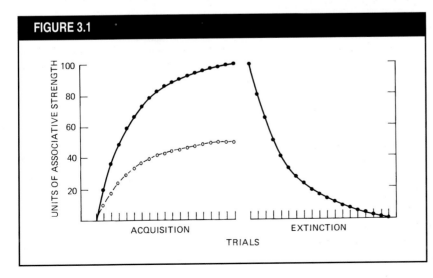

FIGURE 3.1

UNITS OF ASSOCIATIVE STRENGTH

ACQUISITION   EXTINCTION

TRIALS

The changes in associative strength predicted by the Rescorla–Wagner (1972) model during conditioning with a large US (λ = 100 units: solid line) or a small US (λ = 50 units: dashed line), and during extinction for a CS that has been paired with a large US.

must be decided. This term refers to the magnitude of the US, and a value of 0 is appropriate to indicate its absence. The associative strength of the CS, however, does have a value (100 units) and the change in associative strength on the first extinction trial will be given by Equation 3.5.

$$\Delta V = 0.20(0 - 100) \qquad (3.5)$$
$$= -20$$

The first extinction trial will therefore result in the CS losing 20 units of associative strength. Repeatedly applying Equation 3.1 for extinction will, because of the declining value of V, produce progressively smaller losses in associative strength, and result in the curve depicted in the right-hand half of Figure 3.1. Extinction will be complete when the associative strength of the CS has fallen to zero.

The application of Equation 3.1 is not difficult. However, if you feel uneasy with this account of acquisition and extinction, then perform your own calculations to see the effects of changing the values of α and λ on the shape of the learning curve. This will help considerably with understanding what is to follow.

A useful feature of Equation 3.1 is that it captures the essence of what Rescorla and Wagner (1972) consider to be the role of surprise in conditioning. As the associative strength of a CS grows, so it can be said that the CS is becoming a more accurate predictor of the US. When the value of V is low, only a weak US will be expected, but as its value approaches λ, so the expectancy will correspond more and more to the US that is presented.

The implication of this discussion is that the size of the discrepancy $(\lambda - V)$ indicates the extent to which the US is unexpected or surprising. The greater the discrepancy between λ and V, the greater the difference between what is expected and what occurs, and hence the more surprising will the US be. We have seen that conditioning is predicted to be most rapid when $\lambda - V$ has a large value, which is when the US is most unexpected or surprising. Thus, although Equation 3.1 is presented in mathematical terms, it expresses the psychological idea that animals learn most readily about USs that are surprising or unexpected.

A number of factors can influence the course of conditioning; some of these are now described and it is shown how they can be incorporated into the theoretical framework provided by Equation 3.1.

US intensity

One objection that might be raised about Equation 3.1 is that it is impossible to know what value should be assigned to λ. But this is not a serious problem, as the purpose of developing such equations is not to derive exact, quantitative predictions of the sort: "On Trial 4 the CR will be of such a magnitude". Instead, it is concerned more with qualitative statements in which the strength of CR produced by one set of circumstances can be predicted to differ from that recorded in another situation. Suppose we wished to predict the effects of changing the magnitude of the US on conditioning. The fact that we do not know the precise values of λ that should be assigned to USs when they vary in intensity does not matter. All that needs to be said is that this value will be greater for the stronger US. Thus if λ for a strong US is set at 100 units, then a value of 50 units could be employed for one that is weaker.

Equation 3.1 predicts that on the first conditioning trial with the weak US the increment in associative strength will be $0.20 \times (50 - 0) = 10$ units (using the previously selected value for α). Future increments will decline progressively from this value, and conditioning will cease when their combined value is equal to 50. The dotted line in Figure 3.1 portrays this predicted growth of associative strength. Comparing this curve with the solid line, which was calculated with $\lambda = 100$ units, then allows us to conclude what the effects will be of conditioning with different magnitudes of US. Specifically, a strong US should not only result in the more rapid acquisition of a CR, but this response should be ultimately more vigorous than when a weak US is employed. Note that this prediction will always be true no matter what values are ascribed to λ, providing that its value is greater for the stronger US.

The foregoing analysis is reasonably consistent with experimental findings. For instance, Annau and Kamin (1961), using conditioned suppression, found that both the rate of conditioning and the ultimate level of conditioned responding was greater with a strong than with a weak shock US. When examining Figure 3.2, which shows the results from their study, bear in mind that a suppression ratio of 0.50 indicates the absence of a CR, whereas one of 0.00 indicates a CR of maximum strength.

CS intensity

So far little has been said about the the role of α in Equation 3.1. Conditioning is known to progress more rapidly with a strong than with a weak CS, and to accommodate this finding Rescorla and Wagner (1972) proposed that α is set according to the intensity of the CS. With a strong CS α should approach 1, but with a weaker stimulus α should tend towards 0. Figure 3.3 portrays the acquisition curves predicted by Equation 1 with α set at 0.8 (strong CS, solid line) and 0.2 (weak CS, dashed line). The value of λ was 100 units. The effect of changing the magnitude of α is to alter the rate of conditioning but not the ultimate level of conditioned responding. Because the influence of α is confined solely to determining the speed at

which conditioning takes place, it is defined as a learning-rate parameter that reflects the *conditionability* or *associability* of the CS.

The results from a study by Kamin and Schaub (1963), which investigated the influence of CS intensity on the acquisition of conditioned suppression, are presented in Figure 3.4. Three groups were conditioned with the same magnitude of US but with different intensities of a white noise CS. For Group High the CS was 81dB, for Group Medium it was 62.5dB, and for Group Low it was 49dB. The rate of conditioning was directly related to the CS intensity, but this factor did not influence at all the ultimate level of responding.

To leave with the impression that CS intensity never influences the ceiling of responding would be a mistake. Occasionally, the intensity of a CS has been found to determine not only the rate, but also the asymptote of conditioning (e.g. Kamin, 1965). Mackintosh (1974, pp.41–45) provides a good discussion of why changes in CS intensity may occasionally have this effect.

Sometimes two different USs, such as food and water, may support the same ceiling of conditioned responding (which means that they should be

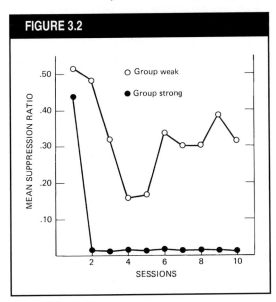

FIGURE 3.2

The acquisition of conditioned suppression to a noise CS by two groups of rats that received either a 0.49 milliamp (Group Weak) or a 0.85 milliamp (Group Strong) shock US (adapted from Annau & Kamin, 1961).

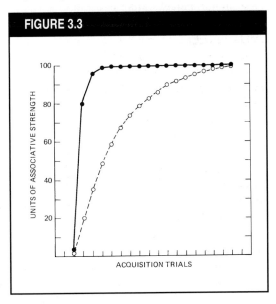

FIGURE 3.3

The change in associative strength predicted by the Rescorla–Wagner (1972) model during conditioning with a relatively intense CS (α = 0.8: solid line) or a weak CS (α = 0.2: dashed line).

FIGURE 3.4

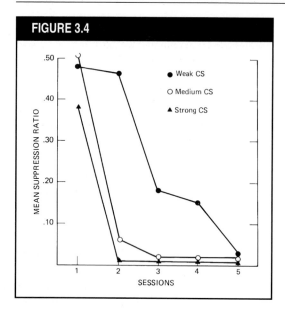

Acquisition of conditioned suppression by groups of rats trained with the same US but with a CS that was weak, medium, or strong (adapted from Kamin & Schaub, 1963).

CONDITIONING WITH A COMPOUND CS

When it comes to conditioning with a compound CS, Rescorla and Wagner (1972) proposed an ingeniously simple modification to Equation 3.1. They retained the principle that conditioning will be most effective with a surprising US—all they did was to extend the factors that can influence surprisingness. Equation 3.1 stipulates that it is the discrepancy between the associative strength of a single CS and λ that determines how surprising the US will be. Rescorla and Wagner (1972) rejected this notion and instead proposed that it is how well

the US is predicted by all the stimuli combined on a given trial that determines whether or not it is surprising. In other words, the value of V to be substituted into right-hand side of Equation 3.1 is not determined by the associative strength of a CS; instead, it reflects the sum of the associative strengths of all the stimuli present on a conditioning trial.

To capture this notion Rescorla and Wagner (1972) suggested Equation 3.6. The term V_{ALL} represents the algebraic sum of the associative strengths of all the CSs that are present on a trial, and it can be said to indicate the extent to which they collectively predict the US. This term also indicates the strength of the CR that can be expected in the presence of these stimuli. The values of V_A, V_B, ... V_X, are determined by the associative strengths of the elements of the compound.

$$V_{ALL} = V_A + V_B + \dots V_X \qquad (3.6)$$

Equation 3.7 shows how this collective associative strength influences conditioning with CS A on a single compound conditioning trial. To understand the effects of this trial on the other stimuli that are present, this equation would have to be used again for each CS in turn. If the intensities of these stimuli are different, then the value of α must change each time the equation is used.

$$\Delta V_A = \alpha_A(\lambda - V_{ALL}) \qquad (3.7)$$

Blocking

It is a relatively simple matter to understand the way in which this equation explains blocking. Consider again the study by Kamin (1969), referred to in Table 3.1, in which conditioning was conducted with a noise (N) prior to compound conditioning with the noise and a light (L). At the end of the first stage of training for Group E the associative strength of the noise will be at the asymptotic value of λ (100 units, say). Equation 3.7 can now be rewritten as Equation 3.8, which shows the increment in associative strength to the light on the first compound trial. The novelty of this stimulus will ensure that V_L is equal to 0 for this trial.

---

represented by the same value of λ), but conditioning with them may progress at different rates. To accommodate this possibility, Rescorla and Wagner (1972) proposed that their equation should include a second learning-rate parameter, ß, which is determined by properties of the US. The factors that influence the value of ß have received scant attention, and no more will be said about this parameter.

$$\Delta V_L = \alpha_L[\lambda - (V_N + V_L)] \quad (3.8)$$
$$= \alpha_L[100 - (100 + 0)]$$
$$= 0$$

On the first—or for that matter any—trial of Stage 2 there will be no change in the associative strength of the light. A rather different state of affairs will hold for the control group, because on the first compound trial both the light and noise will be novel, and the values of V_L and V_N will be zero. Equations 3.9a and 3.9b describe the increments in associative strength that can be expected with these stimuli on the first trial.

$$\Delta V_L = \alpha_L[\lambda - (V_N + V_L)] \quad (3.9a)$$
$$= \alpha_L[100 - (0 + 0)]$$
$$= \alpha_L . 100$$

$$\Delta V_N = \alpha_N[\lambda - (V_N + V_L)] \quad (3.9b)$$
$$= \alpha_N[100 - (0 + 0)]$$
$$= \alpha_N . 100$$

For these subjects the noise and the light will both gain in associative strength, and the latter stimulus will elicit a stronger CR on the test trial than its counterpart in Group E. According to the Rescorla–Wagner model, therefore, blocking is effective because the pretraining with the tone will ensure the US is accurately predicted by the compound. The lack of surprisingness of the US will then prevent the development of a light–US association.

Overshadowing

Some further thought about Equations 3.9a and 3.9b should reveal that conditioning with the noise and light will cease when their combined associative strengths equal λ. As a result, neither V_L nor V_N will alone reach this value, which they would do if they were paired independently with the US. The Rescorla–Wagner model thus predicts that when animals are conditioned with two stimuli in a compound, each will gain less associative strength than if they were separately paired with the same US. In these circumstances the presence of one CS is said to *overshadow* learning about the other. Pavlov (1927) first reported this effect, and it has been demonstrated on many subsequent occasions (e.g. Kamin, 1969).

An interesting feature of the Rescorla–Wagner model is its prediction that the extent to which one stimulus can overshadow another is determined by their relative intensities. Assume that animals are conditioned with a compound comprising a bright light and a low noise. As a result, α_L in Equation 3.9a will be greater than α_N in Equation 3.9b, and the equations predict that on each trial the growth in associative strength to the light will be greater than to the noise. When conditioning eventually reaches asymptote (which will occur when $V_L + V_N = \lambda$), the light will have gained considerably more associative strength than the noise. Compound conditioning with two CSs, therefore, should not necessarily result in each acquiring equal associative strength. Instead, the stimulus that is the more intense will be the one to gain the greater strength. In general, experimental findings conform to this rule, but there are sufficient exceptions to it for at least one author to have been encouraged to seek an alternative explanation for overshadowing (Mackintosh, 1976).

Inhibitory conditioning

One of the great advantages of the Rescorla–Wagner model is that it provides an elegant account for effects of inhibitory conditioning. Consider an experiment in which subjects are first given excitatory conditioning with a tone until its associative strength is at asymptotic value, λ (100 units). They then receive inhibitory conditioning in which tone–US trials are intermixed among presentations of a light–tone compound followed by nothing. What will happen to the associative strength of the light as a result of this training?

Equation 3.10 indicates the change in associative strength that can be expected on the first compound trial. The value of λ is zero because of the absence of the US. V_T is equal to 100 because of the pretraining with the tone, and V_L has a value of 0 due to the novelty of the light. The compound trial will thus reduce the associative strength of the light. Because this stimulus does not possess any strength to lose, we must conclude that the training will endow the light with negative associative strength. In fact, conditioning will continue until V_L is of a sufficient negative value to cancel out the positive strength of the tone, V_T.

$$\Delta V_L = \alpha_L[\lambda - (V_L + V_T)] \qquad (3.10)$$
$$= \alpha_L[0 - (0 - 100)]$$
$$= -\alpha_L \cdot 100$$

Wagner and Rescorla (1972) suggest that any stimulus that possesses negative associative strength will be a conditioned inhibitor, and it is easy to see why this should be. If a stimulus with negative associative strength is paired with a US, then conditioning will at first be without apparent effect, because a number of trials will be needed before the associative strength of the stimulus becomes positive and it can elicit a CR. This effect constitutes a retardation test for conditioned inhibition. As far as the summation test is concerned, bear in mind that Rescorla and Wagner (1972) assume that the associative strength of a compound is made up of the algebraic sum of the associative strengths of the elements (Equation 3.6). If one of the elements has negative associative strength, then the overall associative strength of the compound and the vigour of the CR that is performed in its presence will be less than if that stimulus were absent.

The CS–US contingency

One factor that has been shown to be extremely important in determining associative strength during excitatory conditioning is the degree to which the US occurs in the absence as well as in the presence of the CS, as a study by Rescorla (1968) demonstrates. Rats were trained to press a lever for food in an operant chamber before being given a number of sessions in a different chamber where a 2-minute tone and shock were presented. The effect of these conditioning sessions was ultimately assessed by presenting the tone to the rats while they were again responding for food in the original chamber.

In each conditioning session, for all subjects the probability of the CS being paired with the US was 0.4—that is, the shock was delivered on an average of 4 out of every 10 occasions that the tone was presented. The groups differed in the probability of being shocked during the interval, averaging 8 minutes, between successive tone trials. For Group 0 no shocks were presented in this interval. For Group 0.40 the probability of shock being

presented in each 2-minute segment of the interval was 0.40, which meant that the probability of shock during the CS was the same as at any other time in the session. For the two remaining groups the probability of shock during a 2-minute segment of the interval was either 0.20 (Group 0.20), or 0.10 (Group 0.10). Thus for these subjects there was a chance of being shocked at any time in the session, but US delivery was more likely in the presence than in the absence of the tone.

The effects of this training were revealed by the magnitude of conditioned suppression evoked by the tone in the four groups on the test session (see Figure 3.5). The striking finding was that the strength of conditioning differed dramatically in the four groups, even though the tone–shock pairings were identical for all subjects. What appears to be an important determinant of conditioning, therefore, is the difference between the probability of shock when the CS is present and when it is absent. When this difference is large, as in the case of Group 0, conditioning is very effective. With a smaller difference between these probabilities, conditioning is still effective, but

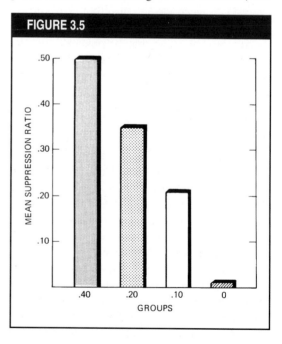

FIGURE 3.5

Mean suppression ratio to the tone CS on the test session for each of the four groups in the study by Rescorla (1968) (adapted from Rescorla, 1968).

correspondingly weaker (Groups 0.20 and 0.10). Finally, when the likelihood of shock is the same whether or not the CS is present, conditioning does not occur (Group 0.40).

Findings such as these are said to demonstrate the importance of *contingency* in conditioning. When the probability of a shock given the presence of a tone is equal to that in the absence of this stimulus, then the contingency between the tone and shock is zero, and conditioning is ineffective. But when the shock is more likely in the presence than the absence of the tone, then there is a positive tone–shock contingency, and excitatory conditioning will take place. A negative contingency between the CS and US can also be envisaged in which the likelihood of the US is greater when the CS is absent than when it is present. An example of such a contingency is provided by the study of Hearst and Franklin (1977), discussed in the previous chapter, in which the probability of food was greater in the absence than in the presence of an illuminated key. The results from that study indicate that when there is a negative CS–US contingency it will result in inhibitory learning.

To account for the importance of the CS–US contingency in determining the outcome of conditioning, Rescorla and Wagner (1972) point out that a CS is necessarily presented in a context that itself can be construed as a stimulus. Even with a single CS, then, conditioning is conducted with a compound in which the experimental context provides the additional stimulus. To return to Rescorla's (1968) study, for some subjects shocks were delivered during the interval between successive presentations of the CS, and this will enable the contextual stimuli to acquire associative strength. The context should then function in a manner analogous to the pretrained element in the earlier example for blocking, and block conditioning to the CS whenever it is presented. It also follows from the model that the more associative strength the blocking stimulus has, the more effective it will be in restricting conditioning to the target CS. Hence the model correctly predicts that increasing the associative strength of the context by increasing the probability of shock in the absence of the CS will reduce conditioning to the CS.

By assuming that the contextual cues can gain in associative strength when they are paired with a US, it is also possible for the model to explain why a negative CS–US contingency should result in inhibitory conditioning. In the study by Hearst and Franklin (1977), the delivery of food in the absence of the key-light will result in the growth of a context–food association. Whenever the key-light is presented against this excitatory context, the absence of food will result in the subject effectively undergoing training for conditioned inhibition.

EVALUATION OF THE RESCORLA–WAGNER MODEL

A great benefit of the Rescorla–Wagner model is that the manner in which it is formulated ensures that it generates testable predictions. The success of the model is revealed by the surprising number of these predictions that have been confirmed. For instance, consider an experiment in which two stimuli, A and B, are separately paired with the same US until V_A and V_B both equal λ. What will happen if the stimuli should then be presented together in a compound accompanied by the same US? With the help of Equation 3.7 spend a few moments calculating the effect of the compound trials on the associative strengths of A and B.

Because both A and B are paired with the US on compound trials, intuition, at least, suggests that this training should not weaken the original learning. According to the model, however, our intuition is wrong. Compound conditioning is, in fact, predicted to reduce to some extent the associative strength of A and B. This prediction has been confirmed in a number of studies (Kremer, 1978; Wagner & Rescorla, 1972).

It would be most convenient if the discussion could be closed at this point with the conclusion that the Rescorla–Wagner model provides the ideal account of the conditions of learning. Unhappily, the perfect learning theory has yet to be developed, and there are numerous results that this particular theory is unable to explain (Miller, Barnet, & Grahame, 1995).

The model provides a good account for many of the facts of compound conditioning, but not all the effects associated with blocking and over-shadowing are consistent with it. A summary of these and related findings can be found in Pearce (1987) and Pearce and Hall (1980). Of particular concern to the present discussion is the discovery that the model does not adequately account for the role of surprise in conditioning. A blocking experiment, using conditioned suppression, by Dickinson, Hall, and Mackintosh (1976) reveals this shortcoming.

A summary of the design is presented in Table 3.2. In Stage 1 two groups received excitatory conditioning in which on every trial a light was followed immediately after its offset by two shocks separated by an interval of 8 seconds. Both groups were then given compound conditioning with the light and a clicker. For Group C the compound was followed by two shocks, again separated by 8 seconds, but for Group E only the first of each pair of shocks accompanied the compound. Apart from the use of double shocks, the method for Group C resembles the conventional blocking design and, in keeping with most blocking studies, the clicker on test trials was found to produce an insubstantial CR.

The outcome for Group E was rather different, because on the test trials the clicker elicited a reasonably strong CR. Blocking for Group E was thus attenuated, and this must have been due to the surprising omission of the second shock during Stage 2. According to the Rescorla–Wagner (1972) model, in this instance effective conditioning with the clicker should definitely not have taken place. To be more specific, for Group E the value of λ in Stage 1, when two shocks followed each trial, will be greater than for the second stage, when only one shock followed each trial. As a consequence, the associative strength of the light at the outset of Stage 2 will be greater than the value of λ for this stage, and the compound trials should reduce the associative strengths of the light and the clicker to some degree. Because the clicker will start by being associatively neutral, Stage 2 is thus predicted to result in this stimulus becoming a conditioned inhibitor, rather than a conditioned excitor.

A further problem with the model relates to the extinction of conditioned inhibition. A conditioned inhibitor is said to possess negative associative strength. According to Equation 3.7, presenting such a stimulus by itself in a context of zero associative strength will result in it gaining positive increments of associative strength. Provided that sufficient trials of this nature are given, the gains will eventually counteract the negative strength and leave the stimulus neutral. However, an extensive investigation by Zimmer-Hart and Rescorla (1974) could find no evidence to support this prediction. Instead, the properties of the conditioned inhibitor were unaffected by the repeated presentation of this stimulus by itself. For a related failure of the model see Baker (1974), and see Rescorla (1979) for a discussion of the ways the model might overcome these difficulties.

Another problem with inhibition is the manner in which it is conceptualised as negative associative strength. There is no objection to this as far as accounting for the retardation and summation tests is concerned. However, we saw in Chapter 2 that occasionally a conditioned inhibitor can elicit its own CRs. How this can be explained by assuming that inhibition is nothing more than negative associative strength is hard to understand.

TABLE 3.2

Summary of the Training Given to the Two Groups of Rats in the Study by Dickinson et al. (1976).

	Stage 1	Stage 2	Test
Group E	Light → Sh + Sh	Clicker + Light → Sh	Clicker 0.27
Group C	Light → Sh + Sh	Clicker + Light → Sh + Sh	Clicker 0.45

Note: The effects of blocking were reduced by the surprising omission of one of a pair of shocks (Sh) during compound conditioning.

We shall also discover in Chapter 5 that there is a problem with the account offered by the Rescorla–Wagner (1972) model for the way in which discriminations are solved.

Despite the shortcomings of the Rescorla and Wagner theory, there are two reasons for taking it seriously. The first reason rests with the the the way in which it is presented. Any attempt to describe the behaviour of an animal with an equation might at first seem unduly optimistic. But once it is appreciated that the theory is concerned only with making qualitative predictions about the relative performance of animals that are treated differently, then the goals of theory can be seen as being reasonable. Furthermore, by being expressed in such formal terms it has been possible to derive testable predictions from the model, and these have led to experiments that on more than one occasion have supported the theory. Even on those occasions when the predictions were not confirmed, the theory has been of value by prompting the development of alternative theories of learning. The Rescorla–Wagner (1972) model, in short, provides an outstanding example of the benefits of a particular style of theorising.

The second reason for taking the theory seriously is that it can now be seen as an important, senior relative of a number of more recent theories of conditioning and associative learning. These theories will be encountered in the next part of this chapter, as well as in Chapter 5. By appreciating the strengths and weaknesses of the Rescorla–Wagner (1972) model, the reasons for the development of its descendants can be readily understood.

PART 2: ATTENTION AND CONDITIONING

Cognitive psychologists have long acknowledged that selective attention plays an important role in the processing of information by humans. They have pointed out that we are often exposed to more sources of information than we can deal with at once, and that some sort of selection is necessary to enable information from one source to be attended to while other information is being ignored. For instance, while you read this textbook, paying attention to the words will probably lead to the sensations in your feet being ignored. But once these sensations have been mentioned, you may concentrate on them momentarily, and this transfer of attention away from the text will disrupt reading. An experimental demonstration of this effect is provided by Brown and Poulton (1961).

People were asked to listen to repeated strings of 8 numbers. The same sequence was presented successively, except that a randomly selected member of the list was changed from one trial to the next. The task for the person was to listen to the sequence and identify the new item. Not surprisingly, performance was very accurate when this was all that subjects were required to do. But when they were asked to identify the changed number and at the same time drive a car through the rural lanes of Cambridgeshire, their accuracy declined considerably. Presumably these people were unable to attend to the task of driving as well as to the list of numbers, and one source of information had to be ignored. Happily for the pedestrians of Cambridgeshire, it was the numerical information that was rejected.

The suggestion has been made on more than one occasion that the attention that animals pay to stimuli can vary. Pavlov raised this possibility by monitoring what is now known as the *orienting response* (OR). In his studies of conditioning, Pavlov (1927, p.12) noted that novel stimuli often elicit an OR, or as he referred to it, an investigatory reflex that

> brings about the immediate response in man and animals to the slightest changes in the world around them, so that they immediately orientate their appropriate receptor organ in accordance with the perceptible quality in the agent bringing about the change, making full investigation of it.

The implication of this statement is that the OR is a consequence of the animal attending to the stimulus, and the vigour of this response may well provide an indication of the attention a stimulus receives. Other methods for determining the amount of attention that a stimulus receives are notably less direct. Hence it has been suggested that the conditionability of a stimulus is not solely determined by its intensity, as the Rescorla–Wagner (1972) model stipulates, but by the attention it receives. If this is correct, then the conditionability of a CS, or its associability with a US, will provide an indication of the attention paid to it.

An experiment by Kaye and Pearce (1987) shows how the the simple experience of being presented repeatedly with a stimulus might influence these measures of attention. Two groups of rats were placed into a conditioning chamber containing a light bulb and a food dispenser. For the first 12 sessions nothing happened for Group Novel, whereas for Group Familiar the bulb was illuminated for 10 seconds at a time at intervals in each session. Both groups were then given a single pretest session in which the light was occasionally illuminated for 10 seconds.

Figure 3.6 shows a typical OR to the light that was performed at the outset of training by Group Familiar. But as the left-hand side of Figure 3.7 reveals, with repeated exposure to the light the frequency with which this response occurred declined progressively across the 12 sessions. Such a decline in the responsiveness to a stimulus as a result of its repeated presentation is referred to as *habituation*. In the extreme right of this side the strength of the OR for both groups is presented for the pretest session. Not surprisingly, it was considerably more vigorous in Group Novel than in Group Familiar, which suggests that the groups differed in the amount of attention they paid to the light. All subjects were then conditioned with the light serving as a signal for food. If the repeated exposure to the light reduced the attention paid to it, then for Group Familiar conditioning should progress relatively slowly. The right-hand side of Figure 3.7 shows the strength of the CR of magazine activity during the light for both groups on the pretest session, when there was no difference, and on each of the four sessions of conditioning. As predicted, conditioning was more

rapid in Group Novel than in Group Familiar. Hence, extended exposure to the light reduced its conditionability in Group Familiar. This effect is known as latent inhibition (see Lubow, 1973)[1] and supports the claim that Group Familiar paid rather little attention to the light as a result of the preexposure stage.

One way of characterising attention is to assume that it is an all-or-none process. A stimulus might either be attended to fully, or not at all. In fact this is a relatively rare theoretical claim. An alternative view is that the amount of attention paid to a stimulus varies along a continuum, and this determines its effectiveness for conditioning as well as the strength of any ORs it might elicit. Such an assumption underlies each of the three theories that we shall now consider. The theories differ in the rules that are believed to govern changes in attention.

WAGNER'S THEORY

Over the course of a series of influential articles, Wagner has developed a complex and extremely comprehensive theory of the memory and learning processes in animals (Wagner, 1976, 1978, 1979, 1981; Wagner & Brandon, 1989; Wagner & Larew, 1985). This theory has been given the acronym SOP because it is concerned with the "Standard Operating Procedures" in memory. At the heart of this theory is the assumption that the representation, or memory, of a stimulus can be in three different states (see Figure 3.8). There is an inactive state where the memory is not modifiable, and it is unable to influence an animal's behaviour. The two remaining, active, states are referred to as A1 and A2 and when a stimulus is represented in these states it may influence behaviour. A stimulus that is in the A1 state could be said to be at the centre of an animal's attention, but when in the A2 state it will be at the periphery of the field of attention. In keeping with our earlier claim that a stimulus must be fully attended to if it is to be learned about readily, Wagner (1981) has proposed that excitatory and inhibitory conditioning is possible only when the CS is represented in the A1 state. The

FIGURE 3.6

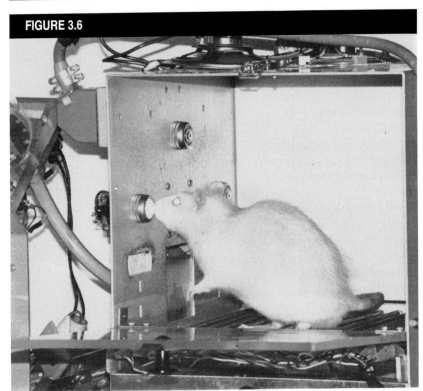

A typical orienting response by a rat to an illuminated bulb (from Kaye, 1983).

FIGURE 3.7

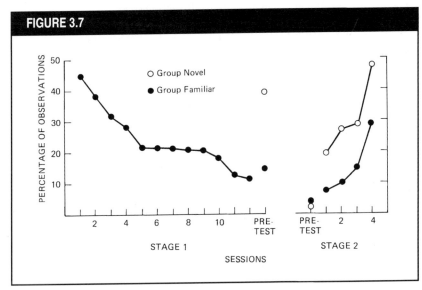

The left-hand side shows the frequency of the OR by rats to a light during 12 sessions of exposure, Group Familiar, and during a single pretest session when this stimulus was first shown to Group Novel. The right-hand side shows, for both groups, the amount of magazine activity in the presence of the light that was recorded during the pretest session and during the next four conditioning sessions (adapted from Kaye & Pearce, 1987).

FIGURE 3.8

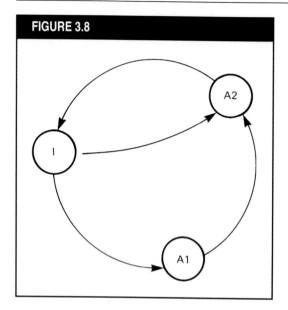

The relationship between the A1, A2, and inactive (I) states of a representation, as envisaged by the SOP model. When in the inactive state, a representation can be excited to the A1 state by presenting the stimulus to which it corresponds. The A2 representation of a stimulus develops either as a result of decay from the A1 state (self-generated representation), or directly from the I state by presenting a stimulus with which it is associated (retrieval-generated representation). Representations are assumed to decay rapidly from the A1 to the A2 state, and then more slowly from the A2 to the inactive state (adapted from Wagner, 1981).

OR to a stimulus will also presumably be strongest in these circumstances.

Information can reside more or less indefinitely in the inactive state, but only for a short while in the active states. More specifically, when information is in the A1 state, it will decay rapidly to the A2 state and then revert rather more slowly to its inactive state. As a result of this relationship the model correctly predicts that conditioning will be more effective with an intermediate rather than short- or long-duration CS (e.g. Smith, 1968). When the CS is too short, conditioning will be poor because there will have been insufficient time for a representation of the CS to be excited from the inactive to the A1 state. And when the CS is too long, the A1 representation that is essential for successful conditioning will have decayed into the A2 state and no longer be capable of entering into

associations. Thus, expressed informally, conditioning with an intermediate duration CS is successful because it is at this point that the stimulus will most fully occupy the animal's attention.

A further feature of the SOP model, and one of particular relevance to this chapter, is the proposal that a representation can be excited to the A1 state from the inactive but not from the A2 state. Thus if an animal is shown a stimulus for which a representation already exists in the A2 state, then an A1 representation of the stimulus will not be activated, and it will effectively be ignored. The two possible routes by which a stimulus can gain access to the A2 state, and hence influence an animal's sensitivity to a stimulus, will be considered separately.

Self-generated A2 representations

The first route has already been mentioned and consists of presenting the stimulus by itself. When it first occurs the stimulus will activate an A1 representation which will then decay rapidly to the A2 representation and, as we have just seen, this A2 representation will then revert slowly to the inactive state. Despite the simplicity of this proposal, it has important implications for both habituation and conditioning.

Habituation, it will be recalled, refers to the decline in responsiveness to a stimulus as a result of its repeated presentation. Suppose that an animal is presented with the same stimulus twice, with a short interval between each presentation. On its first occurrence, the stimulus will be represented in the A1 state and it may elicit a strong response. This state will then decay to the A2 state and the theory predicts that strength of the response will show a corresponding decline. If the stimulus should be presented again while the A2 representation is still active then, because of the principles on which SOP is based, the stimulus will be unable to activate an A1 representation and it will be unable to evoke a strong response. In other words there should be evidence of habituation with the second presentation of the stimulus. However, if the interval between the two presentations of the stimulus is long, then by the time of its second occurrence, the A2 representation of the first occurrence will have decayed to the inactive state. In these conditions, the theory predicts that an A1 representation will be formed of the stimulus on its second appearance and it will elicit a strong response. Thus SOP predicts that habituation is more likely to occur on the second presentation of a stimulus, when the interval between the two presentations is long rather than short.

An experiment that tests these proposals was conducted by Whitlow (1975) who used vasoconstriction (a rapid constriction of the blood vessels) as the measure of responsiveness to a tone. Rabbits were presented with a tone on one occasion, when it elicited a strong response of vasoconstriction, and on a second occasion some time later. In keeping with predictions from SOP, the response on the second trial was significantly stronger with a long rather than a short interval between the two tones.

The implications of this aspect of the SOP model for conditioning is revealed in an experiment by Best and Gemberling (1977). Rats were exposed to a flavour, which was then presented some time later as the CS for taste-aversion conditioning. For Group 3.5, the interval between the flavours was 3.5 hours, and for Group 23.5 it was 23.5 hours. Group Control received just the conditioning trial with no prior exposure to the flavour. On the following day all subjects were given a test trial in which they were allowed to drink the flavoured solutions. Figure 3.9 summarises the results of this test by showing the amount of solution consumed by the three groups. Conditioning was evidently effective with the control group, and with the group exposed to the flavour 23.5 hours before conditioning, as they consumed relatively little. In comparison, conditioning was far less effective for the group exposed to the flavour 3.5 hours before the conditioning trial. This poor conditioning, according to the SOP model, is due to the original exposure to the flavour leaving a memory trace in the A2 state that persisted until the conditioning trial. When the flavour was then presented for this trial, it would be unable to excite an A1 representation of itself, and conditioning should be ineffective. The results from Group 23.5 suggest, not surprisingly, that 23.5 hours is sufficient to

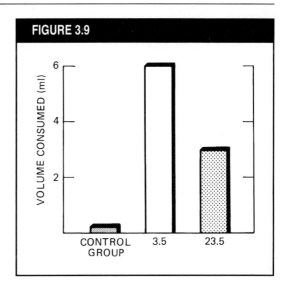

FIGURE 3.9

Mean volume of flavoured solution consumed on a test trial that followed a single flavour-aversion conditioning trial. Two groups were given a single exposure to the flavour either 3.5 or 23.5 hours prior to the conditioning trial, whereas for the control group conditioning was conducted with a novel flavour (adapted from Best & Gemberling, 1977).

allow the A2 trace to decay and permit conditioning when the flavour was again presented.

Retrieval-generated A2 representations

The second route by which a stimulus can gain access to the A2 state, and thus influence attention, is made possible by associative learning. For successful excitatory conditioning, the SOP model requires the simultaneous rehearsal of representations of the CS and the US while they are both in the A1 state. Once conditioning is completed, future presentations of the CS will then be able to excite a representation of the US directly into the A2 state. This is referred to as a retrieval-generated representation, as it is not excited by the US directly but by a CS with which it is associated.

An obvious example of the influence of retrieval-generated representations is provided by blocking. Suppose that stimulus A is paired with a US, prior to trials in which the compound AB is paired with the US. On trials with the compound, the US will be unable to excite an A1 representation of itself, because the presence of A will have activated an A2 representation of this stimulus. Conditioning with B will then be impossible, because it is paired with a representation of a US that is in an unsuitable state for associative learning. What may perhaps be rather less obvious is that a similar account can be developed to explain latent inhibition. Repeatedly presenting a neutral stimulus in a conditioning chamber will, according to the SOP model, result in the growth of a context–stimulus association. Consequently, whenever the animal is returned to the chamber, the sight of it will retrieve a representation of the stimulus to the A2 state. Should the stimulus then be presented in conjunction with a US, learning about this relationship will be difficult because the representation of the CS will be in a state that does not allow excitatory conditioning.

The experiments by Whitlow (1975) and by Best and Gemberling (1977) have also revealed effects that can be attributed to the influence of retrieval-generated A2 representations. In his study with rabbits, Whitlow (1975) discovered that the response to a repeatedly presented tone was greater on the first than on subsequent sessions of testing. This relatively long-term effect was attributed to the growth of a context–tone association during the first session. Subsequent placement of the rabbits into the apparatus should then partially retrieve an A2 representation of the tone and make them less responsive to it whenever it occurred. Thus the SOP model predicts that habituation is the result of the interaction of both short-term (self-generated) and long-term (retrieval-generated) processes.

For the study by Best and Gemberling (1977), inspection of Figure 3.9 reveals that conditioning with Group 23.5 was somewhat less effective than for Group Control. The interval of 23.5 hours between the first exposure to the flavour and the conditioning trial makes it unlikely that this disruption was due to the influence of a self-generated representation. But the pre-exposure trial may well have fostered the growth of a context–flavour association. This would then disrupt conditioning somewhat by ensuring that at least a component of the representation of the flavour was in the A2 state at the time of conditioning. See Westbrook, Bond, and Feyer (1981) for a similar finding.

Some novel predictions

One measure of the value of any theory is the degree to which it generates novel experimental research. In this respect Wagner's theorising has been most successful: A wide range of studies has been designed to test the theory, often with positive results.

We have seen that according to the theory the repeated experience of a stimulus in a specific context will result in the growth of a context–stimulus association and will be responsible for a loss of attention to that stimulus. But such a loss need not be permanent. Suppose the stimulus is subsequently presented in a different context with which it is not associated. The new context should not excite an A2 representation of the stimulus, and it should now be attended to fully. The theory predicts therefore that latent inhibition and habituation will be specific to the context in which the stimulus was exposed. Note that this prediction is confined to the influence of retrieval-generated representations. The more transient effects of self-generated A2 representations should be found in any context, as they depend simply on the recent occurrence of the stimulus concerned.

As far as both latent inhibition and habituation are concerned, there is evidence showing that these effects are specific to the context in which the stimulus was exposed. Lovibond, Preston, and Mackintosh (1984), for example, reported that exposure to a stimulus is more likely to disrupt future conditioning in the same than in a different chamber, whereas Evans and Hammond (1983) found that once habituation has occurred in one context, it is possible to observe dishabituation simply by presenting the stimulus in a different environment.

A related prediction concerns the influence of exposing animals to an experimental context after they have repeatedly been exposed to a stimulus in it. The original exposure will result in the development of a context–stimulus association. Then, just as presenting a CS without a US can weaken a previously formed CS–US association, so a context–stimulus association should be weakened by placing subjects in the apparatus without the stimulus. Such extinction will prevent the context from exciting an A2 representation of the stimulus, so that it should be be attended to when it next occurs. In support of this prediction Wagner (1978, pp.203–204) cites an experiment in which two groups of rabbits were exposed to a series of tones for a single habituation session. One group was then placed into the apparatus for two sessions, in the absence of the tone. Animals from the other group remained in their home cages for this stage. Finally, both groups were returned to the apparatus for a test of their reaction to the tone. Subjects given exposure to the context without the tone, which should have weakened the context–tone association, responded more on these test trials than did those that had spent the previous stage in their home cages.

The successes referred to can be contrasted with a number of failures to support the theory. Latent inhibition is said to be due to the growth of context–CS associations, so that a period of exposure to the apparatus alone after the prior exposure to the CS should weaken these associations and disrupt latent inhibition. Despite a number of tests of this prediction, it has met with very little success (Hall, 1992; Hall & Minor, 1984). In addition, habituating a stimulus and then presenting it in a new context should produce dishabituation, but this does not always occur (Hall & Channell, 1985; Marlin & Miller, 1981). Further results that are inconsistent with Wagner's theorising will also be mentioned later in this chapter. Despite these conflicting findings, the success with which the theory accounts for many of the phenomena associated with latent inhibition and habituation means that it would be unwise to ignore it as an account for the attentional processes of animals.

STIMULUS SIGNIFICANCE

One class of stimuli to which an animal might be expected to attend are those that signal events of biological significance. The animal that rapidly detects a signal for food, for instance, is more likely to survive than one that ignores this stimulus. Given this line of reasoning, several authors have proposed that animals are likely to pay most attention to stimuli that predict important events.

One of the first to make this suggestion was Von Uexkull (1934), who coined the phrase *hunting by search image*. This is meant to imply that when animals are searching for food, their perceptual systems are biased to facilitate the identification of a particular type of food at the expense of not recognising other types. Provided that the food being attended to is in plentiful supply, this should be an efficient strategy for gaining nourishment.

Support for this proposal comes from an experiment by Bond (1983) who presented pigeons with a mixture of two different types of grain on a gravel-based background. When the grains were conspicuous in respect to the background, the birds showed no bias in their choice of grain. A marked bias for one type of grain over another was shown, however, when they were both difficult to distinguish from the background. Thus, if identification of food is difficult, pigeons attend selectively to the features of a single food type to facilitate its discovery. (See also Dawkins, 1971a,b; Plaisted & Mackintosh, 1995)

Another way in which an increase in attention to significant stimuli is believed to influence behaviour is during the course of conditioning and discrimination learning. Lawrence (1949, 1950) first put forward this suggestion, and he supported it with a number of experiments that were said to show that cues that are relevant to the solution of a discrimination, as he put it, acquired distinctiveness. Although the interpretation of these experiments has been called into question (Siegel, 1967), there has been continued theoretical interest in the idea that significant stimuli gain in the attention they are paid during the course of conditioning (Mackintosh, 1975a; Moore & Stickney, 1980; Sutherland & Mackintosh, 1971). In the discussion that follows we shall focus on the most successful of these theories.

Mackintosh's theory

The theory of Mackintosh (1975a) is based on the claim that animals will pay attention to, and hence learn readily about, stimuli that are good predictors of significant events such as food or shock. In other words, stimuli with high associative strength are likely to receive more attention than those with low associative strength. In fact, the theory is not quite this simple. To be attended to fully, a CS must not only be a good predictor of the US, it must be a better predictor than all the other stimuli that are present on a trial.

One important feature of Mackintosh's (1975a) theory is that it provides a different account of blocking to that considered hitherto. The Rescorla–Wagner (1972) model, as well as Wagner's (1981) SOP model, maintain that blocking is due to the US being fully predicted and thus incapable of entering into novel associations. Mackintosh (1975a) has challenged this claim by proposing that blocking is entirely a result of subjects ignoring the stimulus added for compound conditioning.

To understand the application of his theory to blocking, it is essential to emphasise that Mackintosh (1975a) rejects the Rescorla–Wagner (1972) account of compound conditioning. As an alternative, the growth of associative strength to a CS is given by Equation 3.11, which is to be applied when the stimulus is presented either in isolation or in conjunction with other stimuli.

$$\Delta V_A = \alpha_A(\lambda - V_A) \qquad (3.11)$$

According to this equation conditioning with a CS is completely unaffected by the properties of any other stimuli that accompany it. The value of α reflects the amount of attention that the stimulus receives, and the greater its value, the more rapid will conditioning be. The way in which α is calculated need not concern us here, except to note that α will approach 1 when the stimulus is a good predictor of the US relative to other stimuli, and when the stimulus is a relatively poor predictor of the US then α will approach 0.

Consider now a blocking experiment in which a tone is paired with a US prior to conditioning with a light–tone compound. On the first compound trial the attention paid to the light will be relatively high because of its novelty, and Equation 3.11 predicts that it will gain in associative strength. Animals will also have the opportunity of discovering on this trial that the light is a much poorer predictor of the US than the tone. As a result, on future conditioning trials they should pay very little

attention to the light and further increments in associative strength to this stimulus will be slight.

The difference between this account and that provided by the Rescorla–Wagner model for blocking is emphasised by the conflicting predictions they make. As we have seen, the theory of Mackintosh (1975a) asserts that conditioning with the added CS should be normal on the first compound trial. It is only on later trials when the added CS is ignored that the effects of blocking should become evident. In contrast, the Rescorla–Wagner (1972) model predicts that provided the US is fully predicted on the first compound trial, conditioning with the added CS should be impossible.

In keeping with the prediction from his theory, Mackintosh (1975b) has shown that conditioning with the added CS is normal for the first compound-conditioning trial. But there was very little change in the associative strength of this stimulus on subsequent compound trials. More recent experiments, however, have raised doubts about the interpretation of this finding, and it should not be regarded as providing convincing support for the theory. Instead, stronger support can be found in studies which have looked at the influence of surprise on blocking (Dickinson, Hall, & Mackintosh, 1976; Dickinson & Mackintosh, 1979; Mackintosh, Bygrave, & Picton, 1977). One of these studies was described earlier (see p.64), where its results were shown to be incompatible with predictions from the Rescorla–Wagner (1972) model. Essentially the study demonstrated that the surprising omission of one of a pair of shocks after each compound-conditioning trial was sufficient to disrupt blocking. According to the theory, this outcome is due to the surprising omission of one shock arresting the decline in attention to the added stimulus, and hence allowing subjects to learn about its relationship with the shock that was presented. A more detailed presentation of this account can be found in Dickinson and Mackintosh (1979).

Selective association and learned irrelevance

In addition to enhancing our understanding of such effects as blocking, the theory of Mackintosh (1975a) has the merit of pointing to a new way of looking at an effect known as selective association. An assumption that was once common to many theories of learning is that conditioning will be equally effective, no matter what stimuli are paired together. In a discussion of this topic Seligman and Hager (1972) referred to this claim as the principle of equipotentiality, but, they argued, there is abundant evidence to contradict it. For example, Garcia and Koelling (1966) (see Chapter 1, p.12) found that rats associate a novel flavour with subsequent illness much more readily than an auditory–visual compound. This is not simply due to the interoceptive stimulus being more intense and hence a more effective CS than the exteroceptive compound, because the opposite pattern of results was found when the stimuli were paired with shock. Moreover, this pattern of results is not confined to tastes, illness, or rats. Shapiro, Jacobs, and LoLordo (1980) have demonstrated a similar outcome with pigeons. These animals have little trouble in learning that a red light signals food, but they learn with difficulty when the same stimulus is used to signal shock. Conversely, conditioning with a tone progresses more readily when it signals an aversive rather than an appetitive US. The term *selective association* refers to this general finding that some CS–US relationships can be learned about more readily than others.

One explanation for selective association is that it is due to some stimuli, or stimulus dimensions, being more relevant to the occurrence of biologically significant events than others. In the case of the Garcia and Koelling (1966) study, for example, tastes are likely to provide more reliable information than sound about whether or not a certain food is poisonous. Given such naturally occurring relationships, it would be in the animal's best interests to capitalise on them by learning rapidly about those that are most reliable. Animals may also benefit by being disposed to learn little or nothing at all about those relationships that are unlikely in their natural environment (Seligman, 1970; Seligman & Hager, 1972).

Experiments on selective association thus suggest that during conditioning animals will attend most to those stimuli, or dimensions, that in the past have proved reliable predictors of the US concerned. But how do they know which cues are most relevant for a given US? According to Rozin and Kalat (1971), this knowledge is acquired as a result of evolutionary processes. That is, some members of a species may be innately disposed to learn rapidly about the relationship between tastes and illness and hence more likely to survive, and to pass on this characteristic, than those lacking in this respect.

The implication of this suggestion is that selective association will be evident from birth, which is supported by the findings of Gemberling and Domjan (1982). Rats were conditioned when they were only 24 hours old with either illness, induced by an injection of lithium chloride, or electric shock. When illness constituted the US, the consumption of saccharin—but not being placed into a cardboard box—was an effective CS. But when shock was the US, it was being placed into the box, rather than saccharin, that was the more effective US. The rats are unlikely to have learned anything during their first 24 hours of life that would account for this pattern of results. Instead, the most likely explanation for these findings is that rats are genetically disposed to learn about some relationships more easily than about others.

In addition to innate factors, the discovery of an effect known as *learned irrelevance* suggests that an animal's experience may also contribute to selective association. In a typical study Mackintosh (1973) exposed rats to random presentations of a CS and foot shock (Group Random). As the CS was no better a predictor of the US than the contextual stimuli, his theory predicts that attention to the CS will decline. To test this prediction, conditioned suppression training in which the CS and US were paired was then conducted. Figure 3.10 shows that conditioning for this group was considerably less effective than for Group Control, in which the CS and US were both novel at the start of conditioning. A third group, Group Water, was also included in this study. These subjects were given random presentations of the CS and water prior to conditioned suppression training in which the same CS was paired with shock. The intriguing finding from this group is that their pretreatment with the CS had a much less disruptive influence on conditioning than for Group Random. The converse of this effect has also been demonstrated:

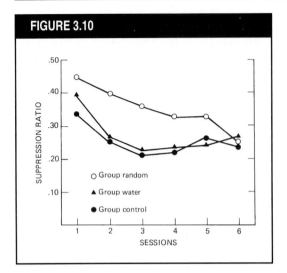

FIGURE 3.10

Acquisition of conditioned suppression by 3 groups of rats trained with a CS that was novel for the start of conditioning (Group Control) or had previously been presented in a random relationship with shock (Group Random) or with water (Group Water) (adapted from Mackintosh, 1973).

Conditioning with water is disrupted to a greater extent by prior random presentations of the CS and water than of the CS and shock. Here then is an example of selective association that is due to the individual's experience, rather than to its evolutionary history.

To explain this pattern of findings, Mackintosh (1973; see also Bennett, Maldonado, & Mackintosh, 1995) proposed that the random pairings of a CS and a US will result in a loss of attention to the CS that is US-specific. Put informally, learning that a CS is irrelevant to the delivery of shock will lead to animals ignoring it when these events are eventually paired. However, should the CS be used to signal a different US, such as water, then attention to it will be restored, and conditioning will progress more readily.

There is, however, an alternative explanation for these findings. The slow conditioning in the test phase of the aforementioned studies may have been due to the CS being a conditioned inhibitor, rather than to it being ignored. In the first stage of the experiment, the random presentation of the CS and foot shock might be thought sufficient to make the former a signal for the absence of the latter, and this inhibitory learning would disrupt conditioning when they were paired together. A problem with

this interpretation is that the probability of shock in the presence of the CS was identical to that in its absence. Such treatment constitutes a zero contingency between the CS and US, whereas I argued earlier that inhibitory learning depends on a negative contingency. In addition, Baker and Mackintosh (1977) have shown that random presentations of the CS and US can also disrupt subsequent inhibitory conditioning with the CS. This outcome is consistent with the claim that animals ignore the CS as a result of the pretraining, and directly opposite to that expected if the CS becomes a conditioned inhibitor because of its random relationship with the US.

The results reported in this section again point to the importance of attentional factors in governing the behaviour of animals. The principal theoretical claim that has been examined is that animals will pay attention to those stimuli that predict important events. Tests of this claim have led to some ingenious experiments that have enhanced considerably our understanding of the factors that influence such effects as blocking. Furthermore, from experimental tests considerable support has been derived of the converse of this claim—that stimuli which are poor predictors of important events will be ignored. In conclusion, however, we should note that it has proved very difficult to demonstrate that the conditionability of a stimulus will be high if it is a good predictor of a US (Siegel, 1967). Indeed, we shall encounter shortly some evidence which stands in direct opposition to this proposal.

PEARCE–HALL THEORY

To introduce the third account of animal attention it may help to return to the experiment of Brown and Poulton (1961), in which people found it difficult to attend to a string of numbers while driving. There was an additional group in this study consisting of policemen with considerable driving experience. They, too, were required to identify the changed member of a list while driving, but they were able to do both tasks without difficulty, even in urban areas. Perhaps this result should not be too surprising, as the popularity of car radios attests to the ability of many people to drive and attend to an unrelated source of information at the same time. The challenge posed by such results is to provide an adequate theory of attention to explain them.

According to a number of authors, people have two modes of attention that can operate simultaneously. One of these is assumed to be of limited capacity and is directed towards tasks that are novel or require conscious control. This type of attention is referred to as *controlled* or *deliberate* (LaBerge & Samuels, 1974; Shiffrin & Schneider, 1977). An example of a task that might be appropriate to this type of attention is the number identification task employed by Brown and Poulton (1961). The other type of attention is more *automatic* and directed towards tasks that are very well practiced and the performance of which is more or less habitual. When learning to drive, it can be assumed that the novelty of the task will demand controlled processing and that there will be little spare capacity available for attending to numbers. With practice, however, automatic processes may be responsible for driving, freeing the controlled processing mechanisms to cope with other tasks.

It is within this framework that the Pearce–Hall (1980) model can be most readily understood. This model is based on the supposition that animals need to attend to a stimulus only while they are learning about its relationship with its consequences. With Pavlovian conditioning, for instance, attention must be paid to the CS to allow it to gain or lose associative strength. But once conditioning has reached a stable asymptote, there will be no further need for the subject to attend to the CS and it can be ignored, at least as far as learning is concerned. This type of attention is analogous to controlled processing in humans. Of course, once learning has ceased, the fact that the stimulus may no longer receive controlled processing does not mean that it will be without influence. Instead, it is assumed that once learning has reached a stable asymptote, the CS will be detected, and the appropriate CR triggered, by automatic processes.

According to Pearce and Hall (1980), therefore, controlled attention will be directed most to those stimuli that need to be learned about. But what sort of stimuli fall into this category? To answer this question we proposed that the surprisingness of the event that follows a CS will determine how much learning remains to be done with that CS. If learning about a CS has reached a stable asymptote, then the US that follows it will not come as a surprise, and no further learning will be needed. In contrast, if learning about the CS–US relationship is still taking place, then the US will to some extent be surprising after each presentation of the CS and thus indicate the need for additional learning. Hence, if the US is surprising on conditioning trial n, then on trial $n + 1$ the CS should receive attention so that learning about its relationship with the US can continue. But if the US that accompanies a CS is entirely predictable, then there is little need for learning and hence little need for attention to be directed towards the CS on future trials.

To present these ideas formally we used the now familiar discrepancy $\lambda - V$. The relationship between this discrepancy on trial n, and the amount of attention paid to the CS on the next trial, α_{n+1}, is given by Equation 3.12

$$\alpha_{n+1} = |\lambda_n - V_n| \qquad (3.12)$$

On trials when the US is surprising, the value of the discrepancy will be large, and attention to the CS will be high on the following trial. But as the CS becomes a better predictor of the US, there will be a smaller difference between λ and V, and attention to the CS will be reduced accordingly.

Implications for the OR

An experiment by Kaye and Pearce (1984) demonstrates the operation of these principles. The aim of the study was to test the Pearce–Hall (1980) theory by using the OR as an index of the attention paid to a light CS during conditioning. Three groups of rats received in a pretest session six presentations of the light, each lasting for 10 seconds, so that their reactions to it when novel could be assessed. Figure 3.11 indicates that attention to the light for this session was comparatively high. The conditions for the groups then differed for the test stage of the experiment, which comprised 14 sessions. In each session, Group None was given a number of exposures to the light entirely in the absence of any US. In these circumstances the events following the light will never be surprising, because from the outset it will not predict a US and none will occur. Accordingly, there will be no need for subjects to attend to the light, and it should very quickly be ignored. Figure 3.11 shows support for this prediction in a rapid decline in the frequency of the OR across sessions. The second group, Group Continuous, received the same number of presentations of the light as the previous group, but each one was followed by a pellet of food. Initially, the low associative strength of the light will ensure that the food with which it is paired is unexpected, and attention to the light should be considerable. As training progresses, however, the CS will gain in associative strength, and as it becomes a better predictor of the US so attention to it will decline. Thus the model predicts that the OR to the light will be high at the start of conditioning but decline gradually thereafter. Once again, these predictions are supported by the results shown in Figure 3.11.

The final group, Group Partial, received the light followed by food on a random 50% of the trials, and on the remaining trials the light was followed by nothing. With this schedule rats will be unable to predict what will follow the CS on each trial, and as a result the occurrence of food, or

its omission, will consistently be surprising. The effect of this should be to sustain attention to the light no matter how many times it is presented. In confirmation of this prediction Figure 3.11 shows that for Group Partial the OR to the light was as vigorous after 14 sessions (84 trials) as when it was novel.

Implications for conditioning

Pearce and Hall (1980) proposed that animals will pay least attention to and hence learn most slowly about those stimuli that have been followed by accurately predicted events, whereas stimuli that have been paired with surprising events should be attended to and learned about readily. To explain the rapid conditioning that often occurs with a novel CS, the theory accepts that the attention paid to a stimulus is high when it is first presented. But once conditioning has commenced, the CS will gain in associative strength and become a progressively more accurate predictor of the US. This will result in a gradual loss of attention to the CS, and the increments in associative strength will therefore be less on later than on earlier trials. Eventually the CS will accurately predict the US, whereupon it will be ignored completely and no further changes in associative strength will be

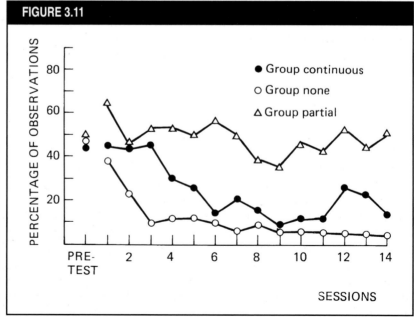

FIGURE 3.11

The frequency with which an OR to a light was recorded for three groups in a pretest session and during the next 14 sessions when the light signalled nothing (Group None), food on every trial (Group Continuous), or food on a randomly determined half of the trials (Group Partial) (adapted from Kaye & Pearce, 1984).

possible. This relationship between attention and learning is summarised by Equation 3.13 in which α is given by Equation 3.12 and S is determined by the intensity of the CS.

$$\Delta V = \alpha \,.\, S \,.\, \lambda \qquad (3.13)$$

The interpretation of the study by Kaye and Pearce (1984) points to the way in which the Pearce–Hall model explains latent inhibition. Attention was said to decline to a stimulus that is repeatedly presented by itself, because it is an accurate predictor of nothing (Group None). If such a stimulus should then be paired with a US, it will gain associative strength more slowly than if it were novel.

Blocking.   The presentation of the Pearce–Hall model so far has been concerned exclusively with the effects of training with a single CS. When applied to compound conditioning, it is assumed that as long as the US is accurately predicted by one stimulus, or a collection of stimuli, then there is no further need for learning and thus no further need for attention to the stimuli present on that trial. As a consequence, Pearce and Hall (1980) stipulate that for conditioning with a compound, attention to each element will be determined by how accurately the US is predicted by all the stimuli that belong to the compound. To incorporate this stipulation into Equation 3.12, the value of V must be determined by the combined associative strength of all the stimuli that are present on a trial.

Quite surprisingly, given the differences between them, the Pearce–Hall model now makes exactly the same predictions about blocking as Mackintosh's theory. On the first compound-conditioning trial the novelty of the added stimulus will ensure it receives attention and that it acquires some associative strength. The subject will also discover on this trial that the stimulus is followed by a US that is totally unsurprising, because its occurrence will be predicted by the other element of the compound. This discovery will ensure that the new stimulus is virtually ignored on the next trial, and further changes in its associative strength will be slight.

Latent inhibition of a CS. The difference between the theories of Mackintosh (1975a) and Pearce and Hall (1980), however, is brought out very clearly by another set of experiments (Hall & Pearce, 1979, 1982a,b; Pearce & Hall, 1979). In one of these (Hall & Pearce 1982a), three groups of rats received conditioned suppression training in which a tone was paired with a moderately strong shock. For Group Novel, the tone was novel at the outset of this stage, and conditioning with it was very rapid (see Figure 3.12). Prior to conditioning with moderately strong shock, Group Pretrain experienced a large number of conditioning trials in which the tone was paired with a relatively weak shock. At the start of conditioning with the weak shock animals should attend to the tone as it gains in associative strength; but once conditioning has

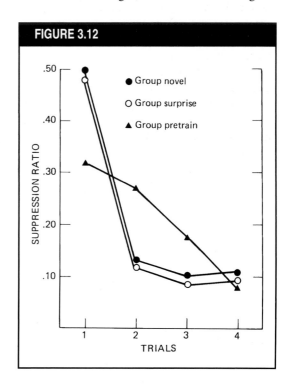

FIGURE 3.12

Acquisition of conditioned suppression to a tone by three groups of rats when it was paired with a strong shock for four test trials. The tone was novel at the outset of this training for Group Novel, but for Groups Pretrain and Surprise it had previously been paired with a weak shock. Group Surprise additionally received two trials with the tone presented alone between the two conditioning stages (adapted from Hall & Pearce, 1982a).

reached asymptote, the Pearce–Hall (1980) theory predicts that the tone should be ignored. This low level of attention to the tone should then ensure that conditioning progresses slowly when it is paired with the large shock for the test phase. In other words, the Pearce–Hall (1980) theory predicts that it should be possible to obtain latent inhibition by repeatedly pairing the CS with a US, as well as repeatedly presenting it by itself. In confirmation of this prediction Figure 3.12 shows that conditioning with Group Pretrain was slow for the test stage. Note that the low suppression ratio on the first trial was probably due to the pretraining with the weak shock.

Subjects in Group Pretrain eventually learned about the relationship between the tone and the large shock, albeit gradually, and this can be explained in the following manner. The low attention paid to the tone on the first trial will permit only a limited increment of associative strength. Of more importance, however, is that subjects will also be provided with the opportunity of discovering that the tone is again followed by a surprising US—in the recent past it accurately predicted a small US, and now suddenly it is followed by a large one. Attention to the tone should therefore be restored and enable better learning about the CS–strong shock relationship in the future. To test this account a third group was included in the study, Group Surprise. These subjects received the same initial training as Group Pretrain, but on the test session two *surprise* trials prior to conditioning with the large shock were included. These trials consisted simply of following the tone by nothing and were intended to alert animals to the fact that the CS is no longer an accurate predictor of shock. Such a manipulation should restore attention to the tone and facilitate conditioning with the larger shock in the final stage. The results confirmed this prediction by showing that Group Surprise conditioned more rapidly than Group Pretrain and at much the same rate as Group Novel. A similar finding, but using appetitive conditioning, has been reported by Wilson, Boumphrey and Pearce (1992).

Turning now to the theory of Mackintosh (1975a), pairing the tone with the weak shock in Group Pretrain should result in the tone eventually being the best available predictor of this US. The theory therefore predicts that the original training with the tone will ensure that it receives considerable attention, and conditioning will progress rapidly when it is paired with the larger shock. By failing to confirm this prediction, the results from Group Pretrain pose a serious challenge to perhaps the most important assumption of the theory. The idea that animals pay a lot of attention to stimuli that signal biologically important events is undoubtedly attractive. On the basis of the findings that have just been discussed, however, we must conclude that if a high level of attention is directed to such stimuli, then it is in order to ensure they elicit appropriate responses, rather than to determine their conditionability.

The results from Group Surprise also have a bearing on the theory developed by Wagner (1981). The way to restore attention to a stimulus according to this theory is to present it in a manner that ensures that it is not represented in the A2 state. We saw earlier that this may be achieved either by exposing subjects to the stimulus in a different context, or by adopting steps to weaken previously formed context–stimulus associations. In the case of Group Surprise, neither of these manipulations was adopted, yet a restoration of attention to the tone was recorded, as revealed by the rapid conditioning in the test phase relative to Group Pretrain. This finding strongly implies that it is how accurately the events following a stimulus are predicted that determines the attention it receives.

Before closing this discussion of the Pearce–Hall model, we should note, with regret, that even this theory has its shortcoming. A clear prediction from the theory is that once a stimulus is ignored, attention to it can be restored only by following it with a surprising event. However, in the discussion of Wagner's theory it was shown that attention to a stimulus can be restored in a number of other ways. It may be restored by presenting the stimulus in a new context, or by placing the subject in the original context and withholding the stimulus for a number of sessions.

Another problem for the theory is posed by Mackintosh's (1973) discovery of learned irrelevance, in which random pairings of a CS and US were found to retard conditioning when they were eventually paired. By being randomly related to the US, the CS can be considered to be an inaccurate predictor of its occurrence. Hence, according to the theory, attention should remain at a high level to this stimulus and facilitate conditioning in the test phase. One possible explanation for the failure to confirm this prediction can be based on the fact that the random presentations of the CS and US will result in the growth of a context–US association. As a consequence, whenever the US is, by chance, paired with the CS, it will be accurately predicted by the contextual stimuli, and attention to the CS will decline because it is followed by an accurately predicted event.

CONCLUDING COMMENTS

The great pity when considering the afore-mentioned three theories of attention is that not one of them is able to explain all the relevant experimental findings. Perhaps we should conclude, therefore, that there is a grain of truth in each of these different theories, and that the attentional processes in animals are more complex than has hitherto been acknowledged. On a more positive note, the development of these theories has led to the discovery of a wide range of experimental findings that now show the importance of attention in animal learning and cognition. Even if they achieve nothing else, the theories will have been of value.

There has been a marked imbalance in the comparative study of attention. A large number of studies have shown habituation in a wide range of species. In contrast, there have been remarkably few attempts to discover whether changes in the conditionability of stimuli can be obtained with species other than mammals. Lubow (1973) reviews experiments showing latent inhibition in goats, dogs, sheep, rats, and rabbits, but beyond this, studies of latent inhibition are rare. There have been several attempts to demonstrate latent inhibition in pigeons, but these have led to conflicting findings (Mackintosh, 1973; Tranberg & Rilling, 1978); others have had no success in their attempts to show latent inhibition in honey-bees (Bitterman, Menzel, Fietz, & Schafer, 1983) or goldfish (Shishimi, 1985). If future research should confirm that changes in attention, as indexed by changes in conditionability, are unique to mammals, then this will be an important discovery. Perhaps selective attention, or some aspects of it, is one capacity that will allow us to differentiate between the cognitive processes of species.

Finally, the experiments described in this chapter demonstrate forcefully that conditioning does not occur automatically whenever the CS and US are paired together. Experiments designed to test the Rescorla–Wagner theory, as well as the theory of Wagner, demonstrate that a US can be effective for conditioning in some circumstances, but not others. Likewise, the experiments considered in the second section of this chapter demonstrate that certain experiences with a CS can alter its effectiveness for conditioning. If future theories of learning are to be successful they must take account of these changes in the properties of both the CS and the US.

NOTE

1. The term "latent inhibition" might imply that the disruption in conditioning to which it refers is the same as that produced by conditioned inhibition. But this is incorrect for two reasons: In Chapter 2 it is proposed that inhibitory conditioning depends on the CS being followed by the omission of an expected US. Latent inhibition, on the other hand, can develop in the absence of an expectancy of a US. Furthermore, latent inhibition has been found to disrupt inhibitory conditioning (e.g. Reiss & Wagner, 1972). Such an outcome should not occur if latent and conditioned inhibition were the same; it is, however, entirely consistent with the view that latent inhibition reflects a loss of attention to the CS.

4

Instrumental Conditioning

Behaviour is often affected by its consequences. Responses that lead to reward are repeated, whereas responses that lead to punishment are withheld. Instrumental conditioning refers to the method of using reward and punishment in order to modify an animal's behaviour. The first laboratory demonstration of instrumental conditioning was provided by Thorndike (1898) who, as we saw in Chapter 1, trained cats to make a response in order to escape from a puzzle box and earn a small amount of fish. Since this pioneering work, there have been many thousands of successful demonstrations of instrumental conditioning, employing a wide range of species, and a variety of experimental designs. Skinner, for example, taught two pigeons, by means of instrumental conditioning, to play ping-pong with each other.

From the point of view of understanding the mechanisms of animal intelligence, three important issues are raised by a successful demonstration of instrumental conditioning. We need to know what information an animal acquires as a result of its training. Pavlovian conditioning was shown to promote the growth of stimulus–stimulus associations, but what sort of associations develop when a response is followed by a reward or punishment? Once the nature of the associations formed during instrumental conditioning has been identified, we then need to

specify the conditions that promote their growth. Surprise, for example, is important for successful Pavlovian conditioning, but what are the necessary ingredients to ensure the success of instrumental conditioning? Finally, we need to understand the factors that determine when, and how vigorously, an instrumental response will be performed.

Before turning to a detailed discussion of these issues, we must be clear what is meant by the term "reinforcer". This word is frequently used to refer to the rewards and punishments that are presented for instrumental conditioning, but different authors use it in different ways. For present purposes the term reinforcer, or *positive reinforcer*, will refer to any event that increases the probability of a response when the event follows that response. An increase in the probability of a response can also result from the removal of a stimulus, such as electric shock, in which case the stimulus is said to be a *negative reinforcer*.

THE NATURE OF INSTRUMENTAL LEARNING

A number of theorists have proposed that instrumental conditioning is effective because it allows animals to learn something about the responses they make and, as we shall see shortly, there is now a wealth of evidence to support this proposal. First, however, we must consider the possibility that instrumental conditioning depends on nothing more than the growth of CS–US associations.

Learning about responses or stimuli?

At first sight, it might seem absurd to suppose that all instrumental responses are a consequence of the growth of CS–US associations. After all, Pavlovian conditioning produces such a limited range of reflexive responses and may lead to maladaptive behaviour (see p.52). But it is not quite as easy to dismiss a Pavlovian account of instrumental conditioning as one might think.

Consider a hungry rat that is placed into a conditioning chamber with a lever. While exploring the apparatus, it might accidentally depress the lever, and food will be delivered. The stimuli perceived by the animal immediately prior to the food will therefore be those related to the lever, and an association might develop between the lever and food. The sight of the lever on a subsequent trial could then elicit an appetitive CR of approach towards the lever. If this should result in the lever being pressed, then food will be delivered, the lever–food association will be further strengthened, and the rat will be more likely to approach the lever in the future.

How accurate is this account? Although during the early stages of training rats often operate a lever by biting it—a response that resembles a consummatory CR—observation of a well-trained rat executing a rapid and efficient series of lever presses before moving to the magazine to collect food makes a Pavlovian account implausible. There is, in addition, experimental evidence that shows even more clearly the inadequacy of a Pavlovian interpretation of instrumental conditioning.

A certain amount of difficulty has been reported in training rats to perform such stereotyped responses as scratching and face-washing to obtain food (Shettleworth, 1975). None the less, the frequency of these responses can be increased by instrumental conditioning, and this finding is difficult to explain if all that animals are capable of is stimulus–stimulus learning. Pearce et al. (1978), for example, increased the frequency with which a rat scratched itself by presenting food every time this response was performed. Scratching bears no similarity to any of the activities that are normally directed towards food, and it is unreasonable to suppose that it is a Pavlovian CR. Instead, a more plausible explanation for this finding is that the rats had learned something about the response.

Studies employing what is known as the bidirectional control also suggest that animals can learn about their responses. This method was used by Grindley (1932), who conducted an experiment with the apparatus depicted in Figure 4.1. A guinea pig was placed into the harness, and when it was facing forwards a buzzer sounded. The buzzer remained on until the guinea pig turned its head in a specified direction, say, to the right. The buzzer was then switched off, and the subject was allowed a single bite on a carrot. A few minutes later the buzzer was switched on for the start of the next trial. At first it took over a minute for the correct response to be made after the onset of the buzzer, but with training the guinea pig learned to turn its head within a second or two of hearing the buzzer.

There is no doubt that this training could result in the growth of a tone–carrot, Pavlovian association, but it seems implausible that a turn of the head to the right should then occur as a Pavlovian CR to the tone. Even if this argument is ignored, a second stage of the experiment allows us to conclude with confidence that the response Grindley (1932) trained was not a CR. For this stage, the subject was trained in exactly the same manner as before, except that it had to turn its head to the left to obtain a reward. Despite some initial difficulty, the guinea pigs soon learned to perform this response swiftly whenever a trial started. Now, if it is assumed that looking to the right was a CR elicited as a result of subjects learning that the buzzer signalled a carrot, then some alternative learning process must have been responsible for the subsequent strengthening of the opposite response of turning the head to the left. The most obvious candidate for this process is one that permits animals to learn about their own behaviour. Thus when the same technique can be used to train opposite responses, then it can be safely concluded that at least one of them is a consequence of instrumental learning.

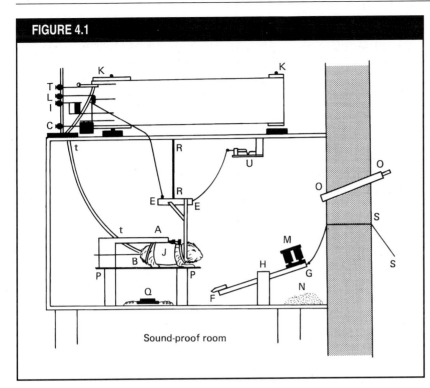

FIGURE 4.1

A sketch of the apparatus used by Grindley (1932) for instrumental conditioning with guinea pigs. A piece of freshly cut carrot was fixed to the lever at the point marked F (adapted from Grindley, 1932).

A rather different experiment that also shows animals are capable of learning about their responses was conducted by Jackson, Alexander and Maier (1980), using a three-arm Y-maze. A rat was placed in one arm of this apparatus and received an electric shock through the grid floor until it moved to the adjacent left arm. A short while later the shock was again turned on, and the same escape response of moving to the adjacent left arm was required. The delivery of shock resulted at first in animals often going to the incorrect, adjacent right arm and perhaps even returning to the original arm before they responded correctly. With continued training, however, the number of such errors declined so that a correct escape response was performed rapidly on nearly every trial. In this task there is no stimulus which the animal can approach consistently in order to escape shock and thus it is difficult to attribute the improvement in performance to Pavlovian conditioning. Instead, the reduction in errors must be attributed to instrumental learning, in which the rats learned to make a specific response whenever the shock was switched on.

The experiments by Grindley (1932) and Jackson et al. (1980) may point to the conclusion that animals are capable of learning about responses, but it does not tell us what this learning consists of. In fact, learning theorists have been concerned with this question for about a century now, and by way of background to the rest of this section a summary of the early attempts to answer this question is presented next.

Historical background

Thorndike (1898) was the first to propose that instrumental conditioning is based on learning about responses. According to his Law of Effect, when a response is followed by a reinforcer, then a stimulus–response (S–R) connection is strengthened. In the case of a rat that must press a lever for food, the stimulus might be the lever itself and the response would be the action of pressing the lever. Each successful lever press would thus serve to strengthen a connection between the sight of the lever and the response of pressing it. As a result, whenever the rat came across the lever in the future, it would be likely to press it and thus gain reward. This analysis of instrumental conditioning has formed the basis of a number of extremely influential theories of learning (e.g. Guthrie, 1935; Hull, 1943).

A feature of the Law of Effect that has proved unacceptable to the intuitions of many psychologists is that it fails to allow the animal to anticipate the goal for which it is responding. The only knowledge that an S–R connection allows an animal to possess is that it must make a particular response in the presence of a given stimulus. The delivery of food after the response will, according to the Law of Effect, effectively come as a complete surprise to the animal. In addition to sounding implausible, this proposal has for many years conflicted with a variety of experimental findings.

One early finding is reported by Tinkelpaugh (1928) who required monkeys to select one of two food wells in order to obtain reward. On some trials the reward was a banana, which was greatly preferred to the other reward, a lettuce leaf. Once the animals had been trained they were occasionally presented with a lettuce leaf when they should have received a banana. The following quote, which is cited in Mackintosh (1974), provides a clear indication that the monkey expected a more attractive reward for making the correct response (Tinkelpaugh, 1928, p.224).

She extends her hand to seize the food. But her hand drops to the floor without touching it. She looks at the lettuce but (unless very hungry) does not touch it. She looks around the cup and behind the board. She stands up and looks under and around her. She picks the cup up and examines it thoroughly inside and out. She had on occasion turned toward the observers present in the room and shrieked at them in apparent anger.

A rather different type of finding that shows animals anticipate the rewards for which they are responding can be found in experiments in which rats ran down an alley, or through a maze, for food. If a rat is trained first with one reward which is then changed in attractiveness, there is a remarkably rapid change in its performance on subsequent trials. Elliott (1928) found that the number of errors

in a multiple-unit maze increased dramatically when the quality of reward in the goal box was reduced. Indeed, the animals were so dejected by this change that they made more errors than a control group that had been trained throughout with the less attractive reward (see Figure 4.2). According to S–R theory, the change in performance by the experimental group should have taken place more slowly, nor should it have resulted in less accurate responding than that shown by the control group. As an alternative explanation, these findings imply that the animals had some expectancy of the reward they would receive in the goal that allowed them to detect when it was made less attractive.

Tolman (1932) argued that findings such as these indicate that rats form R–US associations as a result of instrumental conditioning. That is, they learn that a response will be followed by a particular outcome. There is no doubt that the results are consistent with this proposal, but they do not force us to accept it. Several S–R theorists have pointed out that in these experiments the animals could have anticipated the reward on the basis of CS–US, rather than R–US associations (Hull, 1942; Spence, 1956). In Elliott's (1928) experiment, for example, the animal consumed the reward in the goal box, and it is possible that the stimuli created by this part of the apparatus became associated with food. After a number of training trials, therefore, approaching the goal box would effectively bring the subject into contact with an appetitive CS, which would then activate a representation of the reward and thus permit the animal to detect when its value was changed. Both Hull (1942) and Spence (1956) seized on this possibility and proposed that the strength of instrumental responding is influenced by the Pavlovian properties of the context in which the response is performed.

The debate between S–R theorists and what might be called the expectancy (R–US) theorists continued until quite recently (see for example, Bolles, 1972). In the last 15 years or so, however, experiments have provided new insights into the nature of the associations that are formed during instrumental conditioning. To anticipate the following discussion, these experiments show that both the S–R and the expectancy theorists were correct. The experiments also show that these theorists underestimated the complexity of the information that animals can acquire in even quite simple instrumental conditioning tasks.

Evidence for R–US associations

In order to demonstrate support for an expectancy theory of instrumental conditioning, Colwill and Rescorla (1985) adopted a reinforcer devaluation design (see also Adams & Dickinson, 1981). A single group of rats was trained in the manner summarised in Table 4.1. In the first stage of the experiment subjects were able to make one response (R1) to earn one reinforcer (US1) and another response (R2) to earn a different reinforcer

(US2). The two responses were lever pressing or pulling a small chain that was suspended from the ceiling, and the two reinforcers were food pellets or sucrose solution. After a number of sessions of this training, an aversion was formed to US1 by injecting subjects with a mild poison after they had been allowed free access to it. For the test trials subjects were again allowed to make either of the two responses, but this time neither response led to the delivery of a reinforcer. The results from the experiment are shown in Figure 4.3, which indicates that R2 was performed more vigorously than R1. The figure also shows a gradual decline in the strength of R2, which reflects the fact that neither response was followed by reward. This pattern of results can be most readily explained by

---

FIGURE 4.2

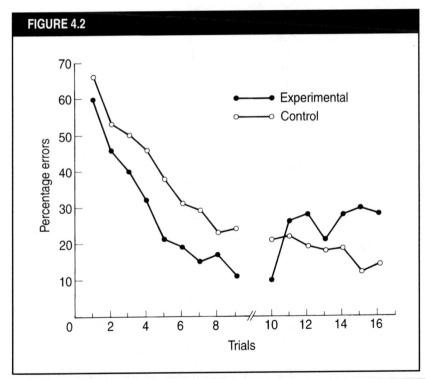

The mean number of errors made by two groups of rats in a multiple-unit maze. For the first nine trials the reward for the control group was more attractive than for the experimental group, but for the remaining trials both groups received the same reward (adapted from Elliott, 1928).

TABLE 4.1

Summary of the Training Given to a Single Group of Rats in an Experiment by Colwill and Rescorla (1985).

Training	Devaluation	Test
R1 → US1	US1 → LiCl	R1 vs. R2
R2 → US2		

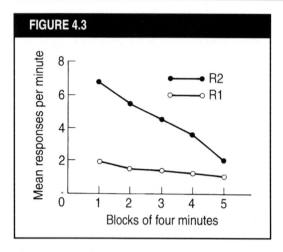

FIGURE 4.3

The mean rates at which a single group of rats performed two responses, R1 and R2, that had previously been associated with two different rewards. Before the test sessions the reward for R1, but not R2, had been devalued. No rewards were presented in the test session (adapted from Rescorla, 1991).

assuming that during their training rats formed R1–US1 and R2–US2 associations. They would then be expected to perform R2 in preference to R1 because of their knowledge that R1 produced a reinforcer that was no longer attractive.

The discussion of the experiment by Elliott (1928) raised the possibility that the context in which instrumental responding occurs may acquire Pavlovian properties and influence the performance of that response. Fortunately, it is difficult to develop a similar explanation for the findings by Colwill and Rescorla (1985). The devaluation training may have altered the associative properties of the context in which instrumental responding occurred. But unless it is accepted that animals learned about the relationship between each response and the reinforcer, it is not clear how a change in these properties could affect one response more than the other.

Evidence for S–R associations

The evidence that instrumental conditioning results in the development of S–R associations is perhaps less convincing than that concerning the development of R–US associations. A re-examination of Figure 4.3 reveals that after the devaluation treatment there remained a tendency to

perform R1. This tendency was sustained even though the response never resulted in the delivery of a reinforcer and, more importantly, it was sustained even though the devaluation training resulted in a complete rejection of US1. The fact that an animal is willing to make a response, even though it will reject the reinforcer that normally follows the response, is just what would be expected if the original training resulted in the growth of an S–R connection. In other words, because an S–R connection does not allow an animal to anticipate the reward it will receive for its responses, once such a connection has formed the animal will respond for the reward even if it is no longer attractive. Thus the results of the experiment by Colwill and Rescorla (1985) indicate that during the course of their training rats acquired both R–US and S–R associations

The reader may be struck by the rather low rate at which R1 was performed, and conclude that the S–R connection is normally of little importance in determining responding. Note, however, that for the test trials there was the opportunity of performing either R1 or R2. Even a slight preference for R2 would then have a suppressive effect on the performance of R1. On the basis of the present results, therefore, it is difficult to draw conclusions concerning the relative contribution S–R and R–US associations to instrumental responding.

To complicate matters even further, there is also some evidence that suggests that the relative contribution of S–R and R–US associations to instrumental behaviour is influenced by the training that is given. Adams and Dickinson (1981) conducted a series of experiments in which rats had to press a lever for food. An aversion to the food was then conditioned by using a technique similar to that adopted by Colwill and Rescorla (1985). If a small amount of instrumental training had been given initially, then subjects showed a marked reluctance to press the lever in a final test session. But if extensive instrumental training had been given initially, then there was little evidence of any effect at all of the devaluation treatment. Adams and Dickinson (1981) were thus led to conclude that R–US associations underlie the acquisition and early stages of instrumental training, but with extended practice this learning is transformed into an S–R habit. There is some debate about the reasons for this change in influence of the two associations, or whether it always takes place (Adams & Dickinson, 1981; Colwill & Rescorla, 1985).

Evidence for S–(R–US) associations

Animals can thus learn to perform a particular response in the presence of a given stimulus (S–R learning), they can also learn that a certain reinforcer will follow a response (R–US learning). The next question to ask is whether this information can be integrated to provide the knowledge that in the presence of a certain stimulus a certain response will be followed by a certain outcome. Table 4.2 summarises the design of an experiment by Rescorla (1991) that was conducted in order to test this possibility.

A group of rats first received discrimination training in which a light or a noise (S1 or S2) was presented for 30 seconds at a time. During each stimulus the rats were required to perform two responses (pulling a chain or pressing a lever), which each resulted in a different reinforcer (food pellets or sucrose solution). The relationship between these responses and the reinforcers was, however, reversed for the two stimuli. Thus in the presence of S1, R1 led to US1 and R2 led to US2; but in S2, R1 led to US2 and R2 led to US1. For the second stage of the experiment, the reinforcer devaluation technique was used to condition an aversion to US2. Finally, test trials were conducted in extinction in which subjects were provided with the opportunity of performing the two responses in the presence of each stimulus. The result from these test trials was quite clear. There was a marked preference to perform R1, rather than R2, in the presence of S1; but in the presence of S2 there was a preference to perform R2 rather than R1. These findings cannot be explained by assuming that the only associations acquired during the first stage were S–R, otherwise the devaluation technique would have been ineffective. Nor can the results be explained by assuming that only R–US associations developed, otherwise devaluation treatment should have weakened R1 and R2 to the same extent in both stimuli. Instead, the results can be most readily explained by assuming that the subjects were sensitive to the fact that the devalued reinforcer followed R2 in S1, and R1 in S2. Rescorla (1991) has argued that this conclusion indicates the development of a hierarchical associative structure that he characterises as S–(R–US). Animals are first believed to acquire an R–US association, and this association in its entirety is then assumed to enter into a new association with S. Whether it is useful to propose that an association can itself enter into an association remains to be seen. There are certainly problems with this type of suggestion (see, for example, Holland, 1992). In addition, as Dickinson (1994) points out, there are alternative ways of explaining the findings of Rescorla (1991). Perhaps the safest conclusion to draw from this experiment is that animals are able to anticipate the reward they will receive for making a certain response in the presence of a given stimulus.

THE CONDITIONS OF LEARNING

There is, therefore, abundant evidence to show that animals are capable of learning about the consequences of their actions. We turn now to consider the conditions that enable this learning to take place.

TABLE 4.2		
Summary of the Training Given to a Single Group of Rats in an Experiment by Colwill and Rescorla (1990).		
Discrimination training	*Devaluation*	*Test*
S1: R1 → US1 and R2 → US2		S1: R1 > R2
	US2 → LiCl	
S2: R1 → US2 and R2 → US1		S2: R2 > R1

Contiguity

One extremely strong influence on instrumental conditioning is the degree of temporal contiguity between the response and the reinforcer. When the reinforcer follows immediately after the response, then conditioning is much more effective than when they are separated by a delay. Even so, instrumental conditioning can be effective when the delay between the response and the reinforcer is substantial. Dickinson, Watt, and Griffin (1992) required groups of rats to press a lever for food. Essentially, each lever press resulted in the delivery of food, but there was a delay before food was delivered that varied for different groups. Even with delays as long as a minute conditioning was successful, although the rats pressed the lever much less rapidly than when the delay was shorter. In this experiment, once the rat had responded a timer was started to ensure the delivery of food after the specified interval. It is thus likely that additional responses were performed during this interval, which would ensure that the interval between a response and the delivery of food was less than the intended interval. A method that overcomes this problem is to impose the constraint that responses during the response–reinforcer interval reset the interval timer, so that the actual interval between a response and food will never be less than the intended value. This method was adopted in a study by Lattal and Gleeson (1990) who found that even with a response–reinforcer interval of 30 seconds there was an increase in the rate of lever-pressing across 20 sessions of training. The results from one rat trained in this manner are shown in Figure 4.4. The remarkable finding from this experiment is that rats with no prior experience of lever pressing can increase the rate of performing this response when the only response-produced stimulus change occurs 30 seconds after a response has been made.

Contingency

In Chapter 3 the CS–US contingency was shown to be an important determinant of the effectiveness of Pavlovian conditioning. That is, conditioning is more effective when the likelihood of the US being delivered is greater in the presence than the absence of the CS. An experiment by Hammond (1980)

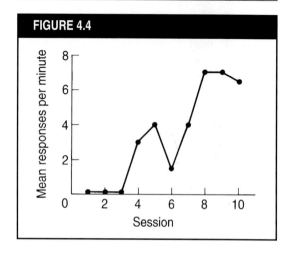

FIGURE 4.4

The mean rate of pressing a lever by a single rat when food was presented 30 seconds after a response (adapted from Lattal & Gleeson, 1990).

demonstrates that the same is true for instrumental conditioning. The training schedule was quite complex, and required that the experimental session was divided into 1-second intervals. If a response occurred in any interval then, for three groups of thirsty rats, water was delivered at the end of the interval with a probability of 0.12. The results from a group that received only this training, and no water in the absence of lever pressing (Group 0), are shown in the left-hand histogram of Figure 4.5. By the end of training this group was responding at more than 50 responses a minute. For the remaining two groups, water was delivered after some of the 1-second intervals in which a response did not occur. For Group 0.08, the probability of one of these intervals being followed by water was 0.08, whereas for Group 0.12 this probability was 0.12. The remaining two histograms show the final response rates for these two groups. Both groups responded more slowly than Group 0. Furthermore, responding was weakest in the group for which water was just as likely to be delivered whether or not a response had been made.

A theoretically uninteresting explanation for the results shown in Figure 4.5 is that the delivery of the free water encouraged animals to remain in the vicinity of the water dispenser, where it would then be difficult to reach and press the lever. Fortunately,

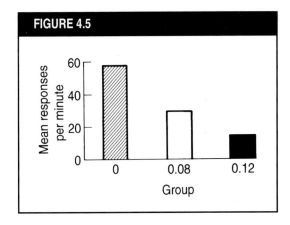

FIGURE 4.5

The mean rates of lever pressing for water by three groups of thirsty rats in their final session of training. The groups differed in the probability with which free water was delivered during the intervals between responses. Group 0 received no water during these intervals, Group 0.08 and Group 0.12, received water with a probability of 0.08 and 0.12, respectively, at the end of each period of 1 second in which a response did not occur (adapted from Hammond, 1980).

this competing response explanation for the effects of degrading the instrumental contingency can be rejected on the basis of results by Dickinson and Mulatero (1989). Rats were trained to make one response, R1, for one reinforcer, US1, and a different response, R2, for a different reinforcer, US2. US1 was also occasionally presented after intervals of 1 second in which neither response was made. A competing response analysis for the effects of the free reinforcer would predict that this manipulation will weaken both R1 and R2 to the same extent. Instead, the free delivery of US1 had a selective effect of disrupting the performance of R1 to a greater extent than R2. Of course, this pattern of results is exactly what would be expected if the contingency between R1 and US1 is an important determinant of the vigour with which R1 is performed.

Associative competition

If two stimuli have been presented together for conditioning, the strength of the CR that each elicits when tested individually is often weaker than if they were presented for conditioning separately. A popular explanation for this overshadowing effect is given by the Rescorla–

Wagner (1972) model that was considered in some detail in the previous chapter. This model stipulates that conditioning with a compound will continue until the combined associative strengths of the components is equal to an asymptotic value, λ, that is set by the US. Provided that one element gains some associative strength, therefore, the other will acquire less than if it alone signalled the US. This theoretical analysis has led to the suggestion that stimuli are in competition with each other for associative strength. The results from a number of instrumental conditioning experiments suggest that responses may also have to compete with stimuli for the associative strength that they gain.

Pearce and Hall (1979; see also St. Claire-Smith, 1979) required rats to press a lever for food on a variable interval schedule, in which only a few responses were followed by reward. For an experimental group each rewarded response was followed by a brief burst of white noise before the food was delivered. The noise did not accompany nonrewarded responses. This burst of noise before food resulted in a substantially lower rate of lever pressing by the experimental than by control groups, which either received similar exposure to the noise (but it always followed nonrewarded responses) or no exposure to the noise at all (see Figure 4.6)

We argued that the most plausible explanation for these findings is that instrumental learning involves the formation of R–US associations and that their strength determines the vigour of instrumental responding. For the control groups the response alone signalled reward, and this should foster a relatively strong R–US association. This association might be weaker for the experimental group, however, because it would be overshadowed by the noise, which also signalled the delivery of food. For a rather different interpretation see Reed (1989).

Associative competition may also be responsible for the contingency effects described earlier. The delivery of a free reinforcer while an animal is responding for the same reinforcer is likely to promote a context–reinforcer association. As this association grows in strength it will restrict the impact of the reinforcer when the animal is rewarded for responding, by effectively blocking

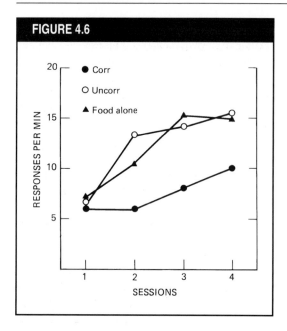

FIGURE 4.6

The mean rates of lever pressing by three groups of rats that received a burst of noise after each rewarded response (Corr), after some nonrewarded responses (Uncorr), or no noise at all (Food alone) (adapted from Pearce & Hall, 1979).

the growth of an R–US association. The R–US association will thus be weaker, and result in slower responding, when some free reinforcers accompany the instrumental training than when all the reinforcers are earned. According to this associative competition analysis, any manipulation that strengthens the context–US association will produce a correspondingly weaker R–US association and further weaken instrumental responding. Thus the orderly results reported by Hammond (1980) can be readily explained by assuming that the strength of the context–US association was directly related to the frequency with which free food was delivered. When this frequency was high, a strong context–food association would allow only a weak R–US association and result in the weak responding that was observed in Group 0.12. In contrast, when this frequency was low a strong R–US would develop and permit a high rate of instrumental responding (Group 0).

A simple test of this analysis can be found in contingency experiments in which a brief stimulus signals the delivery of each free reinforcer. The

brief stimulus should itself overshadow the development of a context–US association and permit the R–US association to develop normally. Responding in these conditions should thus be more vigorous than if the free US is not signalled. In support of this argument, both Hammond and Weinberg (1984) and Dickinson and Charnock (1985) have shown that free reinforcers disrupt instrumental responding to a greater extent when they are unsignalled than when they are signalled. These findings make a particularly convincing case for believing that competition for associative strength is an important influence on the strength of an instrumental response.

The nature of the reinforcer

Perhaps the most important requirement for successful instrumental conditioning is that the response is followed by a reinforcer. But what makes a reinforcer? In nearly all the experiments that have been described thus far, the reinforcer has been food for a hungry animal, or water for a thirsty animal. As these stimuli are of obvious biological importance, it is hardly surprising to discover that animals are prepared to engage in an activity such as lever pressing in order to earn them. However, this does not mean that a reinforcer is necessarily a stimulus that is of biological significance to the animal. As Schwartz (1989) notes, animals will press a lever to turn on a light, and it is difficult to imagine the biological need that is satisfied on these occasions.

Thorndike (1911) appreciated that it was necessary to identify the defining characteristics of a reinforcer, and his solution to this problem was contained within the Law of Effect. He maintained that a reinforcer was a stimulus that resulted in a satisfying state of affairs. A satisfying state of affairs was then defined as (Thorndike, 1913, p.2)

> one which the animal does nothing to avoid, often doing things which maintain or renew it.

In other words, Thorndike effectively proposed that a stimulus would serve as a reinforcer (increase the likelihood of a response) if animals were willing to respond in order to receive that stimulus.

The circularity in this definition should be obvious and has served as a valid source of criticism of the Law of Effect on more than one occasion (e.g. Meehl, 1950). Thorndike was not alone in providing a circular definition of a reinforcer. Skinner has been perhaps the most blatant in this respect, as the following quotation reveals (Skinner, 1953, pp.72–73).

> The only way to tell whether or not a given event is reinforcing to a given organism under given conditions is to make a direct test. We observe the frequency of a selected response, then make an event contingent upon it and observe any change in frequency. If there is a change, we classify the event as reinforcing.

To be fair, for practical purposes this definition is quite adequate. It provides a useful and unambiguous terminology. At the same time, once we have decided that a stimulus, such as food, is a positive reinforcer, then we can turn to a study of a number of issues that are important to the analysis of instrumental learning. For instance, we have been able to study the role of the reinforcer in the associations that are formed during instrumental learning, without worrying unduly about what it is that makes a stimulus a reinforcer. But the definitions offered by Thorndike and Skinner are not very helpful if a general statement is being sought about the characteristics of a stimulus that dictate whether or not it will function as a reinforcer. And the absence of such a general statement makes our understanding of the conditions that promote instrumental learning incomplete.

A particularly elegant solution to the problem of deciding whether a stimulus will function as a reinforcer is provided by the work of Premack (1959, 1962, 1965). He proposed that reinforcers were not stimuli, but opportunities to engage in behaviour. Thus the activity of eating, not the stimulus of food, should be regarded as the reinforcer when an animal has been trained to lever press for food. In order to determine if one activity will serve as the reinforcer for another activity, Premack proposed that the animal should be allowed to engage freely in both activities. For example, a rat might be placed into a chamber containing a lever and a pile of food pellets. If it shows a greater willingness to eat the food than to press the lever, then we can conclude that the opportunity to eat will reinforce lever pressing, but the opportunity to lever press will not reinforce eating.

It is perhaps natural to think of the properties of a reinforcer as being absolute. That is, if eating is an effective reinforcer for one response, such as lever pressing, then it might be expected to serve as a reinforcer for any response. But Premack (1965) has argued this assumption is unjustified. An activity will only be reinforcing if subjects would rather engage in it than in the activity that is to be reinforced. To demonstrate this relative property of a reinforcer, Premack (1971a) placed rats into a running wheel, similar to the one sketched in Figure 4.7, for 15 minutes a day.

When the rats were thirsty, they preferred to drink rather than to run in the wheel, but when they were not thirsty, they preferred to run rather than to drink. For the test phase of the experiment the

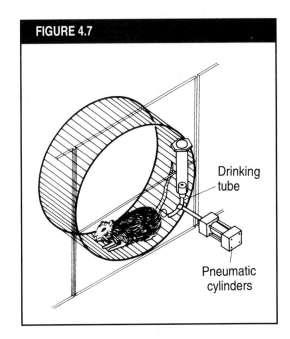

FIGURE 4.7

Drinking tube

Pneumatic cylinders

A sketch of the apparatus used by Premack (1971a) to determine if being given the opportunity to run could serve as a reinforcer for drinking in rats that were not thirsty (adapted from Premack, 1971a).

wheel was locked and the rats had to lick the drinking tube in order to free it and so gain the opportunity to run for 5 seconds. Running is not normally regarded as a reinforcing activity. But because rats that are not thirsty prefer to run rather than drink, it follows from Premack's (1965) argument that they should increase the amount they drink in the wheel in order to earn the opportunity to run. Conversely, running would not be expected to reinforce drinking for thirsty rats, because in this state of deprivation they prefer drinking to running. In clear support of this analysis, Premack (1971a) found that running could serve as a reinforcer for drinking, but only with rats that were not thirsty.

As Allison (1989) has pointed out, Premack's proposals can be expressed succinctly by paraphrasing Thorndike's Law of Effect. For instrumental conditioning to be effective it is necessary for a response to be followed, not by a satisfying state of affairs, but by a preferred response. Despite the improvement this change affords with respect to the problem of defining a reinforcer, experiments have shown that it does not account adequately for all the circumstances where one activity will serve as a reinforcer for another.

Consider an experiment by Allison and Timberlake (1974) in which rats were first allowed to drink from two spouts that provided different concentrations of saccharin solution. This baseline test session revealed a preference for the sweeter solution. According to Premack's proposals, therefore, rats should be willing to increase their consumption of the weaker solution, if drinking it is the only means by which they can gain access to the sweeter solution. In contrast, rats should not be willing to increase their consumption of the sweeter solution, in order to gain access to the weaker one. To test this second prediction, rats were allowed to drink from the spout supplying the sweeter solution, and after every 10 licks they were permitted one lick at the spout offering the less sweet solution. This 10:1 ratio meant that relative to the amount of sweet solution consumed, the rats received less of the weaker solution than they chose to consume in the baseline test session. As a consequence of this constraint imposed by the experiment, Allison and Timberlake (1974) found that rats increased their consumption of the

stronger solution. It is important to emphasise that this increase occurred in order to allow the rats to gain access to the less preferred solution, which, according to Premack's theory, should not have taken place.

Timberlake and Allison (1974) explained their results in terms of an *equilibrium theory* of behaviour. They argued that when an animal is able to engage in a variety of activities, it will have a natural tendency to allocate more time to some than others. The ideal amount of time that would be devoted to an activity is referred to as its *bliss point*, and each activity is assumed to have its own bliss point. By preventing an animal from engaging in even its least preferred activity, it will be displaced from the bliss point and do its best to restore responding to this point.

In the experiment by Allison and Timberlake (1974), therefore, forcing the subjects to drink much more of the strong than the weak solution, meant that they were effectively deprived of the weak solution. Since the only way to overcome this deficit was to drink more of the sweet solution, this is what they did. Of course, as the rats approached their bliss point for the consumption of the weak solution, they would go beyond their bliss point for the consumption of the sweet solution. To cope with this type of conflict, animals are believed to seek a compromise, or state of equilibrium, in which the amount of each activity they perform will lead them as close as possible to the bliss points for all activities. Thus the rats completed the experiment by drinking rather more than they would prefer of the strong solution, and rather less than they would prefer of the weak solution.

By referring to bliss points, we can thus predict when the opportunity to engage in one activity will serve as a reinforcer for another activity. But this does not mean that we have now identified completely the circumstances in which the delivery of a particular event will function as a reinforcer. Some reinforcers do not elicit responses that can be analysed usefully by equilibrium theory. Rats will press a lever in order to receive stimulation to certain regions of the brain, or to turn on a light, or to turn off an electric shock to the feet. I find it difficult to envisage how any measure of baseline activity in the presence of these events would reveal that they will serve as reinforcers for lever pressing. In the next section we shall find that a stimulus which has been paired with food can reinforce lever pressing in hungry rats. Again, simply by observing an animal's behaviour in the presence of the stimulus, it is hard to imagine how one could predict that the stimulus will function as a reinforcer. Our understanding of the nature of a reinforcer has advanced considerably since Thorndike proposed the Law of Effect. However, if we wish to determine with confidence if a certain event will act as a reinforcer for a particular response, at times there will be no better alternative than to adopt Skinner's suggestion of testing for this property directly.

Conditioned reinforcement

The discussion has been concerned thus far with primary reinforcers, that is with stimuli that do not need to be paired with another stimulus in order to function as reinforcers for instrumental conditioning. There are, in addition, numerous studies that have shown that even a neutral stimulus may serve as an instrumental reinforcer by virtue of being paired with a primary reinforcer. An experiment by Hyde (1976) provides a good example of a stimulus acting in this capacity as a conditioned reinforcer. In the first stage of the experiment an experimental group of hungry rats had a number of sessions in which the occasional delivery of food was signalled by a brief tone CS. A control group was treated in much the same way

except that the tone and food were presented randomly in respect to each other. Both groups were then given the opportunity to press the lever in order to present the tone. The results from the eight sessions of this testing are displayed in Figure 4.8. Even though no food was presented in this test phase, the experimental group initially showed a considerable willingness to press the lever. The superior rate of pressing by the experimental compared to the control group strongly suggests that pairing the tone with food resulted in it becoming a conditioned reinforcer.

In the previous experiment the effect of the conditioned reinforcer was relatively short-lasting, which should not be surprising because by being presented in the absence of food it would lose its conditioned properties. The effects of conditioned reinforcers can, however, be considerably more robust if their relationship with the primary reinforcer is maintained, albeit intermittently. Experiments using token reinforcers provide a particularly forceful demonstration of how the influence of a conditioned reinforcer may be sustained in this way. Token reinforcers are typically small plastic discs that are earned by performing some response, and once earned they can be exchanged for food. In an experiment by Kelleher (1958) chimpanzees had to press a key 125 times in order to receive a single token, and when they had collected 50 tokens they were allowed to push them all into a slot in order to receive food. In this experiment, therefore, the

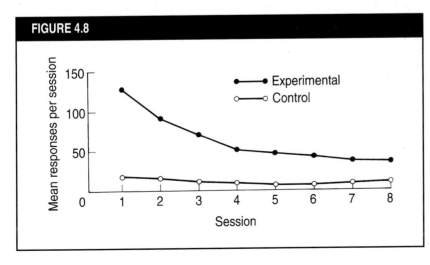

FIGURE 4.8

The mean rates of lever pressing for a brief tone by two groups of rats. For the experimental group the tone had previously been paired with food, whereas for the control group the tone and food had been presented randomly in respect to each other (adapted from Hyde, 1976).

effect of the token reinforcers was sufficiently strong that they were able to reinforce a sequence of more than 6000 responses.

A straightforward explanation for the results of the experiment by Hyde (1976) is that the tone became an appetitive Pavlovian CS and thus effectively served as a substitute for food. The results from experiments such as that by Kelleher (1958) have led Schwartz (1989) to argue that there are additional ways in which conditioned reinforcers can be effective (see also Gollub, 1977). First, they provide feedback that the correct response has been made. Delivering a token after the completion of 125 responses would provide a useful signal that the subject is engaged in the correct activity. Second, conditioned reinforcers might act as a cue for the next response to be performed. Kelleher (1958) observed that his chimpanzees often waited for several hours before making their first response in a session. This delay was virtually eliminated by giving the subject some tokens at the start of the session, thus indicating that the tokens acted as a cue for key pressing. Finally, conditioned reinforcers may be effective because they help to counteract the disruptive effects of imposing a long delay between a response and the delivery of a primary reinforcer. Interestingly, as far as tokens are concerned, this property of the token is seen only when the chimpanzee is allowed to hold the token during the delay. Taken together, these proposals imply that the properties of a conditioned reinforcer are considerably more complex than would be expected if they were based solely on its Pavlovian properties.

THE PERFORMANCE OF INSTRUMENTAL BEHAVIOUR

The experiments considered so far have been concerned with revealing the knowledge that is acquired during the course of instrumental conditioning. They have also indicated some of the factors that influence the acquisition of this knowledge. We turn our attention now to examining the factors that determine the vigour with which an animal will perform an instrumental response. We have already seen that certain devaluation treatments can influence instrumental responding, and so too can manipulations designed to modify the strength of the instrumental association. But there remain a number of other factors that influence instrumental behaviour. In the discussion that follows we shall consider two of these influences in some detail: deprivation state and the presence of Pavlovian CSs.

Deprivation

The level of food deprivation has been shown, up to a point, to be directly related to the vigour with which an animal responds for food. This is true when the response is running down an alley (Cotton, 1953) or pressing a lever (Clark, 1958). To explain this relationship Hull (1943) suggested that motivational effects are mediated by activity in a drive centre. Drive is a central state that is excited by needs and energises behaviour. It was proposed that the greater the level of drive, the more vigorous will be the response that the animal is currently performing. Thus if a rat is pressing a lever for food, then hunger will excite drive, which, in turn, will invigorate this activity.

A serious shortcoming of Hull's (1943) account is the claim that drive is nonspecific, so that it can be enhanced by an increase in any need of the animal. A number of curious predictions follow from this basic aspect of his theorising. For example, the pain produced by electric shock is assumed to increase drive, so that if animals are given shocks while lever pressing for food, they should respond more rapidly than in the absence of shock. By far the most frequent finding is that this manipulation has the opposite effect of decreasing appetitive instrumental responding (e.g. Boe & Church, 1967). Conversely, the theory predicts that enhancing drive by making animals hungrier should facilitate the rate at which they press a lever to escape or avoid shock. Again, it should not be surprising to discover that generally this prediction is not confirmed. Increases in deprivation have been found, in this respect, to be either without effect (Misanin & Campbell, 1969) or to reduce the rate of such behaviour (Leander, 1973; Meyer, Adams, & Worthen, 1969).

In response to this problem more recent theorists have proposed that animals possess two drive centres. One is concerned with energising behaviour that leads to reward, the other is responsible for invigorating activity that minimises contact with aversive stimuli. They may be referred to, respectively, as the positive and negative motivational systems. A number of such dual-system theories of motivation have been proposed (Estes, 1969; Gray, 1975; Konorski, 1967; Rescorla & Solomon, 1967).

The assumption that there are two motivational systems rather than a single drive centre allows these theories to overcome many of the problems encountered by Hull's (1943) theory. For example, it is believed that deprivation states like hunger and thirst will increase activity only in the positive system, so that a change in deprivation should not influence the vigour of behaviour that minimises contact with aversive stimuli such as shock. Conversely, electric shock should not invigorate responding for food as it will excite only the negative system.

But even this characterisation of the way in which deprivation states influence behaviour may be too simple. Suppose that an animal has been trained to lever press for food while it is hungry and then it is satiated before being returned to the conditioning chamber. The account that has just been developed predicts that satiating the animal will reduce the motivational support for lever pressing by lowering the activity in the positive system. The animal would thus be expected to respond less vigorously than one that was still hungry. There is some evidence that supports this prediction (e.g. Balleine, Garner, Gonzalez & Dickinson, 1995), but additional findings by Balleine (1992) demonstrate that dual-system theories of motivation are in need of elaboration if they are to provide a complete account of the way in which deprivation states influence responding.

In one experiment by Balleine (1992), two groups of rats were trained to press a bar for food while they were hungry (H). For reasons that will be made evident shortly, it is important to note that the food pellets used as the instrumental reinforcer were different to the food that was presented at all other times in this experiment. Group H–S was then satiated (S) by being allowed unrestricted access to food for 24 hours, whereas Group H–H remained on the deprivation schedule. Finally, both groups were again given the opportunity to press the bar, but responding never resulted in the delivery of the reinforcer. Because of their different deprivation states, dual-system theories of motivation predict that Group H–H should respond more vigorously than Group H–S in this test session. The mean number of responses made by each group in the test session are shown in the two open histograms in the left-hand side of Figure 4.9, which reveal that this prediction was not confirmed.

The equivalent histograms in the right-hand side of Figure 4.9 show the results of two further groups from this study. They were trained to lever press for food while they were satiated by being fed unrestricted food in their home cages.[1] Group S–S was then tested while satiated, whereas Group S–H was tested while hungry. Once again, despite their different deprivation levels, both groups performed similarly in the test session. When the results of the four groups are compared it is evident that the groups that were trained hungry responded more vigorously on the test trials than those that were trained when they were satiated. But to labour the point, there is no indication that changing deprivation level for the test session had any influence on responding.

To explain these findings Balleine (1992) proposed that the incentive value, or attractiveness, of the reinforcer is an important determinant of how willing animals will be to press for it. If an animal consumes a reinforcer when it is hungry, then that reinforcer may well be more attractive than if it is consumed when the animal is satiated. Thus Group H–H and Group H–S may have responded rapidly in the test session because they anticipated a food that in the past had proved attractive. By way of contrast, the slower responding by Group S–S and S–H can be attributed to them anticipating food that in the past had not been particularly attractive.

Balleine (1992) tested this explanation for his results with two additional groups. Prior to the experiment, Group PreH–S was given reward pellets while it was satiated in order to demonstrate they are not particularly attractive in this

FIGURE 4.9

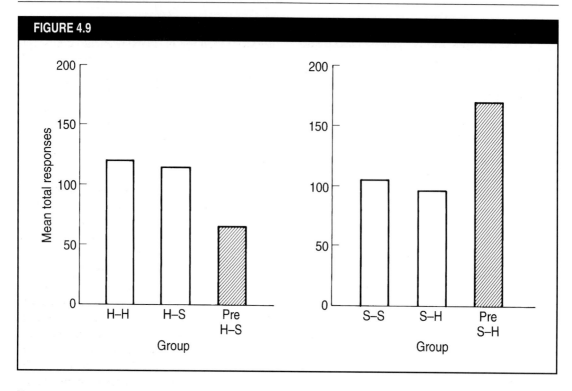

The mean number of responses made by six groups of rats in an extinction-test session (adapted from Balleine, 1992).

deprivation state. The group was then trained to lever press while hungry and received test trials while satiated. On the test trials, the subjects should know that because of their low level of deprivation the reward pellets are no longer attractive and they should be reluctant to press the lever. The results, which are shown by the shaded histogram in the left-hand side of Figure 4.9, confirmed this prediction. The final group to be considered, Group PreS–H, was first allowed to eat reward pellets in the home cage while hungry, instrumental conditioning was then conducted while the group was satiated and the test trials were conducted while the group was hungry. In contrast to Group S–H and Group S–S, this group should appreciate that the reward pellets are attractive when hungry and respond more rapidly than the other two groups during the test trials. Once again the results confirmed this prediction—see the shaded histogram in the right-hand side of Figure 4.9.

By now it should be evident that no simple conclusion can be drawn concerning the way in which deprivation states influence the vigour of instrumental responding. On some occasions a change in deprivation state is able to modify directly the rate of responding, as dual-systems theories of motivation predict. On other occasions, this influence is more indirect by modifying the attractiveness of the reinforcer. An informative account of the way in which these findings may be integrated can be found in Balleine et al. (1995).

Pavlovian–instrumental interactions

Theorists for a long time have been interested in the way in which Pavlovian CSs influence the strength of instrumental responses that are performed in their presence. One reason for this interest is that Pavlovian and instrumental conditioning are regarded as two fundamental learning processes, and it is important to appreciate the way in which they work together to determine how an animal behaves. A second reason was mentioned at the end of Chapter 2, where we saw that Pavlovian CSs tend to elicit reflexive responses that may not always be in the best interests of the animal. If a Pavlovian CS were also able to modulate the vigour of instrumental responding, then this would allow it to have a more general, and more flexible, influence on behaviour than has so far been implied. For example, if a CS for food were to invigorate instrumental responses that normally lead to food, then such responses would be strongest at a time when it is most appropriate—that is, in context where food is likely to occur. The experiments described in the following section show that Pavlovian stimuli can modulate the strength of instrumental responding. They also show that there are at least two ways in which this influence takes place.

Motivational influences. Konorski (1967), it should be recalled from Chapter 2, believed that a CS can excite an affective representation of the US that was responsible for arousing a preparatory CR. He further believed that a component of this CR consists of a change in the level of activity in a motivational system. A CS for food, say, was said to increase activity in the positive motivational system, whereas a CS for shock should excite the negative system. If these proposals are correct, then it should be possible to alter the strength of instrumental responding by presenting the appropriate Pavlovian CS (see also Rescorla & Solomon, 1976).

An experiment by Lovibond (1983) provides good support for this prediction. Hungry rabbits were first trained to operate a lever with their snouts in order to receive a squirt of sucrose into the mouth. The levers were then withdrawn for a number of sessions of Pavlovian conditioning in which a clicker that lasted for 10 seconds signalled the delivery of sucrose. In a final test stage subjects were again able to press the lever, and while they were doing so the clicker was occasionally operated. The effect of this appetitive CS was to increase the rate of lever pressing both during its presence and for a short while after it was turned off. A similar effect has also been reported in a study using an aversive US. Rescorla and LoLordo (1965) found that the presentation of a CS previously paired with shock enhanced the rate at which dogs responded to avoid shock.

In addition to explaining the findings that have just been described, a further advantage of

dual-system theories of motivation is that they are able to account for many of the effects of exposing animals simultaneously to both appetitive and aversive stimuli. For example, an animal may be exposed to one stimulus that signals reward and another indicating danger. In these circumstances, instead of the two systems working independently, they are assumed to be connected by mutually inhibitory links, so that activity in one will inhibit the other (Dickinson & Pearce, 1977).

To understand this relationship, consider the effect of presenting a signal for shock to a rat while it is lever pressing for food. Prior to the signal the level of activity in the positive system will be solely responsible for the rate of pressing. When the aversive CS is presented, it will arouse the negative system. The existence of the inhibitory link will then allow the negative system to suppress activity in the positive system and weaken instrumental responding. As soon as the aversive CS is turned off, the inhibition will be removed and the original response rate restored. Thus by assuming the existence of inhibitory links, dual-system theories can provide a very simple explanation for conditioned suppression. It occurs because the aversive CS reduces the positive motivational support for the instrumental response.

Response-cueing properties of Pavlovian CRs.
In addition to modulating activity in motivational systems, Pavlovian stimuli can influence instrumental responding through a response-cueing process (Trapold & Overmier, 1972). To demonstrate this point we shall consider an experiment by Colwill and Rescorla (1988), which is very similar in design to an earlier study by Kruse, Overmier, Konz, and Rokke (1983).

In the first stage of the experiment, hungry rats received Pavlovian conditioning in which US1 was occasionally delivered during a 30-second CS. Training was then given, in separate sessions, in which R1 produced US1 and R2 produced US2.[2] For the test stage, animals had the opportunity for the first time to perform R1 and R2 in the presence of the CS, but neither response led to a reinforcer. As Figure 4.10 shows, R1 was performed more vigorously than R2.

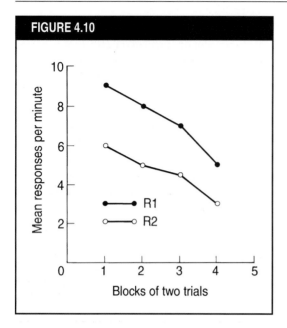

FIGURE 4.10

The mean rates of performing two responses, R1 and R2, in the presence of an established Pavlovian CS. Prior to testing, instrumental conditioning had been given in which the reinforcer for R1 was the same as the Pavlovian US, and the reinforcer for R2 was different to the Pavlovian US. Testing was conducted in the absence of any reinforcers in a single session (adapted from Colwill & Rescorla, 1988).

The first point to note is that it is not possible to explain these findings by appealing to the motivational properties of the CS. The CS should, of course, enhance the level of activity in the positive system. But this increase in activity should then invigorate R1 to exactly the same extent as R2 because the motivational support for both responses will be provided by the same, positive, system.

In developing an alternative explanation for the findings by Colwill and Rescorla (1988), note that instrumental conditioning with the two responses was conducted in separate sessions. Thus R1 was acquired against a background of presentations of US1 and, likewise, R2 was acquired against a background of US2 presentations. If we now accept that the training resulted in the development of S–R associations, it is conceivable that certain properties of the two rewards contributed towards the S component of these associations. For example, a memory of US1 might contribute to the

set of stimuli that are responsible for eliciting R1. When the CS was presented for testing, it should activate a memory of US1, which in turn should elicit R1 rather than R2. In other words, the Pavlovian CS was able to invigorate the instrumental response by providing cues that had previously become associated with the instrumental response.

Concluding comments

The research reviewed so far in this chapter shows that we have discovered a considerable amount about the associations that are formed during instrumental conditioning. We have also discovered a great deal about the factors that influence the strength of instrumental responding. In Chapter 2 a simple memory model was developed to show how the associations formed during Pavlovian conditioning influence responding. It would be helpful if a similar model could be developed for instrumental conditioning, but this may not be an easy task. We would need to take account of three different associations that have been shown to be involved in instrumental behaviour, S–R, R–US, S–(R–US). We would also need to take account of the motivational and response-cueing properties of any Pavlovian CS–US associations that may develop. Finally, the model would need to explain how changes in deprivation can influence responding. It hardly needs to be said that any model that is able to take account of all these factors satisfactorily will be complex and would not fit comfortably into an introductory text. The interested reader is, however, referred to Dickinson (1994) who shows how much of our knowledge about instrumental behaviour can be explained by what he calls an associative-cybernetic model. In essence, this model is a more complex version of the dual-system theories of motivation that we have considered.

Our discussion of the basic processes of instrumental conditioning is now complete. But the topics that we have considered are not the only ones to have been studied by those with an interest in instrumental behaviour. First, there is a long history of research that has been designed to identify the range of species that can be influenced by instrumental training methods. Second, there has been a certain amount of debate as to whether or not it is possible to account for successful Pavlovian conditioning in terms of instrumental principles. Finally, ever since the work of Thorndike (1911) the claim has been made that the apparently sophisticated way in which some animals solve problems can be explained entirely by the Law of Effect. These three topics are reviewed in the remainder of this chapter.

THE COMPARATIVE ANALYSIS OF INSTRUMENTAL CONDITIONING

Thus far instrumental conditioning has been shown to be successful with rats, rabbits, and guinea pigs. How do other species fare when they must respond in a certain way either to gain reward or to minimise contact with an aversive US? Although there are many experiments relevant to this question, we shall look only at a selected few. The results from these studies reveal that the behaviour of a remarkable range of animals can be altered by methods of instrumental conditioning. In many cases, however, the interpretation of these experiments is ambiguous because the results do not allow us to identify the learning that forms the basis of this change in behaviour.

Demonstrations

The first demonstration concerns ants that were trained by Schneirla (1929) to pass through mazes of the sort depicted in Figure 4.11 in order to get from their nest to food, or vice versa. At first the ants made numerous errors, turning in the wrong direction at choice points, and many took more than 200 seconds to complete the maze. After as few as 16 training trials there was a marked improvement in performance: Ants now made one or two errors and completed the maze within 40 seconds. The common fly can also be trained to find its way through a complex maze (Platt, Holliday, & Drudge, 1980).

Instrumental conditioning has also been successful with another invertebrate, the octopus. Dews (1959) taught three subjects, Albert,

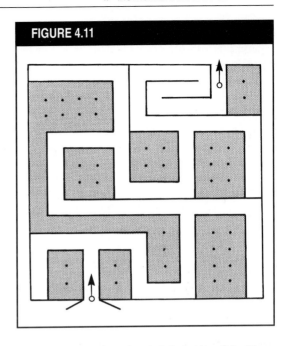

FIGURE 4.11

Plan of a maze used to train ants (adapted from Schneirla, 1929).

Bertram, and Charles, to pull a vertical lever, hinged at the top, for food. Suspended from the bottom of the lever was a distinctive cross that moved in the current of water passing it. All three octopuses learned to pull the lever, although attempts to train them to repeat this response for a single reward were not particularly successful: Once they had pulled the lever towards themselves with their tentacles they were most reluctant to release it for the next response, until food was delivered.

Turning now to vertebrates, Macphail (1982) has summarised many demonstrations of instrumental conditioning with fish, reptiles, amphibians, and mammals. Thus sharks have been trained to push an underwater panel for food (Clark, 1959), alligators will respond correctly in a simple discrimination to escape from heat (Davidson, 1966), indigo snakes will press a panel for water (Kleinginna, 1970), desert iguanas will respond similarly to maintain their temperatures within a restricted range (Kemp, 1969), and toads were able to learn in a single trial to avoid bumblebees after being stung while eating one (Brower, Brower, & Westcott, 1960). There is no need to add mammals to this list of examples—experiments already mentioned in this chapter demonstrate their susceptibility to instrumental conditioning.

Interpretation

Earlier in this chapter an explanation in terms of stimulus–stimulus learning was developed to account for the instrumental conditioning of lever pressing in rats. Although it was shown that this type of account is not appropriate for all studies of instrumental conditioning, it might well apply to at least some of the studies just mentioned. In the octopus experiment, for example, the sight of the cross at the end of the lever might regularly precede the delivery of food. Consequently, pulling the lever might have been nothing more than a CR of approaching and contacting the cross CS. This may seem far-fetched, but it is noteworthy that Dews (1959) was unable to condition the octopuses when the cross was absent. To take a rather different line of argument, in any form of maze some cues will be more closely related in time to food than others, and will therefore become better signals for reward. Accurate performance in a maze may then depend on subjects approaching those stimuli that they have learned are most closely related to food (see Deutsch, 1960, for an account of maze learning in these terms). Thus the performance of Schneirla's (1929) ants may have been due to the occurrence of Pavlovian approach CRs rather than to any instrumental learning.[3]

The obvious counter to this type of interpretation is to employ the bidirectional control, or to condition a response that it would be unreasonable to regard as a CR. In fact, studies with non-mammals that are based on these designs are extremely rare. Perhaps the best demonstration of response learning in a nonmammalian species is provided by Jenkins (1977) using pigeons. A subject was placed into a conditioning chamber, and whenever an 8-second burst of white noise was sounded it had to wave its head to and fro, interrupting two photocell beams, in order to gain food. As there was no localisable CS to attract the pigeon to the correct position or to make it move its head, the most plausible explanation for this finding is that the bird learned to perform a response of moving to a certain location and then waving its head. For a study that suggests that fish are capable of learning about the responses they make see Mandriota, Thompson, and Bennett (1968).

Even though the experiment by Jenkins demonstrates response learning, it fails to reveal anything about the nature of this learning. The pigeons may have acquired R–US associations and anticipated the reward for which they were responding. Alternatively, as the Law of Effect stipulates, the reward may have strengthened an S–R association. Very little additional research has been undertaken to distinguish between these alternatives, although there is one study that suggests R–US associations develop during the course of instrumental conditioning with pigeons (Hall, 1982).

PAVLOVIAN CONDITIONING AS INSTRUMENTAL LEARNING

The impression may well have been created by the organisation of the book so far that Pavlovian conditioning is a more fundamental process than instrumental conditioning. It would be a mistake to accept this view without question. One possibility that has hitherto been ignored is that response learning constitutes the basic learning process, and that relatively few species are capable of acquiring stimulus–stimulus associations. This argument has been advocated most forcefully by Bitterman (1975). He regards fish, among other species, as being capable only of instrumental learning, which for him consists of the formation of S–R associations.

In order to examine this claim a technique must be found that enables us to determine whether or not Pavlovian conditioning has been effective with an animal. There is no doubt that the behaviour of most animals can be influenced by Pavlovian conditioning, but to what extent does this depend on the CS being paired with the US? In order to appreciate the significance of this question, we shall consider again the experiment by Williams and Williams (1969) who examined the effects of an omission schedule on autoshaping. This experiment was mentioned at the end of Chapter 2.

Autoshaping experiments have shown that pigeons will peck a response key whenever it is illuminated if this signals the delivery of food. Thus far it has been unquestioningly accepted that this behaviour depends on the CS being paired with the US. But an alternative explanation is possible. Suppose that when the key is first illuminated the pigeon approaches and by chance pecks it. This response will be followed by food when the light is turned off, and according to the Law of Effect, an S–R connection will be strengthened between the key-light stimulus and the key-peck response. On the next trial the sight of the illuminated key will elicit a tendency to peck at it, so that the food at the end of the trial will further strengthen the S–R bond. Note that this interpretation does not depend on the pigeon being required to peck the key in order to obtain food. It is just that after the pairing of the first response with food, the pigeon is mistakenly led into believing, as it were, that key-pecking is responsible for the delivery of food.

With an omission schedule for autoshaping, food is not delivered on every trial but only on those trials when a peck does *not* occur. As a result, pecking will never be followed by food and there will be no opportunity for reward to strengthen accidentally a key-light–key-peck association. If the foregoing account is correct, then autoshaping with the omission schedule should be ineffective in generating response to the key. In fact, Williams and Williams (1969) found a relatively high rate of responding with this method. The single, acceptable explanation for this outcome is that it was the intermittent pairing of the key-light CS with food that was responsible for the CR.

A reasonable rate of responding with the omission schedule thus provides clear evidence that it is the relationship between the CS and the US that is responsible for occurrence of a CR. How do species other than pigeons fare with this schedule? In the case of mammals there is ample evidence that they are capable of stimulus–stimulus learning. For example, pairing a CS with water for rabbits (Gormezano & Hiller, 1972) or with food for rats (Holland, 1979) on an omission schedule will still elicit a CR on about half the

trials. For other species the evidence is not available: Experiments with the omission schedule have not been conducted, or, if they have, the results have been hard to interpret (e.g. Brandon & Bitterman, 1979).

The foregoing arguments are complex and difficult to present clearly. It is therefore a pity that the rewards for pursuing them are slight. We can be confident that the behaviour of pigeons and mammals is modifiable by instrumental training in which a response is followed by a reinforcer. We can also be certain that the mere pairing of a CS and a US is sufficient to change the behaviour of pigeons and mammals. There is, in addition, abundant evidence to show that the behaviour of virtually all animals is modifiable by either instrumental or Pavlovian techniques. But until the appropriate experiments have been conducted with each of these species, we shall not know what associations result from these methods of training.

THE LAW OF EFFECT AND PROBLEM SOLVING

Animals can be said to have solved a problem whenever they overcome an obstacle to attain a goal. The problem may be artificial, such as having to press a lever for reward, or it might be one that occurs naturally, such as having to locate a new source of food. Towards the end of the last century there was considerable interest in the way in which animals solved problems. Researchers would collect anecdoctes about the problem-solving skills of animals, and then use this information to make inferences about their intellectual processes. On the basis of observations of a cat opening a gate, Romanes (1882), for example, concluded that this skill was acquired through rational imitation that developed as a result of watching humans. Rational imitation in this instance was meant to involve understanding the mechanical properties of the gate together with considerable reasoning power.

Of course, simpler explanations can be developed to explain how animals learn to open gates. It was not long, therefore, before the conclusions about the intelligence of animals of the sort drawn by Romanes were justly criticised. Lloyd Morgan (1894), for example, argued that animals solve problems solely on the basis of learning by trial and error. In support of his argument he carefully observed a fox terrier, Tony, who learned to raise the latch of a gate in order to open it (see Figure 4.12). Lloyd Morgan (1894) was unable to find anything in the way this skill developed that indicated sophisticated reasoning by the dog. Indeed, Tony always raised the latch with the back of his head, rather than with his

muzzle, which would have been the more efficient method. Such a finding is just what would be expected if the discovery of how to open the gate was arrived at by chance, rather than by reasoning.

A more systematic approach to the study of problem-solving by animals was initiated by Thorndike (1898), who embarked on a series of experiments in order "to give the *coup de grace* to the despised theory that animals reason"(p.39). Despite the range of potential problems that can confront an animal, Thorndike (1911) maintained

FIGURE 4.12

Lloyd Morgan's dog, Tony, using trial-and-error learning to open a gate (from Morgan, 1900).

that they are all solved in the same manner. Animals are assumed to behave randomly until by trial and error the correct response is made and reward is forthcoming. As we have seen already, the Law of Effect stipulates that one effect of reward is to strengthen the accidentally occurring response and to make its occurrence more likely in the future. This account may explain adequately the way cats learn to escape from puzzle boxes (see p.19), but is it suitable for all aspects of problem solving?

An early objector to Thorndike's (1911) account of problem solving was Kohler (1925). Thorndike's experiments were so restrictive, he argued, that they prevented animals from revealing their capacity to solve problems by any means other than the most simple. Kohler spent the First World War on the Canary Islands, where he conducted a number of studies that were meant to reveal sophisticated intellectual processes in animals. He is best known for his experiments that, he claimed, demonstrate the importance of insight in problem solving. Many of his findings are described in his book *The mentality of apes,* which documents some remarkable feats of problem solving by animals.

Kohler (1925) believed that a major step in solving any problem is that of insight. Unfortunately it is rather difficult to know what he meant by this term—apparently it is not easy to translate the German word *Einsicht* that Kohler (1925) used. For writers in English, insight is generally regarded as a period of thought followed by a flash of inspiration, when the solution suddenly occurs to the problem-solver. This is rather different from Thorndike's (1911) account of problem solving in which the correct solution is said to be arrived at by chance.

Kohler (1925) cites many instances of what he considers to be evidence of insight in animals. The following three examples might help to convey the meaning of the term. In one experiment, a dog watched Kohler throw some food out of a window before shutting it. The behaviour of the dog is then described as follows (Kohler, 1925, p.26):

The dog jumps once against the window-pane, then stands a moment, her head raised towards the window, looks a second at the observer, when all at once she wags her tail a few times, with one leap whirls round 180°, dashes out of the door and runs round outside, till she is underneath the window where she finds the food immediately.

In another study, Sultan, whom Kohler (1925) regarded as the brightest of a number of apes he worked with, was in his cage, in which there was also a small stick. Outside the cage was a longer stick, which was beyond Sultan's reach, and even further away was a reward of fruit (p.151):

Sultan tries to reach the fruit with the smaller of the sticks. Not succeeding, he tries a piece of wire that projects from the netting in his cage, but that, too, is in vain. Then he gazes about him (there are always in the course of these tests some long pauses, during which the animal scrutinises the whole visible area). He suddenly picks up the little stick once more, goes to the bars directly opposite to the long stick, scratches it towards him with the auxiliary, seizes it and goes with it to the point opposite the objective which he secures. From the moment that his eyes fell upon the long stick, his procedure forms one consecutive whole.

Finally, Kohler (1925) hung a piece of fruit from the ceiling of a cage housing six apes, including Sultan. There was a wooden box in the cage (p.41):

All six apes vainly endeavoured to reach the fruit by leaping up from the ground. Sultan soon relinquished this attempt, paced restlessly up and down, suddenly stood still in front of the box, seized it, tipped it hastily straight towards the objective, but began to climb upon it at a (horizontal) distance of 1/2 metre and springing upwards with all his force, tore down the banana.

In all of these examples there is a period when the animal responds incorrectly; this is then followed by activity which, as it is reported, suggests that the solution to the problem has suddenly occurred to the subject. There is certainly no hint in these reports that the problem was solved by trial and error. Does this mean, then, that Kohler (1925) was correct in his criticism of Thorndike's (1911) theorising?

Unfortunately it is a most frustrating experience reading Kohler's book, because the majority of his experiments are difficult to interpret. The very fact that six apes may be simultaneously engaged in the same problem means it is virtually impossible to understand the problem-solving abilities of any individual. Furthermore, all of his subjects had played with boxes and sticks prior to the studies just described. The absence of trial-and-error responding may thus have been due to the prior experience of the animals. Sultan may, by accident, have learned about the consequences of jumping from boxes in earlier sessions, and he was perhaps doing no more than acting on the basis of his previous learning. This criticism of Kohler's (1925) work is by no means original. Birch (1945) and Schiller (1952) have both suggested that without prior experience with sticks and so forth, there is very little reason for believing that apes can solve Kohler's problems in the manner just described.

An amusing experiment by Epstein, Kirshnit, Lanza, and Rubin (1984) also shows the importance of past experience in problem solving and, at the same time, raises some important issues concerning the intellectual abilities of animals. Pigeons were given two different types of training. They were rewarded with food for pushing a box towards a spot randomly located at the base of a wall of the test chamber. Pushing in the absence of the spot was never rewarded. They were also trained to stand on the box when it was fixed to the floor and peck for food at a plastic banana suspended from the ceiling. Attempts to peck the banana when not standing on the box were never rewarded. Finally, on a test session they were confronted with a novel situation in which the banana was suspended from the ceiling and the box was placed some distance from beneath it. Epstein et al. (1984) report that (p.61):

At first each pigeon appeared to be "confused"; it stretched and turned beneath the banana, looked back and forth from banana to box, and so on. Then each subject began rather suddenly to push the box in what was clearly the direction of the banana. Each subject sighted the banana as it pushed and readjusted the box as necessary to move it towards the banana. Each subject stopped pushing it in the appropriate place, climbed and pecked the banana. This quite remarkable performance was achieved by one bird in 49 seconds, which compares very favourably with the 5 minutes it took Sultan to solve his similar problem.

There can be no doubt that the prior training of the pigeons in this study played an important role in helping them solve the problem. Even so, the study clearly reveals that the pigeons performed on the test session in a manner that extends beyond trial-and-error responding. The act of pecking the banana might have been acquired by trial-and-error learning, and so, too, might the act of moving the box around. But the way in which the box was moved to below the banana does not seem to be compatible with this analysis. This report, as well as those of Kohler (1925), implies that the novel act from its initiation to its conclusion was directed towards the achievement of a specific goal; and, if this is true, then it lies beyond the scope of any trial-and-error analysis.

The description by Epstein et al. (1984) of the pigeons' behaviour bears a striking similarity to Kohler's (1925) account of Sultan's reaction to the similar problem. It might be thought, therefore, that it would be appropriate to account for the pigeons' success in terms of insight. In truth, this would not be a particularly useful approach as it really does not offer an account of the way in which the problem was solved. Other than indicating that the problem was solved suddenly and not by trial and error, the term insight adds very little to our understanding of these results.

I regret that I find it impossible to offer, with confidence, any explanation for the findings by Epstein et al. (1984). But one possibility is that during their training with the blue spot, pigeons learned that certain responses moved the box towards the spot, and that the box by the spot was a signal for food. The combination of these associations would then result in them pushing the box towards the spot. During their training with the banana, one of the things they may have learned is that the banana is associated with food. Then, for the test session, although they would be unable to push the box towards the blue spot, generalisation from their previous training might result in them pushing the box in the direction of another signal for food, the banana.

Whatever the merits of this explanation, the findings by Epstein et al. (1984) forcefully demonstrate that there is more to the problem-solving abilities of animals than simply acting on the basis of trial and error. In subsequent chapters, many other findings will be encountered that confirm this conclusion. Animals that are released from an unfamiliar location, or that are prevented from travelling along a familiar route, do not necessarily act in a random fashion. They are often observed to select a route that is novel and that leads them to their goal (Chapter 8). We shall also encounter experimental studies of transitive

inference (Chapter 7) and analogical reasoning (Chapter 6) that clearly demonstrate that animals do not resort to trial and error when confronted with a novel problem. Thorndike's Law of Effect would thus seem to provide an incomplete account of how animals solve problems. One purpose of the following chapters is to explore in some detail the additional ways in which animals overcome the problems they encounter.

NOTES

1. Rats will learn to respond for food in these conditions, provided that the pellets are of a different flavour to that of the unrestricted food presented in the home cages.
2. In this experiment, the two responses were chain pulling and lever pressing, and the two reinforcers were food pellets and sucrose solution.
3. There is also the possibility that the ants were able to mark the route through the maze by laying a pheromone trail (see Chapter 7).

5

Discrimination Learning

Animals must be able to solve discriminations if they are to survive. There is the need to develop a diet whereby nutritious foods are selected and potentially poisonous substances are avoided. Predators have to be distinguished from less threatening creatures. Animals that form bonds with a single member of the opposite sex must be able to differentiate this chosen individual from all others that belong to the same species. Infants often have to be able to tell between their parents and other adults. And social animals must be able to identify the group to which they belong.

Given this importance of the ability to acquire discriminations, it should not be surprising to discover that it is displayed by, if not all, then very nearly all animals. We saw in Chapter 3, for example, that *Aplysia* will react more strongly to being stimulated on one part of the body than another if the former stimulation is consistently followed by an electric shock. There is also a report that *paramecia*, which consist only of a single complex cell, are capable of forming a discrimination between two tones that differ in frequency (Hennessey, Rucker, & McDiarmid, 1979).

The way in which animals solve discriminations has been the focus of interest now for nearly 100 years. Pavlov (1927) describes an experiment conducted in 1917 in which the presentation of an illuminated circle, but not an illuminated square,

signalled the imminent delivery of food to a hungry dog. Initially, both stimuli were treated similarly, but with continued training a CR of salivation was recorded predominantly in the presence of the circle. Since this study, there has been a persistent interest in the way discriminations are solved. Indeed, the analysis of discrimination learning constitutes one of the more enduring theoretical endeavours in psychology. The fruits of this endeavour are summarised in the first part of this chapter, which is intended to show how our theoretical understanding of discrimination learning has gradually evolved.

Much of our theoretical understanding about discrimination learning has been derived from experiments that use relatively simple stimuli. In this way, the interpretation of experimental findings is presumed to be rendered more straightforward than when more complex stimuli are used. Of course, by focusing on relatively simple discriminations, there is a risk that important principles concerning the solution of complex discriminations will be overlooked. This possibility is made more plausible by the intriguing results of an experiment by Herrnstein, Loveland, and Cable (1976). In each session pigeons were shown a set of 80 different photographic slides, half of which contained pictures of trees. The trees were not especially prominent in the slides—rather, the slides were of scenes that contained trees. The remaining slides were of similar scenes but without trees. Slides were shown one at a time, and pecks at a response key were rewarded with food only in the presence of pictures of trees. The slides were selected from a pool containing more than 500 pictures, and eventually subjects were able to discriminate accurately between the two sets, or categories, of slides. Perhaps the most impressive feature of this study is that the pigeons responded correctly even when they were shown novel photographs. Such a finding has led some authors (e.g. Herrnstein et al., 1976) to propose that pigeons have the ability to acquire concepts. In the second part of this chapter we shall examine the way in which animals solve categorisation problems.

The discriminations that have been mentioned thus far have been based on the presence or absence of a physical feature, such as a circle or a tree. Experimental studies of discrimination learning have also been conducted to determine whether animals can solve problems of a more abstract nature. The conclusions that can be drawn from these experiments will be considered in a further section of this chapter.

THEORIES OF DISCRIMINATION LEARNING

Relational learning and transposition

In many discriminations, the signals for reward and nonreward bear some relationship to each other. One of the earliest theoretical accounts of discrimination learning proposed that an appreciation of this relationship was essential if the discrimination was to be solved (Kinnaman, 1902; Kohler, 1918). Suppose that an animal must approach a white square, but not a black square, in order to obtain food. Kohler (1918) argued that to solve this discrimination animals inspected both stimuli on each trial and then selected the lighter of the two. As a test of this proposal, chickens were trained with two cards, one of which was darker than the other. Pecks at the light card (S+), but not the dark card (S–), were rewarded with food. Once this discrimination had been mastered, a *transposition* test was given in which the subjects

had to choose between the original S+ and an even lighter card. If the original discrimination was solved on the basis of relational information, then Kohler reasoned the new card will be chosen in preference to S+ on the test trials. This prediction was confirmed, even though it meant that subjects rejected the card that they had originally been trained to select. Despite the success of this experiment, we shall see shortly that a number of more recent theorists have preferred to interpret Kohler's findings in other ways.

Hypothesis testing

Figure 5.1 shows a jumping stand that was used for many years to study discrimination learning. The discriminative stimuli, horizontal and vertical stripes, are situated behind ledges that the subject must jump onto from the central platform. If the subject should jump onto the ledge in front of the correct stimulus, then it can push the stimulus card over and gain access to a reward. The position of the discriminative stimuli is normally varied randomly from trial to trial, which ensures that subjects learn food is behind a certain stimulus, rather than in a particular location.

A typical finding in experiments of this sort is that initially the subject, a rat, will adopt a position preference of jumping consistently to one side, even though it will then receive reward on only half the trials. Eventually this preference will weaken and the animal will start to jump more consistently to the correct panel. To explain results such as these, Krechevsky (1932; see also Lashley, 1929), argued that when animals are confronted with a discrimination, they rapidly formulate a single hypothesis, such as "jump to the left", which then guides their behaviour for the following trials. If this hypothesis should prove inadequate, it would eventually be discarded in favour of another one, such as "jump to the vertical stripes". Hypotheses were believed to be tested one at a time, so that while choices were being dictated by one hypothesis, nothing could be learned about the merits of alternative hypotheses.

Evidence against this analysis of discrimination learning can be found in a study by Turner (1968, cited in Sutherland & Mackintosh, 1971). While rats were being trained with a brightness

FIGURE 5.1

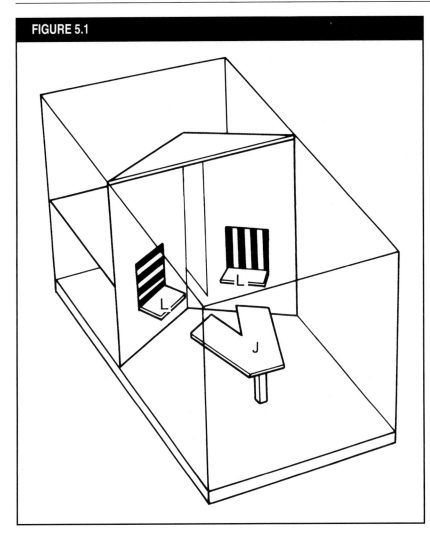

Sketch of a typical jumping stand used for studies of discrimination learning. A rat is placed on the platform (J) and must jump to one of the two ledges (L) (from Sutherland, 1964).

discrimination in a jumping stand, the time taken to jump from the platform was recorded. Turner found that even though the rats adopted a position preference, there was a difference between the latency to jump to S+ or S−. This difference is shown in Figure 5.2, which plots the time rats spent on the platform before jumping to each stimulus, as a function of the trials before the position habit was broken and the discrimination was solved. If choice was guided entirely by a hypothesis about position, then performance should have been unaffected by the nature of the stimulus that the rat was jumping towards. Instead, the results strongly suggest that while the rats were in the grip of their position habit, they none the less learned

something about the black and white stimuli to which they were jumping. Moreover, this learning seems to have taken place gradually and was presumably responsible for the ultimate rejection of the position preference. Not surprisingly, in view of these findings, the idea that discriminations are solved by selecting one hypothesis after another has fallen from popularity.

Spence

The first formal theory of discrimination learning was presented in two classic papers by Spence (1936, 1937). He proposed that if an animal is rewarded for approaching a set of stimuli, then this will result in an increment in the tendency to repeat

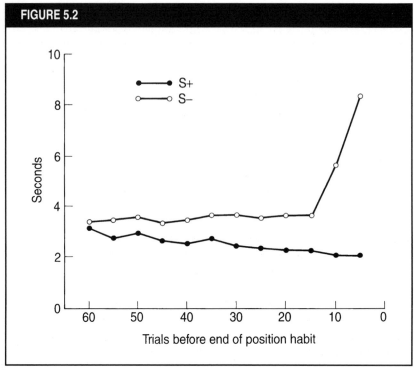

FIGURE 5.2

The mean time spent by rats on the platform in a jumping stand before selecting S+ or S−, as a function of the number of trials before their position habit was broken (adapted from Sutherland & Mackintosh, 1971).

the response to each of these stimuli in the future. Conversely, if the animal should fail to receive reward for approaching a set of stimuli, then the likelihood of repeating the response to any of these stimuli will be reduced. To appreciate the way in which these simple principles operate consider, again, the study by Turner (1968).

In Turner's experiment four different stimuli can be envisaged: There are the relevant bright (S+) and dark (S−) cards, as well as the irrelevant cues associated with the left and the right sides of the jumping stand. If on the first trial the rat jumped to the dark card on the left, then the tendency to jump to the dark card, and to the left, will be strengthened by reward. There are good reasons for believing that positional cues are more salient than brightness cues, so that the increase in approach strength to the left side of the apparatus will be considerably greater than to the dark card (see Sutherland & Mackintosh, 1971, p.90). On the next trial, the dark card might be on the right and the animal should show a position preference by incorrectly jumping to the left. The tendency to approach the light card, and the left side, will then decrease and on the next

trial the animal might well be attracted to the dark card, whatever its position. Depending on the behaviour of the animal, the relative salience of the various stimuli, and the sequence of trials, it should be evident that gradually and inevitably the solution to the discrimination will appear. Moreover, this solution will develop after a position habit has emerged, and then disappeared.

Implicit in the foregoing account is the assumption that animals learn about the absolute properties of stimuli. Spence believed that if animals were given a choice between, say, a black and a white card, they would not use relational information to decide where to jump. Instead, they would simply select the stimulus that had the highest approach strength. In view of the transposition study by Kohler (1918), these proposals might well be regarded as mistaken. But by referring to the effects of stimulus generalisation, Spence (1937) was able to explain transposition in a way that is both elegant and ingenious.

He argued that when animals are presented with a discrimination between two stimuli from the same dimension, say brightness, there will be a measure of generalisation between them. As a consequence, the excitatory tendency to approach S+ (light) will also be elicited by S– (dark), but to a weaker extent; and the inhibitory tendency to avoid S– will be aroused, albeit slightly, by S+. The strength of approach to either stimulus will then be determined by the interaction between these sources of generalisation. Spence (1937) characterised this interaction in the manner shown in Figure 5.3. The training stimuli are placed on the horizontal axis according to their brightness together with a third stimulus, S′, which is even lighter than S+. The larger curve depicts the excitatory generalisation gradient that will develop after a number of rewards have been received for selecting S+, and the smaller curve depicts the inhibitory generalisation gradient that will develop around S–. The strength of approach to any stimulus will then be determined by the difference between these two gradients. As this difference is greater for S+ than S–, the theory correctly predicts that discrimination training will result in a preference for S+ over S–. Now turn to the stimulus S′, which is to the left of S+, the difference between the two generalisation gradients for this new stimulus is greater than for S+. The theory thus predicts that after discrimination training with S+ and S–, if subjects are required to choose between S′ and S+, they will choose the lighter of the two and show transposition.

A related test of Spence's (1936, 1937) theorising was conducted by Hanson (1959) with a successive discrimination, in which the discriminative stimuli were presented at different times, rather than simultaneously. Pigeons were first rewarded for pecking a response key when it was illuminated by light of 550 nanometres (nm) (S+) but not when it was illuminated by light of 590nm (S–). Test trials were then conducted with different colours of light ranging in wavelength from 480 to 620nm. The effects of this training can again be explained by referring to Figure 5.3, but now the difference between the excitatory and inhibitory gradients indicates the strength of responding during a stimulus. Responding during S+ is predicted to be faster than during S–. Of considerably more interest, however, is the prediction that responding during light with a wavelength that is slightly less than that of S+ should result in stronger responding than S+ itself. In confirmation of this prediction, Hanson discovered that the highest rate of responding on the test trials occurred in the presence of light with a wavelength of 540nm. The discovery of such a *peak shift* constitutes an outstanding success of Spence's theory. Further examination of Figure 5.3 suggests that as the wavelength of the test stimuli is reduced below 540nm, so the peak shift will disappear and responding should eventually decline to a lower rate than during S+. Hanson (1959) was also able to confirm these predictions. A summary of the response rates that were recorded during his test trials is shown in Figure 5.4.

Despite this success of Spence's theory, there are a number of problems that it is unable to

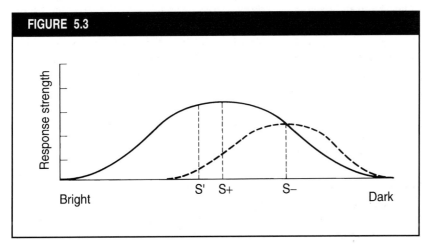

FIGURE 5.3

The gradients of excitation and inhibition that are predicted by the theory of Spence to develop during a discrimination in which reward is presented in the presence of one stimulus (S+) but not another (S–). The stimuli are located on a dimension of brightness (adapted from Spence, 1937).

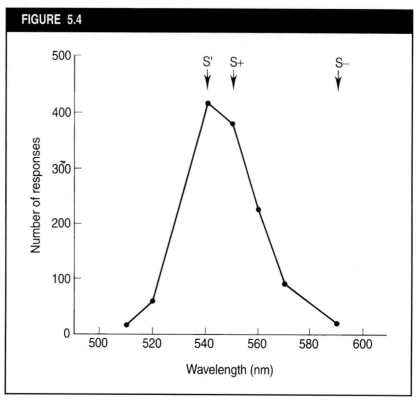

FIGURE 5.4

The number of responses recorded on test trials with key-lights of varying colours, after pigeons have been rewarded for pecking a key when it was illuminated with light of 550 nanometres (S+) but not when it was illuminated wih light of 590 nanometres (S–) (adapted from Hanson, 1959).

overcome. First, an inspection of Figure 5.3 will reveal that many stimuli to the left of S′ will have less of an excitatory influence than S′ itself. Thus, if after training with S+ and S–, a transposition test is conducted with one of these weakly excitatory stimuli and S′, a preference for S′ should be exhibited. In other words, although the original training will have resulted in a preference for the brighter stimulus, the proposed test trial is predicted to result in a preference for the darker stimulus. There have been a number of attempts to demonstrate such a reversal of transposition, but there is no good evidence that it ever occurs (Mackintosh, 1974; Riley, 1968). A second problem is that there are several successful demonstrations of transposition which Spence's theory is unable to explain (see Mackintosh, 1974, p.599). Gonzalez, Gentry, and Bitterman (1954), for example, trained chimpanzees on a discrimination involving three stimuli that varied in size, with food being signalled by only the intermediate stimulus. Spence's theory predicts that if testing is conducted with three new stimuli

that differ in size, and which lie beyond the range of the original stimuli, then transposition will not occur. Instead, the stimulus that is closest to S+ should be preferred because this is the one to which most excitation will generalise. In contrast to this prediction, Gonzalez et al. (1954) found that subjects again preferred the intermediate stimulus, which suggests that on this occasion a relational solution was adopted for the discrimination. Further evidence that animals are able to detect relations between stimuli can be found in experiments by Lawrence and DeRivera (1954). Very often, therefore, animals solve discrimina-tions on the basis of the absolute properties of the stimuli with which they are trained, but in certain circumstances they can respond on the basis of relational information. We shall pursue the implications of this conclusion in a later section of the chapter.

A further shortcoming of Spence's theorising can be appreciated by considering the effects of what is known as a feature-positive discrimination. In an experiment by Wagner (1969), rats were rewarded for lever pressing when a tone and light were presented together for 2 minutes, but they were never rewarded for responding when the tone was presented by itself. The effects of this training are shown in Figure 5.5, which reveals responding was vigorous during the compound and negligible during the tone. Indeed, responding during the tone was no faster than during the interval between trials, when responding never produced food. Perhaps surprisingly, Spence's theory is unable to explain this pattern of results. In essence, his theory provides a nonselective account for the way in which discriminations are solved. This means that learning will take place about a stimulus independently of what has been learned about any other stimulus that is present on a trial. In the case of the feature positive discrimination, therefore, the light will rapidly acquire excitatory strength because every time the light is presented it is paired with food. As a result responding on trials when the light is presented is predicted to be rapid. Turning now to the tone, because this stimulus is paired with food on half the occasions that it occurs, the theory predicts that this stimulus too should

acquire excitatory strength. The intermittent pairing of the tone with food will mean however that the tone acquires less excitatory strength than the light. Even so, the theory unequivocally predicts that the tone will elicit a relatively strong response whenever it is presented, and thus the discrimination will never be properly solved. The results in Figure 5.5 show, however, that the training used by Wagner (1969) resulted in a perfect discrimination.

Rescorla–Wagner theory

In terms of the profound influence it has exerted on the study of discrimination learning, the Rescorla–Wagner (1972) model of conditioning can be seen as the natural successor to the theory of Spence. Indeed, there are a number of similarities between the two theories. They both assume that conditioning can result in the acquisition of either excitatory or inhibitory tendencies, they both assume that changes in these tendencies are gradual, and they both assume that animals learn about the absolute properties of stimuli. The major difference between the theories concerns the rule that is used to determine the extent to which the associative properties of a stimulus will change on any trial. Whereas Spence believed these changes took place independently of the properties of the other stimuli that were present, we saw in Chapter 3 that this is not true for the Rescorla–Wagner (1972) model. As a consequence, this theory is readily able to explain the successful solution of the feature positive-discrimination that poses such a problem for the theory of Spence.

Consider again the experiment by Wagner (1969). Equation 3.7 on p.60 predicts that initially the compound trials will result in the tone and light each gaining associative strength. This strength will be lost to some extent by the tone on the nonreinforced trials, but the light will continue to acquire associative strength on each compound trial until it reaches the asymptotic value, λ. At this point the light will block any additional increments in the associative strength of the tone on the compound trials, and the only effect of further training will be to reduce the associative strength of the tone on nonreinforced trials. Eventually, the

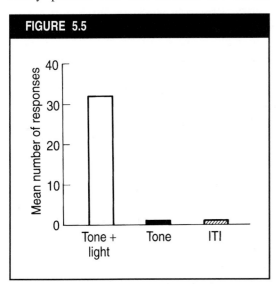

FIGURE 5.5

The mean number of responses that were recorded during a tone–light compound, a tone, and the inter-trial interval (ITI) by a group of rats that had received food for lever pressing only during the compound. The results were collected after 25 sessions of training had been given (adapted from Wagner, 1969).

tone will have no associative strength and responding during this stimulus by itself will be minimal, whereas responding during the tone–light compound will be vigorous. It is not just the outcome of feature-positive discriminations that the Rescorla–Wagner theory is able to predict satisfactorily. There are many other types of discrimination where the theory has proved to be a substantial improvement over its predecessors, particularly where the role of inhibition is concerned. Moreover, by making a few simple modifications to the theory it has been possible to extend its scope considerably.

One useful modification has been to assume that individual stimuli are composed of a variety of elements that represent its different characteristics (Blough, 1975; Rescorla, 1976). These elements are then assumed to gain and lose their associative strength in a manner that is dictated by the Rescorla–Wagner equation. If it is accepted that the elements belonging to one stimulus are shared to some extent by other stimuli, the model is then able to explain stimulus generalisation. In addition, as Blough (1975) has shown, such an extension of the Rescorla–Wagner (1972) theory allows it to explain a wide range of findings associated with discrimination learning, including peak shift.

A second modification was proposed in order to take account of the problem for the theory that is posed by the results from *negative patterning* discriminations (Woodbury, 1943). In a recent example of this discrimination, Rescorla (1972) rewarded rats for pressing a lever in the presence of a tone (T), or a clicker (C), but lever pressing was never rewarded when these stimuli were presented together (C+ CT– T+). The course of acquisition of this discrimination is portrayed in Figure 5.6, which shows that eventually the rate of lever pressing for food was more rapid when the stimuli were presented alone rather than together. The trials in which C and T were individually paired with food can be expected to result in each of them acquiring positive associative strength. Because the Rescorla–Wagner (1972) theory assumes that responding during a compound is determined by the sum of the associative strengths of its components, responding during CT is predicted to be stronger than during either C or T

alone. The theory, therefore, incorrectly predicts that a negative patterning discrimination will be insoluble.

To overcome this problem, Wagner and Rescorla (1972) suggested that when two stimuli are presented together they create a hypothetical, compound-unique, configural cue that is capable of taking part in associative learning just like any other stimulus. Thus the experimental design of Rescorla (1972) can be conceptualised as C+ T+ CTX– where X is the hypothetical stimulus. In these circumstances, the theory now predicts that on the nonreinforced trials with the compound, X will acquire inhibitory properties that will counter the excitatory influence of C and T. As these inhibitory properties grow in strength, they will reduce the level of responding during the compound and result eventually in the discrimination being mastered.

Now that some of the successful predictions from the Rescorla–Wagner theory have been reviewed, we shall examine a finding that is not so readily explained by the theory. The finding was reported by Redhead and Pearce (1995a, see also Pearce, 1994). A group of pigeons received discrimination training in which the stimuli were dots of different colours. Food was delivered on trials when dots of one colour (A) were shown, and when dots of two other colours (B and C) were shown together, but food was never delivered in the presence of dots of all three colours (A, B, and C), thus creating an A+ BC+ ABC– discrimination. The left-hand side of Figure 5.7 shows the results from this experiment, which makes it quite clear that eventually responding during ABC was slower than during either A or BC.

The right-hand side of Figure 5.7 shows the outcome of the discrimination that is predicted by the Rescorla–Wagner model. This prediction was derived from a computer simulation based on the Rescorla–Wagner equation and which incorporated the assumption that compounds generate unique cues. An account of the way in which the simulation was conducted can be found in Pearce (1994). Although the figure shows that responding during ABC will eventually be slow, it also shows that responding during BC is predicted to be consistently stronger than during A. Such a pattern

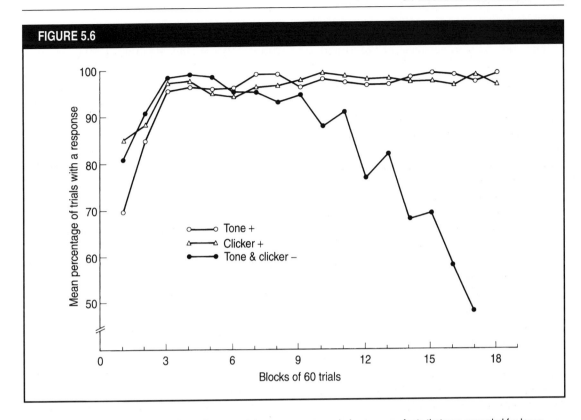

FIGURE 5.6

The mean percentage of trials in which an instrumental response was made for a group of rats that was rewarded for lever pressing during a tone and a clicker when they were presented individually, but not when they were presented together (adapted from Rescorla, 1972).

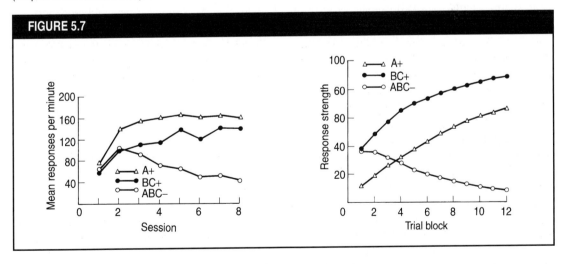

FIGURE 5.7

Left-hand side: The mean rates of responding during three different trials that were presented for eight sessions of discrimination training in an autoshaping experiment. Food was made available after trials with stimulus A, and compound BC, but food was never presented on trials with compound ABC (adapted from Redhead & Pearce, 1995a).
Right-hand side: The response strengths for A, BC, and ABC that are predicted by the Rescorla–Wagner theory for the experiment by Redhead and Pearce (1995a).

of results is anticipated because excitatory conditioning with a compound of two stimuli is expected to progress more readily than with a single stimulus.

The prediction that responding will be more vigorous during BC than A poses two serious problems for the Rescorla–Wagner model. First, this prediction was not confirmed: The left-hand side of Figure 5.7 shows that responding throughout the experiment was faster during A than BC. The second problem is perhaps more serious and requires us to consider the relationship between similarity and discrimination learning. In keeping with common sense, most theorists accept that the difficulty of a discrimination is determined by the similarity of the signals for reward and nonreward. The greater the similarity of these signals, the harder will be the discrimination. The results from the experiment by Redhead and Pearce (1995a) are entirely in keeping with this analysis. Because A has only one element in common with ABC, these signals for reward and nonreward can be regarded as being quite different and the discrimination between them should develop rapidly. On the other hand, BC shares two elements with ABC and these signals for reward and nonreward can be seen as quite similar, so that the discrimination between them should emerge slowly. If similarity exerts an important influence on the ease with which discriminations are solved, then the difference between the rates of responding during A and ABC will be greater than for BC and ABC. The results shown in the left-hand side of Figure 5.7 show that this was true throughout the experiment.

Turning now to the pattern of results predicted by the Rescorla–Wagner theory for the experiment by Redhead and Pearce (1995a), we can see that the discrimination between BC and ABC is predicted to develop more readily than between A and ABC. The theory thus makes the counterintuitive prediction that a discrimination between two sets of stimuli will be easier when they are similar (BC and ABC) than when they are different (A and ABC). I have argued (Pearce, 1994) that by making such a counterintuitive, and incorrect, prediction, the analysis of discrimination learning offered by the Rescorla–Wagner theory is seriously called into question. Moreover, it is not just the results from a single experiment that pose a problem for the theory. Pearce and Redhead (1993; see also Redhead & Pearce, 1995a,b) describe a number of experimental designs for which the Rescorla–Wagner theory predicts that a discrimination will be made easier by enhancing the similarity of the signals for reward and nonreward. The results from all of our experiments contradicted this prediction.

There can be no denying that a large number of successful predictions have been derived from the Rescorla–Wagner model, and that it has thoroughly deserved its considerable influence during the last 25 years or so. None the less, the fact that it occasionally makes counterintuitive, and incorrect, predictions concerning the influence of similarity on discrimination learning suggests that there is a need to seek an alternative theoretical account for the way in which discriminations are solved.

Configural theory

Despite their differences many theories of discrimination learning share a common feature. They assume that when animals are presented with a set of stimuli they learn about each one separately. In the case of the Rescorla–Wagner model, for example, if a US is delivered after a compound, then each element of that compound may enter into an association with the US. It should be apparent that this *elemental* assumption can also be found in the theory of Spence. Despite the popularity of this assumption the theories that have adopted it are unable to explain all that is known about discrimination learning. The possibility must be considered, therefore, that the elemental assumption on which these theories are based is wrong. The next theory to be considered does not incorporate the elemental assumption and, interestingly, it is able to provide an accurate account of the relationship between similarity and discrimination learning.

According to configural theory (e.g. Pearce, 1987, 1994), if a compound stimulus should be presented for conditioning, or a discrimination, then a configural representation will be formed of the entire pattern of stimulation. This representation will then enter into a single association with the outcome of the trial. The association is assumed to develop gradually over trials, and its strength determines the vigour of the CR that will occur to that particular pattern of stimulation. If the pattern of stimulation should change in any way, then a weaker CR will be performed with a vigour that is related to the similarity of the training and test patterns. In other words, responding during the new pattern will be determined by stimulus generalisation from the original pattern.

The application of this theory to discrimination learning can be introduced by referring again to a feature-positive, AB+ B–, discrimination in which food is presented after AB but not B. When AB is first presented a representation of this compound will enter into an association with food. On a subsequent trial with B there will be a measure of generalisation from AB, and a response will occur. Of course, this response will be inappropriate because B signals the absence of food and as a consequence B will enter into an inhibitory association to counter the excitation that generalises from AB. The discrimination will be solved when the excitation aroused by AB is sufficient to generate a normal response, and the inhibition associated with B is sufficient to counter completely the excitation that spreads to it from AB.

This account may seem complex, but it is really no more than a modification of the analysis of discrimination learning developed by Spence (1937). Figure 5.8 shows the way in which these ideas can be accommodated within Spence's (1937) framework. In this figure, distance along the abscissa does not reflect the difference between two stimuli from the same dimension. This distance instead reflects the difference between configurations of stimuli measured in some more complex manner.[1] The figure demonstrates that an AB+ B– discrimination will result in an inhibitory generalisation gradient around B (small curve) and an excitatory gradient around AB (large curve). If the difference between these gradients determines the strength of responding, then it follows that the compound AB, but not the element, B, will elicit a CR.

By emphasising the importance of generalisation between different patterns of stimuli, configural theory is able to provide a straightforward explanation of the results reported by Redhead and Pearce (1995a) that posed such a problem for the Rescorla–Wagner theory. Training with an A+ BC+ ABC– discrimination will result in A and BC entering into excitatory associations. The configuration of ABC will then have to enter into an inhibitory association to counter the generalisation of excitation from A and BC. The inhibition that grows to ABC will generalise to both A and BC, and weaken responding in their presence. Because ABC is more similar to BC than A, more inhibition will generalise to BC than A and thus disrupt responding to a greater extent during BC than A. As the discrimination is being acquired, therefore, A is correctly predicted to elicit a stronger response than BC.

A further advantage of configural theory is that it is able to explain the solution to discriminations, such as negative patterning, without the need to make additional assumptions. Quite simply, a

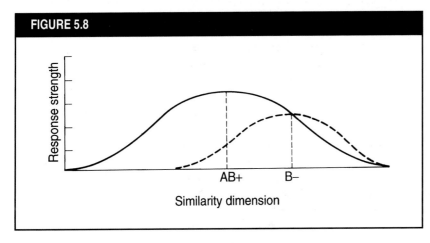

FIGURE 5.8

Response strength

AB+   B–

Similarity dimension

One way in which the theory of Spence (1937) could be developed to provide a configural explanation for the solution of an AB+ B– discrimination.

negative patterning discrimination (A+ B+ AB–) will result in A and B entering individually into excitatory associations. Although the effects of these associations will generalise to AB, the absence of any reward in its presence will result in this compound entering into an inhibitory association that will eventually serve to confine responding to trials with A and B alone.

In summary, configural theory differs from the other theories that have been considered because it is assumed that when two or more stimuli are presented together for conditioning, then only a single association will develop. This association is between a unitary, configural representation of all the stimuli and the US. By making the additional assumption that generalisation will occur between configurations, configural theory can explain most of the findings from the discrimination studies that have been described earlier. The only findings that lie beyond the scope of this theory are those that show animals use relational information to solve discriminations. These findings will be discussed shortly.

We can now close this discussion of the theoretical analysis of simple discriminations. For reasons that are no doubt obvious, I favour a configural account for the way in which discriminations are solved, but not everyone shares my enthusiasm for this type of theory. A number of theorists remain wedded to the idea that elemental associations are responsible for the way in which discriminations are solved (e.g. McLaren, Kaye, & Mackintosh, 1989). Others have argued that both elemental and configural associations may develop during the course of a discrimination (e.g. Kehoe, 1988; Schmajuk & DiCarlo, 1992). It will be interesting to find out which of these approaches proves the most fruitful for enhancing our understanding of discrimination learning.

CATEGORISATION

This section is concerned with understanding the way in which animals solve categorisation problems. We shall see that the theories that were developed to explain the solution of simple discriminations can be used with considerable success to account for the results from experiments with more complex stimuli. Before turning to the theoretical analysis of categorisation, however, some selected experimental findings merit attention. These add little in substance to the findings of Herrnstein et al. (1976) mentioned at the start of the chapter, but they emphasise the remarkable ability of animals to utilise categories.

In one experiment (Cerella, 1979), pigeons were shown the same set of 80 slides in each session. Reward was made available for responding in the presence of 40 slides, which were all silhouettes of oak leaves (see upper row, Figure 5.9), but reward was never presented for responding during the remaining slides, which were silhouettes of other leaves (see lower row, Figure 5.9). Only 24 sessions were needed before the birds displayed a near-perfect discrimination between the two sets of slides. The discrimination was also maintained when 40 novel silhouettes of oak leaves replaced the original set. This last finding is particularly important because it shows that categorisation does not depend merely on remembering how to respond to each training slide (see also Bhatt, Wasserman, Reynolds, & Knauss, 1988; Herrnstein et al., 1976; Schrier & Brady, 1987). Other pigeons were trained with one oak leaf as S+ and 40 other leaves as S–. Even in these circumstances pigeons learned to respond to the category of oak leaf, because a generalisation test with 40 new slides of different oak leaves intermixed among the original S– slides revealed an excellent level of discrimination. There is a limit to the ability of pigeons. Cerella (1980) had difficulty in training them to distinguish one oak leaf from 40 other oak leaves; in fact, two of the four pigeons trained in this manner were unable to learn the discrimination.

There is now ample evidence showing that a large number of species are capable of solving categorisation problems. Indeed, after reviewing some of this evidence, Herrnstein (1990, p.138) was led to conclude that categorisation has "turned up at every level of the animal kingdom where it has been competently sought". Thus studies of categorisation have involved monkeys (e.g. Schrier, Angarella, & Povar, 1984), chinchillas

FIGURE 5.9

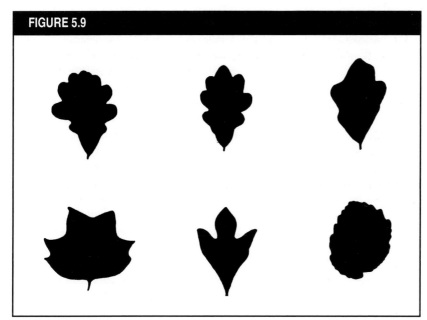

Silhouettes of oak leaves (upper row) and nonoak leaves (lower row) that are representative of the stimuli used in a category learning experiment by Cerella (1979) (from Cerella, 1979).

(Burdick & Miller, 1975), pigeons (e.g. Herrnstein et al., 1976), chickens (Ryan, 1982), quail (Kluender, Diehl, & Killeen, 1987), blue jays (Pietrewicz & Kamil, 1977) and an African grey parrot (Pepperberg, 1983).

A wide variety of categories have been studied in these experiments. Some categories have been based on natural objects: trees, water, people, cats, and flowers (e.g. Bhatt et al., 1988; Herrnstein et al., 1976). Other categories have involved human-made objects: cars, chairs, the letter A in various typescripts, the cartoon character Charlie Brown, and even the paintings of Monet and Picasso (Bhatt et al., 1988; Cerella, 1980; Morgan, Fitch, Holman, & Lea, 1976; Watanabe, Sakamoto, & Wakita, 1995). Most categorisation studies employ visual stimuli, but it is worthwhile describing an experiment by Porter and Neuringer (1984) that provides an example of successful categorisation with auditory stimuli.

While they were in conditioning chambers, pigeons were presented with excerpts of J.S. Bach's Toccatas and Fugues for organ, which alternated with Stravinsky's "Rite of Spring" for orchestra. Pecks on one key were occasionally rewarded during the music by Bach, whereas pecks on another key were rewarded during the "Rite of Spring". Even though the excerpts of music varied

considerably from trial to trial, all subjects eventually displayed a clear discrimination between the two pieces of music. This training might have resulted in the pigeons discriminating between an organ (Bach) and an orchestra (Stravinsky), but the results from a series of generalisation tests suggest this did not occur. The tests consisted of various novel pieces of music by a variety of composers. There was no indication that organ works necessarily resulted in responding on the "Bach" key, or orchestral works on the "Stravinsky" key. Instead, the fairest conclusion to be drawn from these test trials is that subjects were likely to respond on the "Stravinsky" key whenever they heard modern music and on the "Bach" key in the presence of baroque music. In addition to being able to form musical categories, there is also evidence showing that some animals can discriminate between auditory categories based on the phonemes of human speech (Burdick & Miller, 1975; Kluender et al., 1987)

Feature theory

Humans have been said to assign individual stimuli to categories on the basis of the features of which they are composed. That is, membership of a category is determined by whether or not an item possesses some necessary set of defining features (see Smith & Medin, 1981). A similar analysis has been developed to account for categorisation by animals (e.g. D'Amato & Van Sant, 1988; Lea, 1984).

Support for feature theories of categorisation can be found in a study by Cerella (1980) who trained pigeons to peck a key for food in the presence of Charlie Brown cartoons but not other cartoon characters. Once this was achieved, albeit with considerable difficulty, they received generalisation tests with unusual slides of Charlie Brown (see Figure 5.10). These were treated as if they were quite normal instances of the training category. Feature theory is able to explain this finding because the test stimuli contained all the features of the training stimuli, even though they were presented in a novel way.

Further evidence that is consistent with a feature analysis of categorisation can be found in a study by D'Amato and Van Sant (1988) who trained monkeys with photographs showing the presence or absence of humans. Although the monkeys were successful on this problem, test trials revealed a number of interesting errors. For example, any nonperson slide that contained a red patch, such as half a watermelon, or a dead flamingo being carried by a jackal, was likely to be classified as belonging to the person category. One straightforward interpretation of this finding is that the feature of red patch was used to classify the photographs, presumably because it is common to many faces.

If we accept that the presence or absence of a certain feature is responsible for determining how a subject reacts to individual stimuli, then the way in which these features acquire their influence must be specified. One solution to this problem is to look to a theory such as the Rescorla–Wagner (1972) model. Suppose that animals receive trials in which photographs of trees signal food, whereas nontree slides are followed by nothing. Whenever a photograph is presented for a trial, the associative strength of each of its many features can be expected to change. The features that belong to trees will, in general, be present only on reinforced trials and they will steadily acquire associative strength. In contrast, the features that are irrelevant to the solution of the discrimination, for example patches of sky, will occur on both reinforced and nonreinforced trials and the manner in which they acquire associative strength will be erratic. In other words, a categorisation problem can be construed as feature-positive discrimination in which the features that are present only on reinforced trials, specifically those belonging to trees, will gain considerably more associative strength than the features present on both types of trial. Once this has occurred, the discrimination will be solved and even novel photographs will be classified correctly. Rigorous tests of this type of analysis have often proved difficult because of the complex nature of the stimuli that are typically employed in a categorisation experiment. However, the results of

FIGURE 5.10

Examples of the slides used in the generalisation tests by Cerella (1980) (from Cerella, 1982).

an experiment by Huber and Lenz (1993) are entirely consistent with detailed predictions that can be derived from feature theory. Figure 5.11 shows three examples of the stimuli that were employed in this study. Inspection of these figures will reveal that the faces differ on four dimensions: the area above the eyes, the distance between the eyes, the length of the nose, and the area below the mouth. The figures also show, progressively from left to right, the three values that were used to represent each dimension. The features in the left-hand figure were assigned a value of –1, in the centre figure 0, and in the right-hand figure +1.

There were 62 different faces used for the training stage of the experiment. Pigeons were rewarded for pecking a response key in the presence of any face for which the sum of the feature values was greater than zero. A substantially greater level of responding was eventually recorded in the presence of those faces that signalled the availability, rather than the absence of food. The advantage of using artificially created stimuli in this study is that the experimenter knows which features the subjects must use in order to solve the discrimination. It is also possible

to study performance in the presence of different faces, to gain an understanding of the control exerted by these features. In fact, Huber and Lenz (1993) found that there was an extremely orderly relationship between the sum of the feature values of a particular face and the rate of responding that it elicited. This relationship is shown for one pigeon in Figure 5.12, which makes it clear that the more features a face had in common with the right-hand face of Figure 5.11, the faster was responding in its presence.

This experiment demonstrates that not all members of a category are treated equally, with some being classified more readily than others. To explain this pattern of results in terms of a feature theory, such as the Rescorla–Wagner model, we must assume that each of the positive feature values gained positive associative strength during the course of training, and that each of the negative feature values gained negative associative strength. As the theory predicts that the strength of responding during a compound is determined by the sum of the associative strengths of its components, there will be a direct relationship between the rate of responding during a particular

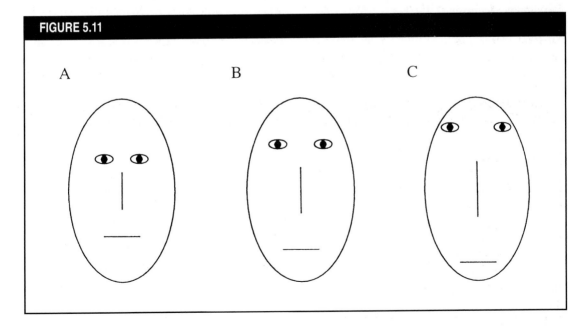

FIGURE 5.11

Examples of three of the faces used by Huber and Lenz (1993) in a categorisation study (adapted from Huber & Lenz, 1993).

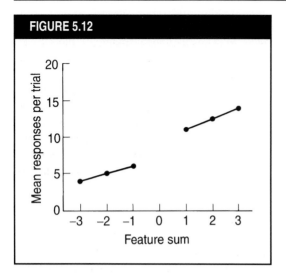

FIGURE 5.12

The mean number of responses on test trials in the categorisation study by Huber and Lenz (1993). The test stimuli are arranged according to the sum of the values of their three features (adapted from Huber & Lenz, 1993).

face and the sum of the values of its component features.

Exemplar theory

A number of authors have argued that the ability of both humans (Hintzman, 1986; Kruschke, 1992; Medin & Schaffer, 1978) and animals (Astley & Wasserman, 1992; Pearce, 1988, 1989, 1991) to categorise objects depends on them remembering each instance or exemplar and the category to which it belongs. Such an account can clearly explain the ability to categorise familiar exemplars, but some additional mechanism is required if this account is to explain the successful categorisation of novel stimuli. Both Pearce (1988, 1991) and Astley and Wasserman (1992) have proposed that this additional mechanism is based on the principles of stimulus generalisation as envisaged by Spence (1937). When a stimulus is presented for the first time in a categorisation problem, there will be generalisation of both excitation and inhibition to it as a result of the training with the previous exemplars. If the new stimulus belongs to the category that signals food, then it is likely that it will bear a strong similarity to many other stimuli that have already been shown and that belong to the

same category. There will, as a consequence, be a considerable generalisation of excitation to this new stimulus. In contrast, the new pattern is unlikely to bear a close resemblance to the members of the nonreinforced category and the generalisation of inhibition that will result from the nonreinforced trials will be slight. The interaction of these sources of excitation and inhibition will leave the new stimulus with a net level of excitation, and it will elicit a response appropriate to the category to which it belongs.

Two points merit emphasis concerning this account of categorisation. The first relates to an argument that may occur to many readers: The account is implausible because it requires that animals remember an unreasonably large number of individual stimuli. In the case of the study by Herrnstein et al. (1976) this number would have to be a sizable proportion of 500. But we shall see in the next chapter that Vaughan and Greene (1984) have demonstrated pigeons are able to remember many hundreds of different photographs.

The second point to make concerns the finding that when the same pool of photographs is used for training with a category discrimination, performance in the presence of these photographs is often better than with novel photographs belonging to the same category (Bhatt et al., 1988; Schrier, Angarella, & Povar, 1984). This result has also been found in experiments with humans, where it is referred to as the *exemplar effect* (Homa, Dunbar, & Nohre, 1991). The implication of this result is that animals can learn about individual training stimuli in a categorisation task, and that this information is at least partially responsible for their successful performance.

Despite the very different assumptions on which they are based, it is often extremely difficult to differentiate between a feature and an exemplar theory in terms of the predictions they make. Consider, for example, the finding by Huber and Lenz (1993) that faces with a net feature sum of, say, 3 elicited faster responding than those with a net feature sum of 1, even though they belonged to the same category. At first sight this finding may appear to be more compatible with a feature than an exemplar analysis of categorisation, but it can be readily explained by the latter. Any face with a net feature sum of 1 will be more similar to the members of the negative category than a face with a net feature sum of 3. The generalisation of inhibition from members of the nonreinforced category will thus be greater to the former instance than the latter, and result in faces with a feature sum of 3 eliciting a higher rate of responding than those with a feature sum of 1. In other words, the reason for the high rate of responding to a +3 face is essentially the same as that offered by Spence's (1937) theory of discrimination learning for the peak shift effect.

Certain results that were reviewed in the first part of this chapter were interpreted as being more consistent with a configural than an elemental theory of discrimination learning. It might be tempting to conclude, therefore, that for the analysis of categorisation experiments the exemplar-based counterpart of configural theory should be viewed more favourably than the feature-based counterpart of elemental theory. Such a temptation should, however, be resisted. The experiments described in the first part of the chapter employed relatively simple designs and their findings may be of little relevance where the evaluation of theories of categorisation is concerned. When complex stimuli are employed, animals may adopt different strategies to solve discriminations than when simple stimuli are employed. In addition, certain categorisation tasks may encourage animals to focus on the components of the stimuli, as feature theory predicts, whereas in other tasks they may focus on more global aspects of the stimuli, as exemplar theory predicts (see Huber & Lenz, 1993). Because of these possibilities, it is difficult to derive any firm conclusions concerning the relative merits of feature and exemplar accounts of categorisation by animals. Instead we shall conclude for the present that the mechanisms that are believed to be responsible for the way animals solve relatively simple discriminations are also likely to be responsible for the way they solve categorisation problems. We turn now to examine whether any additional processes are ever involved in categorisation by animals.

Prototype theory

The results from experimental studies of categorisation by humans have encouraged the proposal that exposure to the members of a category results in the formation of a prototype (e.g. Posner & Keele, 1968; see also Shanks, 1994). The prototype of a category is supposed to be a summary representation that corresponds to the average, or central tendency, of all the exemplars that have been experienced. Once a prototype has been formed it is assumed to be activated whenever an exemplar is presented, and once activated it will elicit the response that is appropriate for the category. The likelihood of the response being performed is assumed to be determined by the extent to which the prototype is activated, which, in turn, is assumed to be related to the degree of similarity between the exemplar and the prototype.

Evidence in support of these proposals comes from the finding that exemplars that bear a close resemblance to the prototype are classified more easily than exemplars that are rather different to the prototype (Posner & Keele, 1968). Although initial attempts to find a similar prototype effect with animals failed (see, for example, Lea & Harrison, 1978; Pearce, 1987; Watanabe, 1988), more recent experiments have been successful (Aydin & Pearce, 1994; Von Fersen & Lea, 1990). But even these successes do not necessarily mean that a prototypical representation is responsible for successful categorisation by animals. It now seems that demonstrations of such an effect with humans can be explained by either a feature (McClelland & Rumelhart, 1985) or an exemplar (Hintzman, 1986; Shin & Nosofsky, 1992) theory of categorisation, and the same may well be true for experiments with animals.

In terms of feature theory, for instance, a stimulus that corresponds to the average of all the members of a category is likely to be composed of elements that occur frequently in that category. If the category in question has been used to signal food, then each of these frequently occurring features will have considerable associative strength, and their combined influence will result in a high rate of responding during the prototypical stimulus. Furthermore, this level of responding is likely to be higher than during stimuli that are only distantly related to the prototype, and that can be expected to possess only a few features with high associative strength. Likewise, in terms of exemplar theory, an exemplar that corresponds to the average of the training patterns will bear a close similarity to these patterns. Responding in the presence of the exemplar can then be expected to be high because of the substantial spread of excitation to it from all the training patterns (see Aydin & Pearce, 1994).

Categorisation as concept formation

The claim has been made occasionally that animals are able to categorise because they possess a concept. Schrier and Brady (1987, p.142), for instance, proposed that monkeys can categorise photographs of people because they possess a "concept *humans* as we commonly understand it". Although it is easy to talk about concepts when they are used by humans, it is rather more difficult to specify what this term means when it applies to animals. Lea (1984) has considered this matter in some detail. He concludes that if animals acquire concepts, then successful categorisation need not depend on the physical similarity of the members of the category. Thus far, successful categorisation of a novel exemplar has been attributed to it bearing some similarity, or sharing common elements, with at least one training stimulus. But if categorisation is based on learning about the significance of concepts, then it should be successful even when the exemplars bear no physical similarity to each other. To help clarify this point, consider the following experiment by Savage-Rumbaugh, Rumbaugh, Smith, and Lawson (1980). Chimpanzees were required to sort a mixed pile of tools and food into two separate piles. Initially they were trained with the same objects, but when test trials were given with new objects they were able to categorise these successfully. It is not easy to argue that this problem was solved on the basis of the physical similarity of the test items to the training items, because it is difficult to identify a set of physical features an object must possess in order to be classified as a tool or as food. Instead, these objects may have been categorised successfully because the subjects possessed the concepts "food"

and "tool". In fact, the chimpanzees had received considerable language training (see Chapter 10) prior to this experiment and it is conceivable that this was responsible for their ability to acquire these concepts. There is, however, an alternative, theoretically less exciting explanation for the results of this experiment.

When a chimpanzee picks up an item of food it may react in some consistent way, such as by salivating. In order to solve the discrimination, therefore, all the animal has to learn is that any object which elicits this reaction must be treated in one way, and objects which do not elicit this reaction must be treated in another way. Such a "mediated generalisation" account is, admittedly, cumbersome but it has a long history (e.g. Osgood, 1953, p.353) and there are good reasons for believing it to be true for both simple (Honey & Hall, 1989) and complex (Wasserman, DeVolder, & Coppage, 1992) discriminations. In view of this possible role of mediated generalisation, it remains an open question as to whether or not success by animals in solving any categorisation problems ever implies the possession of a concept.

RELATIONSHIPS AS DISCRIMINATIVE STIMULI

The majority of the experiments described in this chapter have been confined to discriminations, and categorisation problems, where responding is controlled by the presence or absence of a physical stimulus, or set of stimuli. We now return to consider in some detail the question of whether or not animals can respond on the basis of the relationship between two or more stimuli. Some support for this possibility has already been encountered in the form of a transposition experiment, using chimpanzees, by Gonzalez et al. (1954). In addition to transposition experiments, a number of other techniques have been developed to determine whether or not animals are capable of using relational information to solve discriminations. The results from these experiments are of interest because they highlight the intellectual limitations of certain species. These experiments are also of interest because of the conclusions they suggest concerning the way in which animals represent knowledge.

Sameness

One method that has been developed to study the way in which animals learn about relationships is known as matching to sample or, simply, matching. For this technique a subject is presented with a sample stimulus, and, a short while after it has been turned off, two comparison stimuli are shown, one of which is the same as the sample. To gain reward, the comparison stimulus that matches the sample must be selected. Panel *a* of Figure 5.13 portrays schematically the array of stimuli that might be presented for one trial of a typical matching experiment. There is a sample stimulus, which may be of a particular colour, and two comparison stimuli, one of which will be the same colour as the sample. In order to gain reward the subject must respond to the comparison stimulus that corresponds to the sample. The theoretically interesting account for successful matching is that animals can appreciate that the sample and comparison stimuli are the same, and that this relationship controls the choice of the correct comparison. As is so often the case, however, there are alternative accounts for successful matching, and these must be discounted before we accept that animals can detect and respond to a relationship.

A plausible account for matching can be developed in terms of configural learning. The four panels in Figure 5.13 depict the possible configurations of stimuli that will confront an animal during a typical matching problem. To respond correctly, the left-hand comparison stimuli in panels *a* and *d* must be chosen, and so must the right-hand stimuli in panels *b* and *c*. Note that these are the only possible trials, and that each panel contains a different configuration of sample and comparison stimuli. In order to solve the problem, then, all the animal must do is to associate a specific response with each configuration. For example, configuration *b* would be associated with the response of approaching top-left. Once the four associations have been formed, the problem can be solved successfully on every trial.

In order to test this account of matching, it would be necessary to introduce a new set of sample and comparison stimuli. As there will have been no opportunity to associate the configurations of these stimuli with the correct choices, this change will result in a marked loss of accuracy if such associations are responsible for matching. On the other hand, if the original training resulted in subjects learning to respond according to the relationship between the sample and comparison stimuli, then changing their physical properties should not disrupt responding. Even when the stimuli are novel it will be possible to identify the comparison that is the same as the sample and respond correctly.

Experiments with chimpanzees (Nissen, Blum, & Blum, 1948; Oden, Thompson, & Premack, 1988), rhesus monkeys (Mishkin, Prockop, & Rosvold, 1962), dolphins (Herman & Gordon, 1974), sea lions (Kastak & Schusterman, 1994), and corvids (Wilson, Mackintosh, & Boakes, 1985) have found that after sufficient training on a variety of matching discriminations, these animals can respond correctly on the first trial with a novel set of stimuli. At least some species, therefore,

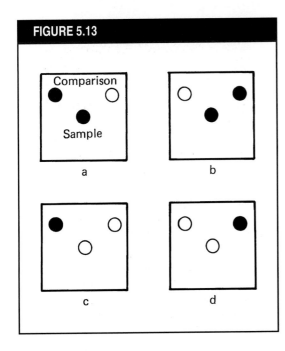

FIGURE 5.13

The four possible configurations of sample and comparison stimuli that can occur in a matching study.

seem capable of solving discriminations on the basis of relational information.

An experiment by Pepperberg (1987) provides rather different evidence that animals can classify novel stimuli on the basis of a judgement about sameness and difference. The single subject in this experiment, Alex, an African grey parrot, had been trained over many years to use vocal English labels to refer to a variety of objects in response to questions posed in spoken English by his trainers.[2] He could also use such categorical labels as "colour" and "shape". For the experiment under consideration, Alex was presented with two objects, such as a red pentagon and a red oval and was asked "What's same?" or "What's different?" (see Figure 5.14). He was then expected to respond by saying the appropriate category label: "colour" for the first question, and "shape" for the second. Performance on these tests, even when the objects had not previously been presented for testing, was considerably better than would be expected on the basis of chance.

It is instructive to contrast the findings that have just been considered with those from a variety of experiments with pigeons. Wilson et al. (1985) trained pigeons with a matching problem before

FIGURE 5.14

Alex making a sameness/difference judgement about two stimuli presented to him by Irene Pepperberg. Photograph by David Linden.

transferring to a second matching problem with novel stimuli. There was no hint of any positive transfer from the first stage of training to the second, which suggests that pigeons relied solely on learning about the absolute properties of the stimuli with which they were trained. Further support for this conclusion can be found from rather different experimental designs that have been used in the hope of encouraging pigeons to use relational information. I have spent many frustrating hours attempting to train pigeons to judge whether or not two adjacent vertical bars were of the same or different heights (Pearce, 1988, 1991). Although I was eventually successful, the method I had to adopt makes it quite likely that the subjects remembered every possible configuration and whether or not it signalled food. A similar conclusion can be drawn from a study by Herrnstein, Vaughan, Mumford, and Kosslyn (1989) who presented pigeons with a discrimination in which a dot was located either *inside* or *outside* a hoop (see Figure 5.15). This was an extremely difficult problem for the birds and, once again, it is more than possible that their success was based solely on remembering the significance of individual training patterns.

Second-order relationships

A rather more complex method for studying relational discriminations is to assess the ability of animals to appreciate second-order relationships. In experiments based on this design animals may be required to judge whether the relationship between one pair of stimuli is the same as, or different to, that between another pair. Thus a subject might be confronted with the pairs AA and BB, or, alternatively, AX and BY, and be expected to indicate same in both cases. In the former instance both pairs contain the same stimuli and in the latter both pairs are composed of different items. Conversely, given AX and BB, the response should indicate that the relationship between the two pairs is different. Success on this type of task would indicate the sophisticated skill of being able to perceive the relationship between relationships.

Premack (1983b) reports an experiment based on this design in which naive chimpanzees were unable to solve this problem, even after 15 sessions of training. This should not be too surprising in the light of his claim that children under 6 years also find it difficult. To reach any firm conclusions on the basis of a single study would be foolish, but this finding begins to suggest that we are reaching the limits of animal intelligence.

Analogical reasoning

If we are reaching the limits of animal intelligence, then it may be a frontier only for untutored animals. Premack (1983b) reports that after receiving language training, which will be described in Chapter 10, Sarah, a chimpanzee, had little difficulty in solving the problem just referred to. An even more impressive demonstration of her capacity to perceive complex relationships is provided by the way she was able to reason analogically (Gillan, Premack, & Woodruff, 1981).

A typical analogical reasoning test for humans would consist of a question like "As dog is to

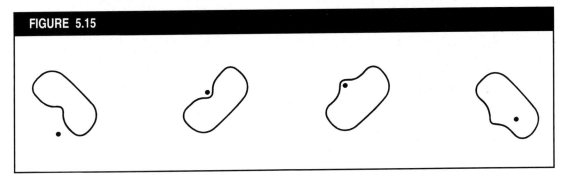

FIGURE 5.15

Four stimuli that are typical of those used in a categorisation study by Herrnstein et al. (1989), based on the abstract relation of insideness (adapted from Herrnstein, 1990).

puppy, so cow is to ... ?" In order to reply correctly, it is necessary to identify the relationship between "dog" and "puppy" and then to select a word that bears the same relationship to "cow": "calf". Analogical reasoning, then, is the ability to judge the equivalence of the relationships between two different sets of stimuli. From the present point of view this capacity is interesting because its existence in any animal would indicate that it can identify relationships that extend beyond sameness and difference.

The stimuli used to study analogical reasoning by Sarah were of two basic types: In several experiments she was presented with a matrix of geometric shapes similar to those shown in the left-hand upper panel of Figure 5.16. Her task was to select from the bottom row a single shape and place it in the vacant space in the matrix so that the relationship in the right-hand column matched that in the left-hand column. In this example the correct shape is the small triangle containing a dot. Sarah was able to perform a variety of problems based on this design with considerable ease. The other stimuli that Sarah was tested with consisted of household objects that were familiar to her. The example in the lower panel of Figure 5.16 is similar in principle to that in the upper panel, and in this instance the correct item to be placed in the space

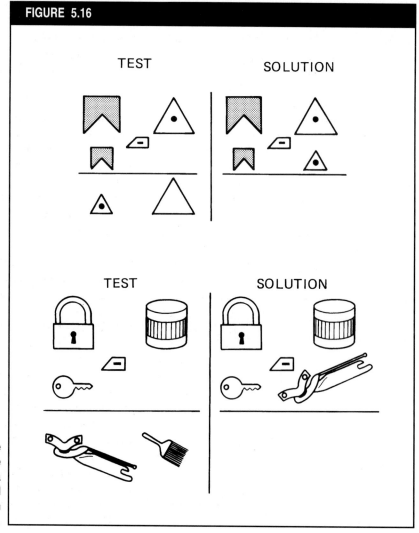

FIGURE 5.16

Two examples of the problems given to the chimpanzee, Sarah, in a study of analogical reasoning (adapted from Gillan et al., 1981).

is the can-opener. Given her success with the geometric shapes, it may not be surprising to learn that Sarah was also very good at solving this sort of problem.

THE REPRESENTATION OF KNOWLEDGE

Many of the findings that have just been discussed are fascinating in their own right, but they are also important because they have implications for our understanding of the way in which animals represent their knowledge. This is a difficult issue about which a great deal of controversy persists as far as human cognition is concerned. It is also a topic that is only infrequently considered in discussions of animal cognition (but see Premack, 1983a,b). None the less, I suspect that until we have discovered how information is stored by animals we shall remain a long way from understanding their cognitive abilities.

The simplest way in which information can be retained about a particular event is by storing a copy of it. The term "concrete code" can be used to refer to this means of storing information. Of course, the copy need not be perfect—a concrete copy may store only a fraction of the information that is available. Premack (1983a) talks about an "imaginal" code when he refers to information that is stored in a concrete way. By this, he implies that a memory of a stimulus is effectively equivalent to an image of it. In Chapter 2, we discussed some experiments by Holland (see pp.39–41) that suggest that rats may use an imaginal code for retaining information about food. Premack (1983a) argues that a concrete code is adequate for retaining information about any physical stimulus. A concrete code could also be used to represent the stimuli used for a categorisation problem, provided it is based on specific objects, such as trees, water, or a person. Premack (1983a) maintains, however, that a concrete code is of limited value when information of a more abstract nature must be retained.

One sort of information that is difficult to represent with a concrete code concerns relationships. I can form an image of a man, and of a boy, but I am unable to form an image of the relationship between the two. For example, the man might be the boy's stepfather, and it is impossible to form a concrete code, or image, of this relationship. The same is also true for other relationships. Thus it is impossible to construct an image, or concrete code, that represents sameness. At first sight, therefore, showing that animals can solve discriminations on the basis of a relationship would appear to imply that they are able to represent knowledge in a more sophisticated manner than that allowed by a concrete code. Although this conclusion holds for certain types of discrimination, Premack (1983a) has argued that it does not necessarily apply to all experimental demonstrations of relational learning. To develop his argument Premack (1983a,b) focuses on the relationship of sameness, and proposes that it can hold at a number of levels. At the most fundamental, there is the similarity that pertains to objects that are physically identical. Suppose that an animal is briefly shown an object, which is presented again a short time later. On its first presentation, the object may leave an enduring concrete copy, or memory, of itself. This copy will then match the object when it is again presented, and according to Premack this will result in a reaction of similarity. Premack does not specify what this reaction consists of, but for want of a better expression, the second presentation of the object could be said to elicit a sensation of familiarity. In the case of physical identity, then, the sensation of familiarity could provide a concrete stimulus for use in solving simple matching problems. For the task summarised in Figure 5.13, a subject might look first at the sample and then at a comparison stimulus. If the latter should elicit a reaction of familiarity, then this could serve as the discriminative stimulus controlling the correct response. Thus, according to Premack (1983b), success on matching tasks, even with novel stimuli, does not require particularly sophisticated intellectual mechanisms.

At another level, Premack (1983a,b) argues there is similarity between relationships, for example, we can talk about the similarity between a dog–puppy and a cow–calf relationship. Premack (1983a) maintains that because of the difference between the four components of these two relationships, it is impossible to construct imaginal codes of the relationships that will allow us to conclude they are the same. These limitations of concrete representations led Premack (1983a) to propose that all relationships, apart from those of physical similarity and difference, must be represented in an abstract code. Premack (1983a) himself says very little about how the abstract code is formed, or about the information it may contain, but the absence of an obvious alternative method for storing information about relationships means that his ideas merit serious consideration.

A further proposal of Premack (1983a) is that most animals are capable of forming concrete representations, but primates alone possess the capacity to form abstract representations. For primates without language training this capacity is said to be poorly developed, yet it is a capacity they all share. Once primates have received language training, however, their capacity to use an abstract system for storing knowledge is presumed to be considerably enhanced. And it is for this reason that Sarah was able to identify second-order relationships and to perform so well on the analogical reasoning test. These claims are based on slender evidence, and they are undoubtedly controversial. But the issues being considered are important and will have to be examined further if the study of animal cognition is to progress.

CONNECTIONIST MODELS OF DISCRIMINATION AND CATEGORISATION

A recent development in the study of human cognition has been the growth of interest in connectionist, or neural net, explanations for various psychological phenomena. In particular, a number of connectionist theories have been shown to account quite adequately for the results from categorisation experiments with humans. One reason for mentioning these theories at this point is that they bear more than a passing similarity to some of the theories that have been examined in this chapter. This raises the possibility that the mechanisms for discrimination and categorisation

in animals and humans might be quite similar, and it is certainly worthwhile spending some time exploring this possibility. We might even hope that experiments that have aided the evaluation of theories of animal discrimination learning are of relevance to theories of learning in humans.

An attractive feature of connectionist network theories is that they operate in a way that bears at least a superficial resemblance to processes that take place in the brain. The brain consists of a very large number of interconnected elements that communicate with each other by means of excitatory and inhibitory signals. In essence, these properties can also be found in neural networks. To understand how these networks operate, we shall start by examining a very simple network and then progress to ones that are more complex.

Single-layer networks.   By now it should be clear that theorists attribute learning in animals to a change in the strength of a connection. In the case of Pavlovian conditioning, this connection can be said to be between an input unit that is responsible for the detection of the CS, and an output unit that is responsible both for the detection of the US and for the performance of the response. This relationship is shown in Figure 5.17. When the CS–US connection is weak, the CS unit will have little impact on the output unit; but when the connection is strong, the CS will strongly excite the output unit and lead to a response even if the US is not presented.

When more than one stimulus is used for an experiment, the simple model in Figure 5.17 must be elaborated. According to Rescorla and Wagner (1972), this elaboration will allow each stimulus to become connected with the US. Figure 5.18 shows the connections that this theory assumes will develop if four different stimuli are used to signal the presence, or absence, of a US. If two or more stimuli are presented together, then Rescorla and Wagner (1972) stipulate that the strength of the CR will be determined by the combined strength of the relevant connections. This network is referred to as a single-layer network, because there is only a single layer of connections.

The single-layer network shown in Figure 5.18 has been used by Gluck and Bower (1988) to

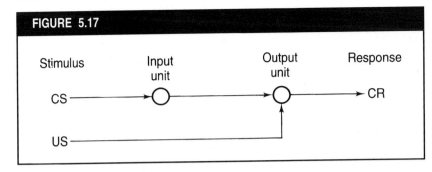

FIGURE 5.17

A simple connectionist network for representing the changes that occur during Pavlovian conditioning with a CS and US. The strength of the connection between the input and output unit increases with repeated pairings of the CS and US.

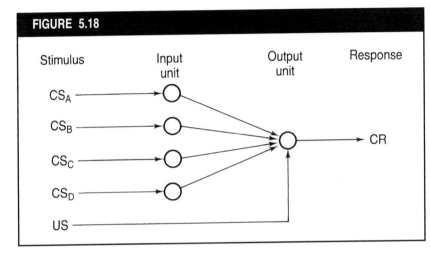

FIGURE 5.18

A development of the network shown in Figure 5.17 to represent the changes that can take place when as many as four stimuli are used for conditioning with a single US (adapted from Gluck & Bower, 1988).

account for categorisation by humans. The purpose of this network was to classify lists of various combinations of four different symptoms on the basis of whether they were indicative of one of two illnesses. Each of the four symptoms activated a different input unit, and when the output unit had a value of $+\lambda$, the network was regarded as classifying a list as being symptomatic of one illness, whereas an output value of $-\lambda$ was construed as being indicative of the other illness. The rule that governed changes in the four connections was the Rescorla–Wagner (1972) rule.[3] By using this rule, the network made much the same predictions for the various lists of symptoms as a group of humans who were given the same problem.

In the discussion of the Rescorla–Wagner (1972) model it was shown that in its most basic form this theory is unable to explain the ability of animals to solve a negative patterning discrimination (A+ B+ AB−). In fact, this is not a

problem that is unique to this particular theory. There have been other attempts to develop single-layer learning networks (e.g. Rosenblatt, 1962), and it has long been appreciated that they are unable to solve negative patterning discriminations, or, as it is more generally known, the *exclusive–or* problem (Minsky & Papert, 1969). That is, many single-layer networks are unable to respond correctly when they are trained with a problem in which an outcome is signalled by either of two events when they are presented separately, but not when they are presented together. Indeed, the Gluck and Bower (1988) network shown in Figure 5.18 is unable to solve this type of problem.

Following the proposals made by Rescorla and Wagner (1972) to deal with this problem, Gluck (1991) has suggested that the network shown in Figure 5.18 can be modified to include compound-unique configural cues as input units. Figure 5.19 shows a network that incorporates this proposal. There are three input units that are

FIGURE 5.19

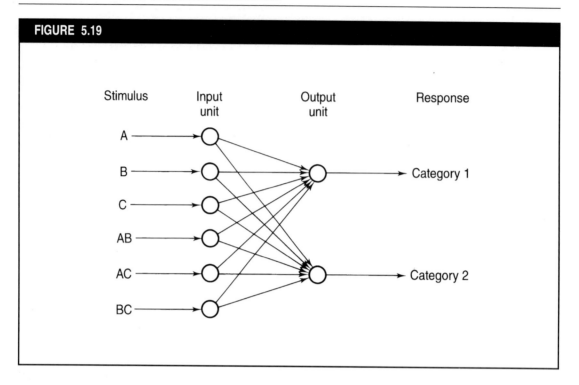

A development of the network shown in Figure 5.18 that allows for the possibility that pairs of stimuli create configural cues, and which allows for more than one output unit (adapted from Gluck, 1991).

activated by three different stimuli, A, B, and C. There are also three input units that are activated only by particular pairs of stimuli. Thus if the compound AB should be presented to the network, then three input units will be activated by A, B, and AB. This network has also been expanded to include two output units. One is expected to fire maximally when members belonging to one category are presented, the other is expected to fire maximally when members belonging to a second category are presented to the network. Although this network appears to be considerably more complex than the one shown in Figure 5.18, it works on exactly the same principles.

The network developed by Gluck (1991) is capable of solving many categorisation problems, but there remain at least two shortcomings with this type of network. First, because it is formally equivalent to the Rescorla–Wagner (1972) model, it makes the same erroneous predictions as that model concerning the outcome of the experiment by Redhead and Pearce (1995a). When this

network is presented with an A+ BC+ ABC– discrimination, it incorrectly predicts that the discrimination between the two similar signals, BC and ABC, will progress more readily than between the two different signals, A and ABC.

The second problem is one that is common to many network theories of learning (McCloskey & Cohen, 1989): The networks proposed by Gluck and Bower (1988) and Gluck (1991) are unduly sensitive to the effects of retroactive interference. That is, if the network is trained to solve one problem, and it is then subsequently required to learn something new, this new learning can have a catastrophic effect on the original learning. An experiment by Pearce and Wilson (1991) will serve to demonstrate this problem; the design of the experiment is summarised in Table 5.1. Rats first received a feature-negative discrimination (A+ AB–) in which food was signalled by one stimulus, A, but not by AB. According to the network model of Gluck and Bower (1989) this training will enable A to excite the output unit to its maximum value of

TABLE 5.1		
Summary of the Training Given to a Single Group in an Experiment by Pearce and Wilson (1991).		
Stage 1	*Stage 2*	*Test stage*
A → Food and	B → Food	A → Food and
AB → Nothing		AB → Nothing

λ, whereas B will have the opposite effect of reducing the level of activation in the same output unit to $-\lambda$. When A and B are then presented together, these effects will cancel each other out, and no response will be observed. For a more detailed presentation of this analysis see pp.61–62.

For the second stage of training, B was repeatedly paired with food until this stimulus elicited a CR of asymptotic magnitude. In terms of the network models of both Gluck and Bower (1988) and Gluck (1991), this training will result in the connection between B and the output unit acquiring an asymptotic value of λ, and thus erase entirely the effect of the original training. To test this interpretation, the subjects were reintroduced to the original discrimination. The first presentation of AB will now allow each of A and B to exert an excitatory influence on the output unit, and an unusually strong response should be observed. In formal terms, the level of activation of the output unit will initially have a magnitude of 2λ. The model thus predicts that not only should pairing B with food erase the effects of the original discrimination, it should actually result in stronger responding during AB than A. In fact, the effects of the excitatory conditioning were far less disruptive on the original discrimination than this prediction implies. There was no evidence of an unusually high level of responding during AB, and the A+ AB− discrimination was re-acquired significantly more rapidly than by a control group.

Multi-layer networks.   Another way for enabling a network to solve the exclusive–or problem is to add a second layer of connections. This strategy has been used to great effect with what is known as a two-layer back-propagation network (e.g. Rumelhart, Hinton, & Williams, 1988). A

relatively simple version of this network is shown in the upper panel of Figure 5.19, which was used by Maki and Abunawass (1991) to simulate the way in which matching-to-sample discriminations are solved. In this network, different input units are activated by red or green light presented on the left, centre, or right response key. A more elaborate example of a two-layer network is shown in the lower panel of Figure 5.20. In both networks the input and output units perform in much the same way as in the networks that we have already considered. There is, in addition, a row of hidden units, each one of which is connected to every input unit and every output unit. Whenever the input layer is activated, each hidden unit will be excited to a level that is determined by the activation that it receives from all the input units. Likewise, the level of activation of each output unit is determined by the activation it receives from all the hidden units. The rules that determine the change in the strength of each connection are rather more complex than we have considered so far. There is also a more complex rule for determining the way in which each hidden unit and output unit is activated. Even so, the point has been made on more than one occasion that there remains a close relationship between the Rescorla–Wagner (1972) model and this type of connectionist network model (Gluck & Bower, 1988; Maki & Abunawass, 1991; Sutton & Barto, 1981).

This relationship is not so close, however, that it prevents the two-layer network from solving the exclusive–or problem. The ability to solve this problem, as well as many other properties, have led various versions of this network to be used to explain the way in which humans categorise, read, acquire language, and so forth. It has even been claimed that the effects of brain damage can be understood by reference to this type of multi-layer network.

FIGURE 5.20

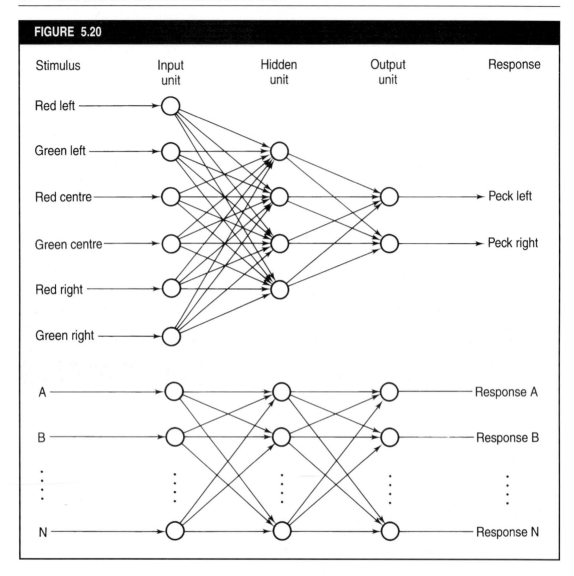

Upper panel: A simple two-layer, back-propagation network that was developed to account for the way in which pigeons solve matching-to-sample discriminations (adapted from Maki & Abunawass, 1991).
Lower panel: A complex two-layer back-propagation network that has proved successful for explaining various aspects of human cognition.

None the less, given its relationship, albeit distant, with the Rescorla–Wagner (1972) model, the back-propagation network has inherited at least some of its problems. Thus McCloskey and Cohen (1989) show forcefully that this type of network is unduly sensitive to the effects of retroactive interference. Likewise, Shanks and Darby (in press) maintain that a back-propagation network is unable to explain the findings by Pearce and Wilson (1991) that have just been mentioned. And Pearce (1994) has argued that a two-layer back-propagation network based on the principles espoused by Maki and Abunawass (1991) occasionally makes the wrong predictions concerning the influence of similarity on discrimination learning.

Exemplar-based networks. I suspect that it will be possible to develop a back-propagation network that overcomes these shortcomings. Even so, a number of theorists have been encouraged to develop a rather different type of multi-layer network. These exemplar-based networks capture many of the principles of configural theories of conditioning (Pearce, 1994) and exemplar theories of categorisation (Kruschke, 1992). Figure 5.21 shows one version of this type of exemplar-based network that was proposed by Pearce (1994). In this network, the role of the units in the hidden layer is more specific than in the two-layer network of Rumelhart et al. (1988). As a result of being exposed to a particular pattern of stimulation, the network will select one hidden unit, or configural unit, which will be activated maximally whenever that pattern is presented again. If the pattern signals a US, then an association will develop between that configural unit and the US output unit. Subsequent presentations of the same pattern will then activate fully the configural unit, which will activate fully the US unit and lead to a CR. If the input pattern should change, then it will only partially activate the configural unit, and lead to a weaker CR. In addition, the new pattern will activate its own configural unit, which will then be capable of entering into its own associations with a US.

Kruschke (1992) shows how a network that is in principle similar to the one in Figure 5.21 is able to account for the outcome of many studies of categorisation with humans, including those reported in the study by Gluck and Bower (1988). Furthermore, Pearce (1994) has shown that an exemplar-based connectionist network is less sensitive to the effects of retroactive interference than the other networks that we have considered. An exemplar-based network is also able to predict the correct influence of similarity on discrimination learning.

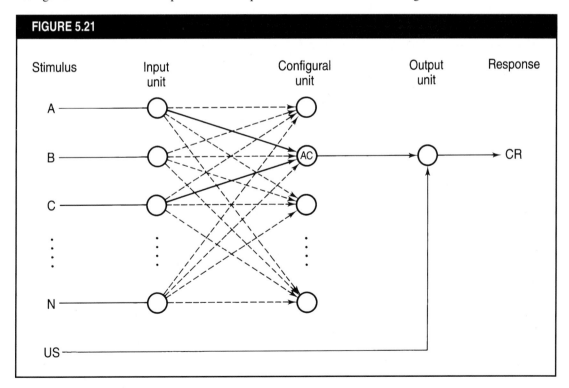

FIGURE 5.21

An exemplar-based connectionist network that has been exposed to trials in which a compound AC is paired with a US. The dashed lines depict potential connections that can become effective whenever a new pattern is presented to the input units (adapted from Pearce, 1994).

These are but a few of the network theories of learning that have been developed (see also Gluck & Myers, 1993; Kehoe, 1988; McLaren et al., 1989; Schmajuk & DiCarlo, 1992). In addition, a number of modifications have been proposed for the models that we have already considered. Until the predictions made by these different models and their variations have been thoroughly tested it would be premature to conclude that one type of network is superior to another. For the present, the main conclusion to draw from this discussion is that there is a growing correspondence between network theories that have been developed to account for learning by animals on the one hand, and humans on the other. Such a development strongly suggests that there are at least some similarities between the ways in which humans and animals are able to form categories and solve discriminations.

NOTES

1. There is a variety of ways in which similarity can be computed. According to Pearce (1987), the similarity between two configurations is determined by the common elements they share. Shepard (1987) has suggested that similarity is determined by distance measured in a multidimensional space.

2. A more detailed account of the training that Alex received can be found in Chapter 10.

3. This rule is formally equivalent to the Widrow–Hoff (1960) rule, which is also known as the least mean squares rule, or the delta rule. Connectionist theories of human learning generally refer to these alternative names.

6

Memory

The study of animal memory is concerned with understanding how information acquired at a particular time is able to influence future behaviour. An example of the role of memory in a naturalistic setting is provided by certain birds who hide food when it is plentiful in the autumn and retrieve it in the winter when supplies are scarce. Unless the birds retained information, or a memory, of where the food had been hidden they would be unable to find it efficiently. An early demonstration of animal memory in the laboratory is provided by Hunter (1914) who allowed raccoons to observe three exits while they were retained in an observation chamber. A light above one exit was then briefly illuminated and some time later the animal was released. If it chose the exit that had been indicated by the light it received reward. With sufficient training the subjects were able to tolerate a delay of as much as 25 seconds between the offset of the light and their release. Such a finding suggests that the raccoons could retain for nearly half a minute a memory of which light had been illuminated.

Once it is established that animals are able to retain information about past events, then a number of interesting questions arise. What sort of information can be retained? How much information can be retained? And for how long is it retained? In attempting to answer questions of this sort, a distinction is often made between two types of memory. One type lasts for relatively short periods of time and concerns information about the immediate past. While in this state the information can take part in associative learning, and it may influence the current performance of the animal. The other type of memory is believed to endure for much longer periods of time. It may consist of the associations that are acquired during the course of either Pavlovian or instrumental conditioning, or it may consist of a representation of some particular event. A number of authors have made this distinction, which is reflected by their use of such terms as primary and secondary memory (James, 1890; Waugh & Norman, 1965), short- and long-term memory (Peterson & Peterson, 1959; Atkinson & Shiffrin, 1968), working and reference memory (Baddeley & Hitch, 1974; Honig, 1978) and, finally, active and inactive memory (Lewis, 1979; Wagner, 1981).

The distinction between two types of memory is also adopted in this chapter, where they are referred to as short- and long-term retention. In the first section we look at the ability of animals to store information over relatively long intervals; we also look at some of the factors that are responsible for the forgetting of this information. The second, and larger section, then examines what is known about short-term retention in animals.

PART 1: LONG-TERM RETENTION

The two outstanding features of long-term retention in humans are its capacity and durability. A moment's reflection should reveal the large capacity of this type of memory as it covers the memories of a life-time. And the durability of human memory is revealed most forcefully by an elderly person's recollections of childhood. These characteristics of large capacity and durability can also be found in studies of long-term retention in animals.

CAPACITY

As far as the amount of information that can be retained by an animal is concerned, the record, at present, is held by Clark's nutcracker. Every autumn these birds collect as many as 33,000 pine seeds and bury them in shallow holes (caches) at an average of 4 seeds per cache. Throughout the winter and spring the birds retrieve these hidden supplies to feed both themselves and their offspring. According to Vander Wall (1982), this requires the nutcrackers to revisit between 2500 and 3750 different caches. Because the seeds are most frequently recovered from caches made by the retriever, these birds are believed to store sufficient information to identify well over 3000 different locations. Even though strategies might be employed to reduce the amount that must be remembered—for instance, by burying a number of seeds close to one another—this still provides a most impressive demonstration of animal memory.

Almost equally remarkable are the results of a series of laboratory experiments involving pigeons (Vaughan & Greene, 1984). Subjects were placed into a conditioning chamber with a clear response key that was about 5cm in diameter. They then received discrimination training in which a series of different slides was projected onto the key. Responding in the presence of some (S+) resulted in the delivery of food, whereas responding in the presence of the remainder (S−) did not. When the slides were first introduced, subjects naturally responded at a similar rate to all of them, but as training progressed, the pigeons came to peck more rapidly at those designated as S+ and more slowly at those designated as S−. This discrimination can only be possible if the pigeons remembered the slides and how to respond in their presence.

In one study the slides between which pigeons successfully discriminated were complex random squiggles of the sort depicted in Figure 6.1. Despite the large number of slides employed (80 S+ and 80 S−), performance was extremely accurate by the

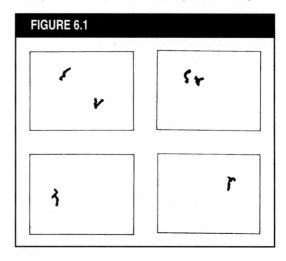

FIGURE 6.1

Examples of the slides used in a study by Vaughan and Greene (1984). Slides in the left-hand column signalled the availability of food, whereas those in the right-hand column signalled its absence (from Vaughan & Greene, 1984).

FIGURE 6.2

Examples of the photographs that were used in a study by Vaughan and Green (1984). Pictures in the left-hand column signalled the availability of food (from Vaughan & Greene, 1984).

end of training, although, it must be admitted, training continued for just on 1000 sessions.

For another experiment the pigeons were shown a large number of ordinary snapshots. Some of the slides that were used are depicted in Figure 6.2. For each pair, one picture was always associated with reward and the other with nonreward. Quite surprisingly, only 18 trials with each of the bottom pair were necessary before the discrimination between them was acquired. Initially, the birds were trained with 40 S+ and 40 S– snapshots, but this does not appear to be close to the upper limit of the number of pictures that pigeons can remember. Once they were discriminating accurately between the original slides a new set of 80 slides was introduced. Training with these was continued until the discrimination had been learned, whereupon a further set of 80 slides was introduced. The experiment continued in this way until the pigeons had been exposed to 320 different pictures, half of which were associated with food. At this point the birds were exposed to all 320 slides—separately of course—and their discrimination between them was very accurate indeed.

DURABILITY

Animals can, therefore, retain large amounts of information. But how is retention affected by the passage of time? One attempt to answer this question can be found in the study by Vaughan and Greene (1984). After the experiment just described, the pigeons were retained in their home cages for 2 years before being returned to the experimental apparatus. Even after this interval the discrimination between the two categories of pictures was still far in excess of that expected by chance. Further evidence of the durability of pigeon memory is provided by Skinner (1950), who demonstrated that they may retain information for as long as 5 years.

The considerably shorter life-span of the rat (2–3 years) than of the pigeon (more than 15 years) means that demonstrations of a long memory with rats are of necessity less impressive. None the less,

there is ample evidence that they are capable of storing information for considerable periods. In an experiment by Hendersen (1985), rats were conditioned with a CS signalling shock that varied in intensity among different groups. To test how well subjects remembered this training, they were made thirsty and placed in chambers where they could lick a tube for water. Once they were licking at a consistent rate the CS was presented without the shock. Figure 6.3 shows the number of licks that were recorded in the presence of the CS for some subjects who were tested 1 day after conditioning and for others who were tested 60 days after conditioning. There is a clear indication that rats were more reluctant to lick when the CS had signalled a strong rather than a weak shock. But what is more important is that there is no hint that the retention interval had any influence on responding. Thus rats are able to remember very accurately for at least 60 days the magnitude of an aversive event that was paired with a CS. A rather similar experiment with rats by Gleitman (1971) found no forgetting of a conditioned response they had acquired 90 days previously.

A very different demonstration of the robustness of animal memory comes from a creature known as the African claw-toed frog. This animal undergoes a metamorphosis, over a period of 35 days, from a limbless tadpole to a young frog that differs only in size from an adult, and this change is accompanied by considerable neural growth. In one study Miller and Berk (1977) trained subjects to move from a black to a white compartment in order to reduce the severity of an electric shock. Both tadpoles and young frogs learned this task with equal facility, but the remarkable finding is that they also showed excellent retention of the task when tested 35 days later. In the former case, of course, they had metamorphosed into frogs by the time of the retention test, but the changes associated with this metamorphosis did nothing to disrupt memory.

Animals can therefore remember for a remarkably long time. But is there any loss of the information that is stored over such periods? One study to look for such forgetting is by Thomas and Lopez (1962), who trained pigeons to peck a key illuminated by a monochromatic light of a

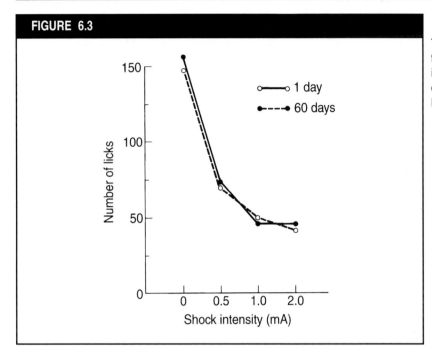

FIGURE 6.3

The retention of conditioned fear as a function of the intensity of shock during conditioning (adapted from Hendersen, 1985).

wavelength of 550 nanometres for food. The memory for this training stimulus was then tested in different groups after retention intervals of 1 minute, 1 day, or 1 week. The method of testing was to present the subjects with the key illuminated by light varying in wavelength from 500 to 600 nanometres. The results from this study are shown in Figure 6.4

The group tested within a minute of being trained responded more rapidly to the original training colour than to any other employed during testing. This indicates that the memory for the original training stimulus remained intact for at least 1 minute. The results from the other groups show that this memory soon decays to some extent. Both groups responded no more rapidly to the original training colour than to its nearest neighbours (540 and 560 nanometres), which suggests that with the passage of time the exact value of the stimulus employed during training was forgotten. This conclusion has been confirmed with a variety of species and training procedures (e.g. Thomas & Riccio, 1979). The implication from this study is that with the passage of time subjects forget the specific attributes of the training stimulus but not its general significance.

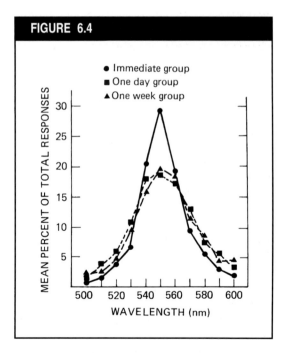

FIGURE 6.4

Mean stimulus generalisation gradients for three groups of pigeons tested at different intervals after they had been trained to peck a key for food when it was illuminated with light of a wavelength of 550 nanometres (adapted from Thomas, 1981).

The previous conclusion applies to a discriminative stimulus that was used for instrumental conditioning. A report by Hendersen, Peterson, and Jackson (1980) suggests that it may also be true for the US in Pavlovian conditioning. Although the results portrayed in Figure 6.3 show that rats are very good at remembering the severity of an aversive event, Hendersen at al. (1980) found that they are not so good at remembering its quality. Rats received conditioning in which a CS was paired for many trials with an aversive airblast. The CS was then presented after a retention interval while the animals were responding in order to avoid shock. With a retention interval of one day the CS had little impact on responding, whereas after 45 days the CS augmented substantially the rate of responding. To explain these results Hendersen et al. (1980) proposed that over the course of the retention interval the memory of the precise nature of the air blast deteriorated. Thus the CS would not be expected to have an effect after a short retention interval, because it would retrieve information about an event that is very different to the one that subjects were seeking to avoid. But after a longer retention interval, the CS would simply signal the imminent delivery of an unspecified aversive event (of certain magnitude), which would encourage responding to avoid any aversive stimulus.

The final experiments to be considered in this section show that forgetting may have a more disruptive effect on inhibitory than excitatory conditioning. Hendersen (1978) and Thomas (1979) trained rats so that one stimulus served as an excitatory CS signalling the delivery of shock, and another stimulus served as an inhibitory CS signalling the omission of shock. The rats then received test trials 25 days after the completion of the initial training. There was no effect of this interval on the strength of responding during the excitatory CS, but there was a considerable loss of influence by the inhibitory CS. The reasons for this greater sensitivity of inhibition than excitation to forgetting are not yet understood.

In addition to the passage of time, a number of other factors have been shown to influence how well material is remembered or recalled. These demonstrations have generally been conducted with the aim of evaluating different theories of long-term retention and will be considered next, along with the theories they were designed to test.

THEORETICAL INTERPRETATION

Two rather different theoretical frameworks have been developed to explain the way in which long-term storage of information takes place. Consolidation or rehearsal theory stresses that information must be rehearsed immediately after it has been presented if it is to be stored adequately. Retrieval theory, on the other hand, holds that information is stored virtually instantaneously and assumes that forgetting is due principally to a failure to find the information at the time of testing.

Consolidation theory

One reason for studying animal memory has been the hope that it will lead to an understanding of the neural processes subserving the acquisition and storage of knowledge in both humans and animals. The assumption underlying much of this work has been that any long-term retention of information must be due to an equally long-term change in the nervous system. According to Hebb (1949), memory storage depends on the virtually permanent formation of circuits of interconnected neurons. These circuits were assumed to be only partially formed at the end of a training trial, and for learning to be complete a period of sustained reverberatory activity (consolidation) in the neural circuit after the trial was deemed essential. Should this activity not occur, or be disrupted, then permanent links in the network would not be formed, and the memory of the trial would be incomplete.

Evidence to support this type of theory came from studies investigating the influence of electro-convulsive shock (ECS) on animal memory. ECS involves the passage through the brain of an electric current of sufficient intensity that it would presumably disrupt any reverberatory activity in a localised collection of cells. Administration of ECS shortly after a training trial should, therefore, inhibit the processes necessary for producing a normal memory of that trial. An experiment by Duncan (1949) was among the first to test this prediction. Rats were placed into a box with a metal grid floor that could be electrified. A light was then turned on for 10 seconds, and this was followed by foot shock (which is not part of the ECS treatment that involves a shock only to the brain). To prevent the foot shock occurring, the rat was required to move from one end of the box to the other while the light was still on, and unless this response was made, foot shock was automatically delivered as soon as the light was turned off. There were 9 groups in the study, 8 of which received ECS at intervals varying from 20 seconds to 14 hours after each daily trial. A control group, which did not receive ECS, quickly learned to avoid the shock, but this learning was very much poorer for the group that received ECS 20 seconds after each trial. Moreover, as the interval between the end of each trial and the administration of ECS was extended, the disruptive influence of this treatment diminished (see Figure 6.5). One explanation for these findings is that ECS immediately after a trial prevents the consolidation of the learning necessary for the successful prevention of shock. Postponing the ECS for a period after each trial

would reduce this disruptive influence and allow more effective learning. A review of more recent experiments on this topic is presented in Lewis (1979).

A prediction that follows from consolidation theory is that repeated exposure to a stimulus might be expected to result in a more accurate memory for it than a single exposure, especially if the stimulus is complex (McLaren, Kaye, & Mackintosh, 1989). The outcome of an experiment by Todd and Mackintosh (1990) is consistent with this prediction. In each session pigeons were shown 20 different photographs, with each photograph being presented twice. Pecking on a response key resulted in the delivery of food, but only during the first presentation of each photograph. When birds were trained with a new set of photographs each day, they eventually showed a higher rate of responding on the first than on the second presentation of each stimulus, but they found this task difficult. As success on this task requires a memory of each photograph to be retained until it is presented again, one reason for the poor performance might be that a single exposure to a photograph resulted in the acquisition of only a poor memory for it. In keeping

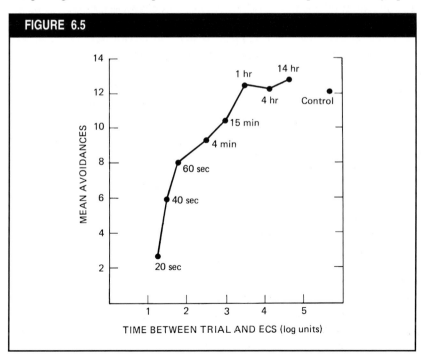

FIGURE 6.5

TIME BETWEEN TRIAL AND ECS (log units)

MEAN AVOIDANCES

Mean number of avoidance responses made by groups of rats that differed in the interval for which the delivery of electro-convulsive shock (ECS) was delayed after each of 18 avoidance training trials. Group Control did not receive ECS (adapted from Duncan, 1949).

with this analysis, additional training revealed that performance on this problem can be improved when the same pool of 20 photographs was used on successive days. The clear implication of this finding is that repeated exposure to the same photographs allowed a precise memory of each of them to consolidate. This precise memory would then facilitate the assessment in a given session as to whether a photograph was being presented for the first or second time.

Retrieval theory

In essence, the long-term retention of information can be subdivided into three stages: The first involves the formation of a memory trace of a particular training episode, the second involves the storage of that information for some time, and the third consists of retrieving the trace when it is required. Consolidation theories place most emphasis on the first two of these stages. They assume that a poor memory is due either to an inadequate trace being formed at the time of training, or to a decay of the memory trace due to the passage of time. In contrast, retrieval theories of memory (Lewis, 1979; Spear, 1973) maintain that the formation of memories is more or less instantaneous and that once formed they remain permanently intact. To account for forgetting and the amnesic effects of ECS, these theories place greatest emphasis on the retrieval process.

Of the various accounts of a retrieval theory of memory that have been proposed, the one considered here is that by Lewis (1979) because it provides the most explicit framework into which a variety of experimental findings can be accommodated. He maintains that the formation of the memory trace is very rapid and once formed it can reside in either Inactive or Active Memory. At the time of acquisition, information is held in Active Memory, where it is assumed to be swiftly coded and elaborated before being stored permanently in Inactive Memory. The purpose of this coding and elaboration is to aid the efficient retrieval of the information from Inactive Memory when it is needed. In order for this retrieval to take place, subjects must be in the presence of some of the stimuli that were present at the time of the training trial. These stimuli serve to retrieve the

memory of the entire trial into Active Memory, and once in this state the information can be further elaborated as well as influence the subject's behaviour. It is important to emphasise that unless information is retrieved from Inactive into Active Memory, it will be of no use to the animal. In some respects these ideas are similar to the views of Wagner that were discussed in Chapter 3.

A simple study supporting many of these proposals is reported by Spear et al. (1980), which also shows that the room in which the training was conducted can serve as a retrieval cue. The apparatus was a two-compartment shuttle box with an open top so that subjects could observe the room in which the experiment was conducted. One compartment was white with a grid floor through which an electric shock could be passed, the other compartment was black; to cross between the two it was necessary to jump over a small hurdle. For the initial stage of the experiment all animals received avoidance training in which they were placed into the white compartment and were given an electric shock if they did not step into the black compartment within 5 seconds. After a number of such trials, subjects rapidly jumped from the white compartment whenever they were placed into it. Some time after the completion of this training the rats were again placed into the white compartment, and the time taken to leave it was recorded. For Group Same the test trials were conducted with apparatus in the same room as that used during training, whereas for Group Different another room was used for the test trial. According to retrieval theory, the sight of the features of the room, which were visible during training, should immediately retrieve the memory of their training for Group Same and result in a rapid exit from the white compartment. On the other hand, the cues provided by the new room for Group Different will not aid such efficient retrieval, and these subjects should take longer than those in Group Same to escape from the white compartment—which is exactly what Spear et al. (1980) observed.

Further support for retrieval theory comes from two additional groups, trained on opposite tasks in the two rooms. Their initial training, in Room X, was designed to teach them to stay in the white compartment: They were placed into this compartment at the outset of each trial, and they were shocked only if they left it. Having learned this, they were then transferred to Room Y, where they had to learn to leave the white compartment in order to avoid shock. Not surprisingly, there was initially some interference from the previous, opposed training, but subjects eventually learned to leave the white compartment rapidly whenever they were placed in it. At the end of this training the rats were again placed into the white compartment for a test trial. Group X received this trial in the room used for the original training, Room X, and Group Y was tested in the room where the animals had been trained to leave the white compartment, Room Y. Retrieval theory predicts that these different rooms should retrieve memories of the different training that was conducted in them: Group X should retrieve a memory of being trained to remain in the white compartment and act accordingly, whereas Group Y should retrieve a memory of its more recent training and move swiftly to the black compartment. In keeping with this analysis, it was found that Group X remained in the white compartment for much longer than Group Y.

Reactivation Effects.   Some surprising results that are consistent with retrieval theory concern the effects of what have come to be known as reactivation treatments. Retrieval theory asserts that after training on a particular task, exposure to even a fraction of the cues that were present at the time of training will retrieve or reactivate information about that episode into Active Memory. Once reactivated, this information can be modified in a variety of ways and thus effectively alter the animal's memory of the original training.

A series of experiments summarised by Gordon (1981) supports this type of analysis. In one experiment (Gordon, Frankl, & Hamberg, 1979, Experiment 1) rats were trained with a procedure identical to that used by Spear et al. (1980) to leave a white compartment to avoid shock. Three days after the successful completion of this training, the subjects were returned to the experimental room for what may be termed reactivation treatment. For one group this consisted of being confined in the white compartment for 15 seconds, and for another

group for 75 seconds. In both cases crossing to the black side was impossible, and shock was never delivered. A third group was not placed into the apparatus for this stage of the experiment. Finally, on the following day all three groups received a single test trial in which they were placed into the white compartment and the time taken to cross to the black side was recorded.

The reactivation treatment had a profound effect on the performance of the three groups (see Figure 6.6). Subjects that had received exposure to the apparatus for 15 seconds were the fastest to leave the white compartment, those receiving no exposure were somewhat slower, whereas those that received 75 seconds of reactivation treatment showed little concern about being in the white compartment. Gordon (1981) interpreted his

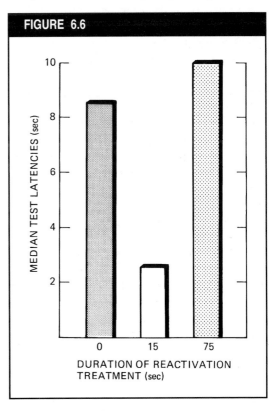

FIGURE 6.6

Median latency to leave a white compartment for three groups of rats that had previously been trained to jump from the compartment to avoid shock. The groups received reactivation treatment of being placed in the white compartment without shock for 0, 15, or 75 seconds before the test trial (adapted from Gordon, 1981).

findings in the following way. Exposure to the apparatus for 15 seconds should reactivate the memory of the avoidance training and may very well result in further elaboration and coding of this memory. On the test trial the memory of the original training should then be rapidly retrieved and result in a swifter avoidance response than for the group that did not receive the reactivation treatment. A similar effect would not be expected for the group that received the reactivation treatment for 75 seconds, as the extended exposure to the white compartment will have modified the memory of the original training to incorporate the information that shocks are now unlikely to occur in the apparatus. The retrieval of this modified memory on the test trial would not produce a particularly vigorous avoidance response.

This may strike the reader as a rather arbitrary explanation. Why is it that a period of elaboration for 15 seconds in the absence of shock should facilitate the retrieval of information on the test trial? One possibility is suggested by the idea that the internal state of an animal provides a component of the information that can be used to retrieve the memory of a training episode (e.g. Spear, 1981). When the interval between the training and test episodes is short, there will be little change in the internal state of the subject and this should not influence the retrieval process. On the other hand, when there is a longer interval between the two episodes, there may very well be a change in the animal's internal state and this will make it more difficult to retrieve the memory of training. In support of this claim Spear et al. (1980) have shown that drugs such as pentobarbitol, which can alter an animal's anxiety level, can serve as influential retrieval cues in memory tasks.

In the study by Gordon et al. (1979) there was a delay between the original training and testing. Perhaps the subjects experienced a change in their internal state over this period, and for those that received no reactivation treatment memory retrieval on the test trial would be hindered. In the case of the group exposed to the apparatus for 15 seconds this treatment would reactivate the training memory and enable it to incorporate information about the subject's current internal state. The internal state on the test trial will thus correspond with the internal state recently incorporated into the memory of the training trial, and this will serve to facilitate the retrieval of the training memory.

A further demonstration of the influence of a reactivation treatment comes from an experiment by Deweer, Sara, and Hars (1980, Experiment 2). Rats were initially trained to run through a maze containing six choice points to collect food. After only five trials the three groups were making as few as two errors per trial, and the time to run through the maze had fallen from some 300 seconds on the first trial to about 50 seconds on the fifth trial. One group (Group Immediate) was given a test trial on the next day, whereas the remaining subjects were not exposed to the apparatus for 25 days. Then, on the test session, one of the remaining groups (Group Delay) was run in the maze in the same manner as during training. The other group also received this test procedure, but just before it the rats were placed into a wire mesh cage beside the maze for 90 seconds (Group Reactivate).

The results from the study are depicted in Figure 6.7, which shows the average time it took the three groups to run through the maze on the final training trial and on the test trial. The first feature to note is that on the test trial Group Immediate ran through the maze considerably more rapidly than Group Delay. This difference demonstrates forgetting by Group Delay. The more important point to note is that there was a similar difference between Group Delay and Group Reactivate on this trial. One explanation for this finding is that the exposure to the room cues prior to testing reactivated a memory of the original training. The presence of this information in Active Memory when the animal was placed into the maze itself should then facilitate running through the maze relative to Group Delay. For the latter subjects a period would be required to reactivate the training memory before they could negotiate the maze successfully.

By using reactivation treatments it has also proved possible to provide a better understanding of why ECS has a disruptive influence on memory. Gordon and Mowrer (1980) trained rats to jump from a white compartment with an avoidance task similar to that described previously and tested their retention three days later. Animals that received

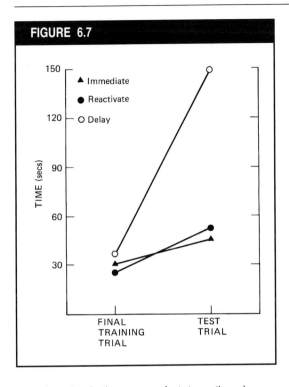

FIGURE 6.7

Mean time taken by three groups of rats to run through a maze on the final training trial and on a subsequent test trial. For Group Immediate the interval between these trials was one day, for the other two groups it was 25 days. Group Reactivate was given reactivation treatment immediately before the test trial (adapted from Deweer et al., 1980).

ECS immediately after the initial training were much slower to respond on this retention test than controls given no ECS. But the deleterious effects of this ECS treatment were completely abolished if animals received a reactivation trial, consisting of brief exposure to the test apparatus, 15 minutes before the retention test.

According to retrieval theory, ECS acts by reducing the elaboration of memory necessary to ensure successful retrieval. The reactivation trial should—albeit with difficulty—have retrieved a memory of the original training and thus allowed it to undergo further elaboration to make it readily available at the time of testing. In keeping with this analysis it was found that reactivation not only alleviated the effects of ECS, but also improved performance relative to the group that had received neither ECS nor the reactivation treatment.

The reactivation treatments mentioned so far can be said to have ameliorated the effects of forgetting about the original training. An experiment by Dekeyne and Deweer (1990) demonstrates that a reactivation treatment can also influence how an animal will react in a situation where it has been trained to make two conflicting responses. The apparatus consisted of a two-compartment box similar to that used by Spear et al. (1980). Rats first received passive avoidance training by being placed into the white compartment and they were given a foot shock if they crossed over into the black compartment. Ten minutes after the completion of this training they received active avoidance training in which they were placed again into the white compartment, and received a shock if they did not swiftly move to the black compartment. For two groups a tone was continuously present during the passive avoidance training, and for another two groups a tone was continuously present during the active avoidance training. The four groups were then returned to the apparatus the following day for testing. One of the groups that received the passive avoidance training in the presence of the tone received a reactivation treatment of exposure to the tone for 90 seconds, 5 minutes before the test trial. When this group was placed in the test apparatus it spent considerably more time in the white compartment than the other group that heard the tone during the passive avoidance training but received no reactivation treatment. Thus the reactivation treatment appears to have reminded the subjects of the passive avoidance training, and encouraged subjects to remain in the white chamber. An opposite effect was obtained with the remaining two groups, which heard the tone during the active avoidance trials. One of these groups also received reactivation exposure to the tone prior to testing, and this treatment was found to reduce the time spent in the white compartment before subjects jumped into the black compartment. In other words, the reactivation treatment for this group appears to have reminded the subjects of their active avoidance training and enouraged them to leave the white compartment as quickly as possible. Taken together, these results demonstrate that the effects of a reactivation treatment can be strongly influenced by the training that accompanied the initial exposure to the reactivation cue.

Concluding comments

The foregoing results provide impressive evidence that reactivation treatments can improve the efficiency of memory recall. We should admit, however, that our understanding of the way retrieval operates is still incomplete. Thus, although efficient memory retrieval might depend on a period of elaboration after a training trial, it is not yet clear how this elaboration should be characterised. There is also some uncertainty about the way in which reactivation is effective. If exposure to the apparatus just before a test trial can activate a training memory, why should this not also occur on the test trial and result in normal performance?

Finally, we should acknowledge that it may not be as easy as I have implied to decide whether a particular pattern of results should be interpreted in terms of consolidation theory or retrieval theory. Suppose that a reactivation treatment improves performance on a subsequent memory test.

According to retrieval theory, this improvement is due to the reactivation treatment making it easier to recover information about the original training. But it is quite conceivable that the reactivation treatment allowed the memory for the original training to be enriched. This proposal, which is more in keeping with consolidation than retrieval theory, would also be expected to enhance performance on the test trial. Unfortunately, it is not easy to choose between these accounts, because there is no clear-cut test for deciding whether an experimental manipulation has affected a consolidation or a retrieval process. Until such a test is developed, we should be cautious about interpreting any of the findings considered in this section as providing unequivocal support for one theory or the other. Instead, the greatest value of this research is for the insights it provides into the factors that influence the ease with which animals can recall information about prior events.

PART 2: SHORT-TERM RETENTION

The study of short-term retention in animals has been conducted with a variety of tasks. They reveal the common outcome that after being exposed to a source of information, subjects are able to utilise it for only a restricted period.

them is to demonstrate that even the most elementary behavioural phenomena rely on the involvement of memory processes. Of course, short-term memory processes are also influential in more complex tasks, and two of these are considered in the second part of this section.

METHODS OF STUDY

In order to determine whether or not an animal has retained information about a previously presented stimulus, the experimenter must provide some sort of recognition test. The stimulus may be presented on a number of occasions, and, if the subject's behaviour to it should change, then this may be due to the existence of a memory of the initial exposure to the stimulus. The repeated presentations could involve the stimulus by itself (habituation), or the stimulus could serve as a signal for a biologically important event (conditioning). These are very simple techniques, and one reason for discussing

Habituation

Hinde (1970, p. 577) defines habituation as "the relatively persistent waning of a response as a result of repeated stimulation which is not followed by any kind of reinforcement".[1] To explain this effect, several authors have proposed that the initial exposure to the stimulus results in the formation of a memory or model of it (Sokolov, 1963; Wagner, 1976). If on subsequent trials the stimulus should match this model, then the reaction to it will be slight. The idea that the memory of a stimulus is important for habituation was raised in Chapter 3, where an experiment by Whitlow (1975) was said to support an account of habituation based on Wagner's (1981) theory, SOP. In reality it is more difficult than I implied at that time to demonstrate the involvement of memory processes in habituation, as we shall see shortly when we discuss further Whitlow's (1975) experiment. First, a few examples should serve to demonstrate the ubiquity of habituation.

Jennings (1906) reports that *paramecia* react to being touched by contracting. With continued touching, however, the number of stimulations needed to produce this response increases to about 20 or 30. In a study of the Pacific sea anemone, Logan (1975) has shown that the contractions produced by a novel strong stream of water are reduced considerably in magnitude after about 30 trials. The three-spined stickleback will respond aggressively to any territorial rivals, but this weakens with the continued presence of the same rival (Peeke & Veno, 1973). Finally, as Whitlow (1975) demonstrated, sounding a relatively loud tone to a rabbit will, among other reactions, produce a pronounced change in the rate of blood flow through the ear, brought about by vasoconstriction, which diminishes with repeated exposure to the tone.

In the experiment by Whitlow (1975) rabbits were placed into a sound- and light-proof chamber. After a while a 1-second tone (S1) was presented, which was followed 30, 60, or 150 seconds later by

another 1-second tone (S2). A resting period then followed (long enough to prevent one trial from influencing the next), which again consisted of the presentation of the pair of tones S1 and S2, separated by one of the three intervals. Training continued in this manner, with S1 and S2 on some trials being identical in frequency and on other trials being different.

The principal findings of the study are shown in Figure 6.8. The vertical axis represents the maximum change in vasoconstriction that was recorded on any trial. When S1 and S2 were identical (left-hand panel) and the interval between them was relatively short, the response to the second member of the pair was weaker than to the first. With a longer interval of 150 seconds, however, the response to the second recovered and was much the same as to the first. Thus the repetition of a tone can result in habituation, provided that the interval between its presentations is relatively short.

As we saw in Chapter 3, Wagner (1976, 1981) explained these findings by proposing that the offset of S1 will leave a decaying representation of itself. If S2 is then presented before this decay is complete—that is, within 150 seconds—and it matches the representation of S1, habituation will be observed. But we need to consider alternative

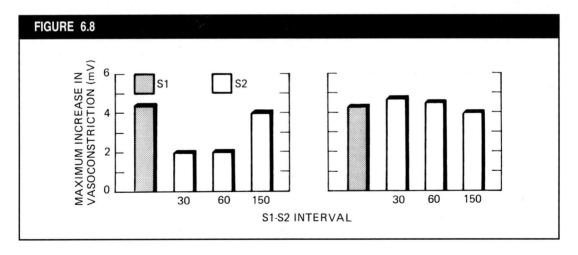

FIGURE 6.8

The maximum response to S1 and S2 in the study by Whitlow (1975) on trials when they were separated by intervals of 30, 60, or 150 seconds. The left-hand panel shows the results when S1 and S2 were identical, the right-hand panel when these stimuli were different. The measure of vasoconstriction is the increase from resting level in the output of a plethysmograph connected to the rabbit's ear (adapted form Whitlow, 1975).

explanations for these results. For a short while after each response, the effector system may be fatigued, so that subsequent presentations of the tone will be unable to induce a large response. The simplicity of this account makes it attractive, and it may even be true for the findings with *paramecia* reported by Jennings (1906). But for the rabbit it is unlikely. The right-hand panel of Figure 6.8 indicates the maximum response to S1 and S2 for the trials when they differed. Although the two different tones elicited the same response in the same effector system, on these trials the response to S2 was as strong as that to S1, no matter how short the interval between them. This finding makes it difficult to believe that the weak response to S2, when it was the same as S1 and followed shortly after S1, was due to effector fatigue.

Yet another explanation for Whitlow's (1975) demonstration of habituation is that once a stimulus has been presented, the cells responsible for its reception become temporarily less sensitive. The occurrence of S2, when it is the same as S1, will then have less of an impact on the central nervous system and may produce a weaker response than S1. The results obtained when S1 and S2 were different are consistent with this interpretation, as the use of different stimuli will presumably excite different receptors.

Fortunately, there is an additional finding by Whitlow (1975), which allows this account to be rejected. Subjects received similar training to that described previously, but the interval between S1 and S2 was always 60 seconds. On half the trials a 2-second distractor, consisting of a flashing light followed by electrotactile stimulation, was presented 20 seconds after S1; on the remaining trials this complex stimulus was omitted. On trials when S1 and S2 were identical, the response to S2 was weak if the distractor was omitted, but when this stimulus was presented, a much stronger response was elicited by S2. In other words, the distractor disrupted habituation with S2; this is usually referred to as dishabituation.

This example of dishabituation is important because it suggests that S2 is capable of eliciting a strong response, even though it is the same as S1 and the interval between them is short. This in turn implies that S2 is as well perceived as S1 even

when they are the same, and that sensory adaptation is not an adequate explanation of habituation. One further possibility, however, is that the distractor enhances the responsiveness of the animal to any stimulus that is presented shortly after it (e.g. Thompson & Spencer, 1966). Thus S2 may have been poorly perceived by the rabbits but still elicited a strong response because of the arousing effects of the distractor. A reason for rejecting this possibility can be found in the impact of the distractor on trials when S1 and S2 were different. The arousing effects of the distractor should also be evident on these trials, yet the response to S2 was much the same on trials with and without the distractor. The account offered by Wagner (1976) for the dishabituating effect of the distractor when S1 and S2 were the same is quite straightforward. It assumes that this stimulus effectively erased the memory of S1, or made subjects forget it, so that when S2 was presented it would not match a representation left by a preceding stimulus.

Taken together, Whitlow's (1975) results strongly suggest that habituation in the rabbit depends on the existence of a memory of the repeatedly presented stimulus. The question is now raised as to whether all instances of habituation are due to the same process. Unfortunately, most investigations of habituation lack the necessary control conditions to enable unambiguous conclusions to be drawn from them. For the present, therefore, we must conclude that habituation, in at least some cases, depends on the ability of animals to remember stimuli for short periods of time. But whether this is true for all, or even the majority, of instances remains to be seen.

Conditioning

Typically in Pavlovian conditioning the CS remains on until at least the onset of the US. This technique is known as delay conditioning. With trace conditioning, the US is presented after the CS has been turned off, and for this training to be successful a memory of the CS must persist until the US occurs. Because trace conditioning is generally ineffective with relatively long trace intervals, it provides us with a method for studying short-term retention. In fact, it was thought originally that trace conditioning could only be effective with intervals extending up to a minute or so. More recent studies, however, have shown that this is incorrect and that the short-term retention of some animals can extend up to several hours. A study by Smith and Roll (1967) demonstrates this point.

Thirsty rats were permitted to drink saccharin solution from a tube in a test chamber for several minutes. Later, at varying intervals, different groups were exposed to X-irradiation to induce illness. The animals were then returned to the chambers after two days, where they could drink either from a tube containing saccharin or from one containing water. Evidence of successful taste-aversion conditioning was revealed by a low consumption of the saccharin solution. The results from this test are shown in Figure 6.9, which shows that even with a trace interval of 12 hours the consumption of saccharin was less than for a control group that was treated identically except that it never received X-irradiation.

In several experiments of this sort rats have been given either water or some other flavour to drink in the interval between consumption of the flavour CS and the onset of illness, so it is quite implausible to suppose that the original flavour could have lingered in the mouth throughout the trace interval (Revusky, 1971). Instead, the more plausible

interpretation of taste-aversion learning over long delays is that a memory trace of the CS persists until the US occurs, and it is the existence of this trace that is responsible for successful conditioning.

The discovery that taste-aversion conditioning is possible with extensive trace intervals prompted a number of authors to suggest that taste-aversion learning is not typical of conditioning in general. Seligman (1970) regards successful conditioning over such long delays as being due to the existence of a specialised taste-learning process. According to Garcia, McGowan, and Green (1972), the mechanism responsible for this learning resides in a neural region that is relatively insulated from stimuli that do not arise from eating and drinking and is specialised to handle long trace intervals.

A variety of arguments have been offered to counter this suggestion (see, for example, Revusky, 1977), but perhaps the most convincing is that other, quite different preparations have also resulted in learning over surprisingly long trace intervals. In an experiment by D'Amato and Buckiewicz (1980), monkeys were allowed to explore a T-maze with a black arm and a striped arm. The next day they were confined in one arm for a minute and then placed into a holding chamber for 30 minutes. On their release they were

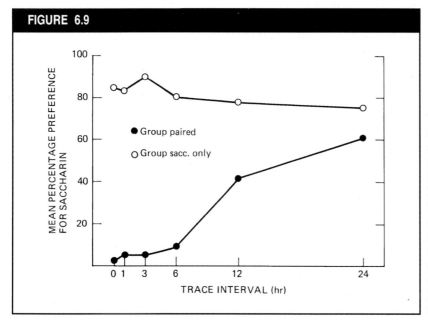

FIGURE 6.9

The preference of rats for drinking from a spout containing saccharin solution rather than water after they had previously received X-irradiation at different trace intervals following the consumption of saccharin solution (Group Paired). For Group Sacc. only, the consumption of saccharin was never followed by X-irradiation (adapted from Smith & Roll, 1967).

put into the start box of the T-maze and allowed to consume 12 raisins. The monkeys were then given a test trial in which they could choose between the two arms of the maze. A control group was treated identically, except that the raisins were not available on their return to the start box. On the choice trial the monkeys that had been fed the raisins showed a significantly greater preference than the controls for the arm in which they had been confined for a minute. The implication from this study is that the monkeys had retained, at least for 30 minutes, a memory of the arm in which they had been confined (CS) and that this became associated with the raisins (US) by the experimental group. D'Amato and Buckiewicz (1980) regarded the preference for the arm in which they had been confined as an example of conditioned attraction consequent on this trace conditioning.

A similar finding has been reported by D'Amato, Safarjan, and Salmon (1981), except that the subjects were rats and they were held in a waste-paper basket before the choice trial in a T-maze. One group was confined in an arm of the T-maze for 40 minutes before being placed into the basket where they were fed after 2 hours. Once they had been fed, they were allowed to choose between the two arms of the maze. As with the monkeys, these subjects exhibited a greater preference for the arm in which they had been confined than a control group that was treated identically except that they were not fed in the waste-paper basket. Once again the explanation offered for this finding is that the memory of the arm of the maze was sustained for 2 hours and associated with the food that was eaten in the basket.

An intriguing study by Thomas, Lieberman, McIntosh, and Ronaldson (1983; see also Lieberman, McIntosh, & Thomas, 1979) identifies one factor that may be important for promoting learning across delays. Rats in Group Control were trained to run through a maze similar to that depicted in Figure 6.10. After entering the choice box from the start box, they were permitted to enter either the black or the white side arm and then pass into the delay box, where they were confined for 2 minutes before being allowed to enter the goal box. Food was available in the goal box only on those trials when the rat had passed through the white

arm. The results for this group are presented in Figure 6.11, which shows that despite a large amount of training there was virtually no increase in the preference for the white arm.

A second group in this study, Group Marker, was treated in much the same way except that both correct responses, of entering the white compartment, and incorrect responses, of entering the black compartment, were "marked" by being followed immediately with a burst of white noise for 2 seconds. This modest procedural change was sufficient to produce a substantial improvement in

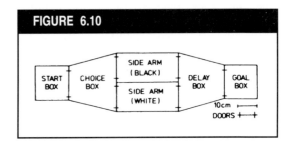

Ground plan of the maze used by Thomas et al. (1983).

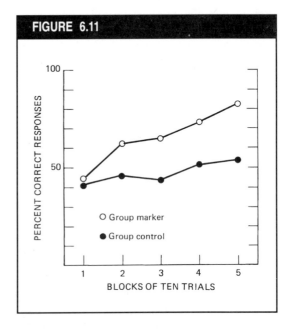

Percentage of correct responses by Group Control and Group Marker, in 10-trial blocks, in the marking study by Thomas et al. (1983) (adapted from Thomas et al., 1983).

FIGURE 6.12

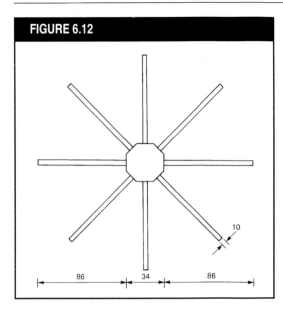

Top view of an 8-arm radial maze (dimensions in centimetres) (from Olton & Samuelson, 1976).

performance (see Figure 6.11). To explain this finding, Thomas et al. (1983) suggested that each burst of noise surprised the rat and resulted in the formation of a relatively salient memory of the response that had produced it. As a consequence, when food is delivered some 2 minutes later, subjects should be more likely in Group Marker than Group Control to remember their choice response and learn about its significance.

The radial maze

One task that has proved extremely popular for the study of short-term memory processes in animals is the radial maze. A diagram of a radial maze, together with the dimensions of its various components, is presented in Figure 6.12, and a photograph of a rat exploring a radial maze can be seen in Figure 6.13. A trial typically starts with a rat being placed into the arena at the centre of the apparatus and with a pellet of food in a hole at the end of each arm. The rat is then allowed to explore the maze where it remains until the food has been collected from each of the eight arms. After a number of such trials with this task rats become very efficient at collecting food and rarely visit the same arm more than once per trial. It has been claimed that in order to perform with this accuracy the rat remembers either the arms that have been visited, or those that remain to be visited.

In order to examine how long information relevant to the solution of radial maze problems can be retained, Beatty and Shavalia (1980a) returned rats to their home cage after they had made four choices in an 8-arm maze. After a given period had elapsed, they were allowed to complete the trial. When this period of removal was 4 hours or less, subjects were still very accurate in selecting the arms they had not previously visited. There was, however, a marked and systematic decline in this accuracy when the delay was extended to 8, 12, and 24 hours.

FIGURE 6.13

A rat exploring a radial maze.

There have also been attempts to establish how much information can be remembered when animals are solving radial maze problems. Olton (1978) has suggested that with an 8-arm maze the animal must remember 7 locations in order to perform perfectly, but this may not be the limit of the rat's memory capacity. Olton, Collison, and Werz (1977) employed a 17-arm maze and found that even in these circumstances rats performed well above a level predicted by chance. Roberts (1979) constructed an 8-arm maze in which 3 subsidiary arms branched off from the end of the principal arms. On each trial, therefore, the subjects had to visit 24 different locations to collect food, and even in these circumstances they soon learned to perform with very few errors. Although these latter findings imply that rats can remember something approaching 24 different locations, an alternative explanation is possible. Observation of the rats in the maze revealed that they adopted stereotyped response patterns that may take the form, for example, of always turning right as they entered the central arena. Such a strategy, which is rarely evident in a more conventional 8-arm maze, would reduce considerably the number of locations that would have to be remembered in order to retrieve all the food efficiently. Thus, whereas the results show that rats are very good at performing in complex mazes, these results may not provide unambiguous information about the capacity of their memory.

Before leaving this discussion of the radial maze a report by Roberts and Van Veldhuizen (1985) merits brief mention. They examined the performance of pigeons in the radial maze. With appropriate training this species made no more errors than rats in an 8-arm maze, and there was no evidence that they adopted a stereotyped response pattern to aid their memory. In addition, in one experiment subjects were forced to select 4 arms before they were confined to the central arena for various intervals up to 6 minutes. When they were then allowed to choose from the 8 arms, they reliably selected those that had not previously been visited. Performance at all delays was above chance, but there was some evidence of forgetting with longer intervals. Thus, as with the rat, pigeons demonstrate a reasonably capacious memory when solving radial maze problems, but it may not be as durable.

Delayed matching to sample (DMTS)

In the previous chapter, the technique of matching to sample was introduced as a means for studying relational learning. A simple modification of this task, known as delayed matching to sample (DMTS), has proved extremely useful for the study of animal memory. However, in contrast to the robust effects just described, the implication of studies with DMTS is that short-term retention is rather poor.

Subjects are presented with one of two stimuli at the beginning of a trial. In the case of pigeons, this could be the illumination of a response key by either red or green light. After a while this *sample* stimulus is turned off and nothing is presented for a period known as the *retention interval*. At the end of this interval two different response keys are illuminated, one with red, the other with green light. These are referred to as the *comparison stimuli*. To gain reward, the pigeon must peck the comparison colour that is the same as the sample presented on that particular trial. Pecks to the other colour normally result in both keys being darkened and no reward. After the completion of the trial, whether the subject is correct or not, there is a period in which nothing happens—the *inter-trial interval*—before the sample is presented for the next trial. In order to gain reward, then, the subject must store information at the time the sample is presented and use it to select the correct response when the comparison stimuli are subsequently available.

Unlike the tasks already considered, DMTS is extremely difficult to learn. Subjects must first be trained with the single sample and two comparison stimuli presented simultaneously. Once they have learned to peck the comparison that matches the sample, the comparison stimuli are presented as soon as the sample is turned off. After considerable training, this 0-second retention interval is gradually extended, but rarely to very long intervals. For example, most researchers use delays of 5 to 10 seconds when pigeons are subjects. In one study, Grant (1976) obtained reasonably accurate performance by pigeons on DMTS with a l-minute retention interval. This was achieved at the expense of considerable effort by both experimenter and subjects, as it required some 17,000 training trials.

Other species fare little better when this technique is adapted for them. D'Amato and O'Neill (1971) found with monkeys that accurate retention was possible for 2 minutes, and with careful training this can be extended to 9 minutes (D'Amato & Worsham, 1972). Using dolphins, accurate DMTS has been achieved with a retention interval of 4 minutes (Herman & Thompson, 1982).

A number of experiments have examined how much information can be stored during the retention interval with DMTS, and their findings suggest that it is relatively little. Riley and Roitblat (1978) employed a version of DMTS in which two samples were projected simultaneously onto the same key at the outset of a trial. Pigeons were required to remember information about both in order to perform accurately. Performance in this instance was inferior to that when only a single sample was used. The implication of this finding is that the memory of pigeons is stretched when they must retain simultaneously information about two items, even for short periods. Although this conclusion has been challenged (Cox & D'Amato, 1982), it is supported by more recent evidence (Langley & Riley, 1993).

The most obvious account of successful delayed matching is that subjects remember the sample until the comparison stimuli are presented, whereupon the comparison stimulus that matches the memory of the sample can be selected (see, for example, Roberts & Grant, 1976). The memory of the sample in this instance is referred to as a retrospective code, because it is of a stimulus that

has already occurred. But this rather obvious view may be wrong, at least under certain circumstances (Gaffan, 1977; Honig, 1978; Roitblat, 1980). As an alternative it may well be that at the time the sample is presented an instruction is retained of the form "peck the green comparison stimulus". Obviously the memory of an inarticulate animal would not encode the information in precisely this way, but the point should be clear that it is knowledge about a mode of responding that is being stored. Because this knowledge relates to how the subject should respond in the future, it is referred to as a prospective code.

Much of the evidence that relates to this proposal is based on experimental procedures that are not among the easiest to describe, or comprehend. In addition, as Grant (1981) concludes from his review of these studies, their interpretation is difficult as they occasionally yield ambiguous findings. Little space will therefore be devoted to this issue, except to describe one set of results that is at least consistent with the claim that pigeons can employ a prospective code. Roitblat (1980) conducted a matching study with three different coloured samples and three line orientations as the comparison stimuli. On any trial a single sample was shown and was followed after a retention interval by the simultaneous presentation of the comparisons on three different keys. Table 6.1 shows the colours and line orientations used, and the way they were paired. Hence, on trials with a blue sample, the subject had to peck the comparison key with a vertical line on it to obtain food.

With extended retention intervals, Roitblat (1980) discovered that pigeons made more errors when the blue and orange samples were used than when red was the sample. This effect, he proposed,

---

TABLE 6.1

Sample Stimuli, Presented Individually, and Comparison Stimuli, Presented Simultaneously, Used in the Experiment by Roitblat (1980).

Sample stimuli	Comparison stimuli
Blue	Vertical (0°)
Orange	Slant (12.5°)
Red	Horizontal (90°)

suggests that they stored a prospective code during the retention interval. The prospective codes on trials with the blue and orange samples will involve information about the vertical and slanting lines. Because these stimuli are rather similar, differing by only 12.5°, any deterioration of the prospective memory during the interval would make it difficult to identify the correct comparison at the end of the trial. On the other hand, when red is the sample, a deterioration of the prospective code for the horizontal comparison might still be expected to permit identification of the correct key, because this comparison stimulus is so different from the other two. Furthermore, if subjects employed a retrospective code, then a different outcome to this study would be anticipated. Any forgetting about the samples would lead to more errors on trials when red and orange rather than blue were used.

Theoretical interpretation

Thus far relatively little has been said about the processes that are responsible for the findings of short-term retention in animals that we have considered. The simplest approach would be to assume that there is a single system concerned with the short-term retention of information. If this is correct, then we might expect a given animal to remember similar amounts of information for similar intervals, irrespective of the task employed. But this has not proved to be the case. Using the radial maze, for example, the impression would be gained that short-term retention is both durable and of large capacity. In stark contrast, if the results from studies of DMTS are taken at face value, then short-term retention in animals would seem to be rather poor. The question is thus raised whether success on the different procedures that have been discussed depends on different memory processes. I do not believe it is possible to answer this question with complete certainty, but I favour the possibility that all the findings we have been reviewing are due to the operation of the same memory system. To account for the variety of outcomes that have been reported we must look to differences in the procedures that led to them.

One reason for the excellent memory revealed by the radial maze is that there are many features that enable the different arms to be identified. They occupy different spatial locations and they will be placed next to different features of the room housing the equipment. In contrast, with DMTS the samples are generally presented in a very similar manner and differ in only a single attribute: usually colour. Perhaps it is easier to remember items that are composed of many distinctive attributes. Support for such a possibility comes from a study by Mazmanian and Roberts (1983) who trained two groups of rats on a radial maze. One group was permitted unrestricted views of the room while running in the maze; for the other, the careful placement of screens allowed only a restricted view of the room. In the latter case, the information available to identify the arms must have been considerably reduced, and, as evidenced by the substantial number of errors, they were very much harder to remember.

A further difference between the various techniques we have discussed is the frequency with which the trials are conducted. Typically, conditioning with long trace intervals is successful only when there is a very long interval between the trials, or in the limiting case when only a single trial is given (e.g. Kaplan, 1984; Smith & Roll, 1967). Trials with the radial maze tend to be performed once a day. In the case of DMTS, 60 or more trials may be presented in a single session with an average inter-trial interval of only 30 seconds. It turns out that massing trials in this way can have a profoundly disruptive effect on performance on this kind of task and may well contribute to the difference between DMTS and the other tasks. To understand why this should be, it is necessary to discuss the factors that are responsible for forgetting. We shall turn to this issue shortly.

Surprisingly, the manner in which reward is delivered might also be responsible for the outcome of a memory experiment. For example, in the radial maze different choice responses lead to rewards in different locations, whereas for delayed matching to sample reward is normally delivered in the same location. As the following experiment shows, this difference might have important consequences.

Williams, Butler, and Overmier (1990) trained two groups of pigeons in apparatus containing a stimulus panel similar to that shown in Figure 6.14.

FIGURE 6.14

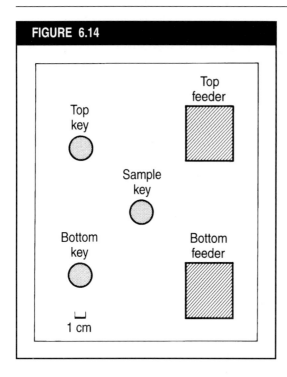

A diagram of the stimulus panel used in the experiment by Williams et al. (1990) (adapted from Williams et al., 1990).

For both groups, the centre sample key was occasionally illuminated with either red or green light for 5 seconds. A short time after the offset of this sample stimulus the top and bottom keys were both illuminated yellow. Pecks to the top key in the presence of yellow resulted in reward being delivered if the red sample had just been presented, whereas if the green sample had been presented reward was presented only if subjects chose the bottom key. For Group Consistent, correct pecks to the top key were always followed by food in the top feeder and, likewise, correct pecks to the bottom key were always followed by food to the bottom feeder. For Group Inconsistent, however, the place where food was delivered was randomly related to the position of the key on which a correct choice response was made. The results from the experiment are presented in Figure 6.15, which shows, for both groups, the percentage of trials on which a correct choice was made as a function of the delay interval between the offset of the sample stimulus and the onset of the yellow illumination of the two choice keys. As far as Group Inconsistent is concerned, the results are similar to those found in more conventional experiments: Subjects were able to tolerate small delays between the darkening

FIGURE 6.15

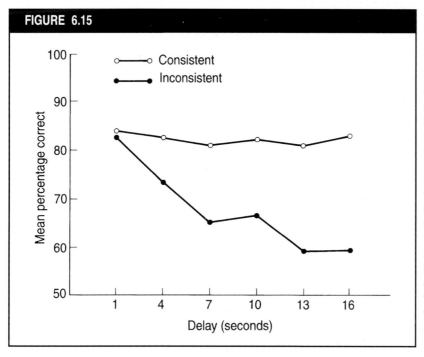

Mean percentage correct choices in a delayed matching experiment by Williams et al. (1990). For Group Consistent, the correct selection of the top and bottom keys shown in Figure 6.15 was followed by food delivered, respectively, to the top and bottom hoppers. For Group Inconsistent there was no systematic relationship between the location of the correct choice response and the hopper to which food was subsequently delivered (adapted from Williams et al., 1990).

of the sample key and the illumination of the choice keys, but as this interval was extended peformance deteriorated to little better than would be expected if the choice keys were selected at random. In contrast, the performance of Group Consistent was accurate for all the delays that were tested.

Thus performance on a memory task is improved when different choice responses are followed by food that is consistently presented in different locations. Various reasons for this effect are reviewed by Linwick et al. (1988) and Williams et al. (1990). For the present, the important conclusion to draw is that the way in which reward is presented might be at least partially responsible for superior short-term retention that is seen with the radial maze rather than with delayed matching to sample.

FORGETTING

In all of the experiments considered in the previous section the retention of information may be short-lived simply because it decays with the passage of time. More detailed consideration of such forgetting, however, suggests an alternative or at least additional explanation. Items are not remembered in isolation—instead they are presented against a background of many other events. It may be that this additional material is responsible for forgetting, either because its presence in memory serves as a source of con-fusion, or because it displaces the representation of the target from memory. In either case the material can be said to induce forgetting by interference.

At a procedural level it is possible to identify two potential sources of interference. *Proactive interference* is said to occur when information acquired prior to the target item disrupts its retention. *Retroactive interference* is used to describe the forgetting of information that occurs because it is followed by something distracting. Although both types of interference may be due to the same process, this distinction is useful, if only because it serves to organise a rather large body of diverse experimental findings. After examining a number of demonstrations of proactive and retroactive interference, we consider the various theories that have been offered to explain these effects.

Proactive interference

A modified DMTS design was adopted by Grant and Roberts (1973) to study proactive interference with pigeons. On control trials, straightforward DMTS with only a single sample was conducted, but at the start of other trials the two different samples were presented in succession, separated by a gap of either 0 or 10 seconds. For these trials subjects were rewarded if they pecked the comparison stimulus that was the same as the more recently presented sample. When the interval between the two samples was 10 seconds, subjects chose the correct comparison with an accuracy equivalent to that when only a single sample was presented. But when the interval between the samples was 0 seconds, there was a significant reduction in the accuracy of matching. Thus the presence of the first sample can be said to have interfered proactively with the memory of the second one, but only when the interval between them was minimal.

A between-trials demonstration of proactive interference with DMTS is provided by Grant (1975). Pigeons were given a single delayed matching trial with two stimuli, X and Y, serving as the comparisons, and X as the sample. Immediately following this trial they received another trial with the same comparison stimuli, but on this occasion Y served as the sample. Performance on the second trial was less accurate in these circumstances than when the first trial was omitted. This finding suggests that when the first trial was given, the memory of the sample persisted into the second trial and made it harder for subjects to identify the correct comparison.

A similar effect has been reported by Olton (1978), who demonstrated that the choices on one trial with the radial maze can influence the errors made on the subsequent trial. (Recall that a trial is defined as being completed when all the arms have been visited). During a trial the subject must keep a record of the arms it has already visited or has still to visit. If this information should be retained, then its presence at the start of a new trial could be extremely disruptive. Normally, trials with the radial maze are conducted at the rate of one a day, and this problem does not occur because the information about one trial is likely to have disappeared long before the start of the next trial. But if the interval between trials is reduced, then the potential for the memories of one trial to interfere proactively with performance on the next one will be increased. In order to test this possibility, Olton (1978) conducted 8 radial maze trials a day with 1 minute between each trial. Figure 6.16 shows the results plotted for 8 successive trials in one day. On Trial 1 rats made very few errors, and it was only when they had visited 7 of the 8 arms that they occasionally made a mistake by revisiting one of the arms. With an increase in the number of trials, performance on the latter part of each trial showed more errors than on the first trial. This deterioration in performance can be regarded as an effect of proactive interference due to the initial training trials.

Retroactive interference

A straightforward demonstration of retroactive interference comes from the study by Whitlow (1975), discussed on p.150, who found that the presentation of a 2-second distractor in the 60-second interval between two identical tones eliminated the habituation normally observed to the second tone. Because it has been argued that habituation results from the persistence of a memory for the first tone, the distractor can be said to have interfered with this memory. Such an effect is referred to as retroactive interference because the distractor disrupted the memory of a previous event.

Retroactive interference has been revealed with pigeons by Grant (1988) using DMTS. During the interval between the offset of the sample and the onset of the comparison stimuli there was an increase in the illumination of the test chamber. This manipulation appears to have interfered retroactively with the memory of the sample because subjects found greater difficulty in identifying the correct comparison stimulus than when there was either no change or a reduction in the level of illumination. Similar effects have been observed with dolphins (Herman, 1975) and monkeys (D'Amato, 1973). A surprising finding is that for monkeys and pigeons the only effective distractor for DMTS is an increase in illumination (D'Amato, 1973; Grant & Roberts, 1976; Kraemer & Roberts, 1984). Thus, for example, retroactive interference does not occur when sounds are presented in the retention interval. This is true for monkeys even when the sounds consist of the vocalisations of other members of the species.

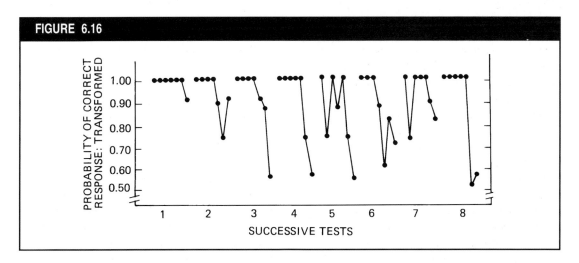

FIGURE 6.16

The corrected mean probability of a correct response for choices on an 8-arm radial maze when 8 test trials were given in succession (adapted from Olton, 1978).

Retroactive interference can also be observed with the radial maze, but here the distracting event must be quite substantial. A typical experiment involves confining a rat to the central arena after it has made 4 forced choices in an 8-arm maze (Beatty & Shavalia, 1980b; Maki, Brokofsky, & Berg, 1979). A variety of events such as lights, sounds, odours, and food are then presented before the subject can continue with the trial. Very often, such treatment has no influence at all on the 4 remaining choices, and more dramatic means of demonstrating retroactive interference are required. One technique that has been tried is to remove the animal from the radial maze after it has made 4 choices and to give it a trial with a different piece of apparatus. Such an interpolated trial can involve another 8-arm maze and be conducted in either the same or a different room. When conducted in the same room, the second maze may be physically superimposed on the first. Despite the similarity of the distracting interpolated trial with the original trial, it is still difficult to demonstrate retroactive interference. Indeed, W.A. Roberts (1981) reports that it is necessary to expose subjects to three identical mazes in different rooms before they display any significant decline in accuracy on the remaining 4 choices of the target trial.

THEORETICAL INTERPRETATION

Two accounts have dominated theorising about short-term retention. According to one, forgetting occurs because once an event has been presented to an animal, information about it gradually, and spontaneously, decays. The other asserts that animals have a limited capacity for the amount of short-term information they are able to retain at the same time. Forgetting then occurs because information about an item is displaced by more recent events. Even though these simple principles can account for many of the effects outlined previously, I shall argue that both accounts are contradicted by certain findings.

Decay theory

Roberts and Grant (1974, 1976) proposed that the presentation of a stimulus activates a representation, or trace, that persists after the stimulus has been removed. But traces do not last indefinitely; as soon as the stimulus ends, the trace starts to decay. The initial strength and persistence of this trace is determined by the intensity and duration of the stimulus concerned. An important feature of this theory is that the strength of a trace is not influenced at all by the presence of other short-term traces. The theory asserts, therefore, that short-term retention is of unrestricted capacity and the number of items stored is determined by the frequency with which they occur in the environment.

In a task such as DMTS it is assumed that if a number of items are in memory when the comparison stimuli are presented, then the one with the strongest trace will determine the subject's choice. Errors will occur if the traces of two samples are present and of equal strength, because it will be difficult to identify the relevant one. This outcome would be expected to occur in the study by Grant and Roberts (1973) when a target sample was preceded by one that was irrelevant. Increasing the interval between the two samples will enhance the discrepancy in the strength of their traces and make it easier to identify the trace of the correct sample. This account thus correctly explains the finding that a distracting sample produces most proactive interference when it is presented immediately before the sample. In a similar way, decay theory can also account for the proactive interference produced by one trial that shortly precedes another (Grant, 1975; Olton, 1978).

A problem with decay theory, as Grant (1981, p.229) has pointed out, is that it does not provide a very good account of the sort of retroactive interference effects reported by Whitlow (1975). In that study presentation of a distractor between a pair of identical tones attenuated habituation to the second tone (see p.150). Because the distractor should not influence the memory of the preceding tone, it is hard to understand why it had this effect. For similar reasons it is not clear why a change in illumination should interfere retroactively with

DMTS. As we shall see, limited capacity theories provide a much better account for this type of interference.

Limited capacity theory

Wagner (1976) has proposed that there is a limit to the number of traces of stimuli that can be retained simultaneously. The introduction of a stimulus, therefore, will not only result in a representation of itself being formed, it will also weaken or displace any previously formed traces. These principles explain the effects of the distractor in the habituation experiment with rabbits by Whitlow (1975).

The retroactive interference effects that posed a problem for decay theory can also be understood within this framework. Presenting a distractor after a target, such as a sample in DMTS, will weaken the trace of the target and make it that much harder for it to be effective at the time of testing. The retroactive interference observed with the radial maze is also consistent with this account. Furthermore, by adding the assumption that existing memory traces can restrict the strength of new traces, this theory can account for many of the effects of proactive interference. Thus it would be difficult to store a list of arms that have been visited during a trial with the radial maze if there already exist numerous traces of arms visited in previous trials.

Despite these successes there remain problems for limited capacity theory. It does not explain why, for pigeons and monkeys, DMTS is susceptible to retroactive interference only when the distractor is a change of illumination. The use of other distractors should also reduce the trace strength of the sample and result in forgetting. In addition, it is not immediately clear why immunity to retroactive interference should be so much greater for tasks such as the radial maze than, say, habituation.

Finally, both decay and limited capacity theory are unable to explain the results obtained by Thomas et al. (1983) using the apparatus depicted in Figure 6.10. Recall that they argued that rats were able to remember which of two responses led to food some 2 minutes later, if this response was followed by a burst of noise for 2 seconds. According to the theories, this manipulation should either have no effect, or it should disrupt the memory for the response. If the effect described by Thomas et al. (1983) genuinely reflects an enhancement of the memory for the choice response, then both theories will be in need of development if they are to accommodate this finding.

Deliberate forgetting

As it has been described, animal memory is a rather passive repository for information, with the short-term duration of a memory trace being determined by its intensity and, perhaps, the number of other traces that are present. Recently a number of authors have suggested that the storage of information may be more flexible than this account implies, and when information is irrelevant to a task it might be discarded by a process of deliberate or active forgetting.

Olton (1978) was among the first to suggest that rats actively forget information that is no longer relevant, supporting this claim by his study of proactive interference that we considered earlier. Olton (1978) was impressed by the small amount of proactive interference when rats were given a series of massed trials on the radial maze—that is, by the accuracy of his rats when they were given several trials in succession (see Figure 6.16). Accordingly, he proposed that rats can erase or reset the contents of memory at the end of each trial. In this way the memory of arms visited on one trial would not be able to interfere with the task of trying to remember which arms had already been visited on a subsequent trial.

Subsequent findings suggest that Olton (1978) may have greatly exaggerated his rats' efficiency. Roberts and Dale (1981) repeated Olton's study, and at the same time they kept a record of the pattern of responding within each trial. Although they were able essentially to replicate Olton's (1978) findings, they discovered that the use of massed trials resulted in rats adopting the response strategy of always choosing the adjacent arm. This outcome indicates that the memories formed on one trial may not be reset at the end of a trial. Instead, in order to overcome the potentially interfering effects of these memories, the rats were forced to find a method that did not involve remembering the arms they had visited. A further observation by Roberts and Dale (1981) is consistent with this interpretation. At the start of a trial rats showed a marked tendency to avoid the arm selected last on the preceding trial. This bias should not be evident if information about the preceding trial had been erased from memory on its completion.

Although there may be little evidence for the deliberate forgetting of information from one trial to the next, it is possible that rats employ deliberate memory strategies within a radial maze trial. Thus far I have followed Olton (1978) and others in assuming that the radial maze task imposes an increasing burden on memory as each trial progresses. After 7 choices, for example, the rat must remember all 7 arms if it is to choose the one unvisited arm. A moment's thought, however, suggests that this is an uneconomical strategy. At this point in the trial, the rat need only remember the one unvisited arm. The most efficient strategy, in terms of minimising the burden on memory, is to remember the arms already visited, in order to avoid them, for the first half of the trial, and the arms that have not been visited, in order to select them, for the second half of the trial. In this way the subject could perform the entire task without having to remember more than half the arms of the maze.

A study by Cook, Brown, and Riley (1985), using a 12-arm radial maze, suggests that rats do indeed adopt this sensible strategy. Once they had learned the problem, they were occasionally removed from the apparatus for a period of 15 minutes after the 2nd, 4th, 6th, 8th, or 10th choice. If they always remembered the arms they had already visited on a trial, then this additional delay should be most difficult to cope with when their memory is most overburdened—that is, after 10 choices. On the other hand, if they remembered the arms that remained to be visited, then the delay should be most disruptive after 2 choices. Instead, they made most errors when the delay was imposed after 6 choices. The implication of this finding is

that the subject's memory is most burdened at the half-way point in a trial, and this is exactly what would be expected if they adopted the strategy just outlined.

Turning now to the pigeon, it has also been suggested that this species is capable of deliberate forgetting. After giving subjects standard DMTS training, Maki and Hegvik (1980) introduced trials in which the sample was immediately followed by one of two stimuli. One stimulus, known as the *remember cue*, signalled that the comparison stimuli would be presented at the end of the retention interval. The other stimulus, the *forget cue*, signalled that the comparison stimuli would not be presented. On these latter trials, then, there was no need to remember the sample, and the forget cue could serve as a signal for the sample to be forgotten. To examine whether the forget cue served this function, subjects were occasionally tricked by being presented with the comparison stimuli at the end of the forget cue trials. If this cue makes pigeons actively forget the sample, then on these test trials they should be very poor at identifying the correct comparison. The results were consistent with this prediction (see also Grant & Soldat, 1995). There are also reasons for believing that, like rats, pigeons remember the choices that have been made during the early trials of a radial maze problem, but later in the trial they remember the choices that remain to be made (Zentall, Steirn, & Jackson-Smith, 1990).

The issue of whether or not animals are capable of deliberately forgetting information is one that has been raised only recently. We should not be surprised, therefore, to find that the interpretation of many of the results in this area is still a matter for debate (e.g. Roper & Zentall, 1993). But if it should be discovered that animals are capable of deliberately forgetting, and perhaps also deliberately remembering, then this would have important implications for our understanding of forgetting in general. We should have to acknowledge that neither decay nor interference theory by themselves can provide an adequate account of forgetting because superimposed on these processes would be deliberate memory strategies that greatly influenced their outcome.

SERIAL POSITION EFFECTS

When humans are given a list of words and asked to recall them immediately, they typically recall the first and last few items correctly but are more likely to make mistakes with the middle of the list. This pattern is referred to as the serial position curve. The good recall of early items is referred to as "primacy", whereas the term "recency" refers to the good recall of the later items. These effects have been extensively studied with humans, but they still remain a matter of theoretical debate. One suggestion is that they reflect the combined influence of proactive and retroactive interference (e.g. Baddeley, 1976). Memory for the items in the middle of the list is said to be poor because of proactive interference from the items they follow, and retroactive interference from the items they precede. In contrast, recall of the extremes of the list should be somewhat better because they will suffer from only one source of interference. If this interpretation is correct, then—because animal memory is disrupted by both proactive and retroactive interference—animals too should manifest serial position effects when required to remember lists.

Recency effects have been relatively easy to demonstrate with a variety of species. Thompson and Herman (1977) presented bottle-nosed dolphins with a list of six sounds, after which they were presented with a test sound. On some trials the test sound was different to those in the list; on others, it was identical to a member of the list, but the position of the one to which it corresponded varied from trial to trial. The task confronting the dolphin was to indicate whether or not the test sound had occurred in the list.

Figure 6.17 shows the accuracy with which this task was performed for the various list positions.

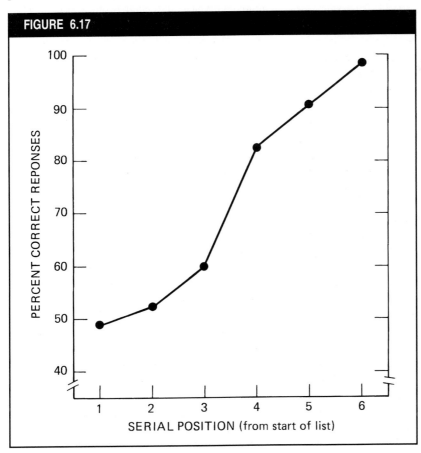

FIGURE 6.17

Percentage of correct recognitions by dolphins of a sound that had previously been presented in a list of six items, according to its serial position (adapted from Thompson & Herman, 1977).

When the test sound was identical to the last member of the list, a recency effect of responding very accurately was revealed. This accuracy declined, however, as the serial position of the sound that matched the test sound moved towards the front of the list. There was, however, no indication of a primacy effect, as performance was very poor when the test sound matched the initial member of the list. Using variations of this technique, similar effects have been revealed with rhesus monkeys (Gaffan, 1977; Gaffan & Weiskrantz, 1980), squirrel monkeys (Roberts & Kraemer, 1981), pigeons (Macphail, 1980), and rats (Roberts & Smythe, 1979).

Successful demonstrations of a primacy effect in list learning by animals have been reported only rarely (e.g. Dimattia & Kesner, 1984; Wright, Santiago, Sands, & Urcuioli, 1984), and some controversy surrounds the way in which several of these findings should be interpreted (Gaffan, 1992). A study by Harper, McLean, and Dalrymple-Alford (1993) shows, however, that it is possible to obtain a robust primacy effect with rats tested in a 12-arm radial maze. Experienced rats were placed into the the central arena of the maze with their access to each arm blocked by a door. The experimenter then opened the door for one arm and allowed the rat to run to the end in order to retrieve a chocolate chip. On returning to the central arena, the door was closed behind the rat and another was opened. Training continued in this manner until the rat had visited 7 arms. Testing then began with the rat being confined to the central arena for 5 seconds before it was offered a choice between two open doors: One provided access to an arm that had just been visited, and one led to an arm that had not been visited on this particular trial. In order to earn food, the subject was required to select the arm that had already been visited. Testing took place over a number of sessions, with a different set of 7 arms being selected by the experimenter for each session.

The curve with solid circles in the left-hand panel of Figure 6.18 shows the accuracy with which subjects selected the familar rather than the novel arm on the test trials. These results are plotted according to the serial position with which the familiar arm was entered in the training list. When

the familiar arm was experienced either early or late in the list of 7 arms, subjects selected it with confidence. But when the arm occupied an intermediate position in the training list, subjects were less likely to select the familiar arm. These results thus constitute a clear demonstration of both a primacy and a recency effect in list learning by rats.

The results by Harper et al. (1993) show that serial position curves are not unique to humans, which implies that similar processes underlie list learning by both humans and animals. Further support for this conclusion can be found in additional findings reported by Harper et al. (1993). Experiments with humans have shown that if a delay is allowed to elapse between the learning of a list and the test trial, then the primacy effect remains but the recency effect is reduced (Glanzer & Cunitz, 1966). Likewise, if humans engage in some activity, such as counting backwards, immediately after they have been exposed to a list then once again testing reveals a disruption in the effect of recency but not primacy (Roediger & Crowder, 1975). Similar effects can be found with rats.

A second group of rats in the study by Harper et al. (1993) was trained in the manner described above, but a delay of 30 seconds elapsed before they received the test trial. The results from these trials are shown by the curve with the open circles in the left-hand panel of Figure 6.18. It is quite evident that extending the interval between training and testing from 5 to 30 seconds reduced the recency effect, and left the primacy effect more or less unaffected. In a second study, the gap between the end of training and testing was always 10 seconds. For a control condition, subjects were simply retained in the central arena for this period, whereas for the experimental condition they were allowed to eat chocolate freely during this period. The results in the right-hand panel of Figure 6.18 show that the control condition (solid circles) resulted in the typical serial position curve, but eating chocolate in the experimental condition (open circles) eliminated the recency component of this curve.

These results by Harper et al. (1993) point to a similarity between the ways in which humans and

FIGURE 6.18

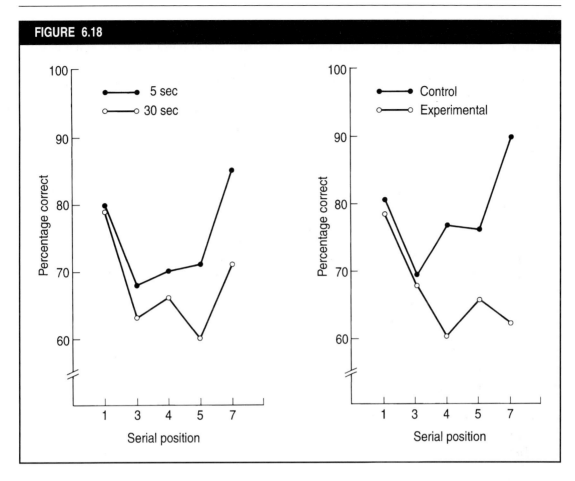

Mean percentages of correct choices of a previously visited arm in a radial maze, from one that had not been visited, as a function of the position of the correct arm in a sequence of 7 previously visited arms. In one experiment (left-hand panel) the choice trial for one group was given 5 seconds after the 7 arms had been visited, but for another group this interval was 30 seconds. In a second experiment (right-hand panel) the choice trial was delayed for 10 seconds during which an Experimental, but not a Control group was allowed to eat chocolate (adapted from Harper et al., 1993).

animals retain information about lists. The results also suggest that the factors that are responsible for the primacy component of the serial position curve are different from those responsible for the recency component.

CONCLUSIONS

In general, there appears to be a striking similarity between the memory processes of different species. For example, using spatial learning tasks, such as the radial maze, short-term retention has

been found to be both capacious and durable for rats (Olton, 1978), pigeons (Roberts & Van Veldhuizen, 1985; Spetch & Edwards, 1986), chimpanzees (Menzel, 1978), a species of the Hawaiian honey-creeper (Kamil, 1978), the savannah sparrow (Moore & Osadchuk, 1982), humming-birds (Healy & Hurly, 1995), and even honey-bees (Brown & Demas, 1994). Similarly, when memory is investigated with DMTS, the results are not very different for species as diverse as pigeons and dolphins. Perhaps even more remarkable is the finding by Menzel (1979) that ECS has the same sort of disruptive influence on learning in bees as it has in rats. Finally, serial position curves have now been obtained in experiments with monkeys (Castro & Larsen, 1992; Wright et al., 1984), rats (Dimattia & Kesner, 1984), and pigeons (Wright et al., 1984).

One finding that is inconsistent with the tone of the preceding paragraph is provided by Roitblat, Tham, and Gollub (1982). They trained Siamese fighting fish in an aquatic 8-arm radial maze and found that successful performance depended on the development of response strategies of swimming down adjacent arms in a clockwise or anti-clockwise direction. When steps were taken to disrupt this strategy, there was a marked deterioration in the efficiency of responding. This finding may be due to the memory system of the Siamese fighting fish being radically different from anything that has been considered so far. But given the generality of the findings discussed in this chapter, it is just as plausible that some more trivial factor was responsible for the inability of these fish to perform efficiently in the maze. Perhaps the construction of the maze was such that it prevented subjects from seeing the spatial cues that surrounded it. We have already seen that this type of restriction will impair the performance of a rat in the radial maze, and the same may also be true for Siamese fighting fish.

Perhaps a more challenging argument to the conclusion that there is rather little difference between the memory processes of animals comes from studies of food-storing birds. In Chapter 8, evidence will be cited that suggests that a brain region known as the hippocampus is involved in spatial memory. It has been found that the relative size of the hippocampus is larger in birds that store

a large amount of food than in birds that store little or no food. For example, the hippocampus is larger relative to the rest of the forebrain in marsh tits, which store food, than great tits, which do not store food (Healy, Clayton, & Krebs, 1994). Accordingly, Krebs (1990) has suggested that this difference between the size of the hippocampus of storers and nonstorers may reflect differences in memory capacity. Attractive as this argument may seem, it should be treated with a measure of caution in the light of a report by Healy (1995). Two food-storing species of tit and two nonstoring species were trained in a delayed nonmatching to sample task. This is similar to DMTS, except that to gain reward the comparison stimulus that differs from the sample must be selected. There was no hint in any measure of memory that the species differed in their abilities on this task. For instance, both storers and nonstorers were able to tolerate delays of up to 100 seconds between the offset of the sample and the onset of the comparison stimuli. For the present, therefore, the most reasonable conclusion to draw is that at least among vertebrates there is very little evidence to suggest that species differ in their ability to remember.

NOTE

1. The term "reinforcement" is used in different ways by different authors. In this instance it refers to any biologically significant event such as food or shock. A rather different definition was developed in Chapter 4.

7

The Representation of Time, Number, and Order

The previous chapters provide a summary of our understanding of the fundamental mechanisms of animal cognition. These mechanisms are responsible for associative learning and memory and, by referring to them, the behaviour of animals in a wide range of settings can be readily explained. One concern now is to determine if these principles are able to explain all aspects of animal learning and cognition. Towards this end, this and the next chapter pursue an issue that was touched on in Chapter 5—the representation of knowledge.

The experiments discussed thus far without doubt indicate that animals can retain information about concrete stimuli, and they may even be able to represent some of the relationships created by these stimuli. But there is no good reason to believe that animals are confined to remembering and learning just about stimuli, or responses. Animals live in a world that changes with time, and where the same event may occur more than once. To deal with these more abstract properties of their environment, animals may develop the capacity to measure the passage of time, and to count. In a rather different vein, associative learning enables animals to learn that one event is paired with another. But it is quite conceivable that they will

also benefit from being able to appreciate the order in which a succession of stimuli occurs, or in which a variety of responses must be performed. The question is thus raised as to whether animals have a capacity for representing the order in which events take place.

These issues are explored in this chapter, which concentrates on the way animals use and represent information about time, number, and serial order. Chapter 8 is then devoted to an examination of the way in which animals use spatial information.

TIME

The behaviour of many animals, both vertebrates and invertebrates, is regulated by time. In order to understand the way in which this regulation takes place, two types of timing have been identified: periodic and interval (Church & Broadbent, 1991). Periodic timing refers to the ability of animals to respond at a particular time. Interval timing refers to the ability of animals to respond on the basis of specific durations.

Periodic timing

Many animals display periodic cycles of activity. Mice, for example, show enhanced levels of activity once every 24 hours. This *circadian rhythm* of their activity is unlikely to be controlled by such external factors as a change in illumination, because it is observed even when this source of stimulation remains constant. Instead, the timing of this change in activity is probably controlled by an internal clock that cycles once every 24 hours (Aschoff, 1955). On a rather grander time scale, Berthold (1978) has proposed that the annual migration of many birds is controlled by a clock that indicates when a year has elapsed.

The properties of an internal, 24-hour clock have been clearly elucidated by Roberts (1965) in an experiment with cockroaches. These insects show an increased level of activity at dusk. To determine if this change in behaviour is controlled by an internal clock, a cockroach was temporarily blinded by coating its eyes with nail varnish. Even though this eliminated any visual cues about the passage of time, the circadian rhythm in activity was sustained, albeit with the slightly shorter period of 23.5 hours. After 30 days of the experiment, therefore, the daily increase in activity was observed 15 hours before dusk. As it is hard to identify any external source of stimulation that would be responsible for this gradual shift in the activity cycle, it seems more than likely that it was controlled by an internal clock. Roberts further discovered that when the nail varnish was peeled from the eyes, and the cockroach's sight was restored, the daily increase in activity did not suddenly revert to occurring just before dusk. Instead, it moved progressively closer to this time at the rate of about an hour a day. The implication of this observation is that even in normal circumstances an increase in activity is controlled by the clock, which required a number of days before it readjusted and again ensured that there was an increase in activity at dusk. A further implication of this finding is that in normal circumstances, any error in the measurement of time by the internal clock is adjusted by entraining it on the external light–dark cycle.

In addition to activity, there is ample evidence to show that feeding can be controlled by an internal clock. Wahl (1932) fed honey-bees at a feeding station every day between 3.00 and 5.00 pm, and they soon concentrated their visits to the station to this 2-hour period. Of course, the timing of these visits could have been due to the bees being insufficiently motivated to seek food until 22 hours had elapsed since their last visit to the feeder. An experiment by Kolterman (1971), however, makes this explanation unlikely. Bees were trained to fly to a feeding station where food was continuously available. For one day only, the feeding beaker was placed on paper that had been soaked in geraniol (an extract from geranium flowers) for two periods of 15 minutes, one at 10.00 am and the other at 11.00 am. Throughout the following day the bees were confronted with a choice between two empty beakers that were scented either with geraniol or with thyme. They consistently preferred the geraniol beaker. The magnitude of this preference, however, was most marked at 10.00 am and 11.00 am and considerably weaker at other test times, including 10.30 am. The marked preference for the geraniol at 10.00 am and 11.00 am must have resulted from the bees' prior experience with the extract at these times. Moreover, it is not at all obvious how the results could be explained by referring to changes in the intensity of an internal state, such as hunger.

These findings can be explained if visits by bees to a feeding station are controlled by some external cue, such as the position of the sun. By making a note of its position whenever food is available, the experiences of one day would enable a return visit to the feeding table at the appropriate times on a subsequent day. Once again, there are good reasons for believing that this explanation is at best incomplete. Wahl (1932) trained bees to leave their hive at the same time every day for food that was a short distance away. Even when this experiment was conducted indoors, and in constant light, the bees reappeared at the feeder 24 hours after their last daily feeding. This result has also been replicated in a salt mine, where the sun could not possibly serve as a cue for the passage of time. Finally, in a study that commenced in France, Renner (1960) trained bees to leave an experimental chamber at a certain time each day for food. They were then flown in their chamber to

New York where it was discovered that they next reappeared for food 24 hours after their last feeding, rather than 29 hours later, which would have been the correct time in New York, as defined by the position of the sun.

If it is accepted that animals have a 24-hour internal clock, then a series of experiments by Bolles and his colleagues has revealed that the use of such a clock is not without its limitations for indicating the time of occurrence of a meal. When rats are reared and housed in conditions that eliminate fluctuations in light, temperature, and so forth, they will show an increase in activity prior to meals that occur regularly once every 24 hours (Bolles & Moot, 1973). However, if the meals are presented regularly every 19 hours, or 29 hours, then this increase in anticipatory activity does not take place, even in animals that are reared in an environment where the light–dark cycle is set to these values (Bolles & de Lorge, 1962; Bolles & Stokes, 1965).

Gallistel (1990) has proposed that this pattern of results can be most readily explained by assuming that rats possess an internal clock that cycles once every 24 hours. If rats are fed every 24 hours, it will be possible for a particular state of the internal clock to be associated with food and, as this state approaches each day, so their activity will increase. There is abundant evidence that shows that although the internal clock can adapt to slight changes in the length of each day (between about 21 and 27 hours), the clock is unable to adapt to the size of change that was adopted in the experiments by Bolles. As a consequence, the state of the clock will be different on each day that the animal is fed. For example, if the internal clock cycles once every 24 hours, and food is delivered every 19 hours, then each meal will be associated with a state of the clock that occurs 5 hours in advance of the state associated with the previous meal. No particular state of the internal clock will thus be reliably associated with food, and there will be no cue to regulate anticipatory feeding activity.

A further interesting conclusion that can be drawn from this research is that the internal clock can be used only to indicate times of day, but not intervals of time. If the clock could be used to measure intervals, then rats would be able to

identify when a period such as 19 hours had elapsed, and anticipatory activity with this interval between meals should be possible. This conclusion may not be surprising. Our everyday experience with clocks reveals that it is much easier to identify the time than it is to calculate the time that has elapsed since a previous reading of the clock. Even so, we shall see shortly that animals are able to perform this sort of calculation, provided that the intervals are considerably shorter than 19 hours.

There is evidence that animals are able to use an internal clock to identify a time of day with considerable precision. Gallistel (1990, pp. 258, 283–286) has argued that for both rats and bees the clock can regulate their daily activities to within 5 or 10 minutes. Unfortunately, very little is known about the way in which the clock can be used so accurately. Both Gallistel (1990) and Church and Broadbent (1991) consider that periodic timing can be achieved with the use of oscillators. By this they mean that timing is based on changes that occur in the animal on a regular basis. The changes could take place within the central nervous system, but regular changes that occur in the circulatory system, hormonal system, or the behavioural system could also be used for timing (Church & Broadbent, 1990; Mistlberger, 1994). If only a single oscillator were used, then it would have to change consistently throughout a 24-hour period and return to its original state at the end of this period. This would be akin to a clock with a single hand that rotated once every 24 hours. The use of such an oscillator would permit the identification of specific times on successive days, but it might be difficult to discriminate between times that are close together. On the other hand, Church and Broadbent (1991) show how a series of oscillators can measure time very precisely. One oscillator would alternate between two states, on and off, every 12 hours. A second oscillator would alternate between these states every 6 hours, and so forth. A particular pattern of activation of the entire bank of oscillators would then permit a certain time to be read, with a precision that is determined by the oscillator with the shortest cycle time. The scant evidence that is available does not allow us to decide how many oscillators animals have at their disposal for timing. Indeed, the evidence does not really allow us to decide if timing is based at all on the use of oscillators.

Interval timing

A clear demonstration of rats timing intervals can be found in an experiment by Church and Gibbon (1982). The rats were placed into an illuminated chamber in which the lights were occasionally turned off for periods that ranged from 0.8 to 7.2 seconds. The lights were then turned on, and a lever was inserted into the chamber. Lever pressing was rewarded after an interval of darkness of 4 seconds, but not after intervals of darkness that were shorter or longer than this value. The centre panel of Figure 7.1 summarises the performance of the group after it had received extensive training on this task. A response on the lever was most probable after 4 seconds of darkness, but for periods that were either shorter or longer than this value there was an orderly decline in this measure of responding.

Additional training was then given that was similar to that just described except that food was presented after either a 2-second or an 8-second interval of darkness. The results for the rats trained with the 2-second signal are shown in the left-hand panel of Figure 7.1, and those for the other group in the right-hand panel. Responding was again most likely after the interval of darkness that signalled food, but relative to the 4-second signal, the slope of the generalisation gradient is steeper

for the 2-second signal, and gentler for the 8-second signal.

These orderly findings forcefully demonstrate that rats are able to remember the durations of stimuli, and whether or not a specific duration signals the availability of food. Indeed, the results shown in the left-hand panel indicate that the rats were able to discriminate between signals that were of either 2 or 3.2 seconds duration. How then is it possible for an animal to remember a specific interval of time? One answer to this question can be found in an information-processing model of timing that was developed by Gibbon, Church, and Meck (1984; see also Gibbon & Church, 1984; Church & Broadbent, 1990), and which is summarised in Figure 7.2.

At the heart of the model lies a pacemaker that generates short-duration pulses at a constant rate. When a signal is presented, a switch directs these pulses to working memory until the signal is turned off. If the pacemaker generates T pulses per second, and the signal is of N seconds duration, then $N \times T$ pulses will be stored in working memory. At the end of the trial, this value is then transferred to reference memory, which will also contain information about whether or not the trial resulted in food.[1] On subsequent trials, the number of pulses in working memory that have been generated during a test stimulus is compared, by means of the comparator, with the contents of reference

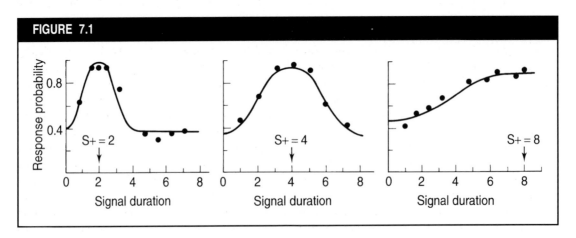

FIGURE 7.1

Mean probability of making a response after a period of darkness that varied in its duration. Responses were followed by food when the preceding period of darkness had been 2 seconds (left-hand panel), 4 seconds (centre panel), and 8 seconds (right-hand panel) (adapted from Church & Gibbon, 1982).

FIGURE 7.2

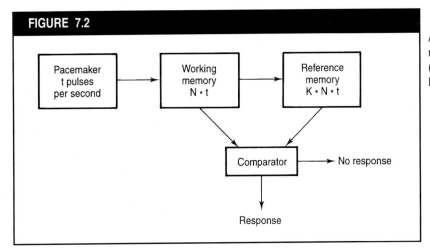

An information-processing model for animal timing (adapted from Church & Broadbent, 1990).

memory. If the value in working memory should correspond closely with the number of pulses stored in reference memory for a stimulus that previously signalled food, then the animal will respond vigorously. But if these values in working and reference memory should differ, then the likelihood of a response after the test stimulus will be reduced.

An interesting conclusion about this decision process in the comparator can be drawn from the results shown in Figure 7.1. If the decision is based on the absolute difference between the values stored in working memory and reference memory, then the slopes of the gradients shown for the three durations of the signal should have been similar. For example, consider a trial with a 2-second test signal for the group trained with a 4-second food signal, and a trial with a 6-second test signal for the group trained with the 8-second food signal. In both cases the difference between the durations of the training and test signals is 2 seconds. If the magnitude of this difference is principally responsible for determining the likelihood of a response rate on a trial, then both groups should show an equivalent discrimination between the two types of signal. However, an inspection of the centre and right-hand panels of Figure 7.1 shows this was not the case. Responding after both the 6- and 8-second test signals was of a similar strength for the group trained with the 8-second food stimulus, but for the group trained with the 4-second food stimulus, the probability of a

response to the 2-second stimulus was considerably less than for a 4-second stimulus. Church and Gibbon (1982; see also Gallistel, 1990) proposed, therefore, that the comparison process is based on the ratio of the values stored in working and reference memory. Specifically, when the ratio of the durations of the test and training stimuli is close to 1, which will be the case when these values are 6 and 8 seconds, then responding during the test stimulus will be similar to that during the training stimulus. But as the value of this ratio moves away from 1, which will be the case with a test stimulus duration of 2 seconds and a training stimulus duration of 4 seconds, then responding on the test trials will be progressively weaker than on the training trials.

Further insights into the way in which animals represent temporal intervals have been provided by *scalar timing theory* (Gibbon, 1977), which is based on the assumption that there is a constant relationship between each unit of remembered time and each unit of actual time. In other words, every interval of actual time is believed to be transformed by multiplying it by a constant, scalar factor, K, in order to determine the interval that is remembered. This fundamental assumption of scalar timing theory can be accommodated into the information-processing model shown in Figure 7.2, by allowing the value $N{\times}T$ in working memory to be transformed to $K{\times}N{\times}T$ when it is transferred to reference memory. Ideally, the value of K would be 1, so that each unit of remembered time will have the same value as each unit of actual time and timing by the animal will always be accurate. This relationship between remembered and actual time is depicted in the left-hand panel of Figure 7.3. In most cases, however, errors will creep into the timing process, and the value of K will differ from 1. If K is less than 1, then the remembered interval of time will be an underestimate of the actual interval, and this will result in the relationship between the two being similar to that shown in the centre panel of Figure 7.3. On the other hand, if K is greater than 1, then remembered time will be an overestimate of actual time (see right-hand panel of Figure 7.3).

An example of the effects of an error in timing can be found in the *peak* procedure (Roberts, 1982). A single rat was trained to lever press for food in the presence of a distinctive stimulus, such as a white noise. On the majority of trials, the first response that occurred after 20 seconds from the onset of the stimulus resulted in the delivery of food and the stimulus was turned off. Responses prior to this point were without effect. In addition, there were occasional test trials in which the stimulus remained on for at least 40 seconds and all responses were without effect, except the last one, which turned the stimulus off. Figure 7.4 shows the results from the test trials after the rat had received considerable training with this

procedure. At the outset of the trial, the rate of responding was slow, but it increased to a maximum at about 20 seconds, whereupon it returned to a low level after 40 seconds had elapsed. This pattern of results is similar to that obtained with the temporal generalisation technique, and it can be explained in a similar way with the information-processing model of timing.

A careful inspection of the results in Figure 7.4 indicates that the peak rate of responding occurred at about 24 seconds, which implies that the rat anticipated food would be delivered later than when it was actually available. To explain this finding, scalar timing theory would assign a value of 1.2 to the scalar factor, K. An important implication of this type of analysis is that the absolute magnitude of errors in timing will increase as the interval being timed becomes larger. Gibbon et al. (1984) have shown that at least for the peak procedure this prediction is correct.

Further tests of scalar timing theory have examined the ability of animals to estimate the mid-point of a temporal interval. Inspection of Figure 7.3 shows that the mid-point (M) of an interval between two actual times (T1 and T2) will also be the mid-point of the remembered interval. This relationship will be true if animals can time accurately (left-hand panel), or inaccurately (centre and right-hand panels). If a way could

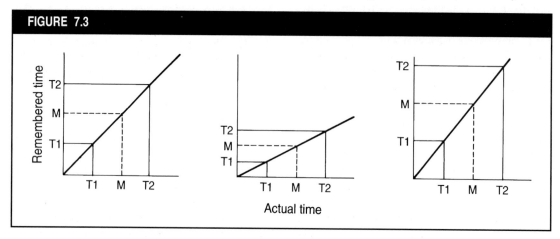

FIGURE 7.3

Three different possible relationships between the duration of remembered time, relative to the passage of actual time. In the left-hand panel the duration of a remembered interval is the same as for the actual interval. In the remaining panels the duration of a remembered interval is either less than the actual interval (centre panel), or greater than this interval (right-hand panel).

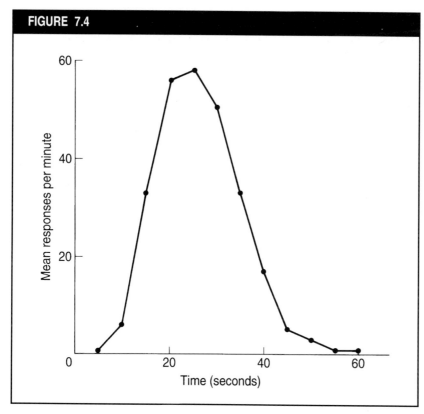

FIGURE 7.4

Mean rate of responding during a 60-second test stimulus for rats who had been rewarded for making a response after 20 seconds from the onset of this stimulus (adapted from Roberts, 1982).

therefore be found for a rat to show that it has calculated it is at the mid-point of a given interval, then, according to scalar timing theory, this mid-point should correspond to the actual mid-point. An ingenious experiment by Gibbon and Church (1981) was designed to test this prediction.

Rats were trained in conditioning chambers containing two levers. On some trials a light was presented and 60 seconds later a response to the left lever produced food; on other trials a tone signalled the availability of food 30 seconds later for responses on the right lever. After extensive training with the stimuli presented separately, the preference exhibited for the levers when the stimuli were combined was examined. When the light and tone were switched on simultaneously, there was a marked preference for the right lever, which is to be expected because responding on this lever should produce food in 30 seconds, whereas a minute would have to elapse before food was made available for responding on the left lever. On other trials the tone commenced 45 seconds after the

onset of the light, and here the preference was reversed. For this to have occurred, the rats must have calculated that the interval before food was available was less for the left (15 seconds) than the right (30 seconds) lever. Of particular interest is the finding that a preference for neither lever was revealed on trials when the tone commenced 30 seconds after the light, which suggests that the rats estimated they were at the mid-point of the light and that food would therefore be available on both levers in 30 seconds.

To be fair, not all experimental results lend such clear support to scalar timing theory. In a study described by Church (1978), rats in test boxes received either short (4 seconds) or long (16 seconds) signals. As soon as the signal had finished, two levers were inserted into the box. Presses on one resulted in food if the short signal had been presented, whereas after the long stimulus, presses on the other lever produced food. Once this discrimination had been learned, generalisation test trials were given with signal durations that varied between the training values. With durations that were near one or other training value, responses tended to be directed towards the appropriate lever; but with intermediate values there was a reduction of this preference. A summary of these results can be seen in Figure 7.5, which shows how the probability of making a "long" response varied with the duration of the interval. The odd feature of the results, from the point of view of scalar timing theory, concerns the point at which the levers were equally preferred. Instead of being at the mid-point of the interval between 4 and 16 seconds, that is, 10 seconds, the equal preference was at the lower value of 8 seconds.

With a little thought, however, it turns out that these findings can be explained by scalar timing theory (Gibbon & Church, 1981). We saw earlier that comparisons between durations are based on their ratio, rather than their absolute difference. On this basis since 16 seconds is twice 8, and 8 is twice

four, it is with a signal of 8 seconds that animals should be undecided as to which lever to press.

One question that can be raised about the information-processing model of timing developed by Gibbon et al. (1984) concerns the way in which temporal information is stored in reference memory. This information could be intimately related to the experimental stimulus that was used to provide the temporal information. For example, in the temporal generalisation experiment described at the beginning of this section the information about duration stored in reference memory could be that a period of darkness of a certain duration signalled the availability of food. On the other hand, the information could be more general, such that duration itself, rather than the duration of a particular stimulus, served as the signal for food. In this latter example, the term "amodal representation" is used, because the representation in reference memory is not confined to the modality of the original training stimulus.

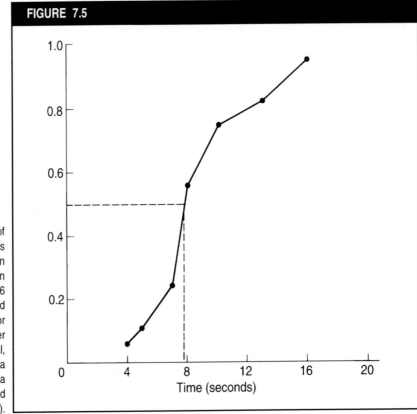

FIGURE 7.5

The mean probability of choosing one of two levers after a signal had been presented that varied in duration between 4 and 16 seconds. Rats had previously received food for responding on one lever after a 4-second signal, and on the other lever (a "long" response) after a 16-second signal (adapted from Church, 1978).

One experiment that demonstrates that temporal information may be stored independently of the modality of the training stimulus was conducted by Meck and Church (1982). Rats were trained on a temporal generalisation task in which they were rewarded for pressing a lever after they had been exposed to a light of medium, but not short or long duration. The solid line in Figure 7.6 indicates that with sufficient training rats learned the discrimination. Meck and Church (1982) then changed the procedure by using white noise rather than light as the temporal signal. The effects of this change are shown by the dashed lines in Figure 7.6, and it is quite evident that the discrimination was as good with this stimulus as with the light. Because there is physically little in common between a tone and a light, it is likely that an amodal representation of duration gained control over responding and permitted the excellent transfer between the two stimuli. For a similar finding with pigeons see Roberts, Cheng, and Cohen (1989).

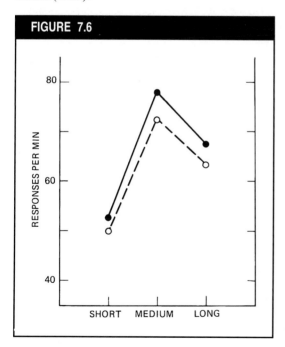

FIGURE 7.6

Average number of responses per minute following the short-, medium-, and long-duration stimuli in the experiment by Meck and Church (1982) (adapted from Meck & Church, 1982).

Many more experiments could be described that bear on the analysis of animal timing developed by Gibbon et al. (1984). Church (1989), for instance, has reviewed a range of studies that shed light on the biological basis of timing and the way in which it is affected by certain drugs. There is a suggestion that the value of K can be reduced by injections of vasopressin, whereas the rate of the pacemaker can be enhanced by metamphetamine (Church, 1984). There is also evidence to suggest that rats are capable of timing two different intervals simultaneously (Meck & Church, 1984), which indicates that the information-processing model of timing is in need of elaboration. More recently, Church and Broadbent (1991) have developed a connectionist model of timing that captures many of the positive attributes of the information-processing model. In addition, this connectionist model can be shown to provide a good account of the way in which animals respond on a fixed interval schedule of reinforcement (Wearden & Doherty, 1995). Overall, this body of research provides clear evidence that animals are capable of timing intervals and, at the same time, it has provided valuable insights into the way in which animals store and utilise information about such intervals.

NUMBER

At the turn of the century a horse named Clever Hans was said to possess remarkable intellectual skills (Pfungst, 1965/1908). In response to being posed an arithmetic question by his trainer, Hans would tap a hoof on the ground for the number of times that corresponded to the correct answer. The problems that Hans solved were not always simple. For example, in response to seeing the expression 1/2 + 2/5 written on a blackboard, he correctly tapped 9, followed after a pause by 10 to indicate the solution 9/10. He was not confined to replying to questions written on the blackboard. When in the presence of a large audience, his trainer might ask Hans to identify the number of people carrying an umbrella and the horse would again reply correctly.

For a while, this behaviour was taken as evidence that horses are capable of mental arithmetic, but a detailed examination of the conditions in which Hans performed yielded a different interpretation. Apparently, Hans' trainer calculated the answer to the problem, and after the correct number of taps he unconsciously moved. This movement, albeit slight, was a sufficient cue for Hans to stop tapping his hoof and coincidentally provide the correct answer.[2]

Interestingly, if the questions were posed to Hans by people other than his trainer, the horse very often produced the correct answer. Apparently, once they have posed a question to an animal humans will commonly adopt a tense posture, which is then relaxed as soon as the correct answer has been reached. Hans was evidently sensitive to these subtle changes in behaviour. Needless to say, Hans was never correct if the questioner did not know the answer.

The study of counting by animals did not cease with Clever Hans. During the last 90 years more than 100 experimental studies of counting by animals have been conducted. These experiments have examined counting by animals in three different ways: counting responses, counting sequentially presented stimuli, and counting simultaneously presented stimuli. After considering examples of each type of study, we shall review the various ways in which their findings can be explained. There are reasonable grounds for believing that at least some animals are able to count in a more honest way than Clever Hans.

FIGURE 7.7

Clever Hans (from Pfungst, 1965).

Responses

Mechner (1958; Mechner & Guevrekian, 1962) required a rat to press a lever for a specified number of responses, before pressing another lever in order to earn food. Although subjects were able to earn reward when the criterion number for first lever presses was as high as 24, they also made many errors. A rather different study of counting responses was conducted by Rumbaugh and Washburn (1993) with a chimpanzee who had been trained to move a cursor on a computer monitor with a joystick. At the start of a trial, an Arabic numeral (1, 2, 3, or 4) was presented on the screen together with an array of coloured rectangles, of which there were often considerably more than four. The chimpanzee was then required to delete the rectangles, by placing the cursor on them, until the number that had disappeared from the screen corresponded to the Arabic numeral. After extensive training the chimpanzee achieved a consistently high level of accuracy on this task. Figure 7.8 shows her performance for each of the numbers with which she was tested. Even though her accuracy declined as the number of rectangles to be deleted increased, the chimpanzee's performance was still in excess of chance for every number.

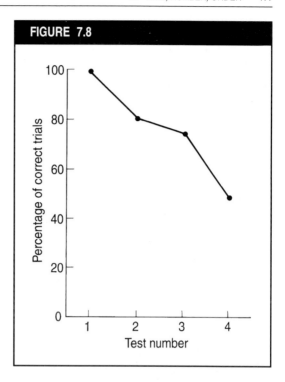

FIGURE 7.8

The percentage of correct trials by a chimpanzee who was required to delete a specified number, from 1 to 4, of rectangles from a computer monitor. The results are from all test trials, and chance performance was calculated to be at 20% (adapted from Rumbaugh & Washburn, 1993).

Sequential stimuli

An ingeniously simple experimental design has been used by Capaldi and Miller (1988) to study the counting of sequential stimuli by rats. The subjects were placed into the start box of a straight alley, about 200 centimetres in length, and required to run to a goal box in order to gain food that was available only intermittently. The trials were conducted in blocks of two different sequences. For the RRRN sequence there were four trials, with reward occurring on all but the last trial. There were five trials in the NRRRN block, of which the middle three led to reward. Typically the interval between each trial of a block was about 15 seconds, and each block was separated by about 15 minutes. The blocks were presented randomly, with the consequence that on the first trial of a block the rat would be unable to anticipate whether or not it would receive food. The speed of running down the alley to the goal box for each trial of the two kinds

of block is shown in Figure 7.9. In both blocks, subjects ran rapidly on every trial except the last. To explain this pattern of results, Capaldi and Miller (1988) argued that the rats counted the number of rewards they had received within a block, and that once they had received three, this served as a cue that the next trial would not result in food. One obvious effect of such a cue would be to reduce the running speed in the final trial of each block.

Another method for studying counting with sequentially presented stimuli was developed by Meck and Church (1983). Rats in a conditioning chamber were presented with either a *few* signal composed of two pulses of white noise, or a *many* signal composed of eight pulses. Two levers were then inserted into the chamber and food was delivered for pressing the left lever after the *few* signal, or the right lever after the *many* lever. The discrimination was mastered with little difficulty.

FIGURE 7.9

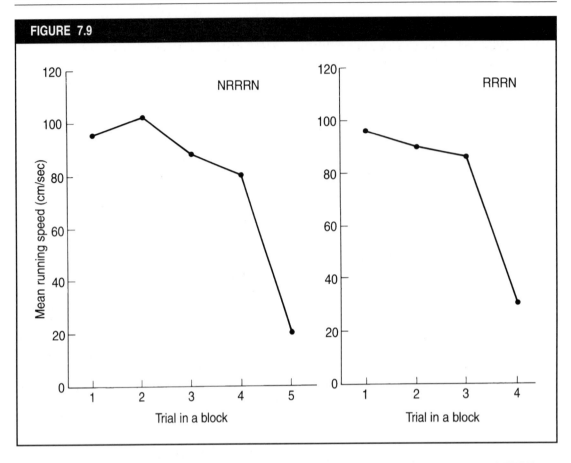

The mean speed of running down an alley by a group of rats for successive trials within a block. On 5-trial blocks (NRRRN) reward was available on trials 2, 3, and 4; and on 4-trial blocks (RRRN) reward was available on trials 1, 2, and 3 (adapted from Capaldi & Miller, 1988).

An explanation that comes to mind for the outcome of this last experiment is based on the ability of rats to time rather than count. Both signals consisted of 0.5-second pulses of white noise, separated by an equivalent period of silence. Thus the duration of the *few* signal was 2 seconds, whereas the *many* signal lasted 8 seconds. In order to confirm that animals had learned about the numerical attributes of the signals, therefore, a test session was conducted with signals that lasted for 4 seconds. To obtain these signals the duration of each of the two pulses of the *few* signal was extended, whereas it was reduced for each of the eight pulses of the *many* signal. Despite these changes, there was a clear preference for the left lever after the *few* signal and for the right lever after the *many* signal.

Now that the possibility has been raised that animals may cheat by using timing processes to solve counting problems, we should consider the extent to which the other findings mentioned earlier can be explained in this way. Although Broadbent, Church, Meck, and Rakitin (1993) have argued that it is possible to explain the results of Mechner (1958) in terms of timing, this explanation is less likely to apply to the remaining studies. In the experiment by Rumbaugh and Washburn (1993), the chimpanzee occasionally paused while she was completing her task. If the Arabic numeral served as a cue to delete rectangles for a given length of time, then pauses during the task should have severely disturbed her performance. In fact, the disruptive effect of these pauses was only slight. Turning to the design by

Capaldi and Miller (1988), it is worth noting that in an experiment by Capaldi (1993) the interval between the trials was varied randomly, rather than remaining constant. Despite making time a very poor indicator for the outcome of any particular trial, rats still ran more slowly on the final, nonreinforced trial than on any of the previous trials.

Our final demonstration of counting with sequentially presented stimuli is provided by a single chimpanzee, Sheba, who received several years of training by Boysen and Berntson (1989). At first, Sheba was shown a tray beside three placards. The tray contained up to three objects and the placards each portrayed either one, two, or three discs. Her task was to select the placard with the same number of discs as objects in the tray. Once she was adept at this task, her training continued in a similar way but with the discs being replaced by the appropriate Arabic numerals. At the end of this training she was able to select correctly the numerals 0, 1, 2, 3, and 4. In the next stage of the experiment, Sheba was allowed into the room depicted in Figure 7.10 where oranges were hidden in as many as three different places. To gain reward,

Sheba was expected to inspect the three locations, and then select the numeral that corresponded to the total number of oranges that she had seen. From the outset of this testing, her performance was very accurate. Finally, this method of testing was repeated, except that Arabic numerals were placed in two of the locations. Once again, from the first session of testing onwards, Sheba responded correctly by selecting the Arabic numeral that corresponded to the *sum* of the two numerals that she had just inspected. The number of trials that she received with each total, the number of times that she was correct with these totals, and the numerals she was shown to create the totals are shown in Table 7.1.

Simultaneous stimuli

As far as counting simultaneously presented stimuli is concerned, successful studies have been reported using monkeys, a chimpanzee, and a parrot. In a study by Terrell and Thomas (1990), monkeys were presented with two randomly constructed polygons that differed in the number of sides they contained (see Figure 7.11). They were rewarded for selecting the one with the

FIGURE 7.10

Experimental setting for a symbol counting task (adapted from Boysen & Berntson, 1989).

TABLE 7.1

Details of the Different Types of Test Trial Used for a Study of Counting by a Chimpanzee.

Sum	Test items	Number of trials	Number of correct trials
1	1 + 0	8	7
2	0 + 2 1 + 1	11	10
3	0 + 3 1 + 2	12	10
4	0 + 4 1 + 3	12	11

Adapted from Boysen and Berntson (1989).

FIGURE 7.11

Examples of the shapes used in the experiment by Terrell and Thomas (1990) (adapted from Terrell & Thomas, 1990).

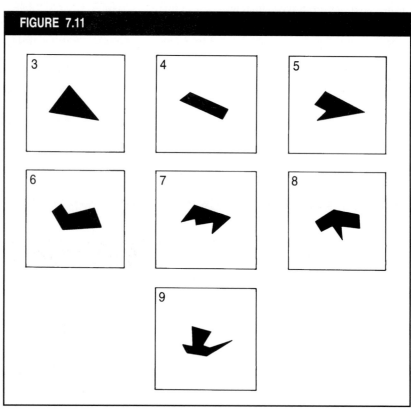

smaller number of sides and discriminated with great accuracy between heptagons and octagons, but not between octagons and nonagons.

Matsuzawa (1985) trained Ai, a chimpanzee, to select an appropriately numbered response key from 1, 2, 3, 4, 5, or 6, whenever she was shown an array of a given object, for example, three blue pencils. With each of these numbers she was eventually accurate on more than 90% of the training trials. She also showed an above-chance level of accuracy when she was presented with an array of novel objects.

Finally, Pepperberg (1994) tested an African grey parrot who had been trained over many years to respond with spoken words to questions that were addressed to him. A more detailed account of this training can be found in Chapter 10, for the present it is sufficient to know that he was able to say in English the numbers 1 to 6. For a typical test trial Alex would be shown an array of 4 purple blocks of wood, intermixed randomly among a number of other objects. The experimenter would then ask "How many purple wood?" and Alex was expected to reply with the correct number. A sample of the questions that were posed to Alex, are shown in Table 7.2. His answers are listed in the right-hand column of the table. Even though a novel array was presented on each test trial, his answers were considerably better than would be expected on the basis of chance.

Theoretical interpretation

There is little doubt that animals are able to respond on the basis of the numerical attributes of stimuli. But how are they able to use this numerical information?

Subitising. When humans are asked to report the number of items in an array, they are able to respond both rapidly and accurately for numbers up to 6. This performance is said to depend on an ability to subitise. Subitising can be contrasted with estimating, which is less accurate, but which can be applied to much larger numbers, or counting, which again can be applied to large numbers but which involves the slow process of enumerating one by one. A number of authors have proposed that subitising does not depend on counting, instead it is regarded as more of a perceptual process where a frequently recurring pattern of stimulation elicits the appropriate numerical response. Although subitising has been offered as an explanation for counting in animals (Davis & Perusse, 1988), others are less than enthusiastic about this proposal (Capaldi, 1993; Miller, 1993). They point to the fact that there is no clear test to determine whether or not subitisation has taken place. There is also the problem of specifying how a particular pattern becomes associated with a given number. At present, it is not possible to decide whether or not animals are capable of subitising. However, we can note that subitising is normally said to occur with simultaneously presented events. It would thus be unreasonable to apply this account to the results obtained with sequentially presented stimuli. Furthermore, because of the relatively high numbers that are involved, the capacity of monkeys

TABLE 7.2		
Examples of the Different Types of Test Trial Used for a Study of Counting by a Parrot.		
1 orange chalk, 2 orange wood, 4 purple wood, 5 purple chalk	How many purple wood?	4
1 yellow block, 2 gray block 4 yellow wool, 6 gray wool	How many yellow block?	1
1 rose wood, 2 blue nail, 3 blue wood, 5 rose nail	How many rose nail?	5
2 gray truck, 3 gray key, 4 orange key, 5 orange truck	How many grey key?	2, 3
1 blue box, 3 green box, 4 blue cup, 6 green cup	How many green cup?	6
1 blue box, 2 green rock, 3 purple plastic key, 4 green plastic key	How many green rock?	2

Note: Singular labels were used for all the questions in order to avoid cueing *one*. Adapted from Pepperberg, 1994.

to discriminate between polygons composed of 7 and 8 sides is difficult to explain by reference to subitising. Finally, subitising is normally assumed to take place when the items to be counted are presented by themselves. The ability of Alex to count the members of one class of objects, when they were intermixed with members of a different class of objects, further demonstrates that, at best, subitising provides an incomplete explanation for the way in which animals count.

Perceptual matching.   Rumbaugh and Washburn (1993) have proposed that perceptual matching may account for the success of animals in a variety of counting experiments. Consider the study by Terrell and Thomas (1990), in which monkeys were able to discriminate successfully between polygons composed of 7 and 8 sides. The experiment involved 37 heptagons and 40 octagons, each of which were presented for many hundreds of trials. Given such extensive training with a limited set of stimuli, subjects could conceivably remember every instance and which response to make in its presence. By matching the current pattern to the appropriate remembered pattern, they would be able to perform accurately on every trial. Although there is no good reason for rejecting this account, it does not explain why subjects were unable to master the discrimination between octagons and nonagons.

Additional findings described earlier can be explained by a perceptual matching account, if it is accepted that animals can remember sequences of events. For example, the rats in the study by Meck and Church (1983) might have formed a memory of the sequence noise–silence–noise, and associated this with pressing the left lever. Subsequent presentations of the *few* stimulus would then activate this memory and lead to the correct response being performed. It is not unreasonable to suppose that explanations based on this type of analysis can also explain the findings by Capaldi and Miller (1988) and Rumbaugh and Washburn (1993).

A clear prediction of a perceptual matching explanation for counting is that animals will be able to respond correctly only with familiar training stimuli. If they are presented with a novel test stimulus, they should not know how to react to it. The results of the experiments with Ai, Alex, and Sheba are thus important because these animals were all able to perform correctly with novel test arrays. Whether or not a perceptual matching account can be developed to explain these findings satisfactorily remains to be seen.

Counting.   If Alex, Ai, or Sheba were human, we would happily explain their behaviour by saying that they counted the number of items that they were shown. But we should be very cautious about using this explanation for animals that have either no, or at best limited, linguistic ability. At the very least, if we are to say that an animal is capable of counting, then we should specify precisely what is meant by this term.

In his discussion of counting Gallistel (1993) draws a distinction between numbers as categories and numbers as concepts. When a number is used as a category, it allows the user to treat groups of things in the same way because they are composed of the same number of items. The groups may have nothing in common whatsoever, other than the number of items of which they are composed. Thus Alex can be said to use number as a category because arrays of, say, six blocks of wood and six pieces of chalk both elicited the same response of "six". The same could be said of Ai. An important consequence of being able to use a number as a category is that it can be accurately applied to any group of things, even when the group is presented to the subject for the first time. Both Alex and Ai were successful in this respect.

To explain successful categorisation on the basis of number Gelman and Gallistel (1978) made use of the term numerons. Numerons are labels that represent numerosities, they are not necessarily written or spoken, and they form an essential part of the counting process. The role of numerons in counting is revealed in the following quotation (Gallistel, 1993, pp. 217–218):

Counting processes obey three constraints: (a) The *one–one* principle: Each item in the set is assigned one and only one numeron ...

(b) the *stable-ordering principle*: The order in which numerons are assigned is always the same. Note that it is the order in which numerons are assigned, not the order in which items are counted, that must be the same from one count to the next; (c) the *cardinal principle*: The final numeron assigned, and only the final numeron, is used as the representative of the numerosity of the set.

Thus all groups of things that are represented by the same numeron will contain the same number of items. By virtue of being represented by the same numeron, the groups can then be treated in the same way, and categorisation on the basis of number will be successful.

When a number is used as a concept, Gallistel (1993) maintains that it is capable of playing an unambiguous role in a mental operation. For example, if I am asked to add together 23 and 36, I am able to do so accurately because I have a concept of the numbers 23 and 36 and I know their role in the operation of addition. Turning once again to the experiments referred to earlier, it would not be justifiable to argue that Alex and Ai used their numbers as concepts. They were never required to perform such operations as addition with the numbers that they employed. On the other hand, the performance of Sheba (Boysen & Berntson, 1989) is compatible with the conclusion that she was able to use numbers as concepts.

The clear way in which this analysis of counting by Gallistel (1993) is presented draws attention to a number of its deficiencies. It does not explain what a numeron is, how a numeron can be acquired, or how one numeron differs from another. Rather little is also said about the way in which the conceptual use of numbers could develop, or about the way in which addition might take place. At present, the results from studies of counting by animals barely allow us to even speculate as to how these issues will be resolved in the future. None the less, a valuable contribution of the analysis of counting developed by Gallistel (1993; Gelman & Gallistel, 1978) is that it provides a framework to guide further research on this topic.

SERIAL ORDER

The aim of this section is to understand the extent to which animals are able to represent serial order. A number of relatively simple experiments have shown that animals can remember the order in which a sequence of stimuli has been presented, or a sequence of responses must be performed. Using a *serial recognition task* Weisman, Wasserman, Dodd, and Larew (1980) presented pigeons with sequences of two colours: red–green, green–red, green–green, and red–red. Pecks on a response key after the first of these sequences resulted in the delivery of food, but reward was never presented after the remaining three sequences. Not many sessions were required before the birds were responding more rapidly after the red–green sequence than any other sequence, which confirms that they were influenced by the order in which the stimuli were presented. Similar results have been reported with sequences of three stimuli by Terrace (1986) and Roitblat, Bever, Helweg, and Harley (1991). In a *response-chaining study*, Balleine et al. (1995) required rats to press a lever and then pull a chain that was suspended from the ceiling in order to gain reward. Subjects had little trouble with learning to execute this sequence.

Successful performance on the serial recognition task has been taken as evidence that animals are able to represent the sequence with which stimuli are presented (Terrace, 1986; Weisman et al., 1980). One way of characterising this knowledge is to assume, using terminology introduced in previous chapters, that a representation of the first element of the correct sequence enters into an association with a representation of the next element and that this chain is retained in long-term memory. By comparing a representation of this chain on subsequent trials with the sequence that is presented, it would be possible to determine whether or not responding will produce reward.

Successful response chaining can be most easily explained if it is accepted that instrumental conditioning results in the growth of S–R associations. In the experiment by Balleine et al. (1995) the conditioning chamber might serve as a discriminative stimulus that elicits the response of lever pressing. A press on the lever will then generate a specific pattern of feedback, which itself could serve as the stimulus that elicits the next component in the sequence, chain pulling.

The ability of animals to learn chains of responses, and to recognise certain sequences of stimuli, can thus be explained by principles that we encountered in earlier chapters. But the use of a rather different task for studying sequence learning has revealed findings that are not so readily explained by these principles. In this task an animal is presented with an array of, say, four stimuli and it must make the same response to each of them in the correct sequence in order to gain reward (Terrace, Straub, Bever & Seidenberg, 1977). Terrace (1986) refers to this task as *simultaneous chaining*. Evidence is accumulating that suggests that pigeons and monkeys solve this problem in different ways. Because of this possibility, we shall examine separately the results from these species.

Pigeons

Studies of simultaneous chaining with pigeons are typically conducted in a test chamber containing a response panel composed of eight response locations arranged in a 4×2 matrix (Terrace, 1987, 1991). Each response location is about 2.5cm in diameter and a coloured circle—red (A) , green (B), blue (C), yellow (D), or violet (E)—can be projected onto any response location. On a typical trial for a well-trained pigeon, five randomly selected locations are simultaneously illuminated with the five colours and the bird must peck the colours in a predetermined sequence, A–B–C–D–E, in order to obtain reward. As the bird progresses through the sequence, there is no change to the array. Thus the five colours remain present until the final one had been pecked. At this point, the entire array is extinguished and food delivered. Any errors of pecking a colour out of sequence result in the array being extinguished and no food is presented.

Those with little experience of training pigeons may be surprised to discover that this is not an easy task for them to learn. Their training must commence with the first pair of items from the list A–B, and when they are able to peck A before B,

they are introduced to the triad A–B–C. Training is then continued with A–B–C–D and finally A–B–C–D–E. The histograms in Figure 7.12 shows the mean number of sessions (with 40 trials in a session) that a group of five pigeons required to master each stage of training. In all, some 120 daily sessions were needed before a satisfactory level of performance was obtained with the five-item list.

The most widely accepted explanation for the way in which pigeons solve this serial problem is by assuming they treat it as a sequence of discriminations (D'Amato & Colombo, 1988; Terrace, 1991). The onset of the array might serve as a cue for pecking A. Once A has been pecked, the action of withdrawing the beak from A would provide a unique pattern of stimulation that could then serve as a cue for pecking B. The feedback generated by withdrawing from B could then serve as a discriminative stimulus for pecking at C, and so forth, until E is pecked. In other words, pigeons are believed to solve the serial learning task by acquiring a chain of responses, where the feedback from one response serves as the cue for the next response.

The strengths, and weaknesses, of this analysis are highlighted by further results reported by Terrace (1987). Once pigeons had been trained on a five-item series, they received test trials with pairs of items from the training sequence, such as AC, CD, and so forth. The results from these tests can be seen in Figure 7.13, which shows the percentage of trials on which the members of each pair were pecked in the correct sequence. Thus A was pecked before B on more than 80% of the trials with AB, whereas B and C were pecked first equally often on trials with BC. The results in Figure 7.13 can be summarised by saying that responding was accurate on any pair that contained either the first item, A, or the last item, E, whereas performance was poor with pairs that were composed of two intermediate items, B, C, or D.

According to the account that has just been developed, the onset of any test array will serve as a discriminative stimulus for pecking A. Subjects should thus peck this stimulus first whenever it occurs in a test pair. Having pecked A, subjects will have no option but to peck its partner second, which

FIGURE 7.12

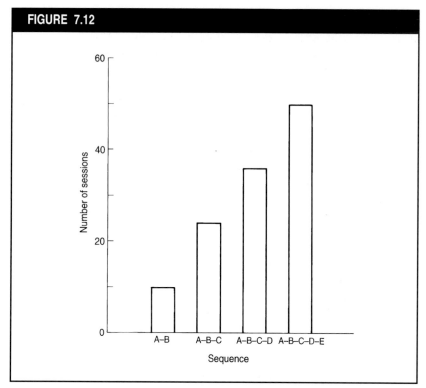

The mean number of sessions of training required for the various stages of a simultaneous chaining experiment with pigeons (adapted from Terrace, 1987).

FIGURE 7.13

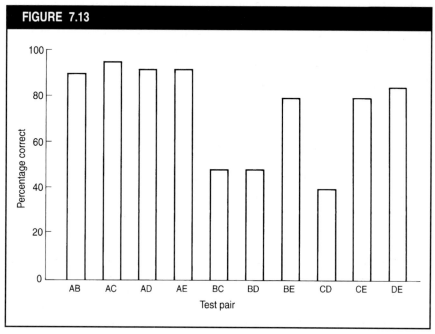

The mean percentage of correct responses on test trials with pairs of stimuli, after pigeons have been trained with the simultaneous chain A–B–C–D–E (adapted from Terrace, 1987).

will then ensure successful completion of the test sequence. The results from the test trials with AB, AC, AD, and AE are consistent with this analysis. Turning now to the trials with BC, BD, and CD, their onset might also elicit a tendency to peck at A. But in the absence of any opportunity to peck this key, the pigeons will lack the stimulation to guide their first response and they should thus choose an item at random. Once again, the results from the trials with these pairs are consistent with a response-chaining analysis. Of course, this analysis also predicts poor performance with the pairs BE, CE, and DE, but the level of accuracy on these trials was much the same as with the pairs containing A. In order to explain these results, therefore, it is generally accepted that the serial training results in a tendency to refrain from pecking E until all the other keys have been pecked (D'Amato & Colombo, 1988; Straub & Terrace, 1981).

In summary, the results of the test trials with the intermediate pairs are important because they suggest that pigeons lacked any detailed knowledge about the structure of the list. If they possessed that knowledge, then they should have preferred, for example, to peck C before D with the pair CD. Their failure to respond in this manner lends considerable support to the overall principles of a response-chaining analysis for serial learning.

Chunking. The results thus far suggest that pigeons perform rather poorly on serial learning tasks, but a considerable improvement can be brought about if the method of training is changed slightly. Terrace (1991) trained a group in the same way as that just described, but the stimuli were different. Instead of receiving five colours, the birds were presented with an array composed of three colours (A, B, C) and two geometric shapes (X, Y). Food was delivered after these stimuli had been pecked in the sequence A–B–C–X–Y. Figure 7.14 shows the number of sessions that were required for each of the training stages in this experiment.

The differences between these results and those for the original group are striking. Training with the four- and five-item sequence was much more efficient, with the result that there was a total of around 60 training sessions. Furthermore, when

test trials were conducted with pairs of stimuli, performance was accurate with each of the 10 possible pairs. In one respect, this pattern of results is not surprising. There are many studies of human memory that show that changing the nature of the items part of the way through a list will facilitate considerably the memory for that list (Brooks & Watkins, 1990; Watkins, 1977).

Terrace (1991) interprets these findings in terms of chunking. By this he means that the use of two types of stimuli encouraged the pigeons to regard the serial task as being composed of two lists, the first containing three items and the second two. Additional studies by Terrace and Chen (1991a,b) lend this proposal considerable support. They also identify some of the factors that influence chunking. Unfortunately these additional studies do not make clear why performance with two successive lists should be better than on a single list, when both problems contain the same number of elements.

We shall see shortly that, compared with pigeons, monkeys find simultaneous chaining problems with five similar elements relatively easy. To explain this outcome, it has been suggested that monkeys are able to remember lists of five items, which then enables them to solve the simultaneous chaining problem without having to resort to the more cumbersome method of response chaining. Perhaps, therefore, pigeons can remember a list of no more than three items. In which case, they could then reduce the A–B–C–X–Y sequence to two manageable lists, and there would be no need to rely on response chaining in order to solve the problem.

Monkeys

D'Amato and Colombo (1988) describe a single experiment with monkeys that was effectively of the same design as the first of the pigeon studies. Of course, the monkeys were not expected to peck at the stimuli, they had to touch them instead. Figure 7.15 shows the mean number of trials that were required by a group of five cebus monkeys to pass through the various stages of training. The monkeys mastered their problem more readily than the pigeons, but this might have occurred because there were five rather than eight response locations

FIGURE 7.14

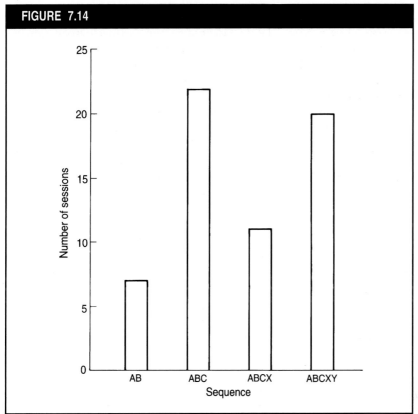

The mean number of sessions of training required in the various stages of a simultaneous chaining experiment with pigeons. Stimuli A, B, and C were colours, and stimuli X and Y were geometric shapes (adapted from Terrace, 1991).

FIGURE 7.15

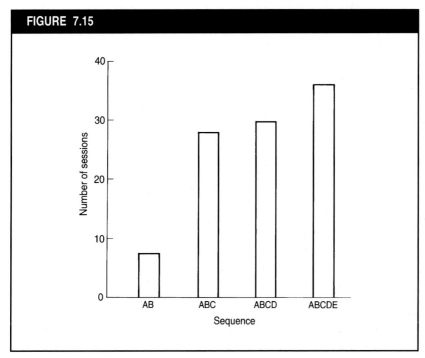

The mean number of sessions of training required for the various stages of a simultaneous chaining experiment with monkeys (adapted from D'Amato & Colombo, 1988).

for the monkeys. When they received their test trials with pairs of stimuli, the monkeys performed accurately with every possible test pair. The fact that the monkeys were able to respond accurately with the pairs composed of the intermediate items (B, C, and D), whereas the pigeons were not, provides compelling evidence that these different species solved the serial-learning task in different ways.

During the test trials a record was kept of the time that elapsed (1) between the onset of the array and when the first response was made, and (2) between the first and second response. The

left-hand panel of Figure 7.16 shows the latency to respond to the first item, as a function of its position in the training list. The nearer the first item was to the beginning of the list, the more rapidly were responses directed at it. The results in the right-hand panel of Figure 7.16 show the time between the responses to the first and second member of each pair, according to the number of items that were missing between them. Thus the results for 0 missing items were for trials with AB, BC, CD, and DE. The response to the second item on these trials occurred fairly soon after the response to the first item. But as the number of

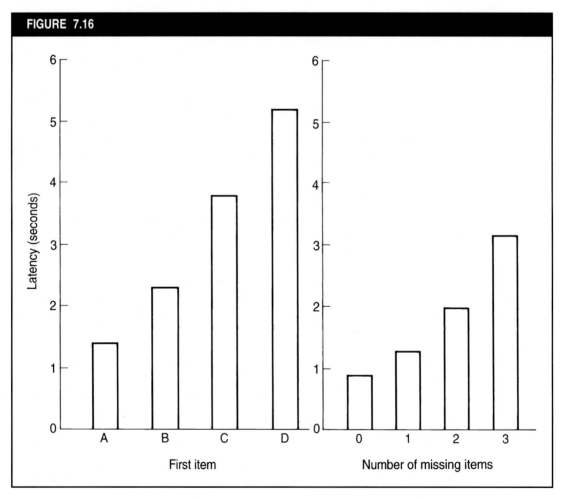

FIGURE 7.16

Left-hand panel: The mean time taken to select the first item of a test pair of stimuli by monkeys, after they were trained with the simultaneous chain A–B–C–D–E.
Right-hand panel: The mean time to select the second item of the test pairs by the same monkeys, as a function of the number of items that separate the members of the pair in the training list (adapted from D'Amato & Colombo, 1988).

missing items increased, so it took longer to respond to the second item, with the consequence that responding to the pair with three missing items, AE, was particularly slow. A moment's reflection will indicate that these last results are surprising because after the response to the first item, there is only one item left to select and this could be achieved at the same speed no matter how many items are missing between the test pair. In view of their surprising nature, it is of some comfort to note that the trends depicted in both panels of Figure 7.16 have been replicated by Swartz, Chen, and Terrace (1991) with cebus monkeys and a four-item list.[3]

The suggestion has been made by several authors that these results indicate that the monkeys retained some representation of the sequence in which the five items had to be selected. Harris and McGonigle (1994) proposed that monkeys will use a stack of rules of the form Touch A, Touch B, Touch C, which are consulted in succession. Alternatively, D'Amato and Colombo (1988; see also D'Amato, 1991) suggested that serial learning depends on the development of an associative chain in which representations of the five stimuli are connected. The chain would then be used to guide the sequence of responding. Despite their differences, these accounts make similar predictions concerning the outcome of test trials with pairs of stimuli. As soon as a pair is presented, the subjects will have to work through their stack of rules, or through their associative chain, until they encounter a relevant rule or representation. At this point the first response can be performed, and it will be correct. If it takes time to inspect each member of the list, then it follows that the latency to the first response will be directly related to its position in the list. On the basis of this analysis, the results in the right-hand panel of Figure 7.16 imply that having made their first response, the monkeys continued to work through their list until they encountered the rule or representation that was appropriate for their second response. In order to explain the difference that we have seen between the serial learning results with pigeons and monkeys, it could then be argued that monkeys, but not pigeons, are able to construct lists. Alternatively, it is possible that both species

are capable of constructing lists, but that these can be longer in monkeys.

Each of these list-learning explanations thus provides a ready explanation for all the results with monkeys, but they both have their shortcomings. The first one (Harris & McGonigle, 1994) does not make clear how a rule such as Peck A is represented, and the second one (D'Amato, 1991) fails to specify how an animal progresses through the associative chain, and how a member of the chain is able to generate a response at the appropriate time. There is also one feature of both accounts that may be a fatal weakness. Neither of them endows the animal with any knowledge of the position of the items in a list. There is nothing in the rule Touch C, or in the representation of C in the associative chain A–B–C–D–E, to indicate that C is the third item in the list. If it could be shown, therefore, that animals can acquire information about the position of items in a list, then each of these accounts would be incomplete. Given the importance of this prediction, it is a pity that there are no published reports of whether or not monkeys are sensitive to the position of items in lists.

Concluding comments

The findings that have been reviewed in this section indicate that further investigation of serial-order problems with animals could reveal a range of important findings. They may allow us to understand more about the way in which the intelligence of monkeys and pigeons differs, and new insights may be gained into the way animals construct and utilise lists or chains in order to execute sequences of responses. Unfortunately, for so long as the the preliminary training in these experiments requires about 100 sessions, the rate at which our understanding of serial-order learning develops is likely to be slow.

TRANSITIVE INFERENCE

When told that A is bigger than B, and that B is bigger than C, few adults have difficulty in reaching the conclusion that A is bigger than C. This type of reasoning, which allows us to combine knowledge about specific relationships in order to infer another relationship, is known as transitive inference. The results from several experiments suggest that animals, too, are capable of solving transitive inference problems. The reason for discussing these experiments now is that their results have been said to depend on the formation of a transitive series, which is similar to the list that is thought to aid the solution of serial-order problems (D'Amato, 1991).

In a study by Gillan (1981; see also McGonigle & Chalmers, 1977, 1986, 1992) three female chimpanzees first received training with five containers, A, B, C, D, and E, each of which was a different colour. A pair of containers was presented to the subject on each trial and her task was to identify the one in which food was hidden. The trials were of the following sort: A+B–, B+C–, C+D–, D+E–, where + denotes the container with food. The spatial relationship between the members of each pair varied irregularly, so that the discriminations could be solved only on the basis of colour. After a number of training sessions performance on all discriminations was consistently accurate, which can be taken to indicate that subjects preferred A to B, B to C, C to D, and D to E. To examine whether these relationships can be combined to lead to a novel inference, Gillan (1981) then gave test sessions that included, for the first time, the pair B and D. If chimpanzees are capable of transitive inference, then combining the knowledge that B is preferred to C with the knowledge that C is preferred to D should lead to the conclusion that B is preferred to D. One chimpanzee, Sadie, performed perfectly on this test by choosing B in preference to D on all 12 test trials. Although the results for the other two chimpanzees were not so good, the success of Sadie shows that at least one chimpanzee can solve transitive inference problems.

This clear demonstration of transitive inference raises the question of how it was achieved. One explanation assumes that chimpanzees have a means of encoding information that allows them to represent the relationship between each pair and also to combine this information. They perhaps learn that "B is preferred to C" and "C is preferred to D", so that the combination of this knowledge

would then lead to the correct conclusion. Fortunately we do not have to worry about presenting this account in detail, because there is already evidence that suggests it is wrong. McGonigle and Chalmers (1992) studied transitive inference in squirrel monkeys using a similar method to that of Gillan (1981). Test trials included novel pairs of items that were either closely or distantly related on the transitive series. When the members of the test pair were closely related on the transitive series (e.g. BD), information about only a few training pairs would be required in order to determine which test item should be selected. In contrast, for pairs that were distantly related on the transitive series (e.g. AE), information about many of the training pairs would need to be consulted before a decision could be made. According to this analysis, therefore, subjects should be quicker at choosing between items that are close rather than far apart on the transitive series. In fact, the results directly contradicted this prediction.

Figure 7.17 shows the time it took subjects to choose a cup on the test trials. The results are

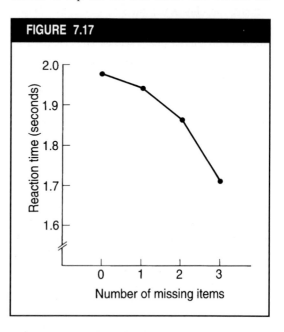

FIGURE 7.17

The time taken to select one of two cups on test trials with stimuli selected from a transitive series comprising five items. The results are arranged according to the number of items that separate the test pair in the transitive series (adapted from McGonigle & Chalmers, 1992).

arranged according to the number of missing items of the transitive series between the two test items. For example, there were no missing items for the test pair AB, and one missing item for the pair AC. As the figure shows, choice of the correct item was faster when the members of a pair were distantly related, with the result, paradoxically, that choices between pairs that had never been given during training—BD, for example—were made more swiftly than those between pairs that were familiar, BC. This finding is known as the *symbolic distance effect* and is often found in experiments with humans (Bryant & Trabasso, 1971; Woocher, Glass, & Holyoak, 1978).

One explanation for the symbolic distance effect is that the information provided during training is reorganised into a transitive series. This suggestion has been made for humans (e.g. Anderson, 1980) as well as animals (D'Amato, 1991; McGonigle & Chalmers, 1986; Roberts & Phelps, 1994). In the experiment by McGonigle and Chalmers (1992), for example, the training with individual pairs will eventually result in the acquisition of the sequence A–B–C–D–E. Once this has been learned, then on any trial all that the subject must do is select the member of the pair of items that is nearer to A in the sequence. A further assumption of this type of explanation is that the representation of the series is meant to have spatial properties. As a consequence, decisions about which item of a pair is nearer to A will be easier, and faster, when the items are far apart, rather than close together in the list.

A worrying finding for this explanation is that pigeons can also solve transitive inference problems, even when five stimuli are involved (Von Fersen, Wynne, Delius, & Staddon, 1991). We have just seen that these animals may not be able to represent a list of five items, which then makes it hard to accept that they created a transitive series of five items. Couvillon and Bitterman (1992) have also expressed doubts about the merits of this type of explanation for the findings by Von Fersen et al. (1991). Because these doubts are relevant to other studies of transitive inference, they are worth considering in some detail.

Pigeons were trained by Von Fersen et al. (1991) in the apparatus shown in Figure 7.18. On any trial,

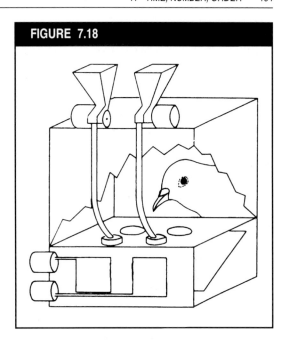

FIGURE 7.18

A sketch of the apparatus used by Von Fersen et al. (1991) to study transitive inference in pigeons. Food can be delivered to two cups through the vertical tubes, and the stimuli were projected onto circular keys in front of the cups (adapted from Von Fersen et al., 1991).

different geometric shapes were presented on the two displays and the bird was required to peck one, but not the other, in order to receive food. In keeping with other studies of transitive inference in animals, the pigeons received the following discriminations: A+B–, B+C–, C+D–, and D+E–, followed at the end of the experiment by test trials with BD. The results from the training trials are given by the solid circles in Figure 7.19, which shows for each pair the percentage of trials on which a correct response was made. The results from the test trials with BD are shown by the histogram in Figure 7.19, which demonstrates that subjects exhibited a considerable preference to peck at B rather than D.

The simplest explanation for the preference of B over D is that the associative strength of B was greater than that of D. This explanation is normally rejected on the basis that both B and D were equally often paired with reward and nonreward. Thus, selection of B was rewarded on trials with BC, but not AB; likewise, selection of D was rewarded on

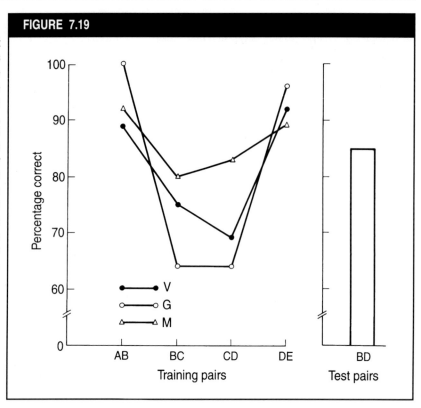

FIGURE 7.19

Mean percentages of correct choices with the various training pairs that were presented in the transitive inference studies of Von Fersen et al. (1991) (V), Gillan (1981) (G), and McGonigle and Chalmers (1992) (M). The results for the test trial with the pair BD in the study by Von Fersen et al. (1991) are shown by the histogram (adapted from Gillan, 1981; McGonigle & Chalmers, 1992; and Von Fersen et al., 1991).

trials with DE but not CD. However, Couvillon and Bitterman (1992) point out that the results shown in Figure 7.19 provide a good reason for believing that the associative strength of B was in fact greater than that of D. Subjects were very accurate on the trials with AB and thus pecked B on about only 13% of the trials with this pair, whereas they incorrectly pecked D on about 33% of the trials with CD. Many more unrewarded pecks were therefore made to D than B and it should hardly be surprising that a preference was exhibited for the latter stimulus on the test trials.[4] Couvillon and Bitterman (1992) show this argument can be developed to explain the symbolic distance effect that was demonstrated in a further experiment with pigeons by Von Fersen et al. (1991).

Couvillon and Bitterman's (1992) argument is valid only when transitive inference training results in a pattern of responding similar to that shown in Figure 7.19 for the study by Von Fersen et al. (1991). If the animals could be trained to respond at the same level of accuracy with each pair, then it would be reasonable to assume that the

associative strengths of all the intermediate stimuli in the transitive series were equal and their account would no longer be appropriate. Interestingly, the pattern of results shown for the training pairs with pigeons in Figure 7.19, is also found with monkeys and chimpanzees. The open circles in Figure 7.19 show the results from the final training sessions with Sadie, in the study by Gillan (1981); and the open triangles show the results for the squirrel monkeys in the study by McGonigle and Chalmers (1992). The results from the three different species bear a remarkable similarity to each other. We must accept therefore that at least for animals, we need look no further than to the principles of associative learning to describe their success with transitive inference (see also, Steirn, Weaver, & Zentall, 1995).

Research on transitive inference has not fulfilled the early promise that was expected of it. The initial studies of transitive inference were intended to demonstrate that at least some animals are capable of a form of reasoning that is found in humans. The experiments were also expected to demonstrate that at least some animals are capable of representing knowledge, and utilising that knowledge, in a way that is considerably more sophisticated than that allowed by current theories of instrumental and Pavlovian conditioning. Until Couvillon and Bitterman's (1992) analysis of transitive inference can be rejected, however, the fundamental principles of conditioning would indeed seem capable of accounting for transitive inference in animals. Research into transitive inference is thus important, if for no other reason, because it shows that until we can be confident that a simple explanation for an experimental finding is inadequate, we should be very cautious about seeking a more sophisticated one.

CONCLUDING COMMENTS

Considerable attention was paid in the first part of this chapter to the ability of insects to utilise temporal information. Cockroaches were said to time daily bursts of activity by virtue of possessing a 24-hour clock, and a similar claim was made to explain patterns of feeding by honey-bees. Such conclusions are of interest in their own right, but they also emphasise three related points concerning the study of animal cognition.

First, they indicate that cognitive processes play an important role in the behaviour of so-called primitive animals, and in the most basic of experimental tasks. Animal cognition is thus not to be found in a restricted selection of species, nor is it confined to methods designed to tax the higher mental capacities. The concern of this area of study is, instead, with the mechanisms that enable animals to store and utilise information gained from their experiences, wherever this may occur.

The second point relates to the tendency, when considering the cognitive processes of animals, to anthropomorphise by imagining that their mental experiences are much the same as our own. It is very hard, if not impossible, to believe that cockroaches have a mental life. A discussion of their cognitive processes, therefore, draws attention to the fact that the study of animal cognition is concerned with information

processing, not with the mental experience or consciousness of animals.

The final point concerns the merits of conducting experiments on animals with relatively simple nervous systems. By using insects, for example, it may be possible to study the fundamental operation of such processes as timing in a way that would be impossible with more sophisticated animals. We have already encountered support for this argument in Chapter 2, where the merits of studying the physiological mechanisms of associative learning with *Aplysia* were presented. In the next chapter we shall consider additional evidence that is in keeping with the spirit of this conclusion. In addition, the fact that periodic timing can be studied at all in insects suggests that this sort of timing does not depend on a particularly sophisticated nervous system.

Of course, it would be naive to believe that there are no limitations to the study of cognitive processes in animals with simple nervous systems. Although there is abundant evidence to suggest that at least some insects are capable of periodic timing, to my knowledge there is no evidence to show that they are capable of timing intervals in the way that has been shown with rats. Moreover, even though bees may be capable of a rudimentary form of counting (Chittka & Geiger, 1995), it would be a rash person indeed who would argue that the numerical skills of Alex the parrot, or Sheba the chimpanzee, will ever be replicated with insects. Indeed, it may well be the case that for each of the topics considered in this chapter, some vertebrates will prove to be more sophisticated than others. The difference between the performance of monkeys and pigeons on serial-order problems already provides good support for this proposal.

Finally, some comment is needed about the general conclusions that can be drawn from the experiments considered in this chapter. The experiments clearly show that animals can respond on the basis of information about time, number, and serial order. The question is then raised as to how animals are able to achieve their success on these tasks and it is here that our lack of knowledge becomes woefully apparent. We have very little evidence to support the claim that periodic timing depends on oscillators, or that interval timing depends on a pacemaker. We know very little about the way in which animals are able to count. And the manner in which animals represent and use information about serial order remains a matter for speculation. We have thus extended considerably our understanding of the information that animals are able to use, but we have discovered rather little about the mechanisms that enable them to make use of this information.

NOTES

1. For present purposes the properties of working memory and reference memory can be regarded as being much the same, respectively as short- and long-term memory, which were considered in Chapter 6.
2. Hans' trainer is said to have believed firmly in the arithmetic ability of his horse. When eventually he was persuaded that this was not the case, he became severely depressed and died a short time later.
3. Further evidence of a difference between the way monkeys and pigeons solve serial-order problems can be found in the report by Terrace (1991) that pigeons do not show these effects. Thus they respond equally rapidly to the first item of a test pair, no matter what position in the list it occupies; they also respond equally rapidly to the second item with no influence at all on the number of missing items (see also D'Amato, 1991, pp. 168–171).
4. The argument of Couvillon and Bitterman (1992) ignores the fact that on the other training trials with B and D, pecks at D resulted in reward on about 96% of the trials with DE, whereas pecks at B resulted in reward on only 75% of the trials with BC. Although this pattern of responding would encourage a preference for D over B, the overall probability of a response being followed by food was still greater for B than D. Couvillon and Bitterman (1992) provide a more formal exposition of this analysis.

8

Navigation

A capacity for navigation should be invaluable for the majority of animals. They will often find themselves in one location and need to move to another in order to obtain food, seek a mate, return to their home, and so forth. This journey could, of course, be haphazard and guided by nothing more than the principle of trial and error. But if the position of the goal is known, then a more efficient way of travelling would be to plot, and then follow a course to the goal. There are a variety of sources of information that could be used to help an animal navigate in this way. In the first part of this chapter we shall examine how animals use these sources of information when the distance that must be travelled is relatively short.

In addition to navigating successfully over short distances, some animals are able to complete journeys that cover considerable distances and that may last for long periods of time. Pigeons are famous for their skill at homing, which allows them to fly hundreds of miles back to their loft after they have been released from an unfamiliar location. Other animals migrate annually over vast distances to a specific location, even when they have never before made that journey. The second part of this chapter will consider how animals are able to travel successfully over such large distances.

A theme that runs through this chapter is that travel through the environment can be controlled by numerous cues, and spatial problems can be solved in a variety of ways. Animals appear to take advantage of this redundancy. They will often refer to different sources of information, and adopt different strategies, depending on the nature of the task that confronts them.

PART 1: SHORT-DISTANCE TRAVEL

METHODS OF NAVIGATION

Pheromone trails

A very simple way in which an animal can find its way is to make use of a scent trail. Some animals possess scent glands that release pheromones. This term was used first by Karlson, and Lüscher (1959) to refer to chemicals that are used for communication, through the sense of smell, among individuals of a given species. Pheromones can be released directly into the air. For example, the female silkworm moth releases the pheromone bombykol from a gland in her abdomen, and the pheromone is then carried away by air currents. If the antenna of a male should detect the pheromone, he will fly upwind until he finds the female and they will copulate. The detection of a single molecule is sufficient to encourage the male to fly, which makes the release of this particular pheromone effective over several kilometres (Shorey, 1976).

Pheromone trails can also guide animals to food. Foraging ants that have discovered a source of food deposit a recruitment trail of pheromones on the ground as they return to the nest. Once it has reached the nest, the ant performs stereotyped responses that stimulate other ants to leave the nest and to pursue the trail. As the recruited ants return to the nest, they too deposit the same pheromone, which strengthens the trail and attracts yet more foragers. As soon as the food source is depleted, the returning ants cease to secrete pheromones and the trail will gradually disappear.

The laying of a pheromone trail leads certain animals into displaying a quite unpleasant behaviour described as urine washing (Shorey, 1976). In order to mark their journey through the branches of a forest the males of some species of loris urinate onto one hand, rub their hands together, and then rub their hands on their feet. The consequent scent trails that are deposited as they move through the branches of the forest allow the route to be retraced, and also permit travel at night. Even worse, the brown bear marks its territory by rolling in its urine and then rubbing itself against a tree. A more efficient, and possibly healthier method would be to urinate directly onto the tree, but for some reason bears have yet to discover this technique.

Dead reckoning

Dead reckoning refers to the method of navigating where no reference is made to landmarks. Instead, a record is kept of one's position in respect to some reference point by taking account of the distance that has been travelled and the changes in direction that have been made. As long as these sources of information are correct, and they are combined in an appropriate manner, they should permit an accurate determination of the current position. An obvious problem with navigating in this way is that

once an error has entered into the calculations as a result of a faulty measurement, there is no means of detecting it and the navigator will have no indication of being lost. Such errors can obviously have serious consequences. In the early years of the Second World War, the pilots of Bomber Command were compelled to use dead reckoning because they could fly with safety only at night when they had no visible landmarks to guide them. The errors that crept into their navigation were occasionally so severe that they bombed cities in England believing them to be in Germany (Hastings, 1979). A more successful example of dead reckoning is described by Gallistel (1990) concerning a 19th-century sailor, Slocum. He sailed 4500 miles across the Pacific without once sighting land and correctly estimated when he was within a few hours of his destination.

The calculations involved in determining position by dead reckoning would seem to be complex but, as the following experiments show, even insects are capable of using this method. Desert ants will search for food in a rather haphazard manner and then find themselves some 100 metres from their nest. Having discovered food, they do not then return along the circuitous path of their outward journey but, instead, they head directly for the nest. One obvious explanation for the way in which they set this course is that they identify some feature associated with the nest, and then head directly towards it. There are, however, good reasons for believing that ants do not necessarily adopt this strategy. If an ant is trapped as it emerges from the nest, and is then released about 5 metres away, it shows every indication of being lost and searches for the nest in all directions (Wehner & Flatt, 1972). As Gallistel (1990, p.60) suggests, "ants do not know where they are, unless they themselves get there". He further proposes that they learn where they are by a process of dead reckoning, which can take place with considerable accuracy as the next experiment shows.

Desert ants were trained on a featureless plain to travel about 20 metres from their nest to a food source (Wehner & Srinivasan, 1981). When they were familiar with this journey, individual ants were picked up as they left the food source and transported about 600 metres before being placed on the ground. At this point, the ants behaved as if they had not been displaced at all. They headed in a compass direction that was the same as the direction of the nest from the food source. Moreover, they continued in this direction for a distance that was virtually the same as the distance between the food source and the nest. When this distance had been travelled they began to search, unsuccessfully of course, for the nest. If the ants had not been displaced, then this journey would have brought them to within half a metre of the nest. It is unreasonable to argue that the ants were following a pheromone trail in this experiment, or that they were orienting towards a particular landmark. Instead, their journey must have been guided by dead reckoning, with the distance and direction of travel being determined relative to the point of release.

Rather little is known about the way in which ants estimate distance, but the sun appears to play an important role in determining the direction in which they will travel. Santchi (1913) placed a shield between the sun and an ant that was marching in a given direction. He then reflected the sun onto the ant from a mirror placed on its opposite side, so that the position of the sun appeared to change from one side of the ant to the other. As a consequence, the ant promptly turned round and marched in the opposite direction. In the experiment by Wehner and Srinivasan (1981), it is thus likely that the position of the sun was used by the ant in order to determine in which direction it should head when it was eventually placed on the ground. Of course, journeys based on the position of the sun must take account of its movement through the sky. Jander (1957) has shown that even ants are able to make allowances for this movement. He interrupted their straight-line journeys by retaining them in a light-proof box for a number of hours. When they were released they continued to head in their original directions, despite a considerable change in the position of the sun.

Another example of dead reckoning is provided by honey-bees. These insects possess a sophisticated method of communication that permits a forager returning to the hive to indicate the distance and direction, as the crow flies, of the source of food it has just collected (see Chapter 10). Von Frisch (1950) was interested in the information that was conveyed when the forager took a detour while returning to the hive from the food source. The detour was forced by the presence of a mountain that was too high for bees to cross directly.

Von Frisch (1950) expected the bee on returning to the hive to indicate the direction and distance of either the first or the second leg of its journey. Instead it communicated the direct route to food, despite never having passed along it. The information for this communication was presumably derived from dead reckoning. Further evidence of dead reckoning in the honey-bee is provided by the fact that once a bee has communicated information about the location of a food supply, the recipients of this knowledge fly in the appropriate direction and for the appropriate distance to the food. Dead reckoning must indicate when the bee has reached the supply of food.

Dead reckoning in the ant and honey-bee is likely to depend on information acquired from the movements they initiate during their journey. Dead reckoning in other animals, gerbils and hamsters, for example, has been said to be influenced also by changes that take place in the vestibular system (Etienne, Lambert, Reverdin, & Teroni, 1993; Mittelstaedt & Mittelstaedt, 1982). To support this proposal, experimenters have moved subjects passively on a turntable in order to displace them from a goal. The subsequent return to the goal then indicated that account was taken of this movement, even though it had not been initiated by the animal. In rats, lesions of the vestibular system have been shown to disrupt their capacity for dead reckoning (Matthews, Ryu, & Bockaneck, 1989).

A series of experiments by Saint Paul (1982) provides further evidence of dead reckoning when an animal is passively transported to a release point. Furthermore, her results indicate that information about the direction and distance of travel is acquired visually. In one experiment, seven geese were taken individually in a cage similar to the one sketched in Figure 8.1 from their home (H) to a place with which they were unfamiliar (S). The dotted line in Figure 8.2 shows this journey and the arrows show the direction in

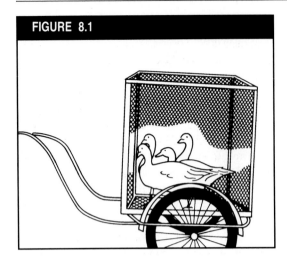

FIGURE 8.1

A sketch of the cart that was used to transport geese in the study by Saint Paul (1982) (adapted from Saint Paul, 1982).

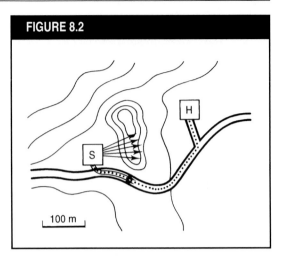

FIGURE 8.2

100 m

The departure direction of seven geese that were transported in an open cart along the route marked by the dotted line from their home, H, to the release point, S (adapted from Saint Paul, 1982).

which each goose headed when it was released from S. Two subjects started to retrace their outward route, but the remainder walked in the direction of home. Of course, those that headed in the direction of home may have been guided by a landmark that was also visible from home. Such an explanation for the initial heading of the geese is made unlikely by the results of a second group. This was treated in exactly the same way as the first group, except that the cart was covered on the outward journey. When released, these subjects showed no systematic tendency to head towards home.

Further evidence that homing by geese does not depend on orientation towards visual landmarks can be found in a second experiment by Saint Paul (1982). Geese were again transported from their home in a wheeled cage. Their home is marked by H in Figure 8.3, and they were taken to A along the route marked by the dotted line. At this point, a cover was placed over the cage and they were wheeled to B. When they were released from B, they followed the route that is marked by the dashed line in Figure 8.3. That is, they headed in the direction that would have taken them from A to H. The implication of this finding is that while travelling from H to A, the geese kept a record of their position in respect to H, based on what they

saw. This record was not altered by the journey in the covered cart, so that when they were eventually released they headed in an entirely inappropriate direction.

Piloting with a single landmark

Piloting refers to the act of setting a course to a goal on the basis of landmarks that are in a known relation to the goal. We have already seen that animals may embark on journeys without making any reference to landmarks but, perhaps not surprisingly, animals can make use of landmarks to determine both the direction and the distance that they will travel.

The simplest form of piloting would be to navigate towards a feature that was located immediately by the goal—a beacon. But very often landmarks are not conveniently situated by a goal, and their use then becomes more complicated. Two related sets of experiments have provided considerable insight into the ways in which bees (Cartwright & Collett, 1983) and gerbils (Collett, Cartwright, & Smith, 1986) use landmarks that are located at a distance from a goal.

The bees were able to enter a white room (4 metres by 4 metres) through a small opening. A single landmark was provided by a black cylinder 4 centimetres wide and 40 centimetres high, and

FIGURE 8.3

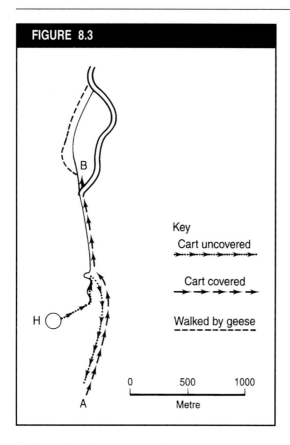

Key

Cart uncovered
▶····▷····▶····▷····▶····▷·

Cart covered
→ → → → →

Walked by geese
----

0   500   1000

Metre

The dashed line shows the route taken by two geese as they walked together from their point of release at B. They had previously been taken from their home (H) to A in an uncovered cart, and then from A to B in a covered cart (adapted from Saint Paul, 1982).

the goal consisted of a drop of sucrose solution placed on a glass slide. For the experiments with gerbils, a circular arena (3.5 metres in diameter) was used. There were black chippings on the floor that made it possible to hide a sprinkling of sunflower seeds just below the surface at a specific location. The landmark consisted of a white cylinder that was 6.3 centimetres wide and 40 centimetres high.

Both gerbils and bees were trained to find food when it was located at a given distance, for example 50 centimetres, and a given compass bearing, say due south from the landmark. Once they had been trained, then even when there was no food in the test area, they persistently searched in the correct location. It is important to note that in these studies

the position of the landmark moved from trial to trial, and that the gerbils were released from different points on the edge of the arena. Thus food could not be found simply by moving a fixed distance and at a fixed orientation from the release point. As a consequence, dead reckoning is unlikely to have guided the animals to their goal. The results suggest, instead, that the animals were using information that food was at a certain distance and a certain compass bearing from the landmark.

The authors say very little about the way in which their subjects derived information about compass bearings. One possibility is that animals have a magnetic sense that allows them to determine directions such as north. Although there are reasons for believing that bees possess a magnetic sense (Walker, Baird, & Bitterman, 1989), there is no good evidence that this source of information is available to gerbils. As an alternative, the animals may have derived their compass bearing from a relatively distant landmark, such as the entrance to the room. Suppose that food is always placed due south of the landmark, and that the entrance to the room is north of the landmark; food could then be found by searching on the side of the landmark that is furthest from the entrance. In any case, the fact the animals persistently searched in the correct location forcefully suggests that they were able to derive the direction of food in respect to the landmark.

As far as deriving information about distance is concerned, bees and gerbils appear to employ different methods. Once bees had been trained to find food at 35 centimetres from a single landmark, test trials were conducted in which the size of the landmark was varied. When the size of the landmark was halved, the bees concentrated their search in an area that was much closer to the landmark. But when the size of the landmark was doubled, they searched at a distance of greater than 35 centimetres from the landmark. On the basis of these findings Cartwright and Collett (1983) proposed that when bees are trained with a single landmark they make a record of the size of its retinal image at the goal. In other words, the bee takes a "retinal snapshot" of the landmark. On subsequent visits to the test area it will then approach the landmark from the appropriate direction and as it does so, a comparison is made between the size of the image of the landmark on the retina and its size in the retinal snapshot. When there is a close correspondence between the two, the bee will then initiate its search for the goal. Providing that the retinal snapshot is reasonably accurate, this simple method should ensure that the bee consistently and accurately returns to the goal.

When a similar experiment was conducted with gerbils, changing the size of the landmark had relatively little effect on where the search for the goal was conducted. The account for the way that bees find food with a single landmark may not, therefore, be appropriate for gerbils. Further support for this conclusion comes from an experiment in which gerbils were again trained to find food near a certain landmark. On test trials, which were conducted in the absence of food, gerbils were released and as soon as they headed towards the goal all the lights in the room were extinguished. By monitoring the movement of the gerbil with the use of infra-red light, it was found that the animal continued on its journey until it reached the correct location, whereupon it began to search for food. In some tests the gerbils covered as much as 2.5 metres yet they still managed to search in the correct region. In contrast to bees, therefore, gerbils appear to know how far they have to travel to food when they set their course on the basis of a landmark, and presumably dead reckoning can inform them when this distance has been travelled. At present we do not know how the distance that must be travelled is gauged.

Piloting with multiple landmarks

When multiple landmarks are located in a consistent relationship to a goal, a variety of ways can be used to pilot towards that goal. Bees exploit a very simple method when they are presented with three landmarks (Cartwright & Collett, 1983). Figure 8.4 shows an array of three landmarks that are each 76cm from the food source and whose compass bearings are 60°, 120°, and 180° from the food source. (For the sake of discussion, these bearings can be assumed to be in respect to the top of the page, which would then have a bearing of

0°.) Bees were readily able to learn to locate food when they were trained with this configuration. It is important to note that although the location of the array was moved from one trial to the next, throughout the experiment, its orientation remained constant. That is, from the food site, the landmarks were always oriented with respect to north as shown in Figure 8.4. There were two types of test trial in this experiment. On some occasions, the distance of the landmarks from the goal was altered, while maintaining their size. On other occasions, the size of the landmarks was altered, while holding their distance from the goal constant. In the light of the results described in the previous section, it is interesting to note that neither of these manipulations had any substantial effect. The bees continued to search in a location that was defined simply by its compass bearings from the three landmarks.

The presence of multiple landmarks, therefore, appears to render their retinal size relatively unimportant as cues for navigation. What seems to be important is their compass bearing from the goal. Thus Cartwright and Collett (1983) have proposed that when a bee is at the goal, it makes a record of the compass bearing of each landmark. On returning to the area in the future, it will then

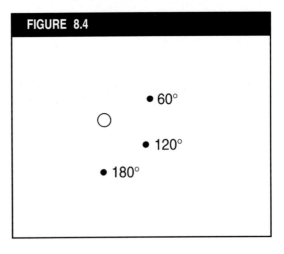

FIGURE 8.4

Plan of the room used by Cartwright and Collett (1983) to study the way in which bees use three landmarks to identify the location of food. The bees were able to enter the room through a small opening. The open circle depicts the location of food, the filled circles depict the three landmarks (adapted from Cartwright & Collet, 1983).

search until it is in a position where the compass bearings of the landmarks match this record. An important feature of this account is that the bee is assumed to rely exclusively on compass bearings, that is bearings in respect to a feature that lies beyond the landmarks themselves. This proposal was tested by repeating the experiment, with the simple change that the orientation of the array depicted in Figure 8.4 varied randomly during training. Thus only occasionally was the angle between the top landmark and north 60°. Each of the three bees that were trained in this way failed completely to show any sign of searching in the correct region for food. The failure of the bees to locate the food suggests, therefore, that they were unable to use information about the relative position of one landmark to another to identify where food could be found.

An experiment with gerbils indicates that, in contrast to bees, they can use information about the relative position of a number of landmarks. Subjects were trained to find food at a point that was near two landmarks. This point is marked by F in Figure 8.5a, which represents the test apparatus; the positions of the landmarks are identified by two circles. Test trials were then given in which one landmark was removed (Figure 8.5b), or the landmarks were placed further apart (Figure 8.5c). With only a single landmark present the subjects searched in the regions marked by S, which were either to the south-west or south-east

of the landmark. This finding suggests that the animals knew about the direction and distance of food from the landmarks, but they did not know which landmark they were being tested with. The results from the test trial with the separated landmarks show that the gerbils again searched in two places, which were defined by the direction and distance of the goal from each of the two landmarks during the training stage. An important implication of this finding is that the landmarks were not treated independently. Thus the gerbils searched to the south-west of the eastern landmark, and to the south-east of the western landmark. Had the landmarks not been identified by their relative position, then the gerbils would have searched both to the south-west and south-east of each landmark.

These findings, together with those from related studies, led Collett et al. (1986) to conclude that gerbils use vectors based on individual landmarks to define the location of a goal. These vectors may be based on a compass bearing, so that they would be of the form "food is at a certain distance and in a certain direction from the landmark". Or, when more than one landmark is available, they may be based on information about the relationship among landmarks. For the experiment just described this might be of the form "food is at a certain distance to the south-west of the easternmost landmark and a certain distance to the south-east of the westernmost landmark". On the basis of his experiments with pigeons, Cheng (1994) has also

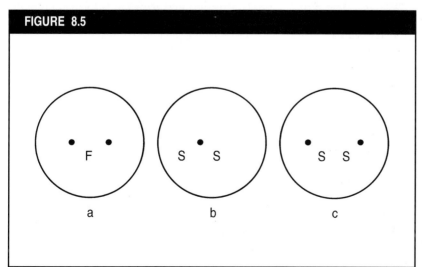

FIGURE 8.5

a
b
c

Plan of the test arena used by Collett et al. (1986) to study the way in which gerbils use two landmarks to locate a hidden source of food (F). One circle (a) depicts the arena used for training the gerbils. The two other circles depict where the gerbils searched (S) for food on test trials with a single landmark (circle b) or with the landmarks more widely separated than during training (circle c) (adapted from Collet et al., 1986).

found that these animals pilot on the basis of information about the relationship among a number of landmarks.

Use of geometric relations

When two or more landmarks are present, they create a geometric shape. Two landmarks create a line, three a triangle, and so forth. A question that has been asked on a number of occasions is whether animals are able to detect this geometric information and to use it to define the location of a goal. For example, in the previous experiment, food in the training stage was near the mid-point of the line between the two landmarks. If this geometric information had been used to define the location of the goal, then on the test trial with the separated landmarks searching would have been concentrated on the region at the mid-point between them. The failure to search in this single place does not mean that gerbils are insensitive to geometric information, some aspect of their training may have discouraged them from utilising it on this occasion. The results that are about to be described from experiments with wasps, rats, and chicks demonstrate that a wide range of species can make use of geometric information.

After laying her eggs in a hole that she has dug in the ground the female digger wasp flies in a series of loops around the hole before departing in search of food. Once a suitable prey has been captured, it is carried some tens of metres to the hole, where it is buried with the eggs (Tinbergen, 1951). In order to determine how the wasp is able to identify the location of the hole from such a distance, a series of experiments was conducted with pine cones. While the wasp was in her hole, Tinbergen (1951) formed a circle of 20 pine cones around its entrance. Then, after the wasp had departed in search of prey, he moved the circle about a foot away from the hole without distorting its shape. On her return the wasp went to the centre of the pine cone circle, which suggests she was using the cones as landmarks to identify her nesting hole.

In a variant of this experiment, Van Beusekom (1948) also constructed a circle of pine cones around the hole while the wasp was in it, but as soon as she flew away, he constructed either a square or an ellipse of cones beside the circle. On returning, the wasp went to the circle rather than to the square, but she selected the circle and the ellipse equally often. This discovery indicates that during her initial flight around the hole the wasp remembers the shape created by the cones. Evidently the representation of this shape is sufficiently precise to permit a distinction between a circle and a square but not between a circle and an ellipse.

A series of experiments by Cheng (1986) shows how rats use geometric information. The experimental apparatus consisted of a black rectangular box with a distinctive panel in each corner. The panels, which were employed as landmarks, differed on the basis of their texture, smell, and visual appearance. The floor of the box was covered with wood chippings to a sufficient depth to allow food to be hidden below their surface. Finally, the entire apparatus was housed in a black sound-attenuating chamber that restricted the sensory information that could be derived from the room in which the experiment was conducted.

On each trial, the rat was placed into the chamber and allowed to explore until it found a small supply of food randomly located on the surface of the floor. After eating the food, the rat was removed from the chamber and placed a short time later into an exact replica of the first chamber with food in the same place, as defined by its relation to the four landmarks, but this time the food was hidden.

The rats searched predominantly in two places on the test trials. They searched either in the correct location or they made, almost as often, what were called *rotational errors*. That is, the rat searched in a place that was diagonally opposite to the correct location. This pattern of results would not be expected if the rats identified the location of food on the basis of the information provided by the landmarks, either individually or as a configuration. Instead, the results suggest that the rat used the shape of the training chamber to define where food was located. When the rat was put into the test chamber there would be two places where food could possibly be buried. According to Gallistel (1990), this preference for only two sites indicates that the rats were able to appreciate the difference between the lengths of the two walls, and that they also have an appreciation of a sense relation (left–right). Thus this experiment provides a clear demonstration that rats are sensitive to the geometric relations contained in the shape of their test environment. The experiment also shows that rats may prefer to use the shape of the test chamber, rather than the landmarks, to define a particular place. We do not know if rats will always display this preference when either type of information can be used to define a particular location, but see Cheng (1986) for additional evidence for the importance of information about the shape of the test area.

Using a similar procedure to that developed by Cheng (1986), Vallortigara, Zanforlin, and Pasti (1990) have shown that recently hatched chicks learn about both landmarks and shape cues when they are trained to find food in an enclosed environment. The apparatus again consisted of a large rectangular chamber with a distinctive landmark in each corner. For their training the chicks were required to find food that was always buried beneath the sawdust floor in the same corner, and beside the same landmark, X. Test trials were then conducted with no food in the chamber. When the apparatus was the same as for the training trials, the chicks consistently searched in the place where food was originally buried. Furthermore, if landmark X was exchanged with the landmark in the diametrically opposite corner, or it was moved to an adjacent corner, then the chicks continued to search near this landmark. Overall, these results indicate that searching by the chicks was controlled by landmark X, no matter what its relationship was with the other landmarks or with the shape of the test chamber.

It would be a mistake to conclude, however, that the chicks were insensitive to the shape of the apparatus. When they were tested with the four landmarks removed, they searched either in the corner where food was normally found, or they made rotational errors and searched in the diametrically opposite corner. Thus chicks can make use of geometric information, but they appear to ignore it when a single landmark can be used to identify the position of food.

HIPPOCAMPAL PLACE CELLS

The results that have been reviewed so far demonstrate forcefully that a specific location can be identified by animals in a variety of ways. This conclusion is further supported by some remarkable findings that have been obtained by recording the activity of nerve cells in a particular region of the brain—the hippocampus. By inserting a small electrode into a single hippocampal cell its electrical activity can be recorded as the animal, normally a rat or a rabbit, moves freely around its environment (O'Keefe, 1979). In a study by O'Keefe and Speakman (1987), rats were trained to find food in the simple maze depicted in Figure 8.6 overleaf. The maze was an elevated wooden cross located in a circular enclosure created from curtains (see Figure 8.7). There were a number of landmarks in the enclosure, which included a cage of two rats, a white card, a light, a fan, a black towel, and an aromatic pen. On any trial, the relationship between the maze and these landmarks remained constant, so that food was always presented at the end of the arm that had the white card on its left and the light on its right. However, the entire configuration of landmarks and the maze itself was rotated from one trial to the next. On any trial a rat would be released from a randomly selected arm and it was expected to run to the goal in order to obtain food. Subjects became adept at this task, which indicates that they used the information provided by the landmarks to identify the location of the goal.

By recording the activity of different cells in the hippocampus, O'Keefe and Speakman (1987) were able to identify a number of "place" cells. These cells were normally inactive, but as the rat passed through a specific part of the maze they fired at a high rate. Figure 8.8 shows the regions of the maze that produced a high rate of firing in two different cells. For one cell, a high burst of activity was recorded only in the goal arm, whereas the second cell fired maximally when the rat was in the arm that was to the left of the goal arm. In both cases, it did not matter in which compass direction the arm was pointing. Thus the cues provided by the

Plan of an elevated maze and the surrounding room used in the experiment by O'Keefe and Speakman (1987) to study the reaction of hippocampal place cells as rats moved through the maze (adapted from O'Keefe & Speakman, 1987).

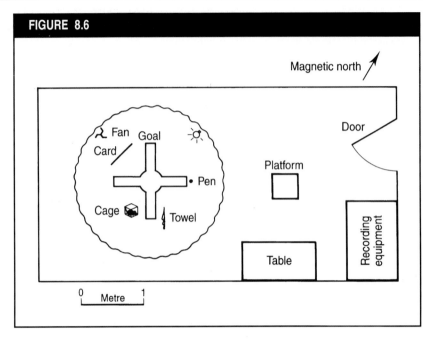

FIGURE 8.6

Magnetic north

Fan Goal

Card

Pen

Cage

Towel

Platform

Door

Recording equipment

Table

0 Metre 1

FIGURE 8.7

A rat exploring an elevated cross maze.

FIGURE 8.8

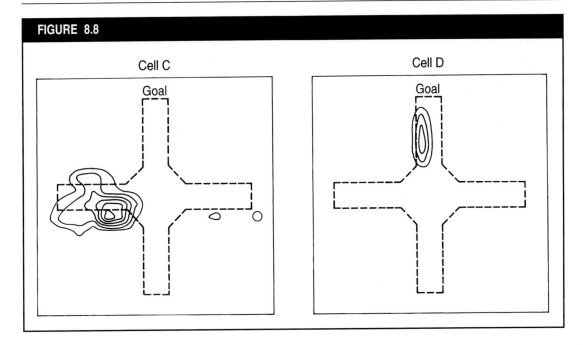

Regions of an elevated maze that produced activity in two different hippocampal cells of a rat. The regions extend further than the maze itself because the rat was able to move its head freely beyond the sides of the apparatus (from O'Keefe & Speakman, 1987).

room, or the orientation of the maze in respect to the room, did not control the activity of the place cells. Instead, the determinant of responding was the position of the arm relative to the landmarks.

By selectively removing landmarks while the animal is in the goal arm, it should be possible to derive a more detailed understanding of the pattern of stimulation that controls the activity of the place cell. Although this strategy was not adopted in the study just referred to, it was employed in a very similar experiment in which there were four landmarks (O'Keefe & Conway, 1978). Removal of the landmarks revealed that some cells depended on one or two specific landmarks in order to be activated, whereas other cells would fire provided any two of the four landmarks were present. A more recent study has shown that certain hippocampal cells are controlled by cues that lie beyond the immediate environment of the maze (O'Keefe & Speakman, 1987). For example, firing was observed whenever the rat entered a particular location in the room, no matter what the configuration of the local landmarks. If these findings have any implications for the way in

which animals represent spatial information, then they confirm the conclusion that can be drawn from the previous sections of this chapter: A variety of potential sources of information can be used to define a specific location.

A further stage of the experiment by O'Keefe and Speakman (1987) demonstrates that the continued presence of the relevant landmarks is not always essential for the firing of place cells. In this stage, the rat was placed on the start arm and prevented from leaving it for about 90 seconds. During the first minute of this period the landmarks could be seen in their correct location, after which they were all removed from the apparatus. The animal was then allowed to leave the start arm, and to select the arm that led to the goal. Even though this choice was determined by cues that were no longer present, subjects were readily able to identify the correct arm. Of more importance, however, was the finding that some of the place cells that were normally controlled by the landmarks continued to fire when the rat entered the appropriate location in the maze. Note, however, that the normal pattern of firing of the place cells was seriously disrupted if the animals were placed into the apparatus in the absence of any landmarks. The firing of the place cells on the memory trial was therefore not due to the influence of some additional landmark that the experimenters failed to remove.

These findings, more than any other, justify naming the relevant hippocampal cells as "place" cells. The findings indicate that the firing of a cell does not require the presence of a particular stimulus, or set of stimuli. Rather, these stimuli are necessary only to define a particular place in the animal's environment. Once this place has been identified it will serve to activate the relevant place cell whenever the animal enters it.

COGNITIVE MAPS

A currently popular proposal is that not only do animals have the ability to define specific places within their environment, but they may also integrate the information about a number of places into a cognitive map (Gallistel, 1990; O'Keefe & Nadel, 1978; Tolman, Ritchie, & Kalish, 1946). Definitions of a cognitive map tend to be rather formal and thus they may not always be easy to understand. A cognitive map has been said to provide animals with

a maplike representation which acts as a framework for organizing its sensory inputs and is perceived as remaining stationary in spite of the movements of the organism (O'Keefe & Nadel, 1979, p.488).

a record in the central nervous system of macroscopic geometric relations among surfaces in the environment used to plan movements through the environment (Gallistel, 1990, p.103).

a global representation of objects within some manifold or coordinate system from which their mutual spatial relationships can be derived but that is, to some extent, independent of the objects themselves (Leonard & McNaughton, 1990, p.365).

Rather than dwell on the interpretation of these definitions, it would not be too misleading to suggest that a cognitive map is rather like an aerial view or plan of the space that is being represented. Very often, the claim that animals possess a cognitive map leads to the same predictions as simpler explanations for their spatial behaviour. There are, however, at least two ways in which an animal that has acquired a cognitive map will be at an advantage over one that has not. One advantage is that such a map should allow an animal to select a novel route to a goal. Another advantage is that the possession of a cognitive map may help it to make a detour around an obstacle.

The selection of a novel route

The earlier discussion of dead reckoning revealed how it is possible for an animal to select a novel route in order to return to where it started its journey. The animal is able to achieve this because dead reckoning allows it to keep a record of its current position in respect to the point where the journey commenced. However, if an animal possesses a cognitive map, then not only should it be able to return directly to the starting point of its present journey, it should also be able to move directly to any place in the environment that is represented on the map. An early attempt to demonstrate this influence of a cognitive map was conducted by Tolman et al. (1946).

A hungry rat was placed into the maze shown on the left-hand side of Figure 8.9 at point A; it then had to pass points C, D, E, F, and G to reach the goal containing food. Once subjects were practised at running along this route, they were placed again at A for a trial in which the maze had been modified to the form depicted on the right-hand side of the figure. On this occasion the original exit from the maze was blocked, and 18 alternative exits were added. Tolman et al. (1946) argued that if animals possessed a cognitive map of the maze, then on the test trial they should be able to deduce from it the direction of the goal relative to the arena and select the exit that most closely corresponded with this direction. On this basis animals were expected to leave the arena through Exit 5.

In support of the claim that rats possess cognitive maps, the majority of subjects did indeed

FIGURE 8.9

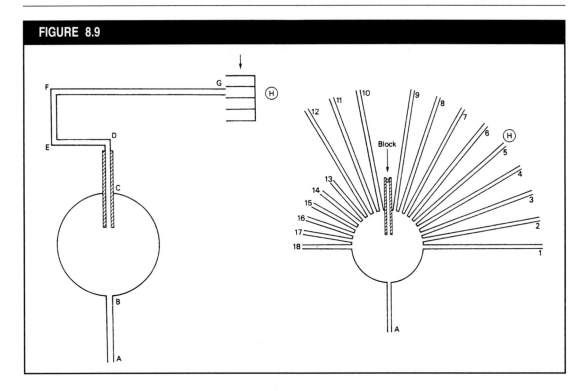

Plans of the mazes used in the two stages of the experiment by Tolman et al. (1946). Throughout the experiment a light bulb was located at H (from Tolman et al., 1946).

leave by Exit 5. But there is a serious shortcoming with the design of this experiment. Throughout the study there was a light bulb, H, suspended over the goal, which was visible from all points of the maze. During their training, rats may have associated the light with food, and on the test trial selected the path that led most directly to it. That is, piloting with the use of a single landmark, rather than taking advantage of a cognitive map, may have been responsible for the result of this experiment.

A study by Morris (1981) provides one of the better attempts to eliminate piloting as a possible means for selecting a novel route. To avoid the problem of giving the location of the goal away by a specific cue, a vat (1.3 metres in diameter) of milky water was used as the maze, and a platform submerged just below the surface was the goal. The apparatus was located in a room with a number of distinctive features that the rat could use as landmarks. After being placed into the vat for several trials, rats soon learned to swim directly to the platform, provided that it remained in the same

position from one trial to the next (see Figures 8.10 and 8.11). To explain this successful detection of the invisible goal, Morris (1981) argued that as a result of their initial training subjects formed a cognitive map. This might represent the position of the platform in the vat and also include features of the experimental room. When placed into the vat, the subject would have to identify its location on the map and then deduce the direction in which to swim to reach the platform.

As a test of this argument, rats were trained to swim to the platform from a specific point on the edge of the vat. The position of the platform was also constant for this training. They were then divided into three groups for testing. Group Control received the same treatment as for the previous stage; Group New-Place was placed at the original point of release and had to find the platform in a new location; and Group Same-Place was required to swim from a novel starting point to the platform, which was not moved. The routes taken by each rat from the time it was released until

FIGURE 8.10

A rat exploring a water maze.

FIGURE 8.11

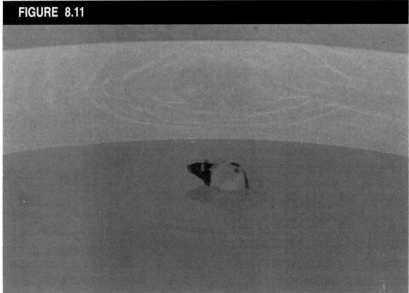

A rat resting on a submerged platform after swimming to it from a release point at the side of a water maze.

the platform was discovered are shown in Figure 8.12.

The control group performed the task without difficulty and swam directly to the platform. The performance for Group New-Place suggests that their problem was very difficult. After a period of swimming around the original location of the goal, the behaviour of these animals was essentially without direction until they came upon the goal by chance. This finding confirms that there were no

hidden cues to give away the position of the platform. The results for rats in Group Same-Place lie between these extremes. They located the platform without too much difficulty, which Morris (1981) regards as evidence that they possessed a cognitive map.

A careful inspection of Figure 8.12 suggests, however, that this conclusion may be unwarranted. Apart from Subject 1, all the animals in Group Same-Place started off by swimming in the wrong

FIGURE 8.12

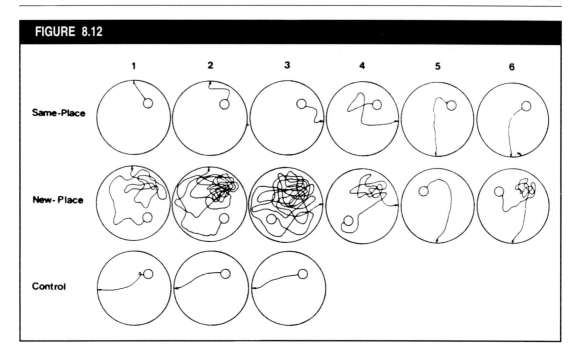

A vertical view of the routes taken on the first test trial by all the rats in the three groups of the study by Morris (1981) (from Morris, 1981).

direction, and there is no obvious reason why the possession of a cognitive map should result in this incorrect behaviour. Admittedly, the rats soon adjusted their course, but this does not provide compelling evidence for the use of a cognitive map. During their training rats will doubtless approach the platform from many angles, and they may well learn a variety of routes to the goal. The landmarks of these routes would be provided by the various configurations of external cues, and success in finding the platform would depend on nothing more than learning to swim in a certain direction relative to a specific landmark. In other words, learning to find the platform may involve nothing more than learning a number of different heading vectors. On the test trial Group Same-Place might set off in a randomly determined direction and swim until a familiar landmark was perceived. At this point they could adjust their course and swim towards the platform. I am not sure how seriously this account should be taken, but Sutherland, Chew, Baker, and Linggard (1987) have shown that place navigation in a water maze is inaccurate when a novel starting point is located on an

unfamiliar route. Thus, if nothing else, the study by Morris (1981) demonstrates that even with a well-designed experiment, convincing evidence for the existence and operation of a cognitive map is hard to obtain.

With this caution in mind we can turn to a study by Gould (1986), which examined whether or not honey-bees possess a cognitive map. Bees were trained to fly from a hive (see the map in Figure 8.13) to a feeding station at A. For testing they were captured as they left the hive and transported in a dark container to a novel place, B, where they were released. All subjects left B in the direction of A and all arrived at A. Moreover, the time taken by many of them suggests that they barely deviated from the straight line between these points. The explanation developed by Gould (1986) for these findings is very similar to one offered by Morris (1981): The honey-bees were assumed to have a cognitive map of the area around the hive and used it to deduce the direction in which they must fly from B in order to get to the food. It is also important to note that when the bees were released from B, the slope of the field was such that they

FIGURE 8.13

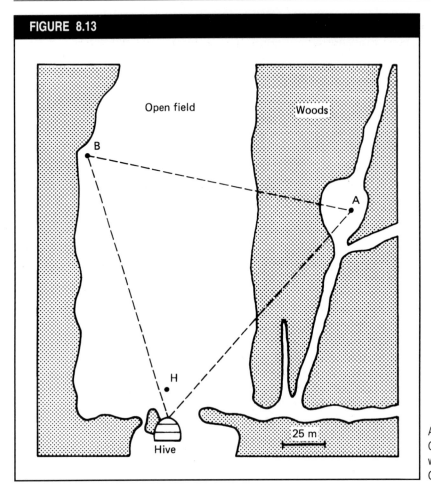

A map of the area used by Gould (1986) for his study with bees (adapted from Gould, 1986).

could not see any of the features surrounding A. Thus it is unlikely that the bees solved this problem by approaching a landmark near the goal. In addition, as there is no reason for believing that the honey-bees had learned to go directly from B to A for food, an explanation for these findings in terms of following a previously learned route is also unacceptable (Gould, 1986).

Not surprisingly, perhaps, the suggestion that honey-bees possess a cognitive map has not gone unchallenged (Dyer, 1991; Menzel, 1990). As an alternative explanation for the findings by Gould (1986), Dyer developed the ideas of Cartwright and Collett (1983) and proposed that bees navigate by travelling at certain angles to the succession of landmarks they encounter on the way to the goal. Consider again the experiment by Gould (1986). Inspection of Figure 8.13 should make it evident

that landmarks, such as the edge of the woods, that were visible from the release site B were also visible from the hive. According to Dyer (1991), the honey-bees would have been able to reach their goal from B simply by using information based on the position and angle at which they normally enter the woods from the hive. This explanation may appear straightforward, but appearances in this instance are deceptive. Gould (1992) and Gallistel (1994) both have shown that in order to determine the route in which to fly from B, the bees would have to perform calculations of considerable complexity. They would also need all the directional information that would be contained in a cognitive map. As a consequence, it is difficult at present to decide if bees used a cognitive map to fly from B, or whether they used a method more similar to that proposed by Dyer (1991). If the results of the next experiment are accepted, then the balance of evidence supports the explanation based on the use of a cognitive map.

Gould (1984) cites a study by Dyer in which foragers were trained to collect food from a boat at the point marked *lake station* in Figure 8.14. On returning to the hive they were unable to attract any recruits with their dance to indicate where the food was located. When the boat was moved to the *shore station*, however, returning foragers were able to send substantial numbers of recruits to collect food. According to Gould (1984, 1988), the explanation for these findings is that bees possess a map of the area around the hive, and when the direction and distance of food is communicated to them by a forager, they identify its position on this map. Because food, for bees, is never found in the middle

of lakes, it would be foolish to leave the hive when the map indicated this to be its predicted location. On the other hand, when food is indicated as being on the far side of the lake, then it makes good sense to search for it. Provided that this result is reliable and not open to alternative interpreta- tion, it provides compelling evidence that bees, at least, possess cognitive maps.

Detour studies

A second strategy that may demonstrate the operation of a cognitive map is first to show the animal a goal and then to place it behind a barrier some distance away. If the subject should select the correct, shortest route to the goal, then this may be because it possesses a cognitive map of the prob- lem area and uses it to determine how to respond.

FIGURE 8.14

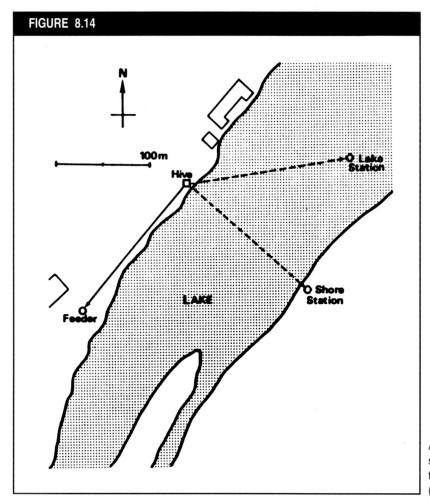

A map of the lake and surrounding area used for the study with bees by Dyer (from Gould, 1984).

FIGURE 8.15

Plans of the apparatus used in the detour studies by Kohler (1925), not to scale. The dogs were placed initially near S and food was near F (adapted from Kohler, 1925).

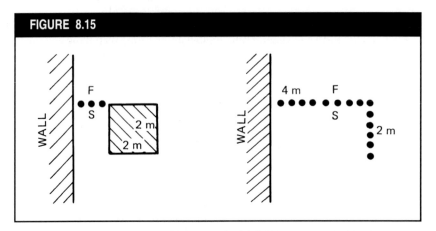

FIGURE 8.16

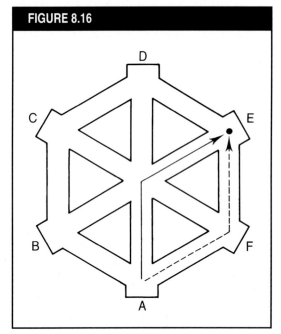

A plan of the circular maze used by Chapuis and Scardigli (1993) to study the way in which hamsters solve detour problems (adapted from Chapuis & Scardigli, 1993).

Figure 8.15 shows the sort of apparatus used by Kohler (1925), who was one of the first to study detour problems. The subject was placed behind the bars at S and could see food being placed on the other side at F. When dogs were tested, their behaviour depended very much on the distance of the food from the barrier. If the food was some distance away, then the dog would immediately run in a smooth loop around the barrier to collect it. When the food was placed by the fence, then the dog would run directly towards it and stay there even though the food was inaccessible.

In describing these experiments, Kohler (1925) failed to provide any indication of the previous training or experiences of the dogs. They may have encountered many natural detour problems and solved them by trial and error. The transfer of learning about these previous successes to the test trial would then account for the animals' behaviour.

A more useful demonstration of the ability of animals to solve detour problems is reported by Chapuis and Scardigli (1993). A plan of their apparatus is shown in Figure 8.16, which can best be described as a collection of alley-ways and chambers joined together in the shape of a wheel. In one experiment, a hamster was placed into Chamber A, and it had to pass along the route identified by the dotted line to obtain food in Chamber E. Locked doors prevented the subject from deviating from this route. After a number of sessions of this training, all the doors in the apparatus were unlocked except the one that allowed the animal to leave Chamber A on its

normal route to food. If hamsters are able to calculate the shortest detour to food, then they should pass along the route marked by the solid line in Figure 8.16. For the three test trials that were conducted, hamsters selected this route significantly more frequently than would be expected on the basis of chance.

An important feature of this experiment is that during the training phase, the maze was rotated relative to the room from one trial to the next. In addition, the chamber that served as the start of the route (Chamber A), was varied from trial to trial. The success of the animals on this detour problem was thus not due to them orienting towards landmarks that lay beyond, or within the maze. A more plausible explanation is that the hamsters formed a map of the shape of their route during the training stage, and then used this map to plot their course to the goal on the test trial.

Before closing this discussion of detour studies, mention should be made of a further study by Kohler (1925), which suggests that chickens may not share the capacity of hamsters to solve detour problems. The chickens were tested in a similar way to the dogs, but they rarely solved the problem. Instead, they persistently tried to reach the food by pushing through the barrier, as Kohler (1925, p.20) comments: "Some particularly ungifted specimens keep on running up against the fence a long while even in the simplest predicaments". Indeed, the chickens were successful only when their attempts to pass through the barrier led them by chance to pass around it. There is little here to encourage the hope that chickens can acquire cognitive maps.

Cognitive maps and the radial maze

In Chapter 6 a number of experiments were described that used a radial maze. In case the details of this apparatus have been forgotten, it is composed of a number of arms, usually 8, that radiate from a central platform and have a small amount of food at the end. When a well-trained rat is placed into this apparatus it will retrieve all the food and make very few errors of running down the same arm more than once. Successful performance on the radial maze has been said to depend on the utilisation of a cognitive map (Gallistel, 1990; Roberts, 1984; Suzuki, Augerinos, & Black, 1980). A cognitive map could be used to keep a record of the arms that have been visited and to guide the subject away from them in the future.

An alternative explanation for the way in which rats solve radial maze problems was first proposed by Olton and Samuelson (1976; see also Brown, 1992, 1993). According to this account, when a rat retrieves food from the end of a maze, it remembers the configuration of landmarks that surround that end. On returning to the central platform, the rat will choose an arm at random and look towards the end. If the landmarks at the end are recognised as

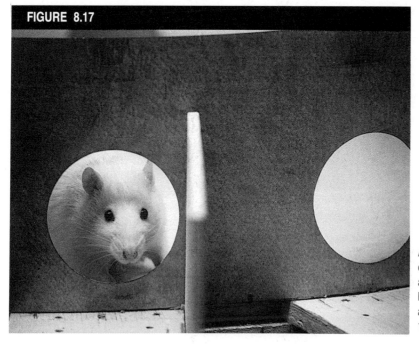

FIGURE 8.17

A rat engaged in visual orientation towards the end of an arm in a radial maze that Brown (1992) defines as a microchoice (from Brown, 1992).

ones that have been recently approached, then the rat will reject the arm and seek an alternative. This account has been difficult to test, because it is normally hard to tell when a rat is looking down an arm. However, Brown (1992) required rats to make what he called a microchoice, or observing response, of peering through a hole (see Figure 8.17), before they entered an arm. He discovered that observing responses were directed to arms on an essentially random basis, which would not be expected if performance was guided by a cognitive map.

But the story does not end here. The results of a more recent study indicate that in certain circumstances the selection of the arms of a radial maze is governed by a cognitive map (Brown, Rish, Von Culin, & Edberg, 1993). Rats were trained in the 12-arm radial maze shown in Figure 8.18,

FIGURE 8.18

The apparatus used by Brown et al. (1993) in order to prevent rats from seeing any extramaze cues when they are confined in the central arena of a radial maze. In order to enter an arm, the rat is required to push open a plywood door that is hinged at the top (from Brown, 1992).

which was unusual because the central platform was contained within a large circular enclosure that prevented rats from seeing the landmarks surrounding the maze. To enter an arm it was necessary to push open a door. In the first half of the trial all the doors were locked, and one door at a time was opened until the rat had been forced to enter 6 arms. The rat was then removed from the maze and returned to the central arena 15 minutes later. At this point, all the doors were unlocked and the rat was required to visit the remaining 6 arms if it was to retrieve the maximum amount of food. Instead of selecting from the 12 arms at random, the rats displayed a strong preference for the arms that remained to be visited. Because the landmarks surrounding these arms could not be seen from the central arena, Brown et al. (1993) conclude that the animals made their choice by consulting a cognitive map. Presumably, the rats oriented themselves with respect to this map as they were returned to the apparatus for the test trials.

There is, therefore, some reason for believing that rats, and honey-bees, acquire cognitive maps. But even if we accept this conclusion, there remain a number of problems with the use of this term. One justification for attributing an experimental outcome to the existence of a cognitive map is that it provides a parsimonious, or simple, account of the animal's behaviour (Menzel, 1978; Morris, 1981). The ease of invoking a cognitive map as an explanation, however, is partly illusory; the explanation seems simple only because it directs attention away from certain very important questions. If it is accepted that an animal possesses a cognitive map, then we need to know how it is constructed, how the animal knows where it is located on the map, and how the map is used to determine the route that is taken. Until these questions can be answered satisfactorily, accounts of behaviour in terms of cognitive maps must be seen as incomplete. At present we are a considerable distance from answering any of them.

PART 2: LONG-DISTANCE TRAVEL

Some of the most remarkable feats of animal navigation are revealed by their capacity to travel long distances, often towards a very localised goal. On some journeys animals find their way to a specific goal, even though they have never previously visited it. They are also able to find their way home over hundreds of miles when they are released in unfamiliar territory. In order to understand how animals are capable of these achievements, the following discussion will look at studies of homing and migration. Both homing and migration have been said to depend on the capacity of animals to detect sources of stimulation that are undetectable by humans. The first part of this section will therefore consider whether or not animals are indeed sensitive to these sources of information.

NAVIGATIONAL CUES

Magnetic fields

Animals might benefit from being able to detect magnetic fields, because the magnetic properties of the earth provide a pervasive source of information for orientation. We have already come across the suggestion that this information would be useful for travelling short journeys, and a number of authors have suggested it would also help with navigation for longer journeys. Thus both Yeagley (1947) and Keeton (1974) have suggested that pigeon homing relies on information provided by the earth's magnetic field. In support of this proposal, pigeon homing is less accurate when there is a magnetic storm (Gould, 1982), or when they are in the vicinity of anomalies in the earth's magnetic field (Walcott, 1978). On the other hand, with a single exception (Bookman, 1977), experimental tests for the ability of pigeons to detect magnetic fields in the laboratory have been unsuccessful. A special section in the 1987 edition of the journal *Animal learning and behavior*, for example, cites four unsuccessful attempts to show that pigeons possess a magnetic sense. There were also two reports of a similar failure with the South American bush opposum and the hamster. In these studies, a change in strength of a magnetic field signalled the availability of reward for making an instrumental response. The possibility is raised, therefore, that pigeons possess a magnetic sense, but they have difficulty in learning about the significance of this information when it signals a US such as shock or food. After all, a change in a magnetic field is hardly likely to signal these events naturally, and it is plausible that animals lack the processes that would allow good conditioning with a magnetic field in an artificial environment. Alternatively, there is good evidence that honey-bees can respond to magnetic field stimuli that signal the imminent delivery of shock. Such learning is confined to flying honey-bees (Walker et al., 1989), which leaves open the possibility that conditioning with pigeons, and even mammals, will be successful with magnetic fields once the correct techniques have been discovered.

Air pressure

A change in altitude will necessarily be accompanied by a change in air pressure. Accordingly, any animals, but in particular birds, that possess the capacity to detect and remember levels of air pressure should be able to compute their altitude. In order to demonstrate that pigeons are capable of utilising this source of information, Delius and Emmerton (1978) used a 10-second change in air pressure to signal the delivery of electric shock. As conditioning progressed, a CR of accelerated heart rate was recorded whenever this stimulus was presented. The change in pressure was slight and indicates that pigeons are sensitive to changes in air pressure that correspond to a vertical displacement of as little as 20 metres.

Rapid fluctuations in air pressure constitute

sound, and if they are of sufficient intensity and within a range of 20–20,000Hz, they will be heard by humans. Below the lower threshold of human hearing, however, there are slowly oscillating changes in air pressure with a frequency as low as 0.1Hz that may be detected by other species. These *infrasounds* can be generated by thunderstorms, magnetic storms, earthquakes, and the impact of air currents on mountain ranges. One important property of infrasound is that it can travel many thousands of kilometres with little attenuation or distortion. Hence sonic booms generated by Concorde crossing the Atlantic have been recorded in New York from a distance of 1000 kilometres (Balachandran, Dunn, & Rind, 1977).

Kreithen (1978) has noted that an ability to detect infrasound would provide valuable meteorological and navigational information for animals. In order to test whether pigeons are sensitive to this sort of stimulation, Yodlowski, Kreithen, and Keeton (1977) conducted a conditioning study in which a burst of infrasound, with a frequency of 0.1Hz, served as a CS paired with shock. Even though the infrasound was inaudible to humans, conditioning with the pigeons was successful.

Pigeons are thus capable of detecting infrasound, but there may be limitations to the use of this source of information, especially for navigation. Infrasound is prone to severe interference by local winds and turbulence, and its source would also be extremely difficult for a stationary animal to localise. Unless animals possess mechanisms for circumventing these problems, infrasound would not be a useful tool for navigation. None the less, as Baker (1984) points out, pigeons would be unlikely to be able to perceive infrasound unless it serves some purpose; and Quine (1982) shows how it would be possible for birds to use infrasound for navigation.

Polarised and ultraviolet light

Human sight is insensitive both to polarised and to ultraviolet light, and for a while it was thought that this constraint applied to all vertebrates. In contrast, insects such as bees have been known for some time to be able to detect both types of light (e.g. Von Frisch, 1950). But a report by Kreithen (1978) now suggests that one vertebrate, the pigeon again, can detect and be conditioned with ultraviolet as well as with polarised light. With both classes of stimuli a CR of an accelerated heart rate was detected when they were used to signal the occurrence of an electric shock. An ability to perceive polarised light is of value for navigation, providing some blue sky is visible, because it allows the sun to be located when it is obscured by clouds. Whether pigeons use it in this way remains to be seen.

HOMING

Homing refers to the ability of animals to return to their nest or loft when they have been taken some distance from it and released. Very often this journey involves travelling across unfamiliar territory. Matthews (1955) has reported that a Manx shearwater released from Boston, Massachusetts, flew more than 3000 miles in 12 days to return to its nest in South Wales. The albatross has been known to home successfully over distances of greater than 4100 miles (Kenyon & Rice, 1958). The feats of the most famous homing bird, the pigeon, do not compare with these reports in terms of distance, but that they can return to their loft on the same day that they are released some 600 miles away is no small achievement (Keeton, 1974). Homing is not confined to birds. Missouri cave bats were able to find their way back to a barn in which they nested, after they had been released 75 miles away in unfamiliar territory (Gunier & Elder, 1971).

Animals are able to use a variety of strategies for homing. To give an indication of these stategies, we will examine a number of explanations that have been developed to account for the homing skills of pigeons.

The use of landmarks

Homing is very much more successful after pigeons have been allowed to explore the area around their loft. This may permit them to identify its location relative to prominent landmarks. Should they then be released from within sight of these landmarks they will be able to use them to

guide their journey towards the loft. In addition, when pigeons are repeatedly released from a distant location, in circumstances that are designed to disrupt their homing ability, they show a marked improvement over successive journeys. This improvement is very likely to reflect a growing reliance on landmarks. According to Bingman (1990), the disruptive conditions include interfering with the sense of smell, anomalies in the earth's magnetic field, and clock-shifting (which will be discussed shortly).

There are, however, good reasons for believing that pigeons are able to home accurately without the use of landmarks. In a study by Keeton (1974), great care was taken to ensure that pigeons were released more than 50 miles from familiar territory. It is highly unlikely that they could perceive any familiar landmarks when released, yet they were able to home without difficulty.

In a more ingenious test of the hypothesis that use of landmarks is not essential for successful homing, Schlicte and Schmidt-Koenig (1971) fitted pigeons with frosted contact lenses. These allowed light to pass through, but the identification of landmarks was restricted to 6 metres. In spite of this enormous handicap, when the pigeons were released 80 miles from their loft they rapidly oriented in the correct direction, and a number actually managed to return. It is well worth reporting Keeton's (1974) observations of the behaviour of the successful birds on their return home, because they strongly imply that homing is possible without the use of landmarks (p.91):

> It was a truly remarkable sight. The birds flew considerably higher than normal, and they did not swoop in for a landing on the loft like normal pigeons. Instead, they came almost straight down in a peculiar helicoptering or hovering flight. Being unable to see the loft itself, they landed in yards or fields in the vicinity, where we picked them up and carried them to the loft.

Thus the use of landmarks appears to be important only when other means of homing are disrupted for some reason, or when the pigeon is very close to its loft (Fuller, Kowalski, & Wiltschko, 1983).

Retracing the outward route

While it is being transported to the release site, a pigeon might acquire information about the terrain through which it passes. This information could then be used to determine the correct direction in which to fly from the release point. In support of this proposal, homing can be influenced by various manipulations to the birds as they are being transported to the release site. These manipulations include transporting birds along different routes to the same release site (Papi, Fiore, Fiaschi, & Benvenuti, 1972); preventing the animals from using their sense of smell (Baldaccini, Benvenuti, Fiaschi, Ioale, & Papi, 1982); and changing the magnetic field that surrounds the bird (Kiepenheuer, 1978). Furthermore, experiments have also shown that when pigeons are released from a particular site, their direction of flight from the site is very much influenced by their route to the site (Baker, 1980, see Figure 8.19).

On the other hand, pigeons are able to home effectively even when they are deeply anaesthetised on the journey to the release site (Walcott & Schmidt-Koenig, 1973). It is highly unlikely that pigeons learn much about the terrain through which they pass while asleep. Thus information acquired on the outward route can influence the return journey, but this information is not essential if the return journey is to be successful.

The map and compass hypothesis

According to Kramer (1952), pigeons possess a map that allows them to determine the direction in which they must fly in order to return home. To be of any value, this information must be converted into a bearing that relates to the environment, which could be achieved, Kramer (1952) argues, if pigeons have a compass. For example, if it was inferred from the map that home lies due west of the release point, the use of a compass would then permit the subject to determine the direction in which it should fly. Obviously pigeons do not possess compasses of the sort that can be purchased in shops, nor do they employ directions like due west, but the position of the sun appears to provide

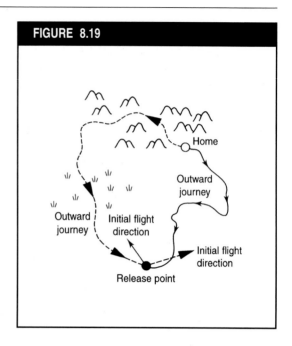

FIGURE 8.19

The initial direction of flight of two groups of pigeons that were taken from the same home to the same release point, along different routes. The different heading directions of the two groups indicate that information acquired on the outward journey can influence the return journey (adapted from Baker, 1980).

an excellent substitute. In fact, quite a lot is now known about the compass component of Kramer's hypothesis, whereas the map component is poorly understood.

The compass is assumed to operate in the following way: On being released, the pigeon observes the position of the sun and by using the information supplied by an internal clock (see Chapter 7) it would then be able to compute any direction it requires. Suppose it needs to fly in a direction that is equivalent to south, then this can be readily computed by extrapolating from the present position of the sun to where it should be at mid-day. Admittedly, this is a complex calculation, but it does not appear to be beyond the capability of pigeons, as experiments on clock-shifting have shown.

An internal clock is generally considered to be set according to the light–dark cycle. Thus by maintaining pigeons in an artificial environment with a light–dark cycle that is out of phase with the external cycle, it should be possible to change the internal clock and influence the accuracy of the sun compass. In a clock-shift experiment, then, pigeons are maintained for a while in conditions where the lights might come on at midnight and be turned off at midday. Assuming that dawn is at 6 am, the internal clock will eventually be ahead of real time by 6 hours. If the pigeon is then released at, say, 9 am real time, the internal clock will inform it that the time is 3 pm. This will lead the bird to infer that the direction of the sun is equivalent to south-west, when in reality it will be south-east, and any computations involving this information will make the bird fly at right angles to the correct route home. A number of experiments have confirmed predictions of this sort (Keeton, 1969), which strongly implicates the involvement of the sun and the internal clock in homing.

Does this mean that pigeons can home only when the sun is shining? Not at all; accurate homing has been reported when the sky is overcast and, on occasions, at night (Keeton, 1974; Lipp, 1983). An obvious candidate for the source of compass information in these circumstances is the earth's magnetic field. Attempts to test this possibility have involved the placement of magnets, or coils that generate magnetic fields, on pigeons in the hope of distorting their magnetic sense. At first these manipulations did not disrupt homing, but Keeton (1974) has argued that this might be because the experiments were conducted on clear days when the sun compass can be used to home successfully. In support of this argument Keeton (1974) has reported that carrying magnets can disrupt homing on overcast days. Similarly, the disruption to homing that is believed to be a consequence of magnetic storms (Gould, 1982) is not found on sunny days (Lednor & Walcott, 1983). However, given the difficulty of demonstrating an ability by pigeons to detect magnetic fields in the laboratory, the role of a magnetic sense in homing should not be accepted without question.

In contrast to the support for the compass component of Kramer's hypothesis, the evidence for the map component is much weaker. Kramer (1952) said rather little about this aspect of his model, which is perhaps not surprising. Because pigeons are capable of homing from a totally unfamiliar location, it is implausible that their success depends on a map that they can have had no opportunity to acquire. As it stands, then, the map and compass hypothesis must be regarded as an incomplete account of homing.

Bicoordinate navigation

Imagine that a pigeon is able to perceive two separate stimulus sources from its loft, and that it can also detect these sources from the release site. The direction and intensity of the sources will be different for these locations, and if the pigeon is sensitive to these differences, then it will be in possession of sufficient information to compute the correct course home by means of bicoordinate navigation. The obvious advantage of this means of homing is that it can readily explain successful homing from unfamiliar territory. And a major obstacle is the specification of stimulus sources that can be detected over many hundreds of miles. As far as the pigeon is concerned, a number of possibilities have been examined. In addition to the earth's magnetic field, researchers have investigated the information supplied by infrasound, lines of coriolis force (Yeagley, 1947, 1951), and smell (e.g. Papi, Ioale, Fiaschi, Benvenuti, & Baldaccini, 1978). None of these possibilities, however, has gained universal acceptance (see Keeton, 1974; Able, 1980; Gould, 1982, for reviews), and bicoordinate navigation should be seen as a possible rather than a likely explanation for homing.

After reviewing the results from a large number of pigeon homing studies, Gould (1982, p.211) concluded that:

> We probably now have nearly all the pieces of the puzzle before us (and, doubtless, several utterly irrelevant ones as well), but for the immediate future, at least, the nature of the animal map sense seems likely to retain its status as the most elusive and intriguing mystery in animal behaviour.

On the basis of the evidence reviewed here, there can be little reason for disagreeing with him.

MIGRATION

Able (1980, p.286) defines migration as "oriented, long-distance, seasonal movement of individuals". It thus differs from homing, as migration need not be oriented towards a specific goal. Although this may make feats of migration less mysterious than homing, they are often just as spectacular. The Arctic tern, for instance, spends a fortnight each year at the North Pole, slightly longer at the South Pole, and the rest of the year travelling between the two. Innate processes and learning both play an important role in successful migration, as the following discussion demonstrates.

Endogenous control

In many cases of migration generations of the same species undertake much the same journey. It is thus possible, as Gwinner (1972) has noted, that the direction and duration of migration is largely under endogenous control and depends rather little on learning. Migration by the loggerhead sea turtle provides an instance of this type of migration.

Loggerhead turtles hatch from eggs that are laid in underground nests on the Atlantic beaches of Florida. The hatchlings climb out of their nests and then scramble towards the sea where they swim between 30 to 50 miles to the Gulf Stream. The Gulf Stream is attractive because it contains relatively few predators and yet provides an abundant supply of food. The turtles then spend the next few years swimming in loops around the Sargasso sea before returning to a beach in Florida, which may be the one on which they were born. A map of this voyage is presented in Figure 8.20.

A series of experiments has revealed how newly hatched turtles are able to find their way to the Gulf Stream. Young loggerhead turtles were placed into a large dish in which it was possible to measure their preferred direction of swimming (Lohman, 1992). When the experimental room was dark, except for the presence of a dim light source, the turtles were observed to swim towards the light. Apparently, newly hatched turtles emerge onto the

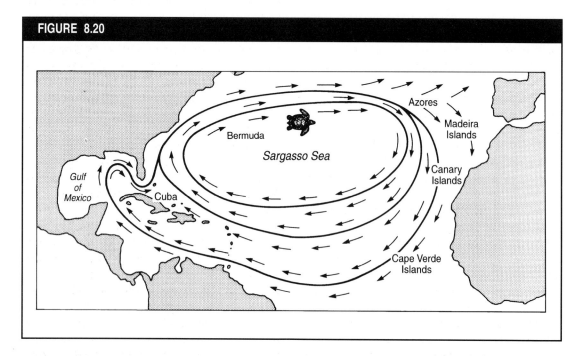

FIGURE 8.20

Migratory paths of sea turtles once they have left their nesting beaches in Florida. The arrows indicate the flow of ocean currents.

beach at night, and reflected light from the moon and stars makes the sea brighter than the land. By being attracted to light, the turtles are thus led towards the ocean. When the room was completely dark, further testing revealed that the turtles had a tendency to swim head on into the waves, and also towards magnetic east (Lohman, 1991). Once they have reached the ocean, the joint influence of these tendencies would then lead to the comparative safety of the Gulf Stream.

As far as navigating around the Sargasso Sea is concerned, this could be accomplished by following the currents (see Figure 8.20). How the turtles are then able to return to their hatching beaches, however, remains a matter of speculation. Chemosensory information, the earth's magnetic field, patterns of wave propagation, and ocean swells have all been suggested as providing landmarks for the return journey. But none of these has received convincing support. On the other hand, the likelihood of turtles using celestial information at night is remote. They are extremely myopic when their heads are above water.

The role of learning

The migration of the indigo bunting provides a good example of the way in which learning interacts with endogenous processes in order to influence the direction of migration (Emlen, 1970). These North American birds migrate southwards in the autumn and northwards in the spring. As the time to migrate approaches, they start to build up fat deposits to provide energy reserves for the forthcoming journey. They also become restless, and if they are held in a cage this restlessness is oriented towards the direction of migration. By keeping a record of this restless activity, it is possible to infer the direction of migration when the bird is released. The restless activity is referred to as *Zugunruhe*.

Emlen (1970) hand-reared indigo buntings in an aviary that was entirely cut off from the outside world, except that the light–dark cycle coincided with that occurring naturally. As autumn approached, two groups spent a number of nights in a planetarium, and a third group remained in the aviary. While they were in the planetarium, the buntings were exposed to a configuration of stars. For one group the configuration rotated around the normal north–south axis, but for the second group it rotated around a different axis. When it was time for the autumn migration, all three groups spent a test session of several hours in the planetarium with the stars motionless. The buntings were retained in small cages that indicated the orientation of their *Zugunruhe*.

The direction of their restless activity was essentially random for those birds that had remained in the aviary until the test session, which suggests they lacked a preferred direction for migration. The remaining birds, on the other hand, did express a preference, but it differed for the two groups. The group for which the stars had rotated around the north–south axis indicated a tendency to migrate southwards. The preferred direction for the other group was also along the axis of rotation they had experienced, but this was obviously not towards the south.

The interpretation of these results is complex yet fascinating. The random behaviour of the buntings that spent all but the test session in the aviary indicates that extended exposure to the stars is essential if they are to migrate in the correct direction. As the groups that were exposed to the stars expressed different orientations of *Zugunruhe*, the movement of the stars must be an important influence on the direction of migration. Why should this be? The apparent movement of the stars is largely due to the rotation of the earth, so that the stars above the equator will seem to move a greater distance than those above the poles. Indeed, the stars that do not move at all, or at least very little, will indicate the direction of north (in the northern hemisphere). Thus by remembering the position of the stars and comparing it with their position some time later, it would be possible to determine which stars have moved the least and therefore which indicate north. Emlen (1970) argues that buntings perform precisely this process when they are in the planetarium, and, by remembering the stars located above the pole, they are able to infer the direction for migration. Of course, this will be southwards only for those birds exposed to the normal rotation of the stars. The ability of buntings to determine the relative motion of stars provides compelling evidence that this species is capable of representing comparatively complex spatial information.

The orientation of migration is thus controlled by the stars, whereas the duration of the journey could be determined either by an internal clock, or when the energy reserves are depleted. Provided that the subject travels at a reasonably constant speed, these factors alone should be sufficient to ensure that it arrives at much the same place as its forefathers (see Able, 1980, for a review).

Obviously, the route will be unfamiliar to a bird on its first migration, but on subsequent journeys, this will not be true. Experiments with starlings have revealed that the knowledge acquired on one journey can influence the course of a subsequent one. In an experiment by Perdeck (1958), starlings were taken from where they were born in Holland and released for migration from Switzerland. When juveniles without any experience of migration were released, the direction of their migration was appropriate for a release site in Holland rather than Switzerland. On the other hand, the adults that were released took account of their displacement and flew towards their usual winter quarters. Presumably this adjustment was possible because of information acquired during the course of previous migrations. But what this information might consist of remains a mystery—it is certainly unlikely to be based on a first-hand experience of Switzerland.

CONCLUDING COMMENTS

Whether they travel over relatively short, or very long distances, animals have a range of strategies available to help them navigate towards their goal. But what determines which strategy will be chosen in any given task? One possibility is that animals do not make any choice and they use all the information that is available to them. O'Keefe and Nadel (1978), for instance, have suggested that the construction of a cognitive map will progress more or less independently of any learning that takes

place about individual landmarks, especially those close to the individual (see Morris, 1981). Another possibility is that animals will rely, for some reason, on one particular source of information for navigation and learn rather little about other, equally useful, sources. In terms presented in Chapter 3, animals might focus their attention on some navigational cues and ignore others.

An experiment by Diez-Chamizo, Sterio, and Mackintosh (1985; see also March, Chamizo, and Mackintosh, 1992) indicates that there is at least some merit in the second possibility. Rats were trained in a rather unusual way in a radial maze. They were placed at the end of one arm and then had to go to the end of another arm in order to receive food. The correct arm was unique because it had a sandpaper floor. Throughout this training, the landmarks provided by various objects in the room, and the shape of the room itself, were made irrelevant by rotating the maze from one trial to the next. In a second stage of the experiment, food was placed again at the end of the sandpaper arm, but the maze was not rotated so that all the cues associated with the room were no longer irrelevant to the solution to the problem. Despite this change in training, subsequent testing revealed that the rats had learned very little about the significance of the cues that lay outside the maze. In contrast, a control group, which received just the second stage, learned a great deal about the significance of the extramaze cues. One way of summarising these results is to say that pretraining with the local landmark of sandpaper blocked the development of a cognitive map based on extramaze cues in the second stage of the experiment.

In contrast to these findings, an experiment that has already been mentioned shows that it is possible for learning to take place simultaneously about two different types of navigational cue. Recall that Vallortigara et al. (1990) trained young chicks to find food near a landmark placed in the corner of a rectangular chamber. Test trials then revealed that the chicks had learned about the significance of the landmark, because they searched near it, no matter where it was located. When the landmark was removed, however, the authors found that the chicks had also learned about the shape of the chamber because searching was either confined to the correct corner, or rotational errors were made. There can be little point in attempting to draw any firm theoretical conclusions from the results of these two, very different, studies. Instead, they serve to emphasise that the analysis of the way in which animals use different sources of navigational information remains an intriguing area for future research.

9

Social Learning

Until now we have concentrated on the behaviour of animals in isolation, but many species live in groups and it is possible that the presence of one animal can influence greatly the knowledge that is acquired by another. The study of social learning is directed at exploring this possibility.

One obvious way in which social learning could benefit an animal is by allowing it to copy what other members of its group have learned through the, possibly painful, process of trial and error. By copying the diet of the adult members of a group, an infant will avoid poisonous substances without having to test them itself. An animal might also learn to avoid predators, not by interacting with them directly, but by observing how other members of the species react to them. And if one member of a group should by chance solve a difficult problem, other members of the group would gain by copying the actions of the problem solver, rather than by having to work through the tedious problem-solving process themselves.

Social learning may not only allow an animal to profit from the experiences of others, it may be important in determining how a group of animals interacts. Most animals engage in some form of communication, and for animals that live in groups this skill could be based on infants learning from adults. Alternatively, living in a group may pose problems that solitary animals rarely face, and animals might need to learn specialised skills in

order to overcome these problems. For example, in groups where some members are dominant over others, subordinate members may need to develop special strategies in order to outwit their superiors, who would otherwise restrict their access to such resources as food or a sexual partner. The proposal has been made that such strategies require an animal to learn about the intentions of other individuals.

The purpose of this chapter is to examine these and other examples of social learning, in the hope of understanding how this type of learning takes place. At first sight, a number of the effects that are described might appear to involve learning processes that we have not yet considered. Perhaps surprisingly, however, many demonstrations of social learning can be understood in terms of the principles that also govern learning in the simpler settings that were considered in earlier chapters.

DIET SELECTION AND FORAGING

For most of us, the selection of a diet might seem to be very much a personal matter that is guided by our own experiences with food. In the case of animals, however, the preferences and food-seeking behaviour of one animal can exert a profound influence on the way in which another looks for food and chooses its diet.

An example of the way in which social learning can influence foraging is provided by a study of Burmese jungle fowl by McQuoid and Galef (1992). Hungry fowl were allowed to explore an enclosure in which four bowls were placed in fixed positions. Food was consistently available in one of these bowls and eventually all the subjects approached this bowl whenever they entered the enclosure. Towards the end of this training, another group of fowl (observers) watched the first group (demonstrators) as they ate from the bowl. When the observers were themselves permitted into the enclosure, they showed a marked preference for the bowl from which the demonstrators had been seen to eat.

This experiment makes it quite clear that animals can learn something about a stimulus, a food bowl, simply by watching another animal eat from it. To explain this outcome, McQuoid and Galef (1992) refer to the mechanism of *stimulus enhancement*, which implies that as a result of watching the demonstrators as they ate, the attention of the observers was drawn to the bowl. This attention would then encourage the observers to approach the bowl and fortuitously lead them to food. Rather little is understood about the factors that promote stimulus enhancement, but we do know that its effects can persist for a relatively long time. Thus the experiment by McQuoid and Galef (1992) was successful even when a period of two days elapsed between observational training and the test trial. It may be of some interest to know that stimulus enhancement effects are not unique to vertebrates. A similar result to that described by McQuoid and Galef (1992) has been reported by Fiorito and Scotto (1992) with octopuses.

A rather different type of social learning can be shown to result in animals acquiring a preference for a particular food, even when they have no opportunity to consume it. In a series of experiments by Galef and his colleagues (see Galef, 1988) a demonstrator rat was allowed to eat food with a distinctive flavour: either cocoa or cinnamon. An observer was then placed in the company of the demonstrator for 30 minutes, but in the absence of any food, before being allowed to

choose between food flavoured with either cocoa or cinnamon. The observers preferred the food that was of the same flavour as that consumed by the demonstrator. This preference has been shown to occur even if the demonstrator eats the flavoured diet up to 4 hours before its encounter with the observer. Likewise, the preference is still evident when an interval of 12 hours has elapsed between the time of the interaction between the rats and the time of testing. Finally, a preference will develop for each of four flavours if the observer should encounter in succession four rats that have individually eaten diets containing one of the four flavours.

One explanation for these remarkably robust effects can be based on the fact that rats are neophobic—they are reluctant to eat food with a novel flavour (Barnett, 1958; Galef, 1970, see Galef, 1988, p. 131). In the experiments that have just been mentioned, the observers had no experience of cocoa- or cinnamon-flavoured food prior to the test trial. The interaction between the rats might thus have allowed the observers to familiarise themselves with the food that the demonstrator has just eaten. Perhaps they detected the odour of the food on the demonstrator's breath, or they may have consumed particles of food that had stuck to the demonstrator's fur. At the time of testing, the observers would then be confronted with a choice between a familiar and a novel flavour, and their neophobia would lead them to select the former. Additional findings reported by Galef (1988) suggest that this explanation is unlikely. Before their encounter with a demonstrator, who had just eaten food flavoured, say, with cinnamon, observer rats were allowed access to plentiful supplies of both cinnamon- and cocoa-flavoured food for two days. Despite this opportunity to overcome their neophobia of both flavours, they still acquired a preference for the cinnamon as a result of their interaction with the demonstrator. The important conclusion to be drawn from this finding is that interacting with a rat that has just eaten food of a particular flavour results in a temporary enhancement of the attractiveness of that food.

A further experiment described by Galef (1988) identifies some of the critical features of the social interaction that are responsible for the acquired preference. The experiment employed the simple apparatus shown in Figure 9.1. An observer rat was placed into the bucket of the apparatus, and an anaesthetised demonstrator was placed into the wire mesh basket. Some demonstrators had food dusted on their faces, and others had food placed directly into their stomachs through a tube. In both cases the observers subsequently showed a preference for the flavoured diet that had just been fed to the demonstrator. However, if the rear end of the demonstrator was dusted with food, and placed foremost in the basket, then only a slight preference for the food was demonstrated. Finally, if a wad of cotton wool, rather than a rat, was placed in the basket, then despite being dusted with food, there was no evidence that this resulted in a change in the attractiveness of the food. Thus the demonstrator does not need to be conscious if it is to encourage the development of a food preference in another rat. But the observer must interact with a rat, and preferably its front rather than rear end.

The foregoing results suggest that a socially acquired food preference depends on the observer being able to smell food at the same time as it smells the demonstrator's breath (Galef, Mason, Preti, & Bean, 1988). Given such a conclusion, Galef and Durlach (1993) then proposed that the smell of the demonstrator serves as a US that enhances a preference for the relevant flavour

through a process of Pavlovian conditioning. However, a serious objection to this proposal is that the preference lasts for only a few hours after the interaction between the two rats. The effects of Pavlovian conditioning normally endure for a much longer time. In addition, there is no evidence that the socially acquired preference is susceptible to weakening by blocking, overshadowing, or latent inhibition (Galef & Durlach, 1993). These effects have come to be regarded as the hallmarks of Pavlovian conditioning, and in their absence it is hard to argue that a socially acquired preference is effectively a conditioned response. For the present, therefore, we must conclude that the way in which a social interaction promotes a food preference is not completely understood.

The ease with which rats acquire food preferences socially might lead one to expect that they can learn in a similar way to avoid food that is poisonous. A moment's reflection, however, should indicate that this means of socially acquiring a food preference will not be very effective for aversion learning. Once a rat has acquired an aversion to a particular food, it will avoid that food, and thus be unlikely to carry any traces of it. When the rat then encounters another rat, it will be unable to convey any information about the type of food that has been avoided, and the aversion will not be transferred. This analysis is supported by the findings from a study by Galef (1988; see also Galef, McQuoid, & Whiskin, 1990), who was unable to demonstrate experimentally a social transfer of an acquired food aversion. Thus whenever rats avoid poisoned bait that has been left for them, this must depend on their neophobia, together with their preference for food that has been eaten by other rats and that is presumably safe. A more detailed discussion of the way in which rats avoid toxic food can be found in Galef and Clark (1971).

The final experiment in this section is an ingenious experiment by Galef (1988) that indicates the potentially important role that socially acquired preferences may play in foraging. Figure 9.2 shows a maze with a start box connected to three goal boxes, A, B, and C. The rats were first trained by being required to run to a goal box to obtain food. The correct goal box varied from day

FIGURE 9.1

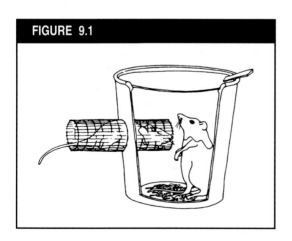

The apparatus used to allow one rat to smell food on an anaesthetised demonstrator rat (from Galef et al., 1985, reprinted by permission of the Psychonomic Society, Inc.).

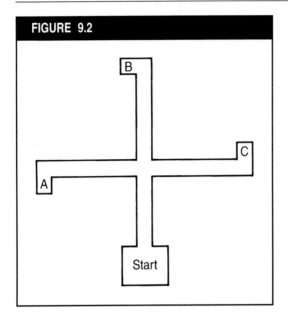

FIGURE 9.2

A plan of the maze used in an experiment by Galef (1988). Rats were allowed to leave the start box in order to find food in one of the three goal boxes. On different days they would find cheese in A, or cinnamon-flavoured food in B, or cocoa-flavoured food in C (adapted from Galef, 1988).

to day, and food of different flavours was presented consistently in the different goals. Thus, depending on which goal box was correct, cheese would be presented in Goal A, cinnamon-flavoured food in Goal B, or cocoa-flavoured food in Goal C. After sufficient training, once a rat had discovered by chance which goal contained food, it developed a strong tendency to return to that goal box for the remainder of the session.

The test stage was conducted in much the same way as the training stage, except that prior to the first trial the rat was confined in the start box with another rat. The second rat had just eaten food of the flavour that was available in the correct goal box. As a result of the interaction between the rats, the likelihood of the experimental rat running directly to the correct goal was enhanced considerably. The implication of these results for understanding the way in which rats find food should be obvious. When a rat returns to the colony after eating food, the information provided by this rat, together with the knowledge that has been acquired of the area around the colony, will be sufficient to enable others to go to what is likely to be an abundant food supply.

FEAR OF PREDATORS

The experiments described in this section demonstrate the importance of social learning for acquiring a fear of potential predators. We will focus on the way in which monkeys acquire their fear of snakes.

When an adult free-ranging monkey suddenly encounters a snake its reaction is quite dramatic. It will attempt to flee from the snake, its facial expressions will indicate fear, it will look at the snake, and it will make specific alarm calls. A monkey that has been reared in the laboratory will, in stark contrast, show none of these reactions. Clearly, a fear of snakes by monkeys is not innate, but acquired through experience. In order to understand what this experience might be, experiments have been conducted in which laboratory-reared monkeys watch the reactions of a wild-reared monkey to a snake (Mineka & Cook, 1988). Typically, as soon as the wild-reared monkey sees the snake it becomes extremely agitated and, on seeing this reaction, the observer responds in a similar way. If the observer should subsequently be exposed to the snake by itself, it will then reveal all the manifestations of being afraid. Further studies have shown that this acquired fear of snakes can be passed on, by allowing another laboratory-reared monkey to observe the originally trained monkey display its fear in the presence of a snake. The acquired fear is also extremely durable and has been shown to persist for at least a year. Interestingly, Mineka and Cook (1988) report that if an observer watched a model that was unafraid of snakes, then the observer did not become afraid of the snake. Indeed, this treatment was found to immunise the observer so that it failed to acquire a fear of snakes when it eventually saw a model react fearfully to a snake.

According to Mineka and Cook (1988), an acquired fear of snakes is a consequence of Pavlovian conditioning, where the snake is the CS, and the model's fear response is the US. In support of this proposal they report that the effectiveness of observational conditioning was directly related to the intensity of the model's reaction to the snake. Such a finding is consistent with the many experiments that show that the effectiveness of Pavlovian conditioning is determined by the magnitude of the US (see Chapter 3). Pavlovian conditioning is known to be disrupted by pre-exposure to the CS (see Chapter 3), and Mineka and Cook (1988) have shown that this is also true for the experiments they describe. If a laboratory-reared monkey is repeatedly exposed to a snake prior to an observational conditioning trial, then the acquired fear of snakes is less than if the prior exposure is omitted.

When they are taken together, the findings described by Mineka and Cook (1988) provide a convincing demonstration of what might be called *observational conditioning*, where the reaction of one animal serves as the reinforcer, or uncon-ditioned stimulus, for Pavlovian conditioning with another animal. For a demonstration of observa-tional conditioning in blackbirds see Curio (1988).

Mineka and Cook (1988) have argued that the highly effective observational conditioning that they have repeatedly demonstrated reflects an innate disposition of monkeys to acquire a fear of snakes. Support for this conclusion comes from an experiment in which laboratory-reared monkeys were able to watch a videotape of a monkey reacting fearfully. After careful editing of this tape the monkey appeared to be showing fear of either a live boa constrictor or brightly coloured flowers. Subsequent testing revealed that the observers who watched the tape of the boa constrictor readily acquired a fear of snakes, whereas those who watched a monkey apparently display a fear of flowers did not themselves become afraid of flowers. This finding is certainly consistent with the notion that monkeys have evolved to associate some stimuli with fear more readily than others.

The alert reader might be concerned that alternative explanations can be developed to explain these results. During their lives the observers may have seen many more flowers than snakes. If this were the case, then latent inhibition could be responsible for the poor conditioning with

flowers. Alternatively, a snake might be a more salient stimulus than a flower for conditioning with any US. Although Cook and Mineka (1990) reject this second possibility, their arguments have not convinced everyone (see Heyes, 1994). Finally, the alert reader might also wonder why monkeys do not simply possess an innate fear of snakes. Until these issues have been dealt with, no firm conclusions should be drawn about innate dispositions for learning about snakes. None the less, these experiments provide a clear demonstration of observational conditioning. They also show how this conditioning can play an important role in learning to avoid predators.

COPYING BEHAVIOUR: MIMICRY

In the experiments that have been discussed so far, the focus of attention has been on the way in which social learning can influence the reactions of an animal to a particular stimulus. We turn now to investigate the way in which social learning can shape the responses that an animal makes. Topics that are of obvious relevance to this issue include mimicry and imitation. But what precisely is meant by these terms? Most psychologists would agree that imitation and mimicry result in animals performing new responses, and that these responses are arbitrary, rather than being closely tied to species-typical reactions to certain stimuli.

Given such a constraint, we can exclude *contagious* behaviour as an example of imitation or mimicry. Contagious behaviour is said to occur when the response of one animal triggers the same response in another animal. Chorusing in dogs and roosters provide two frequently encountered examples of this type of behaviour where the response can hardly be said to be arbitrarily selected. Another example is yawning in humans.

For the purposes of the following discussion, we shall also distinguish between mimicry and imitation. Mimicry will be said to have occurred when the response that is copied does not lead to an immediate, tangible reward. Imitation will be used to refer to responses that have been copied, and that lead to reward.

Mimicry is of interest in its own right, because it can often result in animals behaving in an engaging fashion. Nearly 200 years ago Buffon (1818) reported that several orang-utans dined with humans and mimicked their use of silverware and cups, of pouring drinks, and even touching glasses with their hosts. More recent examples of mimicry by orang-utans can be found in Russon and Galdikas (1993) who observed these animals mimic the human actions of pouring fuel from a can, launching a boat, weeding a garden, and using a paint brush. A chimpanzee has been said to learn through mimicry how to sharpen pencils, use sandpaper, wash dishes (Hayes, 1961; Hayes & Hayes, 1951), and even to wipe its bottom (Goodall, 1986, in Jolly, 1991). There is also ample evidence of vocal mimicry. Parrots and mynah birds are famous for their capacity to mimic human speech. What may not be so well known is that seals have also been said to possess this capacity. A Harbour seal, Hoover, is reputed to have mimicked its human foster parents and produced phrases such as "Hello there" and "How are you?", which were occasionally followed by a belly laugh (cited in Moore, 1992).

More seriously, mimicry is important for theoretical reasons. The ability of an animal to acquire seemingly arbitrary responses, such as a rat pressing a lever, is generally attributed to the influence of instrumental conditioning. The animal is assumed to make the response, or some approximation to it, by trial and error. Should this response then be followed by reward, the likelihood of it being repeated is increased. If mimicry is possible, then it implies that this account of the way in which arbitrary responses are acquired is incomplete. First, it would seem that the form of the response can be acquired through observation, rather than by trial and error. Second, it would seem that reward is not necessary for the response to be performed repeatedly. Thus if mimicry can be reliably demonstrated, then our conclusions concerning the way in which arbitrary responses are acquired would have to be modified considerably.

Given the potential theoretical importance of mimicry, we need to be confident that it really exists. Unfortunately, many of the examples that have been cited were derived from casual observation of the animals, and they are thus open to a variety of interpretations. If a chimpanzee should be seen using sandpaper, does this reflect mimicry, or does it merely reflect the fact that the animal was playing with an object in a way that the observer interprets as mimicry? Alternatively, if an animal should acquire the capacity to say "Hello there", has it copied its trainer, or have its vocalisations been shaped by reward to resemble this human phrase in much the same way as a rat can be trained to press a lever?

An experiment by Moore (1992) provides strong evidence that at least one species, the African grey parrot, has the capacity to mimic humans. The experimenter spent a few minutes every day with the parrot in its room. During this period the experimenter would utter a word or phrase, perform a stereotyped movement in front of the parrot, and then leave. A videotaped record of the parrot's behaviour revealed that during the periods that it was alone it mimicked both the utterance and the action of the experimenter. For example, on leaving the room the experimenter waved good-bye and said "ciao". After a year the bird was heard to say "ciao", and at the same time it waved a foot in the air. As this action was never performed in the presence of the experimenter, its repeated occurrence is unlikely to be due to the influence of an extrinsic reward. Instead, this is but one of many examples reported by Moore (1992) that show that the parrot mimicked both the vocalisations and movements of its trainer.

The ability of the parrot to copy the response of waving is particularly difficult to explain. Conceivably, hearing the word "ciao" allowed a memory of the sound of this word to be stored. In order to mimic the word, the parrot could then modify the sounds it produced until they matched the remembered sound. The parrot may also have stored a visual memory of the experimenter waving as he said "ciao". However, because the parrot's view of its own leg would be very different from the sight of the experimenter waving, this visual memory could not then be used to mould the response of waving a foot in the same way that vocal mimicry could be moulded. Before waving could be copied, some transformation of the visual memory of the experimenter's response would be needed. How this transformation might take place is not known.

Another problem posed by these results is the explanation for why mimicry should occur at all. Moore (1992) has suggested tentatively that mimicry in primates helps them to acquire skills involving tools, whereas in parrots it serves a purely social function. Mimicry also plays an important role in communication. Certain birds, for example, learn their songs by mimicking adult birds. The way in which this learning takes place will be considered in more detail shortly.

COPYING BEHAVIOUR: IMITATION

If a problem is particularly hard for an animal to solve, then it may take a considerable amount of time, or even generations, before the correct response is discovered. Once it has been discovered, other members of the group to which the animal belongs may well benefit from imitating the action of the successful problem solver. Imitation, therefore, can be viewed as a type of social learning that theoretically would be of value to many different species. In fact, despite the considerable benefits that result from an ability to imitate, we shall see that on the whole animals imitate rarely.

Naturalistic evidence

Birds. Blue tits and great tits in Britain are notorious for their ability to break through the foil tops of milk bottles in order to drink the cream at the top (see Figure 9.3). This skill is believed to have originated in a small group (Fisher & Hinde, 1949), and its spread to the rest of the population has been attributed on more than one occasion to imitation (Bonner, 1980). However, the results from a series of experiments by Sherry and Galef (1984, 1990), using black-capped chickadees, suggest that the spread of this annoying habit was promoted by more mundane means than imitation. If a bird should come across a bottle that has already been opened, it will drink the milk. Once it

FIGURE 9.3

A great tit opening a milk bottle. © Michael Leech, Oxford Scientific Films.

has drunk from the bottle, apparently the bird will be very much more likely to break through the foil tops in the future. Pavlovian conditioning provides one explanation for this outcome. While the bird is drinking, the sight of the foil top (CS) may be associated with the cream (US) beneath it. When the bird subsequently sees a foil top it would then be likely to approach and direct CRs of pecking towards it. If these pecks should tear the foil, then the entire sequence of this activity is likely to be strengthened and result in the subject being more willing in the future to tear open foil tops for itself.

Sherry and Galef (1990) report that their subjects were unlikely to open foil tops when they were naive and tested in isolation. Such a finding then raises the question of how the birds came to open foil tops in the first place. In an attempt to answer this question, Sherry and Galef (1990) examined the behaviour of a naive bird that had access to a foil covered container of cream when it could see another naive bird in an adjacent cage. The mere presence of this second bird was sufficient to encourage the first bird to peck at the foil cap and eventually open it. The reasons for this *social facilitation* of pecking are not fully understood, but the presence of the second bird may serve to reduce fear, or to encourage foraging responses, in the experimental subject. But whatever the reason, this type of social facilitation could well be responsible for the origins and perhaps spread of milk-bottle opening among certain birds. There can be little justification for believing that this skill is acquired through imitation.

Primates. The somewhat cumbersome phrase population-specific behavioural traditions is used to describe behaviours that have the following properties (Nagell, Olguin, & Tomasello, 1993):

1. They are acquired through experience, rather than being innate.
2. They are found throughout a well-defined population.
3. They persist from one generation to the next.
4. They are absent in other populations of the same species.

The spread of tearing foil tops by birds might be regarded as a population-specific behavioural tradition. An example of such a tradition in primates is provided by a group of fastidious Japanese macaque monkeys who wash potatoes before eating them (Itani & Nishimura, 1973). Another behavioural tradition has been observed in a group of chimpanzees in the Ivory Coast, who use stones to break open nuts (Boesch, 1991). From the point of view of the present discussion, these behavioural traditions are of interest because their widespread use within a group of primates has been attributed to imitation (Goodall, 1986; Itani & Nishimura, 1973).

There are, however, reasons for believing that these behavioural traditions do not depend on imitation. As far as potato washing is concerned,

Nagell et al. (1993) have suggested that the spread of this habit is due in part to stimulus enhancement. The attention of a naive monkey might be drawn to a potato when it sees another monkey pick one up. The naive monkey may then pick up its own potato and for social reasons follow the experienced monkey into the river. At this point, the naive monkey may learn by accident the benefits that accrue from placing the potato in the water. Although this account may seem contrived, it relies only on processes that are generally accepted to exist (for a similar argument see Byrne, 1995). Moreover, studies of complex skills that develop in colonies of primates have revealed that these skills do not spread easily. Kummer and Goodall (1985) state that "of the many [innovative] behaviors observed, only a few will be passed on to other individuals, and seldom will they spread through the whole troop" (p. 214, quoted in Nagell et al., 1993, p. 185). Such an observation is entirely understandable if the acquisition of a skill depends on the combination of a number of processes, including learning by trial and error. It is not so compatible, however, with the suggestion that primates are willing imitators.[1]

Laboratory studies

An obvious problem with attempts to study imitation in a naturalistic setting is that the history of individual animals is often unknown. Any particular action, or behavioural tradition, can thus be readily explained in a number of ways and often insufficient evidence is available to evaluate them. The experiments described in the next section examined imitation in a laboratory setting. Even though these experiments should ideally be easier to interpret than more naturalistic studies, at least some of them are open to a variety of interpretations.

A straightforward test for learning by imitation in rats was conducted by Huang, Koski, and DeQuardo (1983). At the same time it reveals some of the pitfalls that a study of this kind can encounter. The apparatus consisted of a conventional conditioning chamber with a response lever and a food magazine. A diagonal, transparent partition divided the box into two halves. Three groups of rats were placed individually for 30 minutes into the half that did not contain the lever. Throughout this period an experimental group was able to watch a rat in the other half of the chamber lever press for food. The remaining two groups were controls. For Group Control 1 the other half of the chamber was empty for the 30-minute period, whereas for Group Control 2 the other half of the chamber was occupied by a naive rat that never received reward, even if it accidentally pressed the lever. After this observation period, the rats were permitted access to the lever, which, when pressed, resulted in the delivery of food. The graph in Figure 9.4 shows the mean number of lever presses that were performed in three successive daily sessions by each group. Lever pressing was clearly acquired more readily

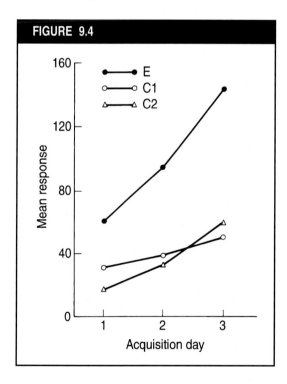

FIGURE 9.4

The mean number of rewarded lever presses made by three groups of rats in three successive test sessions. Prior to testing Group Experimental (E) had observed another rat lever pressing for food, Group Control 1 (C1) had observed an empty operant chamber, and Group Control 2 (C2) had observed a rat that was not rewarded for lever pressing (adapted from Huang et al., 1983).

by the experimental group than by either control group.

The superior performance of the experimental rats may have been due to them learning about lever pressing by virtue of watching the previously trained subjects make this response. But there are at least two other possible explanations for the outcome of the experiment. One explanation appeals to the mechanism of stimulus enhancement that was mentioned earlier in this chapter. Watching a rat spend a great deal of time in the vicinity of the lever may have enhanced the salience of this stimulus for the experimental group. When this group was placed into the test compartment it may have approached the lever out of interest, and pressed it by chance. Any tendency to perform responses in this way would obviously facilitate the acquisition of responding for food. The second explanation is based on observational appetitive conditioning. Browne (1976; see also Parisi & Matthews, 1975) allowed animals to observe, through a partition, an empty compartment where food was occasionally presented after a visual signal. When the animals were allowed access to the compartment, they approached and responded to the signal whenever it was shown. Conceivably, the experimental animals in the study by Huang et al. (1983) associated the sight of the movement of the response lever with the delivery of food. They would then be attracted to the lever when they were placed in the test chamber and this, again, would place them at an advantage over the control animals (see also Denny, Clos, & Bell, 1988).

A rather different procedure for studying imitation in rats has been developed by Heyes and Dawson (1990). Their apparatus is depicted in Figure 9.5, which shows a demonstrator rat in the left compartment of a test chamber and an observer in the right compartment. In order to obtain food the demonstrator had been trained to push the pole in a certain direction, to its left, for example. The position of the pole ensured that the demonstrator was always facing in the direction shown in the figure. After watching the demonstrator respond in this way to earn 50 food pellets, the observer rat was placed in the left-hand compartment. The

FIGURE 9.5

A sketch of the apparatus used to study observational learning in rats, showing the position and orientation of the demonstrator (left) and observer (right) (from Heyes & Dawson, 1990).

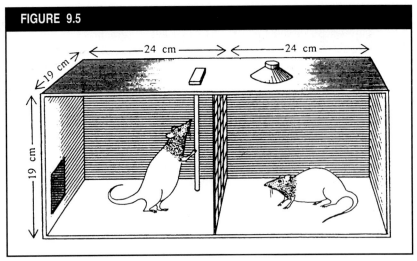

observers showed a reliable tendency to push the pole in the same direction as the demonstrators had pushed it, even though responses in any direction were rewarded.

The observational training can reasonably be said to have taught the observers something about the pole. At the very least, their attention may have been drawn to this stimulus, or they may have learned that a movement of the pole was a signal for food. This learning may then account for the observers approaching the pole in the test phase, but it does not account for the fact that the observers preferred to push the lever in the same direction as the demonstrators. Instead, this particular finding forcefully suggests that during the observational stage, the observers had learned about the response of pushing the pole. But what precisely had the observers learned? One possibility is they learned that moving the pole to a particular place in the apparatus was important. Alternatively, they may have learned that moving the pole in a particular direction, in respect to the body of the demonstrator, was important. A further experiment suggests that this second possibility is correct. The observers were trained in the same way as for the previous experiment, but they were tested with the pole in a new position (Heyes, Dawson, & Nokes, 1992). The plan in Figure 9.6 shows the position of the pole for the first part of the experiment, in which the demonstrators pushed it in the direction L1, but not R1, for food. The plan also shows the

position of the pole for the test phase. In the test session, the observers showed a significant preference for pushing the pole in the direction L2, rather than R2. This result should not occur if rats learned initially to push the pole to a particular location in the chamber. Instead, the results suggest that the observers learned to push the pole in a direction that was defined by its relation to the demonstrator's body.

In order for learning about a response to be regarded as imitation, it must depend on the actions of another animal. Thus far we have seen that the observers learned something about pole pushing, but we do not know that this learning was due to the presence of the demonstrator. Fortunately, Heyes, Jaldow, Nokes, and Dawson (1994) have shown that the effects described earlier do not occur if the observer watches the pole move automatically in the absence of a demonstrator during the observational stage of the experiment.

Taken together, the experiments by Heyes and her colleagues show that animals are capable of learning about a response by observing another animal perform that same response for reward. These findings are important, not only because they provide such a clear demonstration of imitation in animals, but also because they raise interesting questions about the way in which imitation takes place. In the experiments described, the observer rat presumably acquired information through vision, and this information was then used

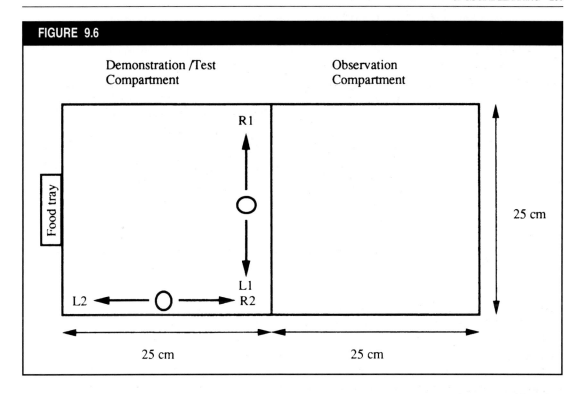

FIGURE 9.6

Demonstration /Test
Compartment

Observation
Compartment

R1

L1
R2

L2

Food tray

25 cm

25 cm

25 cm

A plan of the apparatus used by Heyes et al. (1992) to study observational learning in rats. The plane of movement of the pole during the observation phase is shown by the arrows pointing to L1 and R1, and the plane for the test phase is shown by the arrows pointing to L2 and R2. Responses that moved the pole towards L1 and L2 were treated as being in one direction, and those that moved the pole towards R1 and R2 were treated as being in the opposite direction (from Heyes et al., 1992).

to generate a response. As noted in the discussion of mimicry, the way in which information acquired visually can guide the performance of a new response is not understood at all. There also remains some uncertainty about what exactly the rats learned about the response of pole pushing. In Chapter 5, I argued that instrumental conditioning can result in the development of either S–R or R–US associations. Are similar associations responsible for successful imitation? If they are, then how can a response enter into an association without being performed? These are important questions, and they suggest that further studies of imitation may provide valuable insights into the way animals learn about responses.

In closing this discussion of imitation and mimicry, we can return to a point that was made earlier. Although animals may possess the capacity to copy the behaviour of other animals, they do not necessarily do so. Two examples should serve to

reveal the way in which animals fail to capitalise on any potential they may have for imitation. First, a cebus monkey was allowed to live in the house of a researcher, Gibson (1989). It spent much of its time fastened to a leash, and despite observing on numerous occasions how the leash could be unfastened, the monkey never once performed this response for itself. Second, a small group of vervet monkeys was able to visit a foraging site where there were a number of hollow pieces of bamboo with paper taped over holes that contained food. One monkey developed the knack of removing the paper, but none of the others acquired this skill even though they were at times seen to watch him closely while he retrieved the food (Lefebvre & Palameta, 1988). The contrast between these observations and the findings by Heyes and her colleagues is striking and reveals how poor our understanding is of the factors that promote imitation in animals.

COMMUNICATION

To demonstrate the importance of social learning for communication, I shall focus on two types of communication that have received considerable attention: bird-song and the alarm calls of vervet monkeys. Although learning plays an important role in both types of communication, we shall see that it is constrained by innate factors.

Bird-song development

The vocal communication of birds can be categorised into calls and songs. Bird-calls tend to be brief, almost monosyllabic bursts of sound that last up to a second. They permit individual recognition, serve in courtship, indicate motivational states, and may even serve to convey quite specific information about predators. Domestic chickens have at least two types of alarm call, one for aerial predators and one for ground predators (Klump & Shalter, 1984). Both the form of these calls and their significance is largely determined by inheritance, rather than learning. As a result, there is very little change in the calls from one generation to the next. However, there is a certain flexibility in the use of the calls. As an aid to identification, pairs of American goldfinch are able to modify their flight calls so that they become more similar to each other.

Despite the greater complexity of bird-song—it involves the repetition of a sequence of syllables and notes—the messages it contains appear to be no more complex than those transmitted by bird-calls. Singing is an almost exclusively male activity that serves the purpose of defending their territory from other males, or of attracting females for mating. In contrast to bird-calls, learning is important for song acquisition. This was first made clear in an experiment by Thorpe (1963) who demonstrated that unless young chaffinches heard the song of an adult male chaffinch they could only make a raucous noise when they reached sexual maturity. Subsequent experiments with the white-crowned sparrow by Marler (1970) have shed light on the way in which the song is learned.

The song of the white-crowned sparrow consists of two components: A whistle, which lasts for about 500 to 1000 milliseconds, followed by a trill of much the same length. For sparrows living in the same area there is rather little variation in the structure of either the whistle or the trill. In the case of groups of sparrows from different areas, the construction of these components varies quite considerably. As a consequence, groups of sparrows can be said to possess their own dialects.

The young male white-crowned sparrow leaves the nest at about 10 days of age, and for the next 20 to 100 days he is exposed repeatedly to the adult male song of his father and neighbours. This singing declines in the autumn and winter. The following spring, when he is about a year old and has reached sexual maturity, the young sparrow produces for the first time a good approximation to the local dialect of the adult male song. By acoustically isolating birds of different ages for various intervals, Marler (1970) has shown that the development of the adult song depends on the bird being exposed to it for a period between the ages of 10 to 50 days. A bird that hears the adult song during this period will produce a good copy of it on reaching sexual maturity. One that is not exposed to the adult song at all, or only after the age of 50 days, produces a song that does not correspond even to the basic structure of the species' song. The white-crowned sparrow is also constrained to the type of song it can learn. Marler (1970) found that these birds, when raised in isolation, are unable to learn the songs of other species no matter at what age they hear them.

For the the experiments that have been described, a loudspeaker was used to present recordings of songs to the isolated birds. Rather different conclusions about song learning follow if the experimental subject receives its education from a live tutor that shares the same room. In these conditions, Baptista and Petrinovich (1984, 1986) have shown that song learning by white-crowned sparrows may be more flexible than was originally envisaged. Even if the young bird is older than 50 days when it first hears a song, it may still be able to learn the live tutor's song. In addition, if the live tutor is of a different species, then the subject may acquire the song. Baptista and Petrinovich (1984), for example, found that white-crowned sparrows were able to learn the song of the strawberry finch in this way.

For a chapter on social learning, this effect of a live tutor is interesting because it points to an important social influence on bird-song learning. The beneficial effect of a live tutor is also important because it is difficult to explain with at least one account of the way in which song learning takes place. Marler (1970) has proposed that white-crowned sparrows are born with an auditory template that permits only songs of its own species to pass through into long-term memory. If this were correct, then there should be no reason for a live tutor being more effective than a recording played through a loudspeaker. As an alternative explanation for these results, Petrinovich (1988) has proposed that white-crowned sparrows will learn any song to which they attend. An innate tuning of the sensory pathways is then believed to be responsible for birds paying more attention to the songs of their own, rather than other species. The reason for the superiority of live tutors over tape recordings as a means of teaching is attributed to the different patterns of stimulation that they produce. Live tutors provide a constantly changing pattern of stimulation that makes their songs difficult to ignore. In contrast, the repeated and stereotyped song that is characteristic of a tape recording will be less likely to capture the subject's attention. If this is correct, then it would imply that the presence of a tutor serves no other purpose than to ensure a constantly varying pattern of auditory stimulation. It would be interesting to discover if the tutor's presence served a more important purpose, by allowing the student to hear but not see the live tutor. To my knowledge this experiment has not been conducted, and some uncertainty remains concerning the precise role of a live tutor in the learning of bird-songs.

In closing this discussion of bird-song learning, the achievements of the marsh warbler should not be ignored. This bird constructs its own idiosyncratic song by mimicking and combining the components of the songs of an average of 76 different species of birds (Dowsett-Lemaire, 1979). Some birds are thus more constrained than others in the songs they learn.

Alarm calls in monkeys

Birds are not the only animals to produce alarm calls. Vervet monkeys, which live in troops and inhabit savannah areas of Africa south of the Sahara, also communicate in this way (Struhsaker, 1967). They have a variety of calls, each of which refers to a specific threat and elicits a different reaction from the receiver (see Figures 9.7 and 9.8). If an aerial predator such as an eagle should be spotted, then the alarm call resembles a chuckle that results in the troop either looking up or fleeing into a bush for cover. A threat posed by the appearance of a leopard results in an alarm call of a loud bark that causes the troop to flee for safety in a tree. Any individual that encounters a snake, particularly a python, will call with high-pitched chuttering, whereupon the members of the troop look around and perhaps mob the snake. The approach of baboons, which attack young vervets, also elicits separate and distinctive alarm calls. By playing recordings of these calls to a troop, Cheney and Seyfarth (1988; Seyfarth & Cheney, 1993) revealed that calls in the absence of the relevant predator would still elicit the appropriate response. Thus the possibility can be ruled out that the call serves to elicit a general orienting reaction, which is followed by a specific response as soon as the source of the threat has been identified.

Vervet monkeys have been heard to produce the full repertoire of alarm calls from a very early age, which suggests that the physical properties of the call are genetically determined. Infants also start off by being relatively indiscriminate in the use of alarm calls. They have been heard to produce an eagle alarm call not only to eagles and other aerial predators, but also to pigeons, and even a falling leaf. Erroneous calls by infants are not entirely inappropriate. Eagle alarm calls, for example, were normally given to objects in the air and rarely to terrestrial predators. Vervet monkeys may thus be genetically predisposed to respond to certain classes of stimuli with specific alarm calls. There is, in addition, good reason to believe that learning

FIGURE 9.7

An alert monkey responding to an alarm call.© Eyal Barton, Oxford Scientific Films.

plays an important role in refining the use of alarm calls. Moreover, this learning can be understood with principles that should already be familiar.

In order to investigate the way in which vervet monkeys learn how to respond to the different alarm calls, Seyfarth and Cheney (1986) played a tape of an eagle alarm call whenever they saw an infant wander from its mother. At first, the infant appeared startled, or confused, and searched for its parent. Subsequent presentations of the alarm call then resulted in the infant watching its mother, and eventually the infant copied the mother's reaction to the call of looking up to the sky. It was as if the infant modelled its behaviour on that of its mother.

FIGURE 9.8

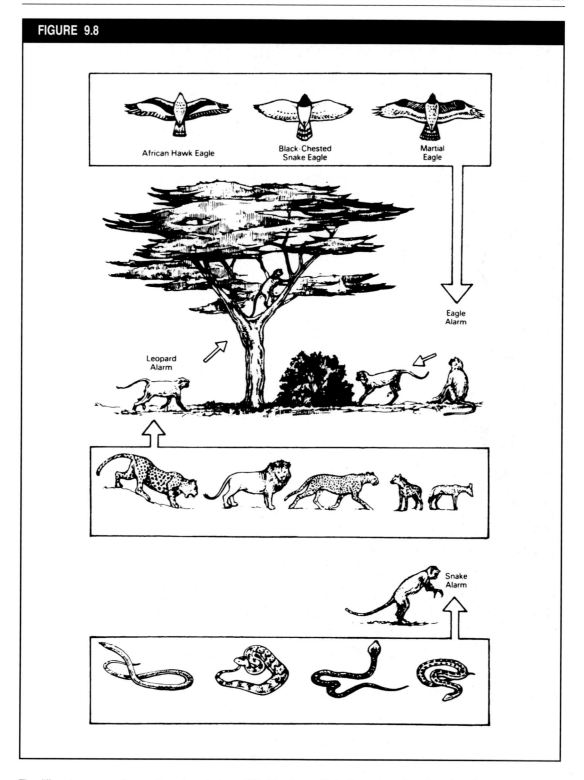

The different responses by vervet monkeys that are elicited by alarm calls for three types of predator (from Bright, 1984).

Thus observational conditioning could be responsible for the ways in which a monkey responds to different alarm calls.

A further role for learning, this time in the production of calls, is indicated by the finding that the indiscriminate production of calls referred to earlier declines as the infant develops. This decline may be explained by the principles of discrimination learning. When an infant was heard to make an eagle alarm call to an eagle other members of the troop looked up and, if they saw an eagle, they also made eagle alarm calls. If the infant's call was inappropriate, perhaps in response to a pigeon, then the adults did not call out. The feedback provided by the adults' calls may thus have served to reinforce correct, but not incorrect, calls by the infant. A report by Caro and Hauser (1992) suggests that additional factors may also influence this process of discrimination learning. Inappropriate alarm calls by infants have been observed to cause their mothers to flee, and then to return and punish the infant by biting or slapping. Whether this punishment was for making an incorrect call, or whether it was for some other reason, remains to be determined.

We shall now consider briefly the significance that the alarm calls of monkeys have for both the sender and the receiver. As far as the significance for the receiver is concerned, hearing an alarm call may well activate a representation of the appropriate predator. Support for this conclusion can be found in an experiment by Cheney and Seyfarth (1988; Seyfarth & Cheney, 1993), which made use of the fact that vervet monkeys make three different calls when they encounter another group of monkeys: a *grunt*, a *wrr*, and a *chutter*. Cheney and Seyfarth (1988) recorded these calls from an individual and then played the *wrr* repeatedly to a selected monkey in the absence of another group. The duration of the individual's reaction to the call was found to diminish as the number of these false alarms increased. In a final stage of the experiment, the subject was tested with either a different group call (a *chutter*), or an alarm call for a leopard. The *chutter* was found to elicit only a weak response, whereas the leopard alarm call elicited a relatively strong response. Cheney and Seyfarth (1988, p. 483) proposed that when a

monkey hears an alarm call, a representation of the threat to which it refers is activated, and this then promotes the relevant response. If the same call should be presented repeatedly in the absence of the threat, then the representation of the threat is believed to become harder to activate. This would then explain why being tested with a *chutter* failed to produce a strong response, it would also explain why the leopard alarm call remained effective. Leopards are so different from a troop of monkeys that a difficulty in activating a representation of the latter would not affect the extent to which a representation of the former could be retrieved.

Turning now to the question of the significance that an alarm call has for the sender, a number of tests have been conducted to determine if these calls are used intentionally. That is, when a monkey sees a predator does it deliberately make a call in order to alert other members of the group to the potential threat? On the basis of the slender evidence that is available, this sort of intentional interpretation is unjustified. Baboons are known to attack young, but not adult, vervet monkeys, with the result that only the infants react with an alarm call when they see a baboon (Bright, 1984). The failure of adults to respond to a baboon is evident even when young vervet monkeys are nearby. If vervet alarm calls were used intentionally, then the adults should call out in these circumstances. In a more experimental study, Seyfarth and Cheney (1993) allowed a mother to watch her infant enter an enclosure in which she knew a threatening individual was hiding. The frequency of alarm calls by the mother was unaffected by whether or not she had been given the information that the infant also knew about the threat. Such a result does nothing to encourage the belief that the alarm calls were used intentionally by the mother to warn her child.

THEORY OF MIND

Humans have been said to possess a theory of mind, which we use to explain behaviour by reference to mental states. To explain why I am walking into a restaurant, for example, I might say it is because I want food. A theory of mind further allows us to attribute mental states to others and then to use this attribution to make inferences about that person's behaviour. In order to explain why my wife insists that we both go to a restaurant, I might say it is because she too wants to eat some food. Finally, a theory of mind allows us to influence the behaviour of others by manipulating their beliefs. If I do not like the restaurant that my wife has selected, then I might attempt to change her behaviour by informing her that rats were recently seen in its kitchens.

In 1978 Premack and Woodruff raised the challenging question of whether or not chimpanzees have a theory of mind. They were asking if chimpanzees, like humans, have an ability to make inferences about the intentions, desires, knowledge, and states of minds of other animals. Of course, this question implies that animals possess mental states, which, itself, is a contentious issue. For the present we shall ignore this issue, and focus on the evidence that has been said to demonstrate that chimpanzees possess a theory of mind. The two sorts of evidence that have been said to reveal a theory of mind, deception and knowledge attribution, will be examined separately.

Deception

Once an animal can appreciate that the actions of other animals are influenced by their knowledge, then one animal could influence the behaviour of another by manipulating the information it receives. Put slightly differently, the way is open for one animal to deceive another. In order to test whether or not chimpanzees possess a theory of mind, Woodruff and Premack (1979) attempted to determine experimentally whether or not chimpanzees are capable of deception.

In this highly original study, a chimpanzee was able to observe a laboratory assistant hide food under one of two containers. The chimpanzee was then placed in such a position that it could not reach the containers and the assistant left the room. Either a *cooperative* or a *competitive* trainer then entered the room. To obtain food with the help of the cooperative trainer, the chimpanzee had to direct the trainer towards the container in which the food was hidden. This was achieved by pointing or

staring at the container. As soon as the trainer had identified the container, he took the food to the chimpanzee.

If the chimpanzee directed the competitive trainer to the container with food, however, the trainer kept the food and the chimpanzee remained hungry. On the other hand, if the competitive trainer was directed to the empty container, then it was the chimpanzee who received food and the trainer who went unrewarded. At least some of the chimpanzees were able to earn food in the presence of both trainers, which suggests that they deliberately misinformed the competitive trainer. A justification for providing such misleading information is that the chimpanzee knew that the trainer would act on it and fail to obtain the food. This line of reasoning is clearly consistent with the proposal that chimpanzees possess a theory of mind.

Unfortunately, the results are open to more than one interpretation. Many training trials were required before the chimpanzees started to deceive the competitive trainer. During their training, therefore, subjects had ample time to learn that certain responses in the presence of the cooperative trainer always resulted in reward, whereas different responses resulted in reward in the presence of the competitive trainer. A discrimination of this sort can be readily explained with conventional principles of associative learning, and there is no reason to believe that this explanation would be inappropriate for the experimental findings. To my knowledge there has been no other test for intentional deception in the laboratory.

If chimpanzees possess a theory of mind, then it is unlikely to be of use only when they are in the psychological laboratory. They should also make use of this theory in more naturalistic settings. Indeed, some authors have argued that the need for a theory of mind has arisen out of the social interaction that occurs in a closely knit group of animals (Humphrey, 1982, 1983). Moreover, the potential for deception is said to be one of the more beneficial consequences of being endowed with a theory of mind (Whiten & Byrne, 1988).

Primates that live in social groups often have strict rules about mating. Dominant males, for example, will generally attempt to prevent their subordinates from mating with the females of a group. In order for these frustrated individuals to fulfil their desires, therefore, they need to deceive their superiors by mating surreptitiously. Alternatively, at times when food is scarce, it may be of benefit to a subordinate member of a group to be secretive about any food that it discovers, so that it is not stolen by a more dominant member. There are numerous reports of individual primates acting in a way that appears to deceive other members of their group. Moreover, many of the perpetrators of these acts of deception have been said to behave in a way that suggests they possess a theory of mind (Byrne & Whiten, 1987; Jolly, 1991). The three examples that follow should help to clarify this line of reasoning.

While Byrne and Whiten (1985, 1987) observed a troop of baboons they noticed a strong adolescent, whom they called Melton, antagonise a younger one. A number of adults in the troop reacted to the screams of the youngster by moving rapidly towards Melton. Instead of fleeing, or showing submission, Melton stood on his hind legs and looked around in a way that is typical when one baboon suddenly notices a predator. The other members of the troop immediately ceased approaching Melton and instead looked in the same direction. As a consequence of this distraction, Melton avoided any punishment that he might have received had the adults reached him. Byrne and Whiten (1985) were unable to see any predator, and they concluded that Melton's behaviour could have been designed to deceive the adults by pretending he had seen a predator. In other words, Melton might have made use of his theory of mind to avoid punishment by encouraging the belief in his chasers that a predator was nearby.

The second example is provided by Kummer (cited in Whiten & Byrne, 1988, p. 236) who also studied a troop of baboons. While he was observing the troop, he noticed an adult female gradually edge towards a rock where she began to groom a junior male. The leader of the troop was seated not too far away, but the position of the rock prevented him from observing the young male that she was grooming. This was fortunate, because the leader rarely permitted such contact. According to Byrne and Whiten (1987), the female was able to appreciate the point of view of the leader and positioned herself in such a way that he would be unable to see the current object of her affections. The cartoon in Figure 9.9, which was taken from Byrne and Whiten (1987), characterises the way in which the female might have used her theory of mind to achieve her goal.

The final example is a quote taken from the observations of de Waal (1982, cited in Whiten & Byrne, 1988).

Dandy and a female were courting each other surreptitiously. Dandy began to make advances to the female, whilst at the same time restlessly looking around to see if any of the other males were watching. Male chimpanzees start their advances by sitting with their legs wide apart revealing their erection. Precisely at this point when Dandy was exhibiting his sexual urge in this way, Luit, one of the older males, unexpectedly came round the corner. Dandy immediately dropped his hands over his penis concealing it from view.

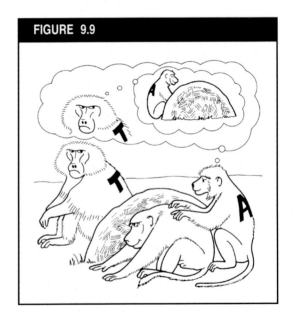

FIGURE 9.9

A cartoon from Byrne and Whiten (1987) depicting how Baboon A might see herself from point of view of the dominant member of the troop, Baboon T (from Byrne & Whiten, 1987).

In this example, Dandy might have been guided by his theory of mind to hide the offending part of his anatomy, and thus encourage the belief in Luit that his intentions towards the female were honourable.

For each example, the interpretation in terms of theory of mind is plausible, but at the same time, alternative explanations for the observed behaviour are easy to develop. Melton may have genuinely seen something that he mistook for a predator. The position adopted by the female observed by Kummer may have served by coincidence to prevent the leader from observing what she was doing. And Dandy may have been doing nothing more than protecting his modesty. Alternatively, at least some of the animals may have learned from past experience that their respective strategies resulted in them avoiding punishment. In which case, learning theory, rather than a theory of mind, could account for the recorded observations. The absence of a detailed record of the previous experiences of these animals makes it impossible to choose between these very different types of explanation. These reports thus provide evidence that suggests, but does not confirm, that some animals possess a theory of mind. A similar argument has been forcefully presented by Yoerg and Kamil (1991).

The alternative explanations that I have presented might be thought unreasonable, but a study by Coussi-Korbel (1994) demonstrates that they should not be taken lightly. She studied deception in a pair of mangabey monkeys: a juvenile male, Rapide, and an adult male, Boss. The study was carried out in a large enclosure containing 40 boxes in which food could be hidden. At the start of a session, Rapide observed food being hidden in two boxes before he and Boss were released into the enclosure. Rapide rapidly discovered that if Boss followed him when he reached the food, he was likely to be displaced by Boss who would eat it. The following quote describes very clearly how Rapide eventually coped with being deprived of food in this way. (Coussi-Korbel, 1994, p. 169)

On being released into the enclosure Rapide struck out in the opposite direction from the food, sat down on a tree trunk at the entrance

of the nonprovisioned zone … Then while Rapide was still on the tree trunk, Boss started exploring the boxes next to the tree trunk. As soon as Boss was engaged in his search Rapide gave Boss a final glance … and set out in a straight line for the food.

The initial activity of Rapide appears to be designed to mislead Boss, but Coussi-Korbel (1994) does not believe that this deceptive behaviour was based on Rapide having any insight into the mental state of Boss. Instead, observations of trial-by-trial behaviour led her to conclude that the response was acquired by chance. The first time that Rapide engaged in what may be termed deceptive behaviour was when he was displaced by Boss from a box containing food. He started to search empty boxes, which encouraged Boss to do the same, but even when it was safe to retrieve the remaining food, Rapide continued with his search of empty boxes. This failure to retrieve the food would not be expected if Rapide had intentionally deceived Boss. On the other hand, the interaction between Rapide and Boss would allow the youngster to learn that when Boss was searching empty boxes it was safe to go to the food.

Perhaps researchers are being too ambitious in looking for evidence of a theory of mind in the deceptive behaviour of animals. If deceptive behaviour should derive from a theory of mind, then it will be the consequence of a complex reasoning process. Consider the example of Melton. The theory of mind interpretation for his behaviour implies that Melton knew, first, that his pursuers intended to punish him, second, that it is possible to instill false beliefs about the presence of predators by adopting a certain posture, and, third, that once false beliefs have been instilled they will disrupt activities guided by previously formed intentions. Perhaps more convincing evidence that animals possess a theory of mind will come from tasks where the theory can be used in a more straightforward fashion.

Knowledge attribution

One potentially simple method for assessing whether or not chimpanzees possess a theory of mind is to determine whether or not they are capable of attributing knowlede to another animal. The design of an experiment that might test this possibility was first suggested by Premack (1988), and put into practice by Povinelli, Nelson and Boysen (1990). One of the four cups shown in Figure 9.10 contains a small piece of food that the chimpanzee is allowed to eat if she correctly identifies the cup that hides it. The chimpanzee does not know which cup hides the food, and to help her with her choice two of her trainers are pointing to two different cups. Immediately prior to this test, the chimpanzee had observed one of the trainers—the guesser—leave the room while the other trainer—the knower—placed food under one

FIGURE 9.10

A chimpanzee chooses one of four cups that might be covering a piece of food. Two trainers are pointing to the cups, one of whom knows where the food is hidden and the other has to guess (from Povinelli, Rulf, and Bierschwale, 1994). Photograph by Donna T. Bierschwale, courtesy of the University of Southwestern Louisiana New Iberia Research Center, Laboratory of Comparative Behavioral Biology.

of the cups, which were hidden from the chimpanzee by a screen. For the test trial the knower was instructed to point to the correct cup, whereas the guesser had to deceive the chimpanzee by pointing to one of the other three, empty cups. If animals are able to attribute mental states, or knowledge, to others, then the chimpanzee should infer that only the knower will be able to identify correctly the cup containing food, and she should thus select the cup to which this person is pointing.

All four subjects tested on this problem showed a preference for the cup identified by the knower, but it required several hundred trials for this preference to be statistically significant in every subject. Although these results are consistent with the proposal that the chimpanzees attributed knowledge to the two trainers, there is, as might by now be expected, a simpler explanation for the successful performance. During their training, the chimpanzees would have often selected a cup that was pointed to by the guesser, and they would not be rewarded. In contrast, the chimpanzee would have received reward on the many trials that she selected the cup pointed to by the knower. The experiment is thus no more than a simple discrimination in which the person who has remained in the room for the longer time is the one who points to the correct cup. This is an unusual discrimination, but there is no reason why it should not be solved on the basis of the principles considered in Chapter 5.

Povinelli et al. (1990) were aware of this possible explanation, which was put to the test in a final stage of their experiment. Once subjects were performing correctly on the task, the method was changed so that a third person baited one of the cups in the presence of the two original trainers. One of the original trainers watched the baiting process closely, while the other was prevented from watching by having his eyes covered in a rather dramatic fashion (see Figure 9.11). The third person then left the room and the two trainers again pointed to two different cups. If chimpanzees are able to attribute knowledge to others, then they should select the cup that is identified by the trainer who observed closely the baiting process. On the other hand, the change in procedure would mean that they should be unable to solve this new

problem if the alternative account developed earlier is correct.

Unfortunately, the results from the test trials are ambiguous. In the 30 trials that were conducted, three of the four subjects showed a significant preference for the cup pointed to by the knower. But this performance was not perfect and the possibility remains that there was a sufficient number of trials for subjects to learn that the trainer who did not cover his head always pointed to the correct cup. If performance had been perfect in this stage, then such an explanation would be untenable. Further discussion on this issue can be found in Heyes (1993) and Povinelli (1994).

The experiment by Povinelli et al. (1990) is undoubtedly of ingenious design. Moreover, given suitable modifications, it may well provide a source of evidence that unequivocally indicates that animals can behave as if they possess a theory of mind. This evidence will not confirm that animals experience and attribute mental states. Instead, it will be compatible with this proposal and, at the same time, be compatible with alternative, nonmentalistic explanations. These alternative explanations may well be complex, and point to new insights into the ways in which the intelligence of animals influences their social behaviour.

SELF-RECOGNITION

The discussion throughout this chapter has been based on the learning that takes places when one animal interacts with another. The final topic to be introduced is devoted to the social learning that might be said to take place when an animal interacts with itself by means of a mirror. As far as humans are concerned, some experience with mirrors is necessary before we appreciate that the image in the mirror is in fact that of our own body. Thus congenitally blind people who have had their sight restored, and young children who have never seen a mirror, both react as if they were seeing another person when they first see a reflection of themselves (Povinelli, Rulf, Landau, & Bierschwale, 1993). But before too much time has passed this reaction is replaced with

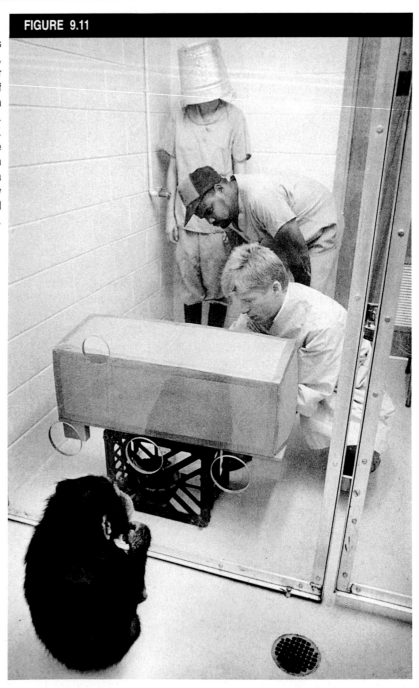

FIGURE 9.11

A chimpanzee watches as one trainer, but not the other, is allowed to see under which of four cups a piece of food is being hidden (from Povinelli et al., 1994). Photograph by Donna T. Bierschwale, courtesy of the University of Southwestern Louisiana New Iberia Research Center, Laboratory of Comparative Behavioral Biology.

self-recognition. How do animals react when they see themselves in a mirror?

The answer to this question depends to some extent on the species that is being tested. When chimpanzees first look in a mirror they treat their reflection as if it were another chimpanzee, but

after several days this response is replaced by more self-directed activities. Indeed, familiarity with a mirror appears to bring out the worst in chimpanzees. They use it to inspect closely the anal-genital area, as well as other hitherto unseen regions of their bodies. They also use the mirror for picking at their teeth, and extracting mucus from their eyes and nose. The photographs in Figure 9.12 indicate some of the less unpleasant ways in which chimpanzees interact with mirrors. Thus, like humans, chimpanzees seem to be able to learn that the image they see in a mirror is that of their own body.

There is also evidence of similar learning with orang-utans (Lethmate & Ducker, 1973; Miles, 1994; Suarez & Gallup, 1981), dolphins (Marten & Psarakos, 1994), and a gorilla (Patterson & Cohn, 1994). Figure 9.13, for example, shows a gorilla, Koko, using a mirror to examine herself (Patterson & Cohn, 1994).

The interpretation of these reports is not straightforward. The pictures shown in Figures 9.12 and 9.13 certainly suggest that the animals appreciated they were looking at their own reflection, but this is not the only possible explanation for their behaviour. A critic might argue that the subjects often engage in the actions shown in the figures, and that it was only by coincidence that they were doing so in front of a mirror when the photographs were taken (Heyes, 1994).

A rather more problematic result for our critic to explain derives from an experimental design developed by Gallup (1970). After chimpanzees appeared to have learned to recognise themselves in a mirror, they were anaesthetised and a mark was made on their foreheads and ears with a nonirritating dye. After recovering from the anaesthetic none of the subjects showed any particular interest in these marks until they saw a mirror, whereupon they were inclined to touch the marks on their heads. Although the way in which these results should be interpreted has been questioned by Heyes (1994), the most popular explanation for the behaviour of the marked chimpanzees is that they used the mirror to direct responses towards their own body. This conclusion is supported by the findings from similar experiments with orang-utans (Lethmate & Ducker, 1973; Suarez & Gallup, 1981) and, particularly forcefully, with a gorilla (Patterson & Cohn, 1994).

Taken together, the results indicate that at least some species can learn to recognise their own bodies in mirrors. Unfortunately, rather little is

known about the factors that are responsible for the transition from treating a reflection as being that of another animal to that of oneself. All that can be said is that the time to make this transition has been reported to take from a few minutes (Povinelli et al., 1993) to a few days (Gallup, 1970). And as far as chimpanzees are concerned, the capacity to recognise their bodies in a mirror does not develop until they are more than four years old (Povinelli et al., 1993).

Other species have been reported to fail to recognise themselves in mirrors. Experiments based on the mark test developed by Gallup (1970) have been unsuccessful with more than a dozen species of Old and New World monkeys (Anderson, 1984), and gibbons (Gallup, 1983). Monkeys also fail to show any of the self-recognition behaviours towards mirrors that have been seen with chimpanzees, orang-utans, and gorillas (Anderson, 1983). Finally, a range of studies has revealed that fish, sea lions, dogs, cats (see Gallup, 1975, for a review), elephants (Povinelli, 1989), and parrots (Pepperberg, Garcia, Jackson, & Marconi, 1995) all react to their own reflections as if they were another animal.

The reason why some animals demonstrate recognition of themselves in mirrors, whereas other do not, remains something of a mystery. One possible explanation is that self-recognition is confined to animals that are able to use information provided by mirrors. However, examples are accumulating of animals being able to use mirrors even though they show no evidence of self-recognition with them. Itakura (1987) reports that monkeys can use a mirror to locate a plastic flower that was suspended above their heads by means of a specially adapted collar (see also Anderson, 1986). Povinelli (1989) describes occasions when an elephant carefully guided its trunk with the help of a mirror in order to retrieve a carrot that was not otherwise visible. And Pepperberg et al. (1995) describe two different experiments in which African grey parrots were able to find hidden objects with a mirror. An obvious puzzle is created by these findings. If an animal is unable to recognise itself in a mirror, how then is it able to use a mirror to guide its own behaviour? Perhaps the animal learns, by trial and

FIGURE 9.12

Examples of the ways in which at least some chimpanzees behave when they are accustomed to seeing their reflection in a mirror (from Povinelli et al., 1993). Photographs by Donna T. Bierschwale, courtesy of the University of Southwestern Louisiana New Iberia Research Center, Laboratory of Comparative Behavioral Biology.

FIGURE 9.13

Koko, a gorilla, making use of a mirror (from Patterson & Cohn, 1994). © Ronald Cohn/The Gorilla Foundation.

error, to make certain movements that manipulate its image in the mirror until a particular configuration is obtained. At this point, as if by coincidence, the animal will also be in physical contact with the goal that it seeks. Put rather differently, the animal may learn to move its image in the mirror in much the same way as humans learn to move a cursor to a particular point on a computer screen by use of a mouse.

A rather different explanation for why only a few species appear to recognise themselves in mirrors has been put forward by Gallup (1970, 1975, 1983), who believes that the use of mirrors for self-directed behaviour depends on self-awareness. Thus a chimpanzee is assumed to be able to use a mirror to locate a spot on its forehead because it knows that it is looking at its own reflection. Moreover, this capacity for self-awareness is said to be confined to great apes (chimpanzees, gorillas, orang-utans) and humans. This argument has by no means gained universal acceptance (e.g. Heyes, 1994). For myself, I am uneasy with Gallup's proposal because I believe it is impossible to know anything about the mental states of animals. How can we, for example, be certain that a chimpanzee has an awareness of self, but a monkey does not? The use of a mirror for guiding self-directed responses might suggest, but it certainly does not confirm, that the animal is self aware.

In closing this discussion of mirror use by animals, therefore, it is reasonably safe to say that some species, but not others, can learn to use mirrors to direct responses towards their own bodies. In other words, they behave as if they believe the image that they see is a reflection of their own body. However, the determination of whether or not they possess such a belief lies beyond the bounds of scientific enquiry.

CONCLUDING COMMENTS

The wide range of experiments reviewed in this chapter demonstrates convincingly that the presence of one animal can influence what another learns. This learning is dependent on a variety of mechanisms. The mere presence of one animal near an object, such as a food bowl or a response lever, might enhance the subsequent attention that an observer of this interaction will pay to the object in the future. This effect is known as stimulus enhancement. Another way an animal can influence what another learns is through social facilitation. Thus the presence of a conspecific can encourage an animal to engage in activities that would not normally be initiated in isolation. These activities need not be directed towards the conspecific, and they may facilitate the discovery of a solution to a problem.

Some uncertainty still surrounds the way in which an observer rat can acquire a food preference by interacting with a rat that has just consumed food. We know that this interaction is not effective because it allows the observer to become familiar with the food, and there are some grounds for believing that the preference is not acquired as a result of associative learning. Perhaps the preference is acquired by a specialised process that has no other purpose. On the other hand, the way in which some animals acquire a fear of stimuli, in particular predators, can be understood in terms of the principles of associative learning.

The principles of associative learning can also be used to explain many demonstrations of mimicry and imitation. There remain a few findings, however, that are not amenable to this type of interpretation. Although these findings imply that an observer is able to copy the responses of another animal, we know very little about how this copying takes place.

Social learning can influence the development of communication among the adults of a species. For certain birds, this learning is responsible for the development of the adult song and is guided by innate predispositions. For vervet monkeys, this learning results in a refinement of the way in which various utterances are used and may depend on the mechanisms of discrimination learning.

Finally, the suggestion has been made that living in social groups has encouraged animals to learn about the intentions, desires, and so forth of other members of their group. This in turn has led to the suggestion that learning from social interactions is based on a theory of mind. Such a claim should be treated with caution. All the evidence that is said to be consistent with it can be explained by the simpler principles of conditioning and discrimination learning.

NOTES

1. An example of a population-specific behavioural tradition in rodents is provided by wild rats living on the banks of the river Po in Italy (Parisi & Gandolfi, 1974). They dive to the river bottom in order to collect molluscs, which they eat. In keeping with the arguments concerning primates, however, there is no evidence that this behavioural tradition depends upon imitation (Galef, 1980).

10

Communication and Language

The most important intellectual capacity possessed by humans is language. By use of the spoken word we are able to live together in large and more or less harmonious social groups; we can teach our children an enormous range of skills; and we can also express our feelings and our thoughts. By use of the written word we have benefited from the knowledge acquired by others over a period of more than 2500 years. Some can also use the written word to create great works of art. Without these and many other benefits of language our lives would be quite different. Indeed, it may not be too far-fetched to say that without language our lives would differ little from those of other animals.

For a variety of reasons it has been argued that language is unique to humans (Chomsky, 1957; Macphail, 1982; Pinker, 1994). The purpose of this chapter is to examine this claim and its implications in some detail. If language is unique to humans, then we should expect to find no evidence of language in the natural communications of animals. By focusing on selected examples of animal communication, this prediction is evaluated in the first part of the chapter. A review of the attempts to teach animals an artificial language is then presented in the second part of the chapter. The proposals made by Macphail (1982) and Chomsky (1957) imply that these attempts will meet with little success.

ANIMAL COMMUNICATION

A definition of communication

The topic of animal communication was touched on in the previous chapter, where the role of learning was examined in the development of bird-song and certain alarm calls. In this section further examples of animal communication will be described briefly in order to demonstrate some of the different ways in which animals are able to communicate with each other.

To define precisely what is meant by animal communication is a surprisingly difficult task that can readily lead to controversy. For present purposes, however, a useful definition is that communication occurs when one organism transmits a signal to another organism that is capable of responding appropriately. By interpreting this statement loosely, a wide range of species can be said to communicate. Thus one of the simplest creatures, the protozoan, can influence the movement of others by secreting a chemical. During courtship the male fruit-fly can stimulate the female by producing a sound with its wings. And the chimpanzee uses a range of sounds, facial expressions, and smell to influence the behaviour of other members of its social group.

The range of information that may be communicated is considerable. The identity of the sender can often be determined from its signals. This information may be rather general and indicate nothing more than the species of the sender, which is still worth knowing in the case of mating signals; alternatively, the identification can be more precise and allow an animal to return to its social group, or a parent to identify and feed its offspring. The motivational state of the sender can also be inferred from the signals it sends. Aggression in cats is indicated by an arching of the back, and the change in bird-song in the spring is a sure sign of the sexual readiness of males. Animals can also communicate about the environment. Many species have an alarm call that indicates the presence of a predator, whereas the honey-bee is famous for her ability to transmit information about the location of food.

In some cases the important component of a signal may be a single feature, such as colour. When the male stickleback is ready to breed, its belly turns red. Should he then enter the territory of another male, the sight of this stimulus will immediately elicit aggression. The importance of the colour red is revealed by Tinbergen's (1953) observation of a stickleback who attempted to attack a red post-office van that passed its aquarium. But even a single feature can convey a variety of information. For instance, Stellar's jay raises its crest during aggressive encounters with other jays, and, according to Brown (1964), the degree to which the crest is raised is directly related to the ferocity of the opponent. A range of intensities of aggression can therefore be signalled by slight adjustments of the crest.

Other definitions of communication have been proposed that are more restrictive than the one given earlier. Slater (1983), for instance, has suggested that an act of communication should, on average, benefit the sender. But this is not always the case. An example of an act of communication where the receiver, but not the sender, benefits is provided by the honey-bee. In brief, after she has returned to the hive a honey-bee will engage in a dance that indicates where she recently found food. Although this dance serves as a valuable source of information for other bees, their response is of no benefit to the dancer. A second example is provided by the alarm calls of vervet monkeys. Apart from

the possibility that the receiver's responses to the calls will confuse the predator, it is difficult to see how the sender can benefit from making an alarm call.

Honey-bee communication

The most complex method of communication by an animal other than humans is believed to have been developed by the honey-bee. The way in which honey-bees transmit information about the location of food is a fascinating topic in its own right. In addition, a brief study of this topic will provide a useful benchmark by which to judge whether or not animal communication can be regarded as language.

On returning to the hive, a worker gives the food she has collected to the other bees, prior to performing a dance on the vertical surface of a comb. If food is within 50 to 100 metres of the hive, then a *round* dance will be observed. The worker remains on the same spot and starts to turn, once to the left, once to the right, and so on for half a minute or more. A sketch of the dance can be seen in the left-hand side of Figure 10.1. This dance indicates to the other workers that food is nearby and the effect it has on them is described by Von Frisch (1950, p. 56):

> During the dance the bees near the dancer become greatly excited; they troop behind her as she circles keeping their antennae close to her body. Suddenly one of them turns away and leaves the hive. Others do likewise, and soon some of the bees appear at the feeding place.

When the food source is more than 100 metres from the hive the returning worker performs a *waggle* dance (see the right-hand side of Figure 10.1). After running a short distance in a straight line while wagging the abdomen rapidly, the bee turns through 360° to the left, and in doing so returns to the start of the straight run. She then again runs in the same straight line, wagging her abdomen, but this time at the end of it turns to the right. By repeating this routine, the waggle dance creates a figure-of-eight pattern. The impressive feature of the waggle dance is that it tells the other workers both the direction and the distance of the

FIGURE 10.1

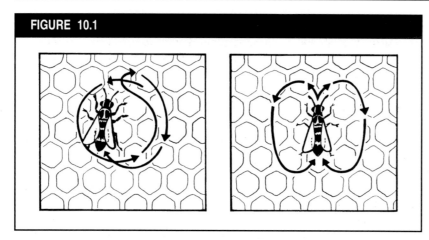

The round dance (left-hand side) and the waggle dance (right-hand side) of the honey-bee (adapted from Von Frisch, 1974).

FIGURE 10.2

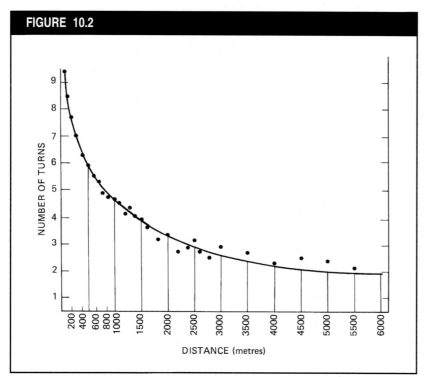

The relationship between the number of turns of the waggle dance, performed during a period of 15 seconds, and the distance of the feeding place (adapted from Von Frisch, 1950).

food. Distance is revealed by the length of the straight run: The further food is from the hive, the longer will be the straight run. As the rate of wagging the abdomen is constant throughout the straight run, it follows that the distance of food is also indicated by the number of wags that are performed on a straight run. Furthermore, because the length of the straight run determines the rate at which the figure of eight can be completed, this measure too provides an indication of the distance of food. An example of this last relationship is presented in Figure 10.2, which was constructed from the observation of 3885 dances performed after the bees had returned from food situated between 100 and 6000 metres from the hive. Apparently the experimenters had to run behind the bees for this study, which Von Frisch (1950, p. 73) described as "rather strenuous and exciting".

The way in which the direction of food is indicated is particularly ingenious. The waggle dance is performed on the vertical surface of a comb, with the direction of the waggle run being at a constant angle to the vertical. This angle corresponds directly to the angle, at the hive, between the direction of the food supply and the direction of the sun (see Figure 10.3). Thus by observing the orientation of the waggle dance on the comb, the workers can calculate the direction in which they must fly from the hive, relative to the sun, in order to reach food.

The analysis offered by Von Frisch of the honey-bee dance has not gone unchallenged. When bees are close to a dancing forager they create squeaks that vibrate the comb and interrupt the

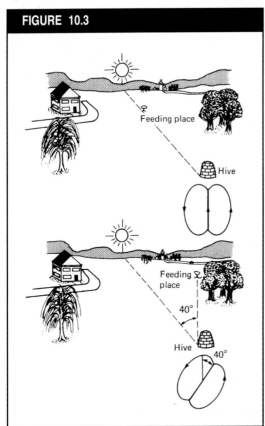

FIGURE 10.3

The way in which the waggle dance indicates the direction of a food source. The angle between the orientation of the dance and the vertical is the same as that between the sun and the food source, as measured at the entrance to the hive (adapted from Von Frisch, 1974).

dance. The forager then distributes small samples of her food to provide information about its taste and smell. Perhaps, therefore, bees learn very little from the dance but, instead, rely on olfactory information to identify the source of food that the dancer has just visited (Wenner, Wells, & Rohlf, 1969). Alternatively, it has been discovered that during her dance, the forager creates a sound like a motorboat by moving her wing muscles in short bursts. Wenner (1967) has argued that it is this sound, rather than the dance, that provides the necessary information about the location of food.

Interesting accounts of the ways in which these alternative explanations have been evaluated can be found in Gould and Gould (1988), and Kirchner and Towne (1994). Kirchner and Towne (1994) describe experiments with a computer-controlled, model bee. The model was made from brass, possessed artificial wings and was able to dispense small samples of food. By simulating a dance, and at the same time dispensing food, and vibrating the wings so that they made the appropriate sounds, the model was able to encourage real bees to leave the hive and search for food in the place indicated by the dance. However, when any one of the three potential sources of information—food, wing sound, or dance—was not available the number of bees that were influenced by the model declined dramatically. Thus it seems that the sounds the dancer makes are important for attracting bees to observe the dance. The sounds may also allow the bees to determine the orientation of the dance if it is performed in the dark. The dance itself provides important information about the direction and distance of food. Additional hints about the taste, smell, and quality of food are then provided by the small samples that are distributed.

Bees from different regions perform slight variations of the waggle dance. For the bees studied by Von Frisch, each waggle of the dance indicated that food was located an extra 45 metres from the hive, for bees in Italy this figure is 20 metres, and for Egyptian bees this figure is 12 metres. From the point of view of the issues raised in the previous chapters concerning communication, it is interesting to note that these differences do not reflect any influence of social learning. For example, if the pupae of one race of bees are placed into the colony of another, then when the bees hatch they persistently behave in a manner that is appropriate to their real sisters and they are not influenced at all by their foster sisters. The details of the way in which the dance is performed and interpreted is thus determined genetically (Gould & Gould, 1988).

The examples referred to constitute only a fraction of what is known about animal communication, yet they serve to demonstrate many of the characteristics of the way in which animals exchange information.

COMMUNICATION AND LANGUAGE

A definition of language

To determine the degree to which animal communication falls short of language, we must first define what is meant by this term. Several authors have done this by listing a set of criteria that an act of communication must fulfil if it is to be regarded as language (Anderson, 1985; Hockett, 1960). Although the following list is by no means exhaustive, it provides a useful framework for evaluating the linguistic skills of animals.

Arbitrariness of units. Language is composed of discrete units, words, which in general are arbitrarily related to the events to which they refer. This characteristic enables different languages to refer to the same object with very different words.

In certain cases, such as alarm calls, animal communication is also composed of discrete units, but in others the signal consists of a coherent unified pattern, as with the dance of the honey-bee. As far as the arbitrariness of the signal is concerned, some instances of communication manifest this property, and some do not. Two examples that fail to meet this criterion are sketched in Figure 10.4. The dogs are displaying submission and aggression, and it is quite apparent that the actions are related to the state they are

FIGURE 10.4

The posture of dogs displaying submission (top) and aggression (bottom) (adapted from Darwin, 1872).

signalling. An example of a more arbitrary relationship between a signal and the information it conveys was enountered in the previous chapter. Vervet monkeys were shown to give different alarm calls to different predators and it is most unlikely that the nature of the predator determines the precise form of the call. In support of this claim, recall that infants must learn to some extent the significance of the calls.

Semanticity. Language allows the transfer of information from one person to another because each word has a specific meaning. We shall presume that a signal, for an animal, has meaning if it can activate a representation of the event to which it relates. We saw in the previous chapter that vervet monkeys appreciate the meaning of the alarm calls that they hear. And the results of an experiment described in Chapter 8 suggest that bees may appreciate the meaning of the communications they receive. Gould (1984) found that bees would leave the hive when the returning forager indicated that food was beside a lake, but they would not leave the hive when they were informed that food was near the middle of the lake. Such an outcome suggests that the forager's dance does not serve simply as a stimulus eliciting flight from the hive. Instead, honey-bees appear to interpret the meaning of the dance—possibly by identifying the potential location of food on a cognitive map—and then decide whether it is worth making the journey.

Displacement. Language allows people to communicate about events that are displaced either in time or in space. The bulk of animal communication lacks this property, because a signal is usually an immediate reaction to an internal state, such as an increase in certain hormones, or an external event, such as the sight of a predator. An obvious exception to this claim is the dance of the honey-bee, in which the precise form of the signal is governed by food that may be several kilometres from the hive.

Productivity. A powerful property of language derives from the fact that it is structured according to rules of grammar, or syntax. By using these rules

an almost infinite number of sentences can be constructed, each of which will convey a different meaning. The productivity criterion refers to this ability to create a large number of meaningful utterances from a limited vocabulary. Examples of animal communication that meet this requirement are scarce, but they do exist. The way in which Stellar's jay signals the intensity of aggression could be said to demonstrate productivity; so, too, could the way in which the honey-bee waggle dance is able to convey information about an almost unlimited number of spatial locations. None the less, in both these cases the range of information that can be transmitted is far more restricted than in human language. In these examples the animals are constrained to communicating about food and aggression. Their rules of production are not sufficiently sophisticated to permit them to converse about a wider range of topics. This may be slightly unfair to the honey-bee, which is able to communicate about the merits of potential sites for a new hive (McFarland, 1985, p. 416).

In addition, to my knowledge animal communication has never met the productivity criterion by combining discrete units, and this may be one characteristic that sets human language apart from the natural communication of every other animal. Where productivity is demonstrated by animals, it is always achieved by varying an attribute of the signal, such as its orientation or intensity.

Language and cooperation

Animal communication therefore differs from human language in a number of ways that are important. But this does not necessarily mean that all animal communication is inferior to language. Much remains to be discovered about the way in which animals communicate, and future research could reveal impressive capacities in this respect. Bottle-nosed dolphins, for instance, are believed to communicate with whistles that are relatively short and vary considerably in frequency (Richards, Wolz, & Herman, 1984). Rather little is known about the function of these signals, and conceivably they may be manifestations of a system approximating language. We should thus acknowledge the possibility that some animal communication meets all the criteria of language, but this has yet to be revealed because of our inability to translate it.

Even though this argument is extremely difficult to refute, because we do not understand the way in which all species communicate, there may be grounds for not taking it too seriously. An important influence of language is that it allows humans to cooperate in extremely complex ways. If it could be shown, therefore, that animals cooperate in complex ways, and that this depends on communication, then we might conclude that the animals concerned possess something akin to language. Of course, there would still remain the task of understanding the communications that passed between the individuals, but at least we could be reasonably confident that our labours in this respect might reveal something of interest. There have been a few studies of cooperation between animals in the laboratory, but none has yet revealed clear evidence that animals possess language.

In 1972 the BBC transmitted a Horizon programme that demonstrated cooperation between a male and a female dolphin, possibly by means of an intelligent communication (details of this and related studies can be found in Bastian, 1961; and Wood, 1973, pp. 113–118). The two dolphins were situated in adjacent pools that allowed them to hear but not to see each other. Occasionally, the female was shown either a steady or an intermittent light, and the male was then required to press one of two paddles in order to earn reward for both of them. Presses by the male on one paddle were rewarded when the steady light was shown to the female, and when the intermittent light was shown, pressing the other paddle led to reward. Despite being unable to see the light, the male eventually responded correctly on the majority of trials. The female emitted different sounds in the presence of the two lights, which is in keeping with the suggestion that the male's success was due to a complex exchange of information.

Boakes and Gaertner (1977) discuss this experiment in some detail, and they propose that the performance of the dolphins can be explained in a rather different way. Suppose that the female, by chance, should make a sound in the presence of one of the lights, and the male should press the correct paddle. Then the female will be rewarded for making the sound during that particular light, and the male will be rewarded for making the response during that particular sound. The next time that the light is presented, the female will be disposed towards making the same sound again and the male will be disposed towards making the correct response. All that is now needed is for the female to make a different sound in the presence of the other light, and the process will repeat itself for the other paddle. In other words, there is no need to look further than the principles of discrimination learning to explain the success of the dolphin pair.

To support their analysis, Boakes and Gaertner (1977) were able to train pairs of pigeons to interact in a similar way to the dolphins. They were also able to show that this was achieved in the manner just described. There have been other studies of cooperation between animals (Epstein, Lanza, & Skinner, 1980; Lubinski & MacCorquodale, 1984; Savage-Rumbaugh, Rumbaugh, & Boysen, 1978), but these too appear to depend on the behaviour of one animal serving as a cue for a certain response from another.

Of course, the possibility remains that the laboratory tests have been inadequate and that animals communicate in sophisticated ways in more naturalistic settings. If this were true, their complex communications should be accompanied by a correspondingly intricate pattern of cooperation. After all, there is little point in engaging in a complex dialogue if it leads nowhere. But to my knowledge there is no naturalistic evidence that groups of animals interact in ways that could be said to be a consequence of a complex communication. For this reason alone, the communications of animals would seem to be very much simpler than that permitted by language.

CAN AN APE CREATE A SENTENCE?

The evidence reviewed thus far provides scant support for anyone wishing to claim that animals possess an intellectual skill akin to language. There remains, however, one line of enquiry to be considered before we can reach any firm conclusions about their linguistic abilities. There has been a variety of attempts to teach animals an artificial language. Although this type of research will reveal little about the way animals communicate naturally, it should provide important insights into their linguistic potential. There is now little doubt that animals can be taught certain features of a language, but there is much dispute as to where the limit of this ability lies. Indeed, the question posed as the title for this section, which is taken from an article by Terrace, Petitto, Sanders, and Bever (1979), captures very precisely a major theoretical issue that occupies this area of research.

There have been a number of attempts in this century to teach language to all of the great apes: chimpanzee, orang-utan, and gorilla. After a brief account of the methods that have been used and the results they have produced, we shall examine critically the conclusions that have been drawn from these studies.

Training methods

One of the earliest attempts to teach an ape language was by William Furness (1916), and the rewards for his endeavours were slight. For many hours he attempted to teach a female orang-utan to speak English, but she was only able to pronounce "papa", "cup", and "th". These were used as the trainer intended, and the ape is reported to have uttered the words "cup cup" shortly before dying of influenza. Some decades later Hayes and Hayes (1951; Hayes, 1961) raised a chimpanzee, Vicki, as if she were a human child, but again despite careful training she was able to speak just four words: "mama", "papa", "cup", "up".

This virtual failure to teach apes to speak is due in part to the fact that their vocal tracts are incapable of producing all the sounds of human speech. Figure 10.5 shows the vocal tracts of a human and a chimpanzee. The structures between the lips and the larynx are of great importance in producing speech, and it is apparent that they differ greatly for the two species. This difference places a considerable limitation on the range of sounds that the chimpanzee can produce—for example the vowel sounds [a], [i], and [u] are said to be impossible for it to pronounce (Lieberman, 1975). Nevertheless, they should be able to articulate some speech sounds and acquire a rudimentary form of spoken language. Passingham (1982) has argued that their inability to do so rests with their failure to imitate the speech that they hear. Why chimpanzees should differ so much from children in this respect has yet to be determined. A possible means for overcoming this barrier to teaching apes a language is to use a medium for communication that does not involve speech. A variety of methods have been tried.

American sign language

Gardner and Gardner (1969; see also Gardner, Gardner, & Van Cantfort, 1989) trained a chimpanzee, Washoe, to communicate by using her hands in much the same way as deaf people do. In fact, Washoe was taught Ameslan, which is the

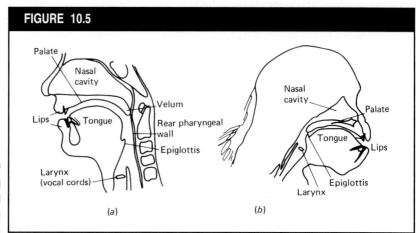

FIGURE 10.5

The adult vocal tract of a human (left-hand side) and a chimpanzee (right-hand side) (adapted from Lieberman, 1975).

principal method for conversation among deaf people in North America. Just as spoken words can be broken down into one or more units, phonemes, so words in Ameslan are constructed from a combination of one or more gestures, cheremes. Each chereme consists of a configuration of the hands placed in a specific position and making a particular action. The words can then be combined to produce sentences by the use of grammatical rules, which differ to some extent from those governing English. Because it possesses these features, Ameslan meets all the requirements for language that were enumerated previously.

By using a variety of techniques, considerable success was achieved with Washoe. At the age of five, after four years of training, she was able to sign 132 different words, which included nouns ("sweet", "key"), pronouns ("me", "you"), and verbs ("tickle", "open"). She was also able to combine these words into strings of up to five in length and used them to give commands to her trainer: "you tickle me", "open key food" (an instruction to open the refrigerator). Washoe was capable of replying to questions posed by her trainer in Ameslan. Thus on one occasion her trainer asked her "What's that?" in the presence of a swan, and was told "Water bird". Following this pioneering work, there have been other attempts to teach apes Ameslan. The most systematic of these has been by Terrace (1979; see especially Terrace et al., 1979), who trained a chimpanzee, Neam Chimpsky—nicknamed Nim. During the course of his training he learned 125 different signs and was observed to combine them into more than 19,000 utterances. Throughout the study a record was kept of these combinations and of the context in which they occurred.

Interestingly, another way of teaching a chimpanzee to use Ameslan was to place an infant in the care of Washoe. This line of research had a rather sad start. When she was about 15, with a vocabularly of 180 signs, Washoe had a child. Her baby became very ill and had to be taken from her in order to receive special care. The treatment was unsuccessful and the baby died. The next day, Washoe's first question to the trainer was the sign "Baby?". The trainer replied "Baby gone, baby finished". Washoe then behaved in a manner that can best be described as grief (Fouts, Hirsch, & Fouts, 1982, p. 170):

> she dropped her arms ... to her lap and she broke eye contact and slowly moved away to a corner of the cage. She was demonstrating all the clinical signs of depression. She continued for the next several days to isolate herself from any interactions with the humans and her signing dropped off to almost nothing. Her eyes appeared to be vacant or distant.

There is, fortunately, a happy ending to this story. A short time later, Washoe was introduced to a 10-month-old infant, Loulis, and rapidly adopted him as her son (see Figure 10.6). They spent a great deal of time together and very soon Loulis started to copy the signs of Washoe. At first, the signs were used in play, but they were eventually used to make spontaneous requests to the trainers, such as "tickle", "drink", "hug". Loulis learned 22 signs from Washoe. Many of the signs were acquired by copying Washoe, but there are one or two reports of Washoe attempting to teach Loulis a sign. On one occasion, Washoe was repeatedly signing "food" as she was being brought some food. She then took Loulis' hand and moulded it into the correct configuration for the food sign. Reports of the development of Loulis as a sign user can be found in Fouts et al. (1982); Fouts, Fouts, and Van Cantfort (1989); and Fouts and Fouts (1989).

There is no doubt that Loulis learned about Ameslan from Washoe, because the trainers were instructed to refrain from signing in his presence. It also seems probable that this learning was based on mimicry and imitation. But how Washoe's role as a teacher should be interpreted remains open to question. She may have been attempting to teach her adopted son to use signs, or she may have been playing with his hands for any one of a number of other reasons.

Plastic tokens

Premack's (1971b, 1976) solution to the problem of the ape's reluctance to speak was to create an artificial language in which the words were plastic objects, which varied in shape, size, colour, and texture. Sarah, Premack's brightest chimpanzee,

FIGURE 10.6

Washoe (left), and her adopted son Loulis (right). Photographs by A. Otley, courtesy Chimpanzee and Human Communication Institute, Central Washington University.

became proficient in the use of about 130 words; these included nouns ("Sarah", "apple", "knife"), verbs ("wash", "draw", "give"), adjectives ("brown"), quantifiers ("all", "none"), and conditionals ("if", "then"). To create a sentence, the words, which had a metal backing, could be placed in a vertical column on a magnetic board (see Figure 10.7). In order for the sentences to be acceptable, the words had to be placed in a grammatically correct sequence.

On some occasions words were placed on the table beside the magnetic board, and the chimpanzee was expected to construct a sentence. If it was correct, then the trainer would place a word representing "correct" on the board, praise the subject verbally, and perhaps give her a jelly bean or similar reward. On trials when the sentence was

wrong, an "incorrect" token was placed on the board, and the trainer might say "No, you dummy".

At other times the trainer placed a sentence on the board, and if it was an instruction, the subject was supposed to obey it—for example, "Sarah give Mary apple". The sentence could also take the form of a question. Two coloured cards might be placed one on top of the other, on the table, and a sentence on the board would ask "? red on green" (is red on green?). The subject was then required to reply by placing a token for either "yes" or "no" on the board.

Lexigrams

Premack's technique has been developed a step further in a project supervised by Rumbaugh (1977), in which the symbols serving as words—or

FIGURE 10.7

One of the chimpanzees, Elizabeth, trained by Premack. The message on the board says, "Elizabeth give apple Amy" (adapted from Premack, 1976).

lexigrams, as they were called—were displayed on a keyboard connected to a computer. Pressing a key resulted in its symbol being projected onto a screen above the console. To create a sentence, the chimpanzee, originally Lana, had to press a sequence of keys that resulted in the display of a string of lexigrams. The sentence had to be structured according to a set of grammatical rules, known as Yerkish, which are not too dissimilar to those governing English. Hence, in order to receive a drink, Lana had to press the lexigrams for "Please machine give juice", in that sequence. Figure 10.8 shows a selection of lexigrams as they are typically arranged on a keyboard. The purpose of the computer was to keep a record of Lana's statements and to dispense films, slides, music, food, sweets, and liquids, when requested. The computer screen could also be used to present instructions to Lana in lexigrams.

Lana is a common chimpanzee (*Pan troglodytes*), but there is another species of chimpanzee, the bonobo (*Pan paniscus*), which is said to be able to modulate their vocalisations to a much greater extent than its near relative. Rumbaugh and Savage-Rumbaugh (1994)

attempted to teach an adult bonobo, Matata, to use lexigrams but they failed dismally. While she was being trained, however, Matata was accompanied by her adopted son, Kanzi. Even though no attempt was made to teach Kanzi, he started to communicate by means of the lexigrams on the keyboard. He requested things, named things, and announced what he was about to do (see Figure 10.9). To explain the success of Kanzi, and the failure of his mother, Rumbaugh and Savage-Rumbaugh (1994) suggest that there is a critical period during early infancy when exposure to language is essential if the effects of language training are to be optimal.

Spoken English

Although apes are very poor at speaking English, they may well be able to comprehend statements that are spoken in English. Fouts et al. (1982) mention in passing that Washoe understood some spoken English. And additional experiments with Kanzi make this point forcefully.

As soon as Kanzi started to use the lexigram keyboard, he received special training. Instead of taking part in formal training sessions for a

FIGURE 10.8

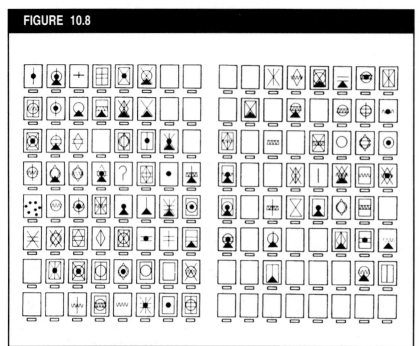

The arrangement of lexigrams on a keyboard. Blank spaces were nonfunctioning keys, or displayed photographs of trainers (from Savage-Rumbaugh et al., 1983).

restricted amount of time each day, he received constant attention and spent his waking hours as a full member of the human social group that worked in the laboratory. He was also spoken to in much the same way as many human parents speak to their children before they can talk. That is, he was spoken to as if he understood everything that was being said. Kanzi continued to receive training in the use of lexigrams, but these were now associated with the appropriate speech sounds. This method of training obviously required a great deal of patience, because it persisted for a number of years. Eventually, however, formal testing with single words and sentences confirmed that Kanzi could understand human speech. In some of the tests he was instructed to "take the can opener to the bedroom", "take the potato outdoors", "go outdoors and get the potato", or "take the potato outdoors and get the apple". He was also tested, and responded correctly, with statements of the sort "get item X from location Y", even if there was an identical item X in front of him. On the basis of his performance Rumbaugh and Savage-Rumbaugh (1994) proposed that Kanzi's comprehension skills are equivalent to those of a child that is $2\frac{1}{2}$ years old. An engaging account of Kanzi's achievements is provided by Savage-Rumbaugh and Lewin (1994).

Assessment of language training with apes

Discreteness and displacement. Of the various criteria that were listed as requisites for language, both displacement and discreteness have been well demonstrated as being met by apes using an unnatural system of communication. Discreteness is revealed by the use of specific gestures or symbols to represent words, and displacement is revealed by conversations involving objects that are not in view. An excellent example of a conversation that meets both of these criteria is provided by Savage-Rumbaugh, Pate, Lawson, Smith, and Rosenbaum (1983). They tested two chimpanzees, Austin and Sherman, who were trained to communicate with an experimenter by a method based on that devised by Rumbaugh (1977). After examining a table of different items of food, the chimpanzee had to walk around a partition to a keyboard, from where the food could not be seen. He then had to request one of the items

FIGURE 10.9

Kanzi using lexigrams on a portable keyboard to communicate with his trainer Sue Savage-Rumbaugh. From *Kanzi: At the brink of the human mind* by E.S. Savage-Rumbaugh & R. Lewin. Reprinted by permission of John Wiley and Sons, Inc.

and wait for permission from the trainer to collect it. Once permission had been granted the chimpanzee returned to the table, picked up the specified food, and took it to the trainer, where it was shared. By requesting food that was out of sight, the subject is clearly communicating about a spatially displaced object.

Semanticity. Considerable effort has been expended in establishing whether or not apes know the meaning of the words they use. It would be as

well to establish at the outset, therefore, what precisely is implied when we say that a word means, or symbolises, something else. In the discussion of natural communication by animals a signal was said to be meaningful if it activated a representation of a particular event. An alternative way of expressing this idea is to say that a signal has meaning if it can serve as a cue for the retrieval of information about the event to which it relates. At this point it is perhaps worth drawing attention to the conclusion drawn in Chapter 2 that after pairing a signal, such as a tone or light, with a US, such as food, the signal then acquires the capacity to activate a representation of the US. As these results were obtained with rats it should not be surprising to discover that apes too can learn the "meaning" of signals.

Indeed, we have already come across evidence that supports this conclusion. The poignant reaction of Washoe to the news of her baby's death, and the ability of Kanzi to execute correctly the instructions he heard, provides compelling evidence that they understood what they were told. Premack (1976, pp. 473–474) describes an experiment that also demonstrates that Sarah understood the meaning of at least one of the words she used. Her training with the word "brown" consisted solely of being told that "Brown colour of chocolate" in the absence of any chocolate. When she was then given four disks of different colours, she responded correctly to the command "Take brown" (Premack, 1976, p. 353). Unless the symbol for chocolate was capable of retrieving information about chocolate, she would not know to which colour the word brown referred.

But there are many reports that suggest chimpanzees do not always understand the words they use. A clear example was provided by Nim. He was quite capable of signing correctly "apple" or "banana" when these fruits were presented one at a time, but when they were given together he was unable to respond correctly if requested to give the trainer an apple. This confusion would not be expected if he understood the meaning of the words he used (Savage-Rumbaugh, 1984).

One explanation for the failure of chimpanzees at times to appreciate the meaning of words may well rest with the way in which they were trained (Savage-Rumbaugh et al., 1983; Savage-Rumbaugh, 1984). Consider one aspect of Sarah's training. She would be seated at her table in the presence of a banana, and if she wrote the sentence "Mary give Sarah banana", the symbol for correct was placed on the board, followed by praise and perhaps something like a jelly baby (Premack, 1976, p. 26). On other trials an apple might be visible, and she would have to request this fruit in order to be given much the same rewards. Thus the effect of this training might be to make the meaning

of the symbols for apple and banana ambiguous, as they were each paired with a variety of rewards. This problem is not unique to Sarah's training. To teach Lana the word "banana", she was given a tray with a slice of banana on it. Using the appropriate lexigrams, the experimenter then constructed the sentence "?What name of this". If she then replied correctly "Banana name of this" she could request from the computer any reward she wanted, including banana. This training might well have taught her to press a certain lexigram in the presence of a banana as an instrumental response that led to reward.

Direct evidence that teaching methods exert an important influence on the effects of language training can be found in an experiment by Savage-Rumbaugh et al. (1980). If some of the details of this experiment should seem familiar, this is because they were mentioned briefly in Chapter 5. Three chimpanzees, Austin, Sherman, and Lana, were separately given a mixed collection of foods and tools and required to sort them into two trays according to these categories. The experiment then progressed through a number of additional training stages, each with its own test trials that were conducted with novel objects. For the second stage, the experimenter held up an object, and the subject had to identify it by pressing the appropriate category key on the computer console. For the third stage the experimenter held up a photograph, and for the fourth a lexigram, and again the chimpanzees had to press a key on the console to categorise the objects that they represented.

Even with this last stage of the experiment both Sherman and Austin performed with a very high level of accuracy on the test trials. Savage-Rumbaugh et al. (1980) maintain that this performance can best be explained by assuming that they knew the meaning of the lexigrams with which they were tested.

An interesting feature of this experiment is that Lana was unable to progress beyond the first stage, which suggests that she did not know the meaning of the lexigrams she used. To understand the success of Austin and Sherman it must be appreciated that their training was different to that for Lana. The two males were taught the meaning of a new lexigram for a particular type of food by being shown a collection of foods, and they were able to use the new symbol to gain access only to the food to which it related. Consequently, responding with the symbol could not be regarded as a means for acquiring any reward; instead, its use was always followed by the same, unique reward. Savage-Rumbaugh et al. (1983) regard this training as being much better suited to teaching the meaning of symbols, and the evident competence of Austin and Sherman in their task supports their trainers in this respect.

Further evidence that Austin and Sherman understood the meaning of the lexigrams they used can be found in a study by Savage-Rumbaugh, Sevcik, and Hopkins (1988). The chimpanzees were shown a lexigram for an object. They were then able to retrieve the object from a box, into which they could not see, and which contained a number of different objects. Unless the chimpanzees knew the meaning of the lexigram, it is difficult to understand how they were able to identify the correct object.

Productivity.   Very often the meaning of a sentence is not just governed by the words it contains; the order in which they occur is also very important. "Jessica hit Tim" is thus completely different in meaning to "Tim hit Jessica", even though both sentences contain the same words. This is possible because all sentences are constructed according to grammatical rules. Not only do these rules constrain the way a sentence can be constructed or interpreted, they also enable a speaker to create an almost unlimited number of meaningful statements from a finite vocabulary. Given the importance of grammar to language, it is understandable that a considerable amount of interest has been directed at the issue of whether or not apes can master these rules. In the following discussion their ability in this respect will be considered separately for language comprehension and production.

Comprehension.   For some of her training Sarah was required to respond on the basis of information provided in the following form of sentence: "Debby give apple Mary ⊃ Sarah insert cracker dish", which is an instruction for Sarah to put a biscuit in a dish if Debby gives Mary an apple. After training with a variety of such sentences, she responded to them correctly, even when novel. Because of the statement's complexity, her success might be taken as evidence that she had used grammatical rules to decode it. Premack (1976) points out, however, that instead of understanding the sentence, Sarah's training could have taught her an alternative means for solving this problem. In all the sentences of this sort that she was given, the first part was always true; in the quoted example Debby, as a matter of course, gave Mary the apple. Thus, to receive reward, Sarah needed only to fulfil the command in the second half of the sentence, and there was no reason for her even to look at the first half. A better test of Sarah's linguistic abilities would have been to examine her response on probe trials in which the "if" condition was not true. Regrettably, as is so often the case with good ideas, this one did not occur to Premack (1976) until it was too late to test it.

Even in the absence of this test Sarah might be said to have understood grammatical rules, because in the example mentioned she put the biscuit in the dish. But Sarah had received extensive training with instructions such as "Sarah insert cracker dish", and she may simply have learned to perform the appropriate action in the presence of a certain configuration of shapes in order to gain reward.

To analyse here the details of all the comprehension tests that have been given to common chimpanzees would be extremely tedious. Suffice it to say that those sentences that have been claimed to reveal the use of grammatical rules by this species are generally open to alternative explanation (Ristau & Robbins, 1982). On the other hand, more encouraging findings can be found in tests with bonobos. I mentioned earlier that one bonobo, Kanzi, was able to respond correctly to spoken instructions. Many of the novel instructions that Kanzi obeyed would have been ambiguous if he was insensitive to their syntactic structure. Even so, he was able to show that he understood them to a degree that is far greater than would be expected on the basis of chance (Savage-Rumbaugh et al., 1993). For some of these tests, Kanzi was required to wear headphones to prevent the person who was assessing his performance from hearing the commands (see Figure 10.10). Examples of instructions that he executed correctly when he first heard them are:

"Make the snake bite Linda."
"Can you throw a potato at the turtle."
"Go outdoors and find the carrot."
"Take the carrot outdoors."
"Pour the Coke in the lemonade."
"Pour the lemonade in the Coke."

It should be apparent that Kanzi's success with this type of test strongly suggests that he has some mastery of the rules with which the instructions were constructed. Of course, we do not know whether it was the special training that Kanzi received, or whether bonobos have a greater potential for acquiring language than chimpanzees, which accounts for the different results from these species.[1]

Production. While being rowed across a pond by Fouts (1975), her trainer, Washoe was shown a swan and asked "what that?" Despite never having been taught the phrase, she replied "Water bird". On another occasion, Washoe's trainer placed a doll in a cup and asked the ape to sign about it. Washoe's reply is quite impressive: "Baby in my drink".

These constitute but two of many examples where an ape has provided a novel utterance that is appropriate to the situation in which it occurred. Moreover, as they consist of a string of words that, for English, are correctly structured, it seems as if Washoe can use grammatical rules to produce sentences. Or does it? Terrace et al. (1979) have argued that they do not justify any sophisticated claims about the linguistic ability of apes.

As far as the water-bird example is concerned, it is not inconceivable that Washoe was replying to the question by identifying, first, a body of water and, second, a bird.

FIGURE 10.10

Kanzi listening to spoken instructions as he participates in a test of language comprehension. Photograph by Mike Nichols.

Before concluding that Washoe was relating the sign *water* to the sign *bird,* one must know whether she regularly placed an adjective *(water)* before, or after, a noun *(bird).* That cannot be decided on the basis of a single anecdote, no matter how compelling the anecdote may seem to an English-speaking observer (Terrace et al., 1979, pp. 895–896).

On examining a film of the "Baby in my drink" incident, Terrace et al. (1979, p. 898) discovered that, perhaps unwittingly, the trainer pointed first to the doll and then to the cup before Washoe started her reply. This information, rather than rules of grammar, was possibly responsible for the way in which Washoe structured her answer.

Lieberman (1984, pp. 240–241) has suggested that these arguments of Terrace et al. (1979) are unduly harsh. He also cites several other examples of novel utterances by chimpanzees, which, he maintains, are harder to discount as examples of rule-governed sequences: "smell fruits" (citrus fruits), "hurt fruit" (a radish), and "drink fruit" (a watermelon). But, once again, although these examples are consistent with a rule such as "adjective before noun", they do not confirm that the chimpanzee was using a rule to generate them. These phrases may have occurred equally often in the reverse order, which would not be expected from a grammatical chimpanzee. I am not sure how seriously this possibility should be taken. It is offered merely to show the difficulty there is in forming conclusions about the grammatical skills of animals when isolated examples are drawn from a large body of multi-word utterances.

In addition to analysing the utterances of apes trained by other researchers, Terrace et al. (1979) also conducted a thorough examination of the strings of words produced by Nim. In total, over an 18-month period, Nim signed 19,203 multi-word utterances, of which there were 5235 different types. Despite this number and variety, the experimenters were unable to conclude that these statements were structured according to a set of rules.

One problem was posed by the limited variety of certain classes of utterance. For example, when the word "more" was used in a two-word utterance, it consistently occupied the first position. Unfortunately, Nim knew no other words to express recurrence, and it is therefore impossible to determine whether this particular pattern reflects a grammatical rule or, more fundamentally, a habit of starting statements with "more". Another difficulty is that Nim often copied the signs of the trainer. He may thus have created grammatically correct sequences by cheating.

It is also instructive to compare the multi-word utterances of Nim with those of children. The term *mean length of utterance* (mlu) refers to the average length of all multi-word utterances made by an individual. Figure 10.11 shows that for a normal child, as well as for one that is deaf and uses Ameslan, there is a sharp increase in mlu with age. In stark contrast, Nim's mlu was maintained at much the same value of about 1.5 throughout his training. If Nim had mastered the rules of grammar, then they would have allowed him to produce increasingly longer sentences. A further difference between Nim and children is that for the latter a long utterance is more informative than a short one. Thus "Sit Daddy" might be elaborated to "Sit Daddy chair". This was very rarely true for Nim, who generated long utterances principally by repeating words. The following utterance by Nim makes it hard to believe that he was grammatical in his use of language: "Give orange me give eat orange me eat orange give me eat orange give me you" (Terrace et al., 1979, p. 895).

Despite these arguments, there is no doubt that apes can produce reliably statements that are grammatically correct. Sarah would consistently write sentences of the form "Give Sarah grape" to indicate that she was to receive, and not give, a grape. But whether these sentences were derived from syntactic rules, or whether they were a consequence of Sarah remembering each of the strings of symbols that had previously led to reward, remains to be determined. In other words, the sight of a grape might have served as a discriminative stimulus controlling the response of placing certain shapes in a fixed sequence.

On a more positive note, Rumbaugh and Savage-Rumbaugh (1994) claim that Kanzi's two-word communications, made with lexigrams

FIGURE 10.11

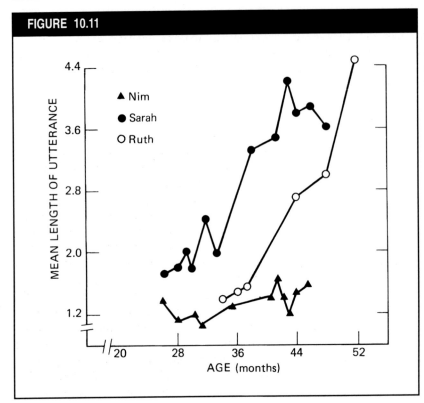

The change in the length of utterance with age for a normal child, Sara, a deaf child, Ruth, and Nim (adapted from Terrace et al., 1979).

and gestures, were structured according to rules. For sentences containing an agent and an action, the action was consistently placed second, whereas for sentences containing an object and an action the action consistently came first. At the very least, these findings suggest that the placement of an action in a sentence was not determined by chance, or by a simple position preference. These two rules could have been acquired from his interaction with his trainers, but he used a further rule which he devised himself. Kanzi would occasionally press in sequence two lexigrams as a request for two actions to be performed in social play, for example "tickle-bite". Rumbaugh and Savage-Rumbaugh (1994) maintain that this sequence reflects the preferred order in which the actions were to take place. Despite these successes, the sentences Kanzi created were considerably less complicated than some of those he was able to comprehend. Thus Savage-Rumbaugh et al. (1993) report that his mlu when communicating with lexigrams was maintained at 1.5.

On the whole, therefore, the evidence that apes can create a sentence is not particularly convincing (see also Ristau & Robbins, 1982). But it would be foolish to assume without reservation that apes will never conquer this apparent barrier between the intelligence of humans and animals. We have seen that the way in which language training is conducted can determine the extent to which it is successful. We have also seen that the age at which training starts may be important. There is thus a real possibility that with the appropriate type of training, apes will improve on the production skills that they have thus far displayed.

One final point: Because of the detailed way in which the study was conducted and analysed, considerable emphasis has justifiably been put on Nim's failure to acquire grammatical skills. There are, however, grounds for being cautious when interpreting the performance of this subject. Undoubtedly the intellectual abilities of individual chimpanzees vary, as they do for humans. Nim may not have been an especially gifted subject, and it would be unwise to regard his results as representative of chimpanzees in general. To support this point, it is noteworthy that Nim had a succession of trainers, which resulted in his repeatedly forming and then breaking close attachments. The influence of these emotional disturbances on his intellectual development is difficult to assess (see Lieberman, 1984, pp. 244–246). There has also been a suggestion that the social context in which Nim was tested was far from perfect (Fouts et al., 1982; O'Sullivan & Yeager, 1989).

LANGUAGE TRAINING WITH OTHER SPECIES

Attempts to teach language to animals have not been confined to the apes. This training has also been conducted with other species, notably a parrot, dolphins, and sea lions. In this section the methods employed for this research, and the results it has revealed, are briefly examined.

Dogs

Although rather little has been learned about the use of language by studying dogs, the skill of a German Shepherd dog, called Fellow, is hard to dismiss. Fellow appeared in a number of films during the 1920s and was reputed to respond to a large number of spoken commands. In a carefully controlled study of his abilities Warden and Warner (1928) discovered that Fellow responded to a total of 53 different commands, including "sit", "stand up", "roll over", "turn around", "lay down" , "lie still", and "put your foot on the chair". If he was told "do that once more" he repeated the last action. In order to eliminate any possibility that Fellow was reacting to subtle actions by his trainer, rather than to spoken commands, he was tested on one occasion in a hotel room while his trainer shouted instructions through the closed door of an adjoining bathroom.

There is, of course, little evidence here to suggest that Fellow possessed any linguistic competence. Instead, his behaviour can be explained quite adequately in terms of S–R theory, where each spoken command serves as the cue for a different response. Even so, the fact that he was able to obey 53 different commands is an impressive achievement by both Fellow and his trainer.

A parrot

Parrots are famous for their capacity to mimic human speech, although normally they say only a few words. In a series of articles Pepperberg (1981, 1983, 1987, 1993) has shown that they can, in fact, acquire a relatively large vocabulary of spoken words, which can be combined to form meaningful multi-word utterances. Her single subject is an African grey parrot, Alex, who was tutored in English. He was trained first to speak the names of objects (e.g. "paper", "key", "grain", "chair", "back", "gym"). Of some interest is the fact that the manner in which correct responses were rewarded differed from that used in the majority of studies with apes. Whenever Alex named an object, he was praised and then allowed to eat it or to play with it. The method of training is also of interest. Alex would be in a position that allowed him to see two trainers. One trainer then asked the other, who adopted the role of a parrot, to name an object; if the trainer's reply was correct, then he or she was praised and expected to play with the object. Merely as a result of watching these interactions, Alex soon entered into the proceedings, as the following extract from a typical session shows (Pepperberg, 1981).

Irene (Pepperberg): Bruce, what's this?
Bruce (a trainer): Pasta. (loudly)
Irene: Good boy! Here you go. (Hands over a piece of pasta)
Alex: (interrupting) ah-ah.
Bruce: Do you want this, Alex? What is it?
Alex: Pah-ah.
Bruce: Better ...
Alex: Pah-ah.
Bruce: No. Irene, what's this?
Irene: Pah-ah.
Bruce: Better!
Irene: Pas-ta. (emphasising the "s" and "t")
Bruce: That's right, tell me what it is again. (offers pasta)

Irene: Pasta! (takes pasta) Pasta! (Alex stretches from his perch on top of the cage, appears to reach for pasta)

Alex: Pa!

Irene: Better... what is it?

Alex: Pah-ah.

Irene: Better!

Alex: Pah-ta.

Irene: Okay, here's the pasta. Good try.

Training in this manner soon became more elaborate, so that Alex's speech eventually included colours, shapes, and numbers, which were often combined with object names. Thus when shown a piece of computer paper for the first time, he was able to identify it as "Four-corner paper". On other trials an object such as a blue triangle might be presented accompanied by the question "What colour?" or "What shape?". His answers were correct with an accuracy that was far in excess of that predicted by chance. These findings are particularly impressive when it is appreciated that Lana was unable to respond correctly on this sort of problem (Savage-Rumbaugh et al., 1983).

Intriguing as these findings may be, they do not show that Alex was capable of understanding or creating sentences. As an alternative, his sentences may have been the product of rote learning sequences of sounds that were produced in the presence of the appropriate discriminative stimuli. Evidence that Alex's linguistic skills might extend beyond this interpretation comes from his use of the phrase "Wanna go". At the outset of his training Alex was unhappy in novel places and consequently spent most of the time in either his cage or his gym, which contained a collection of rods and ropes. When in his cage he was often asked "Wanna go gym?" and this frequently produced a squeaky "yeah" in reply. After a while he spontaneously uttered the phrase "Wanna go gym" and was immediately carried to it. He even modified this phrase to "Wanna go gym-no" when he was in the gym and appeared to want to leave it (as indicated by stretching towards something else).

As he gained in confidence Alex would sit on chairs, shelves, and a trainer's knee. During this time he often heard the names of these perches, but care was taken to ensure that he never heard them in conjunction with the phrase "Wanna go". Despite this constraint, Alex started to say phrases like "Wanna go chair". And if he was taken to a different place he responded either with a "No" or with a repeat of the request.

These findings indicate that Alex is capable of generating novel, meaningful, multi-word utterances (although it is arguable that "wanna go" should be regarded as a single word). Unfortunately the limited number of these utterances makes it difficult to be sure of their origins. They may have been the production of a primitive grammar that contains a rule of the form: "Wanna go" is followed by an object. Alternatively, they may have been produced by chance and strengthened because of the reward that followed.

Dolphins

Herman, Richards, and Wolz (1984; see also Herman, Pack, & Morrel-Samuels, 1993) have presented a carefully documented report of an investigation into the linguistic ability of two dolphins. The results from a very similar study using sea lions, which revealed much the same findings as with dolphins, can be found in Schusterman and Gisiner (1988). Whereas the training for apes, as well as that for Alex, involved both the comprehension and the production of sentences, only the former was tested with dolphins and sea lions.

Herman et al. (1984) trained two bottle-nosed dolphins, Akeakamai and Phoenix, to behave in specific ways according to sequences of signals. For Akeakamai the signals were gestures performed by a person standing by the pool in which the dolphins were tested (see Figure 10.12). The signals for Phoenix were short discrete noises generated by a computer. The training for the two animals differed in a number of other respects, and for the sake of brevity the account that follows concentrates on Akeakamai's treatment and results.

Table 10.1 shows the words that Akeakamai responded to correctly. The list includes objects, actions, agents, and modifiers. After preliminary training, she was instructed in the comprehension of two-word sentences. Examples of these and the longer sentences that were eventually used can be

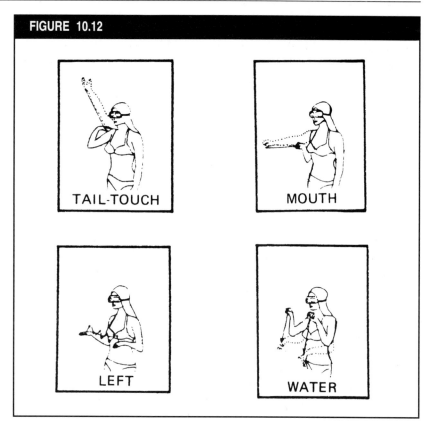

FIGURE 10.12

Examples of some of the gestural signs used for the sentence-comprehension studies with a dolphin, Akeakamai (adapted from Herman et al., 1984).

TAIL-TOUCH

MOUTH

LEFT

WATER

seen in Table 10.2 together with the rules of the artificial syntax that governed their construction. The table also includes a translation of the sentences. Thus two-word sentences were structured according to the rule of object before action, which means that "Phoenix over" is an instruction for Akeakamai to jump over Phoenix. On the most recent test reported, Akeakamai responded correctly to 85% of the possible sentences that can be constructed from this language.

One enormous advantage of this type of training is that it is possible to conduct test trials that provide unambiguous results. For example, during the course of her training Akeakamai was tested with 193 novel sentences when all the objects listed in Table 10.1 were in the pool. The objects thus provided no clue as to how she should respond, yet her performance on these trials was extremely accurate. The most plausible explanation for this outcome is that she had understood the rules that structured the artificial language and could use

them to interpret novel sequences of signals. Support for this important conclusion can be found in other aspects of Akeakamai's performance.

After experiencing many two- and three-word sentences, Akeakamai was suddenly given one containing four words, and she responded correctly. The implication of this finding is that she was able to use the rules relevant to the shorter sentences to understand a more complex syntactic structure. This is precisely the sort of skill that should be demonstrated by an animal that is grammatically competent.

The sample of sentences in Table 10.2 makes it apparent that in some cases their meaning is very much dependent on word order. Although composed of the same signals, the string "Pipe hoop fetch" is a very different instruction to "Hoop pipe fetch". Despite this added complexity Akeakamai was able to react appropriately when given a novel sentence of this sort. In fact, the likelihood of responding correctly was the same as for equivalent sentences with which she was

TABLE 10.1

The Comprehension Vocabulary of a Dolphin, Akeakamai.

Objects

window	speaker	basket	person
net	ball	pipe	frisbee
water	hoop	fish	surfboard
Phoenix			

Actions
tail touch
pectoral touch
mouth (grasp) with mouth
(go) over
(go) under
(go) through
spit (squirt water from mouth at object)
fetch (take one named object to another named object)
in (place one named object in another named object)
toss (throw object)

Agent
Akeakamai (prefix for each sentence)

Modifiers

left	right

Other

no	yes	erase

After Herman et al. (1984).

TABLE 10.2

The Rules of Syntax of the Gestural Language for a Dolphin, Akeakamai.

Rule	*Example*
2-word	
Object + Action	Basket toss (Throw the basket)
	Window tail–touch (Touch the window in the tank with your tail)
3-word	
Modifier + Object + Action	Left person mouth (Touch the person on your left with your mouth)
IO + DO + Action	Pipe hoop fetch (Take the hoop to the pipe)
	Hoop pipe fetch (Take the pipe to the hoop)
4-word	
IO + Modifier + DO + Action	Ball right frisbee fetch (Take the frisbee on your right to the ball)
Modifier + IO + DO + Action	Right basket pipe fetch (Take the pipe to the basket on your right)

IO = Indirect object; DO = Direct object.
After Herman et al. (1984).

familiar. Once again, such an outcome strongly suggests that she was sensitive to the grammatical rules of her language.

The dolphins also demonstrated that they were able to meet some of the other requirements of a linguistic ability. Mastery of the displacement criterion was revealed on numerous occasions. On some trials the instruction related to an object that was hidden from view (spatial displacement), and the dolphin had to find it before responding. On other trials the command was issued as much as 30 seconds before the objects to which it related were thrown into the pool (temporal displacement). Neither of these variants caused much difficulty. A rather different version of this type of test consisted of placing all the objects but one in the pool and then giving a two-word sentence that related to the missing object. Akeakamai would often search for up to nearly a minute for the missing item and then stop, without responding to the other objects. She also rapidly learned to press a paddle to indicate that the designated item was missing.

The way in which dolphins are able to react to sophisticated commands is most impressive and suggests at least a rudimentary understanding of grammatical rules, but some caution is needed when drawing conclusions from this study. As a component of language, production is certainly of equal importance to comprehension and, as yet, there is no evidence that dolphins can produce even the simplest sentence. The study by Herman et al. (1984) suggests that further attempts at language training with dolphins are worthwhile, but the eventual outcome of this research remains uncertain.

THE REQUIREMENTS FOR LEARNING A LANGUAGE

There is, therefore, a need for further research with animals before their ability to use language can be fully appreciated. As a way of gaining an insight into the likely outcome of this research, we can examine the requirements that might be considered necessary if an animal, either human or nonhuman, is to be linguistically proficient. In the discussion

that follows we shall examine the role of innate factors, motivation, and thought, for the acquisition of language.

Language acquisition device

From the point of view advocated by Chomsky (1972; see also Pinker, 1994), the reason for the absence of a clear demonstration of linguistic competence by animals is quite simple. The languages of the world share a striking similarity in the way in which their grammars operate. This suggested to Chomsky (1972) that humans possess an innate device for generating a "universal grammar", from which the grammars of these languages are derived. As apes and other animals do not naturally use language, it would be reasonable to conclude that they do not possess such a device, and this would explain their limitations in sentence construction. Macphail (1982) has also argued that language is a uniquely human phenomenon, but for reasons that are rather different from those of Chomsky (1972). After considering much of the evidence summarised previously, he concluded (p. 312): "humans acquire language (and non-humans do not) not because humans are (quantitatively) more intelligent, but because humans possess some species-specific mechanism (or mechanisms) which is a prerequisite of language-acquisition".

Plausible as these arguments may be, they should not be accepted without further thought. Currently very little is known about the properties of the device that is said to provide humans with their universal grammar. We should, therefore, be cautious in accepting the existence of such a device until we know what it is and how it operates. Furthermore, Chomsky's (1972) proposals have not gone unchallenged. Anderson (1985), for example, maintains that there are constraints on the way in which our cognitive processes operate, and these, in turn, are responsible for the structure of language. Thus it is natural to think of the subject of an action before considering the object, and this constraint may explain why, for three-word sentences, the majority of the world's languages place the subject before the object (Greenberg, 1963). If there are grounds for doubting the existence of a specific language-acquisition device, then we should also doubt the claim that its absence is the reason for the inability of apes to produce a sentence.

Motivation

The claim that humans possess an innate language-acquisition device may not, therefore, be wholly justifiable. But even if it were, the possibility remains that with the right sort of training animals could acquire at least rudimentary language skills. There may, however, be another barrier that restricts animals in their use of language: They may simply be unwilling to communicate with humans—that is, their linguistic shortcomings may be due to a motivational rather than intellectual deficit.

There can be little doubt that young children are extremely willing communicators. In the early stages of language development, they frequently point to objects and name them without any prompting (Locke, 1980). At a later stage they will often initiate a conversation that bears no relevance to what has just been said. Apes, in contrast, have shown themselves to be much more reluctant to engage in spontaneous acts of communication. Hence, rather than to start a conversation, a high proportion of Nim's utterances were imitations of the trainer's previous signs, which is relatively rare in children (Terrace, 1979). Acts of spontaneous pointing and naming are also reported to be uncommon for many language-trained apes (Savage-Rumbaugh, 1984).

Despite what has just been said, there are a number of reports of apes communicating spontaneously, given the appropriate circumstances. A clear example concerns Austin and Sherman. Some time after they had taken part in the categorisation experiment described previously, they began to name objects without being asked to do so. Thus one of the apes would name an object on the keyboard—for instance, "blanket"—and then point to it or give it to the trainer. This behaviour was not specifically trained but, maintains Savage-Rumbaugh (1984), was a consequence of the unique type of language training they had received. There is also a report concerning Nim, which shows that when he was in a more informal setting than the one used for his

training, there was a marked increase in the number of his spontaneous utterances (O'Sullivan & Yeager, 1989). Kanzi, too, would often offer an unsolicited multi-word utterance (Savage-Rumbaugh, McDonald, Sevcik, Hopkins, & Rubert, 1986). On this basis, then, it is likely that an unwillingness to communicate will not prove an impenetrable barrier for training apes to use language.

Some observations by Gardner and Gardner (1974) provide further support for this conclusion. They noticed that Washoe often signed to herself in play, or when looking through a book. "Washoe also signed to herself about her ongoing or impending actions. We have often seen Washoe moving stealthily to a forbidden part of the yard, signing *quiet* to herself" (Gardner & Gardner, 1974, p. 20). Furthermore, these instances of what have been called private signing occur quite frequently. In a detailed investigation of private signing that lasted for 56 hours, Washoe and four other chimpanzees were observed to sign to themselves on more than 350 occasions, using nearly 60 different signs. Finally, the way in which Loulis learned to use signs by copying Washoe suggests at least a rudimentary enthusiasm for communicating in this acquired manner.

Cognition

Language and cognition are intimately related. Without the capacity to think, people would have little need for a language, as they would not have any ideas to communicate; and without certain mental processes we would be unable to produce grammatically correct sentences that are comprehensible to others. Ultimately, therefore, the constraints on language use by animals may be imposed by the limitations of their thought processes. Discussions concerning the nature of animal thought are rare, principally because so little is known about it. We can, however, identify some thought processes that are essential for language and ask whether animals possess them.

Sentence production. Turning first to sentence production, two aspects of thought would seem to be essential. The language user must be able to construct sentences in a correct order. For example, to express the idea in three words that "Tim likes Alex", it is necessary to know that the subject of an English sentence precedes the verb, which, in turn, precedes the object. In Chapter 7, monkeys were shown to be capable of learning to touch in the correct order a number of coloured keys that were displayed simultaneously. Moreover, this ability was sustained when they were tested with a novel subset of the array. Taken together with other findings cited in that chapter, these results provide convincing evidence that monkeys, at least, can represent information about serial order.

A capacity to learn about serial order will, however, be of little use for language if each member of the series is a specific item. Instead, the members of the series need to be categories, so that different exemplars of each category can be placed in the correct position in the sequence and thus allow the creation of novel sentences. In Chapter 6 a number of studies were described that show that animals can classify objects into categories. For example, once a pigeon has been trained to peck a key whenever it is shown a picture of water, then it will do so even in the presence of an unfamiliar picture of water. In general, the categories that have been studied are of objects that share common physical attributes—trees, a particular person, etc.—and this may be insufficient for language. The rules of grammar require that the categories are more abstract, so that events can be classified as subject or object, for example. At present the evidence concerning the ability of animals to acquire abstract categories is, at best, promising rather than convincing (see pp.124–129).

The representation of knowledge. We can now turn to the question of whether animals are capable of representing ideas that merit communication by language. All transitive sentences convey information about the relationship between a subject and an object—for instance, "Alex likes Tim". The same can also be said for intransitive sentences, except that here the relationship is implied: The sentence "Jessica fell over" can be

interpreted as an expression of a relationship between Jessica and the ground. In order to produce a sentence, therefore, animals should be able to represent objects and, more importantly, they should be able to represent the relationships that exist between these objects.

The extent to which animals are capable of comprehending relationships is dealt with in some detail in Chapter 5. According to Premack (1983a,b), the ability to represent any but the most fundamental relationships depends on the possession of an abstract mental code. If his argument is correct, then it follows that language training will only be successful with animals that possess this code because without it they would be incapable of comprehending the relationships on which all sentences are based. Sarah's success with analogical reasoning tasks suggests that she is capable of understanding a wide range of relationships.

On the basis of the slender evidence that is available, some animals have shown that they may possess the fundamental thought processes necessary for language comprehension and production. If further research should confirm this conclusion, then future attempts to train animals in the use of language may well be more successful than the attempts so far. I am certain that humans will always be superior to animals in their use of language, but I suspect that with improved training techniques this difference will be less than authors such as Chomsky (1972) and Macphail (1982) have implied.

NOTE

1.　In this experiment considerable steps were taken to prevent the experimenters from inadvertently helping Kanzi by providing him with subtle cues. The instructions were spoken by a person who could not be seen by Kanzi, and his behaviour was recorded by an observer who was unable to hear the instructions.

11

The Distribution of Intelligence

Two contrasting views of the way in which intelligence is distributed throughout the animal kingdom were presented in the opening chapter of this book. One of these makes the assumption that intelligence is related to brain size or, more precisely, to a cephalisation index (K), which is based on a ratio of the weight of the brain to that of the body. The other, which has been referred to as the Null Hypothesis (Macphail, 1985), asserts that apart from humans all vertebrates are of equal intelligence. We are now in a position to evaluate these very different proposals.

INTELLIGENCE AND BRAIN SIZE

The suggestion that a cephalisation index can provide an indication of intelligence is appealing; after all, it is presumably in the brain that most of the information processing by animals takes place. Moreover, there have been occasional reports that claim to demonstrate a high correspondence between intelligence and some measure of brain size.

One of the earlier sources of support for this claim comes from an experimental method that we have not yet considered: learning-set formation. Experiments that study the formation of learning sets involve a succession of discriminations with different stimuli, and the focus of interest is whether there is an improvement in the rate at which each discrimination is solved. To measure this improvement, a record is kept of the accuracy of responding on the second trial of each problem. If there is an improvement over successive discriminations, then the subject is said to have formed a learning set (Harlow, 1949).

Figure 11.1 shows, for a variety of species, the accuracy on the second trial of a discrimination, as a function of the number of problems that have been given. All six species show an improved performance as their exposure to additional discriminations increases, but this improvement is more marked for some species than others. Passingham (1982) has shown that ranking the species on the basis of their ability to form a learning set corresponds to a ranking based on an index of brain size that is related to the cephalisation index (Riddell, 1979). If it is now assumed that the ability to form learning sets is related to intelligence (McFarland, 1985), then the pattern of results depicted in Figure 11.1 suggests that intelligence depends on brain size.

The foregoing argument is of particular interest to the present discussion because it highlights two pitfalls that will be encountered by any attempt to relate intelligence in animals to their brain size. First, Macphail (1982) and Warren (1973), among others, have argued that comparing results such as

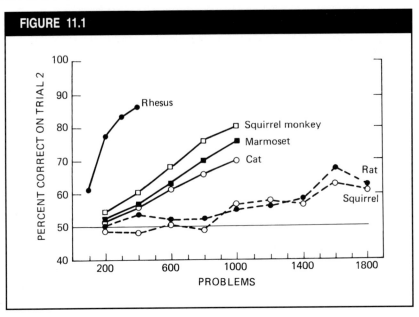

FIGURE 11.1

The mean percentage of correct responses on the second trial of a discrimination, as a function of the number of discrimination problems given, for six different species (from Warren, 1965).

those summarised in Figure 11.1 can be very misleading. The reasons why such a comparison can be misleading were dealt with, in general terms, in Chapter 1 (see pp.11–13). Comparing the speed at which species form learning sets is hampered not only because they possess different perceptual skills and motivational processes, but also because the apparatus in which they are trained is necessarily different. And these differences, rather than variations in intelligence, may well be responsible for the pattern of results summarised in Figure 11.1.

To emphasise this point it is worth looking at the results from two learning-set experiments with dolphins. When a single bottle-nosed dolphin was trained with a series of visual discriminations in which the stimuli differed in shape, Herman, Beach, Pepper, and Stalling (1969) found very little evidence for the formation of a learning set. In contrast, Herman and Arbeit (1973) had little difficulty in training another dolphin to form a learning set when the discriminations involved auditory stimuli. Indeed, by the end of her training, the dolphin was responding with an accuracy of greater than 85% on the second trial of each new discrimination. Thus for dolphins the way in which a learning-set experiment is conducted can have a profound influence on the outcome it reveals. This

conclusion is also bound to be true for other species. Consequently, when an animal shows a reluctance to form a learning set, we should be aware that this may be due to a poorly designed experiment, rather than to a lack of intelligence by the subjects being tested.

The second reason why the study of learning sets may not be a justifiable means for comparing animal intelligence rests with the way intelligence is defined. I argue in Chapter 1 that instead of regarding animal intelligence as a unitary mechanism it may be more useful to see it as being the product of a number of different cognitive processes. Species could then differ in intelligence by possessing different processes, which themselves may operate in different ways. The use of a single measure, such as learning-set formation, is unlikely to test adequately all aspects of information processing by an animal, and any index of intelligence it produces will almost certainly be inaccurate. Indeed, if it is accepted that animal intelligence depends on a collection of capacities that can differ in both degree and kind from one species to the next, then it may not be possible to rank them neatly according to their intelligence. How, for example, would a bee with its sophisticated skills of communication be placed in respect to a bird that can remember the location of thousands of buried pine seeds? Perhaps all we can hope to achieve is to identify and understand the cognitive processes of the species in which we are interested.

Thus even if it were possible to devise a test, or a battery of tests, that could be applied fairly to a range of species, its outcome is unlikely to allow us to rank them according to their intelligence. Once this conclusion is acknowledged, then it is no longer meaningful to try to correlate brain size with intelligence as it is defined here. Indeed, it would not be meaningful to correlate intelligence with any other measure that might, at first sight, appear appropriate.

Despite this cautionary note, research into the relationship between brain size and intelligence has not ceased. But rather than use such crude measures as overall brain size and general intelligence, researchers are focusing more on specific brain regions and specific intellectual skills. The rationale behind this line of work should be obvious: If a region of the brain is responsible for some intellectual skill, then the size of this region may correlate with an individual's capacity for that skill. One line of enquiry that follows from this rationale concerns the size of the hippocampus in birds that do or do not store food. Some birds (Clarks' nutcrackers and willow tits) store many pieces of food for months at a time, and others (magpies and marsh tits) store food for shorter periods of a few hours or days (see Healy, 1995). Interestingly, all these birds have a larger hippocampus than other members of their families that store little or no food. Thus the hippocampus of the great tit is smaller than that of marsh or willow tits, and the hippocampus of the jackdaw is smaller than that of Clark's nutcracker or magpie.

Because food storers need to remember the many locations where they have hidden food, the enhanced size of the hippocampus might endow food storers with superior memory skills relative to those birds that do not store food. Unfortunately, as was mentioned briefly in the conclusion to Chapter 6, several experimental tests of this prediction have not confirmed it. For example, memory tests based on an open-field analogue of the radial maze (Hilton & Krebs, 1990), or delayed nonmatching to sample (Healy, 1995), failed to

find any diffences between the performance of marsh tits and great tits. None of these experiments, however, examined the amount of information that the different species were capable of remembering, and it is perhaps in this respect that storers and nonstorers are most likely to differ (see Healy & Krebs, 1992). One problem with this line of research, and this is not just true for the study of the hippocampus in birds, is that our understanding of the function of most brain regions is rather poor. Until our knowledge in this respect improves, any attempt to relate the size of a brain region to an ability to perform a particular task is obviously going to be difficult.

THE NULL HYPOTHESIS

After reviewing a large body of experimental findings Macphail (1982) concluded that all vertebrates (with the exception of humans) are of equal intelligence. Implausible as this proposal may seem, Macphail (1982, 1985) cites an impressive body of evidence in its support. We turn now to examine the implications of the results cited in the preceding chapters, as well as some others, for the Null Hypothesis. Because there are so many problems with identifying the general intelligence of a species, we shall not use this measure to evaluate the hypothesis. Instead, we shall look at the extent to which the Null Hypothesis can be justified for the various intellectual skills that have been the focus of attention throughout the book.

Associative learning

Macphail (1982) shows that both instrumental and Pavlovian conditioning are effective with an extremely wide range of vertebrate species. We might also add that, as far as I am aware, no vertebrate has ever been shown to be incapable of solving discriminations. On this basis we could conclude, in keeping with the Null Hypothesis, that all vertebrates are capable of associative learning.

But even if this were true, the possibility would remain that the way in which associative learning takes place varies among different species. The effectiveness of Pavlovian conditioning was attributed in Chapter 2 to the development of either CS–US, or CS–R associations. Perhaps CS–R associations are responsible for successful Pavlovian conditioning with some species, whereas for others this success may depend on the growth of CS–US associations, or even both types of association. Brandon and Bitterman (1979) have drawn just such a conclusion by arguing that Pavlovian conditioning results in the formation of only CS–R associations in goldfish. Bitterman (1984) subsequently acknowledged that goldfish can acquire stimulus–stimulus associations, but this does not mean that all vertebrates are capable of forming both types of association. For this conclusion to be accepted, it will be necessary to conduct many well-controlled experiments with a far wider range of species than has hitherto been tested.

Turning now to instrumental conditioning, we saw in Chapter 4 that this can result in the growth of either S–R or R–US associations. Most of this research was conducted with rats and it is far too early to argue with any confidence that a similar conclusion will hold for all vertebrates. We might find, for example, that some vertebrates are capable of acquiring only S–R associations.

Instead of focusing on the types of association that are formed during Pavlovian and instrumental conditioning, a comparison of different species could consider whether they all share the same processes of association formation. Chapter 3 demonstrated the importance of surprise and attention for successful associative learning but, once again, we do not know whether the conclusions drawn in that chapter apply to all vertebrates. The slender evidence that is available suggests, in fact, that they do not.

When a rat is repeatedly exposed to a neutral stimulus, subsequent conditioning is slower than with a novel stimulus. This latent inhibition effect is said to reflect a loss of attention to the familiar stimulus. Although there is little difficulty in demonstrating latent inhibition with many mammals, to my knowledge it has never been demonstrated with goldfish. Indeed, Shishimi (1985) specifically tested them for latent inhibition and was unable to detect it either with excitatory or with inhibitory conditioning, and when both

appetitive and aversive unconditioned stimuli were used. This failure also occurred whether the stimulus was auditory or visual. There seem to be strong grounds for concluding, therefore, that latent inhibition cannot be found in goldfish.

Of course, the possibility remains that Shishimi (1985) did not design his experiments properly. With mammals, at a minimum about 20 trials of exposure to the stimulus are necessary before latent inhibition can be demonstrated. Perhaps goldfish need more exposure than this, and even more than the 160 trials employed in one of the studies by Shishimi (1985). Despite this word of caution, the procedures for both generating and detecting latent inhibition are very simple, and it would be surprising if the various techniques used by Shishimi (1985) were inadequate. There is a possibility that other species are also not susceptible to latent inhibition. Mackintosh (1973) describes an experiment where he failed to demonstrate latent inhibition with pigeons, and I have experienced a similar failure in my laboratory on a number of occasions.

Latent inhibition is said to reflect the influence of attentional processes, which then leads us to the conclusion that mechanisms of attention in rats may differ from those in goldfish and pigeons. Interestingly, there is another source of evidence, based on a different experimental design, which also suggests that the attentional processes of rats and goldfish differ. Chapter 2 shows that, for rats, the effects of blocking can be modified by the surprising omission of a US after each compound conditioning trial (Dickinson et al., 1976). Although there is some dispute about the interpretation of blocking, at least two theories (Mackintosh, 1975a; Pearce & Hall, 1980) attribute the effects of surprising events to their influence on attentional processes. Accordingly, if the mechanisms of attention for goldfish and rats do differ, they might be affected in different ways when a US is unexpectedly omitted after a blocking trial. This prediction has been tested by Gonzalez (1985) who conducted a blocking experiment with goldfish that was similar in design to the one conducted with rats by Dickinson et al. (1976). Although he was able to demonstrate blocking, Gonzalez (1985) found that this effect was not at all disrupted by the surprising omission of a US during compound conditioning. Because of the difficulty of demonstrating latent inhibition with pigeons, it would be interesting to know how they would perform in a blocking experiment similar to that conducted by Gonzalez (1985).

Thus for associative learning, the Null Hypothesis is correct as far as the susceptibility of vertebrates to the techniques of instrumental and Pavlovian conditioning are concerned. But there is insufficient evidence to evaluate this hypothesis when interest is focused on the types of association that are formed as a result of these training methods. In contrast, there is some evidence to suggest that the hypothesis may be wrong as far as the role of attentional processes in learning is concerned.

Memory

The findings from research on the study of animal memory are largely consistent with the Null Hypothesis. These findings were reviewed throughout Chapter 6, and their significance for the Null Hypothesis was evaluated in the conclusion to that chapter. Before leaving the topic of animal memory, however, it is worth looking at a method

known as serial reversal learning because this has revealed results that imply that one species, the rat, has a better memory than another species, the goldfish (Mackintosh, Wilson, & Boakes, 1985). For a serial reversal problem animals are required to solve a discrimination by, say, approaching white and avoiding black. Once the discrimination has been mastered, they are then presented with a reversal of this problem in which they must now approach black and avoid white. When the reversal has been mastered, the original discrimination is reinstated, and so forth.

The results from a study by Mackintosh and Cauty (1971), which compared the performance of rats and goldfish on a serial reversal problem, are shown in Figure 11.2. Both rats and goldfish made fewer errors when they were first presented with the discrimination than when they were confronted with the first reversal. Thereafter, however, the performance of the two species differs: Rats show a much greater improvement across the subsequent reversals than fish. The similarity of the performance at the outset of the experiment suggests that the demands of the task were equivalent for both species, so that it is difficult to attribute the subsequent divergence in the speed of

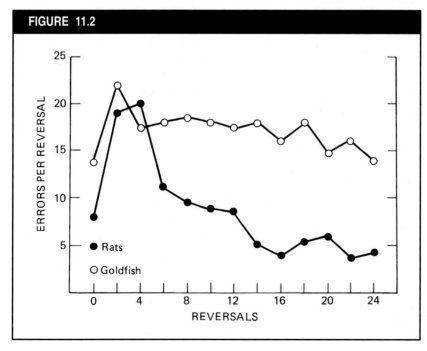

FIGURE 11.2

Number of errors per reversal for groups of rats and goldfish that were given serial reversal training in a study by Mackintosh and Cauty (1971), O = original discrimination (adapted from Mackintosh et al., 1985).

their reversal learning to perceptual, motivational, or other theoretically trivial factors. As an alternative, the possibility is raised that rapid reversal learning depends on an intellectual process that is different for rats and goldfish.

When animals show an improvement across a series of reversal problems, this may be due to the influence of at least two different processes (see Mackintosh, 1974, p. 610). On the one hand, it may be a consequence of learning to attend to the relevant stimuli, so that the appropriate associations change strength rapidly when a reversal is initiated. If this is correct, then the results displayed in Figure 11.2 lend further support to the notion that there is a difference between the attentional processes of rats and goldfish.

On the other hand, successful reversal learning has been said to depend on the ability to remember the outcome of one trial, and to use this information to guide performance on the next trial. Such a strategy would then lead to accurate performance on all trials, except the first, of each reversal. If this is correct, then the results shown in Figure 11.2 imply that the memory processes of rats are more efficient than those of goldfish. There is insufficient knowledge about the memory processes of goldfish to permit a detailed evaluation of this suggestion, but it gains plausibility from studies of alternation learning. In an alternation task an animal may be required to go down an alley for food that is available at the end on alternate trials. If the animal can remember the outcome of the previous trial, then it should be able to anticipate whether or not reward will be delivered on the present trial. Although such anticipation can be readily demonstrated with rats, by discovering that eventually they run faster on rewarded than on nonrewarded trials, a similar effect is very much harder to reveal with goldfish. One explanation for this difference is that unlike rats, goldfish are unable to remember whether or not reward was delivered from one trial to the next (see Mackintosh et al., 1985).

The representation of knowledge

Eventually we may discover that there is rather little difference among the mechanisms of associative learning and memory for most vertebrates. Where a more profound difference may be found is with the sort of knowledge that different animals are able to represent.

The discussion in Chapter 5 focused in some depth on the way in which animals are able to represent knowledge about relationships. In a matching to sample task, animals are required to select one of two comparison stimuli if it is the *same* as a sample stimulus. Although a wide range of species is able to solve this problem if repeated training is given with a restricted set of stimuli, differences begin to emerge when the transfer of this training to new stimuli is examined. Pigeons show extremely poor transfer, whereas corvids, monkeys, and chimpanzees are much better in this respect. According to Premack (1983a,b), successful transfer of matching depends on subjects being able to appreciate the familiarity and novelty of the comparison stimuli in respect to the sample stimulus. Thus, either pigeons are less able than the other species to solve discriminations on the basis of familiarity and novelty, or they are very poor at transferring this strategy from one set of stimuli to a new set. In either case, research is beginning to suggest that there is a difference in the way some species solve matching to sample discriminations.

A further proposal of Premack (1983a,b) is that in order for a true appreciation of the relationship between two stimuli to develop, an animal must possess an abstract code. There are, however, very few demonstrations that suggest that any vertebrate possesses such a code. The capacity of Sarah, a chimpanzee, to solve analogical reasoning problems is one such example. Another example is provided by Alex, a parrot. Recall that Alex might be presented with a red triangle and a red square and be asked "What's same?" or "What's different?". His ability to answer these questions correctly is difficult to explain, unless one accepts that Alex appreciated the relationships of sameness and difference. Thus experiments with Alex and Sarah suggest that at least two species are capable of using an abstract code to represent their knowledge. The lack of relevant research with other species means that it is not strictly justifiable to draw any conclusions about the generality of this skill, but my suspicion is that it will be shown by relatively few vertebrates.

Other types of knowledge that animals could differ in their capacity to represent are time, number, and serial order, which were considered in Chapter 7. There is, in fact, little reason at present for believing that vertebrates differ in their capacity to represent temporal information. And as far as the representation of numerical information is concerned, too few studies have been conducted to permit any firm conclusions to be drawn. Even so, it would be surprising to discover that all vertebrates can match the numerical abilities that have been claimed to be displayed by Sheba, a chimpanzee, and, again, Alex. A particularly strong indication of a difference between species is with the representation of serial order. The work of both Terrace and D'Amato implies that monkeys have much better-developed abilities than pigeons in this respect.

The final way in which vertebrates may differ in their representation of knowledge is revealed by their use of mirrors. The only species to have shown a capacity for self-recognition when they see their reflection are the great apes. Unfortunately, we know very little about the knowledge an animal must possess if it is to direct responses towards itself. The suggestion by a number of authors that it is based on self-awareness is not particularly useful, because it is so difficult to verify.

Language

Only a few species have received language training, which means, yet again, that it is unreasonable to draw conclusions about the generality of the findings of this research to other vertebrates. There is, however, one report that supports the surely reasonable expectation that Kanzi's capacity to respond to spoken sentences (see Chapter 10) will not be found in all vertebrates. Brief mention was made in the previous chapter of a dog called Fellow who responded correctly to a host of spoken commands. He had also received training with the names for a variety of objects with which he was familiar. However, when he was confronted with a collection of these objects, and was instructed to fetch one, he normally performed incorrectly. When Kanzi was given a similar test he performed with a considerable degree of accuracy.

Conclusions

A very important conclusion from the above discussion can be drawn from a critical analysis of the poor performance of Fellow. There are two explanations for Fellow's inability to retrieve the correct object: He may have lacked the necessary linguistic processes to enable him to understand the spoken command, or he may not have received the appropriate training. If his trainer had been more diligent, or used a different methodology, then perhaps Fellow would have matched the skills displayed by Kanzi. Of course, this explanation does not apply solely to the study with Fellow. Whenever there is an indication that one species can perform in a way that is impossible for another species, then a proponent of the Null Hypothesis can argue that this is due to a failure of the experimenter rather than to the intelligence of the animal. Given such an argument, the Null Hypothesis becomes impossible to refute. Even so, if evidence that some species possess an intellectual skill that is absent in other species should continue to grow, then at the very least the plausibility of this hypothesis will be drawn into question. Perhaps as the comparative study of animal cognition develops, so too will demonstrations of animals differing in their intellectual abilities. If this should be the case, then despite the logical difficulty of refuting the Null Hypothesis it is likely to gain few adherents. On the other hand, if this research should reveal only small differences among the intellectual skills of different species, there will be good grounds for taking the hypothesis seriously.

INTELLIGENCE AND EVOLUTION

The final topic to be considered concerns an argument that leads to a conclusion that is diametrically opposite to that of the Null Hypothesis. That is, because of evolutionary pressures, different species will have rather little in common intellectually. During the course of evolution the characteristics of a species will be changed according to the demands imposed on its members by the ecological niche they occupy. This niche can be identified by the relationship of the animal with both other organisms and its physical environment. Because the problems that confront an animal differ markedly from one niche to another, it is understandable why species differ so profoundly in their physical characteristics. Of course, it is not just physical characteristics that are influenced in this way; mental processes will also be modified as a result of evolutionary pressures.

One implication of this discussion is that animals occupying different niches will possess different mental processes. For instance, a capacity to communicate about the location of food will be required only by those animals that need to forage for food cooperatively. We therefore should not expect to find this skill in more solitary animals. Alternatively, an ability to construct a cognitive map may be most likely in animals that forage over distances and must return to a specific location, such as a nest or hive.

A further implication is that even where animals do have mental processes in common, evolutionary processes may result in them becoming specialised in some way. To avoid starving during the winter, Clark's nutcrackers must remember where they have stored a large number of pine seeds. Obviously the birds that are most likely to survive a winter are those with a large and accurate memory. It is therefore plausible that over successive generations there has been an improvement in the memory capacity of this species. Such an improvement would not be expected in species of birds for which the role played by memory in their survival is less critical.

Studies of learning provide a further indication of the way the characteristics of an ecological niche can influence a specific cognitive process. Many animals are capable of associative learning, but very often it is found that a particular species is disposed to learn more readily about some relationships than about others. Moreover, these relationships, such as that between illness and poison, are those that are most likely to occur naturally and are important to the animal's survival. The associative learning mechanisms could therefore be said to be biased in a way that facilitates the acquisition of knowledge that is most likely to be of importance to the animal. The way

in which the white-crowned sparrow is restricted in its song learning provides a further example of the influence of evolution on the learning processes.

On the basis of the foregoing examples and discussion, the argument might be made that Macphail (1982, 1985) is wholly unjustified in proposing that all vertebrates other than humans are of equal intelligence, as they live in such a variety of environments. However, this criticism overlooks the fact that many niches have common characteristics that may be responsible for their occupants possessing similar mental processes (Dickinson, 1980; Revusky, 1977). This point is made in Chapter 1 with the example of Pavlovian conditioning. In many different environments a stimulus will signal the imminent occurrence of an event that is of significance to the animals that live in them. If these relationships can be learned about, then animals will be able to anticipate and prepare themselves for the events. Such a learning ability would be of as much value to insects as to chimpanzees, and we might expect a very wide range of animals to possess this ability. In addition, a number of authors argue convincingly that the laws governing associative learning in many animals are the same (Domjan, 1983; Roper, 1983). Hence, because they face a common problem of needing to predict what will happen to them, many species appear to possess a similar mechanism of associative learning. This argument does not only apply to associative learning; many other cognitive processes that would be of value to a wide range of species can be identified. We are thus in the position of anticipating, on the basis of evolutionary considerations, that animals will possess similar or different cognitive processes, or a mixture of both. Obviously this conclusion is of little help if we wish to draw conclusions about the distribution of different intellectual skills throughout the animal kingdom, as it is impossible to study the environment of an animal and then draw accurate conclusions about its intellectual processes. Instead, as we have seen, the way to understand the intelligence of animals is to experiment on them directly.

Before closing this discussion, some attention should be paid to our own species. Occasionally in this book evidence is cited to suggest that the cognitive processes of humans and animals have much in common. As far as memory is concerned, the distinction between short- and long-term memory is valid for both humans and animals; and when the recall of a list is required, the primacy and recency effects that have been well established with humans can also be reliably shown in animals (see Chapter 6). Further evidence of a similarity in the intellectual processes of humans and animals may be found in the impressive concept-learning skills of animals, which appear to match at least some of those shown by humans. The attentional processes of humans and animals may also operate in fundamentally similar ways—for both it has proved useful to distinguish between two sorts of attention, which may be referred to as automatic and controlled (see Chapter 3). In studies of problem solving it is striking that both animals and humans can find it easier to choose between two members of a transitive series the more distantly they are related. Sarah's ability to reason analogically also hints at there being something in common in the way humans and animals solve

problems. Finally, Premack's (1983a,b) suggestion that primates possess both a concrete and an abstract code for representing knowledge is a claim that has often been made about human cognition (e.g. Anderson, 1980).

How then do the cognitive processes of humans and animals differ? Language undoubtedly provides us with a tremendous intellectual advantage over our fellow creatures, but it is not clear why this is so. The suggestion that there is a language-acquisition device that is unique to humans is questioned in Chapter 10. We also saw that some animals possess a number of the cognitive skills that may be considered essential for language comprehension and production. There is no doubt that there are profound differences between the intellectual processes of humans and animals, but for the present we must withhold judgement on what they might be. We can be sure, however, that as our understanding of animal cognition improves, so we shall discover more about the origins of human intelligence and the ways in which it is unique.

References

Able, K.P. (1980). Mechanisms of orientation, navigation, and homing. In S.A. Gauthreaux (Ed.), *Animal migration, orientation, and navigation* (pp.284–373). New York: Academic Press.

Adams, C.D., & Dickinson, A. (1981). Actions and habits: Variations in associative representations during instrumental learning. In N.E. Spear & R.R. Miller (Eds.), *Information processing in animals: Memory mechanisms* (pp.143–165). Hillsdale, NJ: Lawrence Erlbaum Associates Inc.

Allison, J. (1989) The nature of reinforcement. In S.B. Klein & R.R. Mowrer (Eds.), *Contemporary learning theories: Instrumental conditioning theory and the impact of biological constraints on learning* (pp.13–39). Hillsdale, NJ: Lawrence Erlbaum Associates Inc.

Allison, J., & Timberlake, W. (1974). Instrumental and contingent saccharin-licking in rats: Response deprivation and reinforcement. *Learning and Motivation, 5,* 231–247.

Anderson, J.R. (1980). *Cognitive psychology and its implications,* (1st ed.). San Francisco: Freeman.

Anderson, J.R. (1983). Response to mirror image stimulation and assessment of self-recognition in mirror- and peer-reared stumptail macaques. *Quarterly Journal of Experimental Psychology, 35B,* 201–212.

Anderson, J.R. (1984). The development of self-recognition: A review. *Developmental Psychobiology, 17,* 35–49.

Anderson, J.R. (1985). *Cognitive psychology and its implications,* (2nd ed.). San Francisco: Freeman.

Anderson, J.R. (1986). Mirror-mediated finding of hidden food by monkeys (*Macaca tonkeana* and *M. fascicularis*). *Journal of Comparative Psychology, 100,* 237–242.

Anderson, J.R., Kline, P.J., & Beasley, C.M, (1979). A general learning theory and its application to schema abstraction. In G.H. Bower (Ed.), *The psychology of learning and motivation* (Vol. 13). New York: Academic Press.

Angermeier, W.F. (1984). *The evolution of operant learning and memory.* Basel: Karger.

Annau, Z., & Kamin, L.J. (1961). The conditioned emotional response as a function of intensity of the US. *Journal of Comparative and Physiological Psychology, 54,* 428–432.

Aschoff, J. (1955). Exogene und endogene Komponente der 24 Stunden-Periodik bei Tier und Mensch. *Naturwissenschaften, 42,* 569–575.

Astley, S.L., & Wasserman, E.A. (1992). Categorical discrimination and generalization in pigeons: All negative stimuli are not created equal. *Journal of Experimental Psychology: Animal Behavior Processes, 18,* 193–207.

Atkinson, R.C., & Estes, W.K. (1963). Stimulus sampling theory. In R.D. Luce, R.R. Bush, & E. Galanter (Eds.), *Handbook of mathematical psychology* (Vol. 2, pp.121–268). New York: Wiley.

Atkinson, R.C., & Shiffrin, R.M. (1968). Human memory: A proposed system and its control processes. In K.W. Spence & J.T. Spence (Eds.), *The psychology of learning and motivation* (Vol 2, pp.89–195). New York: Academic Press.

Aydin, A., & Pearce, J.M. (1994). Prototype effects in categorization by pigeons. *Journal of Experimental Psychology: Animal Behavior Processes, 20,* 264–277.

Baddeley, A.D. (1976). *The psychology of memory.* New York: Basic Books.

Baddeley, A.D., & Hitch, G. (1974). Working memory. In G.H. Bower (Ed.), *The psychology of learning and motivation* (Vol. 8, pp.47–90). New York: Academic Press.

Baker, A.G. (1974). Conditioned inhibition is not the symmetrical opposite of conditioned excitation: A test of the Rescorla–Wagner model. *Learning and Motivation, 5,* 369–379.

Baker, A.G., & Mackintosh, N.J. (1977). Excitatory and inhibitory conditioning following uncorrelated presentations of CS and US. *Animal Learning and Behavior, 5,* 315–319.

Baker, R.R. (1980). *The mystery of migration.* London: Macdonald Futura Books.

Baker, R.R. (1984). *Bird navigation: The solution of a mystery?* London: Hodder & Stoughton.

Balachandran, N.K., Dunn, W.L., & Rind, D.H. (1977). Concorde sonic booms as an atmospheric probe. *Science, 197,* 47–49.

Balaz, M.A., Kasprow, W.J., & Miller, R.R. (1982). Blocking with a single compound trial. *Animal Learning and Behavior, 10,* 271–276.

Baldaccini, N., Benvenuti, S., Fiaschi, V., Ioale, P., & Papi, F. (1982). Pigeon orientation: Experiments on the role of olfactory stimuli perceived during the outward journey. In F. Papi & H. Wallraff (Eds.), *Avian navigation.* Berlin: Springer.

Balleine, B. (1992). Instrumental performance following a shift in primary motivation depends on incentive learning. *Journal of Experimental Psychology: Animal Behavior Processes, 18,* 236–250.

Balleine, B.W., Garner, C., Gonzalez, F., & Dickinson, A. (1995). Motivational control of heterogenous instrumental chains. *Journal of Experimental Psychology: Animal Behavior Processes, 21,* 203–217.

Banks, W.P., & Flora, J. (1977). Semantic and perceptual processes in symbolic comparisons. *Journal of Experimental Psychology: Human Perception and Performance, 3,* 278–291.

Baptista, L.F., & Morton, M.I. (1981). Interspecific song acquisition by a white-crowned sparrow. *Auk, 98,* 383–385.

Barnett, S.A. (1958). Experiments on "neophobia" in wild and laboratory rats. *British Journal of Psychology, 49,* 195–201.

Barnett. S.A. (1970). *Instinct and intelligence.* Harmondsworth, UK: Penguin.

Bastian, J. (1961). *Proceedings of the symposium on bionic models of animal sonar systems.* Frascati, Italy.

Batson, J.D., & Best, M.R. (1981). Single-element assessment of conditioned inhibition. *Bulletin of the Psychonomic Society, 18,* 328–330.

Baum, M. (1966). Rapid extinction of an avoidance response following a period of response prevention in the avoidance apparatus. *Psychological Reports, 18,* 59–64.

Beatty, W.W., & Shavalia, D.A. (1980a). Spatial memory in rats: Time course of working memory and effect of anaesthetics. *Behavioral and Neural Biology, 28,* 454–462.

Beatty, W.W., & Shavalia, D.A. (1980b). Rat spatial memory: Resistance to retroactive interference at long retention intervals. *Animal Learning and Behavior, 8,* 550–552.

Bennett, C.H., Maldonado, A., & Mackintosh, N.J. (1995). Learned irrelevance is not the sum of exposure to CS and US. *Quarterly Journal of Experimental Psychology, 48B,* 117–128.

Berthold, P. (1978). Concept of endogenous control of migration in warblers. In K. Schmidt-Koenig & W.T. Keeton (Eds.), *Animal migration. navigation, and homing* (pp.275–282). Berlin: Springer.

Bessemer, D.W., & Stollnitz, F. (1971). Retention of discriminations and an analysis of learning set. In A.M. Schrier & F. Stollnitz (Eds.), *Behavior of nonhuman primates* (Vol. 4, pp.1–58). New York: Academic Press.

Best, M.R., Dunn, D.P., Batson, J.D., Meachum, C. I., & Nash, S.M. (1985). Extinguishing conditioned inhibition in flavour-aversion learning: Effects of repeated testing and extinction of the excitatory element. *Quarterly Journal of Experimental Psychology, 37B,* 359–378.

Best, M.R., & Gemberling, G.A. (1977). Role of short-term processes in the conditioned stimulus preexposure effect and the delay of reinforcement gradient in long-delay taste-aversion learning. *Journal of Experimental Psychology: Animal Behaviour Processes, 3,* 253–263.

Bhatt, R.S., Wasserman, E.A., Reynolds, W.F., & Knauss, K.S. (1988). Conceptual behavior in pigeons: Categorization of both familiar and novel examples from four classes of natural and artificial stimuli. *Journal of Experimental Psychology: Animal Behavior Processes, 14,* 219–234.

Bingman, V.P. (1990). Spatial navigation in birds. In R.P. Kesner & D.S. Olton (Eds.), *Neurobiology of comparative cognition* (pp.423–447). Hillsdale, NJ: Lawrence Erlbaum Associates Inc.

Birch, H.G. (1945). The relation of previous experience to insightful problem solving. *Journal of Comparative Psychology, 38*, 367–383.

Bitterman, M.E. (1965). The evolution of intelligence. *Scientific American, 212*, 92–100.

Bitterman, M.E. (1975). The comparative analysis of learning. *Science, 188*, 699–709.

Bitterman, M.E. (1984). Learning in man and other animals. In V. Sarris & A. Parducci (Eds.), *Perspectives in psychological experimentation* (pp.59–70). Hillsdale, NJ: Lawrence Erlbaum Associates Inc.

Bitterman, M.E., Menzel, R., Fietz, A., & Schafer, S. (1983). Classical conditioning of proboscis extension in honeybees *(Apis mellifera). Journal of Comparative Psychology, 97*, 107–119.

Blough, D.S. (1975). Steady state data and a quantitative model of operant generalization and discrimination. *Journal of Experimental Psychology: Animal Behavior Processes, 1*, 3–21.

Boakes, R.A., & Gaertner, I. (1977). The development of a simple form of communication. *Quarterly Journal of Experimental Psychology, 29*, 561–575.

Boakes, R.A., Poli, M., Lockwood, M.J., & Goodall, G. (1978). A study of misbehavior: Token reinforcement in the rat. *Journal of the Experimental Analysis of Behavior, 29*, 115–134.

Bodoamer, M.D., Fouts, D.H., Fouts, R.S., & Jemsvold, M.L.A. (1994). Functional analysis of chimpanzee *(Pan troglodytes)* private signing. *Human Evolution, 9*, 281–296.

Boe, E.E., & Church, R.M. (1967). Permanent effects of punishment during extinction. *Journal of Comparative and Physiological Psychology, 63*, 486–492.

Boesch, C. (1991). Teaching among wild primates. *Animal Behaviour, 41*, 530–532.

Bolles, R.C. (1971). Species-specific defense reactions. In F.R. Brush (Ed.), *Aversive conditioning and learning* (pp.183–233). New York: Academic Press.

Bolles, R.C. (1972) Reinforcement, expectancy and learning. *Psychological Review, 79*, 394–409.

Bolles, R.C. (1975). *Theory of motivation* (2nd ed.). New York: Harper & Row.

Bolles, R.C., & de Lorge, J. (1962). The rat's adjustment to a-diurnal feeding cycles. *Journal of Comparative and Physiological Psychology, 55*, 760–762.

Bolles, R.C., & Moot, S.A. (1973). The rat's anticipation of two meals a day. *Journal of Comparative and Physiological Psychology, 83*, 510–514.

Bolles, R.C., & Stokes, L.W. (1965). Rat's anticipation of diurnal and a-diurnal feeding. *Journal of Comparative and Physiological Psychology, 60*, 290–294.

Bond, A.B. (1983). Visual search and selection of natural stimuli in the pigeon: The attention threshold hypothesis. *Journal of Experimental Psychology: Animal Behavior Processes, 9*, 292–306.

Bonner, J.T. (1980). *The evolution of culture in animals.* Princeton, NJ: Princeton University Press.

Bookman, M.A. (1977). Sensitivity of the homing pigeon to an earth-strength magnetic field. *Nature, 267*, 340–342.

Boysen, S.T., & Berntson, G.G. (1989). The development of numerical competence in the chimpanzee *(Pan troglodytes). Journal of Comparative Psychology, 103*, 23–31.

Brandon, S.E., & Bitterman, M.E. (1979). Analysis of autoshaping in goldfish. *Animal Learning and Behavior, 7*, 57–62.

Breland, K., & Breland, M. (1961). The misbehavior of organisms. *American Psychologist, 16*, 661–664.

Bright, M. (1984). *Animal communication.* London: British Broadcasting Coporation.

Broadbent, H.A., Church, R.M., Meck, W.H., & Rakitin, B.C. (1993). Quantitative relationships between timing and counting. In S.J. Boysen & E.J. Capaldi (Eds.), *The development of numerical competence: Animal and human models* (pp.171–187). Hillsdale, NJ: Lawrence Erlbaum Associates Inc.

Brooks, J.O., & Watkins, M.J. (1990). Further evidence of the intricacy of memory span. *Journal of Experimental Psychology: Learning, Memory, and Cognition, 16*, 1134–1141.

Brower, L.P., Brower, J.Z., & Westcott, P.W. (1960). Experimental studies of mimicry. 5. The reaction of toads *(Bufo terrestris)* to bumblebees *(Bombus americanorum)* and their robberfly mimics *(Mallaphora bomboides)* with a discussion of aggressive mimicry. *American Naturalist, 94*, 343–355.

Brown, I.D., & Poulton, E.C. (1961). Measuring the spare "mental capacity" of car drivers by a subsidiary task. *Ergonomics, 4*, 35–40.

Brown, J.L. (1964). The integration of agonistic behavior in Stellar's jay *Cyanocitta stelleri* (Gmelin). *University of California Publications in Psychology, 60*, 223–328.

Brown, M.F. (1992). Does a cognitive map guide choices in the radial-arm maze? *Journal of Experimental Psychology: Animal Behavior Processes, 18*, 56–66.

Brown, M.F. (1993). Sequential and simultaneous choice processes in the radial-arm maze. In T.R. Zentall (Ed.), *Animal cognition: A tribute to Donald A. Riley* (pp.153–173). Hillsdale, NJ: Lawrence Erlbaum Associates Inc.

Brown, M.F., & Demas, G.E. (1994). Evidence for spatial working memory in honeybees (*Apis mellifera*). *Journal of Comparative Psychology, 108*, 344–352.

Brown, M.F., Rish, P.A., Von Culin, J.E., & Edberg, J.A. (1993). Spatial guidance of choice behavior in the radial-arm maze. *Journal of Experimental Psychology: Animal Behavior Processes, 19*, 195–214.

Browne, M.P. (1976). The role of primary reinforcement and overt movements in autoshaping in the pigeon. *Animal Learning and Behavior, 4*, 287–292.

Bryant, P.E., & Trabasso, T. (1971). Transitive inference and memory in young children. *Nature, 232*, 456–458.

Buffon, G.L.C., Comte de (1818). *Oeuvres completes de Buffon*. Lacepede, Comte de (Ed.). Paris: Rapet.

Burdick, C.K., & Miller, J.D. (1975). Speech perception by the chinchilla: Discrimination of sustained /a/ and /i/. *Journal of the Acoustical Society of America, 58*, 415–427.

Byrne, R. (1995). *The thinking ape*. Oxford: Oxford University Press.

Byrne, R., & Whiten, A. (1985). Tactical deception of familiar individuals in baboons (*Papio ursinus*). *Animal Behaviour, 33(2)*, 669–673.

Byrne, R., & Whiten, A. (1987). A thinking primate's guide to deception. *New Scientist* (3 Dec.), 54–57.

Capaldi, E.J. (1993). Animal number abilities: Implications for a hierarchical approach to instrumental learning. In S.J. Boysen & E.J. Capaldi (Eds.), *The development of numerical competence: Animal and human models* (pp.191–209). Hillsdale, NJ: Lawrence Erlbaum Associates Inc.

Capaldi, E.J., Hovancik, J.R., & Lamb, E.O. (1975). The effects of strong irrelevant thirst on food-rewarded instrumental performance. *Animal Learning and Behavior, 3*, 172–178.

Capaldi, E.J., & Miller, D.J. (1988). Counting in rats: Its functional significance and the indenpendent cognitive processes that constitute it. *Journal of Experimental Psychology: Animal Behavior Processes, 14*, 3–17.

Carew, T.J., Hawkins, R.D., & Kandel, E.R. (1983). Differential classical conditioning of a defensive withdrawal reflex in *Aplysia californica. Science, 219*, 397–400.

Carew, T.J., Pinsker, H., & Kandel, E.R. (1972). Long-term habituation of a defensive withdrawal reflex in *Aplysia. Science, 175*, 451–454.

Caro, T.M., & Hauser, M.D. (1992). Is there teaching in nonhuman animals? *The Quarterly Review of Biology, 67*, 151–174.

Cartwright, B.A., & Collett, T.S. (1983). Landmark learning in bees: Experiments and models. *Journal of Comparative Physiology, 151*, 521–543.

Castro, C.A., & Larsen, T. (1992). Primacy and recency effects in nonhuman primates. *Journal of Experimental Psychology: Animal Behavior Processes, 18*, 335–340.

Cerella, J. (1979). Visual classes and natural categories in the pigeon. *Journal of Experimental Psychology: Human Perception and Performance, 5*, 68–77.

Cerella, J. (1980). The pigeon's analysis of pictures. *Pattern Recognition, 12*, 1–6.

Cerella, J. (1982). Mechanisms of concept formation in the pigeon. In D.J. Ingle, M.A. Goodale, & R.J.W. Mansfield (Eds.), *Analysis of visual behaviour* (pp.241–262). Cambridge, MA: MIT Press.

Chapuis, N., & Scardigli, P. (1993). Shortcut ability in hamsters (*Mesocricetus auratus*): The role of environmental and kinesthetic information. *Animal Learning and Behavior, 21*, 255–265.

Cheney, D.L., & Seyfarth, R.M. (1988). Assessment of meaning and the detection of unreliable signals by vervet monkeys. *Animal Behaviour, 36*, 477–486.

Cheng, K. (1986). A purely geometric module in the rat's spatial representation. *Cognition, 23*, 149–178.

Cheng, K. (1994). The determination of direction in landmark-based spatial search in pigeons: A further test of the vector sum model. *Animal Learning and Behavior, 22*, 291–301.

Cheng, K., & Gallistel, C.R. (1984). Testing the geometric power of an animal's spatial representation. In H.L. Roitblat, T.G. Bever, & H.S. Terrace (Eds.), *Animal cognition* (pp.409–424). Hilldale, NJ: Lawrence Erlbaum Associates Inc.

Chittka, L., & Geiger, K. (1995). Can honey bees count landmarks? *Animal Behaviour, 49*, 159–164.

Chomsky, N. (1957). *Syntactic structures*. The Hague: Mouton.

Chomsky, N. (1972). *Language and mind* (enlarged edn.). New York: Harcourt Brace Jovanovich.

Church, R.M. (1978). The internal clock. In S.H. Hulse, H. Fowler, & W.K. Honig (Eds.), *Cognitive processes in animal behavior* (pp.277–310). Hillsdale, NJ: Lawrence Erlbaum Associates Inc.

Church, R.M. (1984). Properties of the internal clock. In J. Gibbon & L. Allan (Eds.), *Timing and time perception* (pp.566–582). New York: New York Academy of Sciences.

Church, R.M. (1989). Theories of timing behavior. In R.R. Mowrer, & S.B. Klein. (Eds.), *Contemporary learning theories: Instrumental conditioning theory and impact of biological constraints on learning* (pp.41–71). Hillsdale, NJ: Lawrence Erlbaum Associates Inc.

Church, R.M., & Broadbent, H.A. (1990). Alternative representations of time, number, and rate. *Cognition, 37*, 55–81.

Church, R.M., & Broadbent, H.A. (1991). A connectionist model of timing. In M.L. Commons, S. Grossberg, & J.E.R. Staddon (Eds.), *Neural network models of conditioning and action* (pp.225–240). Hillsdale, NJ: Lawrence Erlbaum Associates Inc.

Church, R.M., & Deluty, M.Z. (1977). Bisection of temporal intervals. *Journal of Experimental Psychology: Animal Behavior Processes, 3*, 216–228.

Church, R.M., & Gibbon, J. (1982). Temporal generalization. *Journal of Experimental Psychology: Animal Behavior Processes, 8*, 165–186.

Church, R.M., LoLordo, V.M., Overmier, J.B., Solomon, R.L., & Turner, L.H. (1966). Cardiac responses to shock in curarized dogs. *Journal of Comparative and Physiological Psychology, 62*, 1–7.

Church, R.M., & Meck, W.H. (1984). The numerical attributes of stimuli. In H.L. Roitblat, T.G. Bever, & H.S. Terrace (Eds.), *Animal cognition* (pp.445–464). Hillsdale, NJ: Lawrence Erlbaum Associates Inc.

Clark, E. (1959). Instrumental conditioning of lemon sharks. *Science, 130*, 217–218.

Clark, F.C. (1958). The effect of deprivation and frequency of reinforcement on variable-interval responding. *Journal of the Experimental Analysis of Behavior, 1*, 221–227.

Collett, T. S., Cartwright, B.A., & Smith, B.A. (1986). Landmark learning and visuo-spatial memories in gerbils. *Journal of Comparative Physiology A, 158*, 835–851.

Colwill, R.M., & Rescorla, R.A. (1985). Instrumental responding remains sensitive to reinforcer devaluation after extensive training. *Journal of Experimental Psychology: Animal Behavior Processes, 11*, 520–536.

Colwill, R.M., Rescorla, R.A. (1988). Associations between the discriminative stimulus and the reinforcer in instrumental learning. *Journal of Experimental Psychology: Animal Behavior Processes, 14*, 155–164.

Colwill, R.M., & Rescorla, R.A. (1990). Effect of reinforcer devaluation on discriminative control of instrumental behavior. *Journal of Experimental Psychology: Animal Behavior Processes, 16*, 40–47.

Cook, M., & Mineka, S. (1990). Selective associations in the observational conditioning of fear in rhesus monkeys. *Journal of Experimental Psychology: Animal Behavior Processes, 16*, 372–389.

Cook, R.G., Brown, M.F., & Riley, D.A. (1985). Flexible memory processing by rats: Use of prospective and retrospective information in the radial maze. *Journal of Experimental Psychology: Animal Behavior Processes, 11*, 453–469.

Corning, W., & Kelly, S. (1972). Platyhelminthes: The turbellarians. In W. Corning, J. Dyal, & A.O.D. Willows (Eds.), *Invertebrate learning* (Vol 1). New York: Plenum.

Corning, W., & Riccio, D. (1970). The planarian controversy. In W. Byrne (Ed.), *Molecular approaches to learning and memory.* New York: Academic Press.

Cotton, J.W. (1953). Running time as a function of food deprivation. *Journal of Experimental Psychology, 46*, 188–198.

Cotton, M.M., Goodall, G., & Mackintosh, N.J. (1982). Inhibitory conditioning resulting from a reduction in the magnitude of reinforcement. *Quarterly Journal of Experimental Psychology, 34B*, 163–181.

Coussi-Korbel, S. (1994). Learning to outwit a competitor in mangabeys (*Cercocebus torquatus torquatus*). *Journal of Comparative Psychology, 108*, 164–171.

Couvillon, P.A., & Bitterman, M.E. (1982). Compound conditioning in honeybees. *Journal of Comparative and Physiological Psychology, 96*, 192–199.

Couvillon, P.A., & Bitterman, M.E. (1992). A conventional conditioning analysis of "transitive inference" in pigeons. *Journal of Experimental Psychology: Animal Behavior Processes, 18*, 308–310.

Couvillon, P.A., Klosterhalfen, S., & Bitterman, M.E. (1983). Analysis of overshadowing in honeybees. *Journal of Comparative Psychology, 97*, 154–166.

Cox, J.K., & D'Amato, M.R. (1982). Matching-to-compound samples by monkeys *(Cebus apella)*: Shared attention or generalization decrement? *Journal of Experimental Psychology: Animal Behavior Processes, 8*, 209–225.

Curio, E. (1988). Cultural transmission of enemy recognition by birds. In T.R. Zentall, & B.G. Galef, Jr. (Eds.), *Social learning psychological and biological perspectives* (pp.75–98). Hillsdale, NJ: Lawrence Erlbaum Associates Inc.

D'Amato, M.R. (1973). Delayed matching and short-term memory in monkeys. In G.H. Bower (Ed.), *The psychology of learning and motivation* (Vol. 7, pp.227–269). New York: Academic Press.

D'Amato, M.R. (1991). Comparative cognition: Processing of serial order and serial pattern. In L. Dachowski & C.F. Flaherty (Eds.), *Current issues in animal learning: Brain, emotion and cognition*, (pp.165–185). Hillsdale, NJ: Lawrence Erlbaum Associates Inc.

D'Amato, M.R., & Buckiewicz, J. (1980). Long delay, one-trial conditioned preference and retention in monkeys *(Cebus apella)*. *Animal Learning and Behavior, 8*, 359–362.

D'Amato, M.R., & Colombo, M. (1988). Representation of serial order in monkeys. *Journal of Experimental Psychology: Animal Behavior Processes, 14*, 131–139.

D'Amato, M.R., & O'Neill, W. (1971). Effect of delay-interval illumination on matching behavior in the capuchin monkey. *Journal of the Experimental Analysis of Behavior, 15*, 327–333.

D'Amato, M.R., Safarjan, W.R., & Salmon, D. (1981). Long-delay conditioning and instrumental learning: Some new findings. In N.E. Spear & R.R. Miller (Eds.), *Information processing in animals: Memory mechanisms* (pp.113–142). Hillsdale, NJ: Lawrence Erlbaum Associates Inc.

D'Amato, M.R., & Salmon, D.P. (1982). Tune discrimination in monkeys *(Cebus apella)* and in rats. *Animal Learning and Behavior, 10*, 126–134.

D'Amato, M.R., & Salmon, D.P. (1984). Processing of complex auditory stimuli (tunes) by rats and monkeys *(Cebus apella)*. *Animal Learning and Behaviour, 12*, 184–194.

D'Amato, M.R., & Van Sant, P. (1988). The Person concept in monkeys *(Cebus apella)*. *Journal of Experimental Psychology: Animal Behavior Processes, 14*, 43–55.

D'Amato, M.R., & Worsham, R.W. (1972). Delayed matching in the capuchin monkey with brief sample durations. *Learning and Motivation, 3*, 304–312.

Darwin, C. (1872). *The expression of emotions in man and animal.* London: John Murray.

Davey, G. (1989). *Ecological learning theory.* London: Routledge.

Davidson, R.S. (1966). Operant stimulus control applied to maze behavior: Heat escape conditioning and discrimination reversal in *Alligator mississippiensis*. *Journal of the Experimental Analysis of Behavior, 9*, 671–676.

Davis, H., & Perusse, R. (1988). Numerical competence in animals: Definitional issues, current evidence, and a new research agenda. *Behavioral and Brain Sciences, 11*, 561–579.

Dawkins, M. (1971a). Perceptual changes in chicks: Another look at the "search image" concept. *Animal Behaviour, 19*, 566–574.

Dawkins, M. (1971b). Shifts of "attention" in chicks during feeding. *Animal Behaviour, 19*, 575–582.

Dekeyne, A., & Deweer, B. (1990). Interaction between conflicting memories in the rat: Contextual pretest cuing reverses control of behavior by testing context. *Animal Learning and Behavior, 18*, 1–12.

Delius, J.D., & Emmerton, J. (1978). Sensory mechanisms related to homing in pigeons. In K. Schmidt-Koenig & W.T. Keeton (Eds.), *Animal migration, navigation, and homing* (pp.35–41). Berlin: Springer.

Denny, M.R., Clos, C.F., & Bell, R.C. (1988). Learning in the rat of a choice response by observation of S-S contingencies. In T.R. Zentall, & B.G. Galef, Jr. (Eds.), *Social learning psychological and biological perspectives* (pp.207–223). Hillsdale, NJ: Lawrence Erlbaum Associates Inc.

Deutsch, J.A. (1960). *The structural basis of behavior.* Cambridge: Cambridge University Press.

de Waal, F. (1982). *Chimpanzee politics.* London: Jonathan Cape.

Deweer, B., Sara, S.J., & Hars, B. (1980). Contextual cues and memory retrieval in rats: Alleviation of forgetting by a pretest exposure to background stimuli. *Animal Learning and Behavior, 8*, 265–272.

Dews, P. (1959). Some observations on an operant in the octopus. *Journal of the Experimental Analysis of Behavior, 2*, 57–63.

Dias, R., Robbins, T.W., & Roberts, A.C. (1996). Dissociation of affective and attentional shifting by selective lesions of the prefrontal cortex. *Nature.*

Dickinson, A. (1977). Appetitive–aversive interactions: Superconditioning of fear by an appetitive CS. *Quarterly Journal of Experimental Psychology, 29*, 71–83.

Dickinson, A. (1980). *Contemporary animal learning theory.* Cambridge: Cambridge University Press.

Dickinson, A. (1985). Actions and habits: The development of behavioural autonomy. In L. Weiskrantz (Ed.), *Animal intelligence* (pp.67–78). Oxford: Clarendon Press.

Dickinson, A. (1994). Instrumental conditioning. In N. J. Mackintosh (Ed.), *Animal learning and cognition* (pp.45–79). San Diego, CA: Academic Press.

Dickinson, A., & Charnock, D.J. (1985). Contingency effects with maintained instrumental reinforcement. *Quarterly Journal of Experimental Psychology, 37B,* 397–416.

Dickinson, A., Hall, G., & Mackintosh, N.J. (1976). Surprise and the attenuation of blocking. *Journal of Experimental Psychology: Animal Behavior Processes, 2,* 313–322.

Dickinson, A., & Mackintosh, N.J. (1979). Reinforcer specificity in the enhancement of conditioning by posttrial surprise. *Journal of Experimental Psychology: Animal Behavior Processes, 5,* 162–177.

Dickinson, A., & Mulatero, C.W. (1989). Reinforcer specificity of the suppression of instrumental performance on a non-contingent schedule. *Behavioral Processes, 19,* 167–180.

Dickinson, A., Nicholas, D.J., & Mackintosh, N.J. (1983). A reexamination of one-trial blocking in conditioned suppression. *Quarterly Journal of Experimental Psychology, 35B,* 67–79.

Dickinson, A., & Pearce, J.M. (1977). Inhibitory interactions between appetitive and aversive stimuli. *Psychological Bulletin, 84,* 690–711.

Dickinson, A., Watt, A., & Griffin, W.J.H. (1992). Free-operant acquisition with delayed reinforcement. *Quarterly Journal of Experimental Psychology, 45B,* 241–258.

Diez-Chamizo, V., Sterio, D., & Mackintosh, N.J. (1985). Blocking and overshadowing between intra-maze and extra-maze cues: A test of the independence of locale and guidance learning. *Quarterly Journal of Experimental Psychology, 37B,* 235–253.

Dimattia, B.V., & Kesner, R.P. (1984). Serial position curves in rats: Automatic versus effortful information processing. *Journal of Experimental Psychology: Animal Behavior Processes, 10,* 557–563.

Domjan, M. (1983). Biological constraints on instrumental and classical conditioning: Implications for general process theory. In G.H. Bower (Ed.), *The psychology of learning and motivation* (Vol. 17, pp.215–277). New York: Academic Press.

Dowsett-Lemaire, F. (1979). The imitative range of the song of the marsh warbler, *Acrocephalus palustris,* with special reference to imitations of African birds. *Ibis, 121,* 453–468.

Dufort, R.H., Guttman, N., & Kimble, G.A. (1954). One-trial discrimination reversal in the white rat. *Journal of Comparative and Physiological Psychology, 47,* 248–249.

Duncan, C.P. (1949). The retroactive effect of electroshock on learning. *Journal of Comparative and Physiological Psychology, 42,* 32–44.

Dyer, F.C. (1991). Bees acquire route-based memories but not cognitive maps in a familiar landscape. *Animal Behaviour, 41,* 239–246.

Eikelboom, R., & Stewart, J. (1979). Conditioned temperature effects using morphine as the unconditioned stimulus. *Psychopharmacology, 61,* 31–38.

Elliott, M.H. (1928). The effect of change of reward on the maze performance of rats. *University of California Publications in Psychology, 4,* 19–30.

Ellison, G.D., & Konorski, J. (1964). Separation of the salivary and motor response in instrumental conditioning. *Science, 146,* 1071–1072.

Emlen, S.T. (1970). Celestial rotation: Its importance in the development of migratory orientation. *Science, 170,* 1198–1201.

Epstein, R., Kirshnit, C.E., Lanza, R.P., & Rubin, L.C. (1984). "Insight" in the pigeon: Antecedents and determinants of an intelligent performance. *Nature, 308,* 61–62.

Epstein, R., Lanza, R.P., & Skinner, B.F. (1980). Symbolic communication between two pigeons *(Columba livia domestica). Science, 207,* 543–545.

Epstein, R., Lanza, R.P., & Skinner, B.F. (1981). "Self-awareness" in the pigeon. *Science, 212,* 695–696.

Estes, W.K. (1969). New perspectives on some old issues in association theory. In N.J. Mackintosh & W.K. Honig (Eds.), *Fundamental issues in associative learning* (pp.162–189). Halifax: Dalhousie University Press.

Etienne, A.S., Lambert, S.J., Reverdin, B., & Teroni, E. (1993). Learning to recalibrate the role of dead reckoning and visual cues in spatial navigation. *Animal Learning and Behavior, 21,* 266–280.

Evans, J.G.M., & Hammond, G.R. (1983). Differential generalization of habituation across contexts as a function of stimulus significance. *Animal Learning and Behavior, 11,* 432–434.

Farah, M.J. (1985). Psychophysical evidence for a shared representational medium for mental images and percepts. *Journal of Experimental Psychology: General, 114,* 91–103.

Finke, R.A. (1980). Levels of equivalence in imagery and perception. *Psychological Review, 87,* 113–132.

Fiorito, G., & Scotto, p.(1992). Observational learning in *Octopus vulgaris. Nature, 256,* 545–547.

Fisher, J., & Hinde, R.A. ((1949). The opening of milk bottles by birds. *British Birds, 42,* 347–357.

Fouts, R.S. (1975). In R.H. Turtle (Ed.), *Society and psychology of primates.* The Hague: Mouton.

Fouts, R.S., & Fouts, D.H. (1989). Loulis in conversation with cross-fostered chimpanzees. In R.G. Gardner, B.T. Gardner, & T.E. Van Cantfort (Eds.) *Teaching sign language to chimpanzees* (pp.293–307). New York: State University of New York Press.

Fouts, R.S., Fouts, D.H., & Van Cantfort, T.E. (1989). The infant Loulis learns signs from cross-fostered chimpanzees. In R. G. Gardner, B.T. Gardner, & T.E. Van Cantfort (Eds.) *Teaching sign language to chimpanzees* (pp.281–292). New York: State University of New York Press.

Fouts, R.S., Hirsch, A.D., & Fouts, D.H. (1982). Cultural transmission of a human language in a chimpanzee mother-infant relationship. In H.E. Fitzgerald, J.A. Mullins, & P. Gage (Eds.) *Child nurturance: III, studies of development in nonhuman primates* (pp.159–193). New York: Plenum.

Fowler, H., & Miller, N.E. (1963). Facilitation and inhibition of runway performance by hind- and forepaw shock of various intensities. *Journal of Comparative and Physiological Psychology, 56,* 801–805.

Franks, J.J., & Bransford, J.D. (1971). Abstraction of visual patterns. *Journal of Experimental Psychology, 90,* 65–74.

Fuller, E., Kowalski, V., & Wiltschko, R. (1983). Orientation of homing pigeons: Compass orientation vs. piloting by landmarks. *Journal of Comparative Physiology A, 153,* 55–58.

Furness, W. (1916). Observations on the mentality of chimpanzees and orangutans. *Proceedings of the American Philosophical Society, 65,* 281–290.

Gaffan, D. (1977). Response coding in recall of colours by monkeys. *Quarterly Journal of Experimental Psychology, 29,* 597–605.

Gaffan, D., & Weiskrantz, L. (1980). Recency effects and lesion effects in delayed non-matching to randomly baited samples by monkeys. *Brain Research, 196,* 373–386.

Gaffan, E.A. (1992). Primacy, recency, and the variability of data in studies of animals' working memory. *Animal Learning and Behavior, 20,* 240–252.

Galef, B.G., Jr. (1970). Aggression and timidity: Responses to novelty in feral Norway rats. *Journal of Comparative and Physiological Psychology, 70,* 370–381.

Galef, B.G., Jr. (1980). Diving for food: Analysis of a possible case of social learning in wild rats (*Rattus norvegicus*). *Journal of Comparative and Physiological Psychology, 94,* 416–425.

Galef, B.G., Jr. (1988). Communication of information concerning diets in social central-place foraging species: *Rattus norvegicus.* In T.R. Zentall, & B.G. Galef, Jr. (Eds.), *Social learning psychological and biological perspectives* (pp.119–140). Hillsdale, NJ: Lawrence Erlbaum Associates Inc.

Galef, B.G., Jr., & Clark, M.M. (1971). Social factors in the poison avoidance and feeding behavior of wild and domesticated rat pups. *Journal of Comparative and Physiological Psychology, 75,* 341–357.

Galef, B.G., Jr., & Durlach, P.J. (1993). Absence of blocking, overshadowing, and latent inhibition in social enhancement of food preferences. *Animal Learning and Behavior, 21,* 214–220.

Galef, B.G., Jr., Kennett, D.J., & Stein, M. (1985). Demonstrator influence on observer diet preference: Effects of simple exposure and the presence of a demonstrator. *Animal Learning and Behavior, 13,* 25–30.

Galef, B.G., Jr., Mason, J.R., Preti, G., & Bean, N.J. (1988). Carbon disulfide: A semiochemical mediating socially induced diet choice in rats. *Physiology and Behavior, 42,* 119–124.

Galef, B.G., Jr., McQuoid, L.M., & Whiskin, E.E. (1990). Further evidence that Norway rats do not socially transmit learned aversions to toxic baits. *Animal Learning and Behavior, 18,* 199–205.

Gallagher, M., & Holland, P.C. (1994). The amygdala complex: Multiple roles in associative learning and attention. *Proceedings of the National Academy of Science, 91,* 11771–11776.

Gallistel, C.R. (1990). *The Organization of learning.* Cambridge, MA: MIT Press.

Gallistel, C.R. (1993). A conceptual framework for the study of numerical estimation and arithmetic reasoning in animals. In S.J. Boysen & E.J. Capaldi (Eds.), *The development of numerical competence: Animal and human models* (pp.211–223). Hillsdale, NJ: Lawrence Erlbaum Associates Inc.

Gallup, G.G., Jr. (1970). Chimpanzees: Self-recognition. *Science, 167,* 86–87.

Gallup, G.G., Jr. (1975). Toward an operational definition of self-awareness. In R.H. Tuttle (Ed.), *Socioecology and psychology of primates* (pp.309–341). The Hague: Mouton.

Gallup, G.G., Jr. (1983). Toward a comparative psychology of mind. In R.L. Mellgren (Ed.), *Animal cognition and behavior* (pp.473–510). Amsterdam: North Holland Publishing Co.

Gallup, G.G., Jr., McClure, M.K., Hill, S.D., & Bundy, R.A. (1971). Capacity for self-recognition in differentially reared chimpanzees. *Psychological Record, 21*, 69–74.

Ganesan, R., & Pearce, J.M. (1988). Effect of changing the unconditioned stimulus on appetitive blocking. *Journal of Experimental Psychology: Animal Behavior Processes, 14*, 280–291.

Garcia, J., & Koelling, R.A. (1966). Relation of cue to consequence in avoidance learning. *Psychonomic Science, 4*, 123–124.

Garcia, J., McGowan, B.K., & Green, K.F. (1972). Biological constraints on conditioning. In A.H. Black & W.F. Prokasy (Eds.), *Classical conditioning II: Current research and theory* (pp.3–27). New York: Appleton-Century-Crofts.

Garcia, J., Rusiniak, K.W., & Brett, L.P. (1977). Conditioning food-illness in wild animals: *Caveant canonici*. In H. Davis & H.M.B. Hurwitz (Eds.), *Operant-Pavlovian interactions* (pp.273–316). Hillsdale, NJ: Lawrence Erlbaum Associates Inc.

Gardner, R.A., & Gardner, B.T. (1969). Teaching sign language to a chimpanzee. *Science, 165*, 664–672.

Gardner, R.A., & Gardner, B.T. (1974). Comparing the early utterances of child and chimpanzee. In A. Pick (Ed.), *Minnesota symposium on child psychology, 8.* Minneapolis, MN: University of Minneapolis Press.

Gardner, R.A., Gardner, B.T., & Van Cantfort, T.E. (1989). *Teaching sign language to chimpanzees.* New York: State University of New York Press.

Gelman, R., & Gallistel, C.R. (1978). *The child's understanding of number.* Cambridge, MA: Harvard University Press.

Gemberling, G.A., & Domjan, M. (1982). Selective association in one-day-old rats: Taste-toxicosis and texture-toxicosis aversion learning. *Journal of Comparative and Physiological Psychology, 96*, 105–113.

Gibbon, J. (1977). Scalar expectancy theory and Weber's law in animal timing. *Psychological Review, 84*, 279–325.

Gibbon, J., & Church, R.M. (1981). Time left: Linear versus logarithmic subjective time. *Journal of Experimental Psychology: Animal Behavior Processes, 7*, 87–108.

Gibbon, J., & Church, R.M. (1984). Sources of variance in an information processing theory of timing. In H.T. Roitblat, T.G. Bever, & H.S. Terrace (Eds.), *Animal cognition* (pp.465–490). Hillsdale, NJ: Lawrence Erlbaum Associates Inc.

Gibbon, J., Church, R.M., & Meck, W.H. (1984). Scalar timing in memory. In J. Gibbon & L. Allen (Eds.), *Timing and time perception, Annals of the New York Academy of Sciences* (Vol. 423, pp.52–77). New York: New York Academy of Sciences.

Gibbs, C.M., Latham, S.B., & Gormezano, I. (1978). Classical conditioning of the rabbit nictitating membrane response: Effects of reinforcement schedule on response maintenance and resistance to extinction. *Animal Learning and Behavior, 6*, 209–215.

Gibson, K.R. (1989). Tool use in cebus monkeys: Moving from orthodox to neo-Piagetian analyses. *Behavioral and Brain Sciences, 12*, 598–599.

Gillan, D.J. (1981). Reasoning in the chimpanzee: II. Transitive inference. *Journal of Experimental Psychology: Animal Behvaior Processes, 7*, 150–164.

Gillan, D.J., Premack, D., & Woodruff, G. (1981). Reasoning in the chimpanzee: I. Analogical reasoning. *Journal of Experimental Psychology: Animal Behavior Processes, 7*, 1–17.

Glanzer, M., & Cunitz, A.R. (1966). Two storage mechanisms in free recall. *Journal of Verbal Learning and Verbal Behavior, 5*, 351–360.

Gleitman, H. (1971). Forgetting of long-term memories in animals. In W.K. Honig & P.H.R. James (Eds.), *Animal memory* (pp.1–44). New York: Academic Press.

Gluck, M.A. (1991). Stimulus generalization and representation in adaptive network models of category learning. *Psychological Science, 2*, 50–55.

Gluck, M.A., & Bower, G.H. (1988). From conditioning to category learning: An adaptive network model. *Journal of Experimental Psychology: General, 117*, 227–247.

Gluck, M.A. & Myers, C.E. (1993). Hippocampal mediation of stimulus representation: A computational theory. *Hippocampus, 3*, 491–516.

Gollub, L. (1977). Conditioned reinforcement: Schedule effects. In W.K. Honig & J.E.R. Staddon (Eds.), *Handbook of operant behavior* (pp.288–312). Englewood Cliffs, NJ: Prentice-Hall.

Gonzalez, R.C. (1985). Personal communication.

Gonzalez, R.C., Gentry, G.V., & Bitterman, M.E. (1954). Relational discrimination of intermediate size in the chimpanzee. *Journal of Comparative and Physiological Psychology, 47*, 385–388.

Goodall, J. (1986). *The chimpanzees of Gombe.* Cambridge, MA: Harvard University Press.

Gordon, W.C. (1981). Mechanisms of cue-induced retention enhancement. In N.E. Spear & R.R. Miller (Eds.), *Information processing in animals: Memory mechanisms* (pp.319–340). Hillsdale, NJ: Lawrence Erlbaum Associates Inc.

Gordon, W.C., Frankl, S.E., & Hamberg, J.M. (1979). Reactivation-induced proactive interference in rats. *American Journal of Psychology, 92*, 693–702.

Gordon, W.C., & Mowrer, R.R. (1980). The use of an extinction trial as a reminder treatment following ECS. *Animal Learning and Behavior, 8*, 363–367.

Gormezano, I. (1965). Yoked comparisons of classical and instrumental conditioning of the eyelid response: And an addendum on "voluntary responders". In W.F. Prokasy (Ed.), *Classical conditioning: A symposium* (pp.48–70). New York: Appleton-Century-Crofts.

Gormezano, I., & Hiller, G.W. (1972). Omission training of the jaw-movement response of the rabbit to a water US. *Psychonomic Science, 29*, 276–278.

Gould, J.L. (1982). The map sense of pigeons. *Nature, 296*, 205–211.

Gould, J.L. (1984). Natural history of honeybee learning. In P. Marler & H.S. Terrace (Eds.), *The biology of learning* (pp.149–180). Berlin: Springer.

Gould, J.L. (1986). The locale map of honey bees: Do insects have a cognitive map? *Science, 232*, 861–863.

Gould, J.L., & Gould, C.G. (1988). *The honey bee.* New York: Scientific American Library.

Grant, D.S. (1975). Proactive interference in pigeon short-term memory. *Journal of Experimental Psychology: Animal Behavior Processes, 1*, 207–220.

Grant, D.S. (1976). Effect of sample presentation time on long-delay matching in the pigeon. *Learning and Motivation, 7*, 580–590.

Grant, D.S. (1981). Short-term memory in the pigeon. In N.E. Spear & R.R. Miller (Eds.), *Information processing in animals: Memory mechanisms* (pp.227–256). Hillsdale, NJ: Lawrence Erlbaum Associates Inc.

Grant, D.S. (1984). Directed forgetting and intratrial interference in pigeon delayed matching. *Canadian Journal of Psychology, 38*, 166–177.

Grant, D.S. (1988). Sources of visual interference in delayed matching-to-sample with pigeons. *Journal of Experimental Psychology: Animal Behavior Processes, 14*, 368–375.

Grant, D.S., & Roberts, W.A. (1973). Trace interaction in pigeon short-term memory. *Journal of Experimental Psychology, 101*, 21–29.

Grant, D.S., & Roberts, W.A. (1976). Sources of retroactive inhibition in pigeon short-term memory. *Journal of Experimental Psychology: Animal Behavior Processes, 2*, 1–16.

Grant, D.S., & Soldat, A.S. (1995). A postsample cue to forget does initiate an active forgetting process in pigeons. *Journal of Experimental Psychology: Animal Behavior Processes, 21*, 218–228.

Gray, J.A. (1975). *Elements of a two-process theory of learning.* London: Academic Press.

Greenberg, J.H. (1963). *Universals of language.* Cambridge, MA: MIT Press.

Grindley, G.C. (1932). The formation of a simple habit in guinea pigs. *British Journal of Psychology, 23*, 127–147.

Gunier, W.J., & Elder, W.H. (1971). Experimental homing of gray bats to a maternity colony in a Missouri barn. *American Midlands Naturalist, 86*, 502–506.

Guthrie, E.R. (1935). *The psychology of learning.* New York: Harper.

Guttman, N., & Kalish, H.I. (1956). Discriminability and stimulus generalization. *Journal of Experimental Psychology, 51*, 79–88.

Gwinner, E. (1972). Endogenous timing factors in bird migration. In S.R. Galler, K. Schmidt-Koenig, G.J. Jacobs, & R.E. Belleville (Eds.), *Animal orientation and navigation* (pp.321–338). Washington: NASA.

Hall, G. (1982). Effects of a brief stimulus accompanying reinforcement on instrumental responding in pigeons. *Learning and Motivation, 13*, 26–43.

Hall, G. (1992). *Perceptual and associative learning.* Oxford: Clarendon Press.

Hall, G., & Channell, S. (1985). Differential effects of contextual change on latent inhibition and on the habituation of an orienting response. *Journal of Experimental Psychology: Animal Behavior Processes, 11*, 470–481.

Hall, G., & Minor, H. (1984), A search for context-stimulus associations in latent inhibition. *Quarterly Journal of Experimental Psychology, 36B*, 146–169.

Hall, G., & Pearce, J.M. (1979). Latent inhibition of a CS during CS-US pairings. *Journal of Experimental Psychology: Animal Behavior Processes, 5*, 31–42.

Hall, G., & Pearce, J.M. (1982a). Restoring the associability of a preexposed CS by a surprising event. *Quarterly Journal of Experimental Psychology, 34B*, 127–140.

Hall, G., & Pearce, J.M. (1982b). Changes in stimulus associability during conditioning: Implications for theories of acquisition. In M.L. Commons, R.J. Herrnstein, & A.R. Wagner (Eds.), *Quantitative analyses of behavior: Acquisition* (pp.221–240). Cambridge, MA: Ballinger.

Hammond, L.J. (1980). The effects of contingencies upon appetitive conditioning of free-operant behavior. *Journal of the Experimental Analysis of Behavior, 34*, 297–304.

Hammond, L.J., & Weinberg, M. (1984). Signaling unearned reinforcers removes suppression produced by a zero correlation in an operant paradigm. *Animal Learning and Behavior, 12*, 371–374.

Hanson, H.M. (1959). Effect of discrimination training on stimulus generalization. *Journal of Experimental Psychology, 58*, 321–334.

Hanson, S.J., & Timberlake, W. (1983). Regulation during challenge: A general model of learned performance under schedule constraint. *Psychological Review, 90*, 261–282.

Harlow, H.F. (1949). The formation of learning sets. *Psychological Review, 56*, 51–65.

Harper, D.N., McLean, A.P., & Dalrymple-Alford, J.C. (1993). List item memory in rats: Effects of delay and task. *Journal of Experimental Psychology: Animal Behavior Processes, 19*, 307–316.

Harris, M.R., & McGonigle, B.O. (1994). A model of transitive choice. *Quarterly Journal of Experimental Psychology, 47B*, 319–348.

Hastings, M. (1979). *Bomber command.* London: Michael Joseph.

Hawkins, R.D., Abrams, T.W., Carew, T.J., & Kandel, E.R. (1983). A cellular mechanism of classical conditioning in *Aplysia*: Activity-dependent amplification of presynaptic facilitation. *Science, 219*, 400–405.

Hawkins, R.D., & Kandel, E.R. (1984). Is there a cell biological alphabet for simple forms of learning? *Psychological Review, 91*, 375–391.

Hayes, C. (1961). *The ape in our house.* New York: Harper.

Hayes, K., & Hayes, C. (1951). The intellectual development of a home-raised chimpanzee. *Proceedings of the American Philosophical Society, 95*, 105–109.

Healy, S.D. (1995). Memory for objects and positions: Delayed non-matching-to-sample in storing and non-storing tits. *Quarterly Journal of Experimental Psychology, 48B*, 179–191.

Healy, S.D. Clayton, N.S., & Krebs, J.R. (1994). Development of hippocampal specialisation in two species of tit (*Parus spp*). *Behavioural Brain Research, 61*, 23–28.

Healy, S.D., & Hurly, T.A. (1995). Spatial memory in rufous hummingbirds (*Selasphorus rufus*): A field test. *Animal Learning and Behavior, 23*, 63–68.

Healy, S.D., & Krebs, J.R. (1992). Comparing spatial memory in tits: Recalling a single positive location. *Animal Learning and Behavior, 20*, 121–126.

Hearst, E. (1972). Some persistent problems in the analysis of conditioned inhibition. In R.A. Boakes & M.S. Halliday (Eds.), *Inhibition and learning* (pp.5–39). London: Academic Press.

Hearst, E., & Franklin, S.R. (1977). Positive and negative relations between a signal and food: Approach-withdrawal behavior. *Journal of Experimental Psychology: Animal Behavior Processes, 3*, 37–52.

Hearst, E., & Jenkins, H.M. (1974). *Sign tracking: The stimulus-reinforcer relation and directed action.* Monograph of the Psychonomic Society, Austin, Texas.

Hebb, D.O. (1949). *The organization of behavior.* New York: Wiley.

Hendersen, R.W. (1978). Forgetting of conditioned fear inhibition. *Learning and Motivation, 9*, 16–30.

Hendersen, R.W. (1985). Fearful memories: The motivational significance of forgetting. In F.R. Brush & J.B. Overmier (Eds.), *Affect, conditioning, and cognition: Essays on the determinants of behavior* (pp.43–53). Hillsdale, NJ: Lawrence Erlbaum Associates Inc.

Hendersen, R.W., Peterson, J.M., & Jackson, R.L. (1980). Acquisition and retention of control of instrumental behavior by a cue signaling an airblast: How specific are conditioned anticipations? *Learning and Motivation, 11*, 407–426.

Hennessey, T.M., Rucker, W.B., & McDiarmid, C.G. (1979). Classical conditioning in *paramecia. Animal Learning and Behavior, 7*, 417–423.

Herman, L.M. (1975). Interference and auditory short-term memory in the bottlenosed dolphin. *Animal Learning and Behavior, 3*, 43–48.

Herman, L.M., & Arbeit, W.R. (1973). Stimulus control and auditory discrimination learning sets in the bottlenose dolphin. *Journal of the Experimental Analysis of Behavior, 19*, 379–394.

Herman, L.M., Beach, F.A., Pepper, R.L., & Stalling, R.B. (1969). Learning-set formation in the bottlenose dolphin. *Psychonomic Science, 14*, 98–99.

Herman, L.M., & Gordon, J.A. (1974). Auditory delayed matching in the bottlenose dolphin. *Journal of Experimental Analysis of Behavior, 21*, 19–29.

Herman, L.M., Pack, A.A., & Morrel-Samuels, P. (1993). Representational and conceptual skills of dolphins. In H.L. Roitblat, L.M. Herman, & P.E. Nachtigall (Eds.), *Language and communication: Comparative perspectives* (pp.403–442). Hillsdale, NJ: Lawrence Erlbaum Associates Inc.

Herman, L.M., Richards, D.G., & Wolz, J.P. (1984). Comprehension of sentences by bottlenosed dolphins. *Cognition, 16*, 129–219.

Herman, L.M., & Thompson, R.K.R. (1982). Symbolic identity, and probed delayed matching of sounds in the bottlenosed dolphin. *Animal Learning and Behavior, 10*, 22–34.

Herrnstein, R.J. (1979). Acquisition, generalization, and discrimination reversal of a natural concept. *Journal of Experimental Psychology: Animal Behavior Processes, 5*, 116–129.

Herrnstein, R.J. (1984). Objects, categories, and discriminative stimuli. In H.T. Roitblat, T.G. Bever, & H.S. Terrace (Eds.), *Animal cognition* (pp.233–262). Hillsdale, NJ: Lawrence Erlbaum Associates Inc.

Herrnstein, R.J. (1985). Riddles of natural categorization, In L. Weiskrantz (Ed.), *Animal intelligence* (pp.129–144). Oxford: Clarendon Press.

Herrnstein, R.J. (1990). Levels of stimulus control. *Cognition, 37*, 133–166.

Herrnstein, R.J., & Loveland, D.H. (1964). Complex visual concept in the pigeon. *Science, 146*, 549–551.

Herrnstein, R.J., Loveland, D.H., & Cable, C. (1976). Natural concepts in pigeons. *Journal of Experimental Psychology: Animal Behavior Processes, 2*, 285–311.

Herrnstein, R.J., Vaughan, W., Jr., Mumford, D.B., & Kosslyn, S.M. (1989). Teaching pigeons an abstract relational rule: Insideness. *Perception and Psychophysics, 46*, 56–64.

Herrnstein, R.J., & de Villiers, P.A. (1980). Fish as a natural category for people and pigeons. In G.H. Bower (Ed.), *The psychology of learning and motivation* (Vol. 14, pp.60–97). New York: Academic Press.

Heyes, C.M. (1993). Anecdotes, training, trapping, and triangulating: Do animals attribute mental states? *Animal Behaviour, 46*, 177–188.

Heyes, C.M. (1994). Social learning in animals: Categories and mechanisms. *Biological Review, 69*, 207–231.

Heyes, C.M., & Dawson, G.R. (1990). A demonstration of observational learning using a bidirectional control. *Quarterly Journal of Experimental Psychology, 42B*, 59–71.

Heyes, C.M., Dawson, G.R., & Nokes, T. (1992). Imitation in rats: Initial responding and transfer evidence. *Quarterly Journal of Experimental Psychology, 45B*, 81–92.

Heyes, C.M., Jaldow, E., Nokes, T., & Dawson, G.R. (1994). Imitation in rats (*Rattus norvegicus*): The role of demonstrator action. *Behavioural Processes, 32*, 173–182.

Hilgard, E.R., & Bower, G.H. (1966). *Theories of learning* (3rd ed.). New York. Appleton-Century-Crofts.

Hilton, S.C., & Krebs, J.R. (1990). Spatial memory in four species of *parus*: Performance in an open-field analogue of a radial maze. *Quarterly Journal of Experimental Psychology, 42B*, 345–368.

Hinde, R.A. (1970). *Animal behaviour: A synthesis of ethology and comparative psychology.* New York: McGraw-Hill.

Hinde, R.A., & Stevenson-Hinde, J. (1973). *Constraints on learning.* London: Academic Press.

Hintzman, D.L. (1986). 'Schema abstraction' in a multiple trace memory. *Psychological Review, 93*, 411–428.

Hockett, C.F. (1960). The origin of speech. *Scientific American, 203*, 89–96.

Holland, P.C. (1977). Conditioned stimulus as a determinant of the form of the Pavlovian conditioned response. *Journal of Experimental Psychology: Animal Behavior Processes, 3*, 77–104.

Holland, P.C. (1979). Differential effects of omission contingencies on various components of Pavlovian appetitive conditioned behavior in rats. *Journal of Experimental Psychology: Animal Behavior Processes, 5*, 178–193.

Holland, P.C. (1981). Acquisition of representation-mediated conditioned food aversions. *Learning and Motivation, 12*, 1–18.

Holland, P.C. (1990). Event representation in Pavlovian conditioning: Image and action. *Cognition, 37*, 105–131.

Holland, P.C. (1992). Occasion setting in Pavlovian conditioning. In D.L. Medin (Ed.), *The psychology of learning and motivation* (Vol. 28, pp.69–125). San Diego, CA: Academic Press.

Holland, P.C., & Rescorla, R.A. (1975). The effects of two ways of devaluing the unconditioned stimulus after first- and second-order appetitive conditioning. *Journal of Experimental Psychology: Animal Behavior Processes, 1*, 355–363.

Holland, P.C., & Ross, R.T. (1981). Associations in serial compound conditioning. *Journal of Experimental Psycho- logy: Animal Behavior Processes, 7*, 228–241.

Holland, P.C., & Straub, J.J. (1979). Differential effects of two ways of devaluing the unconditioned stimulus after Pavlovian appetitive conditioning. *Journal of Experimental Psychology: Animal Behavior Processes, 5*, 65–78.

Homa, D., Dunbar, S., & Nohre, L. (1991). Instance frequency, categorization, and the modulating effect of experience. *Journal of Experimental Psychology: Learning, Memory, and Cognition, 17*, 444–458.

Honey, R.C., & Hall, G. (1989). Acquired equivalence and distinctiveness of cues. *Journal of Experimental Psychology: Animal Behavior Processes, 15*, 338–346.

Honig, W.K. (1978). Studies of working memory in the pigeon. In S.H. Hulse, H. Fowler, & W.K. Honig (Eds.), *Cognitive processes in animal behavior* (pp.211–248). Hillsdale, NJ: Lawrence Erlbaum Associates Inc.

Huang, I., Koski, C.A., & DeQuardo, J.R. (1983). Observational learning of a bar-press by rats. *The Journal of General Psychology, 108*, 103–111.

Huber, L., & Lenz, R. (1993). A test of the linear feature model of polymorphous concept discrimination with pigeons. *Quarterly Journal of Experimental Psychology, 46B*, 1–18.

Hull, C.L. (1943). *Principles of behavior.* New York: Appleton-Century-Crofts.

Hull, C.L. (1952). *A behavior system.* New Haven, CT: Yale University Press.

Hulse, S.H., Cynx, J., & Humpal, J. (1984). Cognitive processes of pitch and rhythm structures by birds. In H.L. Roitblat, T.G. Bever, & H.S. Terrace (Eds.), *Animal cognition* (pp.183–198). Hillsdale, NJ: Lawrence Erlbaum Associates Inc.

Humphrey, N.K. (1982). Consciousness: A just-so story. *New Scientist* (19 Aug.), 474–478.

Humphrey, N.K. (1983). *Consciousness regained.* Oxford: Oxford University Press.

Hunter, W.S. (1914). The delayed reaction in animals and children. *Behavior Monographs, 2*, No. 6.

Hyde, T.S. (1976). The effect of Pavlovian stimuli on the acquisition of a new response. *Learning and Motivation, 7*, 223–239.

Itakura, S. (1987). Mirror guided behavior in Japanese monkeys (*Macaca fuscata fuscata*). *Primates, 28*, 149–161.

Itani, J., & Nishimura, A. (1973). The study of infrahuman culture in Japan. In E. Menzel (Ed.), *Precultural primate behavior* (pp.127–141). Basel, Switzerland: Karger.

Jackson, R.L., Alexander, J.H., & Maier, S.F. (1980). Learned helplessness, inactivity, and associative deficits: Effects of inescapable shock on response choice escape learning. *Journal of Experimental Psychology: Animal Behavior Processes, 6*, 1–20.

James, W. (1890). *The principles of psychology.* New York: Holt.

Jander, R. (1957). Die optische Richtungsorientierung der roten Waldameise (*Formica rufa L.*). *Zeitschrift für vergleichende Physiologie, 40*, 162–238.

Jenkins, H.M. (1977). Sensitivity of different response systems to stimulus-reinforcer and response reinforcer relations. In H. Davis & H.M.B. Hurwitz (Eds.), *Operant-Pavlovian interactions* (pp.47–62). Hillsdale, NJ: Lawrence Erlbaum Associates Inc.

Jennings, H.S. (1906). *Behavior of the lower organisms.* New York: Columbia University Press.

Jerison, H.J. (1969). Brain evolution and dinosaur brains. *American Naturalist, 103*, 575–588.

Jerison, H.J. (1973). *Evolution of the brain and intelligence.* New York: Academic Press.

Jolly, A. (1991). Conscious chimpanzees? A review of recent literature. In C.A. Ristau (Ed.), *Cognitive ethology: The minds of other animals* (pp.231–252). Hillsdale, NJ: Lawrence Erlbaum Associates Inc.

Kamil, A.C. (1978). Systematic foraging by a nectar feeding bird, the amakihi *(Loxops virens). Journal of Comparative and Physiological Psychology, 92*, 388–396.

Kamil, A.C., & Mauldin, J.E. (1975). Intraproblem retention during learning-set acquisition in blue jays *(Cyanocitta cristata). Animal Learning and Behavior, 3*, 125–130.

Kamin, L.J. (1965). Temporal and intensity characteristics of the conditioned stimulus. In W.F. Prokasy (Ed.), *Classical conditioning: A symposium* (pp.118–147). New York: Appleton-Century-Crofts.

Kamin, L.J. (1969). Selective association and conditioning. In N.J. Mackintosh & W.K. Honig (Eds.), *Fundamental issues in associative learning* (pp.42–64). Halifax: Dalhousie University Press.

Kamin, L.J., & Schaub, R.E. (1963). Effects of conditioned stimulus intensity on the conditioned emotional response. *Journal of Comparative and Physiological Psychology, 56,* 502–507.

Kandel, E.R., & Hawkins, R.D. (1992). The biological basis of learning and individuality. *Scientific American, 267,* 62–71.

Kaplan, P.S. (1984). Importance of relative temporal parameters in trace autoshaping: From excitation to inhibition. *Journal of Experimental Psychology: Animal Behavior Processes, 10,* 113–126.

Karlson, P., & Lüscher, M. (1959). "Pheromones": A new term for a class of biologically active substances. *Nature, 183,* 55–56.

Karpicke, J., Christoph, G., Peterson, G., & Hearst, E. (1977). Signal location and positive versus negative conditioned suppression in the rat. *Journal of Experimental Psychology: Animal Behavior Processes, 3,* 105–118.

Kastak, D., & Schusterman, R.J. (1994). Transfer of visual identity matching-to-sample in two Californian sea lions (*Zalophus californianus*). *Animal Learning and Behavior, 22,* 427–453.

Kaye, H. (1983). *The influence of Pavlovian conditioning on the orienting response in the rat.* Unpublished Ph.D. thesis, University College, Cardiff.

Kaye, H., & Pearce, J.M. (1984). The strength of the orienting response during Pavlovian conditioning. *Journal of Experimental Psychology: Animal Behavior Processes, 10,* 90–109.

Kaye, H., & Pearce, J.M. (1987). Hippocampal lesions attenuate latent inhibition of a CS and of a neutral stimulus. *Quarterly Journal of Experimental Psychology, 39B,* 107–125.

Keeton, W.T. (1969). Orientation by pigeons: Is the sun necessary? *Science, 165,* 922–928.

Keeton, W.T. (1974). The orientational and navigational basis of homing in birds. *Advances in the Study of Behaviour, 5,* 47–132.

Kehoe, E.J. (1988). A layered network model of associative learning: Learning to learn and configuration. *Psychological Review, 95,* 411–433.

Kelleher, R.T. (1958). Fixed-ratio schedules of conditioned reinforcement with chimpanzees. *Journal of the Experimental Analysis of Behavior, 1,* 281–289.

Kemp, F.D. (1969). Thermal reinforcement and thermoregulatory behaviour in the lizard *Dipsosaurus dorsalis:* An operant technique. *Animal Behaviour, 17,* 446–451.

Kendrick, D.F., Rilling, M., & Stonebraker, T.B. (1981). Stimulus control of delayed matching in pigeons: Directed forgetting. *Journal of the Experimental Analysis of Behavior, 36,* 241–251.

Kenyon, K.W., & Rice, D.W. (1958). Homing of Laysan albatrosses. *Condor, 60,* 3–6.

Kettner, R.E., & Thompson, R.F. (1982). Auditory signal detection and decision processes in the nervous system. *Journal of Comparative and Physiological Psychology, 96,* 328–331.

Kiepenheuer, J. (1978). Pigeon navigation and the magnetic field: Information collected during the outward journey is used in the homing process. *Naturwissenschaften, 65,* 113.

Kinnaman, A.J. (1902). Mental life of two macacus rhesus monkeys in captivity. *American Journal of Psychology, 13,* 98–148.

Kirchner, W.K., & Towne, W.F. (1994). The sensory basis of the honeybee's dance language. *Scientific American, 277*(6), 52–59.

Kleiginna, P.R. (1970). Operant conditioning in the indigo snake. *Psychonomic Science, 18,* 53–55.

Kluender, K.R., Diehl, R.L., & Killeen, P.R. (1987). Japanese quail can learn phonetic categories. *Science, 237,* 1195–1197.

Klump, G.M., & Shalter, M.D. (1984). Acoustic behavior of birds and mammals in the predator context. *Zeitschrift für Tierpsychologie, 66,* 189–226.

Kohler, W. (1918). Nachweis einfacher Structurfunktionen beim Schimpansen und beim Haushuhn. *Abh. d. König, Preuss. Ak. d. Wissen. Phys. Math. Klasse, 2,* 1–101. [Translated and condensed as "Simple structural functions in chimpanzees and chicken".] In W.D. Ellis (1969), *A source book for Gestalt psychology.* London: Routledge & Kegan Paul.

Kohler, W. (1925). *The mentality of apes.* London: Routledge & Kegan Paul.

Kolterman, R. (1971). 24-Stunden-Periodik in der Langzeiterrinerung an Duft-und Farbsignale bei der Honigbiene. *Zeitschrift für vergleichende Physiologie, 75,* 49–68.

Konorski, J. (1948). *Conditioned reflexes and neuron organization.* Cambridge: Cambridge University Press.

Konorski, J. (1967). *Integrative activity of the brain.* Chicago: University of Chicago Press.

Kraemer, P.J., & Roberts, W.A. (1984). Short-term memory for visual and auditory stimuli in pigeons. *Animal Learning and Behavior, 12*, 275–284.

Kramer, G. (1952). Experiments on bird orientation. *Ibis, 94*, 265–285.

Krechevsky, I. (1932). Hypotheses in rats. *Psychological Review, 39*, 516–532.

Krebs, J.R. (1990). Food-storing in birds: Adaptive specialization in brain and behaviour? *Philosophical Transactions of the Royal Society of London, B, 329*, 153–160.

Kreithen, M.L. (1978). Sensory mechanisms for animal orientation - Can any new ones be discovered? In K. Schmidt-Koenig & W.T. Keeton (Eds.), *Animal migration, navigation and homing* (pp.25–34). Berlin: Springer.

Kreithen, M.L., & Keeton, W.T. (1974). Detection of changes in atmospheric pressure by the homing pigeon, *Columba livia. Journal of Comparative Physiology, 89*, 73–82.

Kremer, E.F. (1978). The Rescorla–Wagner model: Losses of associative strength in compound conditioned stimuli. *Journal of Experimental Psychology: Animal Behavior Processes, 4*, 22–36.

Kroodsma, D.E. (1978). Aspects of learning in the ontogeny of bird song: Where, from whom, when, how many, which and how accurately? In G. Burghardt & M. Bekoff (Eds.), *The development of behavior: Comparative and evolutionary aspects* (pp.215–230). New York: Garland.

Kruschke, J.K. (1992). ALCOVE: A connectionist model of human category learning. In R.P. Lippmann, J.E. Moody, & D.S. Touretzky (Eds.), *Advances in neural information processing systems* (Vol. 3, pp.649–655). San Mateo, CA: Morgan Kaufmann.

Kruse, J.M., Overmier, J.B., Konz, W.A., & Rokke, E. (1983). Pavlovian conditioned stimulus effects upon instrumental choice behaviour are reinforcer specific. *Learning and Motivation, 14*, 165–181.

Kummer, H., & Goodall, J. (1985). Conditions of innovative behavior in primates. *Philosophical Transactions of the Royal Society of London, 308*, 203–214.

LaBerge, D., & Samuels, S.J. (1974). Towards a theory of automatic information processing in reading. *Cognitive Psychology, 6*, 293–323.

Langley, C.M., & Riley, D.A. (1993). Limited capacity information processing and pigeon matching-to-sample: Testing alternative hypotheses. *Animal Learning and Behavior, 21*, 226–232.

Lashley, K.S. (1929). *Brain mechanisms and intelligence: A quantitative study of injuries to the brain.* Chicago: University of Chicago Press.

Lattal, K.A., & Gleeson, S. (1990). Response acquisition with delayed reinforcement. *Journal of Experimental Psychology: Animal Behavior Processes, 16*, 27–39.

Lawrence, D.H. (1949). Acquired distinctiveness of cues: I. Transfer between discriminations on the basis of familiarity with the stimulus. *Journal of Experimental Psychology, 39*, 770–784.

Lawrence, D.H. (1950). Acquired distinctiveness of cues: II. Selective association in a constant stimulus situation. *Journal of Experimental Psychology, 40*, 175–188.

Lawrence, D.H., & DeRivera, J. (1954). Evidence for relational transposition. *Journal of Comparative and Physiological Psychology, 47*, 465–471.

Lea, S.E.G. (1984). In what sense do pigeons learn concepts? In H.T. Roitblat, T.G. Bever, & H.S. Terrace (Eds.), *Animal cognition* (pp.263–276). Hillsdale, NJ: Lawrence Erlbaum Associates Inc.

Lea, S.E.G., & Harrison, S.N. (1978). Discrimination of polymorphous stimulus sets by pigeons. *Quarterly Journal of Experimental Psychology, 30B*, 521–537.

Leander, J.D. (1973). Effects of food deprivation on free-operant avoidance behavior. *Journal of the Experimental Analysis of Behavior, 19*, 17–24.

Lednor, A.J., & Walcott, C. (1983). Homing pigeon navigation: The effects of in-flight exposure to a varying magnetic field. *Comparative Biochemistry and Physiology, 76A*, 665–671.

Lefebvre, L., & Palameta, B. (1988). Mechanisms, ecology, and population diffusion of socially learned, food-finding behavior in feral pigeons. In T.R. Zentall & B.G. Galef, Jr. (Eds.) *Social learning: Psychological and biological perspectives* (pp.141–164). Hillsdale, NJ: Lawrence Erlbaum Associates Inc.

Leonard, B., & McNaughton, B.L. (1990). Spatial representation in the rat: Conceptual, behavioral, and neuropsychological perspectives. In R.P. Kesner & D.S. Olton (Eds.), *Neurobiology of comparative cognition* (pp.363–422). Hillsdale, NJ: Lawrence Erlbaum Associates Inc.

Lethmate, J., & Ducker, G. (1973). Untersuchungen zum Selbsterkennen im Spiegel bei Orang-utans und einigen anderen Affenarten. *Zeitschrift für Tierpsychologie. 33*, 248–269.

Lewis, D.J. (1979). Psychobiology of active and inactive memory. *Psychological Bulletin, 86*, 1054–1083.

Lieberman, D.A., Davidson, F.H., & Thomas, G.V. (1985). Marking in pigeons: The role of memory in delayed reinforcement. *Journal of Experimental Psychology: Animal Behavior Processes, 11*, 611–624.

Lieberman, D.A., McIntosh, D.C., & Thomas, G.V. (1979). Learning when reward is delayed: A marking hypothesis. *Journal of Experimental Psychology: Animal Behavior Processes, 5*, 224–242.

Lieberman, P. (1975). *On the origins of language.* New York: Macmillan.

Lieberman, P. (1984). *The biology and evolution of language.* Cambridge, MA: Harvard University Press.

Linwick, D., Overmier, J.B., Peterson, G.B., & Mertens, M. (1988). Interaction of memories and expectancies as mediators of choice behavior. *American Psychologist, 101*, 313–334.

Lipp, H.P. (1983). Nocturnal homing in pigeons. *Comparative Biochemistry and Physiology, 76A*, 743–749.

Locke, A. (1980). *The guided reinvention of language.* London: Academic Press.

Logan, C. (1975). Topographic changes in responding during habituation to waterstream stimulation in sea anemones *(Anthopleura elegentissima). Journal of Comparative and Physiological Psychology, 89*, 105–117.

Lohman, K.J. (1991). Magnetic orientation by hatchling loggerhead sea turtles. *Journal of Experimental Biology, 155*, 37–49.

Lohman, K.J. (1992). How sea turtles navigate. *Scientific American, 266*(1), 82–88.

LoLordo, V.M. (1979). Selective associations. In A. Dickinson & R.A. Boakes (Eds.), *Mechanisms of learning and motivation* (pp.367–398). Hillsdale, NJ: Lawrence Erlbaum Associates Inc.

Lovibond, P.F. (1983). Facilitation of instrumental behavior by a Pavlovian appetitive conditioned stimulus. *Journal of Experimental Psychology: Animal Behavior Processes, 9*, 225–247.

Lovibond, P.F. Preston, G.C., & Mackintosh, N.J. (1984). Context specificity of conditioning, extinction and latent inhibition. *Journal of Experimental Psychology: Animal Behavior Processes, 10*, 360–375.

Lubinski, D., & MacCorquodale, K. (1984). "Symbolic communication" between two pigeons *(Columba livia)* without unconditioned reinforcement. *Journal of Comparative Psychology, 98*, 372–380.

Lubow, R.E. (1973). Latent inhibition. *Psychological Bulletin, 79*, 398–407.

McClelland, J.L., & Rumelhart, D.E. (1985). Distributed memory and the representation of general and specific information. *Journal of Experimental Psychology: General, 114*, 159–188.

McCloskey, M., & Cohen, N.J. (1989). Catastrophic interference in connectionist networks: The sequential learning problem. In G. Bower (Ed.), *The psychology of learning and motivation* (Vol. 24, pp.109–165). San Diego, CA: Academic Press.

McFarland, D. (1985). *Animal behaviour.* Bath: Pitman.

McGonigle, B.O., & Chalmers, M. (1977). Are monkeys logical? *Nature, 267*, 694–696.

McGonigle, B.O., & Chalmers, M. (1986). Representations and strategies during inference. In T. Myers, K. Brown, & B. McGonigle (Eds.), *Reasoning and discourse processes* (pp.141–164). London: Academic Press.

McGonigle, B.O., & Chalmers, M. (1992). Monkeys are rational. *Quarterly Journal of Experimental Psychology, 45B*, 189–228.

McLaren, I.P.L., Kaye, H., & Mackintosh, N.J. (1989). An associative theory of the representation of stimuli: Applications to perceptual learning and latent inhibition. In R.G.M. Morris (Ed.), *Parallel distributed processing: Implications for psychology and neurobiology* (pp.102–130). Oxford: Clarendon Press.

McQoid, L.M., & Galef, B.G., Jr. (1992). Social influences on feeding site selection by Burmese fowl *(Gallus gallus). Journal of Comparative Psychology, 106*, 136–141.

Mackintosh, N.J. (1973). Stimulus selection: Learning to ignore stimuli that predict no change in reinforcement. In R.A. Hinde & J. Stevenson-Hinde (Eds.), *Constraints on learning* (pp.75–100). London: Academic Press.

Mackintosh, N.J. (1974). *The psychology of animal learning.* London: Academic Press.

Mackintosh, N.J. (1975a). A theory of attention: Variations in the associability of stimuli with reinforcement. *Psychological Review, 82*, 276–298.

Mackintosh, N.J. (1975b). Blocking of conditioned suppression: Role of the first compound trial. *Journal of Experimental Psychology: Animal Behavior Processes, 1*, 335–345.

Mackintosh, N.J. (1976). Overshadowing and stimulus intensity. *Animal Learning and Behavior, 4*, 186–192.

Mackintosh, N.J. (1983). *Conditioning and associative learning.* Oxford: Oxford University Press.

Mackintosh, N.J., Bygrave, D.J., & Picton, B.M.B. (1977). Locus of the effect of a surprising reinforcer in the attenuation of blocking. *Quarterly Journal of Experimental Psychology, 29,* 327–336.

Mackintosh, N.J., & Cauty, A. (1971). Spatial reversal learning in rats, pigeons, and goldfish. *Psychonomic Science, 22,* 281–282.

Mackintosh, N.J., & Cotton, M.M. (1985). Conditioned inhibition from reinforcement reduction. In R.R. Miller & N.E. Spear (Eds.), *Information processing in animals: Conditioned inhibition* (pp.89–111). Hillsdale, NJ: Lawrence Erlbaum Associates Inc.

Mackintosh, N.J., & Dickinson, A. (1979). Instrumental (type II) conditioning. In A. Dickinson & R.A. Boakes (Eds.), *Mechanisms of learning and motivation* (pp.143–169). Hillsdale, NJ: Lawrence Erlbaum Associates Inc.

Mackintosh, N.J., & Holgate, V. (1969). Serial reversal training and nonreversal shift learning. *Journal of Comparative and Physiological Psychology, 67,* 89–93.

Mackintosh, N.J., Wilson, B., & Boakes, R.A. (1985). Differences in mechanisms of intelligence among vertebrates. In L. Weiskrantz (Ed.), *Animal intelligence* (pp.53–66). Oxford: Clarendon Press.

Macphail, E.M. (1980). Short-term visual recognition memory in pigeons. *Quarterly Journal of Experimental Psychology, 32B,* 521–538.

Macphail, E.M. (1982). *Brain and intelligence in vertebrates.* Oxford: Clarendon Press.

Macphail, E.M. (1985). Vertebrate intelligence: The null hypothesis. In L. Weiskrantz (Ed.), *Animal intelligence* (pp.37–51). Oxford: Clarendon Press.

Macphail, E.M. (1993). *The neuroscience of animal intelligence.* New York: Columbia University Press.

Maki, W.S., & Abunawass, A.M. (1991). A connectionist approach to conditional discriminations: Learning, short-term memory, and attention. In M.L. Commons, S. Grossberg, & J.E.R. Staddon (Eds.), *Neural network models of conditioning and action* (pp.241–278). Hillsdale, NJ: Lawrence Erlbaum Associates Inc.

Maki, W.S., Brokofsky, S., & Berg, B. (1979). Spatial memory in rats: Resistance to retroactive interference. *Animal Learning and Behavior, 7,* 25–30.

Maki, W.S., & Hegvik, D.K. (1980). Directed forgetting in pigeons. *Animal Learning and Behavior, 8,* 567–574.

Malott, R.W., & Sidall, J.W. (1972). Acquisition of the people concept in pigeons. *Psychological Reports, 31,* 3–13.

Mandriota, F.J., Thompson, L., Bennett, M.V.L. (1968). Avoidance conditioning of the rate of electric organ discharge in mormyrid fish. *Animal Behaviour, 16,* 448–455.

March, J., Chamizo, V.D., & Mackintosh, N.J. (1992). Reciprocal overshadowing between intra-maze and extra-maze cues. *Quarterly Journal of Experimental Psychology, 45B*(1), 49–63.

Marler, P. (1970). A comparative approach to vocal learning: Song development in white-crowned sparrows. *Journal of Comparative and Physiological Psychology, 71* (Supplement), 1–25.

Marlin, N.A., & Miller, R.R. (1981). Associations to contextual stimuli as a determinant of long-term habituation. *Journal of Experimental Psychology: Animal Behavior Processes, 7,* 313–333.

Marten, K., & Psarakos, S. (1994). Evidence of self-awareness in the bottlenose dolphin (*Tursiops truncatus*). In S.T. Taylor, R.W. Mitchell, & M.L. Boccia (Eds.), *Self-awareness in animals and humans* (pp.361–379). New York: Cambridge University Press.

Matsuzawa, T. (1985). Use of numbers by a chimpanzee. *Nature, 315,* 57–59.

Matthews, B.L., Ryu, J.H., & Bockaneck, C. (1989). Vestibular contribution to spatial orientation: Evidence of vestibular navigation in an animal model. *Acta Otolaryngolica, 468,* 149–154.

Matthews, G.V.T. (1955). *Bird navigation.* London: Cambridge University Press.

Mazmanian, D.S., & Roberts, W.A. (1983). Spatial memory in rats under restricted viewing conditions. *Learning and Motivation, 12,* 261–281.

Mechner, F. (1958). Probability relations within response sequences under ratio reinforcement. *Journal of the Experimental Analysis of Behavior, 1,* 109–122.

Mechner, F., & Guevrekian, L. (1962). Effects of deprivation upon counting and timing in rats. *Journal of the Experimental Analysis of Behavior, 5,* 463–466.

Meck, W.H., & Church. R.M. (1982). Abstraction of temporal attributes. *Journal of Experimental Psychology: Animal Behavior Processes, 8,* 226–243.

Meck, W.H., & Church, R.M. (1983). A mode control model of counting and timing processes. *Journal of Experimental Psychology: Animal Behavior Processes, 9,* 320–334.

Meck, W.H., & Church, R.M. (1984). Simultaneous temporal processing. *Journal of Experimental Psychology: Animal Behavior Processes, 10,* 1–29.

Medin, D.L., & Schaffer, M.M. (1978). A context theory of classification learning. *Psychological Review, 85,* 217–238.

Meehl, P.E. (1950). On the circularity of the law of effect. *Psychological Bulletin, 47,* 52–75.

Menzel, E.W. (1978). Cognitive mapping in chimpanzees. In S.H. Hulse, H. Fowler, & W.K. Honig (Eds.), *Cognitive processes in animal behavior* (pp.375–422). Hillsdale, NJ: Lawrence Erlbaum Associates Inc.

Menzel, E.W., & Halperin, S. (1975). Purposive behavior as a basis for objective communication between chimpanzees. *Science, 189,* 652–654.

Menzel, R. (1979). Behavioural access to short-term memory in bees. *Nature, 241,* 477–478.

Menzel, R. (1990). Learning, memory, and "cognition" in honey bees. In R.P. Kesner, & D.S. Olton (Eds.), *Neurobiology of comparative cognition* (pp.237–292). Hillsdale, NJ: Lawrence Erlbaum Associates Inc.

Menzel, R.M., & Erber, J. (1978). Learning and memory in bees. *Scientific American, 239,* 80–88.

Meyer, M.E., Adams, W.A., & Worthen, V.K. (1969). Deprivation and escape conditioning with various intensities of shock. *Psychonomic Science, 14,* 212–214.

Miles, H.L.W. (1994). ME CHANTEK: The development of self-awareness in the signing orangutan. In S.T. Taylor, R.W. Mitchell, & M.L. Boccia (Eds.), *Self-awareness in animals and humans* (pp.254–272). New York: Cambridge University Press.

Miller, D.J. (1993). Do animals subitize? In S. J. Boysen & E. J. Capaldi (Eds.), *The development of numerical competence: Animal and human models* (pp.149–169). Hillsdale, NJ: Lawrence Erlbaum Associates Inc.

Miller, R.R., Barnet, R.C., & Grahame, N.J. (1995). Assessment of the Rescorla–Wagner model. *Psychological Bulletin, 117,* 363–386.

Miller, R.R., & Berk, A.M. (1977). Retention over metamorphosis in the African claw-toed frog. *Journal of Experimental Psychology: Animal Behavior Processes, 3,* 343–356.

Mineka, S., & Cook, M. (1988). Social learning and the acquisition of snake fear in monkeys. In T. R. Zentall, & B.G. Galef, Jr. (Eds.), *Social learning psychological and biological perspectives* (pp.51–74). Hillsdale, NJ: Lawrence Erlbaum Associates Inc.

Minsky, M.L., & Papert, S. (1969). *Perceptrons: An introduction to computational geometry.* Cambridge, MA: MIT Press.

Misanin, J.R., & Campbell, B.A. (1969). Effects of hunger and thirst on sensitivity and reactivity to shock. *Journal of Comparative and Physiological Psychology, 69,* 207–213.

Mishkin, M., Prockop, E.S., & Rosvold, H.E. (1962). One-trial object-discrimination learning in monkeys with frontal lesions. *Journal of Comparative and Physiological Psychology, 55,* 178–181.

Mistlberger, R.E. (1994). Circadian food-anticipatory activity: Formal models and physiological mechanisms. *Neuroscience and Behavioral Reviews, 18,* 171–195.

Mittelstaedt, H., & Mittelstaedt, M. L. (1982). Homing by path integration. In F. Papi & H.G. Wallraff (Eds.), *Avian navigation* (pp.290–297). Berlin: Springer.

Moore, B.R. (1973). The role of directed Pavlovian reactions in simple instrumental learning in the pigeon. In R.A. Hinde & J. Stevenson-Hinde (Eds.), *Constraints on learning* (pp.159–186). London: Academic Press.

Moore, B.R., (1992). Avian imitation and a new form of mimicry: Tracing the evolution of complex learning. *Behavior, 122,* 231–263.

Moore, J.W. (1972). Stimulus control: Studies of auditory generalization in the rabbit. In A.H. Black & W.F. Prokasy (Eds.), *Classical conditioning II: Current research and theory* (pp.206–320). New York: Appleton-Century-Crofts.

Moore, J.W., & Stickney, K.J. (1980). Formation of attentional-associative networks in real time: Role of the hippocampus and implications for conditioning. *Physiological Psychology, 8,* 207–217.

Moore, R.F., & Osadchuk, T.E. (1982). Spatial memory in a passerine migrant. In F. Pappi & H.G. Wallraff (Eds.), *Avian navigation.* Berlin: Springer.

Morgan, C.L. (1894). *An introduction to comparative psychology.* London: Scott.

Morgan, C.L. (1900). *Animal behaviour.* London: Edward Arnold.

Morgan, M.J., Fitch, M.D., Holman, J.G., & Lea, S.E.G. (1976). Pigeons learn the concept of an "A". *Perception, 5,* 57–66.

Morris, R.G.M. (1981). Spatial localization does not require the presence of local cue. *Learning and Motivation, 12,* 239–260.

Nagell, K., Olguin, R. S., & Tomasello, M. (1993). Processes of social learning in the tool use of chimpanzees (*Pan troglodytes*) and human children (*Homo sapiens*). *Journal of Comparative Psychology, 107,* 174–186.

Nissen, H.W., Blum, J.S., & Blum, R.A. (1948). Analysis of matching behavior in chimpanzees. *Journal of Comparative and Physiological Psychology, 41,* 62–74.

North, A.J. (1959). Discrimination reversal with spaced trials and distinctive cues. *Journal of Comparative and Physiological Psychology, 52,* 426–429.

Oden, D.L., Thompson, R.K.R., & Premack, D. (1988). Spontaneous transfer of matching by infant chimpanzees (*Pan troglodytes*). *Journal of Experimental Psychology: Animal Behavior Processes, 14,* 140–145.

O'Keefe, J. (1979). A review of the hippocampal place cells. *Progress in Neurobiology, 13,* 419–439.

O'Keefe, J., & Conway, D.H. (1978). Hippocampal place units in the freely moving rat: Why they fire when they fire. *Experimental Brain Research, 31,* 573–590.

O'Keefe, J., & Conway, D.H. (1980). On the trail of the hippocampal engram. *Physiological Psychology, 8,* 229–238.

O'Keefe, J., & Nadel, L. (1978). *The hippocampus as a cognitive map.* Oxford: Clarendon Press.

O'Keefe, J., & Speakman, A. (1987). Single unit activity in the rat hippocampus during a spatial memory task. *Experimental Brain Research, 68,* 1–27.

Olds, J., & Milner, P. (1954). Positive reinforce-ment produced by electrical stimulation of septal area and other regions of rat brain. *Journal of Comparative and Physiological Psychology, 47,* 419–427.

Olton, D.S. (1978). Characteristics of spatial memory. In S.H. Hulse, H. Fowler, & W.K. Honig (Eds.), *Cognitive processes in animal behavior* (pp.341–373). Hillsdale, NJ: Lawrence Erlbaum Associates Inc.

Olton, D.S., Collison, C., & Werz, M. (1977). Spatial memory and radial arm maze performance of rats. *Learning and Motivation, 8,* 289–314.

Olton, D.S., Meck, W.H., & Church, R.M. (1987). Separation of hippocampal and amygdaloid involvement in temporal memory dysfunctions. *Brain Research, 404,* 180–188.

Olton, D.S., & Samuelson, R.J. (1976). Remembrance of places past: Spatial memory in rats. *Journal of Experimental Psychology: Animal Behavior Processes, 2,* 97–116.

Osgood, C.E. (1953). *Method and theory in experimental psychology.* New York: Oxford University Press.

O'Sullivan, C., & Yeager, C.P. (1989). Communication context and linguistic competence: The effects of social setting on a chimpanzee's conversational skill. In R.G. Gardner, B.T. Gardner, & T.E. Van Canfort (Eds.), *Teaching sign language to chimpanzees* (pp.281–292). New York: State University of New York Press.

Papi, F., Fiore, L., Fiaschi, V., & Benvenuti, S. (1972). Pigeon homing: Outward journey detours influence the initial orientation. *Monitore Zoologico Italiano, 7,* 129–133.

Papi, F., Ioale, P., Fiaschi, V., Benvenuti, S., & Baldaccini, N.E. (1978). Pigeon homing: Cues detected during the outward journey influence initial orientation. In K. Schmidt-Koenig & W. Keeton (Eds.), *Animal migration, navigation, and homing* (pp.65–77). Berlin: Springer.

Papousek, H. (1977). Entwicklung der Lernfähigkeit im Säuglingsalter. In Nissen (Ed.), *Intelligenz, Lernen und Lernstörungen.* Berlin: Springer.

Parisi, T., & Matthews, T.J. (1975). Pavlovian determinants of the autoshaped keypeck response. *Bulletin of the Psychonomic Society, 6,* 527–529.

Parisi, V., & Gandolfi, G. (1974). Further aspects of the predation by rats on various mollusc species. *Bollettino di Zoologia, 41,* 87–106.

Passingham, R.E. (1982). *The human primate.* San Francisco: Freeman.

Patterson, F.G.P., & Cohn, R.H. (1994). Self-recognition and self-awareness in lowland gorilla. In S.T. Taylor, R.W. Mitchell, & M.L. Boccia (Eds.), *Self-awareness in animals and humans* (pp.254–272). New York: Cambridge University Press.

Pavlov, I.P. (1927). *Conditioned reflexes.* New York: Oxford University Press.

Payne, R.B. (1981). Song learning and social interaction in indigo burnings. *Animal Behaviour, 29,* 688–697.

Pearce, J.M. (1987). A model for stimulus generalization in Pavlovian conditioning, *Psychological Review, 94,* 61–73.

Pearce, J.M. (1988). Stimulus generalization and the acquisition of categories by pigeons. In L. Weiskrantz (Ed.), *Thought without language* (pp.132–152). Oxford: Oxford University Press.

Pearce, J.M. (1989). The acquisition of an artificial category by pigeons. *Quarterly Journal of Experimental Psychology, 41B,* 381–406.

Pearce, J.M. (1991). The acquisition of abstract and concrete categories by pigeons. In L. Dachowski & C. Flaherty (Eds.), *Current topics in animal learning: Brain, emotion and, cognition* (pp.141–164). Hillsdale, NJ: Lawrence Erlbaum Associates Inc.

Pearce, J.M. (1994). Similarity and discrimination: A selective review and a connectionist model. *Psychological Review, 101*, 587–607.

Pearce, J.M., Colwill, R.M., & Hall, G. (1978). Instrumental conditioning of scratching in the laboratory rat. *Learning and Motivation, 9*, 255–271.

Pearce, J.M., & Hall, G. (1978). Overshadowing the instrumental conditioning of a lever press response by a more valid predictor of reinforcement. *Journal of Experimental Psychology: Animal Behavior Processes, 4*, 356–367.

Pearce, J.M., & Hall, G. (1979). Loss of associability by a compound stimulus comprising excitatory and inhibitory elements. *Journal of Experimental Psychology: Animal Behavior Processes, 5*, 19–30.

Pearce, J.M., & Hall, G. (1980). A model for Pavlovian learning: Variations in the effectiveness of conditioned but not of unconditioned stimuli. *Psychological Review, 87*, 532–552.

Pearce, J.M., Kaye, H., & Hall, G. (1982). Predictive accuracy and stimulus associability: Development of a model for Pavlovian learning. In M.L. Commons, R.J. Herrnstein, & A.R. Wagner (Eds.), *Quantitative analyses of behavior: Acquisition* (pp.241–256). Cambridge, MA: Ballinger.

Pearce, J.M., Montgomery, A., & Dickinson, A. (1981). Contralateral transfer of inhibitory and excitatory eyelid conditioning in the rabbit. *Quarterly Journal of Experimental Psychology, 33B*, 45–61.

Pearce, J.M., Nicholas, D.J., & Dickinson, A. (1982). Loss of associability by a conditioned inhibitor. *Quarterly Journal of Experimental Psychology, 33B*, 149–162.

Pearce, J.M., & Redhead, E.S. (1993). The influence of an irrelevant stimulus on two discriminations. *Journal of Experimental Psychology: Animal Behavior Processes, 19*, 180–190.

Pearce, J.M., & Wilson, P.N. (1991). Failure of excitatory conditioning to extinguish the influence of a conditioned inhibitor. *Journal of Experimental Psychology: Animal Behavior Processes, 17*, 519–529.

Peeke, H.V.S., & Veno, A. (1973). Stimulus specificity of habituated aggression in three-spined sticklebacks *(Gasterosteus aculeatus)*. *Behavioral Biology, 8*, 427–432.

Pepperberg, I.M. (1981). Functional vocalizations by an African Grey parrot *(Psittacus erithacus)*. *Z. für Tierpsychologie, 55*, 139–160.

Pepperberg, I.M. (1983). Cognition in the African Grey parrot: Preliminary evidence for auditory/vocal comprehension of the class concept. *Animal Learning and Behaviour, 11*, 179–185.

Pepperberg, I.M. (1987). Interspecies communication: A tool for assessing conceptual abilities in the African Grey parrot *(Psittacus arithacus)*. In G. Greenberg & E. Tobach (Eds.), *Language cognition, consciousness: Integrative levels* (pp.31–56). Hillsdale, NJ: Lawrence Erlbaum Associates Inc.

Pepperberg, I.M. (1993). Cognition and communication in an African Grey parrot *(Psittacus erithacus)*: Studies on a nonhuman, nonprimate, nonmammalian subject. In H.L. Roitblat, L.M. Herman, & P.E. Nachtigall (Eds.), *Language and communication: Comparative perspectives* (pp.221–248). Hillsdale, NJ: Lawrence Erlbaum Associates Inc.

Pepperberg, I.M. (1994). Numerical competence in an African Grey parrot. *Journal of Comparative Psychology, 108*, 36–44.

Pepperberg, I.M., Garcia, S.E., Jackson, E.C., & Marconi, S. (1995). Mirror use by African Grey parrots *(Psittacus erithacus)*. *Journal of Comparative Psychology, 109*, 182–195.

Perdeck, A.C. (1958). Two types of orientation in migratory starlings, *Sturnus vulgaris L.* and chaffinches, *Fringilla coelebs L.* as revealed by displacement experiments. *Ardea, 46*, 1–37.

Peterson, L., & Peterson, M.J. (1959). Short-term retention of individual verbal items. *Journal of Experimental Psychology, 58*, 193–198.

Petrinovich, L. (1988). The role of social factors in white-crowned sparrow song development. In T.R. Zentall & B.G. Galef, Jr. (Eds.), *Social learning: Psychological and biological perspectives* (pp.255–278). Hillsdale, NJ: Lawrence Erlbaum Associates Inc.

Pfungst, O. (1965). *Clever Hans: The horse of Mr Van Osten*. New York: Holt. (German original, 1908).

Pietrewicz, A.T., & Kamil, A.C. (1977). Visual detection of cryptic prey by blue jays. *Science, 195*, 580–582.

Pinker, S. (1994). *The language instinct*. New York: Penguin.

Platt, S.A., Holliday, M., & Drudge, O.W. (1980). Discrimination learning of an instrumental response in individual *Drosophila melanogaster*. *Journal of Experimental Psychology: Animal Behavior Processes, 6*, 301–311.

Plaisted, K.C., & Mackintosh, N.J. (1995). Visual search for cryptic stimuli in pigeons: Implication for the search image and search rate hypotheses. *Animal Behaviour, 50*, 1219–1232.

Porter, D., & Neuringer, A. (1984). Music discriminations by pigeons. *Journal of Experimental Psychology: Animal Behavior Processes, 10*, 138–148.

Posner, M.I., & Keele, S.W. (1968). On the genesis of abstract ideas. *Journal of Experimental Psychology, 77,* 353–363.

Povinelli, D.J. (1989). Failure to find self-recognition in Asian elephants (*Elephas maximus*) in contrast to their use of mirror cues to discover hidden food. *Journal of Comparative Psychology, 103,* 122–131.

Povinelli, D.J. (1994). Comparative studies of animal mental attributions: A reply to Heyes. *Animal Behaviour, 48,* 239–241.

Povinelli, D.J., Nelson, K.E., & Boysen, S.T. (1990). Inferences about guessing and knowing by chimpanzees (*Pan troglodytes*). *Journal of Comparative Psychology, 104,* 203–210.

Povinelli, D.J., Rulf, A.B., & Bierschwale, D.T. (1994). Absence of knowledge attribution and self-recognition in young chimpanzees (*Pan troglodytes*). *Journal of Comparative Psychology, 108,* 74–80.

Povinelli, D.J., Rulf, A.B., Landau, K.R., Bierschwale, D.T. (1993). Self-recognition in chimpanzees (*Pan troglodytes*): Distribution, ontogeny, and patterns of emergence. *Journal of Comparative Psychology, 107,* 347–372.

Premack, D. (1959). Toward empirical behavior laws: I. Positive reinforcement. *Psychological Review, 66,* 219–233.

Premack, D. (1962). Reversibility of the reinforcement relation. *Science, 136,* 235–237.

Premack, D. (1965). Reinforcement theory. In D. Levine (Ed.), *Nebraska symposium on motivation* (pp.123–180). Lincoln: University of Nebraska Press.

Premack, D. (1971a). Catching up with common sense, or two sides of a generalization: Reinforcement and punishment. In R. Glaser (Ed.), *The nature of reinforcement* (pp.121–150). New York: Academic Press.

Premack, D. (1971b). Language in chimpanzees? *Science, 172,* 808–822.

Premack, D. (1976). *Intelligence in ape and man.* Hillsdale, NJ: Lawrence Erlbaum Associates Inc.

Premack, D. (1983a). Animal cognition. *Annual Review of Psychology, 34,* 351–362.

Premack, D. (1983b). The codes of man and beasts. *The Behavioral and Brain Sciences, 6,* 125–167.

Premack, D. (1988). "Does the chimpanzee have a theory of mind?" revisited. In R.W. Byrne & A. Whiten (Eds.), *Machiavellian intelligence* (pp.160–179). Oxford: Clarendon Press.

Premack, D., & Woodruff, G. (1978). Does the chimpanzee have a theory of mind? *Behavioral and Brain Sciences, 4,* 515–526.

Quine, D.B. (1982). Infrasounds: A potential navigational cue for homing pigeons. In F. Papi & H.G. Wallraff (Eds.), *Avian navigation* (pp.373–376). Berlin: Springer.

Rashotte, M.E., Griffin, R.W., & Sisk, C.L. (1977). Second-order conditioning of the pigeon's key peck. *Animal Learning and Behavior, 5,* 25–38.

Redhead, E.S., & Pearce, J.M. (1995a). Similarity and discrimination learning. *Quarterly Journal of Experimental Psychology, 48B,* 46–66.

Redhead, E.S., & Pearce, J.M. (1995b). Stimulus salience and negative patterning. *Quarterly Journal of Experimental Psychology, 48B,* 67–83.

Reed, P. (1989). Influence of interresponse time reinforcement on signalled-reward effect. *Journal of Experimental Psychology: Animal Behavior Processes, 15,* 224–231.

Reed, S.K. (1972). Pattern recognition and categorization. *Cognitive Psychology, 3,* 382–407.

Reiss, S., & Wagner, A.R. (1972). CS habituation produces a "latent inhibition effect" but no active "conditioned inhibition". *Learning and Motivation, 3,* 237–245.

Renner, M. (1960). Contribution of the honey bee to the study of time sense and astronomical orientation. *Cold Spring Harbor Symposium on Quantitative Biology, 25,* 361–367.

Rescorla, R.A. (1967). Pavlovian conditioning and its proper control procedures. *Psychological Review, 74,* 71–80.

Rescorla, R.A. (1968). Probability of shock in the presence and absence of CS in fear conditioning. *Journal of Comparative and Physiological Psychology, 66,* 1–5.

Rescorla, R.A. (1969). Pavlovian conditioned inhibition. *Psychological Bulletin, 72,* 77–94.

Rescorla, R.A. (1972). "Configural" conditioning in discrete-trial bar pressing. *Journal of Comparative and Physiological Psychology, 79,* 307–317.

Rescorla, R.A. (1976). Stimulus generalization: Some predictions from a model of Pavlovian conditioning. *Journal of Experimental Psychology: Animal Behavior Processes, 2,* 88–96.

Rescorla, R.A. (1979). Conditioned inhibition and extinction. In A. Dickinson & R.A. Boakes (Eds.), *Mechanisms of learning and motivation,* (pp.83–110). Hillsdale, NJ: Lawrence Erlbaum Associates Inc.

Rescorla, R.A. (1980). *Pavlovian second-order conditioning*. Hillsdale, NJ: Lawrence Erlbaum Associates Inc.

Rescorla, R.A. (1981). Within-signal learning in autoshaping. *Animal Learning and Behavior, 9,* 245–252.

Rescorla, R.A. (1991). Associative relations in instrumental learning: The Eighteenth Bartlett Memorial Lecture. *Quarterly Journal of Experimental Psychology, 43B,* 1–23.

Rescorla, R.A., & LoLordo, V.M. (1965). Inhibition and avoidance behavior. *Journal of Comparative and Physiological Psychology, 59,* 406–412.

Rescorla, R.A., & Solomon, R.L. (1967). Two-process learning theory: Relationship between Pavlovian conditioning and instrumental learning. *Psychological Review, 88,* 151–182.

Rescorla, R.A., & Wagner, A.R. (1972). A theory of Pavlovian conditioning: Variations in the effectiveness of reinforcement and nonreinforcement. In A.H. Black & W.F. Prokasy (Eds.), *Classical conditioning H: Current research and theory* (pp.64–99). New York: Appleton-Century-Crofts.

Revusky, S.H. (1971). The role of interference over a delay. In W.K. Honig & P.H.R. James (Eds.), *Animal memory* (pp.155–213). New York: Academic Press.

Revusky, S. H. (1977). Learning as a general process with an emphasis on data from feeding experiments. In N.W. Milgram, L. Krames, & T.M. Alloway (Eds.), *Food aversion learning* (pp.1–51). New York: Plenum.

Richards, D.G., Wolz, J.P., & Herman, L.M. (1984). Vocal mimicry of computer-generated sounds and vocal labeling of objects by a bottlenosed dolphin, *Tusiops truncatus. Journal of Comparative Psychology, 98,* 10–28.

Riddell, W.I. (1979). Cerebral indices and behavioral differences. In M.E. Hahn, C. Jensen, & B.C. Dudek (Eds.), *Development and evolution of brain size* (pp.89–111). New York: Academic Press.

Riley, D.A. (1968). *Discrimination learning*. Boston, MA: Allyn and Bacon.

Riley, D.A. (1984). Do pigeons decompose stimulus compounds? In H.L. Roitblat, T.G. Bever, & H.S. Terrace (Eds.), *Animal cognition* (pp.333–350). Hillsdale, NJ: Lawrence Erlbaum Associates Inc.

Riley, D.A., & Roitblat, H.L. (1978). Selective attention and related cognitive processes in pigeons. In S.H. Hulse, H. Fowler, & W.K. Honig (Eds.), *Cognitive processes in animal behavior* (pp.249–276). Hillsdale, NJ: Lawrence Erlbaum Associates Inc.

Ristau, C.A., & Robbins, D. (1982). Language in the great apes: A critical review. *Advances in the Study of Behaviour, 12,* 141–255.

Rizley, R.C., & Rescorla, R.A. (1972). Associations in second-order conditioning and sensory preconditioning. *Journal of Comparative and Physiological Psychology, 81,* 1–11.

Roberts, S. (1981). Isolation of an internal clock. *Journal of Experimental Psychology: Animal Behavior Processes, 7,* 242–268.

Roberts, S. (1982). Cross-modal use of an internal clock. *Journal of Experimental Psychology: Animal Behavior Processes, 8,* 2–22.

Roberts, S.K. (1965). Photoreception and entrainment of cockroach activity rhythms. *Science, 148,* 958–960.

Roberts, W.A. (1979). Spatial memory in the rat on a hierarchical maze. *Learning and Motivation, 10,* 117–140.

Roberts, W.A. (1981). Retroactive inhibition in rat spatial memory. *Animal Learning and Behavior, 9,* 566–574.

Roberts, W.A. (1984). Some issues in animal spatial memory. In H.L. Roitblat, T.G. Bever, & H.S. Terrace (Eds.), *Animal cognition* (pp.425–443). Hillsdale, NJ: Lawrence Erlbaum Associates Inc.

Roberts, W.A., Cheng, K., & Cohen, J.S. (1989). Timing light and tone signals in pigeons. *Journal of Experimental Psychology: Animal Behavior Processes, 15,* 23–35.

Roberts, W.A., & Dale, R.H.I. (1981). Remembrance of places lasts: Proactive inhibition and patterns of choice in rat spatial memory. *Learning and Motivation, 12,* 261–281.

Roberts, W.A., & Grant, D.S. (1974). Short-term memory in the pigeon with presentation time precisely controlled. *Learning and Motivation, 5,* 393–408.

Roberts, W.A., & Grant, D.S. (1976). Studies of short-term memory in the pigeon using the delayed matching-to-sample procedure. In D.L. Medin, W.A. Roberts, & R.T. Davis (Eds.), *Processes in animal memory.* Hillsdale, NJ: Lawrence Erlbaum Associates Inc.

Roberts, W.A., & Kraemer, P.J. (1981). Recognition memory for lists of visual stimuli in monkeys and humans. Animal Learning and Behavior, 9, 587–594.

Roberts, W.A., & Phelps, M.T. (1994). Transitive inference in rats: A test of the spatial coding hypothesis. *Psychological Science, 6,* 368–374.

Roberts, W.A., & Smythe, W.E. (1979). Memory for lists of spatial events in the rat. *Learning and Motivation, 10,* 313–336.

Robert, W.A., & Van Veldhuizen, N. (1985). Spatial memory in pigeons on the radial maze. *Journal of Experimental Psychology: Animal Behavior Processes, 11,* 241–260.

Roediger, H.L., & Crowder, R.G. (1976). The spacing of lists in free recall. *Journal of Verbal Learning and Verbal Behavior, 14,* 580–602.

Roitblat, H.L. (1980). Codes and coding processes in pigeon short-term memory. *Animal Learning and Behavior, 8,* 341–351.

Roitblat, H.L., Bever, T.G., Helweg, D.A., & Harley, H.E. (1991). On-line choice and representation of serially structured stimuli. *Journal of Experimental Psychology: Animal Behavior Processes, 17,* 55–67.

Roitblat, H.L., Tham, W., & Gollub, L. (1982). Performance of *Betta splendens* in a radial arm maze. *Animal Learning and Behavior, 10.* 108–114.

Romanes, G.J. (1882). *Animal intelligence.* London: Keegan Paul.

Romer, A.S. (1966). *The vertebrate body.* Philadelphia, PA: W.B. Saunders.

Romer, A.S., & Parsons, T.S. (1977). *The vertebrate body* (5th edn.). Philadelphia, PA: W.B. Saunders.

Roper, K.L., & Zentall, T.R. (1993). Directed forgetting in animals. *Psychological Bulletin, 113,* 513–532.

Roper, T.J. (1983). Learning as a biological phenomenon. In T.R. Halliday & P.J.B. Slater (Eds.), *Animal behaviour: Genes, development and learning* (pp.178–212). Oxford: Blackwell.

Rosch, E. (1973). On the internal structure of perceptual and semantic categories. In T.E. Moore (Ed.), *Cognitive development and the acquisition of language.* New York: Academic Press.

Rosenblatt, F. (1962). *Principles of neurodynamics.* Washington, DC: Spartan Books.

Rozin, P., & Kalat, J.W. (1971). Specific hungers and poisoning as adaptive specializations of learning. *Psychological Review, 78,* 459–486.

Rumbaugh, D.M. (1977). *Language learning by a chimpanzee: The LANA project.* New York: Academic Press.

Rumbaugh, D.M., & Savage-Rumbaugh, E.S. (1994). Language in comparative perspective. In N.J. Mackintosh (Ed.), *Animal learning and cognition* (pp.307–333). San Diego, CA: Academic Press.

Rumbaugh, D.M., & Washburn, D.A. (1993). Counting by chimpanzees and ordinality judgements by macaques in video-formatted tasks. In S.J. Boysen & E.J. Capaldi (Eds.), *The development of numerical competence: Animal and human models* (pp.87–106). Hillsdale, NJ: Lawrence Erlbaum Associates Inc.

Rumelhart, D.E., Hinton, G.E., & Williams, R.J. (1988). Learning internal representations by error propagation. In D.E. Rumelhart & J.L. McClelland (Eds.), *Parallel distributed processing* (Vol. 1, pp.318–362). Cambridge, MA: MIT Press.

Russell, I.S. (1979). Brain size and intelligence: A comparative perspective. In D.A. Oakley & H.C. Plotkin (Eds.), *Brain behaviour and evolution* (pp.126–153). London: Methuen.

Russon, A.E., & Galdikas, B.M.F. (1993). Imitation in free-ranging orangutans (*Pongo pygmaeus*). *Journal of Comparative Psychology, 107,* 147–161.

Ryan, C.W.E. (1982). Concept formation and individual recognition in the domestic chicken (*Gallus gallus*). *Behavior Analysis Letters, 2,* 213–220.

Saint Paul, U.V. (1982). Do geese use path integration for walking home? In F. Papi and H.G. Wallraff (Eds.), *Avian navigation* (pp.298–307). New York: Springer.

Santchi, F. (1913). Comment s'orient les fourmis. *Revue Suisse de Zoologie, 21,* 347–426.

Savage-Rumbaugh, E.S. (1984). Acquisition of functional symbol usage in apes and children. In H.L. Roitblat, T.G. Bever, & H.S. Terrace (Eds.), *Animal cognition* (pp.291–310). Hillsdale, NJ: Lawrence Erlbaum Associates Inc.

Savage-Rumbaugh, E.S., & Lewin, R. (1994). *Kanzi: At the brink of the human mind.* New York: Wiley.

Savage-Rumbaugh, E.S., McDonald, K., Sevcik, R.A., Hopkins, W.D., & Rubert, E. (1986). Spontaneous symbol acquisition and communication by pygmy chimpanzees *(Pan paniscus). Journal of Experimental Psychology: General, 115,* 211–235.

Savage-Rumbaugh, E.S., Murphy, J., Sevcik, R.A., Brakke, K.E., Williams, S.L., & Rumbaugh, D.M. (1993). Language comprehension in ape and child. *Monographs of the Society for Research in Child Development, 58,* 1–221.

Savage-Rumbaugh, E.S., Pate, J.L., Lawson, J., Smith, T., & Rosenbaum, S. (1983). Can a chimpanzee make a statement? *Journal of Experimental Psychology: General, 112,* 457–492.

Savage-Rumbaugh, E.S., Rumbaugh, D.M., & Boysen, S.L. (1978). Symbolic communication between two chimpanzees *(Pan troglodytes). Science, 201,* 641–644.

Savage-Rumbaugh, E.S., Rumbaugh, D.M., Smith, S.T., & Lawson, J. (1980). Reference - The linguistic essential. *Science, 210*, 922–925.

Savage-Rumbaugh, E.S., Sevcik, R.A., & Hopkins, W.D. (1988). Symbolic cross-modal transfer in two species of chimpanzees. *Child Development, 59*, 617–625.

Schiller, P.H. (1952). Innate constituents of complex responses in primates. *Psychological Review, 59*, 177–191.

Schlicte, H.J., & Schmidt-Koenig, K. (1971). Zum Heimfindevermögen der Brieftaube bei erschwerter optischer Wahrnehmung. *Naturwissenschaften, 58*, 329–330.

Schmajuk, N.A., & DiCarlo, J.J. (1992). Stimulus configuration, classical conditioning, and hippocampal function. *Psychological Review, 99*, 268–305.

Schneirla, T.C. (1929). Learning and orientation in ants. *Comparative Psychology Monographs, 6*, No. 29.

Schrier, A.M. (1966). Transfer by macaque monkeys between learning set and repeated-reversal tasks. *Perceptual and Motor Skills, 23*, 787–792.

Schrier, A.M., Angarella, R., & Povar, M.L. (1984). Studies of concept formation by stumptailed monkeys: Concepts humans, monkeys, and letter A. *Journal of Experimental Psychology: Animal Behavior Processes, 10*, 564–584.

Schrier, A.M., & Brady, P.M. (1987). Categorization of natural stimuli by monkeys (*Macaca mulatta*): Effects of stimulus set size and modification of exemplars. *Journal of Experimental Psychology: Animal Behavior Processes, 13*, 136–143.

Schull, J. (1979). A conditioned opponent theory of Pavlovian conditioning and habituation. In G. Bower (Ed.), *The psychology of learning and motivation: Vol 13.* (pp.57–90).

Schusterman, R.J., & Gisiner, R. (1988). Artificial language comprehension in dolphins and sea lions: The essential cognitive skills. *Psychological Record, 38*, 3–18.

Schwartz, B. (1989). *The psychology of learning and behavior.* New York: W.H. Norton.

Seligman, M.E.P. (1970). On the generality of the laws of learning. *Psychological Review, 77*, 406–418.

Seligman, M.E.P., & Hager, J.L. (1972). *Biological boundaries of learning.* New York: Appleton-Century-Crofts.

Seyfarth, R.M., & Cheney, D.L. (1986). Vocal development in vervet monkeys. *Animal Behavior, 34*, 1640–1658.

Seyfarth, R.M., & Cheney, D. (1993). Meaning, reference, and intentionality in the natural vocalizations of monkeys. In H.L. Roitblat, L.M. Herman, & P.E. Nachtigall (Eds.), *Language and communication: Comparative perspectives* (pp.195–219). Hillsdale, NJ: Lawrence Erlbaum Associates Inc.

Seyfarth, R.M., Cheyney, D.L., & Marier, P. (1980). Vervet monkey alarm calls: Semantic communication in a free-ranging primate. *Animal Behaviour, 28*, 1070–1094.

Shanks, D.R. (1994). Human associative learning. In N.J. Mackintosh (Ed.), *Animal learning and cognition* (pp.335–368). San Diego, CA: Academic Press.

Shanks, D.R., & Darby, R. (in press). Connectionist models of categorization and generalization. In Z. Dienes (Ed.), *Connectionism and human learning.* Oxford: Oxford University Press.

Shapiro, K.L., Jacobs, W.J., & LoLordo, V.M. (1980). Stimulus-reinforcer interactions in Pavlovian conditioning of pigeons: Implications for selective associations. *Animal Learning and Behavior, 8*, 586–594.

Sheafor, P.J. (1975). "Pseudoconditioned" jaw movements of the rabbit reflect associations conditioned to contextual background cues. *Journal of Experimental Psychology: Animal Behavior Processes, 1*, 245–260.

Shepard, R.N. (1987). Toward a universal law of generalization for psychological science. *Science, 237*, 1317–1323.

Sherman, J.E. (1979). The effects of conditioning and novelty on the rat's analgesic and pyretic response to morphine. *Learning and Motivation, 10*, 383–418.

Sherry, D.F., & Galef, B.G., Jr. (1984). Cultural transmission without imitation: Milk bottle opening by birds. *Animal Behaviour, 32*, 937–938.

Sherry, D.F., & Galef, B.G., Jr. (1990). Social learning without imitation: More about milk bottle opening by birds. *Animal Behaviour, 40*, 987–989.

Shettleworth, S.J. (1975). Reinforcement and the organization of behavior in golden hamsters: Hunger, environment, and food reinforcement. *Journal of Experimental Psychology: Animal Behavior Processes, 1*, 56–87.

Shiffrin, R.M., & Schneider, W. (1977). Controlled and automatic human information processing: II. Perceptual learning, automatic attending and a general theory. *Psychological Review, 84*, 127–190.

Shin, H.J., & Nosofsky, R.M. (1992). Similarity-scaling of dot-pattern classification and recognition. *Journal of Experimental Psychology: General, 121,* 278–304.

Shishimi, A. (1985). Latent inhibition experiments with goldfish (*Carassius auratus*). *Journal of Comparative Psychology, 99,* 16–327.

Shorey, H.H. (1976). *Animal communication by pheromones.* New York: Academic Press.

Siegel, R.K., & Honig, W.K. (1970). Pigeon concept formation: Successive and simultaneous acquisition. *Journal of the Experimental Analysis of Behavior, 13,* 385–390.

Siegel, S. (1967). Overtraining and transfer processes. *Journal of Comparative and Physiological Psychology, 64,* 471–477.

Siegel, S. (1977). Morphine tolerance acquisition as an associative process. *Journal of Experimental Psychology: Animal Behavior Processes, 3,* 1–13.

Skard, O. (1950). A comparison of human and animal learning in the Stone multiple T-maze. *Acta Psychologica, 7,* 89–109.

Skinner, B.F. (1938). *The behavior of organisms.* New York: Appleton-Century-Crofts.

Skinner, B.F. (1950). Are theories of learning necessary? *Psychological Review, 57,* 193–216.

Skinner, B.F. (1953). *Science and human behavior.* New York: Macmillan.

Slater, P.J.B. (1983). The study of communication. In T.R. Halliday & P.J.B. Slater (Eds.), *Communication.* Oxford: Blackwell.

Slater, P.J.B., & Ince, S.A. (1982). Song development in chaffinches: What is learnt and when? *Ibis, 124,* 21–26.

Smith, E.E., & Medin, D.L. (1981). *Categories and concepts.* Cambridge, MA: Harvard University Press.

Smith, J.C., & Roll, D.L. (1967). Trace conditioning with X-rays as the aversive stimulus. *Psychonomic Science, 9,* 11–12.

Smith, M.C. (1968). CS-US interval and US intensity in classical conditioning of the rabbit's nictitating membrane response. *Journal of Comparative and Physiological Psychology, 69,* 226–231.

Sokolov, Y.N. (1963). *Perception and the conditioned reflex.* Oxford: Pergamon Press.

Solomon, R.L., & Corbit, J.D. (1974). An opponent-process theory of motivation: 1. Temporal dynamics of affect. *Psychological Review, 81,* 119–145.

Spear, N.E. (1973). Retrieval of memory in animals. *Psychological Review, 80,* 163–175.

Spear, N.E. (1981). Extending the domain of memory retrieval. In N.E. Spear & R.R. Miller (Eds.), *Information processing in animals: Memory mechanisms* (pp.341–378). Hillsdale, NJ: Lawrence Erlbaum Associates Inc.

Spear, N.E., Smith, G.J., Bryan, R., Gordon, W., Timmons, R., & Chiszar, D. (1980). Contextual influences on the interaction between conflicting memories in the rat. *Animal Learning and Behavior, 8,* 273–281.

Spence, K.W. (1936). The nature of discrimination learning in animals. *Psychological Review, 43,* 427–449.

Spence, K.W. (1937). The differential response to stimuli varying within a single dimension. *Psychological Review, 44,* 430–444.

Spence, K.W. (1956). *Behavior theory and conditioning.* New Haven, CT: Yale University Press.

Spetch, M.L., & Edwards, C.A. (1986). Spatial memory in pigeons (*Columba livia*) in an open-field feeding environment. *Journal of Comparative Psychology, 100,* 266–278.

St. Claire-Smith, R. (1979). The overshadowing of instrumental conditioning by a stimulus that predicts reinforcement better than the response. *Animal Learning and Behavior, 7,* 224–228.

Steirn, J.N., Weaver, J.E., & Zentall, T.R. (1995). Transitive inference in pigeons: Simplified procedures and a test of value transfer theory. *Animal Learning and Behavior, 23,* 76–82.

Straub, R.O., & Terrace, H.S. (1981). Generalization of serial learning in the pigeon. *Animal Learning and Behaviour, 9,* 454–468.

Stretch, R.G., McGonigle, B., & Morton, A. (1964). Position-reversal learning in the rat: Trials/problem and intertrial interval. *Journal of Comparative and Physiological Psychology, 57,* 461–463.

Struhsaker, K. (1967). Auditory communication among vervet monkeys (*Cercopithecus aethiops*). In S.A. Altman (Ed.), *Social communication among primates* (pp.281–324). Chicago: University of Chicago Press.

Suarez, D., & Gallup, G.G., Jr. (1981). Self-recognition in chimpanzees and orangutans, but not gorillas. *Journal of Human Evolution, 10,* 175–188.

Sutherland, N.S. (1964). The learning of discrimination by animals. *Endeavour, 23,* 69–78.

Sutherland, N.S., & Mackintosh, N.J. (1971). *Mechanisms of animal discrimination learning.* New York: Academic Press.

Sutherland, R.J., Chew, G.L., Baker, J.C., & Linggard, R.C. (1987). Some limits on the use of distal cues in place navigation by rats. *Psychobiology, 15*, 48–57.

Sutton, R.S., & Barto, A.G. (1981). Toward a modern theory of adaptive networks: Expectation and prediction. *Psychological Review, 88*, 135–170.

Suzuki, S., Augerinos, G., & Black, A.H. (1980). Stimulus control of spatial behavior on the eight-arm maze in rats. *Learning and Motivation, 11*, 1–18.

Swartz, K.B., Chen, S., & Terrace, H.S. (1991). Serial learning by rhesus monkeys: I. Acquisition and retention of multiple four-item lists. *Journal of Experimental Psychology: Animal Behavior Processes, 17*, 396–410.

Terrace, H.S. (1979). *Nim*. New York: Knopf.

Terrace, H.S. (1986). Positive transfer from sequence production to sequence discrimination in a nonverbal organism. *Journal of Experimental Psychology: Animal Behavior Processes, 12*, 215–234.

Terrace, H.S. (1987). Chunking by a pigeon in a serial learning task. *Nature, 325*, 149–151.

Terrace, H.S. (1991). Chunking during serial learning by a pigeon: I. Basic evidence. *Journal of Experimental Psychology: Animal Behavior Processes, 17*, 81–93.

Terrace, H.S., & Chen, S. (1991a). Chunking during serial learning by a pigeon: II. Integrity of a chunk on a new list. *Journal of Experimental Psychology: Animal Behavior Processes, 17*, 94–106.

Terrace, H.S., & Chen, S. (1991b). Chunking during serial learning by a pigeon: III. What are the necessary conditions for establishing a chunk? *Journal of Experimental Psychology: Animal Behavior Processes, 17*, 107–118.

Terrace, H.S., Petitto, L.A., Sanders, R.J., & Bever, T.G. (1979). Can an ape create a sentence? *Science, 206*, 891–902.

Terrace, H.S., Straub, R.O., Bever, T.G., & Seidenberg, M.S. (1977). Representation of a sequence by a pigeon. *Bulletin of the Psychonomic Society, 10*, 269.

Terrell, D.F., & Thomas, R.K. (1990). Number-related discrimination and summation by squirrel monkeys (*Saimiri sciureus* and *S. boliviensus boliviensus*) on the basis of the number of sides of polygons. *Journal of Comparative Psychology, 104*, 238–247.

Theios, J., Lynch, A.D., & Lowe, W.F., Jr. (1966). Differential effects of shock intensity on one-way and shuttle avoidance conditioning. *Journal of Experimental Psychology, 72*, 294–299.

Thomas, D.A. (1979). Retention of conditioned inhibition in a bar-press suppression paradigm. *Learning and Motivation, 10*, 161–177.

Thomas, D.A., & Riccio, D.C. (1979). Forgetting of a CS attribute in a conditioned suppression paradigm. *Animal Learning and Behavior, 7*, 191–195.

Thomas, D.R. (1981). Studies of long-term memory in the pigeon. In N.E. Spear & R.R. Miller (Eds.), *Information processing in animals: Memory mechanisms* (pp.257–290). Hillsdale, NJ: Lawrence Erlbaum Associates Inc.

Thomas, D.R., & Lopez, L.J. (1962). The effect of delayed testing on the generalization slope. *Journal of Comparative and Physiological Psychology, 44*, 541–544.

Thomas, G.V., Lieberman, D.A., McIntosh, D.C., & Ronaldson, P. (1983). The role of marking when reward is delayed. *Journal of Experimental Psychology: Animal Behavior Processes, 9*, 401–411.

Thompson, R.F., Berger, T.W., & Madden, J. (1983). Cellular processes of learning and memory in the mammalian CNS. *Annual Review of Neuroscience, 6*, 447–491.

Thompson, R.F., & Spencer, W.A. (1966). Habituation: A model phenomenon for the study of neuronal substrates of behavior. *Psychological Review, 73*, 16–43.

Thompson, R.K.R., & Herman, L.M. (1977). Memory for lists of sounds by the bottle-nosed dolphin: Convergence of memory processes with humans? *Science, 195*, 501–503.

Thorndike, E.L. (1898). Animal intelligence: An experimental study of the associative processes in animals. *Psychological Monographs, 2* (4, Whole No. 8).

Thorndike, E.L. (1911). *Animal intelligence: Experimental studies*. New York: Macmillan.

Thorndike, E.L. (1913). *Educational psychology: The psychology of learning* (Vol. 2). New York: Teacher's College.

Thorpe, W.H. (1963). *Animal intelligence: Experimental studies*. New York: Macmillan.

Timberlake, W. (1983). The functional organization of appetitive behavior: Behavior systems and learning. In M.D. Zeiler & P. Harzem (Eds.), *Advances in analysis of behavior*, Vol 3: *Biological factors in learning* (pp.177–221), Chichester: Wiley.

Timberlake, W. (1994). Behavior systems, associationism, and Pavlovian conditioning. *Psychonomic Bulletin and Review, 1*, 405–420.

Timberlake, W., & Allison, J. (1974). Response deprivation: An empirical approach to instrumental performance. *Psychological Review, 81*, 146–164.

Timberlake, W., & Grant, D.S. (1975). Autoshaping in rats to presentation of another rat predicting food. *Science, 190,* 690–692.

Tinbergen, N. (1951). *The study of instinct.* Oxford: Clarendon Press.

Tinbergen, N. (1953). *The herring gull's world.* London: Collins.

Tinkelpaugh, O.L. (1928). An experimental study of representative factors in monkeys. *Journal of Comparative Psychology, 8,* 197–236.

Todd, I.A., & Mackintosh, N.J. (1990). Evidence for perceptual learning in pigeons' recognition memory for pictures. *Quarterly Journal of Experimental Psychology, 42B,* 385–400.

Tolman, E.C. (1932). *Purposive behavior in animals and men.* New York: Century.

Tolman, E.C. (1948). Cognitive maps in rats and men. *Psychological Review, 55,* 189–208.

Tolman, E.C., Ritchie, B.F., & Kalish, D. (1946). Studies in spatial learning. I. Orientation and the short-cut. *Journal of Experimental Psychology, 36,* 13–24.

Tranberg, D.K., & Rilling, M. (1978). Latent inhibition in the autoshaping paradigm. *Bulletin of the Psychonomic Society, 11,* 273–276.

Trapold, MA., & Overmier, J.B. (1972). The second learning process in instrumental learning. In A.H. Black & W.F. Prokasy (Eds.), *Classical conditioning II: Current research and theory* (pp.427–452). New York: Appleton-Century-Croft.

Turner, C. (1968). *Models of discrimination learning.* Unpublished doctoral thesis, Oxford University.

Vallortigara, G., Zanforlin, M., & Pasti, G. (1990). Geometric modules in animals' spatial representations: A test with chicks (*Gallus gallus domesticus*). *Journal of Comparative Psychology, 104,* 248–254.

Van Beusekom, G. (1948). Some experiments on the optical orientation in *Philanthus triangulum.* Fabr. *Behavior, 1,* 195–225.

Vander Wall, S.B. (1982). An experimental analysis of cache recovery in Clark's nutcracker. *Animal Behaviour, 30,* 84–94.

Van Sommers, P. (1962). Oxygen-motivated behavior in goldfish (*Carassius auratus*). *Science, 137,* 678–679.

Vaughan, W., Jr., & Greene, S.L. (1984). Pigeon visual memory capacity. *Journal of Experimental Psychology: Animal Behavior Processes, 10,* 256–271.

Von Fersen, L., & Lea, S.E.G. (1990). Category discriminations by pigeons using five polymorphous features. *Journal of the Experimental Analysis of Behavior, 54,* 69–84.

Von Fersen, L., Wynne, C.D.L., Delius, J.D., & Staddon, J.E.R. (1991). Transitive inference formation in pigeons. *Journal of Experimental Psychology: Animal Behavior Processes, 17,* 334–341.

Von Frisch, K. (1950). *Bees, their vision, chemical senses, and language.* Ithaca, NY: Cornell University Press.

Von Frisch, K. (1974). Decoding the language of the bee. *Science, 185,* 663–668.

Von Uexkull, J. (1934). *Streifzüge durch die Umwelten von Tieren und Menschen.* Berlin: Springer. Translated in C.H. Schiller (Ed.), *Instinctive behavior.* London: Methuen.

Wagner, A.R. (1969). Stimulus validity and stimulus selection in associative learning. In N.J. Mackintosh & W.K. Honig (Eds.), *Fundamental issues in associative learning* (pp.90–122). Halifax: Dalhousie University Press.

Wagner, A.R. (1976). Priming in STM: An information-processing mechanism for self-generated and retrieval-generated depression in performance. In T.J. Tighe & R.N. Leaton (Eds.), *Habituation: Perspectives from child development, animal behavior, and neurophysiology* (pp.95–128). Hillsdale, NJ: Lawrence Erlbaum Associates Inc.

Wagner, A.R. (1978). Expectancies and the priming of STM. In S.H. Hulse, H. Fowler, & W.K. Honig (Eds.), *Cognitive processes in animal behavior* (pp.177–209). Hillsdale, NJ: Lawrence Erlbaum Associates Inc.

Wagner, A.R. (1979). Habituation and memory. In A. Dickinson & R.A. Boakes (Eds.), *Mechanisms of learning and motivation* (pp.53–82). Hillsdale, NJ: Lawrence Erlbaum Associates.

Wagner, A.R. (1981). SOP: A model of automatic memory processing in animal behavior. In N.E. Spear & R.R. Miller (Eds.), *Information processing in animals: Memory mechanisms* (pp.5–47). Hillsdale, NJ: Lawrence Erlbaum Associates Inc.

Wagner, A.R., & Brandon, S.E. (1989). Evolution of a structured connectionist model of Pavlovian conditioning (AESOP). In S.B. Klein & R.R. Mowrer (Eds.), *Contemporary learning theories: Pavlovian conditioning and the status of traditional learning theory* (pp.149–189). Hillsdale, NJ: Lawrence Erlbaum Associates Inc.

Wagner, A.R., & Larew, M.B. (1985). Opponent processes and Pavlovian inhibition. In R.R. Miller & N.E. Spear (Eds.), *Information processing in animals: Conditioned inhibition* (pp.223–265). Hillsdale, NJ: Lawrence Erlbaum Associates Inc.

Wagner, A.R., & Rescorla, R.A. (1972). Inhibition in Pavlovian conditioning: Application of a theory. In R.A. Boakes & M.S. Halliday (Eds.), *Inhibition and learning* (pp.301–336). London: Academic Press.

Wahl, O. (1932). Neue Untersuchungen über das Zeitgedächtnis der Bienen. *Zeitschrift für vergleichende Physiologie, 18*, 709–717.

Walcott, C. (1978). Anomalies in the earth's magnetic field increase the scatter of pigeons vanishing bearings. In K. Schmidt-Koenig & W.T. Keeton (Eds.), *Animal migration, navigation, and homing* (pp.143–151). Berlin: Springer.

Walcott, C., & Schmidt-Koenig, K. (1973). The effect of anesthesia during displacement on the homing performance of pigeons. *Auk, 90*, 281–286.

Walker, M.M., Baird, D.L., & Bitterman, M.E. (1989). Failure of stationary but not flying honeybees (*Apis mellifera*) to respond to magnetic field stimuli. *Journal of Comparative Psychology, 103*, 62–69.

Ward, J.P., Yehle, A.I., & Doerflein, R.S. (1970). Cross-modal transfer of a specific discrimination in the bushbaby *(Galago senegalensis). Journal of Comparative and Physiological Psychology, 73*, 74–77.

Warden, C.J., & Warner, L.H. (1928). The sensory capacities and intelligence of dogs, with a report on the ability of the noted dog "Fellow" to respond to verbal stimuli. *Quarterly Review of Biology, 3*, 1–28.

Warren, J.M. (1965). Primate learning in comparative perspective. In A.M. Schrier, H.F. Harlow, & F. Stollnitz (Eds.), *Behaviour of nonhuman primates: Modern research trends* (pp.249–281). New York: Academic Press.

Warren, J.M. (1973). Learning in vertebrates. In D.A. Dewsbury & D.A. Rethlingshafer (Eds.), *Comparative psychology: A modern survey* (pp.471–509). New York: McGraw-Hill.

Wasserman, E.A. (1973). Pavlovian conditioning with heat reinforcement produces stimulus-directed pecking in chicks, *Science, 181*, 875–877.

Wasserman, E.A., DeVolder, C.L., & Coppage, D.J. (1992). Nonsimilarity-based conceptualization in pigeons via secondary or mediated generalization. *Psychological Science, 3*, 374–379.

Watanabe, S. (1988). Failure of visual prototype learning in the pigeon. *Animal Learning and Behavior, 16*, 147–152.

Watanabe, S., Sakamoto, J., & Wakita, M. (1995). Pigeons' discrimination of paintings by Monet and Picasso. *Journal of the Experimental Analysis of Behavior, 63*, 165–174.

Watkins, M.J. (1977). The intricacy of memory span. *Memory and Cognition, 5*, 529–534.

Waugh, N.C., & Norman, D.A. (1965). Primary memory. *Psychological Review, 72*, 89–104.

Wearden, J.H., & Doherty, M.F. (1995). Exploring and developing a connectionist model of animal timing: Peak procedure and fixed-interval simulations. *Journal of Experimental Psychology: Animal Behavior Processes, 21*, 99–115.

Wehner, R., & Flatt, I. (1972). The visual orientation of desert ants, *Cataglyphis bicolor*, by means of territorial cues. In R. Wehner (Ed.), *Information processing in the visual system of arthropods* (pp.295–302). New York: Springer.

Wehner, R., & Menzel, R. (1990). Do insects have cognitive maps? *Annual Review of Neuroscience, 13*, 403–414.

Wehner, R., & Srinivasan, M.V. (1981). Searching behaviour of desert ants, genus *Cataglyphis (Formicidiae, Hymenoptera). Journal of Comparative Physiology, 142*, 315–338.

Weisman, R.G., Wasserman, E.A., Dodd, P.W.D., & Larew, M.B. (1980). Representation and retention of two-event sequences in pigeons. *Journal of Experimental Psychology: Animal Behavior Processes, 6*, 312–325.

Wells, G.P. (1950). Spontaneous activity cycles in polychaete worms. *Symposium of the Society of Experimental Biology, 4*, 127–142.

Wells, G.P. (1967). Training flatworms in a Van Oye maze. In W. Corning & S. Ratner (Eds.), *Chemistry of learning: Invertebrate research.* New York: Plenum.

Wenner, A.M. (1964). Sound communication in honeybees. *Scientific American, 210*, 116–124.

Wenner, A.M. (1967). Honeybees: Do they use distance information contained in their dance maneuver? *Science, 155*, 847–849.

Wenner, A.M., Wells, P.H., & Rohlf, F.J. (1969). Honeybee recruitment to food sources: Olfaction or language? *Science, 164*, 84–86.

Wesley, F. (1961). The number concept: A phylogenetic review. *Psychological Bulletin, 58*, 420–428.

Westbrook, R.F., Bond, N.W., & Feyer, A.M. (1981). Short- and long-term decrements in toxicosis-induced odor-aversion learning: The role of duration of exposure to an odor. *Journal of Experimental Psychology: Animal Behavior Processes, 7*, 362–381.

Whiten, A., & Byrne, R.W. (1988). Tactical deception in primates. *Behavioral and Brain Sciences, 11*, 233–273.

Whitlow, J.W., Jr. (1975). Short-term memory in habituation and dishabituation. *Journal of Experimental Psychology: Animal Behavior Processes, 1*, 189–206.

Widrow, G., & Hoff, M.E. (1960). Adaptive switching circuits. *Institute of Radio Engineers, Western Electronic Show and Convention, Convention Record, 4*, 96–104.

Williams, B.A. (1971). The effects of intertrial interval on discrimination reversal learning in the pigeon. *Psychonomic Science, 23*, 241–243.

Williams, B.A., (1994). Blocking despite changes in reinforcer identity. *Animal Learning and Behavior, 22*, 442–457.

Williams, D.A., Butler, M.M., & Overmier, J.B. (1990). Expectancies of reinforcer location and quality as cues for a conditional discrimination. *Journal of Experimental Psychology: Animal Behavior Processes, 16*, 3–13.

Williams, D.A.. Overmier, J.B., & LoLordo, V.M. (1992). A reevaluation of Rescorla's early dictums about Pavlovian conditioned inhibition. *Psychological Bulletin, 111*, 275–290.

Williams, D.R., & Williams, H. (1969). Auto-maintenance in the pigeon: Sustained pecking despite contingent non-reinforcement. *Journal of the Experimental Analysis of Behavior, 12*, 511–520.

Wilson, B., Mackintosh, N.J., & Boakes, R.A. (1985). Transfer of relational rules in matching and oddity learning by pigeons and corvids. *Quarterly Journal of Experimental Psychology, 37B*, 313–332.

Wilson, P.N., Boumphrey, P., & Pearce, J.M. (1992). Restoration of the orienting response to a light by a change in its predictive accuracy. *Quarterly Journal of Experimental Psychology, 44B*, 17–36.

Wood, F.G. (1973). *Marine mammals and man, the navy's porpoises and sea lions.* Washington, DC: R.B. Luce.

Woocher, F.D., Glass, A.L., & Holyoak, K.J. (1978). Positional discriminability in linear orderings. *Memory and Cognition, 6*, 165–175.

Woodbury, C.B. (1943). The learning of stimulus patterns in dogs. *Journal of Comparative Psychology, 35*, 29–40.

Woodruff, G., & Premack, D. (1979). Intentional communication in the chimpanzee: The development of deception. *Cognition, 7*, 333–362.

Wright, A.A., Santiago, H.C., Sands, S.F., & Urcuioli, P.J. (1984). Pigeon and monkey serial probe recognition: Acquisition, strategies, and serial position effects. In H.L. Roitblat, T.G. Bever, & H.S. Terrace (Eds.), *Animal cognition* (pp.353–374). Hillsdale, NJ: Lawrence Erlbaum Associates Inc.

Yeagley, H.L. (1947). A preliminary study of a physical basis of bird navigation. *Journal of Applied Physiology, 18*, 1035–1063.

Yeagley, H.L. (1951). A preliminary study of a physical basis of bird navigation. II. *Journal of Applied Physiology, 22*, 746–760.

Yerkes, R.M., & Morgulis, S. (1909). The method of Pavlov in animal psychology. *Psychological Bulletin, 6*, 257–273.

Yodlowski, M.L., Kreithen, M.L., & Keeton, W.T. (1977) Detection of atmospheric infrasound by homing pigeons. *Nature, 265*, 725–726.

Yoerg, S.I., & Kamil, A.C. (1991). Integrating cognitive ethology with cognitive psychology. In C. A. Ristau (Ed.), *Cognitive ethology: The minds of other animals* (pp.271–290). Hillsdale, NJ: Lawrence Erlbaum Associates Inc.

Zentall, T.R., Steirn, J.N., & Jackson-Smith, P. (1990). Memory strategies in pigeons' performance of a radial-arm-maze analog task. *Journal of Experimental Psychology: Animal Behavior Processes, 16*, 358–371.

Zimmer-Hart, C.L., & Rescorla, R.A. (1974). Extinction of Pavlovian conditioned inhibition. *Journal of Comparative and Physiological Psychology, 86*, 837–845.

Author Index

Able, K.P., 219, 220, 222
Abunawass, A.M., 133, 134
Adams, C.D., 85, 86, 87
Adams, W.A., 94
Alexander, J.H., 83
Allison, J., 92
Anderson, J.R., 16, 191, 247, 257, 275, 287
Angarella, R., 118, 122
Angermeier, W.F., 11, 13
Annau, Z., 58, 59
Arbeit, W.R., 280
Aschoff, J., 168
Astley, S.L., 122
Atkinson, R.C., 137
Augerinos, G., 213
Aydin, A., 123, 124

Baddeley, A.D., 137, 163
Baird, D.L., 199, 216
Baker, A.G., 64, 74
Baker, J.C., 209
Baker, R.R., 216, 218
Balachandran, N.K., 216
Baldaccini, N., 218, 219
Balleine, B., 95, 96, 183
Banks, W.P., 2, 8, 10
Baptista, L.F., 236, 237
Barnet, R.C., 63
Barnett, S.A., 11, 226

Barto, A.G., 133
Bastian, J., 259
Batson, J.D., 46
Baum, M., 12
Beach, F.A., 280
Bean, N.J., 227
Beatty, W.W., 153, 160
Bell, R.C., 233
Bennett, C.H., 73
Bennett, M.V.L., 100
Benvenuti, S., 218, 219
Berg, B., 160
Berger, T.W., 14
Berk, A.M., 140
Berntson, G.G., 179, 180, 183
Berthold, P., 168
Best, M.R., 46, 69, 70
Bever, T.G., 183, 184, 260, 261, 268, 269, 270
Bhatt, R.S., 118, 119, 122
Bierschwale, D.T., 244, 245, 246, 247, 248
Bingman, V.P., 217
Birch, H.G., 104
Bitterman, M.E., 13, 79, 100, 101, 112, 124, 191, 192, 193, 194, 199, 216, 282
Black, A.H., 213
Blough, D.S., 114
Blum, J.S., 125
Blum, R.A., 125
Boakes, R.A., 53, 125, 126, 259, 283, 284

Bockaneck, C., 197
Boe, E.E., 94
Boesch, C., 232
Bolles, R.C., 12, 22, 84, 169
Bond, A.B., 71
Bond, N.W., 70
Bonner, J.T., 231
Bookman, M.A., 216
Boumphrey, P., 78
Bower, G.H., 11, 130, 131, 132, 133, 135
Boysen, S.L., 259
Boysen, S.T., 179, 180, 183, 244, 245
Brady, P.M., 118, 124
Brakke, K.E., 267, 270
Brandon, S.E., 66, 101, 282
Breland, K., 53
Breland, M., 53
Brett, L.P., 51
Bright, M., 239, 240
Broadbent, H.A., 167, 169, 170, 171, 175, 178
Brokofsky, S., 160
Brooks, J.O., 186
Brower, J.Z., 99
Brower, L.P., 99
Brown, I.D., 65, 75
Brown, J.L., 254
Brown, M.F., 162, 165, 213, 214, 215
Browne, M.P., 233
Bryan, R., 144, 145, 146, 147
Bryant, P.E., 191
Buckiewicz, J., 151, 152
Buffon, G.L.C., 230
Burdick, C.K., 119
Butler, M.M., 156, 157, 158
Bygrave, D.J., 72
Byrne, R., 232, 241, 242

Cable, C., 107, 108, 118, 119, 122
Campbell, B.A., 94
Capaldi, E.J., 22, 177, 178, 179, 181, 182
Carew, T.J., 35, 37
Caro, T.M., 240
Cartwright, B.A., 198, 199, 200, 201, 210
Castro, C.A., 166
Cauty, A., 283

Cerella, J., 118, 119, 120
Chalmers, M., 190, 191, 192
Chamizo, V.D., 222
Channell, S., 71
Chapuis, N., 212
Charnock, D.J., 90
Chen, S., 186, 189
Cheney, D.L., 237, 238, 240
Cheng, K., 175, 201, 202, 203
Chew, G.L., 209
Chiszar, D., 144, 145, 146, 147
Chittka, L., 193
Chomsky, N., 253, 275, 277
Christoph, G., 48
Church, R.M., 14, 48, 49, 94, 167, 169, 170, 171, 172, 173, 174, 175, 177, 178, 182
Clark, E., 99
Clark, F.C., 94
Clark, M.M., 227
Clayton, N.S., 166
Clos, C.F., 233
Cohen, J.S., 175
Cohen, N.J., 132, 134
Cohn, R.H., 247, 248
Collett, T.S., 198, 199, 200, 201, 210
Collison, C., 154
Colombo, M., 184, 186, 187, 188, 189
Colwill, R.M., 12, 82, 85, 86, 87, 97, 98
Conway, D.H., 205
Cook, M., 228, 229
Cook, R.G., 162
Coppage, D.J., 124
Corbit, J.D., 48, 49
Cotton, J.W., 94
Cotton, M.M., 47
Coussi-Korbel, S., 243
Couvillon, P.A., 191, 192, 193, 194
Cox, J.K., 155
Crowder, R.G., 164
Cunitz, A.R., 164

D'Amato, M.R., 120, 151, 152, 155, 158, 184, 186, 187, 188, 189, 190, 191, 194
Dale, R.H.I., 161, 162
Dalrymple-Alford, J.C., 164
Darby, R., 134

Darwin, C., 2, 3, 257
Davey, G., 51
Davidson, R.S., 99
Davis, H., 181
Dawkins, M., 71
Dawson, G.R., 233, 234, 235
de Lorge, J., 169
de Waal, F., 242
Dekeyne, A., 147
Delius, J.D., 191, 192, 216
Demas, G.E., 165
Denny, M.R., 233
DeQuardo, J.R., 232, 233
DeRivera, J., 112
Deutsch, J.A., 100
DeVolder, C.L., 124
Deweer, B., 146, 147
Dews, P., 99, 100
Dias, R., 14
DiCarlo, J.J., 118, 136
Dickinson, A., 33, 34, 45, 47, 64, 72, 85, 86, 87, 88, 89, 90, 95, 97, 98, 183, 282, 286
Diehl, R.L., 119
Diez-Chamizo, V., 222
Dimattia, B.V., 164, 166
Dodd, P.W.D., 183
Doherty, M.F., 175
Domjan, M., 73, 286
Dowsett-Lemaire, F., 237
Drudge, O.W., 99
Ducker, G., 247
Dunbar, S., 122
Duncan, C.P., 143
Dunn, D.P., 46
Dunn, W.L., 216
Durlach, P.J., 227
Dyer, F.C., 210, 211

Edberg, J.A., 214, 215
Edwards, C.A., 165
Eikelboom, R., 51
Elder, W.H., 217
Elliott, M.H., 84, 85 , 86
Emlen, S.T., 221
Emmerton, J., 216
Epstein, R., 104, 105, 259

Erber, J., 11
Estes, W.K., 95
Etienne, A.S., 197
Evans, J.G.M., 70

Farah, M.J., 44
Feyer, A.M., 70
Fiaschi, V., 218
Fietz, A., 79
Finke, R.A., 44
Fiore, L., 218
Fiorito, G., 226
Fisher, J., 231
Fitch, M.D., 119
Flatt, I., 196
Flora, J., 2, 8, 10
Fouts, D.H., 261, 262, 263, 271
Fouts, R.S., 261, 262, 263, 268, 271
Fowler, H., 22
Frankl, S.E., 145, 146
Franklin, S.R., 32, 33, 46, 63
Fuller, E., 217
Furness, W., 260

Gaertner, I., 259
Gaffan, D., 155, 164
Gaffan, E.A., 164
Galdikas, B.M.F., 230
Galef, B.G., 226, 227, 228, 231, 251
Gallagher, M., 14
Gallistel, C.R., 169, 171, 182, 183, 196, 202, 206, 210, 213
Gallup, G.G., 247, 250
Gandolfi, G., 251
Ganesan, R., 45
Garcia, J., 12, 51, 73, 151
Garcia, S.E., 247
Gardner, B.T., 260, 276
Gardner, R.A., 260, 276
Garner, C., 95, 183
Geiger, K., 193
Gelman, R., 182, 183
Gemberling, G.A., 69, 70, 73
Gentry, G.V., 112, 124
Gibbon, J., 170, 171, 172, 173, 174
Gibbs, C.M., 28

Gibson, K.R., 235
Gillan, D.J., 127, 128, 190, 192
Gisiner, R., 272
Glanzer, M., 164
Glass, A.L., 191
Gleeson, S., 88
Gleitman, H., 140
Gluck, M.A., 130, 131, 132, 133, 135, 136
Gollub, L., 94, 166
Gonzalez, F., 95, 183
Gonzalez, R.C., 112, 124, 282, 283
Goodall, G., 47, 53
Goodall, J., 230, 232
Gordon, J.A., 125
Gordon, W., 144, 145, 146, 147
Gordon, W.C., 145, 146
Gormezano, I., 28, 48, 101
Gould, C.G., 256, 257
Gould, J.L., 209, 210, 211, 215, 219, 256, 257, 258
Grahame, N.J., 63
Grant, D.S., 51, 52,. 154, 155, 158, 159, 160, 162
Gray, J.A., 95
Green, K.F., 151
Greenberg, J.H., 275
Greene, S.L., 122, 138, 139, 140
Griffin, R.W., 42, 43
Griffin, W.J.H., 88
Grindley, G.C., 82, 83
Guevrekian, L., 177
Gunier, W.J., 217
Guthrie, E.R., 22, 23, 84
Gwinner, E., 220

Hager, J.L., 3, 73
Hall, G., 12, 30, 46, 56, 64, 71, 72, 74, 75, 76, 77, 78, 82, 89, 90, 100, 124, 282
Hamberg, J.M., 145, 146
Hammond, G.R., 70,
Hammond, L.J., 88, 89, 90
Hanson, H.M., 111, 112
Harley, H.E., 183
Harlow, H.F., 279
Harper, D.N., 164
Harris, M.R., 189

Harrison, S.N., 123
Hars, B., 146, 147
Hastings, M., 196
Hauser, M.D., 240
Hawkins, R.D., 35, 36, 37
Hayes, C., 230, 260
Hayes, K., 230, 260
Healy, S.D., 165, 166, 281
Hearst, E., 32, 33, 46, 48, 52, 63
Hebb, D.O., 142
Hegvik, D.K., 162
Helweg, D.A., 183
Hendersen, R.W., 140, 141, 142
Hennessey, T.M., 107
Herman, L.M., 125, 155, 159, 163, 258, 272, 273, 274, 275, 280
Herrnstein, R.J., 107, 108, 118, 119, 122, 127
Heyes, C.M., 229, 233, 234, 235, 245, 247, 250
Hilgard, E.R., 11
Hiller, G.W., 101
Hilton, S.C., 281
Hinde, R.A., 3, 148, 231
Hinton, G.E., 133, 135
Hintzman, D.L., 122, 123
Hirsch, A.D., 261, 263, 271
Hitch, G., 137
Hockett, C.F., 257
Hoff, M.E., 136
Holland, P.C., 14, 39, 40, 41, 42, 44, 87, 101, 129
Holliday, M., 99
Holman, J.G., 119
Holyoak, K.J., 191
Homa, D., 122
Honey, R.C., 124
Honig, W.K., 137, 155
Hopkins, W.D., 267, 276
Hovancik, J.R., 22
Huang, I., 232, 233
Huber, L., 121, 122, 123
Hull, C.L., 22, 84, 94, 95
Humphrey, N.K., 241
Hunter, W.S., 137
Hurly, T.A., 165
Hyde, T.S., 93, 94

Ioale, P., 218
Itakura, S., 247
Itani, J., 232

Jackson, E.C., 247
Jackson, R.L., 83, 142
Jackson-Smith, P., 162
Jacobs, W.J., 73
Jaldow, E., 234
James, W., 137
Jander, R., 197
Jenkins, H.M., 52, 100
Jennings, H.S., 149, 150
Jerison, H.J., 9, 10, 15
Jolly, A., 230, 242

Kalat, J.W., 73
Kalish, D., 206, 207
Kamil, A.C., 119, 165, 243
Kamin, L.J., 45, 55, 58, 59, 60, 61
Kandel, E.R., 35, 36, 37, 38
Kaplan, P.S., 156
Karlson, P., 195
Karpicke, J., 48
Kastak, D., 125
Kaye, H., 14, 39, 66, 67, 75, 76, 77, 118, 136, 143
Keele, S.W., 123
Keeton, W.T., 215, 216, 217, 219
Kehoe, E.J., 118, 136
Kelleher, R.T., 93, 94
Kemp, F.D., 99
Kenyon, K.W., 217
Kesner, R.P., 164, 166
Kettner, R.E., 14
Kiepenheuer, J., 218
Killeen, P.R., 119
Kinnaman, A.J., 108
Kirchner, W.K., 256
Kirshnit, C.E., 104, 105
Kleinginna, P.R., 99
Kluender, K.R., 119
Klump, G.M., 236
Knauss, K.S., 118, 119, 122
Koelling, R.A., 12, 73

Kohler, W., 103, 104, 108, 110, 212, 213
Kolterman, R., 168
Konorski, J., 44, 45, 46, 47, 48, 49, 51, 95, 97
Konz, W.A., 97
Koski, C.A., 232, 233
Kosslyn, S.M., 127
Kowalski, V., 217
Kraemer, P.J., 159, 163
Kramer, G., 218, 219
Krebs, J.R., 166, 281
Krechevsky, I., 108
Kreithen, M.L., 216
Kremer, E.F., 63
Kruschke, J.K., 122, 135
Kruse, J.M., 97
Kummer, H., 232, 242, 243

LaBerge, D., 75
Lamb, E.O., 22
Lambert, S.J., 197
Landau, K.R., 245, 247, 248
Langley, C.M., 155
Lanza, R.P., 104, 105, 259
Larew, M.B., 66, 183
Larsen, T., 166
Lashley, K.S., 108
Latham, S.B., 28
Lattal, K.A., 88
Lawrence, D.H., 71, 112
Lawson, J., 124, 264, 266, 267, 272
Lea, S.E.G., 119, 120, 123, 124
Leander, J.D., 94
Lednor, A.J., 219
Lefebvre, L., 235
Lenz, R., 121, 122, 123
Leonard, B., 206
Lethmate, J., 247
Lewin, R., 264, 265
Lewis, D.J., 137, 143, 144
Lieberman, D.A., 152, 153, 161, 271
Lieberman, P., 260, 269
Linggard, R.C., 209
Linwick, D., 158
Lipp, H.P., 219
Locke, A., 276

Lockwood, M.J., 53
Logan, C., 149
Lohman, K.J., 220, 221
LoLordo, V.M., 33, 48, 49, 73, 97
Lopez, L.J., 140
Loveland, D.H., 107, 108, 118, 119, 122
Lovibond, P.F., 70, 97
Lowe, W.F., 12
Lubinski, D., 259
Lubow, R.E., 66, 79
Lüscher, M., 195
Lynch, A.D., 12

MacCorquodale, K., 259
Mackintosh, N.J., 47, 56, 59, 61, 64, 70, 71, 72,
    73, 74, 78, 79, 84, 108, 110, 112, 118, 125,
    126, 136, 143, 152, 153, 161, 222, 282, 283,
    284
Macphail, E.M., 10, 11, 14, 36, 37, 99, 164, 253,
    275, 277, 279, 281, 286
Madden, J., 14
Maier, S.F., 83
Maki, W.S., 133, 134, 160, 162
Maldonado, A., 74
Mandriota, F.J., 100
March, J., 222
Marconi, S., 247
Marler, P., 236, 237
Marlin, N.A., 71
Marten, K., 247
Mason, J.R., 227
Matsuzawa, T., 180
Matthews, B.L., 197
Matthews, G.V.T., 217
Matthews, T.J., 233
Mazmanian, D.S., 156
McClelland, J.L., 123
McCloskey, M., 132, 134
McDiarmid, C.G., 107
McDonald, K., 276
McFarland, D., 258, 279
McGonigle, B.O., 189, 190, 191, 192
McGowan, B.K., 151
McIntosh, D.C., 152
McLaren, I.P.L., 118, 136, 143
McLean, A.P., 164

McNaughton, B.L., 206
McQuoid, L.M., 226, 227
Meachum, C.I., 46
Mechner, F., 177, 178
Meck, W.H., 14, 170, 172, 174, 175, 177, 178,
    182
Medin, D.L., 120, 122
Meehl, P.E., 91
Menzel, E.W., 165, 215
Menzel, R., 79, 165, 210
Menzel, R.M., 11
Mertens, M., 158
Meyer, M.E., 94
Miles, H.L.W., 247
Miller, D.J., 177, 178, 179, 181, 182
Miller, J.D., 119
Miller, N.E., 22
Miller, R.R., 63, 71, 140
Milner, P., 22
Mineka, S., 228, 229
Minor, H., 71
Minsky, M.L., 131
Misanin, J.R., 94
Mishkin, M., 125
Mistlberger, R.E., 169
Mittelstaedt, H., 197
Mittelstaedt, M.L., 197
Montgomery, A., 45, 47
Moore, B.R., 48, 230, 231
Moore, J.W., 28, 71
Moore, R.F., 165
Moot, S.A., 169
Morgan, C.L., 102
Morgan, M.J., 15, 119
Morgulis, S., 21
Morrel-Samuels, P., 272
Morris, R.G.M., 207, 208, 209, 215, 222
Mowrer, R.R., 146
Mulatero, C.W., 89
Mumford, D.B., 127
Murphy, J., 267, 270
Myers, C.E., 136

Nadel, L., 206, 222
Nagell, K., 232
Nash, S.M., 46

Nelson, K.E., 244, 245
Neuringer, A., 119
Nicholas, D.J., 33, 34
Nishimura, A., 232
Nissen, H.W., 125
Nohre, L., 122
Nokes, T., 234, 235
Norman, D.A., 137
Nosofsky, R.M., 123

O'Keefe, J., 203, 204, 205, 206, 222
O'Neill, W., 155
O'Sullivan, C., 271, 276
Oden, D.L., 125
Olds, J., 22
Olguin, R.S., 232
Olton, D.S., 14, 153, 154, 158, 159, 160, 161,
    162, 165, 213
Osadchuk, T.E., 165
Osgood, C.E., 124
Overmier, J.B., 33, 48, 49, 97, 156, 157, 158

Pack, A.A., 272
Palameta, B., 235
Papert, S., 131
Papi, F., 218, 219
Papousek, H., 11
Parisi, T., 233
Parisi, V., 251
Passingham, R.E., 260, 279
Pasti, G., 203, 222
Pate, J.L., 264, 266, 267, 272
Pavlov, I.P., 21, 22, 24, 33, 42, 48, 61, 65, 107
Pearce, J.M., 12, 14, 29, 30, 33, 34, 45, 46, 47,
    56, 64, 67, 74, 75, 76, 77, 78, 82, 90, 97, 114,
    115, 116, 117, 122, 123, 124, 127, 132, 133,
    134, 135, 136, 282
Peeke, H.V.S., 149
Pepper, R.L., 280
Pepperberg, I.M., 119, 126, 180, 181, 247, 271
Perdeck, A.C., 222
Perusse, R., 181
Peterson, F.G.P., 247, 248
Peterson, G., 48
Peterson, G.B., 158

Peterson, J.M., 142
Peterson, L., 137
Peterson, M.J., 137
Petitto, L.A., 260, 261, 268, 269, 270
Petrinovich, L., 236, 237
Pfungst, O., 175, 176
Phelps, M.T., 191
Picton, B.M.B., 72
Pietrewicz, A.T., 119
Pinker, S., 275
Pinsker, H., 35
Platt, S.A., 99
Poli, M., 53
Porter, D., 119
Posner, M.I., 123
Poulton, E.C., 65, 74, 75
Povar, M.L., 118, 122
Povinelli, D.J., 244, 245, 246, 247, 248
Premack, D., 91, 92, 125, 127, 128, 129, 130,
    241, 244, 261, 262, 263, 266, 267, 277, 284,
    287
Preston, G.C., 70
Preti, G., 227
Prockop, E.S., 125
Psarakos, S., 247

Quine, D.B., 216

Rakitin, B.C., 178
Rashotte, M.E., 42, 43
Redhead, E.S., 114, 115, 116, 117, 132
Reed, P., 89
Reiss, S., 79
Renner, M., 168
Rescorla, R.A., 31, 33, 34, 42, 43, 44, 46, 56,
    57, 58, 59, 60, 61, 62, 63, 64, 65, 66, 72, 79,
    85, 86, 87, 89, 95, 97, 98, 113, 114, 115, 116,
    117, 120, 121, 130, 131, 132, 133, 134
Reverdin, B., 197
Revusky, S.H., 151, 286
Reynolds, W.F., 118, 119, 122
Riccio, D.C., 141
Rice, D.W., 217
Richards, D.G., 258, 272, 273, 274, 275
Riddell, W.I., 279

Riley, D.A., 112, 155, 162
Rilling, M., 79
Rind, D.H., 216
Rish, P.A., 214, 215
Ristau, C.A., 267, 270
Ritchie, B.F., 206, 207
Rizley, R.C., 42, 43, 44
Robbins, D., 267, 270
Robbins, T.W., 14
Roberts, A.C., 14
Roberts, S., 173
Roberts, S.K., 168
Roberts, W.A., 154, 155, 158, 159, 160, 161,
    162, 164, 165, 175, 191, 213
Roediger, H.L., 164
Rohlf, F.J., 256
Roitblat, H.L., 155, 166, 183
Rokke, E., 97
Roll, D.L., 151, 156
Romanes, G.J., 19, 101, 102
Romer, A.S., 4, 5
Ronaldson, P., 152, 153, 161
Roper, K.L., 162
Roper, T.J., 286
Rosenbaum, S., 264, 266, 267, 272
Rosenblatt, F., 131
Ross, R.T., 42
Rosvold, H.E., 125
Rozin, P., 73
Rubert, E., 276
Rubin, L.C., 104, 105
Rucker, W.B., 107
Rulf, A.B., 244, 245, 246, 247, 248
Rumbaugh, D.M., 124, 177, 178, 182, 259, 262,
    263, 264, 266, 267, 269, 270
Rumelhart, D.E., 123, 133, 135
Rusiniak, K.W., 51
Russon, A.E., 230
Ryan, C.W.E., 119
Ryu, J.H., 197

Safarjan, W.R., 152
Saint Paul, U.V., 197, 198, 199
Sakamoto, J., 119
Salmon, D., 152
Samuels, S.J., 75

Samuelson, R.J., 153, 213
Sanders, R.J., 260, 261, 268, 269, 270
Sands, S.F., 164, 166
Santchi, F., 197
Santiago, H.C., 164, 166
Sara, S.J., 146, 147
Savage-Rumbaugh, E.S., 124, 259, 263,
    264, 265, 266, 267, 269, 270, 272,
    276
Scardigli, P., 212
Schafer, S., 79
Schaffer, M.M., 122
Schaub, R.E., 59, 60
Schiller, P.H., 104
Schlicte, H.J., 217
Schmajuk, N.A., 118, 136
Schmidt-Koenig, K., 217, 218
Schneider, W., 75
Schneirla, T.C., 99, 100
Schrier, A.M., 118, 122, 124
Schull, J., 49
Schusterman, R.J., 125, 272
Schwartz, B., 90, 94
Scotto, P., 226
Seidenberg, M.S., 184
Seligman, M.E.P., 3, 73
Sevcik, R.A., 267, 270, 276
Seyfarth, R.M., 237, 238, 240
Shalter, M.D., 236
Shanks, D.R., 123, 134
Shapiro, K.L., 73
Shavalia, D.A., 153, 160
Sheafor, P.J., 31
Sherman, J.E., 51
Sherry, D.F., 231
Shettleworth, S.J., 82
Shiffrin, R.M., 75, 137
Shin, H.J., 123
Shishimi, A., 79, 282
Shorey, H.H., 196
Siegel, S., 49, 50, 51, 71, 74
Sisk, C.L., 42, 43
Skard, O., 11
Skinner, B.F., 91, 93, 140, 259
Slater, P.J.B., 254
Smith, B.A., 198, 201
Smith, E.E., 120

Smith, G.J., 144, 145, 146, 147
Smith, J.C., 151, 156
Smith, M.C., 68
Smith, S.T., 124, 266
Smith, T., 264, 266, 267, 272
Smythe, W.E., 164
Sokolov, Y.N., 148
Soldat, A.S., 162
Solomon, R.L., 48, 49, 95, 97
Speakman, A., 203, 204, 205
Spear, N.E., 144, 145, 146
Spence, K.W., 84, 109, 110, 111, 112, 113, 116, 117, 122, 123
Spencer, W.A., 150
Spetch, M.L., 165
Srinivasan, M.V., 196, 197
Staddon, J.E.R., 191, 192
Stalling, R.B., 280
St. Claire-Smith, R., 89
Steirn, J.N., 162, 192
Sterio, D., 222
Stevenson-Hinde, J., 3
Stewart, J., 51
Stickney, K.J., 71
Stokes, L.W., 169
Straub, J.J., 39, 40, 41
Straub, R.O., 184, 186
Struhsaker, K., 237
Suarez, D., 247
Sutherland, N.S., 71, 108 109, 110
Sutherland, R.J., 209
Sutton, R.S., 133
Suzuki, S., 213
Swartz, K.B., 189

Teroni, E., 197
Terrace, H.S., 183, 184, 185, 186, 187, 189, 194, 260, 261, 268, 269, 270, 276
Terrell, D.F., 179, 180, 182
Tham, W., 166
Theios, J., 12
Thomas, D.A., 141, 142
Thomas, D.R., 140, 141
Thomas, G.V., 152, 153, 161
Thomas, R.K., 179, 180, 182
Thompson, L., 100

Thompson, R.F., 14, 150
Thompson, R.K.R., 125, 155, 163
Thorndike, E.L., 19, 20, 21, 22, 23, 81, 83, 90, 92, 93, 99, 102, 103, 104
Thorpe, W.H., 236
Timberlake, W., 51, 52, 92
Timmons, R., 144, 145, 146, 147
Tinbergen, N., 202, 254
Tinkelpaugh, O.L., 84
Todd, I.A., 143
Tolman, E.C., 23, 24, 84, 206, 207
Tomasello, M., 232
Towne, W.F., 256
Trabasso, T., 191
Tranberg, D.K., 79
Trapold, M.A., 97
Turner, C., 108, 109, 110
Turner, L.H., 48, 49

Urcuioli, P.J., 164, 166

Vallortigara, G., 203, 222
Van Beusekom, G., 202
Van Cantfort, T.E., 260, 261, 262
Van Sant, P., 120
Van Veldhuizen, N., 154, 165
Vander Wall, S.B., 138
Vaughan, W., 122, 127, 138, 139, 140
Veno, A., 149
Von Culin, J.E., 214, 215
Von Fersen, L., 123, 191, 192
Von Frisch, K., 197, 216, 254, 255, 256
Von Uexkull, J., 71

Wagner, A.R., 56, 57, 58, 59, 60, 61, 62, 63, 64, 65, 66, 68, 70, 71, 72, 78, 79, 89, 112, 113, 114, 116, 117, 120, 121, 130, 131, 132, 133, 134, 137, 148, 149, 150, 161
Wahl, O., 168
Wakita, M., 119
Walcott, C., 216, 218, 219
Walker, M.M., 199, 216
Warren, J.M., 11, 279, 280
Washburn, D.A., 177, 178, 182

Wasserman, E.A., 118, 119, 122, 124, 183
Watanabe, S., 119, 123
Watkins, M.J., 186
Watt, A., 88
Waugh, N.C., 137
Wearden, J.H., 175
Weaver, J.E., 192
Wehner, R., 196, 197
Weinberg, M., 90
Weiskrantz, L., 164
Weisman, R.G., 183
Wells, P.H., 256
Wenner, A.M., 256
Werz, M., 154
Westbrook, R.F., 70
Westcott, P.W., 99
Whiskin, E.E., 227
Whiten, A., 241, 242
Whitlow, J.W., 69, 70, 148, 149, 150, 159, 160, 161
Widrow, G., 136
Williams, B.A., 45
Williams, D.A., 33, 156, 157, 158
Williams, D.R., 52, 100, 101

Williams, H., 52, 100, 101
Williams, R.J., 133, 135
Williams, S.L., 267, 270
Wilson, B., 125, 126, 283, 284
Wilson, P.N., 78, 132, 133, 134
Wiltschko, R., 217
Wolz, J.P., 258, 272, 273, 274, 275
Woocher, F.D., 191
Wood, F.G., 259
Woodbury, C.B., 114
Woodruff, G., 127, 128, 241
Worsham, R.W., 155
Worthen, V.K., 94
Wright, A.A., 164, 166
Wynne, C.D.L., 191, 192

Yeager, C.P., 271, 276
Yeagley, H.L., 215, 219
Yerkes, R.M., 21
Yodlowski, M.L., 216

Zanforlin, M., 203, 222
Zentall, T.R., 162, 192
Zimmer-Hart, C.L., 33, 34, 64

Subject Index

Addition,
    by a horse, 176
    by a chimpanzee, 179
Alarm calls,
    in domestic chickens, 236
    in vervet monkeys, 237-240
Alex, an African grey parrot, 126, 181, 193,
    271-273
Alpha conditioning, 36
Alternation learning, 284
American sign language (Ameslan), 260-261,
    268-269
Analgesia, induced by morphine, 49
Analogical reasoning, 127-129
Anaxagoras, 10
Appetitive Pavlovian conditioning with rats,
    39-41, 45, 51
    influence on OR, 76
    latent inhibition of, 66
Aristotle, 2
Artificial intelligence, 16
Asymptote, 28
Associability, 59
    and CS intensity 59
Automatic processing, 75
Autoshaping, 29, 52
    form of CR and, 47
    and omission schedule, 101
    and second-order conditioning, 42
Avoidance behaviour, 142, 144

    and ECS, 142-143, 146-147
    and retrieval cues, 145-147

Backpropagation, 133
Bidirectional control, 82
Bird-song development, 236-237
Bliss point, 92
Blocking, 45, 55
    attenuation of, by surprise, 64, 282
    by contextual stimuli, 63
    theories of, 60, 72, 77
    in a radial maze, 222
    and socially acquired food preferences, 227

Categorisation
    with auditory stimuli, 119
    based on concepts, 124
    by various species, 118-119
    with visual stimuli, 119, 120
Cephalisation index, 9-10, 279-281
Circadian rhythm,
    in activity, 168
    in feeding, 168-169
Classical conditioning, see Pavlovian
    conditioning
Clever Hans, 16, 175-177
Cognitive map,
    in bees, 209-211

definitions of, 206
in hamsters, 212
in rats, 206-209, 213-215
Coelenterates, 3, 25
Communication,
    definition of, 253-254
    in dolphins, 258-259
    in honey-bees, 254-257
    see also alarm calls
Concepts, role in categorisation, 124
Conditioned attraction, 151-152
Conditioned emotional response (CER), see
    conditioned suppression
Conditioned excitation, see excitatory
    conditioning
Conditioned inhibition, see inhibitory
    conditioning
Conditioned response (CR), 27
    behaviour systems analysis of, 51
    compensatory, 48
    consummatory, 47, 53
    drug tolerance as, 49
    magazine activity as, 39
    preparatory, 48, 53
Conditioned stimulus (CS), 21, 27
    air pressure as, 216
    drug injection as, 49
    intensity of, 59
    magnetic field as, 216
    polarised and ultraviolet light as, 216-217
Conditioned suppression, 29, 33, 34, 47
    blocking of 55
    and conditioned inhibition, 33
    and latent inhibition of a CS, 77
    and learned irrelevance, 74
    role of CS intensity, 59
    role of CS-US contingency, 62
    role of US intensity, 58
    and second-order conditioning, 43-44
Configural cues, role in
    Connectionist networks, 131
    Rescorla-Wagner theory, 114
Configural theory
    application to categorisation, 122-123
    application to discrimination learning, 116-118
    as a connectionist network, 135
Contagious behaviour, 229

Context
    role in habituation, 70-71
    role in latent inhibition, 70-71
Contextual variables, 13
Contiguity,
    influence on instrumental conditioning, 88
    influence on Pavlovian conditioning,
        150-151
Contingency
    influence on instrumental conditioning, 88
    influence on Pavlovian conditioning, 62-63
Controlled processing, 75
Counting,
    explanations of, 181-3
    of responses, 177
    of sequential items, 177-179
    of simultaneous items, 179-180
Critical period,
    for bird-song development, 236
    for language acquisition in chimpanzees, 263

Dead reckoning,
    in ants, 197
    in honeybees, 197,
    in geese, 197-198
Deception, 241-243
Delayed matching to sample (DMTS), 154-156,
    159, 160
Deprivation
    influence on instrumental behaviour, 22, 94-96
Dishabituation, 150
Drive, 22, 94

Equipotentiality, principle of, 73
Escape response, 83
Evolution
    of intelligence, 3-8, 285-287
    by natural selection, 2-3
    of primates, 6-7
    of vertebrates, 5
Excitatory conditioning, 28
    as CS-US learning, 38-41
    neural model of, 35
    as S-R learning, 38, 40, 41
Exclusive-or problem, 131

Exemplar effect, 122
Exemplar-theory of categorisation, 122-123, 124
    as a connectionist network, 135
Extinction, 28, 30, 57
    of conditioned inhibition, 64
Eye-blink conditioning, 28, 45, 47

Feature-negative discrimination, 132
Feature-positive discrimination, 112-113, 117, 120
Feature theory of categorisation, 119-122, 123
Forgetting, 141-142
    and consolidation, 142-144
    decay theory of, 160
    deliberate, 161-162
    limited capacity theory of, 161
    and reactivation effects, 144-147
    see also Proactive interference *and*
        Retroactive interference

Generalisation, 29
Generalisation decrement, 29
Geometric spatial relationships, 202-204, 222
Great Chain of Being, 2, 3

Habituation, 66, 68-69, 70, 148-150
Hippocampus,
    place cells in, 203-207
    size of, in birds, 281
Homing, explanations of, 217-219

Imitation, 101, 231-235
Inhibitory conditioning, 28, 32, 61-62, 64
    disrupted by latent inhibition, 79
    disrupted by learned irrelevance, 74
    forgetting of, 142
    representation of, 44-47, 63-65
    responses recorded during, 32, 46
    retardation test for, 33
    summation test for, 34
Insight, 103-105.

Instrumental conditioning,
    and influence of Pavlovian conditioning, 96-98
    as CS-US learning, 82, 98, 100
    as R-US learning, 84-86, 98, 282
    as S-R learning, 19-21, 22-24, 82-84, 86, 97-98, 282
    purposive nature of, 23
    of stereotyped responses, 82
    with various species, 99
Intelligence,
    and brain size, 8-10, 279-281
    evolution of, 3-8, 285-287
    information processing as, 13
    learning as, 11-13, 281-283
    phylogeny and, 3

Jaw movement conditioning, 31

Landmarks,
    for estimation of direction, 200, 201
    for estimation of distance, 200, 201
    and hippocampal place cells, 205
    role of, in homing, 217-218
Language,
    acquisition device, 275-6
    definition of, 257-258
    motivation for use of, 276
Language training methods,
    with apes, 260-263
    with dolphins, 272-275
    with a parrot, 271-271
Latent inhibition, 66, 79
    of a CS, 77
    role of context, 70, 78
    and socially acquired food preferences, 227
    theories of, 70, 77
    in various species, 79, 282
Law of Effect, 20, 83, 90,
    and problem solving, 101-105
Learned irrelevance, 73-74
Learning sets, 279-280
Lloyd Morgan's canon, 15

Magnetic fields
    and conditioning, 199
    role in navigation, 199, 215-216
Marking, 152
Matching to sample, 125, 133
Mental states,
    and deception, 241-243
    and knowledge attribution, 243-245,
    and mirror use, 245-250
Migration,
    by indigo bunting, 221-22
    by loggerhead turtle, 220-221
Mimicry, 229-231
Mirror use,
    in children, 245
    and self-awareness, 250
    in various species, 247,
Misbehaviour during conditioning, 53
Morphine tolerance, 49
Motivational interactions, 97

Natural selection, 2
Negative patterning discrimination, 114, 117, 131
Null hypothesis of animal intelligence, 11,
    165-166, 281-285

Observational conditioning, 229
Omission schedule, 52, 101
Orienting response (OR), 65, 67, 75-76
Overshadowing, 61
    of instrumental response, 89
    and socially acquired food preferences, 227

Pavlovian conditioning
    and CS duration, 68
    and CS intensity, 59
    as CS-US learning, 24, 38-41, 282
    interaction with instrumental behaviour, 96-98
    physiology of, 14, 35-37
    as S-R learning, 22, 38, 40, 41, 100-101, 282
    techniques of, 21, 28-30
    and US intensity, 59
Peak shift, 111
Pheromone, 195

Population-specific behavioural tradition, 232, 251
Proactive interference, 158-159
Prototype theory of categorisation, 123-124
Protozoa, 3, 25

Radial maze, 153
    blocking in, 222
    and cognitive map, 213-215
Reactivation effects, 145-148
Representation, 15
    abstract, 129-130, 284
    affective, 44-47, 97
    amodal, 174
    concrete, 44, 129-130
    of knowledge in others, 241-245
    of relationships, 129-130, 277,284-5
    of self, 245-250
    specific, 44-47
Reinforcer
    conditioned, 93-94
    definitions of, 81, 90-93
    token, 93
Relationships,
    as discriminative stimuli, 108, 112, 124-129
    representation of, 129-130
Rescorla-Wagner theory, 56-63, 72, 89
    application to discrimination learning, 113-116
    application to categorisation, 120, 121
    as a connectionist network, 130-2
    evaluation of, 63-65
Retroactive interference, 132, 134, 159

Sameness concept, 125-127
    in various species, 126
Scala Naturae, 2
Scalar timing theory, 171-173
Search image, 71
Second-order conditioning, 42-44
Second-order relationships, 127
Selective association, 72-73
Sensory preconditioning, 42-44

Sentence,
    comprehension, 267-268
    production, 268-270, 276-277
Serial conditioning, 42,
Serial learning,
    and chunking, 186
    different tests for, 183-184
    and language, 277
    in monkeys, 186-189
    in pigeons, 184-186
Serial position curve, 163-165
Serial reversal problem, 283-284
Short-term retention,
    and forgetting, 158-160
    prospective and retrospective codes of, 155
    theories of, 66-69, 160-163
    in various species, 165-166
Social facilitation, 232
Socially acquired,
    food preferences, 226-228
    fear of predators, 228-229
S-R theory, 20, 22-23, 84
Standard Operating Procedures (SOP) theory of
    memory, 66-71, 78, 148
Stimulus enhancement, 226
Suppression ratio, 30
Systematic variation, 13

Taste aversion conditioning, 12, 30, 51, 73
    to alter value of instrumental reinforcer, 85, 87
    to alter value of Pavlovian US, 39-41
    influence of CS preexposure, 69, 70
    over long intervals, 151
Timing,
    and amodal representations, 175
    information processing model of, 171,
    of intervals, 170
    periodic, 168-170
Trace conditioning, 151
Transitive inference, 189-193
Transposition, 108, 110, 112, 124
Truly random control, 31

Unconditioned stimulus (US), 21, 27, 59
    representation of, in excitatory conditioning,
        44-45
    representation of, in inhibitory conditioning,
        45-47

Water maze, 207-209

Zugunruhe, 221